This guide to the coast path from Plymouth to Poole (217¼ miles) covers the third part, the South Devon and Dorset section, of the 630-mile South-West Coast Path and is the final book in this series. The first edition was walked, researched and written by **HENRY STEDMAN** (above left) and **JOEL NEWTON** (right) accompanied by Henry's dog, **DAISY** (below): two parts trouble to one part Parson's Jack Russell. They also researched and wrote the two other books in this SWCP series, plus numerous other Trailblazer guides.

This **third edition** was rewalked and updated by Henry – and Daisy went too, as usual. He's been writing guidebooks for more than 25 years and is the author or co-author of over a dozen Trailblazer titles including *Kilimanjaro*, *Inca Trail*, *Coast to Coast Path*, *Hadrian's Wall Path*, *London LOOP* and all three books in the *South-West Coast Path* series. When not travelling, he lives in Battle, East Sussex, editing and arranging climbs on Africa's highest mountain through his company, Kilimanjaro Experts.

T0048983

Dorset & South Devon Coast Path (SWCP Part 3)

First edition: 2013; this third edition 2023

Publisher Trailblazer Publications
The Old Manse, Tower Rd, Hindhead, Surrey, GU26 6SU, UK
info@trailblazer-guides.com, ⌨ trailblazer-guides.com

British Library Cataloguing in Publication Data
A catalogue record for this book is available from the British Library

ISBN 978-1-912716-34-0

© Trailblazer 2013, 2018, 2023: Text and maps

Series Editor: Anna Jacomb-Hood
Editor & layout: Anna Jacomb-Hood **Cartography**: Nick Hill
Proof-reading: Jane Thomas **Index**: Anna Jacomb-Hood
Photographs (flora): C4 Row 1 right, © Jane Thomas; all others © Bryn Thomas
All other photographs: © Henry Stedman unless otherwise indicated

The maps in this guide were prepared from out-of-Crown-copyright Ordnance Survey maps amended and updated by Trailblazer.

Acknowledgements

From Henry Thank you to everyone I met on the trail who stopped to pass on their advice and information, or simply to pause awhile to chat. It all made for a very lovely trip. In addition, I'm grateful to everyone who wrote into Trailblazer with their updates and recommendations for the book, in particular Alan Cadwallader, David Mallinson, Helen Older, Gordon Rhodes, David Schache, Paul Southward, Janine Watson and Roland Thorpe. And, of course, thanks, as ever, to all at Trailblazer: Anna Jacomb-Hood for editing, layout and the index, Jane Thomas proof-reading and Nick Hill for the maps.

A request

The author and publisher have tried to ensure that this guide is as accurate and up to date as possible. Nevertheless, things change. If you notice any changes or omissions that should be included in the next edition of this book, please write to Trailblazer (address above) or email us at ⌨ info@trailblazer-guides.com. A free copy of the next edition will be sent to persons making a significant contribution.

Warning: coastal walking and long-distance walking can be dangerous

Please read the notes on when to go (pp13-16) and on outdoor safety (pp80-3). Every effort has been made by the authors and publisher to ensure that the information contained herein is as accurate and up to date as possible. However, they are unable to accept responsibility for any inconvenience, loss or injury sustained by anyone as a result of the advice and information given in this guide.

Updated information will be available on: ⌨ **trailblazer-guides.com**

Photos – Front cover and this page The stretch west of Durdle Door contains some of the steepest – and most spectacular – sections on the entire South-West Coast Path.
Previous page: Taking a breather on the way out of Osmington Mills, with the tombolo leading to Portland in the distance.

Printed in China; print production by D'Print (☎ +65-6581 3832), Singapore

Above: The first serious river crossing on this section of the South-West Coast Path – across the River Yealm that separates Wembury from Newton Ferrers and Noss Mayo. Thankfully, a ferry operates for half of the year, saving you a lengthy diversion to the nearest foot crossing.
Below: Pausing to take in magnificent Blackpool Sands, near Stoke Fleming.

Dorset & South Devon
COAST PATH

SW COAST PATH PART 3 – PLYMOUTH TO POOLE

97 large-scale maps (1:20,000)
& guides to 48 towns and villages

PLANNING – PLACES TO STAY – PLACES TO EAT

HENRY STEDMAN & JOEL NEWTON

TRAILBLAZER PUBLICATIONS

INTRODUCTION

About the Dorset & South Devon Coast Path

PART 1: PLANNING YOUR WALK

Practical information for the walker

Budgeting 30

Itineraries

What to take

Getting to and from the path

PART 2: THE ENVIRONMENT & NATURE

Flora and fauna

PART 3: MINIMUM IMPACT WALKING & OUTDOOR SAFETY

Minimum impact walking

Outdoor safety

ABOUT THIS BOOK

This guidebook contains all the information you need. The hard work has been done for you so you can plan your trip without having to consult numerous websites and other books and maps. When you're all packed and ready to go, there's comprehensive public transport information to get you to and from the trail and detailed maps (1:20,000) to help you find your way along it. This guide includes:

● All standards of accommodation with reviews of campsites, bunkhouses, hostels, B&Bs, guesthouses and hotels
● Walking companies if you want an organised tour and baggage-transfer services if you just want your luggage carried
● Itineraries for all levels of walkers
● Answers to all your questions: when to go, degree of difficulty, what to pack, and how much the whole walking holiday will cost
● Walking times in both directions and GPS waypoints
● Cafés, pubs, tearooms, takeaways, restaurants and food shops
● Rail, bus and taxi information for all places along the path
● Street plans of the main towns both on and off the path
● Historical, cultural and geographical background information

POST COVID NOTE

This edition of the guide was researched after the Covid pandemic but is liable to more change than usual. Some of the hotels, cafés, pubs, restaurants and tourist attractions may not survive the further hardships caused by rising fuel prices and inflation. Do forgive us where your experience on the ground contradicts what is written in the book; please email us – info@trailblazer-guides.com so we can add your information to the updates page on the website.

❏ MINIMUM IMPACT FOR MAXIMUM INSIGHT

Man has suffered in his separation from the soil and from other living creatures ... and as yet he must still, for security, look long at some portion of the earth as it was before he tampered with it.
Gavin Maxwell, *Ring of Bright Water*, 1960

Why is walking in wild and solitary places so satisfying? Partly it is the sheer physical pleasure: sometimes pitting one's strength against the elements and the lie of the land. The beauty and wonder of the natural world and the fresh air restore our sense of proportion and the stresses and strains of everyday life slip away. Whatever the character of the countryside, walking in it benefits us mentally and physically, inducing a sense of well-being, an enrichment of life and an enhanced awareness of what lies around us.

All this the countryside gives us and the least we can do is to safeguard it by supporting rural economies, local businesses, and low-impact methods of farming and land-management, and by using environmentally sensitive forms of transport – walking being pre-eminent.

PART 4: ROUTE GUIDE AND MAPS

APPENDICES

INTRODUCTION

This book covers the last 217¼ miles (350km) of the South-West Coast Path (SWCP), Britain's longest national trail until they get round to completing the England Coast Path – if they ever do. The walk described begins on the Devon–Cornwall border, at Plymouth and, having navigated Devon's entire southern

This book covers the last 217¼ miles of the 630-mile South-West Coast Path

coastline, enters the county of Dorset at Lyme Regis, before finishing at South Haven Point, overlooking Poole Harbour. Together with the two other books in this series, the entire 630 miles of the SWCP is covered.

There are few, if any, stretches of the British coastline that can offer the walker such variety, such interest – and such beauty – as this third and final leg of the coast path. From sun-drenched promenades to wild, remote cliff-tops, through ancient 'apple-pie' villages, tiny thatched hamlets and smart, friendly Georgian resorts, this path has it all. Indeed it is difficult to think of another section of any national trail that so comprehensively lives up to that well-worn cliché of the travel industry: that there is something for everyone. For historians the trail begins – most appropriately, given the many famous journeys that

Durdle Door with its iconic limestone arch draws the crowds on a sunny day.

Above: The St Christopher Medallion Sculpture on Breakwater Hill is one of several sculptures you pass as you negotiate your way through Plymouth. St Christopher is the patron saint of travellers, of course – most appropriate if you're just setting off on the trail!

have departed from the same spot – at the Mayflower Steps, in Plymouth's timeless Barbican district, and passes through such fascinating towns as medieval Dartmouth, home to the UK's only Royal Naval college, and Teignmouth, the last place in mainland England to be successfully invaded by a foreign power. Castles, caves, barrows, burial mounds, ships, stone circles, historic harbours and old hostelries – all lie on the path and all offer something to intrigue and captivate the history buff.

Similarly, geologists also have plenty that they'll find engrossing – and indeed you don't need to be an expert in stone or strata to enjoy them. Not only is the English Riviera the home of a Global Geopark but across the River Exe there's the Jurassic Coast World Heritage Site, where the very rocks you step on can take you on a 185-million-year geological journey. Steep and precipitous cliffs of orange, grey and white change their hue with each passing geological era; and if these don't 'rock' your world, within these very cliffs are fossils of strange and unfamiliar beasts that once dominated the Earth: a long-vanished land of soaring ptero-

---

THE SOUTH-WEST COAST PATH (SWCP)

As the crow flies, the distance between Minehead (the official start point of the

South-West Coast Path) and South Haven Point (the official end point) is only around 90 miles long. So why would anyone wish to spend weeks on end walking the 630-mile coastal route between the same two points? The answer is simple: the SWCP is one of the most beautiful trails in the UK.

Around 70% of those 630 miles are spent either in national parks or regions that have been designated as Areas of Outstanding Natural Beauty. The variety of places crossed by the SWCP is extraordinary too: from sunkissed beaches to sandy burrows, holiday parks to fishing villages, esplanade to estuary, on top of windswept cliffs and under woodland canopy, the scenery that one travels through has to be the most diverse of any of the national trails.

Maintaining such a monumental route is no easy task, with thousands of signposts and waymarks, hundreds of bridges, gates and stiles, and more than 25,000 steps! The task of looking after the trail falls to a dedicated team from the official body, Natural England (see p56). Another important organisation, and one that looks after the rights of walkers, is the South-West Coast Path Association (see box p48), a charity that fights for improvements to the path and offers advice, information and support to walkers. They also campaign against many of the proposed changes to the path and

dactyls rather than swooping peregrines, where plesiosaurs, not porpoises, cruised the seas, and the endemic scelidosaurus once roamed where sheep now ruminate.

The wildlife of today is not without its merits either, from the lovely deer of Lulworth to otters in Axmouth. And while man has done more than his fair share of shaping and utilising the land you pass through, he has also been careful to protect it too, with numerous Sites of Special Scientific Interest, several nature reserves and no fewer than three Areas of Outstanding Natural Beauty – with each encompassing mile after mile of epic panoramas, jagged sea stacks, and bountiful, beckoning beaches. There are also such spectacular delights as the curious Undercliffs, moulded by landslides and decorated by the free hand of nature into a truly English jungle; the south

Above: The eastern end of the coast path is marked with this sculpture at Sandbanks, near Poole.

coast's highest point, Golden Cap; and the iconic natural architecture of Durdle Door, Stair Hole and Lulworth Cove.

But if all the above sound a bit too worthy, for those after less cerebral pleasures the path also cuts through such quintessential seaside resorts as Exmouth, Sidmouth and the English Riviera (Torquay, Paignton and Brixham) – a land of doughnuts and dodgems, arcades and amusements, candy floss and crazy golf.

help to ensure that England's right-of-way laws (which ensure that the footpath is open to the public – even though it does, on occasion, pass through private property) are fully observed.

History of the path
In 1948 a government report recommended the creation of a footpath around the entire South-West peninsula to improve public access to the coast which, at that time, was pretty dire. It took until 1973 for the Cornwall Coast Path to be declared officially open and another five years for the rest of the South-West Coast Path to be completed. The section covered in this book, Dorset & South Devon, is the third part that most coastal walkers complete, though it was one of the earliest sections opened to the public, back in 1974.

The origins of the path, however, are much older than its official designation. Originally, the paths were established – or at least adopted, as the paths themselves had been connecting coastal villages for centuries – by the local coastguards in the 19th century; they needed a path that hugged the shoreline closely to aid them in their attempts to spot and prevent smugglers from bringing contraband into the country. The coastguards were unpopular in the area as they prevented the locals from exploiting a lucrative if illegal activity, to the extent that it was considered too dangerous for them to stay in the villages; as a result, the authorities were obliged to build special cottages for the coastguards that stood (and, often, still stand) in splendid isolation near the path – but well away from the villages. (*cont'd on p10*) (cont'd from p9) The lifeboat patrols also used the path to look out for craft in distress (and on one famous occasion used the path to drag their boat to a safe launch to rescue a ship in distress). When the coastguards' work ended in 1856, the Admiralty took over the task of protecting England's shoreline and thus the paths continued to be used.

The route – Minehead (Somerset) to Poole Harbour (Dorset)

The SWCP officially begins at Minehead in Somerset (its exact starting point marked by a sculpture that celebrates the trail), heads west right round the bottom south-west corner of Britain then shuffles back along the south coast to South Haven Point, on the tip of Shell Bay, overlooking Poole Harbour in Dorset.

On its lengthy journey around Britain's south-western corner the SWCP crosses national parks such as Exmoor as well as regions that have been designated Areas of Outstanding Natural Beauty (including North, South and East Devon AONB and the Cornwall and Dorset AONBs) or Sites of Special Scientific Interest (Braunton Burrows being just one example – an area that also enjoys a privileged status as a UNESCO Biosphere Reserve), and even two UNESCO World Heritage sites: the Jurassic Coast of East Devon and Dorset, which you pass through in this book, and the old mining landscape of Cornwall and West Devon. Other features passed on the way include the highest cliffs on mainland Britain (at Great Hangman – also the highest point on the coast path at 318m/1043ft, with a cliff-face of 244m), the largest sand-dune system in England (at Braunton Burrows), England's most westerly point (at Land's End) and Britain's most southerly (at the Lizard), the 18-mile barrier beach of Chesil Bank, one of the world's largest natural harbours at Poole, and even the National Trust's only official naturist beach at Studland!

The path ends at South Haven Point, its exact finish marked by a second SWCP sculpture. The path also takes in four counties – Somerset, Devon, Cornwall and Dorset – and connects with over 15 other long-distance trails, including the newly formed England Coast Path. The southern section from Plymouth to Poole also forms part of the 3125-mile long European E9 Coastal Path that runs on a convoluted route from Portugal to Estonia.

Walking the South-West Coast Path

In terms of difficulty, there are those people who, having never undertaken such a trail before, are under the illusion that coastal walking is a cinch; that all it involves is a simple stroll along mile after mile of golden beach, the walker needing to pause only to kick the sand out from his or her flipflops or buy another ice-cream. The truth, of course, is somewhat different, for coastal paths tend to stick to the cliffs above the beaches rather than the beaches themselves (which is actually something of a relief, given how hard it is to walk across sand or shingle). These cliffs make for some spectacular walking. But given the undulating nature of Britain's coastline, and the fact that the course of the SWCP inevitably crosses innumerable river valleys, each of which forces the walker to descend rapidly before climbing back up again almost immediately afterwards, they also make for some exhausting walking too. Indeed, it has been estimated that anybody who completes the entire SWCP will have climbed more than four times the height of Everest (35,031m to be precise, or 114,931ft) by the time they finish!

Given these figures, it is perhaps hardly surprising that most people take around six to eight weeks to complete the whole route and few do so in one go. Indeed, it is not unusual for people to take years or even decades to complete the whole path, taking a week or two here and there to tackle various sections until the whole trail is complete.

The wild flowers are coming into bloom, lambs are skipping in the meadows and the grass is green and lush.

Of course, finding a dry week in spring is not easy but occasionally there's a mini-heatwave at this time. Another advantage with walking at this time is that there will be fewer walkers and finding accommodation is relatively easy, though do check that the hostels, campsites and B&Bs are open. Easter is the exception; the first major holiday in the year when people flock to the coast.

Summer

Summer, on the other hand, can be a bit *too* busy, at least in the towns and tourist centres, and over a weekend in August can be both suffocating and insufferable. Still, the chances of a prolonged period of sunshine are of course higher at this time of year than any other, the days are longer, and all the facilities and public transport are operating. Our advice is this: if you're flexible and want to avoid seeing too many people on the trail, avoid the school holidays, which basically means ruling out the tail end of July, all of August and the first few days of September. Alternatively, if you crave the company of other walkers, summer will provide you with the opportunity of meeting plenty, though do remember that you **must book your accommodation in advance**, and note that particularly at this time some places won't offer accommodation for a stay of less than two nights. Despite the higher-than-average chance of sunshine, take clothes for any eventuality – it will probably still rain at some point.

Autumn

September is a wonderful time to walk; many tourists have returned home and the path is clear. The weather is often sunny too, at least at the beginning of September. The first signs of winter will be felt in October but there's nothing really to deter the walker. In fact there's still much to entice you, such as the colours of the heathland, which come into their own in autumn; a magnificent blaze of brilliant purples and pinks, splashed with the occasional yellow flowers of gorse (it is more usual in spring but can thrive in autumn).

By the end of October, however, the weather will begin to get a little wilder and the nights will start to draw in. Most campsites and some B&Bs and hostels may close. Winter is approaching ...

Winter

November can bring crisp clear days which are ideal for walking, although you'll definitely feel the chill when you stop on the cliff tops for a break. Winter temperatures rarely fall below freezing but the incidence of gales and storms definitely increases. You need to be fairly hardy to walk in December and January and you

Whatever the weather there are numerous welcoming pubs to detain you along the way.

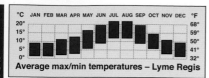

Average max/min temperatures – Lyme Regis

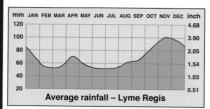

Average rainfall – Lyme Regis

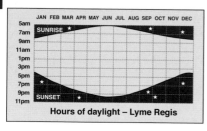

Hours of daylight – Lyme Regis

may have to alter your plans because of the weather. By February the daffodils and primroses are already appearing but even into March it can still be decidedly chilly if the sun is not out.

While winter is definitely the low season with many places closed, this can be an advantage: very few people walk at this time of year, giving you long stretches of the trail to yourself. When you do stumble across other walkers they are as happy as you to stop and chat. Finding B&B accommodation is easier as you will rarely have to book more than a night ahead (though it is still worth checking in advance as some B&Bs close out of season), but if you are planning to camp, or are on a small budget, you will find places to stay much more limited.

WEATHER

Before departing on your walk, tell yourself this: at some point on my walk it is going to **rain**. That's not to say it will, but at least if it does you won't be too disappointed and will hopefully have come prepared for this, clothes-wise. Besides, walking in the rain can be fun, at least for a while: the gentle drumming of rain on hood can be quite relaxing, the path is usually quiet, and if it really does chuck it down at least it provides an excuse to linger in tearooms and have that extra scone. And as long as you dress accordingly and take note of the safety advice given on pp80-3, walking in moderate rain is no more dangerous than walking at any other time – though do be careful, particularly on exposed sections, if the path becomes slippery or the wind picks up.

DAYLIGHT HOURS

If walking in winter, autumn or even early spring, you must take account of how far you can walk in the available light. It won't be possible to cover as many miles as you would in summer. Conversely, in the summer months there is enough available light until at least 9pm. Remember, too, that you will get a further 30-45 minutes of usable light before sunrise and after sunset depending on the weather.

Opposite: Looking east along the coastline towards Durdle Door.

Above: Start Point Lighthouse (see p131), built in 1836, is open to the public in the summer months. **Below**: Daisy taking the ferry across the River Avon (see p114) which separates Bigbury-on-Sea from Bantham.

Above: The Dartmouth Steam Railway runs for over six miles along the coast between Paignton and Kingswear, passing above the colourful beach huts at Goodrington Sands on the way. **Below**: Looking down on the fishing boats by the cosy village of Beer (see p214).

Another joy of the coast path is the food, with fish in Brixham so fresh you can taste the salt of the ocean. Crab sandwiches, pints of real ale and cream teas galore can be savoured all along the path, especially in the thatched villages of Beer, Abbotsbury and West Lulworth, all of which prove that nature doesn't have the monopoly on beauty and defy you not to change your plans and spend a night in their cosy embrace.

Of course such rewards aren't gained without a fight and there are a couple of tough stretches of walking that must be completed before you can say you've conquered the path. But those of you who started the beginning of the SWCP in Minehead will know that, whatever the hardships faced, the treasures of this endlessly fascinating path are always worth any effort expended.

INTRODUCTION

How difficult is the path?

The South-West Coast Path is just a (very, very) long walk, so there's no need for crampons, ropes, ice axes, oxygen bottles or any other climbing paraphernalia, because there's no actual climbing involved. All you need to complete the walk is some suitable clothing, a bit of money, a rucksack full of determination and a half-decent pair of calf muscles.

Below: Looking across sheep-filled fields to Burgh Island (see p114) and its Art Deco hotel, the inspiration for the setting for Agatha Christie's *And Then There Were None*.

Signposting is good: look for the acorn symbol

The part of the SWCP that is covered by this book is perhaps the one with the most variety. Topographically speaking, there are plenty of steep ups-and-downs as well as large flat areas of walking on seaside promenades. While the Riviera (see box p150) provides walkers with an unbroken swathe of civilisation, this book is bookended by two remote sections where settlements are scarce and amenities are few and far between. These two sections, from Mount Batten Point to Salcombe and from Lulworth Cove to Swanage, require a little advanced planning to ensure you have something to eat and somewhere to rest your head for the night. Still, with the path well signposted (look for the acorn symbol) all the way along and the sea keeping you company for the entire stretch, it's difficult to get lost (though it's always a good idea to take a compass or GPS unit, just in case).

As with any walk, you can minimise the risks by preparing properly. Your greatest danger on the path is likely to be from the weather, which can be so unpredictable in this corner of the world, so it is vital that you dress for inclement conditions and always carry a set of dry clothes with you. Not pushing yourself too hard is important too, as over-exertion leads to exhaustion and all its inherent dangers (see pp80-3), so plan an itinerary that matches your abilities rather than your (over-) ambitions.

In terms of orientation, the South-West Coast Path is very well signposted, so you shouldn't lose your way. However, we think that the distances the signposts have written on them can be of questionable accuracy so are not always to be trusted; indeed sometimes even the spelling on the signposts is wrong. But in terms of helping you find your way, the signposts on the SWCP do a terrific job and the trail authorities are to be congratulated both on this and on the maintenance of the trail in general.

How long do you need?

People take an average of around 18 days to complete the walk

People take an average of around 18 days to complete the walk; count on three weeks in total to give you time to travel there and back. Of course, if you're fit there's no reason why you can't go a little faster, if that's what you want to do, and finish the walk in 15 days or even less, though you will end up having a different sort of trek from most of the other people on the trail. For whilst theirs might be a fairly relaxing holiday, yours will be more of a sport. What's more, you won't have much time to laze in the sun on the beaches, scoff scones in tearooms, visit an attraction or two, or sup local beers under the shade of a pub parasol.

There's nothing wrong with the fast approach, of course, but do make sure you **don't push yourself too fast, or too far.** That road leads only to exhaustion, injury or, at the absolute least, an unpleasant time.

See pp34-5 for some suggested itineraries covering different walking speeds

When deciding how long to allow for the trek, those intending to camp and carry their own luggage shouldn't underestimate just how much a heavy pack can slow them down. On p34 and p35 there are some suggested itineraries covering different walking speeds. If you have only a few days, don't try to walk it all; concentrate instead on one area such as the coast path through Dorset, the Riviera (see box p150), or the less-demanding section from Plymouth to Salcombe or Dartmouth.

When to go

SEASONS

'My shoes are clean from walking in the rain.' **Jack Kerouac**

Britain is a notoriously wet country and South-West England does nothing to crush that reputation. Few walkers manage to complete the walk without suffering at least one downpour; two or three per walk are more likely, even in summer. That said, it's equally unlikely that you'll spend a week in the area and not see any sun at all; even the grumpiest of walkers will have to admit that, during the **walking season** at least, there are more sunny days than showery ones.

The season starts at Easter and builds to a crescendo in August, before steadily tailing off in October. Few people attempt the entire path after the end of October though there are still plenty of people on day walks. Many places close in November for the winter.

There is one further point to consider when planning your trip. Firstly, remember that most people set off on the trail at a weekend. This means that **you'll find the trail quieter during the week** and as a consequence you may find it easier to book accommodation.

Spring

Find a dry fortnight in springtime (around the end of March to mid June) and you're in for a treat.

There are lots of chances to reward yourself with ice-cream. Don't expect portions to always be this generous!

❏ FESTIVALS AND ANNUAL EVENTS

Note that Covid meant some of these festivals haven't happened for a while, or have been on a smaller scale, so do check in advance.

April/May
● **Brixham Pirate Festival** (🖥 brixhampirates.com) Live music, historic re-enactments and very large gathering of pirates. Held late April to early May
● **Lyme Regis Fossil Festival** (**fb**; mostly free) A weekend of fossil-hunting walks, talks, displays and a fossil fair. Also held late April to early May
● **Dart Music Festival, Dartmouth** (🖥 dartmusicfestival.co.uk) Held in early May

May/June
● **Teignmouth Folk Festival** (🖥 teignmouthfolk.co.uk) Held in mid June
● **Dawlish Arts Festival** (🖥 dawlishartsfestival.org.uk) Festival of arts, crafts, theatre, classical music, gospel and jazz; held over several weeks between late May and early June
● **Shaldon Festival** (🖥 shaldonfestival.co.uk) 4-5 days of classical music in late June
● **Wessex Folk Festival, Weymouth** (🖥 www.wessexfolkfestival.com/) Free festival at the harbourside in Weymouth generally held in the first week of June but at the time of research it seems no-one had agreed to organise it so check in advance.

June/July
● **Budleigh Music Festival, Budleigh Salterton** (🖥 budleighmusicfestival.co.uk) Week-long classical music festival in late June to early July
● **Camp Bestival, Lulworth Castle** (🖥 campbestival.net) Music, comedy and many other events held over a long weekend in late July.
● **Exmouth Festival** (🖥 exmouthfestival.co.uk) Also in late July an annual 4-day festival of music, theatre, film and dance, showcasing local talent.
● **Paignton Festival** (🖥 paigntonfestival.com) Nine-day-long festival of music, dance, games and shows, held on Paignton Green over late July to early August.
● **Sidmouth Folk Festival** (🖥 sidmouthfolkfestival.co.uk) Long-running week-long folk music festival held between late July and early August.

August
● **Shaldon Water Carnival** (🖥 www.shaldonwatercarnival.co.uk) First Saturday in August.
● **British Firework Championships, Plymouth** (🖥 britishfireworks.co.uk) Held in mid August
● **Burton Bradstock Festival of Music & Art** (🖥 burtonbradstockfestival.com) Three days of classical, jazz and world music in mid to late August

September
● **Seafest (The Dorset Seafood Festival, Weymouth** (🖥 dorsetseafood.co.uk) Popular festival that was previously held in July but now early to mid September
● **Swanage Folk Festival** (🖥 swanagefolkfestival.com) Annual weekend-long shindig (early to mid Sep) with numerous musicians, dance & music workshops.
● **International Agatha Christie Festival** (🖥 iacf-uk.org) Week-long celebration (in mid September) of the author's works in and around Torquay.

October
● **Dartmouth Food Festival** (🖥 dartmouthfoodfestival.com) In mid to late October

Above: View across the Dart to Kingwear. **Below left**: The path takes you through the remarkable Axmouth to Lyme Regis Undercliffs National Nature Reserve (see p220) – the closest you'll get to a jungle in Britain. **Below right**: Jacob's Ladder (p205), the steps that give access to the beach, was originally built in 1870. There's a more modern walkway round the base.

Above left: Approaching Golden Cap on a summer's evening. At 191m (627ft), it's the highest point on the south coast of England. **Above right**: Passing the Radar Monument, St Aldhelm's Head (see p300). **Below**: The Great Globe at Durlston Castle was constructed in 1887 and, weighing about 40 tonnes, is said to be one of the largest stone spheres in the world.

Right: The chalk cliffs west of Durdle Door provide trekkers with some of the most challenging gradients on the entire South-West Coast Path. **Inset**: Who says dogs don't have a sense of humour? For Daisy, the Scratchy Bottom sign is always a highlight of the trail.

LULWORTH
COVE 3
DURDLE DOOR 1½

THE WARREN
SCRATCHY
BOTTOM 1¼

Above: The lighthouse at Portland Bill (see p267). **Below**: You may wish to avert your eyes as you hurry along the beach at Studland.

🌸 **The National Trust**

NATURISTS
MAY BE SEEN
BEYOND
THIS POINT

PLANNING YOUR WALK

Practical information for the walker

ROUTE FINDING

 For most of its length the coast path is well signposted. At confusing junctions the route is usually indicated by a finger-post sign with 'coast path' written on it. At other points, where there could be some confusion, there are wooden waymark posts with an acorn symbol and a yellow arrow to indicate in which direction you should head. The waymarking is the responsibility of the local authorities along the trail who have a duty to maintain the path. Generally they do a good job but occasionally you will come across sections of the trail where waymarking is ambiguous, or even non-existent. But with the detailed trail maps and directions in this book – not to mention the fact that you always have the sea to one side! – it would be hard to get really lost.

❏ **USING GPS WITH THIS BOOK**

I never carried a compass, preferring to rely on a good sense of direction ... I never bothered to understand how a compass works or what it is supposed to do ... To me a compass is a gadget, and I don't get on well with gadgets of any sort. **Alfred Wainwright**

While Wainwright's acolytes may scoff, other walkers will accept GPS technology as an inexpensive, well-established if non-essential, navigational aid, particularly since most people use sat-nav in a car. With a clear view of the sky, a **GPS receiver** will establish your position as well as elevation in a variety of formats, including the British OS grid system, anywhere on earth to an accuracy of within a few metres.

These days most **smartphones** have a GPS receiver built in and mapping software available to run on it (see box p45). Dedicated gadget-buyers can invest in a separate **GPS unit** such as a Garmin.

The maps in the route guide include numbered waypoints; these correlate to the list on pp314-15, which gives the grid reference as well as a description. You can download the complete list of these waypoints for free as a GPS-readable file (that doesn't include the text descriptions) from the Trailblazer website: ☐ trailblazer-guides.com.

Bear in mind that most people who tackle this path do so perfectly successfully without using GPS.

ACCOMMODATION

The trail guide (Part 4) lists a fairly comprehensive selection of places to stay along the length of the trail. You have two main options: camping or using B&Bs/guesthouses/hotels. Few people stick to just one of these options the whole way, preferring, for example, to camp most of the time but spend the odd night in B&B accommodation, or perhaps use hostels where possible (as there are only a few on this stretch of the path) but splash out on a B&B where necessary.

When booking accommodation that is far from the path, remember to ask if a pick-up and drop-off service is available (usually only B&Bs provide this service); at the end of a tiring day it's nice to know a lift is available to take you to your accommodation rather than having to traipse another two or three miles off the path to get to your bed for the night.

The facilities' table on pp32-5 provides a quick snapshot of what type of accommodation is available in each of the towns and villages along the way, while the tables on p34 and p35 provide some suggested itineraries. The following is a brief introduction to what to expect from each type of accommodation.

Camping

There are campsites all the way along this section of the South-West Coast Path, meaning it's entirely feasible to camp the whole way, although not many people

---

❑ SHOULD YOU BOOK YOUR ACCOMMODATION IN ADVANCE?

With the exception of campsites, which rarely need booking, it's essential that you have your night's accommodation booked by the time you set off in the morning. Nothing is more deflating than to arrive at your destination at the day's end only to find that you've then got to walk a further five miles or so, or even take a detour, because everywhere is booked. For this reason, it would pay to cast an eye over the list of festivals and events (see box p14) in towns and villages on the path as accommodation will be particularly hard to find at those times. Note that, as well as the annual events mentioned, a number of the towns, especially those near estuaries such as Dartmouth, host regattas, during which time they can also become very busy.

Outside the high season (ie the summer period coinciding with the long school holidays in the UK), and particularly in April/May or September, as long as you're flexible and willing to take what's offered, with maybe even a night or two in a hostel if that's all there is, you should get away with booking **B&B-style accommodation** just a few nights in advance, or indeed just the night before. If planning to walk in the high season (and also over a weekend) you should book as soon as you can, especially if you want to stay in a particular place. That said, many places don't accept advance bookings for one night in the peak season/at weekends so actually for this route it may be hard to book in advance for a single-night stay. Online booking is also often for a minimum of two nights so for anything less than this you may have to contact the place direct.

If planning to stay in **hostels**, it's worth checking in advance that they will be open (though most on this route are open all year). It's also well worth phoning at least one night before, and well before that if it's a weekend or the peak season, to make sure the hostel isn't fully booked.

Campers have more flexibility and can usually just turn up and find a space there and then, though ringing in advance adds some peace of mind.

camp every single night for the whole walk. You're almost bound to get at least one night where the rain falls relentlessly, soaking equipment and sapping morale, and it is then that some campers opt to spend the next night drying out in a hostel or B&B. There are, however, many advantages with camping. It's more economical, for a start, with most campsites charging £10 or so per person for hikers (though, rarely, some large holiday parks can charge double and even triple that in high season. Thankfully, most have a special hiker's rate – just make sure you tell them that you're walking the SWCP to secure that rate. There's rarely any need to book either, except possibly in the very high season, and even then you'd be very unlucky not to find somewhere.

Campsites vary; some are just a quiet corner of a farmer's field, while others are full-blown holiday parks with a few spaces put aside for tents. Showers are nearly always available, occasionally for a fee though more often than not included in the rate. Note that **wild camping** (ie not in a regular campsite) is not allowed. However, in all honesty we meet quite a few hikers who do, and none, to our knowledge, have got into any trouble for doing so. This may have something to do with the fact that they are careful to set up camp late in the evening and leave without trace early in the morning.

Camping is fabulous fun, but it's not an easy option; the route is wearying enough without carrying your accommodation around with you. You could look into employing a baggage-transfer company (see p28), though this rather negates two of the main advantages of camping – affordability and flexibility – as it will cost you more and means you have to tell the company, at least a day before, of your next destination – and stick to it – so that you and your bag can be reunited every evening. The best thing to do is to just pack as lightly as possible – bring nothing but the absolute essentials.

Hostels

Hostels can be great places to stay in when you get the chance, especially if you want to meet your fellow walkers to swap stories and compare blisters. Unfortunately, it isn't possible to plan to stay in a hostel (or bunkhouse) every night on this walk. There are only five places with hostels: Plymouth, Beer, Portland, West Lulworth and Swanage.

As well as the independent hostels at Plymouth and Portland, there are three YHA (Youth Hostel Association) hostels en route at Beer, Lulworth Cove, and Swanage. If you associate YHAs with cold, crowded dorms, uncomfortable beds and lousy food, be prepared to think again. Many of them provide good meals (breakfast is usually served 7.30-9am and evening meals 6-8pm) and a number are also licensed, but if you prefer to self-cater most have a fully equipped kitchen and some have a shop selling emergency groceries, snacks and souvenirs. In addition they now have a whole range of extra facilities from drying rooms to televisions and wi-fi/internet access.

Dorms usually have bunk beds sleeping 4-6 people but increasingly, hostels also have some private rooms. **Do note that, at the time of writing, only the dorm at YHA Swanage was open; YHA Beer and YHA Lulworth Cove were only offering private rooms**. Hopefully by the time you read this that situation may have changed – but do check their website for the latest. Toilet and shower facilities are still generally shared (but are usually very clean, especially at YHAs) but all YHA hostels on this route have at least one room with en suite facilities.

The curfew (usually 11pm) can be annoying but many YHA hostels now utilise access codes on their doors to offer residents 24hr access.

Most of the hostels on this path are open all year but at certain times the YHA hostels are only open to pre-booked sole-use groups. In fact at any time of the year they may be fully booked with schools or other groups, so contact the YHA or the relevant hostel to check the situation.

The YHA operates flexible pricing so rates vary according to demand and some other factors and therefore may be much higher than the rates quoted in this guide. However, if you're walking alone hostels probably work out far cheaper than B&Bs, even taking into account the added cost of breakfast (£5.95/9.95 continental/cooked), but if there are two or more of you it can be just as expensive as staying in a B&B; see also opposite.

Hostel membership & bookings You don't have to be a YHA member to stay at YHAs, but it does give you a discount (currently 10% per night); this is applicable to both the rate and meals and is valid for a member booking for up to 16 people at the same time. Despite the name, anybody of any age can join the YHA. This can be done at any hostel or by contacting the **Youth Hostels Association of England and Wales** (☎ 01629-592700, 🖳 yha.org.uk). Annual membership costs £20 (or £15 if paying by direct debit).

YHA hostels are easy to book online, but booking by phone through the central switchboard often involves spending a frustrating amount of time on hold. If you're able to call the hostel direct, do so.

Bed and breakfast accommodation

Bed and Breakfasts (**B&Bs**) are a great British institution and many of those along the South-West Coast Path are absolutely charming. Nearly all the B&Bs on this route have either en suite rooms or rooms with private facilities. (In this book we have stated where a B&B has rooms with shared facilities, so rare are they on the trail.)

The rooms usually contain either a double bed (known as a double room), or two single beds (known as a twin room, though these can sometimes be pushed together to create a double bed). Triple rooms are for three people and quad rooms are for four or more. Triple/quad rooms usually contain a double bed and either a single bed or a bunk bed; occasionally there are three or four single beds.

Note that in winter some B&Bs close; for those that stay open, make sure beforehand that they will have their heating in your room turned on!

Increasingly B&B proprietors are able to cater for specific dietary requirements – eg if you're vegetarian, or have to have a gluten-free diet – but you need to tell the B&B owner beforehand. The rate includes breakfast, of course; otherwise, they would just be a 'B', rather than a B&B.

Some B&Bs provide an **evening meal**, particularly if there is no pub or restaurant nearby. Others may offer you a lift to a local eatery, while some will expect you to make your own arrangements. Check the situation when you book.

The difference between a B&B and a **guesthouse** is minimal, though some of the better guesthouses are more like hotels, offering evening meals and a lounge for guests. **Pubs** and **inns** also offer bed and breakfast accommodation and prices are generally no more than in a regular B&B.

Hotels usually *do* cost more than B&Bs, however, and some can be a little perturbed with a bunch of smelly trekkers turning up and treading mud into their carpet. Most on the South-West Coast Path, however, are used to seeing trekkers and welcome them warmly.

There are also branches of chain hotels such as Premier Inn and Travelodge in or near many of the towns/cities en route. The smart, clean rooms are double or twin and most can sleep additional children but not more than two adults. At **Premier Inn** hotels (🖥 premierinn.com) rates typically cost from £35 per night if paid at the time of booking but can go up to £150 or more for a flexible booking and in the peak season. They **do not allow dogs** though they offer **free wi-fi**. Breakfast costs at least an extra £7.50 (or from £9.50 for a full English).

The accommodation offered by their rivals **Travelodge** (🖥 travelodge .co.uk) is very similar – Saver rates start from £29 per room per night but expect to pay double that or more for a flexible booking and in the summer months. **Dogs are allowed** (£20 per stay) and wi-fi is free for 30 minutes or £3 for 24hrs). Breakfast is an additional cost (from £8.99 or unlimited for £17.98) but it isn't available at all branches.

Still, both chains are happy to accept one-night bookings, which gives them a big advantage amongst walkers.

Rates Rates in this guide are quoted on a **per person** (pp) basis, assuming two people are sharing a room. Solo walkers should note: single rooms are not easy to find and you will often end up in a double/twin room and are likely therefore to have to pay a **single occupancy rate**. This is often the room rate less about £10, or may even be the actual room rate in peak season. B&B accommodation in this guide starts at around £30pp for the most basic B&Bs (from £25pp room only), rising to around £60pp for the most luxurious places; most charge around £35-50pp. Rates in guesthouses, pubs and inns are similar to B&Bs but hotel tariffs start at around £50pp and can go up to £200pp for a room with a sea view in the summer. Note that at some hotels the rate is room only.

Most places have their own website and offer online/email **booking** but for many you will need to phone to book a room especially for a single-night stay. Most places ask for a deposit (about 50%) which is generally non-refundable if you cancel at short notice. Some places may charge 100% if the booking is for one night only and many require a stay of at least two nights for an advance booking. Always let the owner know as soon as possible if you have to cancel your booking so they can offer the bed to someone else.

Hotels and guesthouses generally take credit or debit cards but most smaller B&Bs only accept payment by bank transfer or cheques by post for the deposit; the balance can be settled with cash, a further bank transfer or a cheque.

Airbnb

The rise and rise of Airbnb (⌨ airbnb.co.uk) has seen private homes and apartments opened up to overnight travellers on an informal basis. While accommodation is primarily based in cities, the concept is spreading to tourist hotspots in more rural areas, but do check thoroughly what you are getting and the precise location. While the first couple of options listed may be in the area you're after, others may be far too far afield for walkers. At its best, this is a great way to meet local people in a relatively unstructured environment, but do be aware that these places are not registered B&Bs, so standards may vary, yet prices may not necessarily be any lower than for a normal B&B.

FOOD AND DRINK

[See also box on pp24-5] Stay in a B&B and you'll be filled to the gills with a cooked **'full-English' breakfast**. This tends to follow a choice of cereals that will have been laid out for you to graze on while you wait for the main event, which usually consists of a plateful of eggs, bacon, sausages, mushrooms, tomatoes and possibly baked beans or black pudding, with toast and butter, and all washed down with coffee, tea and/or juice. Enormously satisfying the first time you try it, by the fourth or fifth morning you and your arteries may start to prefer a lighter continental breakfast; many places now offer these.

If you have had enough of these cooked breakfasts and/or plan an early start, ask if you can have a **packed lunch** instead of breakfast. Your landlady or hostel can usually provide one at an additional cost (unless it's in lieu of breakfast), though of course there's nothing to stop you preparing your own lunch (a penknife is very handy for this), or going to a pub (see below) or café.

Whatever you do for lunch, don't forget to leave some room for a **cream tea** (see box p24) or two, a morale, energy and cholesterol booster all rolled into one delicious package. To describe it as simply a pot of tea accompanied by scones served with cream and jam is to totally ignore the history, ceremony and joy of this Titan of teatime. The jury is out on whether you should put the jam on first (the Cornish method) or the cream (the Devon orthodoxy) – but either way, do not miss the chance of at least one cream tea on your trip.

Pubs are as much a feature of the walk as seagulls and sheep, and in some cases they are as much a tourist attraction as any castle or cove. Most pubs have become highly attuned to the desires of trekkers and offer lunch and evening meals (often with a couple of local dishes and usually some vegetarian options), some locally brewed real ales (and/or ciders), a garden to relax in on hot days

---

❏ **OPENING DAYS & HOURS**
The opening days and hours for pubs, restaurants and cafés mentioned in Part 4 are as accurate as possible but the shortage of staff and the increasing costs incurred in running a business – let alone if the weather is bad, or there is no demand – means that places will close early or not open at all so it is essential to check in advance, especially if there are few eating places in the area. See also box p85.

and a roaring fire to huddle around on cold ones. The standard of the food varies widely, though is usually served in big portions, which is often just about all trekkers care about at the end of a long day. In many of the villages the pub is the only place to eat out. Note that pubs may close in the afternoon, especially in the winter months, so check in advance if you are hoping to visit a particular one, and also if you are planning lunch there as food serving hours can change.

That other great British culinary institution, the **fish 'n' chip shop**, can be found in virtually every town on the trail. As well as these, there are **restaurants** and **takeaways** in the larger towns en route and also in some of the villages.

Self-catering

There is a food shop of some description in most of the places along the route, though most are small (and often combined with a post office) and whether you'll be able to find precisely what you went in for is uncertain. If self-catering, therefore, your menu for the evening will depend upon what you found in the store that day. Part 4 details what shops are on the path.

Drinking water

Be careful: on a hot day in some of the remoter parts after a steep climb or two you'll quickly dehydrate, which is at best highly unpleasant and at worst mightily dangerous. Always carry some water with you and in hot weather drink 3-4 litres a day. Don't be tempted by the water in the streams; if the cow or sheep faeces in the water don't make you ill, the run-off chemicals from the pesticides and fertilisers almost certainly will. Using iodine or another purifying treatment will help to combat the former, though there's little you can do about the latter.

It's a lot safer to fill up from taps instead, all of which are safe to drink from in England, including those in public toilets (although the annoying rise in automated warm-water hand-washing machines makes re-filling water bottles an impossible task). Look out for handy **water taps** located on some tourist beaches along the coast path, and note that, in Dorset particularly, rows of beach huts often have a water tap behind them. We've marked some water taps on our maps.

MONEY

It's important to carry both cash and card (debit and/or credit) with you. Some places only accept card these days, and their number is growing. But by the same token, some of the older places, or places without a ready internet connection, only accept cash (including at least one of the ferries that transport you across the many rivers you'll encounter along the way).

Thankfully, getting money out isn't too tricky. There are several **banks** on the trail and most are equipped with an **ATM** (cash machine). You'll also find ATMs in many shops and stores though these tend to charge (typically £1.85) to withdraw money. You can also withdraw money over the counter at **post offices** (providing your bank is affiliated – see p27). Another way of getting money in your hand is to use the **cashback** system; find a store or a pub that will accept a debit card and ask them to advance cash against the card. Some will, especially if you buy something. *(Money cont'd on p26)*

PLANNING YOUR WALK

❑ FOOD AND DRINK IN DEVON AND DORSET

Traditional food

As a major centre of farming and fishing, it's not surprising that the South-West is an important food supplier to the rest of Britain and can boast some fine local specialities.

Say 'Devon' to most Brits and in addition to images of sparkling coastlines and rolling hills, the county's name will also conjure up the delights of **clotted cream** – best enjoyed as part of a traditional **cream tea** with a scone or two and some whortleberry jam. This is certainly a speciality, **whortleberry** being the local name for the wild bilberry (though they go by several other names including blueberry, heidelberry, huckleberry, hurtleberry and wimberry) and locally they're called 'worts' or 'urts'.

Dairy products as a whole are plentiful in this corner of the country including delicious yoghurts and ice-cream. **Blue Vinney** is Dorset's most renowned cheese, best eaten with some **Dorset knob biscuits** (today made by only one producer, Moores Biscuits, based near Bridport), or for something sweeter you could try **Dorset apple cake** – and, just to make sure that no artery is left unclogged, enjoy it with a dollop of Dorset clotted cream.

From the sea, **South Devon crab** is reputed to be the tastiest in the world and **smoked eels** are a speciality in these parts too. The county's mature farmhouse cheeses, ice-creams and cottage loaves ensure that, no matter how hard you push yourself on the walk, you won't lose too much weight. Even if you're on a tight budget the ubiquitous fish & chips can be satisfying if cooked with fresh fish. At the other end of the scale there are plenty of fine-dining restaurants around the coast offering mouth-watering dishes concocted from locally caught fish.

Beer

The process of brewing beer is believed to have been in Britain since the Neolithic period and is an art local brewers have been perfecting ever since.

Real ale (also known as cask ale) is beer that has been brewed using traditional methods. Real ales are not filtered or pasteurised, a process which removes and kills all the yeast cells, but instead undergo a secondary fermentation in their casks at the pub, which enhances the natural flavours and brings out the individual characteristics of the beer. It's served at cellar temperature with no artificial fizz added, unlike keg beer which is pasteurised and has the fizz added by injecting nitrogen dioxide.

● **Devon** Devon is thought to have approximately over 60 breweries and micro breweries operating within its borders. Amongst the more celebrated is **Dartmoor Brewery** (🖳 dartmoorbrewery.co.uk), family owned, situated in the centre of the national park and the highest brewery in England (at 1400ft/427m above sea level). From this vantage point they brew their famous Jail Ale (4.8%), as well as Dartmoor IPA (4%).

Closer to the coast at Honiton, **Otter Brewery** (🖳 otterbrewery.com) produces five regular brews including their easy-drinking 'session' ale, Otter Bitter (3.6%), and the ever-popular Otter Ale (4.5%). Meanwhile, based near Kingsbridge, **South Hams Brewery** (🖳 southhamsbrewery.co.uk) is located above Start Bay and brews, amongst others, Devon Pride (3.8%) and Wild Blonde (4.4%).

Located in Newton Abbot, **Teignworthy Brewery** (🖳 teignworthybrewery.com) produces six regular cask ales including Beachcomber (4.5%) and Reel Ale (4%) as well as more than 20 seasonal ales. For the brave, their Cor Bugga! is a dizzying 6.2%!

Based in Paignton, **Bays Brewery** (🖳 baysbrewery.co.uk) produces three permanent beers – Bays Gold (4.3%), Devon Dumpling (5.1%) and Topsail (4%). Behind The Albert Inn in Totnes, you'll find **Bridgetown Brewery** (🖳 albertinntotnes.com/bridgetown-brewery).

The beers from **Branscombe Vale Brewery** (🖥 www.branscombebrewery.co.uk), in Branscombe, include a bitter (Branoc 3.8%) and a Pale Ale (Golden Fiddle 4%).

● **Dorset** Real ale aficionados are just as well catered for over the border in Dorset. Scattered along the coast path you will come across **Hall & Woodhouse** (🖥 hall-woodhouse.co.uk) pubs which stock several of their own-brewed Badger Ales, including Tanglefoot (5%) and Fursty Ferret (4.4%).

Just by the Devon–Dorset border, **Lyme Regis Brewery** (🖥 lymeregisbrewery .com) operates from premises near the old Town Mill in Lyme Regis. Beers include Cobb (3.9%) and Town Mill (4.5%).

Heading east, **Palmers Brewery** (🖥 palmersbrewery.com), based in Bridport, has been perfecting ale for over 225 years. Calling on such experience they produce five fine ales including Dorset Gold (4.5%), Copper Pale Ale (3.7%) and Tally Ho! (5.5%), a strong dark ale which was first brewed in 1949.

Weymouth's **Dorset Brewing Company**'s (🖥 dbcales.com) award-winning ales include Durdle Door (5%), Jurassic (4.2%), and even a lager titled Chesil (4.1%).

Inland from here, in the Dorset village of Piddlehinton, **Piddle Brewery** (🖥 piddlebrewery.co.uk) produces four year-round cask ales including Piddle (4.1%) and the more hoppy Cocky (4.3%), while right at the end of your walk, why not celebrate with a pint from **Isle of Purbeck Brewery** (🖥 isleofpurbeckbrewery.com), which produces beers from its brewery beside Bankes Arms (p305) in Studland. Ales to look for include Fossil Fuel (4.1%) and Purbeck IPA (4.8%).

Ciders and perries

A pint of cider on this section of the walk is almost as obligatory as blisters. **Scrumpy**, or rough cider, is a particular form of cider, easy to differentiate from the weaker, more mass-market keg ciders, being cloudy, fizz-free and with bits floating in it too! The only thing to remember before drinking scrumpy is that it should be done so in moderation – it's powerful stuff. After you've drunk it, you'll be lucky to remember anything at all. Perries are similar to ciders but are produced from perry pears as opposed to apples.

● **Devon** Look out for products from **Sandford Orchards** (🖥 sandford orchards.co.uk), such as the cloudy Devon Scrumpy (6%), and their biggest seller, the sparkling and clear Devon Red (4.5%). **Branscombe Vale Brewery** (see above) also offers ciders including a sea-cider (4.5%).

● **Dorset** Meanwhile, in Dorset, look for ciders fermented at **Marshwood Vale Cider** (🖥 marshwoodvalecider.com), such as the Dorset Tit (6%). An honourable mention must also go to Purbeck Cider Company's (🖥 purbeckcidercompany.co.uk) **Katy Perry**, made with perry pears and Katy apples (the variety of apple chosen presumably so they could justify the name rather than any considerations of flavour).

Other cider companies you may come across on the walk, though which are actually based in neighbouring counties, include Herefordshire's Westons Cider (🖥 westons-cider.co.uk), producers of such classics as Westons Old Rosie (6.8%), and Orchard Pig (🖥 orchardpig.co.uk) in Somerset.

The Square and Compass, in Worth Matravers (p296), is also very proud of the cider they stock and with good reason as they press their own ciders in the back garden, including the Sat Down BeCider (7.2%); they also host an annual cider festival in November.

(Money, cont'd from p23) Most local shops, cafés and pubs accept cards these days, but few B&Bs do so it's important to carry plenty of **cash** with you, though do keep it safe and out of sight (preferably in a moneybelt).

Though they are becoming almost obsolete now, a **cheque book** could prove very useful as back-up if you have one, so that you don't have to keep on dipping into your cash reserves, especially as most B&Bs don't accept credit/debit cards.

❑ INFORMATION FOR FOREIGN VISITORS

● **Currency** The British pound (£) comes in notes of £50, £20, £10 and £5, and coins of £2 and £1. The pound is divided into 100 pence (usually referred to as 'p', pronounced 'pee') which comes in silver coins of 50p, 20p, 10p and 5p, and copper coins of 2p and 1p.

● **Money** Up-to-date **rates of exchange** can be found on 🖳 xe.com/currencyconverter, at some post offices, or at any bank or travel agent.

● **Business hours** Most **village shops** are open Monday to Friday 9am-5pm and Saturday 9am-12.30pm, though some open as early as 7.30/8am; many also open on Sundays but not usually for the whole day. Occasionally you'll come across a local shop that closes at lunchtime on one day during the week, usually a Wednesday or Thursday; this is a throwback to the days when all towns and villages had an 'early closing day'. **Supermarkets** are open Monday to Saturday 8am-8pm (often longer) and on Sunday from about 9am to 5 or 6pm, though main branches of supermarkets generally open 10am-4pm or 11am-5pm only on Sundays.

Main **post offices** generally open Monday to Friday 9am-5pm and Saturday 9am-12.30pm though where the branch is in a shop PO services are sometimes available whenever the shop is open; **banks** typically open at 9.30/10am Monday to Friday and close at 3.30/4pm, though in some places both post offices and banks may open only two or three days a week and/or in the morning, or limited hours, only. **ATMs (cash machines)** located outside a bank, shop, post office or petrol station are open all the time, but any that are inside will be accessible only when that place is open. However, ones that charge, such as Link machines, may not accept foreign-issued cards.

Pub hours are less predictable as each pub may have different opening hours. However, most pubs on the Path open daily 11am-11pm (some close at 10.30pm on Sunday) but **some close in the afternoon** especially in the winter months.

The last entry time to most **museums and galleries** is usually half an hour, or an hour, before the official closing time.

● **National holidays** Most businesses in the South-West are shut on 1st January, Good Friday and Easter Monday (March/April), first and last Monday in May, last Monday in August, 25th December and 26th December.

● **School holidays** State-school holidays in England are generally as follows: a one-week break late October, two weeks over Christmas and the New Year, a week mid February, two weeks around Easter, one week at the end of May/early June (to coincide with the bank holiday at the end of May) and five to six weeks from late July to early September. Private-school holidays fall at the same time, but tend to be slightly longer.

● **Documents** If you are a member of a National Trust organisation in your country bring your membership card as you should be entitled to free entry to National Trust properties and sites in the UK (see p44).

Getting cash at post offices

Several banks have agreements with the Post Office allowing customers to make cash withdrawals free of charge using a debit card at branches throughout the country. Given that many towns and villages have post offices but may not have banks, this is a very useful facility.

You can find a full list of participating banks and a list of post office branches with an ATM on the Post Office website (🖳 postoffice.co.uk, click on Everyday banking and then scroll down to the relevant link.

● **EHICs and travel insurance** Until 31st December 2020 the **European Health Insurance Card** (EHIC) entitled EU nationals (on production of an EHIC card) to necessary medical treatment under the UK's National Health Service (NHS) while on a temporary visit here. However, this is not likely to be the case for EU nationals now, especially once their EHIC card has expired; check on 🖳 nhs.uk/nhs-services (click on: 'Visiting-or-moving-to-England') before you come to the UK. However, the EHIC card was never a substitute for proper medical cover on your travel insurance for unforeseen bills and for getting you home should that be necessary. Also consider getting cover for loss or theft of personal belongings, especially if you're staying in hostels, as there may be times when you have to leave your luggage unattended.

● **Weights and measures** In Britain milk is sold in pints (1 pint = 568ml), as is beer in pubs, though most other **liquids** including petrol (gasoline) and diesel are sold in litres. **Distances** on road and path signs are given in miles (1 mile = 1.6km) rather than kilometres, and yards (1yd = 0.9m) rather than metres. The population remains divided between those who still use inches (1 inch = 2.5cm), feet (1ft = 0.3m) and yards and those who are happy with millimetres, centimetres and metres; you'll often be told that 'it's only a hundred yards or so' to somewhere, rather than a hundred metres or so. Most **food** is sold in metric weights (g and kg) but the imperial weights of pounds (lb: 1lb = 453g) and ounces (oz: 1oz = 28g) are frequently displayed too. The **weather** – a frequent topic of conversation – is also an issue: while most forecasts predict temperatures in Celsius (C), many people continue to think in terms of Fahrenheit (F; see the temperature chart on p16 for conversions).

● **Smoking** The ban on smoking in public places relates not only to pubs and restaurants, but also to B&Bs, hostels and hotels. These latter have the right to designate one or more bedrooms where the occupants can smoke, but the ban is in force in all enclosed areas open to the public – even if they are in a private home such as a B&B. Should you be foolhardy enough to light up in a no-smoking area, which includes pretty well any indoor public place, you could be fined £50, but it's the owners of the premises who carry the can if they fail to stop you, with a potential fine of £2500.

● **Time** During the winter, the whole of Britain is on Greenwich Mean Time (GMT). The clocks move one hour forward on the last Sunday in March, remaining on British Summer Time (BST) until the last Sunday in October.

● **Telephone** The international country access code for Britain is ☎ 44 followed by the area code minus the first 0, and then the number you require.

If you're using a **mobile (cell) phone** that is registered overseas, consider buying a local SIM card to keep costs down. Also remember to bring a universal adaptor so you can charge your phone. See box p43.

● **Emergency services** For police, ambulance, fire or coastguard dial ☎ 999 or ☎ 112.

PLANNING YOUR WALK

OTHER SERVICES

Thanks to the rise of smartphones, internet cafés seem to be a thing of the past. Most pubs, cafés and B&Bs also have **free wi-fi** for customers who have their own devices. Towns have at least one **supermarket** and most villages have a **grocery/convenience store**. You'll sometimes find a **phone box** near these shops, though you will almost definitely need a credit or debit card as many phone boxes no longer accept coins. Calls from a phone box cost a minimum of 60p (including a 40p connection charge; thereafter 10p a minute).

There are **outdoor equipment shops** in most large towns en route.

WALKING COMPANIES

It is, of course, possible to turn up with your boots and backpack at Plymouth and just start walking, with little planned save for your accommodation (see box on p18). The following companies, however, are in the business of making your holiday as stress-free and enjoyable as possible. Several companies offer what are known as **self-guided holidays** (see opposite), where your accommodation, transport at the start/end of the walk and baggage transfer along the trail are arranged for you. Detailed information and maps are also provided as a matter of course, thereby allowing you to just turn up and start marching! These are useful for those who simply don't have the time to organise their trip,

No matter how much information is provided by the self-guided companies – or indeed this book – the chances are you will learn and appreciate much more in the company of an experienced and knowledgeable guide. **Guided walking tours** (see opposite) are ideal for those who want the extra safety, security and companionship that comes with walking in a group.

Accommodation, meals, transport to and from the trail and baggage transfer are usually included in the price. Be warned, however, that the standards of accommodation, the distances walked each day and the age of the clients that companies attract often vary widely, so do check each company carefully to make sure you choose that one that is right for you.

Baggage transfer

For those who don't fancy being burdened while on the path, it is possible to arrange to have your luggage transferred to the end of each day's destination.

The only baggage company on the SWCP is the aptly named **Luggage Transfers** (☎ 01326-567247, 🖳 luggagetransfers.co.uk), who cover the whole of the path. Visit their website for further information.

Alternatively, some of the taxi companies listed in this guide can provide a similar service within a local area if you want a break from carrying your bags for a day or so. Also, don't rule out the possibility of your B&B/guesthouse owner taking your bags ahead for you. Some are happy to do so and, depending on the distance, they may make no charge at all, or charge £10-15; this may be less than a taxi so is worth enquiring about.

Self-guided holidays

The companies listed below offer **tailor-made holidays** in addition to the packages mentioned.

● **Absolute Escapes** (☎ 0131-610 1210, 💻 absoluteescapes.com; Edinburgh) Offer walks along the path from Plymouth to Exmouth, Exmouth to Lyme Regis and Lyme Regis to Poole.
● **Celtic Trails** (☎ 01291-689774, 💻 celtictrailswalkingholidays.co.uk; Chepstow) Long-established company that offers the whole path and in sections.
● **Contours Walking Holidays** (☎ 01629-821900, 💻 contours.co.uk; Derbyshire) Offer the path in sections and its entirety; also dog-friendly walks.
● **Encounter Walking** (☎ 01208-871066, 💻 encounterwalkingholidays.com; Cornwall) Offer walks along the entire path and in sections.
● **Footpath Holidays** (☎ 01985-840049, 💻 footpath-holidays.com; Wiltshire) Operate a range of walking holidays including inn-to-inn itineraries for the whole path and single-centre holidays from the Purbeck peninsula, Dartmouth and Sidmouth. They also offer short breaks.
● **Great British Walks** (☎ 01600-713008, 💻 great-british-walks.com; Monmouth) Have a variety of itineraries which can be adapted to suit the customer.
● **High Point Holidays** (☎ 01749-321032, 💻 highpointholidays.co.uk; Somerset) Offer a range of walks (4-7 days) along the Jurassic Coast Path.
● **Let's Go Walking!** (☎ 01837-880075, 💻 www.letsgowalking.co.uk; North Tawton, Devon) Offer walks along the entire path and in parts.
● **Macs Adventure** (☎ 0141-530 8886, 💻 macsadventure.com; Glasgow) Have walks covering the whole SWCP including Plymouth to Brixham, Exmouth to Lyme Regis, Lyme Regis to Poole, with varying itineraries to suit.
● **Nearwater Holidays** (☎ 01326-279278, 💻 nearwaterwalkingholidays.co.uk; Truro) Walks covering the whole path as well as sections.
● **Mickledore** (☎ 017687-72335; 💻 www.mickledore.co.uk; Keswick, Cumbria) Offer a range of holidays along the entire length of the South-West Coast Path.
● **Responsible Travel** (☎ 01273-823700, 💻 www.responsibletravel.com/holidays/england; Brighton) Offer walks along the whole path.
● **Walkers Britain** (formerly Sherpa Expeditions; ☎ 020-8875 5070, 💻 www.walkersbritain.co.uk; London) Offer 8-day holidays from Lyme Regis to Lulworth Cove.
● **Walk the Trail** (☎ 01326-567252, 💻 www.walkthetrail.co.uk; Helston) Holidays of any itinerary length from short breaks to the entire SWCP and all routes in between.

Group/guided walking tours

● **Footpath Holidays** (see above) Fully guided tours in South Devon and in Dorset on the Purbeck peninsula.
● **Ramblers Walking Holidays** (☎ 01707 331133, 💻 www.ramblersholidays.co.uk; Herts) Offer two itineraries: The Isle of Purbeck and South West Dorset and the Jurassic Coast.

PLANNING YOUR WALK

Budgeting

England is not a cheap place to go travelling and the accommodation providers on the South-West Coast Path are more than used to seeing tourists and charge accordingly. You may think before you set out that you are going to try to keep your budget to a minimum by camping every night and cooking your own food but it's a rare trekker who sticks to this rule. Besides, the B&Bs and pubs on the route are amongst the path's major attractions and it would be a pity not to sample the hospitality in at least some. If you really want to keep costs to a minimum, consider walking out of season when accommodation rates are often cheaper.

If the only expenses of this walk were accommodation and food, budgeting for the trip would be a piece of cake. Unfortunately, in addition there are all the little extras that push up the cost: beer, cream teas, stamps and postcards, internet use, phone costs, buses here and there, ferry rides, baggage transfer, laundry, souvenirs, entrance fees ... it's surprising how much all of these things add up.

CAMPING

You can survive on less than £20 per person (pp) if you use the cheapest campsites (or wild camp), don't visit a pub, avoid all museums and tourist attractions, and cook all your own food from staple ingredients. Even then, unforeseen expenses will probably nudge your daily budget above this figure. Include the occasional pint, and perhaps a pub meal every now and then, and the figure will be nearer £25-30pp a day.

HOSTELS

Rates at the hostels (both independent and YHA) en route start from £13pp but are likely to be much higher in peak season; YHA rates are now very fluid depending on demand. Breakfast at hostels is about £7.50 and a two-course evening meal (where available) may cost £12-15. This means that, overall, it can cost around £35-40pp per day, or £45-55pp to live in a little more comfort and enjoy the odd beer or two. However, since it isn't possible to stay in a hostel or bunkhouse every night on this section of the coast path, anticipate a higher daily budget if you choose to stay in a B&B.

B&Bs, PUBS, GUESTHOUSES AND HOTELS

B&B rates start at around £30pp (based on two sharing) per night but can be twice or even three times this, particularly if you are walking by yourself and are thus liable to pay a single occupancy supplement (see p21). Add on the cost of lunch and dinner and you should reckon on about £50-55pp minimum per day. Staying in a guesthouse or hotel would probably push the minimum up to £55-60pp.

Itineraries

Part 4 of this book has been written from west to east, though there is of course nothing to stop you from tackling it in the opposite direction, and there are advantages in doing so – see below.

To help plan your walk see the **colour maps and gradient profiles** (at the end of the book) and the **table of town and village facilities** (pp32-5), which gives a run-down on the availability of services including accommodation for both directions.

You could follow one of the suggested itineraries (see p34 & p35) which are based on preferred type of accommodation and walking speeds or, if tackling the entire walk seems a bit ambitious, you can tackle it a day or two at a time. To help you, we discuss the highlights of the Dorset & South Devon Coast Path on pp36-8 and you can use public transport to get to the start and end of the walk. The public transport map and service details are on pp52-5.

Once you have an idea of your approach turn to Part 4 for detailed information on accommodation, places to eat and other services in each village and town on the route. Also in Part 4 you will find summaries of the route to accompany the detailed trail maps.

WHICH DIRECTION?

It's more common for walkers attempting the entire SWCP to start from Minehead and finish at South Haven Point and this is the way the route is described in Part 4. Furthermore, the prevailing wind usually comes from the west so, by walking in this direction, you'll find you have the weather behind you for the section described in this book, pushing you on rather than driving in your face. That said, if this is your first taste of the coast path – and you think you're going to continue one day and complete the rest of the 630-mile trek – you may prefer to start at South Haven Point and finish at Plymouth.

Those who prefer to swim against the tide of popular opinion and walk east to west should find it easy to use this book too.

SUGGESTED ITINERARIES

The itineraries in the boxes on p34 and on p35 are based on different accommodation types (camping and B&B-style accommodation), with each divided into three alternatives depending on your walking speed. They are only suggestions so feel free to adapt them. **Don't forget** to add your travelling time before and after the walk.

VILLAGE & TOWN FACILITIES & DISTANCES
Plymouth to Poole Harbour

PLACE* & DISTANCE* APPROX MILES / KM	BANK ATM	POST OFFICE	INFO	EATING PLACE	FOOD SHOP	CAMP-SITE	HOSTEL BUNK	B&B HOTEL
Plymouth	✔	✔	TIC	✔✔	✔		H	✔✔
Wembury 10¾ / 17.25	ATM			✔	✔			✔
(Noss Mayo/N Ferrers +1/1.5) ATM				✔✔				✔
Ch'boro/Bigbury 15¼ / 24.5 ATM£				✔✔	✔	✔(Bigbury)		✔
Outer Hope 5 / 8	ATM£	✔		✔✔	✔			✔✔
Salcombe 8 / 13	ATM	✔	TIC	✔✔	✔	✔(1½ miles)		✔✔
East Prawle T/O 5¾ / 9.25 (E Prawle+¾/1)				✔	✔	✔✔		
Beesands 6½ / 10.5				✔✔				✔
Torcross 1/1.5		(✔)		✔✔				
Slapton T/O 2½ / 4 (Slapton+¾/1)				✔	✔	✔		✔
Strete 3½ / 5.75		✔		✔	✔			✔✔
Stoke Fleming 2½ / 4		✔		✔✔	✔	✔		✔✔✔
Dartmouth 4¼ / 6.75	✔	✔	TIC	✔✔	✔			✔✔✔
Kingswear FERRY		✔	VC	(✔)	✔			
Brixham 11 / 17.75	ATM	✔	TIP	✔✔	✔	✔		✔✔✔
Paignton 5¾ / 9.25	✔	✔	TIP	✔✔	✔	✔(Goodrington)		✔✔✔
Torquay 2¾ / 4.5	✔	✔	TIC	✔✔	✔			✔✔✔
St Marychurch 6 / 9.75	ATM	✔		✔✔	✔			✔
Maidencombe 2 / 3.5				✔✔				
Shaldon 3¼ / 5.25		✔	TIC	✔✔	✔	✔(1 mile)		✔✔
Teignmouth FERRY	✔	✔	TIP	✔✔	✔			✔✔✔
Dawlish 3¾ / 6	✔	✔		✔✔	✔			✔✔✔
Dawlish Warren 1¾ / 2.75 ATM£				✔✔	✔			✔
Cockwood/Starcross 2½ / 4				✔✔	✔			✔
Exmouth FERRY	✔	✔	TIC	✔✔	✔	✔ (1 mile)		✔✔✔
Budleigh Salterton 5½ / 9 ATM		✔	TIC	✔✔	✔	✔		✔✔
Ladram Bay 4¾ / 7.75				✔	✔	✔		
Sidmouth 2¾ / 4.25	✔	✔	TIC	✔✔	✔			✔✔✔
Branscombe Mouth 6½ / 10.5				(✔)				✔
Beer 2¼ / 3.5		✔		✔✔	✔	✔✔	YHA	✔✔✔
Seaton 1½ / 2.5	ATM	✔	TIC	✔✔	✔	✔(¾ mile)		✔✔✔
Lyme Regis 7 / 11.25	✔	✔		✔✔	✔	✔ (¼ mile)		✔✔✔
Charmouth 3 / 4.75				✔✔	✔	✔✔		✔✔✔
Seatown/(Chideock) 4¼ (½) / 6.75 (1)		✔		✔✔	✔	✔		✔
Eype Mouth 2 / 3.25			TIP	(✔)	✔	✔✔		✔
West Bay 1¼ / 2 ATM£				✔✔	✔	✔§		✔✔✔
Btn Bradst'k T/O 1¾ / 3 (BB+¼) ATM£ ✔				✔	✔	✔		✔✔✔
West Bexington 3¾ / 6				✔				✔
Abbotsbury 3¾ / 6	ATM	✔	TIP	✔✔	✔	✔✔		✔✔✔
Fortuneswell/Portland 13 / 21		✔		✔✔	✔	✔(P'land)	H/B(P'land)	✔✔✔
Weymouth 14¾ / 23.75	✔	✔	TIC	✔✔	✔			✔✔✔

cont'd on p34

NOTES *PLACE & *DISTANCE Places in **bold** are on the path; places in brackets and not in bold – eg (Noss Mayo) – are a short walk off the path. DISTANCE is given from the place above. Distances are between **places on the route** or to the **main turnoff (T/O)** to places in brackets. For example the distance from Torcross to the turnoff for Slapton is 2½ miles. Bracketed distances eg (+¾) show the additional distance in miles off the route – eg Slapton is ¾ mile from the Coast Path.

VILLAGE & TOWN FACILITIES & DISTANCES
Poole Harbour to Plymouth

PLACE* & DISTANCE* APPROX MILES / KM	BANK ATM	POST OFFICE	INFO	EATING PLACE	FOOD SHOP	CAMP-SITE	HOSTEL BUNK	B&B HOTEL
South Haven Point								
Swanage 7½ / 12	ATM	✔	TIC	✔✔	✔		YHA/H	✔✔
Worth Matravers T/O 4¾ / 7.75 (Worth M +1/1.6)				✔		✔		✔
Kimmeridge T/O 8¼ /¼13.5 (Kimmeridge+¾/1.2)				✔		✔		✔
Lulworth 7 / 11	ATM£			✔✔	✔	✔	YHA	✔✔
Osmington/Os Mills 6¼ / 10				✔		✔		✔
Weymouth 4¾ / 7.75	✔	✔	TIC	✔✔	✔			✔✔
Fortuneswell/Portland 14¾ / 23.75	✔			✔✔	✔	✔(P'land)	H/B(P'land)	✔✔
Abbotsbury 13 / 21	ATM	✔	TIP	✔✔	✔	✔✔✔		✔✔
West Bexington 3¾ / 6				✔				✔
Btn Bradst'k T/O 3¾ / 6 (BB+¼)	ATM£	✔		✔	✔	✔		✔✔
West Bay 1¾ / 3	ATM£			✔✔	✔	✔§		✔✔
Eype Mouth 1¼ / 2			TIP	(✔)	✔	✔✔		✔
Seatown/(Chideock) 2 (½) / 3.25 (1)		✔		✔✔	✔	✔		✔
Charmouth 4¼ / 6.75				✔✔	✔	✔✔		✔✔
Lyme Regis 3 / 4.75	✔	✔		✔✔	✔	✔ (¼ mile)		✔✔
Seaton 7 / 11.25	ATM	✔	TIC	✔✔	✔	✔(¾ mile)		✔✔
Beer 1½ / 2.5		✔		✔✔	✔	✔✔	YHA	✔✔
Branscombe Mouth 2¼ / 3.5				(✔)				✔
Sidmouth 6½ / 10.5	✔	✔	TIC	✔✔	✔			✔✔
Ladram Bay 2¾ / 4.25				✔	✔	✔		
Budleigh Salterton 4¾ / 7.75	ATM	✔	TIC	✔✔	✔	✔		✔
Exmouth FERRY	✔	✔	TIC	✔✔	✔	✔ (1 mile)		✔✔
Cockwood/Starcross 5½ / 9		✔		✔✔	✔			✔
Dawlish Warren 2½ / 4	ATM£			✔✔	✔			✔
Dawlish 1¾ / 2.75	✔	✔		✔✔	✔			✔✔
Teignmouth 3¾ / 6	✔	✔	TIP	✔✔	✔			✔✔
Shaldon FERRY		✔	TIC	✔✔	✔	✔(1 mile)		✔
Maidencombe 3¼ / 5.25				✔✔				
St Marychurch 2 / 3.5	ATM	✔		✔✔	✔			
Torquay 6 / 9.75	✔	✔	TIC	✔✔	✔			✔✔
Paignton 2¾ / 4.5	✔	✔	TIP	✔✔	✔	✔(Goodrington)		✔✔
Brixham 5¾ / 9.25	ATM	✔	TIP	✔✔	✔	✔		✔✔
Kingswear FERRY		✔	VC	(✔)	✔			
Dartmouth 11 / 17.75	✔	✔	TIC	✔✔	✔			✔✔
Stoke Fleming 4¼ / 6.75		✔		✔✔	✔	✔		✔✔
Strete 2½ / 4		✔		✔	✔			✔
Slapton T/O 3½ / 5.75 (Slapton+¾/1)				✔✔	✔	✔		✔
Torcross 2½ / 4		(✔)		✔✔				
Beesands 1/1.5				✔✔				✔
East Prawle T/O 6½ / 10.5 (E Prawle+¾/1)				✔✔	✔		✔✔	*(cont'd on p35)*

PLANNING YOUR WALK

B&B/HOTEL/CAMPSITE/EATING PLACE ✔ = one place   ✔✔ = two   ✔✔✔ = three or more
EATING PLACE (✔) = seasonal or open daytime only   **POST OFFICE** limited hours = (✔)
HOSTEL/BUNK YHA = YHA hostel   H = independent hostel   B = Bunkhouse
CAMPSITE Bracketed distance eg (½) shows mileage from Coast Path; § = limited opening
INFO TIC/P = Tourist Info Centre/Point   VC = Visitor Centre
BANK/ATM ✔ = bank+ATM   ATM = ATM only   ATM£ = ATM with withdrawal charge

VILLAGE & TOWN FACILITIES & DISTANCES
Plymouth to Poole Harbour

PLACE* & DISTANCE* APPROX MILES / KM	BANK ATM	POST OFFICE	INFO	EATING PLACE	FOOD SHOP	CAMP-SITE	HOSTEL BUNK	B&B HOTEL
Osmington/Os Mills 4¾ / 7.75				✔		✔		✔
Lulworth 6¼ / 10	ATM£			✔✔	✔	✔✔	YHA	✔✔
Kimmeridge T/O 7 / 11 (Kimmeridge+¾/1.2)				✔✔		✔		✔
Worth Matravers T/O 4½ / 7.5 (Worth M +1/1.6)				✔✔	✔			✔
Swanage 8½ / 13.75	ATM	✔	TIC	✔✔	✔		YHA/H	✔✔
South Haven Point 7½ / 12				*(for key and notes see previous page)*				

CAMPING

Relaxed			Medium			Fast		
Place	**Approx Distance**		**Place**	**Approx Distance**		**Place**	**Approx Distance**	
Night	miles	km		miles	km		miles	km
0 Plymouth			Plymouth			Plymouth		
1 Wembury±	10¾	17.25	Wembury±	10¾	17.25	Wembury±	10¾	17.25
2 Bigbury	15¼	24.5	Bigbury	15¼	24.5	Bigbury	15¼	24.5
3 Salcombe*	12½	20	Salcombe*	12½	20	East Prawle*	18½	29.75
4 East Prawle*	7	11.25	East Prawle*	7	11.25	Stoke Flm'g	13¼	21.25
5 Slapton*	8¾	14	Stoke Fleming	13¼	21.25	Brixham	15¼	24.5
6 Stoke Fleming	4½	7.25	Brixham	15¼	24.5	Shaldon*	16½	26.5
7 Brixham	15¼	24.5	Goodrington*	4½	7.5	Budleigh Sn*	13½	21.75
8 Goodrington*	4½	7.5	Shaldon*	12½	20	Seaton*	17¼	27.75
9 Shaldon*	12½	20	Exmouth*	8	13	Seatown	14¼	23
10 Exmouth*	8	13	Budleigh Sn*	5½	9	East Fleet	19¼	31
11 Budleigh Sn*	5½	9	Beer	16	25.5	Portland Bill 20		25.75
12 Ladram Bay∆	7	11.25	Charmouth	11½	18.5	Durdle Door 12		25.75
13 Beer	9	14.5	West Bay§	7	11.25	Kimmeridge§§	7¼	11.75
14 Charmouth	11½	18.5	East Fleet	16½	26	Worth Matrvs	5½	8.75
15 West Bay§	7	11.25	Portland Bill	10¼	16.5	S Haven Pt†	13½	21.5
16 West Fleet*	14	22.5	Osmington M#	15½	31.5			
17 Portland Bill	12½	20	Durdle Door	6¼	10	**Notes**: The Relaxed and		
18 Fortuneswell#∞	5¾	9.2	Kimmeridge§§	7¼	11.75	Medium itineraries are		
19 Osmington M	9¾	15.75	Worth Matrvs	5½	8.75	similar in places because		
20 Durdle Door	6¼	10	S Haven Point†	13½	21.5	there are no other options.		
21 Kimmeridge*§§	7¼	11.75						
22 Worth Matrvs	5½	8.75				† No campsite or other accommodation at South Haven		
23 S Haven Point†13½		21.5				Pt. Cross to Sandbanks for bus to Poole/B'mouth (p309).		

± Pilgrims Rest campsite at Wembury has closed; either head to Brixton, if walking around the Yealm, or take a B&B for this night .... or hope the campsite has reopened.

∆ Ladram Bay There may be a minimum 2-/3-night stay requirement.

After Isle of Portland circuit   ∞ = B&B only option

* On this chart the distance from the path to the campsite is **not** included in the mile counts. The campsites that are a quarter of a mile or more off the path are marked with an asterisk; consult the route guide for the actual distances. Remember to factor these in when calculating the distance you will walk for any one stage.

§ Campsite only open in July & Aug   §§ Distance via Lulworth Ranges

VILLAGE & TOWN FACILITIES & DISTANCES
Poole Harbour to Plymouth

PLACE* & DISTANCE* APPROX MILES / KM	BANK ATM	POST OFFICE	INFO	EATING PLACE	FOOD SHOP	CAMP-SITE	HOSTEL BUNK	B&B HOTEL
Salcombe 5¾ / 9.25	ATM	✔	TIC	〰	✔	✔(1½ miles)		〰
Outer Hope 8 / 13	ATM£	✔		〰	✔			〰
Ch'boro/Bigbury 5 / 8	ATM£			〰	✔	✔(Bigbury)		✔
(Noss Mayo/N Ferrers +1/1.5)	ATM			〰	✔			✔
Wembury 15¼ / 24.5	ATM	✔		✔	✔			✔
Plymouth 10¾ / 17.25	✔	✔	TIC	〰	✔		H	〰

(for key and notes see previous page)

STAYING IN B&B-STYLE ACCOMMODATION

	Relaxed			Medium			Fast	
Night	**Place**	**Approx Distance** miles km	**Place**		**Approx Distance** miles km	**Place**		**Approx Distance** miles km
0	Plymouth		Plymouth			Plymouth		
1	Wembury¡	10¾ 17.25	Wembury¡		10¾ 17.25	Wembury¡	10¾	17.25
2	Bigbury	15¼ 24.5	Bigbury		15¼ 24.5	Bigbury	15¼	24.5
3	Hope Cove	5 8	Salcombe		13 21	Salcombe	13	21
4	Salcombe	8 13	Beesands		11¾ 19.25	Stoke Flem'g	18¾	30
5	Beesands	11¾ 19.25	Dartmouth		11¼ 18.25	Brixham	15¼	24.5
6	Dartmouth	11¼ 18.25	Brixham		11 17.5	Maidencombe	16	26.5
7	Brixham	11 17.75	Torquay		8½ 13.75	Exmouth	11¼	18.25
8	Torquay	8½ 13.75	Teignmouth		11¼ 18.25	Sidmouth	12½	20
9	Teignmouth	11¼ 18.25	Exmouth		8 13	Seaton	10¼	16.5
10	Exmouth	8 13	Sidmouth		12½ 20	Seatown	14¼	23
11	Budleigh Sn	5½ 9	Seaton		10¼ 16.5	Abbotsbury	12½	20
12	Sidmouth	7 11.25	Lyme Regis		7¼ 11.75	Fortuneswell	13	21
13	Beer	8¾ 14	West Bay		10 16	Weymouth#	14¾	23.75
14	Lyme Regis	8½ 13.75	Abbotsbury		9½ 15.25	Lulworth	11	17.75
15	Seatown	7¼ 11.5	Fortuneswell		13 21	Kimmeridge§§	7¼	11.75
16	Abbotsbury	12½ 20	Weymouth#		14¾ 23.75	Swanage	13½	21.75
17	Fortuneswell	13 21	Lulworth Cove		11 17.75	S Haven Pt†	7½	12
18	Portland Bill	4 6.5	Kimmeridge§§		7¼ 11.75			
19	Weymouth	8 13	Swanage		13½ 21.75			
20	Lulworth	11 17.75	S Haven Pt†		7½ 12			
21	Kimmeridge§§	7¼ 11.75						
22	Swanage	13½ 21.75						
23	S Haven Point†	7½ 12						

\# After Isle of Portland circuit

§§ Distance via Lulworth Ranges

¡There is only one B&B in Wembury but another option in Noss Mayo a mile away

† There is no B&B accommodation at South Haven Point. From there cross to Sandbanks for a bus to Poole or Bournemouth (p309).

PLANNING YOUR WALK

THE BEST DAY AND WEEKEND WALKS

We think that this leg of the South-West Coast Path is the most varied of the three and thus deserves to be walked in its entirety. But, if you don't have the time for that, the following will allow you to savour at least some of the joys of this walk.

The routes below are designed to link up with public transport (see pp52-5) at both their start and finish; the only places where there are no services are West Bexington and Kimmeridge. (Bigbury-on-Sea, too, has one bus per week only, on a Friday.) The lack of services to Kimmeridge is particularly annoying as it sits at the end of possibly the most spectacular stage, over the Lulworth Ranges. But if you have a weekend free you can take one path through the ranges on one day – then walk back to Lulworth Cove on the alternative (inland) trail the next.

Note that services are often seasonal and not always daily so check in advance before you plan any of these walks.

Day walks

● **Bigbury-on-Sea to Salcombe** **13 miles/21km (see pp114-23)**
One of the remotest sections on the path, but just divine, beginning at pretty Bigbury and culminating in a saunter round Bolt Tail and Bolt Head, with Hope Cove a lovely place for lunch.

● **Brixham to Torquay** **8½ miles/13.6km (see pp155-61)**
For those who fancy an easy, largely horizontal day strolling from one seaside resort to the next, with a camera in one hand and an ice-cream in the other, this is the heart of the English Riviera.

● **Exmouth to Sidmouth** **12½ miles/20km (see pp195-204)**
Not the easiest of walks, but one that takes in some spectacular scenery, refreshments at Budleigh Salterton – and the gateway to a World Heritage Coast.

● **Sidmouth to Seaton** **10¼ miles/16.5km (see pp208-18)**
A tough trek but the rewards are ample, with the settlements of Branscombe Mouth and Beer lovely places to recover after some stiff strolling on undulating, natural terrain.

● **Seaton to Lyme Regis** **7 miles/11.5km (see pp219-24)**
One of the best – if not the best – walk on the path, taking in the sublime natural beauty of the phenomenon known as the Undercliffs.

● **Lyme Regis to Seatown (& Chideock)** **7¼ miles/11.75km (see pp230-5)**
A short (3hr) and relatively easy walk through some lovely coastal scenery culminating in a conquest of the south coast's highest point, Golden Cap.

● **Portland Circuit** **9¾ miles/15.75km (see pp262-9)**
One of the oddest walks on the path, beginning and ending at Fortuneswell and taking in prisons, housing estates and boulder fields as well as some lovely walking on this idiosyncratic isle.

● **Weymouth to Lulworth Cove** **11 miles/17.75km (see pp275-85)**
A contender for the most photogenic walk in the book with a straightforward stroll to Osmington Mills followed by the tough chalk rollercoaster leading to delightful Durdle Door and lovely Lulworth.

PLANNING YOUR WALK

● **Lulworth Cove to Kimmeridge Bay   7¼ miles/11.75km (see pp285-94)**
Cliff-top strolling doesn't get more awe-inspiring than this stiff hike through the ranges; just make sure you go when they're open (usually weekends only). Transport from Kimmeridge Bay is limited but the walk can be combined with the first of the alternative routes around the ranges (13½ miles/21.75km) for one very long but immensely satisfying circular walk.

Weekend walks
● **Salcombe to Dartmouth   23 miles/37km (see pp125-45)**
One of the best couple of days on the South Devon coastline, very diverse with some fairly strenuous climbing in places, lots of easy flat walking too – and plenty of places for refreshments on the way.
● **Sidmouth to Lyme Regis   17½ miles/28.2km (see pp208-24)**
Dreamy landscapes, pretty beaches, remote combes, lovely villages and the delightful Undercliffs to finish. This reasonably taxing but short walk is packed with interest.
● **Lyme Regis to Abbotsbury   19½ miles/31.4km (see pp229-46 & pp250-5)**
Once past Charmouth this difficult-in-places stroll takes in some delicious Dorset countryside, with Golden Cap and Chesil Beach just two of the many highlights on the way. Abbotsbury is the perfect end to any walk, too.
● **South Dorset Ridgeway (West Bexington to Osmington)**
17 miles/27.4km (see pp247-50)
For those who are fed up with coastal walking but love burial barrows, hillforts, stone circles and other prehistoric constructions. A lovely, lovely walk.
● **Lulworth Cove to Swanage   20¾ miles/33.4km (see pp285-301)**
Arguably the best weekend walk on the path, though only if the ranges are open (which they usually are at weekends). Spectacular, wild, remote, delightful hiking through the Isle of Purbeck, bookended by two lovely settlements. Your calf muscles may curse that you undertook such a testing trek – but your eyes, and your soul, will be forever grateful.

PLANNING YOUR WALK

❑ **CROSSING RIVERS**

As you may expect from a coastal walk, the path from Plymouth to South Haven Point (Poole Harbour), particularly Plymouth to Exmouth, is interrupted fairly frequently by rivers that bisect the path on their way down to the sea. The coast path uses ferries to cross these waterways which actually provide a welcome relief (and a sit-down!) from all your exertions. In summer, getting a ferry is generally not a problem (though some don't operate daily and some only operate limited hours); but walk outside the high season and it's a different story: in places, particularly at the beginning of the walk, the ferries do not run all year. In these instances, trekkers must either resort to (often infrequent) public transport, or take a lengthy diversion inland to a point where the river can be crossed, then return to the coastline to pick up the path again.

In this book we describe these alternative walking routes at the appropriate places in the guide – as well as looking at the public transport options. Remember to add extra days to your trek should you need to take any of these alternative routes.

SIDE TRIPS

The SWCP isn't the only walking trail to meander through Devon and Dorset.
Indeed, at times the coast path is bisected by other trails or even shares its route
with other paths.

A glance at an OS map will give you an idea of the many paths in the region
but below is a brief description of the main ones you may encounter.

● **The Two Moors Way** Known as **Devon's Coast to Coast**, previously this
hike was formed of two separate trails – the **Erme-Plym Trail** that began in
Wembury on the South Devon coast and travelled as far north as Ivybridge
(15 miles in all) where The Two Moors Way began. However, they now both
seem to have been combined under the banner of Two Moors Way (⌨ twom-
oors way.org). From Ivybridge, climbing onto Dartmoor can be strenuous.
The trail then heads north, traversing the length of Dartmoor to Drewsteignton
before passing through Morchard Bishop and Witheridge, eventually entering
Exmoor from the south before culminating in Lynmouth – near the start of the
SWCP, of course. Splendid scenery and real solitude are just two of the joys
of this trip.

❏ THE SOUTH-WEST COAST PATH PASSPORT

In line with a couple of other national trails, the South-West Coast Path has introduced a 'passport; to allow you to record your progress along the trail. The idea,
inspired by Spain's Camino de Santiago pilgrim trail, is a simple one.

The first thing to do is visit the South-West Coast Path Organisation's website
(⌨ www.southwestcoastpath.org.uk) where, for the princely sum of £6.50, you can
buy your own Coast Path passport. In it, you'll find the names of over 100 places,
from tourist offices to pubs to local attractions, that you'll find all the way along the
South-West Coast Path. At each of these places you'll be able to stamp your passport
to show that you have visited. Thus, as you do more and more of the trail, so your
passport will fill with stamps – and thus you'll have some record of how much of the
trail you've completed – and how much you still have left to do!

The National Trail along Hadrian's Wall was the first to introduce the system in
the UK – though to give you an idea of the difference in magnitude between the two
paths, where Hadrian's Wall merely has six stamping points, the South-West Coast
Path has more than 100!

One potential problem with the system is that it is almost impossible to get all
100, due to the fact that some of the stamping points are not open year-round and with
some of them you'll probably end up arriving after they've closed for the day.

Nevertheless, it's an interesting way to record your progress. The stamps themselves, too, are interesting. There are seven designs, each reflecting the heritage, history or nature of the area it represents; for example, Somerset and North Devon has
the picture of a pony, while the West Cornwall stamp features a tin mine.

The scheme has been introduced in time for the path's 50th anniversary in 2023.
As well as raising funds for the path, it is hoped the scheme will also encourage people to explore the path and the places it passes through in greater detail, as well as
encourage interaction between walkers and locals.

● **Avon Estuary Walk** A pretty 7½- to 8½-mile hike (Bigbury-on-Sea to Bantham) which circumvents the need to catch a ferry across the River Avon (see pp116-17).

● **John Musgrave Heritage Trail** A 35-mile inland trail that bypasses Torbay by linking Brixham with Maidencombe, crossing the River Dart twice and taking in Totnes and plenty of splendid Devonshire countryside as it does so. Established in 2005 in memory of John Musgrave, a local walking enthusiast and former chair of the South Devon Group of Ramblers.

● **Templer Way** An 18-mile path that links Haytor on Dartmoor with the coast at Teignmouth, following the journey taken by the granite quarried there during the 19th century on its way to being exported; Templer was the family name of those responsible for the canals and tramways that formed the granite's route.

● **Exe Estuary Trail** This cycle path and walkway around the River Exe (Dawlish to Exmouth; see pp181-92) is useful when the ferry between Starcross and Exmouth is not operational – though it's a decent-enough stroll in its own right too.

● **Monarch's Way** (🖥 monarchsway.50megs.com) A whopping 625-mile route which follows in the footsteps of King Charles II who, having been defeated at the Battle of Worcester in 1651, was being pursued by Cromwell's Parliamentarians. The Way passes through the Cotswolds and the Mendips before arriving on the south coast at Charmouth. It then follows the coast path around Bridport before going inland and finally traversing the South Downs to Shoreham – from where the monarch escaped to France.

● **Macmillan Way** (🖥 macmillanway.org) This 290-mile path links England's east coast and Boston in Lincolnshire with Chesil Beach and Abbotsbury in Dorset; the path also has tributaries leading off the main route to Banbury, Bath and Barnstaple. Set up in aid of Macmillan Cancer Support, so far over £350,000 has been raised from walkers' sponsorship!

● **The Jubilee Trail** Launched in 1995, this 90-mile path connects the Somerset and Hampshire borders and in doing so slices through Dorset, purposefully following, wherever possible, what were previously little-known pathways. The jubilee of the title is the 60th anniversary of the founding of the Ramblers' Association, now called Ramblers (see box p48).

● **The Hardy Way** This 212-mile trail passes through the Dorset countryside that inspired Thomas Hardy's semi-fictional Wessex, the backdrop to his novels. It starts at his birthplace, Higher Bockhampton, and ends at Stingford Church where his heart is buried; both are near Dorchester.

● **The Purbeck Way** (🖥 www.dorsetcouncil.gov.uk/sport-leisure/walking/walking-in-purbeck/the-purbeck-way) A Y-shaped, 28-mile pathway, this time passing through the stunning and varied scenery of the Isle of Purbeck, starting at Wareham Quay and ending either at Ballard Down (east of Swanage), or Chapman's Pool (near St Aldhelm's Head).

TAKING DOGS ALONG THE PATH

The South-West Coast Path is a dog-friendly path but taking a dog does require some planning: it is a long walk and some places have restrictions on whether dogs can go on a beach or not, and regulations that a dog must be on a lead and owners must clean up after their dog.

See pp311-13 for detailed information on long-distance walking with a dog and p29 for self-guided holidays with a dog. Also worth looking at are 🖳 www .visitdevon.co.uk/explore/dog-friendly and 🖳 dorsetdogs.org.uk.

What to take

'When you have worn out your shoes, the strength of the shoe leather has passed into the fiber of your body. I measure your health by the number of shoes and hats and clothes you have worn out.'   **Ralph Waldo Emerson**

Deciding how much to take can be difficult. Experienced walkers know that you should take only the bare essentials but at the same time you should ensure you have all the equipment necessary to make the trip safe and comfortable.

KEEP YOUR LUGGAGE LIGHT

Veteran backpackers know that there is some sort of complicated formula governing the success of a trek, in which the enjoyment of the walk is inversely proportional to the amount carried.

Carrying a heavy rucksack slows you down, tires you out and gives you aches and pains in parts of your body that you didn't even know existed. It is imperative, therefore, that you take a good deal of time packing and that you are ruthless when you do; if it's not essential, don't take it.

HOW TO CARRY IT

If you are using the baggage-transfer service, you must check what their regulations are regarding the weight and size of the luggage you wish them to carry.

Even if you are using this service, you will still need to carry a small **daypack**, filled with those items that you will need during the day: water bottle or pouch, this book, sun-screen, sun hat, wet-weather gear, some food, camera, money and so on.

If you have decided to forego the baggage-transfer service you will have to consider your **rucksack** even more carefully. Ultimately its size will depend on where you are planning to stay and how you are planning to eat. If you are camping and cooking for yourself you will probably need a 65- to 75-litre rucksack, which should be large enough to carry a small tent, sleeping bag, cooking equipment and food. Those not carrying their home on their back should find a 40- to 60-litre rucksack sufficient.

When choosing a rucksack, make sure it has a stiffened back and can be adjusted to fit your back comfortably. Don't just try the rucksack out in the shop: take it home, fill it with things and then try it out around the house and take it out for a short walk. Only then can you be certain that it fits. Make sure the hip belt and chest strap (if there is one) are fastened tightly as this helps distribute the weight more comfortably with most of it being carried on your hips. Carry a small daypack inside the rucksack as this will be useful to carry things in when leaving the main pack at the hostel or B&B.

Most rucksacks these days have a **waterproof rucksack cover** 'built in' to the sack, but they tend to be thin and unable to cope with sustained rain or big downpours so consider buying an extra separate one too. Lining your bag with a **bin liner** is another sensible, cut-price idea. It's also a good idea to keep everything wrapped in plastic bags and put these in a bin-bag inside the rucksack. That way, even if it does pour with rain, everything should remain dry.

FOOTWEAR

Boots
Many hikers swear that only a decent pair of strong, durable trekking boots are good enough to survive the rigours of trails such as the South-West Coast Path. In fact, it's perfectly feasible (and often a lot more comfortable, particularly in summer) to complete the walk in a pair of trainers, as long as they have a good grip. They won't, of course, be waterproof, but they tend to dry quickly (far quicker than other, heavier footwear), so you should always be able to start your walk each morning with dry shoes. If you do go down the hiking boot route, make sure your boots are waterproof: these days most people opt for a synthetic waterproof lining (Gore-Tex or similar), though a good-quality leather boot with dubbin should prove just as reliable in keeping your feet dry.

Whatever footwear you choose, the most important thing to remember is to make sure that your shoes/boots are properly worn in before you start your trip. Never start a multi-day hike like this in brand-new shoes!

Hiking-boot wearers will probably want an extra pair of shoes or trainers to wear off the trail. This is not essential but if you are using the baggage-transfer service and you've got room in your luggage, why not?

Flipflops are handy to bring along for wearing around campsites or for using in shared shower blocks.

Socks
If you haven't got a pair of the modern hi-tech walking socks, the old system of wearing a thin liner sock under a thicker wool sock is just as good. Bring a few pairs of each.

CLOTHES

In a country notorious for its unpredictable climate it is imperative that you pack enough clothes to cover every extreme of weather, from burning hot to bloomin' freezing. Modern hi-tech outdoor clothes come with a range of fancy names and brands but they all still follow the basic two- or three-layer principle, with an inner base layer to transport sweat away from your skin, a mid-layer for warmth and an outer layer to protect you from the wind and rain.

A thin lightweight **thermal top** of a synthetic material is ideal as the base layer as it draws moisture (ie sweat) away from your body. Cool in hot weather and warm when worn under other clothes in the cold, pack at least one thermal top. Over the top in cold weather a mid-weight **polyester fleece** should suffice. Fleeces are light, more water-resistant than the alternatives (such as a woolly jumper), remain warm even when wet and pack down small in rucksacks; they are thus ideal trekking gear.

Over the top of all this a **waterproof jacket** is essential. 'Breathable' jackets cost a small fortune but they do prevent the build-up of condensation.

Leg wear

Many trekkers find trekking **trousers** an unnecessary investment; any light, quick-drying trouser should suffice. Jeans are heavy and dry slowly and are thus not recommended. A pair of waterproof trousers *is* more than useful, however, while on really hot sunny days you'll be glad you brought your **shorts**. Thermal **long johns** take up little room in the rucksack and could be vital if the weather starts to close in. **Gaiters** are not essential but, again, those who bring them are always glad they did, for they provide extra protection when walking through muddy ground and when the vegetation around the trail is dripping wet after bad weather or morning dew.

Underwear

Three or four changes of underwear is likely to be sufficient. Because backpacks can cause bra straps to dig painfully into the skin, women may find a **sports bra** more comfortable.

Other clothes

You might want to consider a woolly **hat** and **gloves** – you'd be surprised how cold it can get up on the cliffs even in summer – and don't forget a sun hat! **Swimwear** is also worth bringing if you fancy taking advantage of some of the wonderful beaches, and quirky outdoor lidos, en route.

TOILETRIES

Once again, take the minimum. **Soap**, **towel**, **toothbrush** and **toothpaste** are pretty much essential (although those staying in B&Bs will find that most provide soap and towels anyway). Some **toilet paper** could also prove vital on the trail, particularly if using public toilets (which occasionally run out).

Other items: **razor**; **deodorant**; **tampons/sanitary towels** and a high factor **sun-screen** (see p83) should cover just about everything.

❏ **MOBILE PHONE RECEPTION AND INTERNET CONNECTIONS**
Mobile phone reception and 3G/4G coverage is much better than on the Cornwall section of the SWCP, but there are still some areas in South Devon and Dorset where you won't get any signal at all, so make sure that you don't need to rely solely on your phone or mobile device.

Most B&Bs, cafés and pubs have free wi-fi access for customers, as do some larger campsites (though often with a daily charge). You can also get free wi-fi at all public libraries but they sometimes charge for internet use on their computer terminals.

FIRST-AID KIT

A small first-aid kit could prove useful for those emergencies that occur along the trail. This kit should include **aspirin** or **paracetamol**; **plasters** for minor cuts; Compeed, Second Skin or some other **treatment for blisters**; a **bandage** or elasticated joint support for supporting a sprained ankle or a weak knee; **antiseptic wipes**; **antiseptic cream**; **safety pins**; **tweezers** and **scissors**. One reader also recommended bringing a **tick remover**, as he picked up several along the way. We guess he was just unlucky as we've never had a problem, but a remover is not a bad idea, and if you've got a dog it's pretty much essential (for what to pack if you're walking with your dog, please see pp311-13).

GENERAL ITEMS

Everybody should have a **water bottle or pouch**, some **emergency food**, **sunglasses**, a **map** (though this book has that covered), a **torch** (particularly if walking during shorter winter days, or if camping), a **whistle** for emergencies (see p81 for details of the international distress signal), **spare batteries and/or chargers** for all your devices, a **penknife** and an ordinary **wristwatch** with an alarm (if that phone battery might not always be charged). A **walking pole** or **sticks** will take the strain off your knees.

It is a good idea to carry a **tide table** with you; they can be purchased for about £1.30 from newsagents or TICs in coastal areas. Tide times are also available online at 🖥 www.tidetimes.org.uk. If you know how to use it properly, you may find a **compass** handy, at least for when you're heading off the trail.

Some people like to bring a book, for days off or on train and bus journeys, as well as a **camera**, a pair of, **binoculars** and a **radio** or **iPod/MP3 player**

Of course, a **smartphone** and its various apps can play the role of many of the above, including torch, book, camera, compass, watch, radio, iPod and tide table. Just remember to bring a power pack to keep it charged.

CAMPING GEAR

Campers will find a **sleeping bag** essential. A two- to three-season bag should suffice for summer. In addition, they will also need a decent bivvy bag or **tent**, a **sleeping mat**, a **towel** (microfleece travel towels are the best), fuel and **stove**, and a camping **cookware** set.

MONEY

Both banks and ATMs (cash machines) are fairly common along the Dorset & South Devon Coast Path. Not everybody accepts **debit** or **credit cards** as payment – though most hotels, restaurants, cafés and pubs now do and also many B&Bs/guesthouses. But you should still carry a fair amount of **cash** with you, just to be on the safe side. Traditionalists may still want to carry a **cheque book** from a British bank, and admittedly they are useful in those places where debit/credit cards are not accepted. But few people use cheques these days.

Crime on the trail is thankfully rare but it's always a good idea to carry your money safely in a **moneybelt**.

DOCUMENTS

National Trust and English Heritage memberships as well as student cards and YHA hostel cards could all save you money on the trail. Some sort of ID, such as a driving licence, could also prove useful. You'll probably need to show photographic ID when you check into all YHA hostels and most independent hostels.

MAPS

It would be perfectly possible to walk long stretches of the coastal path unaided by map or compass. Just keep the sea to your right (or left, depending on which way you're heading) and you can't go too far off track. The hand-drawn maps in this book, though, which cover the trail at a scale of 1:20,000, will hopefully provide sufficient aid in areas where navigation is slightly more problematic.

Having extra maps with you will paint a more fulfilling picture of your surroundings and will allow you to plan more effectively for any accommodation or other facilities that lie off the trail. **Ordnance Survey** (🖥 shop.ordnancesurvey.co.uk) produce their maps to two scales: the 1:25,000 Explorer series in orange and the 1:50,000 Landranger in pink (which is less useful for trekking purposes). Alongside the paper versions they also produce an 'Active' edition of both, which is 'weatherproof' (covered in a lightweight protective plastic coating). Those needed for the stretch of the SWCP covered by this book are Explorer: Outdoor Leisure OL20 *South Devon*; OL44 *Torquay & Dawlish*; OL115 *Exmouth & Sidmouth*; OL116 *Lyme Regis & Bridport*; and OL15 *Purbeck & South Dorset*.

If you don't feel that such precise cartography is needed the Landranger may be a more suitable choice; of the fourteen to cover the SWCP you will need the following six: 201 *Plymouth & Launceston*; 202 *Torbay & South Dartmoor*; 192 *Exeter & Sidmouth*; 193 *Taunton & Lyme Regis*; 194 *Dorchester & Weymouth*; and 195 *Bournemouth & Purbeck*.

The **AZ Adventure Series** (🖥 collins.co.uk/pages/a-z/) has five booklets with OS maps, each to a scale of 1:25,000, for the whole of the SWCP; the main difference from standard OS maps is that the booklets have an index. The South Devon map covers Plymouth to Lyme Regis and the Dorset one covers Lyme Regis to South Haven Point.

❏ DIGITAL MAPPING

There are numerous software packages now available that provide Ordnance Survey (OS) maps for a PC, smartphone, tablet or GPS. Maps are downloaded into an app from where you can view, print and create routes on them.

Memory Map (🖥 memory-map.co.uk) currently sell OS Explorer 1:25,000 and Landranger 1:50,000 mapping covering the whole of Britain with prices from £19.99 for a one year subscription. **Anquet** (🖥 anquet.com) has the full range of OS 1:25,000 maps covering all of the UK from £28 per year annual subscription.

Or you can go to the original source itself: for a subscription of £4.99 for one month or £28.99 for a year (on their current offer) **Ordnance Survey** (🖥 ordnance survey.co.uk) allows you to download and use their UK maps (1:25,000 scale) on a mobile or tablet without a data connection for a specific period.

Maps.me is free and you can download any of its digital mapping to use offline. You can install the Trailblazer waypoints for this walk on its mapping but you'll need to convert the .gpx format file to .kml format before loading it into maps.me. Use an online website such as 🖥 gpx2kml.com to do this then email the kml file to your phone and open it in maps.me.

Harvey (🖥 harveymaps.co.uk) currently use the US Avenza maps app for their SWCP 3 *Plymouth to Poole Harbour* map (1:40,000 scale, $14.99).

It is important to ensure any digital mapping software on your smartphone uses pre-downloaded maps, stored on your device, and doesn't need to download them on-the-fly, as this may be expensive and will be impossible without a signal. Remember that battery life will be significantly reduced, compared to normal usage, when you are using the built-in GPS and running the screen for long periods.

Harvey Maps (🖥 harveymaps.co.uk) produce a series of maps that cover all the designated National Trails to a scale of 1:40,000. For full coverage of the SWCP you will need three maps, but if you are intending to walk the section covered by this book the *Plymouth to Poole Harbour* map is sufficient. This, of course, will save on weight and cost compared to buying the four OS maps, though the OS has more detail and will show you what is further inland.

While it may be extravagant to buy all the OS maps, public libraries in Britain have some OS maps and members can, of course, borrow these for free.

RECOMMENDED READING

Below is a by no means exhaustive but hopefully helpful introduction to some of the literature relating to the coast path.

Guidebooks

It doesn't include any maps, but if you're willing to carry a separate book the most detailed guide to the accommodation, tide tables and other useful information on the entire SWCP is the South-West Coast Path Association's companion to the path, called *The Complete Guide To The South-West Coast Path*, which at the time of research cost £18 (free to members; see box p48). Alongside this annual guide they also produce and sell pamphlets for each section (£2) which can be found in tourist information centres en route or ordered online (🖥 south westcoastpath.org.uk).

Flora, fauna and geology

For identifying obscure plants and peculiar-looking beasties as you walk, Collins and New Holland publish a pocket-sized range to Britain's natural riches. Both series contain a wealth of information.

The **Collins Gem** series are tough little books; current titles include guides to *Trees*, *Birds*, *Mushrooms*, *Wild Flowers*, *Wild Animals*, *Insects* and *Butterflies*. In addition, for any budding crustacean connoisseur there is a *Seashore* book; there is also a handbook to the *Stars*, which could be of particular interest for those who are considering sleeping under them. Also in the Collins series, there's an adapted version of Richard Mabey's classic bestseller *Food for Free* – great for anyone intent on getting back to nature, saving the pennies, or just with an interest in what's edible outside of a supermarket. You could also consult *Wild Food: Foraging for Food in the Wild*, written by Jane Eastoe and published by the National Trust. **New Holland's Concise** range covers many of the same topics as the Gem series, comes in a waterproof plastic jacket and also includes useful quick reference foldout charts.

There are also several field guide **apps**; one to consider for identifying birds is: 🖥 merlin.allaboutbirds.org.

For books that are more **specific to the walk**, *Wildlife of the Jurassic Coast* (Coastal Publishing) by Bryan Edwards is available in local tourist information offices, while *Where to Watch Wildlife in Devon* (Bossiney Books) by Robert Hesketh is one of the several books dealing with the nature in that county.

If you need help grappling with the complex **geology** (see pp58-63) you'll encounter, *The Official Guide to the Jurassic Coast: Dorset and East Devon's World Heritage Coast (Walk Through Time Guide)* by Denys Brunsden is available both locally and online, while *Dorset and East Devon: Landscape and Geology* (The Crowood Press) by Malcolm Hart is another reasonable take on the subject. You'll probably also be interested in *Discover Dorset Fossils* (The Dovecote Press) by Richard Edmonds, or the tiny but useful paperback *Finding Fossils in Lyme Bay* by Robert Coram.

A Guide to Fossil Collecting in England and Wales, by Craig Chapman and Steve Snowball, is an excellent beginner's guide and can be bought from the UK Fossils website (🖥 ukfossils.co.uk).

Autobiography

The Salt Path by Raynor Winn is the true story of a couple's attempt to walk the entire SWCP after they had lost their family home over a legal dispute. With the husband, Moth, also wrestling with a terminal diagnosis, theirs is an extraordinary tale as they attempt, against all the odds, homeless and bankrupt, to conquer Britain's longest national trail. If you feel that life needs more affirming, this is the book to take with you.

With the Falklands War imminent Mark Wallington set off to walk the SWCP in an attempt to impress a girl that he had met at a party. Accompanied by the more-loathed-than-loved Boogie the dog, man and beast survive all that the path can throw at them on a diet of tinned soup and Kennomeat. *Travels with Boogie: 500 Mile Walkies* is Wallington's humorous account of his own time spent on the trail. If you have walked and camped, or have ever walked a long distance with a dog, many of the author's anecdotes will ring true – a light-hearted and thoroughly enjoyable read. Another dog goes walking in *Two feet, four paws*, Spud Talbot-Ponsonby's tale of her time circumnavigating Britain.

The Tarka Trail is a local path named after Henry Williamson's much-loved *Tarka the Otter*, just one of many books in which Williamson's extraordinary ability to evoke the Devonshire countryside gilds every page.

History

One thousand years of farming, quarrying and the Home Guard are crammed into Felicity Goodall's *Lost Devon* (Birlinn Ltd), which is good for those with an interest in the lost heritage of the county.

Derrick Warren's *Curious Devon* (The History Press) examines the quirkier side of the county, as does his *Curious Dorset*, while for something a little darker there's John Van Der Kiste's *Grim Almanac of Devon* (The History Press) that recounts 366 of the county's more macabre episodes. A more general tome on Dorset is Cecil North Cullingford's *A History of Dorset*.

One of the most entertaining reads on one aspect of the history of this coastline is *The Dinosaur Hunters: A True Story of Scientific Rivalry and the Discovery of the Prehistoric World* (Fourth Estate) by Deborah Cadbury, detailing the work of Mary Anning, Gideon Mantell et al and their rivalry in the 19th century.

Fiction

The two counties have been blessed with bestselling authors. Thomas Hardy began the trend, his novels and short stories nearly always set in his fictional Wessex – which is essentially Dorset and the surrounding counties but with the names changed. Hardy's hometown of Dorchester, for example, became 'Casterbridge' in his novels, while Weymouth is 'Budmouth' in his novel *Far from the Madding Crowd*, and is also Eustacia Vye's hometown in *The Return of the Native*. Portland, by the way, is the 'Isle of Slingers'.

Hardy's book sales, however, are outstripped by those of another home-grown talent, Agatha Christie. Once again her homeland features prominently in her books; indeed, the Imperial Hotel at her home town of Torquay appears in three of her novels, *Peril at End House*, *The Body in the Library* and *Sleeping Murder*, while Burgh Island is the setting for two of her thrillers, *And Then There Were None* and *Evil Under the Sun*.

Thomas Hardy's practice of changing local place-names (while otherwise remaining true to the local geography) was emulated by his fellow Victorian, J Meade Falkner, in his most famous work, *Moonfleet* (Vintage). Written at the end of the 19th century, this children's story is set in a small Dorset village (based on East Fleet behind Chesil Beach) and involves smuggling, kidnapping – and an awful lot of intrigue. Falkner stayed in Abbotsbury while he wrote the novel.

Set in the same location, though this time in 1962, before the sexual revolution really took off, *On Chesil Beach* (Vintage) is by one of Britain's most celebrated contemporary novelists, Ian McEwan, and concerns the wedding night of two twenty-somethings, their fears and dreams.

❑ SOURCES OF FURTHER INFORMATION

Online information

● 🖳 **www.southwestcoastpath.org.uk** The site for the **South-West Coast Path Association (SWCPA)**, a registered charity that exists to support users of the path. This is the first place to come for info on the path, with details about river crossings and army ranges (or Military Training Areas as they call them), as well as lots of information on accommodation, itineraries and distance and timing calculators. The Association is also very active politically, pressurising government bodies to ensure that the path is well maintained along its length. Membership is available at £27.50/35.50 for single/joint membership and includes a copy of their guidebook and twice-yearly magazine as well as monthly e-newsletters.

● 🖳 **www.nationaltrail.co.uk/en_GB/trails/south-west-coast-path** The official and most useful website to Britain's longest national trail. Good for background information, it also has the latest news on the path. While it covers a lot of the same ground as the website above, we get the feeling that this site struggles to keep all their information up to date and their interactive maps often don't work as well as they could.

● 🖳 **jurassiccoast.org** Website dedicated to Britain's first natural World Heritage Site with good explanations on the geology of the region and just why it is of such global importance.

● See also p57 for details of the websites for the various Areas of Outstanding Natural Beauty on this section of the path. These are good for background information on the geology, flora and fauna of the region.

Tourist information centres (TICs) and points (TIPs)

As one of the busiest tourist areas of the country, the South-West is reasonably well served by **tourist information centres**: Plymouth (see p90); Salcombe (see p123); Dartmouth (see p142); Torquay (see p162); Shaldon (see p172); Exmouth (see p192); Budleigh Salterton (see p200); Sidmouth (see p204); Seaton (see p216); Weymouth (see p270); and Swanage (see p300).

There are also some **tourist information points** where it is possible to pick up leaflets about local attractions. TIPs are often at caravan parks and may also be in libraries, where there isn't a tourist information centre. Some attractions have a **visitor centre** with information about that particular place.

For general information see: 🖳 www.visitdevon.co.uk and/or 🖳 www.visitdorset.com.

Organisations for walkers

● **Backpackers' Club** (🖳 backpackersclub.co.uk) A club aimed at people who are involved or interested in lightweight camping through walking, cycling, skiing and canoeing. Members receive a quarterly magazine, access to a comprehensive information service (including a library) as well as long-distance path and farm-pitch directories. Membership costs £20 per year, family £30.

● **The Long Distance Walkers' Association** (🖳 ldwa.org.uk) An association of people with the common interest of long-distance walking. Membership includes a journal, *Strider*, three times per year giving details of challenge events and local group walks as well as articles on the subject. Individual membership costs £18 a year (£15/26 without/with Strider for non-UK residents) whilst family membership is £25.50 a year; a £3 discount is offered for those who pay by direct debit.

● **Ramblers** (formerly Ramblers' Association; 🖳 www.ramblers.org.uk) Looks after the interests of walkers throughout Britain. They publish a large amount of useful information including their quarterly *Walk* magazine, also available in pdf and audio format.

Further west, Lyme Regis is the home of Sarah Woodruff, better known as *The French Lieutenant's Woman* (Vintage Classics) in the novel by John Fowles. She spends her days on The Cobb, staring out to sea, in disgrace because of her affair with the Frenchman Varguennes, who, unbeknown to her until later, was already married; it is while standing there that she is spied by Charles Smithson and his fiancée, Ernestina Freeman, and a close relationship between Charles and Sarah ensues. The novel is perhaps most remarkable in that the author offers three different endings. It was made into a film in 1981 starring Jeremy Irons and Meryl Streep.

For something much lighter, PG Wodehouse's *Thank you, Jeeves* (Arrow) is the first to feature the eponymous butler-cum-hero; indeed, the story begins with Jeeves leaving Bertie Wooster's service because of the latter's incessant playing of the banjolele, finding employment instead with Bertie's old chum Lord 'Chuffy' Chuffnell. Bertie retreats to one of Chuffy's cottages in Dorset – and the usual wonderfully entertaining chaos ensues.

Getting to and from the Coast Path

All the major towns along the coast path are reasonably well served by rail and/or coach services from the rest of Britain. Travelling by train or coach is the most convenient way to get to the trail and also the best for the environment. It can also be an enjoyable experience in itself. How many of us have fond memories of relaxing to the regular rattle of the train wheels while sleepily watching the scenery pass by?

NATIONAL TRANSPORT

By train
The main Devon line (operated by GWR) runs from London Paddington through Exeter to **Plymouth**, with branch lines connecting major towns on the coast path. There are several services every day as well as a night train (the Night Riviera, Sun-Fri). Cross Country operates services from Scotland, the North-East, Manchester and the Midlands to Bournemouth, Exeter and Plymouth. To access Dorset from London, including **Poole** and **Weymouth**, South Western Railway run regularly and direct from London Waterloo. See box p51 for contact details and service summaries.

National rail enquiries (☎ 0345-748 4950, 🖳 nationalrail.co.uk) is the only number or website you really need to find out all timetable and fare information. The 'Buy now' button on the website transfers you to the relevant train operator's website where you can buy tickets online.

Rail **tickets** are generally cheaper if you book them well in advance and also if you buy online. Most discounted tickets carry some restrictions (such as travelling on a particular train) so check what they are before you purchase

❏ **GETTING TO BRITAIN**

● **By air** The best international gateway to Britain for the Dorset & South Devon Coast Path is London; its most convenient airports are Heathrow (🖳 www.heathrow .com) and Gatwick (🖳 gatwickairport.com).

Exeter Airport (🖳 exeter-airport.co.uk), Southampton (🖳 southamptonairport .com) and Bournemouth (🖳 bournemouthairport.com) are closer to the walk and have international flights, mostly from Europe.

● **From Europe by train** Eurostar (🖳 eurostar.com) operates a high-speed passenger service via the Channel Tunnel between Paris, Brussels and Lille and London. The Eurostar terminal in London is at St Pancras International with connections to the London Underground and to all other main railway stations in London. Trains to Dorset and Devon leave from Paddington station (Great Western Railway) and also from Waterloo (South Western Railway); see box opposite for details.

There are also various rail services from mainland Europe to Britain; for more information contact your national rail provider or Railteam (🖳 railteam.eu).

● **From Europe by coach** Eurolines (🖳 eurolines.com) have a wide network of long-distance bus services to London (Victoria Coach station).

● **From Europe with a car** There are **ferry services** that operate between: the major European ports and those in Britain. Look at 🖳 ferrysavers.com or 🖳 www.directfer ries.com for a full list of companies and services.

Eurotunnel (🖳 eurotunnel.com) operates 'le shuttle', a **shuttle train service** for vehicles via the Channel Tunnel between Calais and Folkestone up to four times an hour (35 mins).

them. It is best to buy tickets through the relevant companies or at any rail station. However, they can also be bought online at 🖳 thetrainline.com.

It is possible to buy a train ticket that includes bus travel at your destination: for further information visit the **Plusbus** website (🖳 www.plusbus.info).

If you think you'll want a **taxi** when you arrive consult the town guides included in this book, many of which have taxi numbers in their transport sections. Alternatively, visit 🖳 traintaxi.co.uk.

By coach
National Express (☎ 0871-781 8181, 🖳 nationalexpress.com) is the principal coach (ie long-distance bus) operator in Britain. Travel by coach is usually cheaper than by rail but does take longer. See box opposite for details of services to Devon and Dorset.

To get the cheapest fares you need to book in advance. You can purchase tickets from coach and bus station ticket offices, National Express agents (including post offices and some tourist information centres), directly from the driver (though not always, so do check with locals in advance), by telephone (not advisable as expensive), or online. An easier option is to print your ticket yourself at home or, of course, have it on your smartphone. Known as an e-ticket, you should be able to do this direct from the National Express website.

Megabus (🖳 uk.megabus.com) provides low-cost coach services to Poole and Plymouth.

By car

The route options for driving to Dorset and Devon depend largely on your starting point; the main problem is that the roads can get very crowded in the summer

---

❏ RAIL SERVICES

Note: not all stops are listed and not all trains stop at all stops listed

GWR (Great Western Railway; ☎ 0345-700 0125, 🖳 gwr.com)
- London Paddington to Penzance via Reading, Taunton, Exeter St Davids, Newton Abbot, Totnes & **Plymouth**, summer Mon-Sat 1/hr, winter Mon-Fri 1/hr Sat & Sun 7-8/day; additional services from Newton Abbot
  At Newton Abbot some train divide for **Paignton** via Torre & **Torquay**
- Exeter St David's to **Paignton** via **Dawlish**, **Teignmouth**, Newton Abbot, Torre & **Torquay**, 5/day
- Exmouth (The Riviera Line) to **Paignton** via Exeter, **Starcross**, **Dawlish Warren**, **Dawlish**, **Teignmouth**, Newton Abbot, Torre & **Torquay**, Mon-Sat 1-2/hr, Sun approx 1/hr
- Exeter St David's to **Exmouth** (The Avocet Line) via Exeter Central, **Topsham**, **Exton**, Lympstone Commando & Lympstone Village, Mon-Sat 1-2/hr, Sun 1/hr; note some stops are request only
- Barnstaple to Exeter (The Tarka Line), Mon-Sat approx 1/hr
- Penzance to **Plymouth** via Truro, St Austell, Par & Bodmin Parkway, 1-2/hr
- Gloucester/Bristol Temple Meads to **Weymouth** via Bath Spa, Frome, Castle Cary & Dorchester West, Mon-Sat 6-7/day, Sun 3-4/day

South Western Railway (☎ 0345-600 0650, 🖳 southwesternrailway.com)
- London Waterloo to **Weymouth** via Southampton, Bournemouth, Poole, Wareham, Wool & Dorchester South, Mon-Sat 1-2/hr, Sun 1/hr (not all services stop at every station)
- London Waterloo to Exeter via Salisbury, Crewkerne, Axminster & Honiton (not all services stop at every station), daily 1/hr

Cross Country Trains (☎ 0844-811 0124, 🖳 crosscountrytrains.co.uk)
- Birmingham to **Plymouth** via Bristol, Taunton, Exeter St David's, Newton Abbot & Totnes, Mon-Sat 10/day, Sun 5/day
- Birmingham to Bournemouth via Oxford, Reading, Winchester & Southampton, Mon-Fri 8/day, Sat 6/day, Sun 5/day

USEFUL NATIONAL EXPRESS SERVICES

Note: not all stops are listed
- **035** London to Poole via Bournemouth, 8/day; also to **Swanage** (1/day) and **Weymouth** (2/day)
- **101** Birmingham to **Plymouth** via Bristol, Taunton & Exeter, 3/day
- **102** Birmingham to **Plymouth** via Bristol, Exeter, **Torquay** & **Paignton**, 2/day
- **104** Birmingham to Penzance via Bristol, Exeter & **Plymouth**, 1/day
- **106** Birmingham to Penzance via Bristol, Taunton, Exeter & **Plymouth**, 1/day
- **404** London Victoria to Penzance via Heathrow Airport, Exeter, Newton Abbot, **Torquay**, **Paignton**, Totnes & **Plymouth**, 1/day
- **501** London Victoria to Totnes via Heathrow Airport, Exeter, Newton Abbot, **Torquay** & **Paignton**, 4/day
- **504** London Victoria to Penzance via Heathrow, Exeter and **Plymouth**, 5/day

PLANNING YOUR WALK

months. You can get detailed driving directions to the quiet country lanes of Dorset and Devon from the AA website (🖳 theaa.com/route-planner/index.jsp) by clicking on the route planner. Parking your car can be a problem; there are long-stay car parks in Plymouth, Bournemouth and Poole but this means you will have to go back to the car park at the end of your walk. Overall it's probably easier and cheaper and certainly better for the environment to use public transport.

LOCAL TRANSPORT

Bus services

Both Devon and Dorset have reasonable public transport networks linking most of the coastal villages. This is great news for the walker as it opens up the possibility of walking along the coast path from a fixed base. Note, however, that the stretch between Wembury and Salcombe has very limited public transport options, as does the stretch between Lulworth Cove and Swanage.

Timetables Three timetables cover **southern Devon**. If walking the whole path you will need all of them. Starting from Plymouth you will need: South Hams (pink), which covers Plymouth to Torquay; Teignbridge (blue), which covers Brixham to the Exe Estuary and Exeter; and East Devon (green), that covers Exeter and Exmouth to Lyme Regis.

Once in **Dorset** you will need the Southern Dorset Area timetable only.

In both counties you can pick the timetables up for free from bus stations, railway stations and tourist information centres. The timetables for Devon can also be either ordered online or downloaded from Devon County Council (🖳 traveldevon.info/bus/timetables). Unfortunately, the route planner facility for Dorset County Council takes you to travelling for the south-west (see below). The service numbers of the most useful buses are given in the table on pp54-5 so you can then flip straight to the page you need in the actual timetable.

Bus companies and customer helplines If the contact details in the box on pp54-5 prove unsatisfactory, traveline (🖳 traveline.info) has public transport information for the whole of the UK or, just for the south-west (🖳 traveline sw.com, or on their app).

Public transport at a glance

The public transport map (opposite) and the services tables (boxes p51 and pp54-5) are designed to make it easy for you to plan your day using public transport. Use the map to see which towns are covered by each service and then turn to the table to check that service's frequency. Take time to read the table carefully: some services run only one day a week, while others don't run at weekends. The definition of a summer service depends on the company and the route; in some cases it is from Easter to October but in others it's May/July to September – again, always check before you plan to use a summer service.

Note that bus services do change from year to year. Use this information as a rough guide and confirm details with the bus operators before travelling.

For information about tide timetables, see p80.

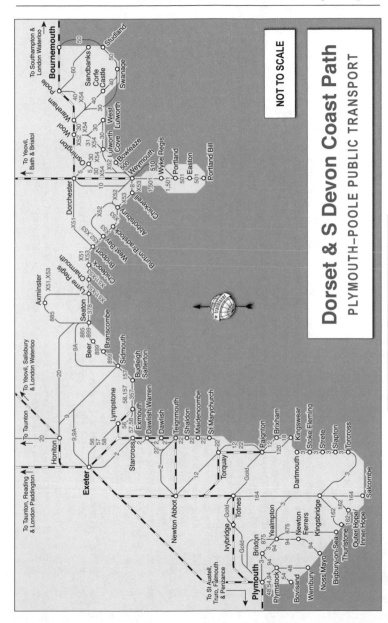

Dorset & S Devon Coast Path
PLYMOUTH–POOLE PUBLIC TRANSPORT

NOT TO SCALE

☐ BUS SERVICES

Note: not all stops are listed. Also that details about the relevant ferry services on this section of the SWCP are provided in Part 4.

Bus services

No	Operator	Route and frequency details
1	First	Weymouth to Portland via Wyke Regis, Fortuneswell, Easton & Southwell, Mon-Sat 3-4/hr, Sun 2-3/hr
2	SSW	Newton Abbot to Exeter bus station via Teignmouth, Dawlish, Dawlish Warren & Starcross, Mon-Sat 2/hr, Sun 1/hr
3	SSW	Plymouth to Dartmouth via Brixton, Yealmpton, Aveton Gifford, Kingsbridge, Torcross, Slapton, Slapton Turn, Strete, Blackpool & Stoke Fleming, Mon-Sat approx 1/hr, Sun 4/day Kingsbridge to Dartmouth
5	More	(Damory 5) Weymouth to Dorchester via Osmington, Mon-Sat 4/day
8	First	Weymouth to Chickerell, Mon-Sat 2/hr, Sun1/hr
9	SSW	Exeter to Honiton via Sidmouth, Mon-Sat 1/hr, Sun Sidmouth to Honiton 2/day & Exeter to Sidmouth 5/day in the evening
9A	SSW	Exeter to Seaton via Sidmouth & Sidford, Mon-Sat 1/hr, Sun 7/day
10	First	Poundbury to Weymouth via Dorchester, Mon-Sat 3-4/hr, Sun 2/hr
12	SSW	Newton Abbot to Brixham via Torquay & Paignton, Mon-Sat 4-6/hr, Sun 4/hr
18	SSW	Kingswear to Brixham, daily 1/hr
20	Dline	Taunton to Seaton via Honiton, Mon-Sat 3/day
22	SSW	Dawlish Warren to Paignton via Teignmouth, Shaldon, Maidencombe, St Marychurch & Torquay, Mon-Sat 1/hr plus 2/hr St Marychurch to Paignton, Sun 1/hr
30	More	(Breezer) Weymouth to Swanage via Osmington, Durdle Door (Holiday Park), Lulworth Cove, West Lulworth, Wool railway station & Wareham, late May to mid Sep daily 6/day
31	More	(Breezer) Wool railway station to Lulworth Cove via Durdle Door, late May to mid Sep daily 5-8/day
40	More	(Breezer) Swanage to Poole via Corfe Castle & Wareham rail station, mid Mar-late Oct daily 1/hr, late Oct-mid Mar Mon-Sat 1/hr, Sun 6/day
48	PC Bus	Plymouth to Wembury via Plymstock, Mon-Sat 11-12/day
50	More	(Breezer) Swanage bus station to Bournemouth station via Studland, Shell Bay (ferry) & Sandbanks (ferry), late May-mid Sep daily 1-2/hr, mid Sep-late May daily approx 1/hr
54	PC Bus	Plymouth to Bovisand via Plymstock, Hooe Lake & Jennycliff, late July-early Sep daily 8/day
56	SSW	Exeter St David's station to Exmouth via Exeter bus station, Exeter Airport & Lympstone, Mon-Sat 10/day
57	SSW	Exeter bus station to Brixington via Topsham, Lympstone & Exmouth, Mon-Sat 2/hr, Sun 1/hr

58	SSW	Exeter to **Budleigh Salterton** via **Lympstone**, Brixington & **Exmouth**, Mon-Fri 5/day
60	More	(Breezer) **Sandbanks** (ferry) to Poole via Canford Cliffs, mid Mar-late Oct daily 2/hr, late Oct-mid Mar Mon-Sat 12/day, Sun 10/day
94	THC	**Plymouth** bus station to **Noss Mayo** via Plymstock, **Brixton, Yealmpton & Newton Ferrers**, Mon-Sat 2-3/day
120	SSW	**Paignton** bus station to **Kingswear** (for ferry to Dartmouth), Mon-Sat 1/hr
157	SSW	**Exmouth** to **Sidmouth** via **Budleigh Salterton**, Mon-Sat 1/hr, Sun 4/day
162	THC	Kingsbridge bus station circular route via Thurlestone, **Outer Hope & Inner Hope**, Mon-Sat 3/day
164	THC	Totnes circular route to **Salcombe** via Kingsbridge bus station, Mon-Fri 15/day, Sat 12/day, Sun 3-4/day
357	SSW	**Exmouth** to **Budleigh Salterton**, daily 1/hr
378	AVMT	**Seaton** to **Lyme Regis**, Easter-end Oct Mon-Sat 4-5/day, end Oct-Easter Mon-Fri 2/day
501	First	(Portland Coaster) **Weymouth** (Pavilion) to **Portland Bill** via **Wyke Regis, Fortuneswell, Portland** & Easton, late May to early Sep daily 4/day, Sep weekends only
875	THC	**Bigbury-on-Sea** to **Plymouth** via **Challaborough & Yealmpton**, 1/week on a Friday
885	AVMT	Axminster to **Seaton**, Mon-Sat 9-11/day, 7/day continue to/start from Beer Cross and 4/day to **Beer**
899	AVMT	**Sidmouth** to **Seaton** via Sidford, **Branscombe. Beer Quarry Caves & Beer**. Mon-Sat 3-4/day plus Mon-Fri 2/day during term-time but a direct service from Sidford to Seaton (though 1/day calls at Beer Cross)
Gold	SSW	**Plymouth** to **Paignton** via Ivybridge & Totnes, Mon-Sat 2/hr, Sun 1/hr
X51	First	(Jurassic Coaster) **Weymouth** to Axminster via Dorchester South, **Bridport, Chideock, Charmouth & Lyme Regis.** Apr-early Oct daily 6-7/day, early Oct-Mar Mon-Sat 7/day
X52	First	(Jurassic Coaster) Bridport to Wool station via **West Bay, Abbotsbury, Weymouth, Durdle Door & Lulworth Cove.** Jun-early Oct daily 5/day
X53	First	(Jurassic Coaster) Axminster to **Weymouth** via **Lyme Regis, Charmouth, Chideock, Bridport, West Bay, Burton Bradstock**, Swyre, **Abbotsbury**, Portesham & Chickerell, Apr-early Oct Mon-Sat 5/day plus 1/day Lyme Regis to **Weymouth**, Sun 3/day + 1/day Bridport to Weymouth, Oct-Mar Mon-Sat 6/day
X54	First	(Jurassic Coaster) **Weymouth** to Poole via **Osmington, Durdle Door, Lulworth Cove,** Wool railway station & Wareham, daily 5/day plus Mon-Sat 1/day as far as Wareham only, Oct-Mar Mon-Fri 4/day

Operator contact details: AVMT (Axe Valley Mini Travel; ☎ 01297-625959, 🖳 avmtbustimes.wixsite.com/mysite); **Dline** (Dartline; ☎01392-872900, 🖳 www.dartline-coaches.co.uk); **First** (First in Wessex Dorset & South Somerset; 🖳 www.firstgroup.com/wessex-dorset-south-somerset); **More** (More Bus; ☎ 01202-338420, 🖳 www.morebus.co.uk/); **SSW** (Stagecoach South West; 🖳 www.stagecoachbus.com) **THC** (Tally Ho Coaches; ☎ 0300 012 0179, 🖳 www.tallyhoholidays.co.uk/Service-details); **PC Bus** (Plymouth Citybus; ☎ 01752-662271, 🖳 www.plymouthbus.co.uk)

2 THE ENVIRONMENT & NATURE

Conserving the Dorset & South Devon Coast Path

Britain is an overcrowded island and England is the most densely populated part of it. As such, the English countryside has suffered a great deal of pressure from both over-population and the activities of an ever more industrialised world. Thankfully, there is some enlightened legislation to protect the surviving pockets of forest and heathland.

Beyond these fragments, it is interesting to note just how much man has altered the land he lives on. Whilst the aesthetic costs of such intrusions are open to debate, what is certain is the loss of biodiversity that has resulted. The last wild boar was shot a few centuries ago; add to its demise the extinction of bear and wolf as well as, far more recently, a number of other species lost or severely depleted and you get an idea of just how much an influence man has over the land and how that influence is all too often used negatively.

There is good news, however. In these enlightened times when environmental issues are quite rightly given more precedence, many endangered species, such as the otter, have increased in number thanks to the active work of voluntary conservation bodies. There are other reasons to be optimistic; the environment is no longer the least important issue in party politics and this reflects the opinions of everyday people who are concerned about issues such as conservation on both a local and global scale.

CONSERVATION SCHEMES – WHAT'S AN AONB?

It is perhaps the chief joy of this walk that much of it is spent in an Area of Outstanding Natural Beauty. But what exactly is this designation and what protection do designations such as this actually confer?

Natural England (🖥 gov.uk/government/organisations/natural-england) is the single body responsible for identifying, establishing and managing National Parks, AONBs, NNRs, SSSIs and Special Areas of Conservation (SACs), see below.

National parks
The highest level of landscape protection is the designation of land as a national park. There are 15 in Britain of which nine are in

England (🖳 www.nationalparksengland.org.uk). This designation recognises the national importance of an area in terms of landscape, biodiversity and as a recreational resource. It does not signify national ownership and these are not uninhabited wildernesses, making conservation a knife-edged balance between protecting the environment and the rights and livelihoods of those living in the park. There are, alas, no national parks on this stretch of the coast path.

Areas of Outstanding Natural Beauty
The second level of protection is Area of Outstanding Natural Beauty (AONB; 🖳 landscapesforlife.org.uk), of which there are 33 wholly in England including three relevant to this section of the SWCP: South Devon (🖳 southdevonaonb.org .uk); East Devon (🖳 eastdevonaonb.org.uk); and Dorset (🖳 dorsetaonb.org.uk).

The primary objective of AONBs is conservation of the natural beauty of a landscape. As there is no statutory administrative framework for their management, this is the responsibility of the local authority within whose boundaries they fall.

As well as many AONBs this section of coast is also blessed with its very own **Geopark** (see box p150), of which there are only eight in the UK.

Incidentally, around 33% of the English coastline has been defined a **Heritage Coast**. This is a non-statutory designation but it shows that the designated area is of interest because of its scenic beauty, wildlife or general heritage; South Devon, East Devon, West Dorset and Purbeck are all Heritage Coasts.

National Nature Reserves and Sites of Special Scientific Interest
The next level of protection includes National Nature Reserves (NNRs) and Sites of Special Scientific Interest (SSSIs).

There are 225 **NNRs** in England, of which Slapton Ley, Berry Head, Dawlish Warren, Axmouth to Lyme Regis Undercliffs, Durlston Head and Studland, are all covered by this book.

There are over 4000 **SSSIs** in England. SSSIs are a particularly important designation as they have some legal standing. They are managed in partnership with the owners and occupiers of the land who must give written notice before initiating any operations likely to damage the site and who cannot proceed without consent from Natural England. There are plenty of SSSIs along this stretch of the SWCP, including 13 on the Jurassic Coast alone.

Special Area of Conservation (SAC; 🖳 jncc.gov.uk/our-work/special-areas-of-conservation-overview/) is an international designation which came into being as a result of the 1992 Earth Summit in Rio de Janeiro, Brazil. This European-wide network of sites is designed to promote the conservation of habitats, wild animals and plants, both on land and at sea. More than 200 land sites in England have been designated as SACs including South Hams, Lyme Bay & Torbay, Dawlish Warren, Chesil Beach, Studland to Portland, and Studland Dunes.

Campaigning and conservation organisations
A number of voluntary organisations started the conservation movement in the mid 19th century and they are still at the forefront of developments. Independent of government but reliant on public support, they can concentrate

THE ENVIRONMENT & NATURE

their resources either on acquiring land which can then be managed purely for conservation purposes, or on influencing political decision-makers by lobbying and campaigning.

Managers and owners of land include well-known bodies such as the **National Trust** (NT; 🖥 nationaltrust.org.uk) that owns over 600 miles of coastline including Wembury, Noss Mayo, South Milton Sands in South Hams, Bolberry Down, East Soar, Overbecks Garden and Mill Bay near Salcombe, Little Dartmouth, Brownstone & Coleton Camp, Sandy Beach near Exmouth, Branscombe, Sidmouth countryside, the highest point on England's south coast at Golden Cap, Burton Bradstock, Ringstead Bay, Corfe Castle, and, at the very end of the walk, Studland Bay.

Other charitable organisations fighting, at least in part, to protect England's coastline include the **Royal Society for the Protection of Birds** (RSPB; 🖥 rspb .org.uk), the **CPRE** (The Countryside Charity; 🖥 cpre.org.uk) and the **Woodland Trust** (🖥 woodlandtrust.org.uk).

The Wildlife Trusts (🖥 wildlifetrusts.org) are the umbrella organisation for the 46 wildlife trusts in the UK that manage nature reserves and run marine conservation projects. The sole purpose of the **Marine Conservation Society** (🖥 mcsuk.org) is to protect the seas and shores as well as the wildlife in and around them so they also run marine conservation projects.

Geology

EONS, ERAS AND PERIODS

The Earth is four and a half billion years old, give or take the odd million years. To make such a huge timespan more manageable, geologists have divided these four and a half billion years into four different **eons**, with each at least half a billion years or more in length; the **Phanerozoic eon** (from 570 million years to the present day) is the most relevant for this walk.

These eons are then further subdivided into **eras**, each spanning several hundred million years – and the cliffs, rocks and fossils found along this 217¼-mile stretch of coast date from three of these eras: the **Palaeozoic** (570-250 million years ago), the **Mesozoic** (250-65 million years ago), and the **Cenozoic** (65 million years ago to the present day).

Without wishing to complicate matters any further, these geological eras are further divided into **periods**. The length of each period varies because the divisions aren't arbitrary, but are defined by distinctive changes in the types of rocks and fossils that can be found in the layers. As you probably know, when you look at a cliff-face you'll notice that it has lines running horizontally through it. These lines are layers of sediment that have been laid down over time, with the oldest at the bottom and the newest at the top.

Geology of the coastline

Triassic
Cretaceous
Jurassic

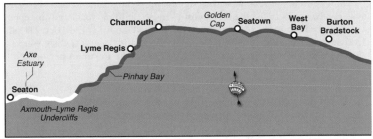

Sidmouth
High Peak
Salcombe Hill
Easterly dip in layers of rock
Branscombe
Beer
Exmouth
Budleigh Salterton
Ladram Bay
Beer Head
Orcombe Point
Otter Estuary

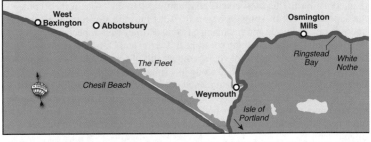

Charmouth
Golden Cap
Seatown
West Bay
Burton Bradstock
Lyme Regis
Axe Estuary
Pinhay Bay
Seaton
Axmouth–Lyme Regis Undercliffs

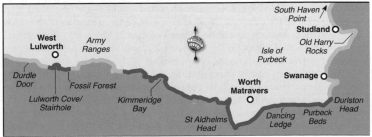

West Bexington
Abbotsbury
Osmington Mills
The Fleet
Ringstead Bay
White Nothe
Chesil Beach
Weymouth
Isle of Portland

South Haven Point
West Lulworth
Army Ranges
Studland
Isle of Purbeck
Old Harry Rocks
Durdle Door
Fossil Forest
Swanage
Lulworth Cove/ Stairhole
Kimmeridge Bay
Worth Matravers
St Aldhelms Head
Dancing Ledge
Purbeck Beds
Durlston Head

THE ENVIRONMENT & NATURE

Geologists are able to identify how long ago each of those layers was formed, and from the type of rock and fossils found in each layer they can determine what the terrain and the climate were like – and what creatures roamed the Earth at that time.

Palaeozoic era

The Palaeozoic era is divided into six main periods. Starting from the oldest they are: the Cambrian, Ordovician, Silurian, Devonian, Carboniferous and Permian.

The **Cambrian period** stretched for 70 million years (570-500 million years ago) and was characterised by the first shellfish and, for the first time, fossils which can be found in great numbers. On the other hand the Permian period spans only 30 million years (280-250 million years ago) and is characterised by the widespread existence of reptiles and amphibians.

On this walk you'll come across significant geological evidence of two of these Palaeozoic periods: the **Devonian** (415-360 million years ago) is represented by the limestone sites between Plymouth and the River Exe (Berry Head, Daddyhole Cove, Hope's Nose); while the red cliffs near Dawlish Warren, which are actually fossilised sand dunes, date from the **Permian period** (290-250 million years ago).

The Mesozoic Era and the Jurassic Coast

The Mesozoic era is the one that will be of most interest to the walker on this route. It is divided into three periods, **Triassic**, **Jurassic** and **Cretaceous** and it's fair to say that these periods could be described – by the layman at least – as the most interesting of all geological periods, when the great dinosaurs roamed the Earth (the Mesozoic is commonly called the 'Age of the Reptiles'), the supercontinent of Pangaea began the split into the separate continents we know today, and birds and mammals also made their first appearance.

So what is it that makes the coastline of Devon and Dorset so special to geologists today? Well, there is, of course, the wealth of fossils and rocks from each of these periods that can be found along this stretch of southern British shoreline. Perhaps, more importantly, this evidence is both exposed and readily accessible.

The erosion so prevalent along most coastlines is partly responsible for this, the millennia of wind, weather and waves exposing the various strata of the three periods. But in part this is also due to a geological phenomenon called an **unconformity**.

At some point during the Cretaceous period, rocks were first tilted then eroded, leading to the complete disappearance on certain stretches of the coast of Jurassic rock. As such, in certain places (such as at Sidmouth) on the coast there are Cretaceous rocks (ie the youngest rocks of the Mesozoic era) lying directly atop Triassic rocks (ie the oldest rocks).

Thus, while geology is impossible to escape and there are several sites between Plymouth and Exmouth that are of interest to rock-hounds, the subject becomes truly spectacular once you arrive at Orcombe Point (see Map 41, p197), just east of Exmouth, and the official start of the Jurassic Coast that's marked, as you will discover, by a geoneedle unveiled by the then Prince

Charles, now King Charles III. The following is a site-by-site guide to the coast, organised by geological period.

Triassic Period (250-200 million years ago) During this period Devon was located near to the centre of a super-continent: Pangaea. The county was part of a huge, hot and arid desert through which seasonal flash floods would sweep, depositing large amounts of sediment – mud and stone – as they carved their way through the landscape.

The red and orange rock that you see at the western end of the Jurassic Coast is indicative of the harsh, barren conditions in which they were formed. The few creatures that survived the mass extinction at the end of the Permian period began to dominate during the Triassic period; dinosaurs also began to evolve at this time. The period ended as it had begun, however, with a mass extinction – volcanic activity, an asteroid strike and climate change are all held up as possible culprits.

❏ WHERE TO SEE EVIDENCE OF THE TRIASSIC PERIOD

● **Orcombe Point** The red mudstone and sandstone at Orcombe provide evidence of the harsh desert environment of the Triassic.

● **Budleigh Salterton** Here one finds Triassic pebble-beds overlain with red sandstone.

● **Otter Estuary** Formed of Triassic sandstone; a fossilised 'Devon rhynchosaur', a stocky dinosaur up to 2m in length with a powerful beak, was also found buried here.

● **Ladram Bay** The impressive red sea stacks here are made of Triassic sandstone, the result of erosion by the sea.

● **Sidmouth to Beer** This stretch provides a great example of the unconformity (see opposite), with the cliff's colours changing from orange Triassic rock to the white chalk of the Cretaceous period.

● **The Undercliffs** Beginning at the Axe estuary in the late Triassic period, 7 miles and 25 million years later you arrive near Pinhay Bay in the early Jurassic! Just to complete the Mesozoic set, landslips also expose Cretaceous chalk.

Jurassic Period (200-140 million years ago) As sea levels rose and tropical oceans flooded the deserts, Pangaea began to split, with the landmass that would become the modern-day Americas separated from that which would become Europe, while in between these continents the Atlantic Ocean formed. With an increase in the length and number of coastlines, the continental climate changed from desert to tropical, lush forests, allowing life to thrive. Birds first took to the wing at this time, dinosaurs stalked the land and mammals also first entered the fray.

This is also the period of the **ammonite**, one of the most common fossils found on beaches today. Luckily for all these creatures, there was no mass extinction at the end of the Jurassic period.

Ammonite

❏ **WHERE TO SEE EVIDENCE OF THE JURASSIC PERIOD**

● **Beaches** At Lyme Regis, Charmouth and Seatown you can hunt the ancient fossilised remains of marine reptiles below the Jurassic Blue Lias cliffs.
● **Portland** One huge slab of Jurassic rock.
● **Weymouth to Ringstead Bay** The geological folds and faults en route consist of Jurassic clays, limestones and sandstones.
● **Osmington Mills** The fossilised burrows and markings of marine animals can be seen on the beach here.
● **Durdle Door/Stair Hole/Lulworth Cove** Jurassic limestone and Cretaceous chalk prove more resistant than the clays and sands that the sea has eroded away, leaving these impressive natural wonders.
● **Fossil Forest** Near Lulworth Cove, this is one of the most complete records of a fossil forest in the world.
● **Kimmeridge Bay** The clay found in these cliffs now gives its name to this type of rock the world over: Kimmeridgian. Meanwhile, the rocks found here were once the base of a tropical ocean.

Cretaceous Period (140-65 million years ago) The most important event in this period occurred midway through it: the South-West of England tilted eastwards, the Atlantic expanded and the whole area became covered by one vast ocean. Billions of algae living in the sea prospered before their skeletons sank to the sea floor to form chalk – the youngest rock of this period (the Latin for chalk is *creta*).

Hospitable conditions on land enabled the largest and most ferocious of dinosaurs to flourish; flowering plants also began to develop. Another mass extinction at the end of the period, however, led to the end of the reptiles' reign; the dawn of the Cenozoic era – and the reign of the mammals – was upon us.

Cenozoic era
The Cenozoic era is divided into two periods, the **Tertiary** (65-1.8 million years ago) and the **Quaternary** (1.8 million years ago to the present day). During the Tertiary period mammals began to dominate the Earth and great

❏ **WHERE TO SEE EVIDENCE OF THE CRETACEOUS PERIOD**

● **High Peak, Salcombe Hill and Branscombe** Due to the unconformity, upper Greensand (ie Cretaceous sandstone) and chalk lie directly on top of distinctively red Triassic mudstone.
● **Beer Head** Here's an anomaly: chalk cliffs in the midst of red Triassic rocks.
● **Golden Cap** Upper greensand lies directly on top of darker Jurassic clay on this, the SWCP's highest peak; the greensand supposedly glowing at night.
● **White Nothe** Cretaceous chalk and sandstone on top of Jurassic clay.
● **The Purbeck Beds** Here you'll find a fossilised record of mammal evolution at the dawn of the Cretaceous Period with the fossils of fish, amphibians, reptiles and even dinosaur footprints; mixture of Cretaceous and Jurassic rock.
● **Old Harry Rocks** Impressive chalk stacks.

shifts in the terrain led to the formation of some of the great mountain ranges, such as the Alps. The great folds in the terrain that run through the Isle of Purbeck, near the end of the walk, were also formed at this time.

The above is obviously a remarkably simplified description of the geology of the area. For those who wish to delve deeper there are several very good books (see Recommended reading, p46).

Flora and fauna

With a varied topography that encompasses a full range of landscapes from windblasted moor to wetland marsh, hogback cliffs to wooded valleys, muddy estuaries to mobile sand dunes, you can begin to appreciate why the South-West can boast such a rich and varied countryside, with several unique species of flora and thriving populations of mammals and birds that, elsewhere in the UK, struggle to survive.

The following is not in any way a comprehensive guide – if it were, you would not have room for anything else in your rucksack – but merely a brief run-down of the more commonly seen flora and fauna on the trail, together with some of the rarer and more spectacular species.

TREES

Like most of Britain, Dorset and Devon would once have been covered in woodland and forest. Much of this woodland has of course long since vanished, having been cleared by our ancestors. Less than 10% of Dorset, for example, is covered in woodland today; and the figure is even lower – around 6% – in East Devon.

However, some of that cleared woodland grew back again several hundred years ago and is now known as ancient woodland. The presence of bluebells, wood anemones and other particular flowering plants are indicators that there has been tree cover for a very long time (the estimate we hear most frequently is 'over 400 years').

Despite man's interference, there are some surprisingly fine patches of woodland on the coast path. The most interesting species is the **oak** (family

❏ **Oak leaves showing galls**
Oak trees support more kinds of insects than any other tree in Britain and some affect the oak in unusual ways. The eggs of gall-flies cause growths known as galls on the leaves. Each of these contains a single insect. Other kinds of gall-flies lay eggs in stalks or flowers, leading to flower galls, growths the size of currants.

THE ENVIRONMENT & NATURE

name *Quercus*), which was originally planted as coppice or scrub. Oak wood-land is a diverse habitat and not exclusively made up of oak. In Dorset the most prolific species of oak is **sessile oak** (*Quercus petraea*). Unfortunately, the two counties have been hit in recent years by a disease know colloquially as 'sudden oak death', and many of the trees have had to be felled to prevent further spread.

Another tree affected by disease in recent years is the **ash** (*Fraxinus excelsior*). Ash dieback disease first appeared on these shores in 2012 and has now spread right across Britain including Devon and Dorset. In Denmark, where the disease appears to have originated, up to 90% of trees have been infected.

Other trees that flourish here include **downy birch** (*Betula pubescens*), its relative the **silver birch** (*Betula pendula)*, **holly** (*Ilex aquifolium*) and **hazel** (*Corylus avellana*) which has traditionally been used for coppicing (the periodic cutting of small trees for harvesting).

BUTTERFLIES AND MOTHS

Butterflies are an unexpected treat on the SWCP. Not only are they numerous, but there are several different varieties too. Portland alone plays host to two butterfly reserves, Broadcroft Quarry and the Perryfields Reserve (both, alas, off the path), home of the rare and fussy silver-studded blue and the island's very own **moth**, the Portland ribbon wave. Small blues, chalkhill blues and common blues are also present, and migrants such as clouded yellow and painted lady may also put in an appearance.

The most famous butterfly in the region is the orange and brown heath fritillary, which has declined rapidly over the last 30 years in the UK, but which is thriving in the combes of north Devon and around Thurlestone.

FLOWERS

The extraordinary geology of the area ensures that a wide diversity of plants is able to thrive too. Whatever ground a plant prefers, be it chalk, clay, shingle, woodland mulch or the acid soils below Golden Cap and the dunes of Studland Beach, there is something for them on this stretch of southern British coastline. Spring is the time to come and see the spectacular displays of colour on the South-West Coast Path, when most of the flowers are in bloom.

Alternatively, arrive in August and you'll see the heathers carpeting patches of the moors in a blaze of purple flowers, picked out with the brilliant yellow of the gorse bush; the latter will have been a feature of the landscape since spring.

Woodland and hedgerows

From March to May **bluebells** (*Hyacinthoides non-scripta*) proliferate in some of the woods along the trail, providing a wonderful spectacle.

The white **wood anemone** (*Anemone nemorosa*) – wide open flowers when sunny but closed and drooping when the weather's dull – and the yellow **primrose** (*Primula vulgaris*) also flower early in spring. **Red campion** (*Silene dioica*), which flowers from late April, can be found in hedgebanks along with **rosebay willowherb** (*Epilobium angustifolium*) which also has the name fireweed due to its habit of colonising burnt areas.

Peacock *Inachis io*

Small Tortoiseshell *Aglais urticae*

Chalkhill Blue *Polyommatus/Lysandra coridon*

Brimstone *Gonepteryx rhamni*

Common Blue *Polyommatus icarus*

Painted Lady *Vanessa cadui*

Small Copper *Lycaena phlaeas*

Red Admiral *Vanessa atalanta*

Meadow Brown *Maniola jurtina*

Large Garden/ Cabbage White *Pieris brassicae*

Clouded Yellow *Colias croceus*

Harebell
*Campanula
rotundifolia*

Rosebay Willowherb
*Epilobium
angustifolium*

Foxglove
Digitalis purpurea

Early Purple Orchid
Orchis mascula

Forget-me-not
Myosotis arvensis

Dog Rose
Rosa canina

Bell Heather
Erica cinerea

Heather (Ling)
Calluna vulgaris

Red Campion
Silene dioica

Bluebell
*Hyacinthoides
non-scripta*

Germander Speedwell
Veronica chamaedrys

Herb-Robert
Geranium robertianum

Ramsons (Wild Garlic)
Allium ursinum

Meadow Cranesbill
Geranium pratense

Common Dog Violet
Viola riviniana

Common Centaury
Centaurium erythraea

In scrubland and on woodland edges you will find **bramble** (*Rubus frutico-sus*), a common vigorous shrub responsible for many a ripped jacket thanks to its sharp thorns and prickles. **Blackberry** fruits ripen from late summer to autumn. Fairly common in scrubland and on woodland edges is the **dog rose** (*Rosa canina*) which has a large pink flower, the fruits of which are used to make rose-hip syrup.

Look out, too, on the water in streams or rivers for the white-flowered **water crow-foot** (*Ranunculus penicillatus pseudofluitans*) which, because it needs unpolluted, flowing water, is a good indicator of the cleanliness of the stream.

Other flowering plants to look for in wooded areas and in hedgerows include the tall **foxglove** (*Digitalis purpurea*) with its trumpet-like flowers, **for-get-me-not** (*Myosotis arvensis*) with tiny, delicate blue flowers, and **cow parsley** (*Anthriscus sylvestris*), a tall member of the carrot family with a large globe of white flowers which often covers roadside verges and hedge banks.

Heathland and scrubland

There are three species of heather. The most dominant is **ling** (*Calluna vulgaris*) with tiny flowers on delicate upright stems. The other two species are **bell heather** (*Erica cinera*) with deep purple bell-shaped flowers and **cross-leaved heath** (*Erica tetralix*) with similarly shaped flowers of a lighter pink, almost white colour. Cross-leaved heath prefers wet and boggy ground. As a result, it usually grows away from bell heather which prefers well-drained soils.

Heather is an incredibly versatile plant which is put to many uses. It provides fodder for livestock, fuel for fires, an orange dye and material for bedding, thatching, basketwork and brooms. It is still sometimes used in place of hops to flavour beer and the flower heads can be brewed to make good tea. It is also incredibly hardy and thrives on the denuded hills, preventing other species from flourishing. Indeed, at times, highland cattle are brought to certain areas of the moors to graze on the heather, allowing other species a chance to grow.

On Portland there is also the **Portland sea lavender** (*Limonium recurvum*), a purple-flowered species first discovered in 1832, that flowers in abundance on the cliff edges on the eastern side of Portland just north of the Bill between July and August – and which doesn't exist anywhere else in the world.

Grassland

There is much overlap between the hedge/woodland-edge habitat and that of pastures and meadows. You will come across **common birdsfoot-trefoil** (*Lotus corniculatus*), **Germander speedwell** (*Veronica chamaedrys*), **tufted** and **bush vetch** (*Vicia cracca* and *Vicia sepium*) and **meadow vetchling** (*Lathyrus pratensis*) in both. Often the only species you will see in heavily grazed pastures are the most resilient.

Of the thistles, in late summer you should come across the **melancholy thistle** (*Cirsium helenoides*) drooping sadly on roadside verges and hay meadows. Unusually, it has no prickles on its stem. The **yellow rattle** is aptly named, for the dry seedpods rattle in the wind, a good indication for farmers that it is time to harvest the hay.

Gorse
Ulex europaeus

Meadow Buttercup
Ranunculus acris

Marsh Marigold (Kingcup)
Caltha palustris

Bird's-foot trefoil
Lotus corniculatus

Water Avens
Geum rivale

Tormentil
Potentilla erecta

Primrose
Primula vulgaris

Ox-eye Daisy
Leucanthemum vulgare

Cotton Grass
Eriophorum angustifolium

Common Ragwort
Senecio jacobaea

Hemp-nettle
Galeopsis speciosa

Cowslip
Primula veris

Yellow Rattle
Rhinanthus minor

Rowan (tree)
Sorbus aucuparia

Sea Holly
Eryngium maritimum

Scarlet Pimpernel
Anagallis arvensis

Self-heal
Prunella vulgaris

Thrift (Sea Pink)
Armeria maritima

Common/Spear Thistle
Cirsium vulgare

Common Hawthorn
Crataegus monogyna

Sea Campion
Silene maritima

Honeysuckle
Lonicera periclymemum

Yarrow
Achillea millefolium

Hogweed
Heracleum sphondylium

Other widespread grassland species include **harebell** (*Campanula rotundifolia*), delicate yellow **tormentil** (*Potentilla erecta*) and **devil's-bit scabious** (*Succisa pratensis*). Also keep an eye out for orchids such as the **fragrant orchid** (*Gymnaadenia conopsea*) and **early purple orchid** (*Orchis mascula*).

Dunes

Dunes are formed by wind action creating a fragile, unstable environment. Among the first colonisers is **marram grass** (*Ammophila arenaria*) which is able to withstand drought, exposure to wind and salt spray and has an ability to grow up through new layers of sand that cover it.

Other specialist plants are **sea holly** (*Eryngium maritimum*), **sea spurge** (*Euphorbia paralias*) and **sea bindweed** (*Calystegia soldanella*). The one thing that these seemingly indomitable plants can't tolerate is trampling by human feet; stay on the path which is nearly always well marked through dunes.

BIRDS

In and around the fishing villages

The wild laugh of the **herring gull** (*Larus argentatus*) is the wake-up call of the coast path. Perched on the rooftops of the stone villages, they are a reminder of the link between people and wildlife, the rocky coast and our stone and concrete towns and cities. Shoreline scavengers, they've adapted to the increasing waste thrown out by human society.

Despite their bad reputation it's worth taking a closer look at these fascinating, ubiquitous birds. How do they keep their pale grey and white plumage so beautiful feeding on rubbish? Nobel-prize-winning animal behaviourist Nikko Tinbergen showed how the young pecking at the red dot on their bright yellow bills triggers the adults to regurgitate food. In August the newly fledged brown young follow their parents begging for food. Over the next three years they'll go through a motley range of plumages, more grey and less brown each year till they reach adulthood. But please don't feed them and do watch your sandwiches and fish & chips – they are quite capable of grabbing food from your hand.

Village harbours are a good place for lunch or an evening drink after a hard day on the cliffs. Look out for the birds who are equally at home on a rocky shore or in villages, such as the beautiful little black-and-white **pied wagtail** (*Motacilla alba*) with its long, bobbing tail. Also looking black from a distance as they strut the beach are **jackdaws** (*Corvus monedula*). Close up, however, they are beautiful with a grey nape giving them a hooded look and shining blue eyes. They are very sociable: you will often see them high up in the air in pairs or flocks playing tag or performing acrobatic tricks.

Small, dark brown and easy to miss, the **rock pipit** (*Anthus petrosus*) is one of our toughest birds, as it feeds whilst walking on the rocks between the land and the sea. They nest in crevices and caves along the rocky coastline.

Seen on or from the sea cliffs

Walking on the coastal path leads you into a world of rock and sea, high cliffs with bracken-clad slopes, exposed green pasture, dramatic drops and headlands,

Above, clockwise from top left: **1**. Oystercatchers **2**. Curlew **3**. Razorbill **4** Pied wagtail 5. Redshank **6**. Black headed gull **7**. Puffin (All ©BT) 8. Herring gull (©HS)

sweeping sandy beaches and softer country around the estuaries. The vertiginous swoops of the path mean it's often possible to be at eye level, or even look down on, birds and mammals. Watch for **kestrels** (*Falco tinnunculus*), hovering on sharp brown wings, before plummeting onto their prey. Such prey includes twittering **linnets** (*Carduelis cannabina*), with their bright red breasts and grey heads. Linnets often fly ahead of you, perching on gorse and fences, as may stunning **stonechats** (*Saxicola torquata*). With black, white and orange colouring, stonechats are common on heath and

STONECHAT
L: 135MM/5.25"

grassy plains where you may hear their distinctive song, which is not dissimilar to two stones being clacked together.

At eye level the black 'moustache' of the powerful slate-grey-backed **peregrine** (*Falco peregrinus*) is sometimes visible. At a glance it can be mistaken for a pigeon, its main prey. But the power and speed of this, the world's fastest bird, soon sets it apart. In the late summer whole families fly over the cliffs. In mid winter look for them over estuaries where they hunt ducks and waders. Despite the remote fastness of the cliffs, peregrines have suffered terribly. Accidental poisoning by the pesticide DDT succeeded where WWII persecution for fear they would kill carrier pigeons failed, and they were almost extinct by the end of the 1960s. Their triumphant return means not only a thriving population on their traditional sea cliffs, but more and more nesting in our cities on man-made cliffs, such as tower blocks and cathedrals. Coast-path walkers have seen them swooping around the Undercliffs near Lyme Regis.

Cliff ledges, a kind of multi-storey block of flats for birds, provide nesting places safe from marauding land predators such as foxes and rats. It's surprising just how close it's possible to get to **fulmars** (*Fulmarus glacialis*), which return

GUILLEMOT
L: 450MM/18"

to their nesting ledges in February for the start of the long breeding season that goes on into the autumn. Only in the depth of winter are the cliffs quiet. Fulmars are related to albatrosses and like them are masters of the air. You can distinguish them from gulls by their ridged, flat wings as they sail the wind close to the waves with the occasional burst of fast flapping. Fulmars are incredibly tenacious at holding their nesting sites and vomit a stinking oily secretion over any intruders, including rock-climbers! The elegant **kittiwake** (*Rissa tridactyla*), the one true seagull that never feeds on land, is another cliff nester, identified by its 'dipped in ink' black wingtips.

Black above, white below, **manx shearwaters** (*Puffinus puffinus*) make globe-encircling journeys as they sail effortlessly just above even the wildest sea.

Small and fast on hard-beating wings, black and white **guillemots** (*Uria troile*) and **razorbills** (*Alca torda*) shoot out from their nesting ledges hidden in the cliffs. Guillemots have a long thin bill and razorbills a heavy half circle bill. Large colonies of guillemots, kittiwakes, razorbills, and a few **puffins** (*Fratercula arctica*) inhabit the cliff ledges near Durlston Head, just before Swanage. Purbeck also has several small colonies of puffins.

Less lovely in most people's eyes, though undeniably magnificent, the big, rapacious **great black-backed gulls** (*Larus marinus*) cruise the nesting colonies for prey. Star of the sea show, however, has to be the big, sharp-winged, Persil-white **gannets** (*Morus bassanus*) cruising slowly for fish, then suddenly plunging with folded wings into the sea. Their strengthened skulls protect them from the huge force of the impact with the water. Gannets, together with storm petrels, shearwaters and skuas are often seen from Portland Bill.

Two birds more familiar from the artificial cliffs of our cities can be seen here in their natural habitat – **house martins** (*Delichon urbica*), steely-blue backed like a **swallow** (*Hirundo rustica*), but with more V-shaped wings and a distinctive white rump, and **rock doves** (*Columba livia*). These are so mixed with **town pigeons** (*Columba livia domestica*) it's hard to say if any 'pure' wild birds remain. But many individuals with the characteristic grey back, small white rump and two black wing bars can be seen.

Where the path drops steeply to a rocky bay, **oystercatchers** (*Haematopus ostralegus*), with their black and white plumage and spectacular carrot-coloured bill, pipe in panic when they fly off. This is also a good spot to get close to **shags** (*Phalacrocorax aristotelis*) and **cormorants** (*Phalacrocorax carbo*), common all round the coast, swimming low and black in the water. Shags are smaller and are always seen on the sea – cormorants are also on rivers and estuaries – and in the summer have a crest whilst cormorants have a white patch near their tail and a white face. Close up, these oily birds shine iridescently: shags are green, cormorants are purple. They are a primitive species and, since their feathers are not completely waterproof, both have to dry their bodies after time in the sea. Their heraldic pose, standing upright with half-spread wings on drying rocks, is one of the special sights of the coast path.

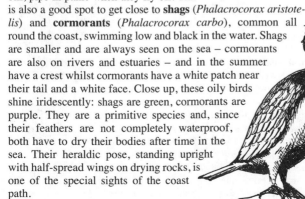

CORMORANT
L: 900MM/36"

SHAG
L: 710MM/28"

THE ENVIRONMENT & NATURE

In pastures, combes and woods

The one species that enjoys more publicity than any other on the coast path is the **cirl bunting** (*Emberiza cirlus*). Its rarity and declining numbers – by 1989 there were only 118 breeding pairs – led to the establishment of some large conservation efforts and you'll come across several cliff-top fields on the trail that have been entirely given over to their protection. Labrador Bay (four miles south of Teignmouth), Prawle Point, Maidencombe, Berry Head, Wembury, Jenny Cliff, and Stoke Point near Noss Mayo, are all good places to spot this smallish bird with a yellow-streaked head and green breast band – like a small yellowhammer. The programme is ongoing but there are now thought to be more than one thousand pairs. They are also found at Slapton Ley National Nature Reserve (see p135), where you may also spot **Cetti's warblers** (*Cettia cetti*) and **Greater crested grebes** (*Podiceps cristatus*).

SKYLARK
L: 185MM/7.25"

On your walk you'll find that the path frequently rises up onto rich green pasture. **Skylarks** (*Alauda arvensis*) soar tunefully – almost disappearing into the spring sky, while in winter small green-brown **meadow pipits** (*Anthus pratensis*) flit weakly, giving a small high-pitched call.

Spring also brings migrant **wheatears** (*Oenanthe oenanthe*): they are beautiful with their grey and black feathers above, buff and white below, and unmistakable when they fly and show their distinctive white rump. **Buzzard** (*Buteo buteo*) soar up with their tilted, broad round wings, giving their high, wild 'ke-oow' cry.

Ravens (*Corvus corax*) cronk-cronk over the cliffs and are distinguished from more common **carrion crows** (*Corvus corone*) by their huge size and wedge-shaped tail.

In the woods you'll find all three native species of **woodpecker** – **green**, **great** and **lesser spotted** (*Picus viridis* and *Dendrocopos major* and *minor* respectively); the two latter are very much wedded to the woods, while the former, with its laughing call, can often be seen on the moors looking for insects.

In spring, familiar birds such as **robins** (*Erithacus rubecula*), **blackbirds** (*Turdus merula*), **blue** and **great tits** (*Parus major* & *caeruleus*), **chaffinches** (*Fringila coelebs*) and **dunnocks** (*Prunella modularis*) are joined by the small green **chiffchaff** (*Phylloscopus collybita*); it's not much to look at but is one of the earliest returning migrants and unmistakably calls its own name in two repeated notes.

GREEN WOODPECKER
L: 330MM/13"

In and around estuaries

Descending to the long walk round the estuaries you move into a different, softer world of shelter and rich farmland. Best for birds in winter, they are a welcome refuge from the ferocity of the worst weather for wildlife and people.

There are large flocks of ducks – whistling **wigeon** (*Anas penelope*), a combination of grey and pinky brown, with big white wing patches in flight – and waders like the brown **curlew** (*Numenius arquata*) with its impossibly long, down-curved beak and beautiful sad fluting call, evocative of summer moors.

The **redshank** (*Tringa totanus*), **greenshank** (*Tringa nebularia*), golden and grey **plover** (*Pluvialis sp.*), and black-tailed and bar-tailed **godwit** (*Limosa sp.*) can also be seen in winter.

Look out for the big black, white and chestnut **shelduck** (*Tadorna tadorna*), and for the tall grey **heron** (*Ardea cinerea*), hunched at rest or extended to its full 175cm as it slowly, patiently stalks fish in the shallows.

A real rarity ten years ago, another species of heron, the stunning white **little egret** (*Egretta garzetta*), is now unmissable on estuaries. Here the more common gull is the nimble **black-headed gull** (*Larus ridibundus*), with its elegant cap, dark in summer but pale in winter. In summer, terns come: the big **sandwich tern** (*Sterna sandvicensis*) with its shaggy black cap and loud rasping call, and the smaller sleeker **aerobatic common tern** (*Sterna hirundo*).

MAMMALS

The south-west is blessed with wildlife. The Lulworth Ranges play host to two of our largest mammal species, one native, one imported. The former is the **roe deer** (*Capreolus capreolus*), the most common of deer species in England. It is quite easy to distinguish from the other species, mainly due to its diminutive size (standing around 65cm to the shoulder), red-brown coat in summer and small antlers (around 25cm), white rump and short tail. Its nocturnal habits, however, mean that you will still be lucky to see one.

Britain's only other native deer, the **red deer** (*Cervus elaphus*), is also present in Devon and Dorset, mainly in Exmoor but also in patches throughout the two counties.

The exotic **sika deer** (*Cervus nippon*) also thrives in the Lulworth Ranges. They are believed to have come from herds that arrived in 1895 at Hyde House and the following year at Brownsea Island in Poole Harbour. Few people realised that the deer could swim to the mainland; together with further escapees from Hyde House they were able to establish themselves on the ranges and nearby areas. Considered sacred in Japan – where they originally hail from – they find the conditions so benign on the ranges that they are now having to be culled before their numbers become unmanageable.

The South-West, in particular Exmoor, is also renowned as the spiritual home of the **otter** (*Lutra lutra*). The county was the home of the author Henry Williamson – creator of *Tarka the Otter* – and Devon today is proud to be associated with this most graceful of British carnivores. It wasn't always like this, however, and for much of the 20th century (and before) the otter was persecuted because it was (wrongly) believed to have an enormously detrimental effect on fish stocks. Today the otter is enjoying something of a renaissance thanks to concerted conservation efforts. At home both in salt water and fresh water, they are a good indicator of an unpolluted environment. It is unlikely that you'll spot one on your walk, although there are records of sightings all along the path. The Erme River, which you wade across on the path, is a particularly good spot to see one, according to records, and Devon is renowned as one of the otter's main strongholds.

Seeing any of the above requires patience and no little amount of luck. One creature that you will definitely see along the walk, however, is the **rabbit** (*Oryctolagus cuniculus*). Most of the time you'll get nothing more than a brief and distant glimpse of their white tails as they race for the nearest warren at the sound of your footfall, since they're timid by nature. Because they are so numerous, however, the laws of probability dictate that you will, at some stage during your walk, get close enough to observe them without being spotted. Trying to take a decent photo of one of them, however, is a different matter.

If you're lucky you may also come across **hares** (*Lepus europaeus*), often mistaken for rabbits but much larger, more elongated and with longer ears and back legs. There are populations of hares all over the arable parts of the South-West – look out for them around the Lulworth Ranges and the Kimmeridge area – though nowhere are they common.

Like the otter, the **water vole** (*Arvicola terrestris*) has both been a major character in a well-known work of fiction (in this case 'Ratty' from Kenneth Grahame's classic children's story *Wind in the Willows*) and has suffered a devastating drop in its population. Their numbers had originally declined due to the arrival in the UK countryside of the mink from North America, which successfully adapted to living in the wild after escaping from local fur farms. Unfortunately, the mink not only hunts water voles but is small enough to slip inside their burrows. Thus, with the voles afforded no protection, the mink was able to wipe out an entire riverbank's population in a matter of months. (Incidentally, this is another reason why protecting the otter is important as they kill mink.) A programme is now in place in which the water vole and its habitat is not only protected but the mink are being trapped and killed.

Another native British species that has suffered at the hands of a foreign invader is the **red squirrel** (*Sciurus vulgaris*), a small, tufty-eared native that has been usurped by its larger cousin from North America, the **grey squirrel** (*Sciurus carolinensis*). The only place where it might be possible to see the red squirrel is on Brownsea Island in Poole Harbour – at the very end of the coast path.

The ubiquitous **fox** (*Vulpes vulpes*) is now just as at home in the city as it is in the country. While usually considered nocturnal, it's not unusual to encounter one during the day. Another creature of the night that you may occasionally see is the **badger** (*Meles meles*). Relatively common throughout the British Isles, these sociable mammals with their distinctive black-and-white striped muzzles live in large underground burrows called setts, appearing around sunset to root for worms and slugs.

The nocturnal **bat**, of which there are 17 species in Britain, is protected by law. Your best chance of spotting one is at dusk while there's still enough light in the sky to make out their flitting forms as they fly along hedgerows, over rivers and streams and around street lamps in their quest for moths and insects. The commonest species in Britain is the **pipistrelle** (*Pipistrellus pipistrellus*).

Do also keep a look out for other fairly common but little seen species such as the carnivorous **stoat** (*Mustela erminea*), its diminutive cousin the **weasel** (*Mustela nivalis*), the **hedgehog** (*Erinaceus europaeus*) – these days, alas, most commonly seen as roadkill – and any number of species of **voles**, **mice** and **shrews**.

Out at sea

The high cliffs are also a great place from which to look out over the sea. Searching for seals is an enjoyable and essential part of cliff walking. You'll spot lots of grey lobster-pot buoys before your first seal, but it's worth the effort. **Atlantic grey seals** (*Halichoerus grypus*) relax in the water, looking over their big Roman noses with doggy eyes, as interested in you as you are in them.

Twice the weight of a red deer, a big bull can be over 200kg. On calm, sunny days it's possible to follow them down through the clear water as they dive, as elegant in their element as they are clumsy on land. Seals generally come ashore only to rest, moult their fur, or to breed. Devon is your best chance of seeing one, though there are small pockets of them as far east as Poole and beyond.

A cliff-top sighting of Britain's largest fish is also a real possibility, but is more chilling than endearing! **Basking sharks** (*Cetorhinus maximus*) can grow to a massive 36ft (11 metres) and weigh seven tonnes, and their two fins, a large shark-like dorsal fin followed by a notched tail fin, are so far apart it takes a second look to be convinced it's one fish. But these are gentle giants cruising slowly with open jaws, filtering microscopic plankton from the sea. You are most likely to see one during late spring and summer when they feed at the surface during calm, warm weather. You are most likely to spy them in the waters off Cornwall, though they do bask in the waters of Devon and Dorset too. Look out for coloured or numbered tags, put on for research into this sadly declining species, and report them to the website given in the box below.

❏ REPORTING WILDLIFE SIGHTINGS

Report basking shark or marine turtle sightings to the website of the Marine Conservation Society (🖳 mcsuk.org). Remember to note any tags you've spotted. Reports are greatly appreciated. If you see any of the other large marine creatures – such as dolphins, whales or seals – you can report them online through Seaquest Southwest, part of the Devon Biodiversity Records Centre (🖳 dbrc.org.uk). With any report give the location, number and the direction they were heading in.

If you come across a stranded marine animal such as a dolphin or porpoise, don't approach it but contact either British Divers Marine Life Rescue (office hours ☎ 01825-765546, 🖳 bdmlr.org.uk) or the RSPCA hotline (☎ 0300-123 4999 daily 8am-8pm, 🖳 rspca.org.uk).

THE ENVIRONMENT & NATURE

Taking a longer view and with some good luck, watch the sea for dolphins, porpoises or even a whale. **Harbour porpoises** (*Phocoena phocoena*) and **bottlenose dolphins** (*Tursiops truncatus*) both visit the offshore waters. One such dolphin, nicknamed George, has been turning up along the Dorset coast for years and even became something of a tabloid celebrity when he settled in the waters off Beer one summer.

Other cetaceans you may catch a glimpse of are **Risso's dolphins** (*Grampus griseus*), **common dolphins** (*Delphinus delphis*), **striped dolphins** (*Stenella coeruleoalba*), **orcas** or **killer whales** (*Orcinus orca*) and **pilot whales** (*Globicephala melaena*) but, be warned, they are fiendishly difficult to tell apart: a brief glimpse of a fin is nothing like the 'whole animal' pictures shown in field guides.

REPTILES

Dorset and Devon both have populations of all six British reptile species: smooth snake, grass snake, adder, sand lizard, common lizard and slow worm. Of the above, by far the rarest is the **sand lizard**, though wonderfully Dorset is its stronghold. Unremarkable most of the time, during the mating season the male's sides become a vivid green. Confined largely to the heathlands of Dorset, there is a small population on Studland on the last day of the walk.

The **adder** (*Vipera berus*) is the only poisonous snake of the three. They pose very little risk to walkers – indeed, you should consider yourself extremely fortunate to see one, providing you're a safe distance away. They bite only when provoked, preferring to hide instead. The venom is designed to kill small mammals such as mice, voles and shrews, so deaths in humans are very rare but a bite can be extremely unpleasant and occasionally dangerous to children or the elderly. You are most likely to encounter them in spring when they come out of hibernation and during the summer when pregnant females warm themselves in the sun. They are easily identified by the striking zigzag pattern on their back. Should you be lucky enough to encounter one (they enjoy basking on clifftops and on the moors), enjoy it but leave it undisturbed.

The **grass snake** (*Natrix natrix*) is the largest British species, growing up to over a metre in length. Olive-grey in colour with short black bars down each side and orange or yellow patches just below the head, they are harmless, relying not on venom or biting for defence but instead give off a foul odour if disturbed.

The **slow-worm** (*Anguis fragilis*) must be one of the more unusual creatures in the British Isles – a reptile that is called a worm, looks like a snake but is actually a legless lizard! Silver-grey with a dark line down the centre of the back and along each side, it is common in Devon and Dorset, where it feeds on slugs, worms and insects.

MINIMUM IMPACT & OUTDOOR SAFETY

3

Minimum impact walking

By visiting this rural corner of England you are having a positive impact, not just on your own well-being but on local communities as well. Your presence brings money and jobs into the local economy and also pride in and awareness of the region's environment and culture.

However, the environment should not just be considered in terms of its value as a tourist asset. Its long-term survival and enjoyment by future generations will only be possible if both visitors and local communities protect it now. The following points are made to help you reduce your impact on the environment, encourage conservation and promote sustainable tourism in the area.

ECONOMIC IMPACT

Rural businesses and communities in Britain have been hit hard in recent years by a seemingly endless series of crises. Most people are aware of the countryside code – not dropping litter and closing the gate behind you are still as pertinent as ever – but in light of the economic pressures that local countryside businesses are under, there is something else you can do: **buy local**.

Look and ask for local produce (see box pp24-5) to buy and eat. Not only does this cut down on the amount of pollution and congestion that the transportation of food creates – so-called 'food miles' – but also ensures that you are supporting local farmers and producers, the very people who have moulded the countryside you have come to see and who are in the best position to protect it. If you can find local food which is also organic so much the better.

Money spent at local level – perhaps in a market, or at the greengrocer, or in an independent pub – has a far greater impact for good in that community than the equivalent spent in a branch of a national chain store or restaurant. It would be going too far advocate that walkers boycott the larger supermarkets, which after all do provide local employment, but it's worth remembering that smaller businesses in rural communities rely heavily on visitors for their very existence. If we want to keep these local shops and post offices, we need to use them.

ENVIRONMENTAL IMPACT

A walking holiday in itself is an environmentally friendly approach to tourism. The following are some ideas on how you can go a few steps further in helping to minimise your impact on the environment while walking the Coast Path.

Use public transport whenever possible

While we recognise that public transport along this section of the South-West Coast Path is not great, using it is preferable to taking a car as it benefits everyone: visitors, locals and the environment.

Never leave litter

Leaving litter shows a total disrespect for the natural world and others coming after you. As well as being unsightly, litter kills wildlife, pollutes the environment and can be dangerous to farm animals. Please carry a plastic bag so you can dispose of your rubbish in a bin in the next village. It would be very helpful if you could pick up litter left by other people too.

● **Is it OK if it's biodegradable?** Not really. Apple cores, banana skins, orange peel and the like are unsightly, encourage flies, ants and wasps and ruin a picnic spot for others.

● **The lasting impact of litter** A piece of orange peel left on the ground takes six months to decompose; silver foil 18 months; a plastic bag 10 years; clothes 15 years; and an aluminium can 85 years.

Respect all wildlife

Care for all wildlife you come across along the path; it has as much right to be there as you. As tempting as it may be to pick wild flowers, leave them in place so the next people who pass can enjoy them too. Don't break branches off or damage trees in any way. If you come across wildlife, keep your distance and don't watch for too long. Your presence can cause considerable stress, particularly if the adults are with young, or in winter when the weather is harsh and food is scarce. Young animals are rarely abandoned. If you come across young birds, keep away so that their mother can return.

Outdoor toiletry

As more and more people discover the joys of walking in the natural environment issues such as how to go to the loo outdoors rapidly gain importance. How many of us have shaken our heads at the sight of toilet paper strewn beside the path, or even worse, someone's dump left in full view? Human excrement is not only offensive to our senses but, more importantly, can infect water sources.

Where to go The coast path is a high-use area and many habitats will not benefit from your fertilisation. As far as 'number twos' are concerned try whenever possible to use public toilets. There is no shortage of public toilets along the coast path and they are all marked on the trail maps. However, there are those times when the only time is now.

If you have to go outdoors help the environment to deal with your deposit in the best possible way by following a few simple guidelines.

● **Choose your site carefully** It should be at least 30 metres away from running water and out of reach of the high tide and not on any site of historical or archaeological interest. Carry a small trowel or use a sturdy stick to dig a small hole about 15cm (6") deep to bury your faeces in. Faeces decompose quicker when in contact with the top layer of soil or leaf mould; by using a stick to stir loose soil into your deposit you will speed decomposition up even more. Do not squash it under rocks as this slows down the decomposition process. If you have to use rocks as a cover make sure they are not in contact with your faeces.

● **Pack out toilet paper and tampons** Toilet paper takes a long time to decompose whether buried or not. It is easily dug up by animals and may then blow into water sources or onto the trail. The best method for dealing with used toilet paper is to pack it out. Put it in a paper bag placed inside a plastic bag and then dispose of it at the next toilet. Tampons and sanitary towels also need to be packed out in a similar way. They take years to decompose and may also be dug up and scattered about by animals.

ACCESS

Britain is a crowded cluster of islands with few places where you can wander as you please. Most of the land is a patchwork of fields and agriculture and the environment through which the Dorset & South Devon Coast Path marches is no different. However, there are countless public rights of way, in addition to the main trail, that criss-cross the land.

This is fine, but what happens if you feel a little more adventurous and want to explore the moorland, woodland and hills that can also be found near the walk. Access to the country-side has always been a hot topic in Britain. In the 1940s soldiers coming back from the Second World War were horrified and dis-gruntled to find that landowners were denying them the right to walk across the moors; iron-ically the very country that they had been fighting to protect. Since then it has been an ongoing battle and it is a battle that was final-ly won (for the most part) as new legislation came into force in 2005 granting public access to thousands of acres of Britain's wildest land.

Old milestone in miles, furlongs and poles. In case you've forgotten, 40 poles make one furlong and eight furlongs equal one mile.

All those who enjoy access to the countryside must respect the land, its wildlife, the interests of those who live and work there and other users; we all share a common interest in the countryside. Knowing your rights and responsibilities gives you the information you need to act with minimal impact.

❑ THE COUNTRYSIDE CODE

The Countryside Code, originally described in the 1950s as the Country Code, was revised and relaunched in 2004, in part because of the changes brought about by the CRoW Act (see opposite); it has been updated several times since, the last time in 2022. The Code seems like common sense but sadly some people still appear to have no understanding of how to treat the countryside they walk in. A summary of the latest Code (🖳 gov.uk/government/publications/the-countryside-code), launched under the banner 'Respect. Protect. Enjoy.', is given below.

Respect other people
● be considerate to those living in, working in and enjoying the countryside
● leave gates and property as you find them
● do not block access to gateways or driveways when parking
● be nice, say hello, share the space
● follow local signs and keep to marked paths unless wider access is available

Protect the natural environment
● take your litter home – leave no trace of your visit
● do not light fires and only have BBQs where signs say you can
● always keep dogs under control and in sight (see also pp311-13)
● dog poo – bag it and bin it – any public waste bin will do
● care for nature – do not cause damage or disturbance

Enjoy the outdoors
● check your route and local conditions
● plan your adventure – know what to expect and what you can do
● enjoy your visit, have fun, make a memory

Rights of way

As a designated National Trail the coast path is a public right of way. A public right of way is either a footpath, a bridleway or a byway. The Dorset & South Devon section of the South-West Coast Path is a footpath for almost all its length which means that anyone has the legal right to use it on foot only.

Rights of way are theoretically established because the owner has dedicated them to public use. However, very few paths are formally dedicated in this way. If members of the public have been using a path without interference for 20 years or more the law assumes the owner has intended to dedicate it as a right of way. If a path has been unused for 20 years it does not cease to exist; the guiding principle is 'once a highway, always a highway'.

On a public right of way you have the right to 'pass and repass along the way' which includes stopping to rest or admire the view, or to consume refreshments. You can also take with you a 'natural accompaniment', which includes a dog, but it must be kept under close control (see box above).

Farmers and land managers must ensure that paths are not blocked by crops or other vegetation, or otherwise obstructed, that the route is identifiable and the surface is restored soon after cultivation. If crops are growing over the path you have every right to walk through them, following the line of the right of way as closely as possible.

If you find a path blocked or impassable you should report it to the appropriate highway authority. Highway authorities are responsible for maintaining footpaths. In Devon and Dorset the highway authorities are the respective county councils. The council is also the surveying authority with responsibility for maintaining the official definitive map of public rights of way.

Wider access

The access situation to land around the coast path is a little more complicated. Trying to unravel and understand the seemingly thousands of laws and acts is never easy in any legal system. Parliamentary Acts give a right to walk over certain areas of land such as some, but by no means all, common land and some specific places such as Dartmoor and the New Forest. However, in other places, such as Bodmin Moor and many British beaches, right of access is not written in law. It is merely tolerated by the landowner and could be terminated at any time.

Some landowners, such as the Forestry Commission, water companies and the National Trust, are obliged by law to allow some degree of access to their land. There are also a few truly altruistic landowners who have allowed access over their land and these include organisations such as the RSPB, the Woodland Trust, and some local authorities. Overall, however, access to most of Britain's countryside is forbidden to Britain's people, in marked contrast to the general rights of access that prevail in other European countries.

Right to roam

For many years groups such as Ramblers (see box p48) and the British Mountaineering Council (🖳 thebmc.co.uk) campaigned for new and wider access legislation. This finally bore fruit in the form of the Countryside and Rights of Way Act of November 2000, colloquially known as the CRoW Act, which granted access for 'recreation on foot' to mountain, moor, heath, down and registered common land in England and Wales. In essence it allows walkers the freedom to roam responsibly away from footpaths, without being accused of trespass, on about four million acres of open, uncultivated land.

There may be a good reason why you shouldn't take a short cut.

On 28th August 2005 the South-West became the sixth region in England and Wales to be opened up under this act; however, restrictions may still be in place from time to time – check the situation on 🖳 www.gov.uk/right-of-way-open-access-land/use-your-right-to-roam.

Outdoor safety

AVOIDANCE OF HAZARDS

Swimming

If you are not an experienced swimmer or familiar with the sea, plan ahead and swim at **beaches** where there is a lifeguard service, such as Exmouth, Teignmouth and Dawlish Warren. On such beaches you should swim between the red and yellow flags as this is the patrolled area.

Don't swim between black and white chequered flags as these areas are only for surfboards. A red flag flying indicates that it is dangerous to enter the water. If you are not sure about anything ask one of the lifeguards; after all they are there to help you.

If you are going to swim at unsupervised beaches never do so alone and always take care; some beaches are prone to strong rips. Never swim off headlands or near river mouths as there may be strong currents. Always be aware of changing weather conditions and tidal movement (see box below). The South-West has a huge tidal range and it can be very easy to get cut off by the tide.

If you see someone in difficulty do not attempt a rescue until you have contacted the coastguard (see p82). Once you know help is on the way try to assist the person by throwing something to help them stay afloat. Many beaches have rescue equipment located in red boxes; these are marked on the trail maps.

For a safer place to swim, look out for outdoor swimming pools, known as **lidos**. Plymouth's Art-Deco, salt-water Tinside Lido (p88) is a striking example, but there's also a small lido in Teignmouth (p177).

There are also free-to-use **sea-water lidos** by Plymouth's Royal William Yard (p88) at Devil's Point Tidal Pool, and just outside Brixham at Shoalstone Seawater Pool (p152).

❏ **TIDES**

Tides are the regular rise and fall of the ocean caused by the gravitational pull of the moon. They are actually very long waves which follow the path of the moon across the ocean. Twice a day there is a high tide and a low tide and there are approximately 6¼ hours between high and low water.

Spring tides (derived from the German word *springen* meaning 'to jump') are tides with a very large range that occur just after the full- and new-moon phases when the gravitational forces of the sun and the moon line up. Spring tides occur twice every month; high tides then are higher and low tides lower than normal. **Neap tides** occur halfway between each spring tide and are tides with the smallest range, so you get comparatively high low tides and low high tides. They occur at the first and third quarters of the moon when the sun, moon and earth are all at right angles to each other, hence the gravitational forces of the sun and moon are weakened.

Walking alone

If you are walking alone you must appreciate and be prepared for the increased risk. It is always a good idea to leave word with somebody about where you are going; you can always ring ahead to book accommodation and let them know you are walking alone and what time you expect to arrive. Don't forget to contact whoever you have left word with to let them know you've arrived safely. Carrying a mobile phone can be useful though you cannot rely on getting good reception everywhere on the path (see box p43).

Safety on the coast path

Sadly every year people are injured walking along the trail, though usually it's nothing more than a badly twisted ankle. Landslides are rare but not unknown (see p219). Parts of the path can be pretty remote, however, and it certainly pays to take precautions when walking. Abiding by the following rules should minimise the risks.

● Avoid walking on your own if possible.

● Whether or not you are alone make sure that somebody knows your plans for every day you are on the trail. This could be a friend or relative whom you have promised to call every night or the B&B or hostel you plan to stay in at the end of each day's walk. That way, if you fail to turn up or call, they can raise the alarm.

● If the weather closes in suddenly and fog or mist descends while you are on the trail and you become uncertain of the correct trail, do not be tempted to continue. Just wait where you are and you'll find that mist often clears, at least for long enough to allow you to get your bearings.

If you are still uncertain and the weather does not look like improving, return the way you came to the nearest point of civilisation and try again another time when conditions have improved.

● Always fill your water bottle or pouch at every available opportunity and ensure you have some food such as high-energy snacks.

● Always carry a map, torch, whistle and wet-weather gear with you.

● Wear footwear with good grip.

● Be extra vigilant with children.

● Always keep dogs on leads on clifftops.

● Avoid walking and sitting directly below steep unstable-looking cliffs where possible.

Dealing with an accident

● Use basic first aid to treat the injury to the best of your ability.

● Try to attract the attention of anybody else who may be in the area. The **international distress (emergency) signal** is six blasts on a whistle, or six flashes with a torch.

● If possible leave someone with the casualty while others go to get help. If there are only two people, you have a dilemma. If you decide to get help, leave all spare clothing and food with the casualty.

● In an emergency dial ☎ 999 and ask for the coastguard. They are responsible for dealing with any emergency that occurs on the coast or at sea. Make sure you know exactly where you are before you call.

● Report the exact position of the casualty and their condition. However, before you call work out exactly where you are; on the app **What3words** (🖳 what3 words.com) the world is divided into three-metre squares and each has its own three-word geocode so it makes it easy to tell people where you are.

WEATHER AND WEATHER FORECASTS

The trail suffers from extremes of weather so it's vital that you always try to find out what the weather is going to be like before you set off for the day. It is a good idea to pay attention to **wind and gale warnings**.

The wind on any coastline can get very strong and if it is strong it is advisable not to walk, particularly if you are carrying a pack which can act as a sail. If you are on a steep incline or above high cliffs it is also dangerous.

Even if the wind direction is inland it can literally blow you right over (unpleasant if there are gorse bushes around!), or if it suddenly stops or eddies (a common phenomenon when strong winds hit cliffs) it can cause you to lose your balance and stagger in the direction in which you have been leaning, ie towards the cliffs!

Another hazard on the coast is **sea mist or fog** which can dramatically decrease visibility. If a coastal fog blows over take extreme care where the path runs close to cliff edges.

Most hotels, some B&Bs and TICs will have pinned up somewhere a summary of the **weather forecast**. Alternatively you can get a forecast through 🖳 bbc.co.uk/weather, or 🖳 metoffice.gov.uk/weather.

Pay close attention to the weather forecast and alter your plans for the day accordingly. That said, even if the forecast is for a fine sunny day, always assume the worst and pack some wet-weather gear.

BLISTERS

It is important to break in new boots/shoes before embarking on a long trek. Make sure they are comfortable and try to avoid getting them wet on the inside. Air your feet at every opportunity, keep them clean and change your socks regularly; using talcum powder can help to keep them dry. If you feel any hot spots, stop immediately and apply a few strips of zinc oxide tape and leave it on until the 'hot spot' is pain free or the tape starts to come off.

If you have left it too late and a blister has developed you should surround it with Compeed or any other blister kit to protect it from abrasion. Popping it can lead to infection. If the skin is broken keep the area clean with antiseptic and cover with a non-adhesive dressing material held in place with tape.

HYPOTHERMIA, HYPERTHERMIA & SUNBURN

Also known as exposure, **hypothermia** occurs when the body can't generate enough heat to maintain its normal temperature, usually as a result of being wet, cold, unprotected from the wind, tired and hungry. It is usually more of a problem in upland areas such as on the moors. Hypothermia is easily avoided by wearing suitable clothing, carrying and eating enough food and drink, being aware of the weather conditions and checking the morale of your companions.

Early signs to watch for are feeling cold and tired with involuntary shivering. Find some shelter as soon as possible and warm the victim up with a hot drink and some chocolate or other high-energy food. If possible give them another warm layer of clothing and allow them to rest until feeling better.

If allowed to worsen, strange behaviour, slurring of speech and poor coordination will become apparent and the victim can easily progress into unconsciousness, followed by coma and death. Quickly get the victim out of any wind and rain, improvising a shelter if necessary. Rapid restoration of bodily warmth is essential and best achieved by bare-skin contact: someone should get into the same sleeping bag as the patient, both having stripped to their underwear, putting any spare clothing under or over them to build up heat. Send urgently for help.

Hyperthermia occurs when the body generates too much heat, eg heat exhaustion and heatstroke. Not ailments that you would normally associate with England, these are serious problems nonetheless.

Symptoms of **heat exhaustion** include thirst, fatigue, giddiness, a rapid pulse, raised body temperature, low urine output and, if not treated, delirium and finally a coma. The best cure is to drink plenty of water. The darker your urine the more you should drink.

Heatstroke is more serious. A high body temperature and an absence of sweating are early indications, followed by symptoms similar to hypothermia (see above) such as a lack of coordination, convulsions and coma. Death will follow if treatment is not given instantly. Sponge the victim down, wrap them in wet towels, fan them and get help immediately.

The sun in the South-West can be very strong. The best way to avoid **sunburn** – and the extra risk of developing skin cancers that sunburn brings – is to keep your skin covered at all times in light, loose-fitting clothing, and to cover any exposed areas of skin in sunscreen (with a minimum factor of 30). Sunscreen should be applied regularly throughout the day. Don't forget your lips, nose, ears, the back of your neck, and even under your chin to protect you against rays reflected from the ground. Most importantly of all, always wear a hat!

ROUTE GUIDE & MAPS

Using this guide

While this guide has been divided into stages, each of which approximates a day's walk, they are meant as a guide only. To plan an itinerary that better suits your pace, fitness and the time you have available, please see the 'Suggested itineraries' section on pp34-5.

The **route summaries** below describe the trail between significant places and are written as if walking the coast path from Plymouth to South Haven Point (Poole Harbour). To enable you to plan your own itinerary, **practical information** is presented clearly on the trail maps. This includes walking times, all places to stay, camp and eat, as well as shops where you can buy supplies. Further service **details** are given in the text under the entry for each place.

For a condensed overview of this information see the town and village facilities table on pp32-5.

TRAIL MAPS   [see key map inside cover; symbols key p316]

Scale and walking times

The trail maps are to a scale of 1:20,000 (1cm = 200m; $3^{1}/_{8}$ inches = one mile). Walking times are given along the side of each map and the arrow shows the direction to which the time refers. Black triangles indicate the points between which the times have been taken. **See the note on walking times in the box opposite**.

The time-bars are a tool and are not there to judge your walking ability. There are so many variables that affect walking speed, from the weather conditions to how many beers you drank the previous evening. After the first hour or two of walking you will be able to see how your speed relates to the timings on the maps.

Up or down?

Other than when on a track or bridleway the trail is shown as a dotted line. An arrow across the trail indicates the slope; two arrows show that it is steep. Note that the arrow points towards the higher part of the trail. If, for example, you are walking from A (at 80m) to B (at 200m) and the trail between the two is short and steep it would be shown thus: A – – – >> – – – – B. Reversed arrow heads indicate a downward gradient.

GPS waypoints

The numbered GPS waypoints refer to the list on pp314-16.

❏ **IMPORTANT NOTE – WALKING TIMES**

Unless otherwise specified, **all times in this book refer only to the time spent walking**. You should add 20-30% to allow for rests, photos, checking the map, drinking water etc, not to mention time simply to stop and stare. When planning the day's hike count on 5-7 hours' actual walking.

ACCOMMODATION

Apart from in large towns where some selection of places has been necessary, almost every place to stay that is within easy reach of the trail is marked on the map, and details of each place are given in the accompanying text.

The number of **rooms of each type** is indicated as follows: **S** = single bed, **T** = twin beds, **D** = double bed, **Tr** = triple room (for three people) and **Qd** = quad (for four). Note that most of the Tr/Qd rooms have a double bed and one/two single beds or bunk beds; thus for a group of three or four, two people may have to share the double bed but the room can also be used as a double or twin. Unless specified, B&B-style accommodation is either en suite or has private facilities.

Rates quoted are **per person** (pp) based on two people sharing a room for a one-night stay; rates are almost always discounted for longer stays. Where a single room (sgl) is available the rate for that is quoted if different from the per person rate. The rate for single occupancy (sgl occ) of a double/twin is generally higher, and the rate for three or more sharing a room may be lower. Unless specified, rates are for B&B. At some places the only option is a room rate; this will be the same whether one or two people share.

Many places do not accept **advance bookings** for a single-night stay at peak times; the minimum is often two, or even, three nights. However, if you turn up on the day, or even call a few nights before, they may accept a booking.

Some B&Bs don't accept **credit/debit cards** but all hotels do.

The text also mentions whether the premises have **wi-fi** (WI-FI); if a **bath** is available (🛁) in, or for, at least one room; and whether **dogs** (🐾) are welcome. Most places will not take more than one dog in a room and also accept them subject to prior arrangement. Many make an additional charge (usually per night but occasionally per stay) while others may require a deposit which is refundable if the dog doesn't make a mess. See also pp311-13.

❏ **FOOD AND DRINK PLANNING**

Remember, to plan ahead: certain stretches of the walk are virtually devoid of eating places (Kingswear to Brixham, Seaton to Lyme Regis, Lulworth Cove to Kimmeridge Bay and from there to Swanage, as well as the South Dorset Ridgeway) so read ahead about the next day's walk to make sure you never go hungry.

The **opening days and hours** for pubs, restaurants and cafés mentioned are as accurate as possible but many factors mean these may change (see box p22) so it is always essential to check especially if there are few options.

ROUTE GUIDE AND MAPS

Prices for **camping** vary from site to site. Some charge per pitch (and sometimes with an additional charge for a second person), some per person. Note that the larger holiday parks, whose priorities lie with longer-stay families and groups, do still often have special rates for hikers that are cheaper than the rates advertised on their websites, so if calling up to reserve a tent pitch, always make it clear that you are walking the coast path. However, you rarely need to book campsites in advance, especially if you're walking alone, though calling ahead the morning before you arrive is good for peace of mind.

Other features

Features are marked on the map when pertinent to navigation. In order to avoid cluttering the maps and making them unusable not all features have been marked each time they occur.

The route guide

PLYMOUTH   [map p93]

'*Plymouth is indeed a town of considera-*
tion, and of great importance to the public.
The situation of it between two very large
inlets of the sea, and in the bottom of a
large bay [...] is very remarkable for the
advantage of navigation.'
            Daniel Defoe, *A Tour through the*
            Whole Island of Great Britain

Lying between the mouths of the rivers Plym and Tamar, Plymouth is a modern city with a rich and eventful past. The city's growth and prosperity are forever indebted to its proximity to – and relationship with – the sea. Not just as the famous departure point of the Pilgrim Fathers (see box p89) but also as a hub for trade (the commercial dockyards are amongst the largest in Europe) and, foremost, as a vital naval base, with a tradition that dates back to the very inception of the Royal Navy. No surprise, therefore, that there is much to see and do in this historic city.

The first record of habitation in the area, Sudtone (Saxon for 'South Farm'), situated on the site of the present-day Barbican, can be found in the Domesday Book (1086). Initially just a small fishing village, its strategically important location soon brought prosperity and – despite bouts

of plague, cholera and smallpox trimming the ever-burgeoning population as well as a concerted attempt at destruction by the Luftwaffe during the Plymouth Blitz – the town has continued to swell in size.

Much of this success is down to its situation at the mouths of two rivers, a crucial location that the nascent Royal Navy in the 17th century was quick to recognise. Her Majesty's Naval Base (HMNB) Devonport opened in 1690, with further docks being built in 1727, 1762 and 1795. Isambard Kingdom Brunel then designed the Great Western Docks (1844-50) and in 1854 the Keynham Steam Yard, built for the construction of steam ships, was also completed. It's hardly surprising, then, that most of the town's defining moments are sea based, from the defeat of the Spanish Armada (1588; see box opposite) to the sailing of the Mayflower (1620; see box p89) as well as the heroic resistance the city showed in WWII when, despite 59 German bombing sorties, it still played a full part in the Battle of the Atlantic and was a major embarkation point on D-Day.

Unfortunately, where the Luftwaffe flattened Plymouth some ugly buildings have sprouted and a large chunk of the town is actually fairly nondescript and pretty much devoid of charm. Thankfully, the **seafront** remains one of the more interesting and beautiful parts; and the area around the **Mayflower Steps**, known as **The Barbican**, is one of Plymouth's oldest, prettiest and most vibrant, with plenty of bars and restaurants in which to conduct any last-minute planning for your walk.

What to see and do

The Hoe The green expanse that separates the modern-day city centre from the sea, The Hoe is best known for playing host to Francis Drake's game of bowls in 1588 (see box below). It is also the place where, during the Plymouth Blitz of WWII, Nancy Astor, MP for the city and great friend of TE Lawrence (of Arabia) danced with servicemen, defiantly proclaiming that the city would go on despite the bombing.

Lighthouse lovers will be impressed by the red-and-white-striped **Smeaton's Tower** (see box p88).

Other notable sites on The Hoe include a three-tier **belvedere** (a structure that was deliberately designed to command a view), built in 1891, and the **Drake Statue** (1884), sculpted by one of the Victorian era's most pre-eminent producers of commemorative statues, Joseph Boehm.

❏ FRANCIS DRAKE, THE SPANISH ARMADA AND THAT FAMOUS GAME OF BOWLS

The Elizabethan era was a time of turmoil. The major European powers were often at war, with religion frequently the cause. The two main protagonists at this time were Protestant England and Catholic Spain. The latter controlled the Netherlands where Protestant ideals were popular. England, as was their wont, aided the Dutch Protestants who were being hunted by the Spanish Inquisition, and it was this decision – as well as the beheading of the Catholic Mary Queen of Scots, ordered by the Protestant Queen Elizabeth I in 1587 – that led to King Philip II of Spain's decision to 'defend Catholicism' by invading England.

One of Queen Elizabeth I's most feared seamen was Sir Francis Drake. A buccaneering adventurer and hero to the English, to the Spanish he was a constant thorn in their side. Conducting his own personal Protestant crusade, by 1588 he had already harassed and harried many Spanish boats in the West Indies, occupied the ports of Cadiz and Corunna, destroying 37 Spanish ships as he did so, and plundered the treasures of Spain wherever he found them, describing his wish to 'singe the king of Spain's beard'.

King Philip II's Spanish Armada set sail from Lisbon in May 1588; their ships were attacked by English and Dutch boats throughout their journey. Struggling through, the Spanish were eventually spotted off The Lizard and the news of their arrival swiftly reached Plymouth, where the English navy was waiting. Famously, Drake purportedly scoffed on being told of the arrival of the Armada, and chose to finish his game of bowls, claiming he could do so and defeat the Spanish. A much-debated incident, if it did actually happen it is possible that Drake would have known that the tide of the Tamar was against him – so preventing his boats from accessing the Channel until it turned – and thus recognised that he had ample time to complete his game.

History doesn't record whether Drake won his game of bowls. The outcome of the battle, however, is certain. Fighting between the Spanish and English navies went on for eight days before the Spaniards finally had to admit defeat, their navy beaten, burnt and scattered. To make matters worse, because of westerly winds many of the defeated boats couldn't return straight home, but instead had to sail around the tip of Scotland and down the coast of Ireland where they were further battered by storms – as well as being attacked by the English in Ireland. Drake meanwhile sailed home a hero, his legend forever cemented in English naval history for establishing England's dominance of the Atlantic – and refusing to end a game of bowls.

Many **war memorials** also adorn the area, fittingly so when one considers the number of servicemen and women to have departed from the city on various campaigns and missions over the years.

Overlooked by the Smeaton Tower is **Tinside Lido** (☎ 01752-261915, 💻 ply mouthactive.co.uk/centres/tinside-lido; see the website for details; free), a striking Art Deco outdoor swimming pool that opened in 1935. Following years of neglect the pool became a Grade II-listed building before being renovated and reopened in 2005. If that's not quirky enough for you, consider taking a bracing dip in the small, sea-fed **tidal pool** by Royal William Yard.

The Hoe is also the site of the **British Firework Championships** (see p14) in August. It is a competition between the country's professional firework companies that, for two nights, light up the skies above Devon.

The Royal Citadel At The Hoe's eastern end is the Royal Citadel. A large and impressive limestone fort, it was built in the late 1660s on the orders of Charles II in response to the second Dutch War (1664-7). Encompassing a previous fort that Drake had requested to be built in the 16th century, its guns bear down on the town as well as out to sea, most likely as a reaction to Plymouth's Parliamentarian leanings during the English Civil War.

Still militarily operational today, you can only visit the fort on **guided tours** (💻 www.english-heritage.org.uk/visit/places/royal-citadel-plymouth; £12.50), which are available from April to October on Tuesday, Thursday & Sunday at 2pm and last for around two hours. You have to book and pay online at least a day before – for details visit the website. Note that as The Citadel is still a working fort, tours may be cancelled without notice and that photography is also prohibited.

❑ PLYMOUTH'S HISTORY IN AND OUT OF THE BOX

Recently revamped at a cost of £46 million, and now known as **The Box** (☎ 01752-304774, 💻 theboxplymouth.com; Tue-Sun & bank holidays 10am-5pm; free), Plymouth's premier **museum and art gallery** is entered through an eye-catching cuboid facade. The complex now houses a *café*, shop and bar as well as a series of new galleries and exhibition spaces, including its elevated 'archive in the sky'. Highlights include some of the earliest depictions of Plymouth (sketches and watercolours dating from the 1600s) plus, in the '100 Journeys' exhibition, effects belonging to two of the city's heroes: a side drum (the oldest in the UK) that was once Francis Drake's; and a pair of skis owned and used by Robert Falcon Scott in his 1902 Antarctic expedition.

The Box also manages two key historic sights in Plymouth. On The Hoe, **Smeaton's Tower** was originally the third lighthouse to be put on Eddystone Rocks 14km south-west of Rame Head. Built in 1759, it was dismantled in 1882 and the upper portions reconstructed on The Hoe. Named after its builder John Smeaton, at 72ft high it offers striking views of Plymouth Sound and the city from its lantern room.

Close to The Barbican on New St is **Elizabethan House**. Built in the late 1500s, it retains much of its original structure but underwent major restoration as part of Plymouth's Mayflower 400 commemorations. It's been home to merchants, businessmen, fishermen, washerwomen and dressmakers, survived the Blitz and slum clearances in the early 1900s and presents a fascinating journey through the history of Plymouth.

Both Smeaton's Tower and Elizabethan House are open Mar/Apr-end Oct Tue-Sun and bank holidays 10am-5pm, weekends only rest of year for Smeaton's Tower; £5 for one, £8 for both).

❏ THE MAYFLOWER AND THE PILGRIM FATHERS

Most visitors to Plymouth – and certainly every American tourist in the city – are aware that amongst the first and most famous Europeans to settle in America (a group now celebrated as the Pilgrim Fathers) set sail from Plymouth in 1620. What is less well-known, perhaps, is the background to their emigration... and why they felt compelled to head for the New World in the first place.

The pilgrimage has its roots in Henry VIII's rejection of the Catholic Church back in 1534, an act that led to England becoming a Protestant country for the first time. Puritanism, the ideology followed by the Pilgrim fathers, emerged soon afterwards during the reign of Henry VIII's daughter, Elizabeth I. As the name suggests, the Puritans felt that Henry VIII's Church of England was neither strict nor pious enough for their rather fanatical tastes. This stance angered both Elizabeth and her successor, James I, and it wasn't long before the Puritans were being persecuted for their beliefs.

In 1609 a number of Puritans headed for Leiden in the Netherlands to seek a land where they could practise their faith in peace. Unfortunately, whilst the persecutions were less common, they were still unhappy with the tolerance and levity of their Dutch hosts; and more worrying still for the Puritans was the way their offspring were being assimilated into Dutch culture. There seemed to be only one solution: to build their own community, away from the persecution and profanity (as they saw it) of Europe, in the New World.

Plymouth's role in their story is actually both fortuitous and fairly minor. Setting sail from Southampton in *The Mayflower* and *The Speedwell* in August 1620, they only docked in Plymouth due to a storm that damaged the already old and leaking boats as they navigated The Channel. Fully stocked, and with the decision made to leave *The Speedwell* behind, a total of 102 passengers and crew (not all of whom were Puritans) finally left the city on 6th September 1620, reaching Cape Cod 66 days later to found the community they had dreamed of, in Massachusetts.

Alas, the Pilgrim Fathers' travails didn't end there. Weakened by their journey and unprepared for winter, half of them died within the first four months of landing. However, those who did survive owed their survival to the natives, a relationship cemented in the Pilgrims' first harvest of 1621 – a ceremony which would go on to become the basis for the American festival of Thanksgiving.

The Barbican The Barbican is the old harbour area of the city and the heart of the old town. Fortuitously escaping much of the bombing inflicted on Plymouth during WWII, the mazes of narrow **cobbled streets** (reputed to be the most extensive collection of cobbled thoroughfares in the UK) still exist in the originally medieval layout of what was then the town of Sutton. The former location of Plymouth's fish market, the area is now more of a draw to those seeking art, antiques and alcohol.

Speaking of the latter, if Plymouth marks the end of your walk, and you feel that a celebratory tipple is in order, the venerable **Plymouth Gin Distillery** (☎ 01752-665292, 🖵 plymouthdistillery.com; Mon 11am-5pm, Tue-Sat to 5.30pm, Sun noon-5pm), on Southside St, has been knocking out grade-A booze to discerning punters since 1793 and runs hour-long distillery **tours** (contact the distillery for details; from £15) round its building, which partly dates back to the early 15th century. The building, incidentally, and more than a little ironically, was also where the Puritan Pilgrim Fathers supposedly spent their last night before embarking for America.

Only a couple of minutes away is **Elizabethan House** (see box opposite); it is kitted out in suitable period furniture.

Next to the pedestrian walkway which crosses Sutton Harbour, the **Mayflower Steps** commemorate the Pilgrim Fathers' departure for the New World in 1620. The steps consist of a portico that was built in 1934 and a platform hanging out over the water's edge.

Nearby, above the tourist information centre (see column opposite) and open the same hours, you will find the **Mayflower Museum** (Apr-Oct Mon-Sat 9am-5pm, Sun 10am-4pm, Nov-Mar Mon-Fri 9am-5pm, Sat 10am-4pm; £5), covering three floors telling the story of the Pilgrim Fathers. It also has a balcony from which you can gaze out over the bustle below.

Not technically part of The Barbican but just across the walkway from the Mayflower Steps is the **National Marine Aquarium** (Map 1; ☎ 0844-893 7938, ▣ national-aquarium.co.uk; daily summer 10am-6pm, rest of year to 5pm; £20.50-25 includes free entry for 12 months). The UK's largest, it houses a tank that contains 2.5 million litres of water! The Atlantic Ocean display, as it is known, is home not only to tiger and nurse sharks, stingrays and barracuda but also a full-sized replica of a WWII plane. There are regular talks and feedings as well as a 4D cinema.

Services

As you'd expect, Plymouth has just about every amenity you need. The **tourist information centre** (☎ 01752-306330, ▣ visit plymouth.co.uk; **fb**; same days/hours as Mayflower Museum, see column opposite) is handily placed right by the Mayflower Steps on the Barbican and is one of the friendliest and most helpful on the walk.

There are two handy **supermarkets** on Notte St: Tesco Express (6am-11pm; ATM outside), and Co-op (daily 6am-11pm; ATM inside). For **camping/trekking** supplies head to nearby New George St, northwest of the Saint Andrew's Cross Roundabout, where you'll find Millets (No 40; Mon-Sat 9am-6pm, Sun 10am-4pm) and Trespass (No 34; Mon-Sat 9am-5.30pm, Sun 10.30am-4.30pm). There are

---

❑ THE COAST PATH THROUGH PLYMOUTH

While the route for this book starts at the Mayflower Steps, the South-West Coast Path begins way back in Minehead, in Somerset, and thus on its way travels through the centre of Plymouth. Initially this 2¾-mile trail is a little confusing, the lack of coast path signs not helping. That said, the city has worked hard to add some quirky features to what is already a walk stuffed with points of interest.

The path begins at **Cremyll Ferry** by Admiral's Hard. Having wiped your feet on the welcome mat positioned there, you come to a fried breakfast expertly rendered in wool on the wall of *Elvira's Café* (**fb**; Mon-Thur & Sat 8am-2.30pm, Fri 7.30am-2.30pm, Sun 8.30am-2.30pm) – look just below the main sign for the café. Said to be the home of the fry-up, the café has also been immortalised in a Beryl Cook painting. Unsurprisingly, the breakfasts here are particularly good. Close by you come to the **Codeword Pavement**, where messages between sailors and their loved ones at home have been carved, in shorthand, into the pavement.

Taking a right before The Vine pub, onto Strand St and then a left onto Cremyll St leads to **Royal William Yard**. Named after King William IV (who stands overlooking the entrance), the yard was built, mostly from reclaimed land, to supply the navy with beef, biscuits and beer – with a brewery, bakery and slaughterhouse on site. The path goes on a circuit of the yard, allowing walkers to explore its historic buildings (some of which now house cafés and restaurants), before climbing steps to head through the ramparts and on to the **Artillery Tower**, built to protect the harbour and yard but now a *restaurant* (see p95).

There's a small **tidal pool** (see p88) that you can swim in, just beside the tower, while nearby is *The Hutong Café* (**fb**; Wed-Mon 7.30am-2.30pm), which has a

plenty of **ATMs** near here too, in what is largely a pedestrianised shopping zone; there are also banks in Plymouth. The most convenient **launderette** is Hoegate Laundromat (☎ 01752-223031; Mon-Fri 8.30am-5pm, Sat 9am-1pm) at 55 Notte St.

Transport

Plymouth City Buses' 48 & 54 **bus** services run to Wembury and Bovisand and Tally Ho Coaches' No 94 operates to Noss Mayo and their 875 to Bigbury-on-Sea but only Fri 1/day. Note that getting public transport to most coastal destinations between Plymouth and Salcombe and then from there to Torcross is not easy. However, Stagecoach's No 3 journeys inland and then along the coast between Torcross and Dartmouth. If you want to avoid an area so devoid of public transport Stagecoach's Gold service will take you to Paignton. See pp53-5 for more details.

Plymouth railway station is an easy 10-minute walk north of Royal Parade; walk straight up Armada Way and follow the signs. GWR trains call at the station; see box p51 for details.

Plymouth Coach Station is at 165 Armada Way, off Mayflower St. For details of National Express coach services see box p51 and for Megabus p50.

The **ferry to Mount Batten Point** (see box p96) leaves from just south of Mayflower Steps. Close by is the departure point for **Cawsand Ferry** (🖳 www.ply mouthboattrips.co.uk/ferries/cawsand-ferry/; Apr-end Oct daily 9am, 10.30am, noon, 1.30pm, 3pm & 4.30pm; 30 mins; £5 one-way; 🐾), which shuttles passengers to the village of Cawsand in Cornwall.

For a **taxi**, try Need-a-Cab (☎ 01752-666222, 🖳 needacab247.com) or Ship to Shore Door to Door (☎ 07500-894492, 🖳 www.ship2shoredoor2door.com).

Where to stay

Hostels At the time of research long standing *Plymouth Backpackers* (☎ 01752-371536, 🖳 www.plymouthbackpackers.co .uk; 1 x female 4-, 6-, male 8- and 10-bed

---

modern European-café menu, but takes its inspiration from the cafés found in the traditional alleyways of old Beijing, where the owners used to live (*hutong* means 'narrow lane' in Chinese).

From the Artillery Tower, the route takes a left and leads past the smart Georgian terraces of Durnford St, where Sir Arthur Conan-Doyle worked as a doctor – which explains the **Sherlock Holmes' quotes** in the pavement. A hard right after **Stonehouse Barracks** leads you onto Millbay Rd, with Millbay Docks on the right. To return to the waterfront you need to turn right onto West Hoe Rd, which you follow all the way to The Barbican, passing the lovely **Tinside Lido** (see p88) on your right and both **The Hoe** (see p87) and **The Royal Citadel** (see p88) on your left.

There are still some quirky little sights on the way, including a **cross** in the pavement to celebrate 1999's total eclipse of the sun and a marble **scallop shell** in the wall near the start of The Barbican, which celebrates the fact that Plymouth was one of only two English ports licensed by the king from which pilgrims were allowed to embark when heading to Santiago de Compostela on the Way of St James. The shell is the symbol of St James, the patron saint of pilgrims. Another patron saint is celebrated in the same wall a little further down: **Stella Maris, the Virgin, Star of the Sea**, patron saint of seafarers, was rescued from a lost cargo of marble and now sits illuminated by the pole star shining above.

Pilgrims would pray to these saints for protection during their journeys; although your journey is mostly land based, it can't hurt to ask for their help on your forthcoming expedition, just in case.

dorms all en suite, 5T shared facilities; WI-FI; 🐾), at 102 Union St, had new owners and they weren't sure whether the room breakdown would stay the same for 2023. Rates (dorm bed from £20pp, £40 for a private room) include a continental breakfast and they have a self-catering kitchen.

Chain hotels The most central of Plymouth's several *Premier Inns* (City Centre, Derry's Cross; ☎ 0330 175 9006, 🖳 premierinn.com; WI-FI) is at one end of Royal Parade. Also in the Derry's Cross area, is a branch of *Travelodge* (☎ 0871-984 6251, 🖳 travelodge.co.uk; WI-FI; 🐾); see p21 for more details.

B&Bs Plymouth has plenty of B&Bs; a useful resource is 🖳 visitplymouth.co.uk/accommodation. Many are well situated for both the path and the city sights. Two of the most convenient for the Cremyll ferry are

> **Where to stay: note**
> Unless specified, B&B-style accommodation is either en suite or has private facilities.

The Firs (☎ 01752-300010, 🖳 thefirsin plymouth.co .uk; WI-FI; 1S shared facilities, 1D/1T/2Tr all en suite; 🐾; £42.50-60pp, sgl from £65), at 13 Pier St; and *The Caraneal* (☎ 01752-663589, 🖳 caraneal plymouth.co.uk; WI-FI; 2T/4D; from £35pp, sgl occ £45), at 12-14 Pier St.

More central, Citadel Rd has numerous B&B options all along its length. At the road's eastern end, close to The Barbican, is the aptly named *Barbican Reach Guest House* (☎ 01752-220021, 🖳 barbicanreach .co.uk; 1S/3D/1Tr; WI-FI; £45-55pp, sgl occ from £80), at No 225, with super clean rooms and a friendly welcome.

PLYMOUTH MAP KEY

Where to stay
5 Plymouth Backpackers
6 Duke of Cornwall Hotel
7 Travelodge
8 Premier Inn
11 The Firs
12 The Caraneal
17 Caledonia Guesthouse
18 Tudor Guest House
19 The Kynance
20 Invicta Hotel
22 George Guest House
34 Barbican Reach Guest House

Where to eat & drink
1 Elvira's Café
2 The Hutong
3 Artillery Tower
13 By the Park Deli-Café
14 The Waterfront

Where to eat & drink *(cont'd)*
15 The Wet Wok
16 Maritimo
21 Gypsy Moth
25 Yukisan
26 Favourite Food
28 Eastern Eye
29 Arribas
30 Barbican Steakhouse
31 The Thai House
32 The Bottling Plant
33 Barbican Kitchen (in Plymouth Gin Distillery)
35 Barbican Pasty Co
36 The Ship
37 Rakuda Bar & Pizzeria
38 The Village Restaurant
39 The Navy Inn
40 The Flower Café
42 Jacka Bakery)
43 Mad Merchant Coffee House
44 Harbourside

Where to eat & drink *(cont'd)*
45 Himalayan Spice
46 Monty's Café
48 Pier Master's House

Other
4 Aldi
9 Millets
10 Trespass
23 Tesco Express & ATM
24 Co-op
27 Hoegate Laundromat
33 Plymouth Gin Distillery
41 Elizabethan House & Gardens
47 Tourist Office & Mayflower Museum

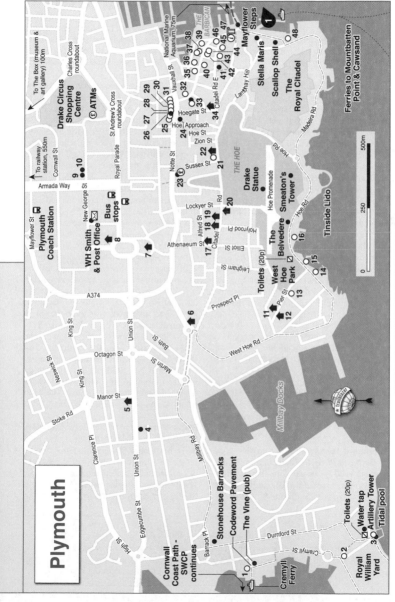

Plymouth

Further along, facing Hoe Park, is *The George Guesthouse* (☎ 01752-661517, 🖥 georgeguesthouse.com; 1S/2T/2Tr/1Qd, some en suite; 🐾), at No 161, which offers very competitive rates but for room only (from £32.50pp, sgl £40).

Towards the western end of Citadel Rd, there are more options such as *The Kynance* (☎ 01752-266821, 🖥 kynance house.co.uk; 2S/6D/8T/2Tr/2Qd; ☛; WI-FI; 🐾; from £45pp, sgl/sgl occ £65/75), at 107-11; *Caledonia Guesthouse* (☎ 01752-229052; 4D/1T all en suite, 1S/2T shared facilities; WI-FI; from £35pp room only, sgl/sgl occ £60), at No 27 Athenaeum St; and *Tudor Guest House* (☎ 01752-661557, 🖥 tudorhouseplymouth.co.uk; WI-FI; 2S shared facilities, 1T/4D/1Tr all en suite; from £40pp, sgl/sgl occ £42/55) at No 105 Citadel Rd.

Hotels The closest hotel to the Cremyll Ferry is the grand, 150-year-old *Duke of Cornwall Hotel* (☎ 01752-275850, 🖥 the dukeofcornwall.co.uk; 11S/61D or T; WI-FI; 🐾) on Millbay Rd. You can get rooms from £40pp (sgl £55, sgl occ room rate) in winter, but expect to pay at least double that in season. Nearer to The Hoe is *Invicta Hotel* (☎ 01752-664997, 🖥 invictahotel.co .uk; 4S/8D/6D or T/4Qd; ☛; 🐾; WI-FI; from £50pp, sgl/sgl occ £80), 11/12 Osborne Place.

Where to eat and drink
The Barbican is the place to go for food, though there are also some nice waterside spots right on the coast path along Hoe Rd.

Snacks & takeaways For **pasties**, head to *Barbican Pasty Co* (daily 9am-4.30pm), on Southside St, or get your **fish & chips** fix at *Harbourside* (**fb**; daily 11am-10.30/11pm), at 35 Southside St. *B-Bar* (🖥 barbicantheatre.co.uk/bbar; food daily noon-9pm; eat in or takeaway) is a **Thai** noodle bar inside Barbican Theatre on Castle St, or get **kebabs** from *Favourite Food* (🖥 favouritefood.co.uk; Mon-Sat 4-8.55pm, Sun 3.45-8.55pm) at 53 Notte St.

Cafés There's a great choice of places for coffee, cake, breakfast or a light lunch, from cute and friendly to whimsical and eccentric including; *Jacka Bakery* (38 Southside St; **fb**; Wed-Mon 8.30am-2.30pm) with the best bread in the city; the long-established *Monty's Café* (13 The Barbican; **fb**; daily 8am-4pm) with stand-out all-day breakfasts; and *The Flower Café* (46 Southside St; **fb**; Mon-Sat 10am-4pm, Sun to 5pm), perfect for tea and cake in their small back garden.

Hidden away in the cobbled back streets is the quirky *Mad Merchant Coffee House* (37 New St, 🖥 themadmerchants coffeehouse.com; **fb**; Tue-Sun 10am-4pm), with a gorgeous flower-filled back garden and arguably the best cream teas in the city.

If you're following the coast path from the Cremyll Ferry round to the Barbican, just a short diversion off it, at 26 Pier St, is the small deli-café *By The Park* (**fb**; Tue-Fri 9.30am-4.30pm, Sat & Sun to 5pm). Close by, right on the path, is *The Waterfront* (🖥 waterfront-plymouth.co.uk; food 9am-10pm, drinks to 11pm), with an art deco frontage and outstanding views from a large waterside terrace. The food (seafood and pub grub) is excellent.

Pubs & bars On Southside St, *The Navy Inn* (☎ 01752-301812; **fb**; WI-FI; 🐾; food daily noon-6pm) has won awards for its food. It's a traditional pub with a seemingly ordinary pub-grub menu, but the results are excellent, and the atmosphere always lively, particularly if the football's on. An

---

SYMBOLS USED IN TEXT

☛ Bathtub in, or for, at least one room;   WI-FI means wi-fi is available
🐾 Dogs allowed; for accommodation subject to prior arrangement (see p313)
fb signifies places that have a Facebook page (for latest opening hours)

added bonus is the upstairs terrace with waterfront views.

Opening out onto the waterfront, *The Ship* (☎ 01752-667604, 🖳 theshipplymouth.co.uk; WI-FI; 🐾 ground floor only; food Mon-Sat noon-9pm, Sun to 8pm) does very good food (mains £10-15) – the fish & chips are superb. Practically next door, *Rakuda Bar & Pizzeria* (☎ 01752-221155, 🖳 rakudabar.com; food daily noon-9pm) has the same great outdoor seating spot as The Ship for your pasta, pizza and cocktails.

Away from the tourists, *Gipsy Moth* (☎ 01752-219183, 🖳 gipsymoth.co.uk; WI-FI; 🐾; **fb**; food Mon-Sat 9.30-11.30am, noon-3pm & 5-9pm, Sun noon-6pm) is a shiny, glittery place serving tapas (dishes £6-7) and pub food with roasts on Sunday.

Restaurants Next door to The Navy Inn, *The Village Restaurant* (☎ 01752-667688, 🖳 thevillagerestaurantplymouth.co.uk; **fb**; daily 11.30am-10.15pm; mains £14-24), at No 32 Southside St, is an excellent seafood restaurant which also does a terrific roast beef on Sundays. Also on Southside St, *Barbican Kitchen* (☎ 01752-604448, 🖳 barbicankitchen.com; **fb**; food Wed-Sat noon-2pm, Tue-Fri 6-9pm, Sat 5-9pm; mains £15-32) is in **Plymouth Gin Distillery** (see p89) and serves delights such as slow-cooked Devon lamb shoulder, and roasted sea bream. Opposite, inside the distillery's former bottling house is *The Bottling Plant* (☎ 01752-511511, 🖳 the bottlingplant.co.uk; **fb**; WI-FI; 🐾; food Mon-Thur 9am-9pm, Fri & Sat to 9.30pm, Sun 10am-8.30pm). With period furniture and portraits of the past, the atmosphere certainly demands an afternoon cream tea, if not a gin or two. Mains cost £13-25 and they also do a good range of breakfasts.

With a fabulous harbourside location, *Pier Masters House* (☎ 01752-651410, 🖳 piermastershouse.com; **fb**; food daily 8am-10pm) is a fine choice for a meal. Its huge wood-decked terrace jutting out over the water is a very popular spot on summer evenings, and its menu (mains £12.50-26.95) of seafood, burgers and steaks doesn't disappoint. It's also open nice and early for breakfasts (full English £10.50).

A short walk away, on Notte St, *Barbican Steakhouse* (☎ 01752-222214, 🖳 barbicansteakhouse.com; **fb**; daily 5-10pm) does a side-busting 'half a calf', – a 20oz rump steak for £24.95.

For **Indian** cuisine, eat in or takeaway, there's *Eastern Eye* (☎ 01752-262948, 🖳 easterneyeplymouth.com; daily 5-11pm), at 57 Notte St, or the excellent *Himalayan Spice* (☎ 01752-252211, 🖳 himalayanspice.net; Sun-Thur 6-11pm, Fri & Sat to 11.30pm), housed in a 16th-century building at 31 New St.

For **Thai** food, head to *Thai House* (☎ 01752-661600, 🖳 thethaihouseplymouth.com; **fb**; Mon-Sat 5-10.30pm, Sun to 9.30pm) at 63 Notte St. Eat **Mexican** at *Arribas* (☎ 01752-603303, 🖳 v7.arribasmexican.com; **fb**; daily 5-10pm) at No 58. At No 51 is long-standing **Japanese** restaurant *Yukisan* (☎ 01752-250240, 🖳 yukisan.co.uk; Mon, Wed & Thur noon-2.30pm & 5-10pm, Fri & Sat noon-10.30pm, Sun to 9.30pm).

There are plenty of **Chinese** options in town, though perhaps the most unusual is *The Wet Wok* (☎ 01752-664456, 🖳 wetwok.com; daily noon-2pm & 6-10pm) hidden away down a flight of steps leading to a secret perch overlooking Plymouth Sound. Service is quick (ideal for passing walkers), and the food is tasty.

Also on Hoe Rd, and also overlooking the Sound, is the cute wine and **tapas** bar *Maritimo* (☎ 01752-222938, 🖳 maritimoplymouth.co.uk; **fb**; food daily noon-9pm), with a relaxed atmosphere and more great views.

Further afield, but worth the walk, *Artillery Tower* (☎ 01752-257610, 🖳 artillerytower.co.uk; Wed-Sat 7-11pm, last arrivals 8pm; booking essential), is one of the more discreet places in the city; indeed, you may well have walked right past it without knowing on the way into the centre from the Cremyll ferry. Evening meals are from £60/67 for two/three courses, and may include mains such as peppered haunch of venison with red cabbage and pineapple pickle. The restaurant is located in a 15th-century defensive tower on the sea wall and overlooks Plymouth Sound.

PLYMOUTH TO WEMBURY   [MAPS 1-6]

For such a lovely trek, this initial **10¾-mile (17.25km; 4¼hrs)** leg is a bit of an inauspicious start. True, there may be the occasional stroller who will swoon at this saunter through the city's unsung suburbs and praise the opportunity it provides to plod through Plymouth's less picturesque parts. But for most people the start of their 217¼-mile odyssey is little more than a fairly mundane trudge through an unappealing industrial estate followed by an only-slightly-more-interesting hike through the suburban sprawl that precedes Mount Batten Point.

You can, of course, opt to take the ferry (see box below) from The Barbican to Mount Batten Point, and if time is short this would be a good decision. It does, after all, completely cut out the dullest stretch of this stage (possibly, some may argue, of the entire SWCP), and leaves you with just its more appetising latter half along the eastern edge of Plymouth Sound and on past Heybrook Bay to Wembury.

But if you do have the time – and you're serious about completing the walk described in this book – you should probably attempt the whole stage, from Mayflower Steps to Wembury: taking a short-cut before you've even begun walking is no way to begin a challenge such as this. And besides, the path is not entirely without interest. There's the signage, for one thing, which for some unknown reason is by far the best on the entire coast path. Why anyone designed such a variegated array of signposts and waymarks is anyone's guess – but the fact is the path is marked with signposts made from huge recycled navigation beacons, some Communist-style iron star plaques and even giant metal sycamore keys. It's all rather bizarre – but they do serve to provide much-needed distractions for this stage. The city authorities have also gone to some length to provide interest to this section and are to be applauded for their efforts. On the first half of this stage, for example, you'll come across a wall of poetry and a rhino sculpture.

After Mount Batten Point matters improve and the countryside for the first time starts to dominate. While the bucolic beauty of this stage's second half is still interrupted on occasion – most noticeably by the holiday park at Bovisand – it is, on the whole, a largely rustic, gentle ramble, and much more characteristic of the trek to come. So strap on those boots, tighten the shoulder straps and get going: you've got 217¼ miles to go and these paths don't walk themselves.

Before you set off, though, make sure you check the ferry times (see box below and p105) for this section of the path; and if you do want to get across the Yealm today, make sure you complete this stage and are at the ferry slip by 4pm.

❏ **THE FERRY TO MOUNT BATTEN POINT**

The ferry to Mount Batten Point (boat ☎ 07930-838614, 🖳 mountbattenferry.co.uk; £2, 🐾 free) is not actually part of the coast path – though many trekkers treat it as such to cut out the rather dull walking through Plymouth. Crossings depart every 15-30 minutes (end Apr-early Oct Mon-Fri 8am-10pm, Sat & Sun 9am-10pm; rest of year Mon-Fri 8am-6.15pm, Sat & Sun 9am-6.15pm), and take around 10 minutes.

The route

Beginning at the **Mayflower Steps**, the path leaves the busy delights of The Barbican behind by crossing the lock gates that secure Sutton Harbour, passing the huge **National Marine Aquarium** on the left on its way to the **Wallsend** and Cattedown **industrial estates**. (You may be surprised to find that the former is actually an SSSI, see p57, a disused quarry clearly showing the development of Devonian Plymouth limestone.) It's not the only surprise on this section of the trail: the **giant 'rocket' SWCP waypoint** leading you on to **Breakwater Hill** was once a navigational beacon for sailors and now serves much the same purpose for landlubbing trekkers. A section of speeding through an industrial estate, past a quirky **SWCP bench**, then separates you from **Laira Bridge** and a crossing of the Plym. A **poetry wall** (Map 2) lines busy Billacombe Rd, which brightens an otherwise unpleasant stretch.

You leave this thoroughfare at **Oreston Rhino**, a sculpture which celebrates the prehistoric fossils of lion, ox, elephant, hippo, camel and, yes, rhino, that have been found in the caves near the city. Heading down Breakwater Rd, it's not long before the banks of **Hooe Lake** are reached, which you then hug most of the way to the neat suburb of Turnchapel (see p98). On the way you pass **Radford Castle**, originally built for the 'keep-

Oreston Rhino sculpture

er', a member of staff of nearby Radford House, who was responsible for looking after the estate's moorings and quays. Shortly after, by Hooe Green, a pub, *The Royal Oak* (☎ 01752-401111; **fb**; **food** Wed-Sat noon-3pm & 5-8pm, Sun noon-5pm; WI-FI; 🐾) has a **plaque** on its wall facing the path – one of several such plaques that decorate the walls around here. It is a large-scale re-creation of

ROUTE GUIDE AND MAPS

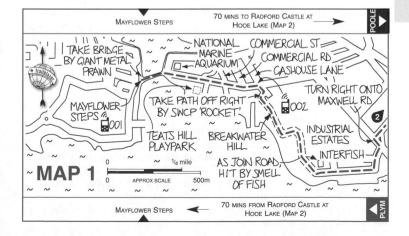

MAYFLOWER STEPS

70 MINS TO RADFORD CASTLE AT HOOE LAKE (MAP 2)

POOLE

TAKE BRIDGE BY GIANT METAL PRAWN

trailblazer

NATIONAL MARINE AQUARIUM

COMMERCIAL ST
COMMERCIAL RD
GASHOUSE LANE

TURN RIGHT ONTO MAXWELL RD

MAYFLOWER STEPS 001

TAKE PATH OFF RIGHT BY SWCP 'ROCKET'

002

INDUSTRIAL ESTATES

INTERFISH

TEATS HILL PLAYPARK

BREAKWATER HILL

MAP 1

0 ¼ mile
0 APPROX SCALE 500m

AS JOIN ROAD, HIT BY SMELL OF FISH

MAYFLOWER STEPS

70 MINS FROM RADFORD CASTLE AT HOOE LAKE (MAP 2)

PLYM

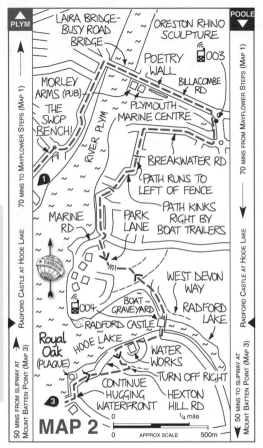

a medallion issued by John Smeaton (see box p88), builder of Eddystone Lighthouse, which he gave to his highly skilled workers to prevent them being taken by press-gangs – hired thugs employed to force men into the military service. The pub dates from 1799 and welcomes coast-path walkers. It overlooks Hooe Green and the corner of the harbour, otherwise known as Hooe Lake. Plymouth City Bus 54 stops here; see box pp53-5.

You'll soon pass through the delightfully colourful, narrow streets of **Turnchapel**, where two fine pubs – the cool-blue *Boringdon Arms* (☎ 01752-402053, 🖥 boringdon-arms.net; **food** Mon-Sat noon-3pm & 6-9pm, Sun noon-3pm; WI-FI; 🐾), which does **B&B** (3T/1Tr share facilities, 1Tr/1Qd both en suite; from £35pp inc for sgl occ) and the bright-yellow *Clovelly Bay Inn* (☎ 01752-402765, 🖥 www.clovellybay inn.co.uk; fb; 🐾; **food** Mon-Thur 6-9pm, Fri & Sat noon-3pm & 6-9pm, Sun noon-3.30pm, bar similar hours) – vie for your attention.

It's not long before you arrive at **Mount Batten Point** (see box p100). You'll find several more places to eat round here though we advise holding off until you're strolling on the **Jennycliffs** and reach the no-frills, but very popular *Jennycliff Café* (Map 3; ☎ 01752-402358; fb; WI-FI; 🐾; daily 9am-4pm), with the best views over the Sound and a great-value menu including omelettes (£6.20-6.50), full breakfasts (£5.20-6.50), baguettes, baked potatoes, and pasties (£5.60-5.90) so huge they could constitute a danger to shipping. Plymouth City Bus 54 stops at Jennycliff; see box pp53-5.

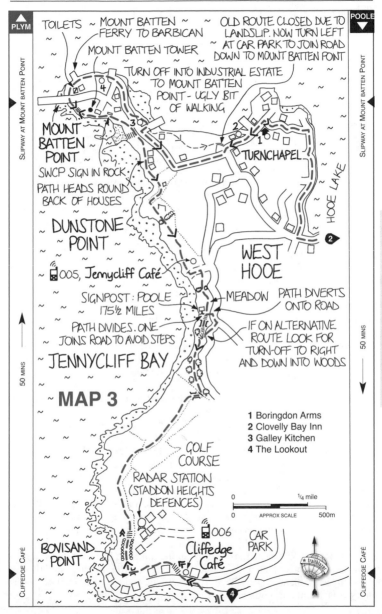

TOILETS ~ MOUNT BATTEN ~
FERRY TO BARBICAN

OLD ROUTE CLOSED DUE TO
LANDSLIP. NOW TURN LEFT
AT CAR PARK TO JOIN ROAD
DOWN TO MOUNT BATTEN POINT

MOUNT BATTEN TOWER

TURN OFF INTO INDUSTRIAL ESTATE
TO MOUNT BATTEN
POINT- UGLY BIT
OF WALKING

MOUNT
BATTEN
POINT

TURNCHAPEL

SWCP SIGN IN ROCK

PATH HEADS ROUND
BACK OF HOUSES

DUNSTONE
~ POINT

HOOE LAKE

005, Jenycliff Café

WEST
HOOE

SIGNPOST: POOLE
175½ MILES

MEADOW

PATH DIVERTS
ONTO ROAD

PATH DIVIDES. ONE
JOINS ROAD TO AVOID STEPS

IF ON ALTERNATIVE
ROUTE LOOK FOR
TURN-OFF TO RIGHT
AND DOWN INTO WOODS

JENNYCLIFF BAY

MAP 3

1 Boringdon Arms
2 Clovelly Bay Inn
3 Galley Kitchen
4 The Lookout

GOLF
COURSE

RADAR STATION
(STADDON HEIGHTS
DEFENCES)

0   ¼ mile
0   500m
APPROX SCALE

006
Cliffedge
Café

CAR
PARK

BOVISAND
~ POINT

trailblaze

50 MINS

50 MINS

❏ **MOUNT BATTEN POINT**

Though today it seems little more than an unprepossessing pimple of grassy rock, Mount Batten Point actually has a lengthy history, as a few of its old buildings may suggest. Indeed, excavations indicate that this spot was the location for the very earliest trade the British had with Europe. From the late Bronze Age right through to the Roman era, archaeologists at Mount Batten Point have found evidence of a market that led some to suggest that this spot could be the 'Tamaris' mentioned by Ptolemy in his *Geographica* (often cited as the world's earliest guide book). The most obvious building here today, however, the austere **Mount Batten Tower**, is significantly younger, having been constructed in 1652 to protect the burgeoning new settlement around Plymouth Harbour.

Skip forward a few hundred years and the waters off Mount Batten Point were used to test the first sea-plane models, and an air station was subsequently established here. A **monument in the shape of a propellor** from a Sunderland flying boat, situated at the very end of the point, celebrates the RAF's tenure.

After Mount Batten Point the path changes character and finally becomes the rustic ramble you were hoping for. True, Plymouth is still a huge looming presence over your right shoulder. The large naval contingent in the Sound and the helicopters swooping overhead further ensure that you aren't free of the city shackles just yet. But climbing away from Mount Batten Point the path is soon dodging amongst woods and meadows rather than warehouses and marinas.

This rural idyll is interrupted by naval defences near **Bovisand Point**, which is home to the cosy *Cliffedge Café* (**fb**; daily 9am-5.30pm, winter to 4pm) and its neighbouring holiday park – which in turn plays host to *Café Bovisands* (Map 4; ☎ 01752-862679; **fb**; 🐾; Tue-Sun 10am-4pm) and a **shop** (generally Apr-Sep 10am-4pm). But it's not long before you are once again away from civilisation on a reasonably flat path heading via **Heybrook Bay** to round **Wembury Point**.

The island out to sea, by the way, is **Great Mewstone**, now uninhabited but once occupied by one Sam Wakeman, who was exiled there for seven years as punishment for some misdemeanour and paid his rent by supplying rabbits for the table of the local manor. There is a painting of the island by JMW Turner, dated 1816, which is now in the National Gallery of Ireland, Dublin.

With **Wembury Marine Conservation Area** to the right, rising ground to the left and an easy flat path ahead, it's a pleasant final stretch to *The Old Mill Café* (☎ 01752-863280; **fb**; WI-FI; 🐾 on lead; Apr-end Oct daily 10.30am to 4/5pm – check in advance; Nov-Mar weekends & hols 11am-4pm), a 150-year-old watermill turned eatery. The small **Wembury Marine Centre** (☎ 01752-862538, 🖳 wemburymarinecentre.org; Apr-Oct Tue-Sun 10am-4.30pm; free) next door gives a kid-friendly introduction to the coastline conservation.

The road to Wembury runs steeply up the hill from here – or you can continue along the coast path to the mouth of the Yealm, from where a slightly flatter path heads inland to the village. Alternatively, you can carry on down to the ferry launch and the continuation of the trail.

WEMBURY [map p102, top]

An unassuming little place nestling in the shadow of Plymouth and its suburbs, Wembury has been around for a long time – some flint tools have been found hereabouts which proves that man has been stomping around since at least the Mesolithic era (10,000-4000BC).

(cont'd on p104)

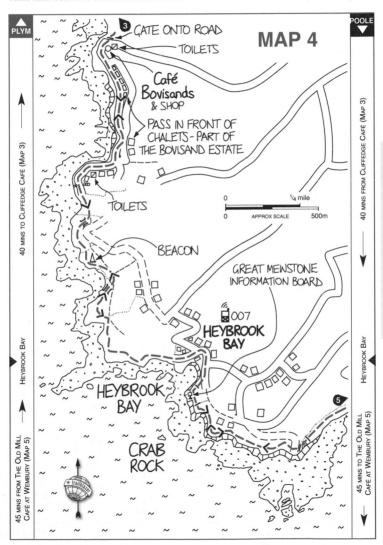

PLYM

POOLE

GATE ONTO ROAD

TOILETS

MAP 4

Café
Bovisands
& SHOP

PASS IN FRONT OF
CHALETS - PART OF
THE BOVISAND ESTATE

TOILETS

0   ¼ mile
0   500m
APPROX SCALE

BEACON

GREAT MEWSTONE
INFORMATION BOARD

007

HEYBROOK
BAY

HEYBROOK
BAY

CRAB
ROCK

5

trailblazer

40 MINS TO CLIFFEDGE CAFÉ (MAP 3)

HEYBROOK BAY

45 MINS FROM THE OLD MILL
CAFÉ AT WEMBURY (MAP 5)

40 MINS FROM CLIFFEDGE CAFÉ (MAP 3)

HEYBROOK BAY

45 MINS TO THE OLD MILL
CAFÉ AT WEMBURY (MAP 5)

ROUTE GUIDE AND MAPS

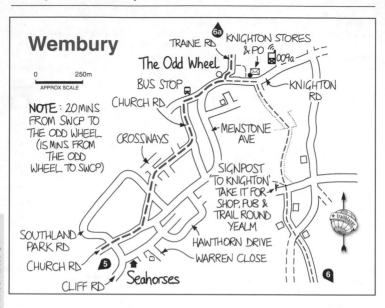

Wembury

0   250m
APPROX SCALE

NOTE: 20 MINS
FROM SWCP TO
THE ODD WHEEL
(15 MINS FROM
THE ODD
WHEEL TO SWCP)

6a

TRAINE RD

KNIGHTON STORES
& PO

009a

The Odd Wheel

BUS STOP

CHURCH RD

KNIGHTON
RD

MEWSTONE
AVE

CROSSWAYS

SIGNPOST
'TO KNIGHTON'
TAKE IT FOR
SHOP, PUB &
TRAIL ROUND
YEALM

SOUTHLAND
PARK RD

HAWTHORN DRIVE

CHURCH RD   5

WARREN CLOSE

CLIFF RD

Seahorses

6

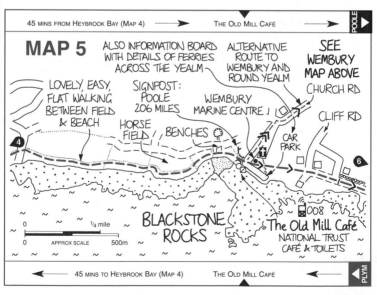

45 MINS FROM HEYBROOK BAY (MAP 4) ⟶   THE OLD MILL CAFÉ ⟶   **POOLE ▶**

MAP 5

ALSO INFORMATION BOARD
WITH DETAILS OF FERRIES
ACROSS THE YEALM

ALTERNATIVE
ROUTE TO
WEMBURY AND
ROUND YEALM

SEE
WEMBURY
MAP ABOVE

CHURCH RD

LOVELY, EASY,
FLAT WALKING
BETWEEN FIELD
& BEACH

SIGNPOST:
POOLE
206 MILES

WEMBURY
MARINE CENTRE

CLIFF RD

HORSE
FIELD

BENCHES

CAR
PARK

4

6

0   ¼ mile

0   APPROX SCALE   500m

BLACKSTONE
~ ROCKS ~

008

The Old Mill Café
NATIONAL TRUST
CAFÉ & TOILETS

◀   45 MINS TO HEYBROOK BAY (MAP 4)   THE OLD MILL CAFÉ ◀   **PLYM ▲**

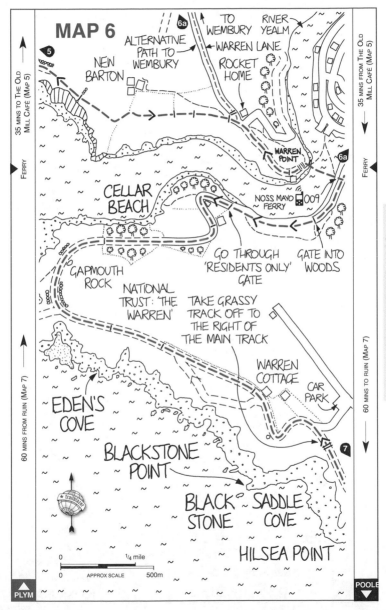

MAP 6

5

FERRY

TO WEMBURY

RIVER YEALM

ALTERNATIVE PATH TO WEMBURY

NEW BARTON

WARREN LANE

ROCKET HOME

6a

WARREN POINT

6a

FERRY

CELLAR BEACH

NOSS MAYO FERRY   009

GAPMOUTH ROCK

GO THROUGH 'RESIDENTS ONLY' GATE

GATE INTO WOODS

NATIONAL TRUST: 'THE WARREN'

TAKE GRASSY TRACK OFF TO THE RIGHT OF THE MAIN TRACK

WARREN COTTAGE

CAR PARK

EDEN'S COVE

7

BLACKSTONE POINT

BLACK STONE

SADDLE COVE

HILSEA POINT

trailblazer

0   ¼ mile

0   APPROX SCALE   500m

PLYM

POOLE

(cont'd from p101) Little happens here in Wembury but it's a pleasant-enough place, if a little too uphill from the coast for most tired trekkers. **Knighton Stores** (daily 7am-7pm, Sun 8am-6pm) is well stocked, and doubles up as the **post office** (same hours).

Plymouth Citybus's No 48 **bus** service (see pp53-5) travels to Plymouth.

For **accommodation**, your choice is limited to just *Seahorses* (☎ 01752-863038,

📧 jackiecurtis147@gmail.com; 1T; 🛏; WI-FI; from £45pp, sgl occ £50), at 10 Hawthorn Park Rd.

For **food**, the village pub, *The Odd Wheel* (☎ 01752-862504; **fb**; food summer Mon-Sat noon-8.30pm, Sun to 7.30pm, rest of year check **fb** page; WI-FI; 🐾) does some great dishes including a mean Sunday roast. Also stocks a selection of real ales.

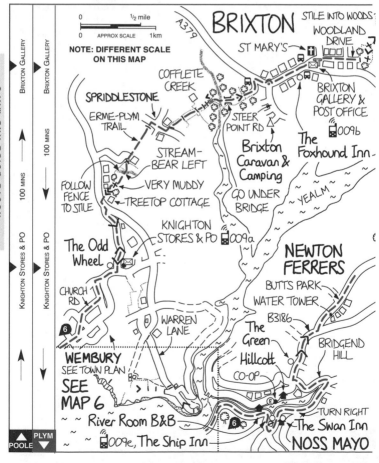

ROUTE GUIDE AND MAPS

BRIXTON GALLERY

100 MINS

KNIGHTON STORES & PO

PLYM
POOLE

TACKLING THE YEALM

Ferry and bus details

For the coast path you need the Warren Point to Noss Mayo service (the service from Warren Point to Newton Ferrers will still get you across the river, but further away from the coast path than the Noss Mayo one). The **ferry** (☎ 07817-132757; £4; 🐕 free) operates daily from Easter/Apr to the end of September 10am-4pm but at times this may be restricted to 10am-noon & 3-4pm. If you miss the ferry, and don't want to walk around the estuary, you can take Plymouth City **Buses'** No 48 from Wembury to Plymstock then change for Tally Ho Coaches No 94 to Noss Mayo; see pp53-5.

Walking around the Yealm [Map 5 p102, Map 6a]

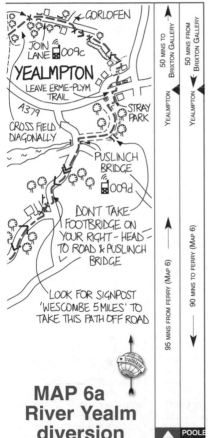

**MAP 6a
River Yealm
diversion**

ROUTE GUIDE AND MAPS

The **9-mile (14.5km; 4hrs)** diversion is not without its attractions including some pleasant walking on the **Erme-Plym Trail** (see pp22-3). However, overall there are times, particularly when you reach the Devonshire village of Brixton, that the coast path seems an awfully long way away and it won't be long before you'll be yearning for the sound of the sea again.

The trail begins by The Odd Wheel pub, at the eastern end of Wembury, where a small country lane, Traine Rd, runs north away from the village to Wembury Rd. Opposite the junction here, the Erme-Plym Trail continues along a pathway down the side of Treetop Cottage (Map 6a), through a forest, across an open field with a pond, and on to a wooded track towards tiny **Spriddlestone**. Turn right then left and continue across **Cofflete Creek** to the busy A379, where you turn right to reach the historic village of **Brixton**. **Camping** is available at *Brixton Caravan & Camping* (☎ 01752-402732, 🖳 www.brixton-caravan-camping-park.co.uk; 🐕; £7 per pitch, £5pp) and there is a local **post office** (Mon-Fri 9am-noon) but no shop.

Brixton also has a standout pub: *The Foxhound Inn* (☎ 01752-880271, 🖳 foxhoundinn.co.uk; **fb**; WI-FI; 🐕; food daily noon-2pm,

Sun-Thur 6-8pm, Fri & Sat 6-9pm), an award-winning 200-year-old real-ale pub with one beer – Redcoat – that's brewed by the landlord and always on tap. Stagecoach's No 3 and Tally Ho's No 94 call in Brixton (see pp53-5).

From Brixton the path continues along the Erme-Plym Trail which you rejoin beside Brixton Stores post office-cum-gallery (don't be tempted to walk along the A379 as it has no pavement), heading through fields of crops and pheasants on your way to a small country lane that you join at **Gorlofen**. This you leave via a steep climb up a field, rejoining the A379 at **Yealmpton**. Stagecoach's No 3 and Tally Ho's No 94 & 875 call here (see pp53-5).

A lovely stretch now follows as you say goodbye to the Erme-Plym for the last time, briefly heading west back along the A379 then down **Stray Park** to the end to reach a lovely wooded track on the right that heads, via some charmingly overgrown quarry works, to **Puslinch Bridge**, where you actually cross the Yealm. Much of the next section is, alas, on roads (albeit quiet country roads) as you climb steeply out of the valley, diverting off the road briefly to cross a couple of fields before returning to the tarmac for the long but hilly straight stretch to the **Water Tower** at Butts Park and the B3186 leading down (right) to **Newton Ferrers** (see below).

Sticking to the road, you skirt the end of Newton Creek to reach the even tinier settlement of **Noss Mayo** (see below) – at the end of which, of course, lies the **ferry launch** and a reunion with the coast path.

NOSS MAYO & NEWTON FERRERS
[Map 6a, pp104-5]
Separated by a narrow tidal creek, these tidy twin villages lie on the estuary of the River Yealm. **Newton Ferrers** is the larger of the two. Originally called *Niwetone*, the village was given as a gift to the Norman Ferrers family – hence the name. Here you'll find a Co-op **supermarket** (daily 7am-10pm) with a free **ATM**, as well as *The Green* (☎ 01752-872313, 🖥 thegreen deli.co.uk; **fb**; 🐾 on lead; Tue-Thur & Sat 8.30am-4pm, Fri to 7pm, Sun 10am-3pm), a lovely deli and café as you head north out of the village on Parsonage Rd.

Hillcott (book through 🖥 airbnb.co .uk; 2D; ☛; WI-FI; 🐾) offers self-catering **accommodation**. It is opposite the Co-op and is a lovely place, an entire cottage that's available through Airbnb. The problem is that they require a two- or three-night minimum stay.

If you would prefer to stay nearer to the path you should head to the quieter, and ever-so charming **Noss Mayo**, which clings tightly to the edge of a side creek. The ferry across the Yealm calls in at the edge of the village, about 10 minutes' walk from the centre. Here you'll find *River Room B&B*

(1D; 🐾; from £50pp, sgl occ room rate), a self-contained studio room with a shower room (accessed from across a terrace), a kettle and a microwave, and stunning views of the estuary. Again, it's a lovely spot, but they prefer *three-night* minimum stays and also bookings must be through Airbnb.

For **food**, *The Swan Inn* (☎ 01752-873115, 🖥 www.swaninnnossmayo.com; **fb**; WI-FI; 🐾) is one of two great pubs in Noss Mayo, which look out at each other from across the creek. Their **food** (Tue 5-8.30pm, Wed-Sat noon-3pm & 5-8.30pm, Sun noon-3pm & 5-8pm) is hearty and reasonably priced and they have a covered outdoor seating area equipped with heaters, blankets and hot water bottles – so you can enjoy the views whatever the weather. The other pub, *The Ship Inn* (☎ 01752-872387, 🖥 www.nossmayo.com; **fb**; 🐾; food daily noon-9.30pm), also has a smashing location, but is more of a gastro-pub, with mains costing £14-20. Both stock real ales.

Tally Ho Coach's No 94 **bus service** calls at both Newton Ferrers & Noss Mayo and also at Yealmpton (en route to Plymouth) where you can connect with Stagecoach's No 3; see pp53-5.

WEMBURY TO BIGBURY-ON-SEA   [MAPS 6-11]

This **15¼-mile (24.5km; 5½hrs)** stage is fairly typical of the South Devon section of the SWCP. There are a couple of river crossings (including one, uniquely for this stretch of the coast path, that you have to wade across), an excellent café to stop at for lunch, and a quiet village at the end of your hike with a very quirky pub. And with mile after mile of lovely scenery to delight the eyes and lift the soul, this is very much in keeping with this county's ability to inspire and entertain.

There are, however, some possible problems on the trail. The first is that this is actually one of the quietest stretches on the entire path, with the café at Mothecombe the only place to eat at before Challaborough and Bigbury. The second problem is the crossing of the Erme: with no ferry, the only way to tackle it is to wade across – which, according to the noticeboards dotted about, **is possible only an hour either side of low tide**. It's important, therefore, that you find out when this will be and keep a close eye on your progress against the clock. Mistime your arrival and you'll have to arrange a taxi, or walk around – and given that this walk around the estuary is almost entirely on roads without pavements, this is one estuary diversion you really don't want to have to do.

The route
Having crossed the Yealm, your next task on the trail is to follow an old carriage drive west round **Gapmouth Rock** (Map 6) then east on **Revelstoke Drive** past various old ruins (including a **ruined signal station**) to Stoke Beach. This is a really lovely stretch; fairly straightforward on gentle, grassy Revelstoke Drive, wooded in places, with delicious sea views every now and then on your right. Passing above the **Church of St Peter the Poor Fisherman** – which dates back to the 12th century and is once again, following extensive repairs in the 1970s, used for services occasionally – the path reaches the drive to Stoke House and, soon after, at **Beacon Hill** (note the ruined look-out by the path), becomes even more strenuous – though, if anything, more gorgeous too.

The main feature on this approach to the River Erme is undoubtedly **St Anchorite's Rock**, a huge tor gazing silently out over the sea. An *anchorite* is an old term for a hermit and it is probable that a hermitage was established near here at some point in the dim and distant past.

Not long afterwards the mouth at **Mothecombe** (Map 9) is reached, from where you can head inland to wait for low tide at the excellent café, *Schoolhouse* (☎ 01752-830552, 🖳 schoolhouse-devon.com; WI-FI; 🐾; food daily 10am-4pm, summer Fri & Sat 5-8pm). Sit in the garden or (possibly only in the winter months) at long shared tables inside the rustic barn-like main room, while you gorge on breakfasts, burgers and sandwiches, and Italian mains including pizzas (£13-16). Most of the menu is available as takeaway. Don't forget to keep an eye on the time and tide, though. It would be a shame to miss your only chance of fording the Erme for the sake of a coffee.

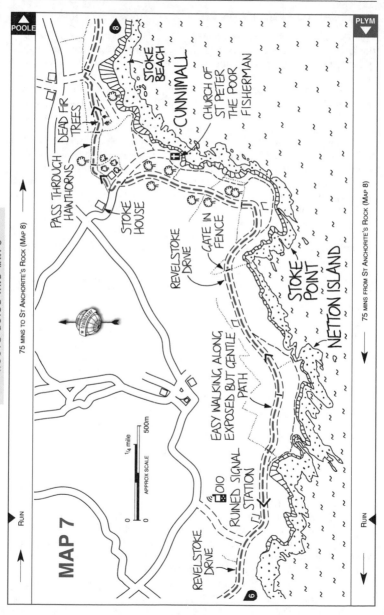

MAP 7

POOLE

PLYM

RUIN

75 MINS TO ST ANCHORITE'S ROCK (MAP 8)

PASS THROUGH HAWTHORNS

DEAD FIR TREES

STOKE BEACH

8

CUNNIMALL

STOKE HOUSE

CHURCH OF ST PETER THE POOR FISHERMAN

REVELSTOKE DRIVE

GATE IN FENCE

STOKE POINT

NETTON ISLAND

EASY WALKING ALONG GENTLE PATH EXPOSED BUT

RUINED SIGNAL STATION

REVELSTOKE DRIVE

6

RUIN

75 MINS FROM ST ANCHORITE'S ROCK (MAP 8)

¼ mile

500m

APPROX SCALE

0

0

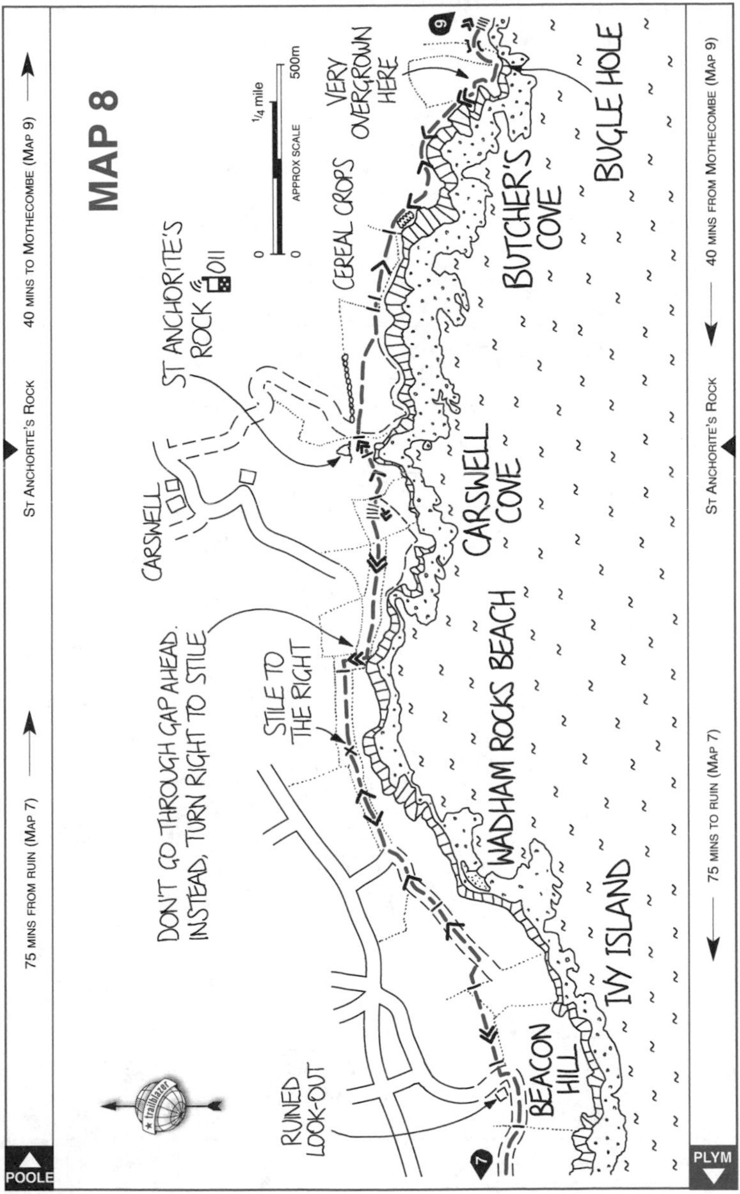

MAP 8

POOLE

CARSWELL

ST ANCHORITE'S ROCK

ST ANCHORITE'S ROCK

CEREAL CROPS

VERY OVERGROWN HERE

9

BUGLE HOLE

BUTCHER'S COVE

CARSWELL COVE

WADHAM ROCKS BEACH

IVY ISLAND

DON'T GO THROUGH GAP AHEAD. INSTEAD, TURN RIGHT TO STILE

STILE TO THE RIGHT

BEACON HILL

RUINED LOOK-OUT

7

PLYM

0   ¼ mile

0   500m

APPROX SCALE

TACKLING THE ERME   [Map 9; Map 9a]

Wading across Assuming you are here an hour either side of low tide you can wade across the river; the best place is clearly signposted. The terrain underfoot is sandy and, on occasion, pebbly too – but it doesn't take more than a few minutes at most to cross.

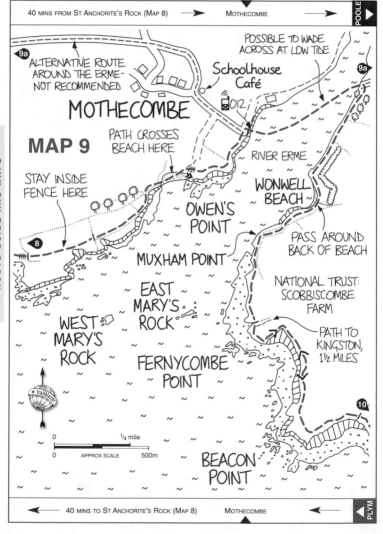

40 MINS FROM ST ANCHORITE'S ROCK (MAP 8) → MOTHECOMBE → POOLE

POSSIBLE TO WADE ACROSS AT LOW TIDE

Schoolhouse Café

012

9a ALTERNATIVE ROUTE AROUND THE ERME- NOT RECOMMENDED

9a

MOTHECOMBE

MAP 9

PATH CROSSES BEACH HERE

RIVER ERME

STAY INSIDE FENCE HERE

WONWELL BEACH

8

OWEN'S POINT

PASS AROUND BACK OF BEACH

MUXHAM POINT

NATIONAL TRUST: SCOBBISCOMBE FARM

EAST MARY'S ROCK

PATH TO KINGSTON, 1½ MILES

WEST MARY'S ROCK

FERNYCOMBE POINT

★ trailblazer

10

0   ¼ mile

0   APPROX SCALE   500m

BEACON POINT

40 MINS TO ST ANCHORITE'S ROCK (MAP 8) ← MOTHECOMBE ← PLYM

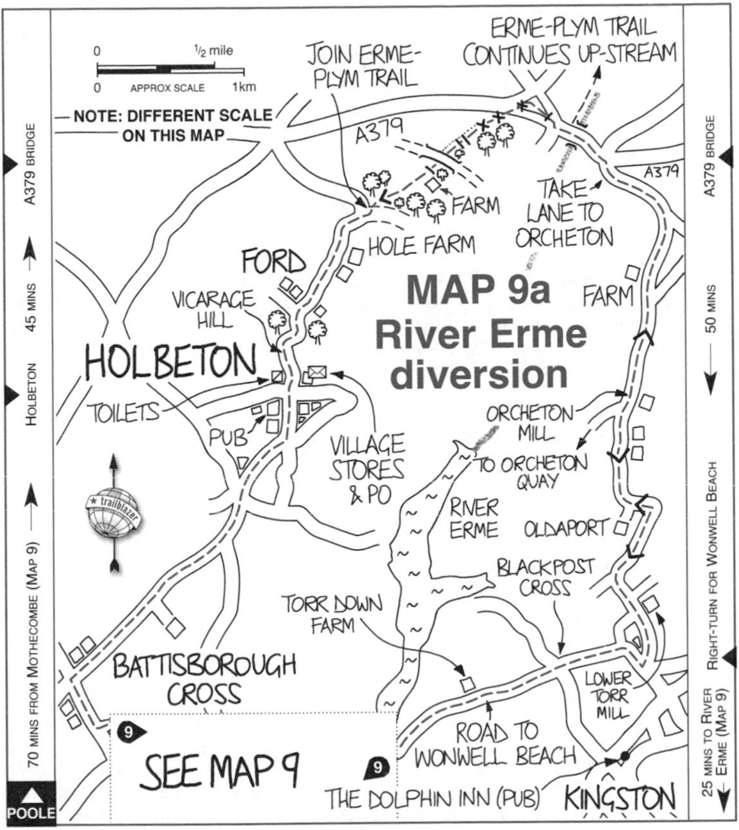
0 ½ mile
0 APPROX SCALE 1km
NOTE: DIFFERENT SCALE ON THIS MAP
JOIN ERME-PLYM TRAIL
ERME-PLYM TRAIL CONTINUES UP-STREAM
A379
A379
FARM
TAKE LANE TO ORCHETON
HOLE FARM
FORD
MAP 9a
River Erme
diversion
FARM
VICARAGE HILL
HOLBETON
TOILETS
PUB
VILLAGE STORES & PO
ORCHETON MILL
TO ORCHETON QUAY
RIVER ERME
OLDAPORT
BLACKPOST CROSS
TORR DOWN FARM
BATTISBOROUGH CROSS
LOWER TORR MILL
ROAD TO WONWELL BEACH
SEE MAP 9
THE DOLPHIN INN (PUB)
KINGSTON
trailblazer
POOLE
70 MINS FROM MOTHECOMBE (MAP 9)
HOLBETON 45 MINS A379 BRIDGE
A379 BRIDGE 50 MINS
RIGHT-TURN FOR WONWELL BEACH
25 MINS TO RIVER ERME (MAP 9)

By taxi A taxi will cost £30-35. Since it's quite a way from any of the taxi offices to Mothecombe it is advisable to book a taxi in advance. Be aware that the taxi driver may not know where you are and also may not know the route. For those using the What3words app (see p82), the location where the path joins the road before dropping down to the beach is 'gearing,estuaries.road'. For a **taxi** try Wembury Cars (☎ 01752-881651).

Walking around the Erme

This is the least pleasant of the riverside diversions in the book – so either of the above options is far more preferable.

The walk **(8¾ miles; 3hrs 10 mins)** begins – and largely continues – along roads, both upriver and back down the other side again. Hopefully Maps 9 and 9a make the correct route clear. Don't be tempted by some attractive-looking footpaths leading off the roads in what seems to be the correct direction; trust us when we say that they don't lead to anywhere useful. It goes without saying that you need to be careful as most of these country lanes have no pavements. The OL20 Ordnance Survey map is useful to find your way, though it's not particularly difficult. Follow the road west out of Mothecombe, turning right at **Battisborough Cross**, continue north for a couple of miles to **Holbeton** before following Vicarage Hill to the left of the Village Stores (**fb**).

The even tinier village of **Ford** is your next destination, again signposted, north of which is **Hole Farm**. Continuing north, eventually you'll hit the Erme-Plym Trail which you should take right to join the A379. Thankfully, your stay on this road lasts for only a few hundred metres, where a lane to the right is signed to Orcheton.

Follow this for another couple of miles down past **Orcheton Mill** and its nearby quay, then **Oldaport**, Clyng Mill, the turn-off to Waster and Shearlangstone, and so on to Torr Rock and **Lower Torr**. Finally a road to the right is signposted to **Wonwell Beach** (if you reach Kingston you've walked too far), your destination for this walk, and reachable after taking a left where the road forks past the row of pink cottages, passing Blackpost Cross and Torr Down Farm on your way down to the east bank of the Erme.

There's no let-up in the beauty of the walking after the Erme, though there are no major sites – just more miles of magnificence to meander through, including **Muxham Point** and **Beacon Point**, both of which have wonderful panoramic views, and the cliffs of **Westcombe** and **Ayrmer Cove**.

Finally, you find yourself trudging, weary but happy, into **Challaborough** and its neighbour, **Bigbury-on-Sea**.

CHALLABOROUGH & BIGBURY-ON-SEA [Map 10; Map 11, p115]

These two conjoined settlements probably wouldn't linger in the memory for too long, were it not for the curious Burgh Island that sits just offshore (see box p114).

Challaborough, which is dominated by Challaborough Bay Holiday Park (no camping), is home to: *The Waterfront* (food Thur-Mon 9am-9pm, Tue & Wed 9am-3pm & 5-9pm), a restaurant-café run by the holiday park; *Fryer Tucks* (Easter/Apr to end Oct Mon 5-9pm, Tue-Sun noon-9pm), a no-frills fish-&-chips restaurant that's been going for more than 20 years; and a handy Nisa Local **supermarket** (Tue-Thur & Sat-Sun 8am-6pm, Mon & Fri to 7pm). The **ATM** in the holiday park charges for withdrawals.

Tally Ho Coaches No 875 **bus** calls at both places; see pp53-5 for details.

Facilities in **Bigbury** are few but **campers** can pitch a tent at the welcoming *Mount Folly Farm* (☎ 01548-810267, 🖥 bigburyholidays.co.uk; 🐾 on lead; walkers from £9pp inc shower), which is right on the coast path, where the path turns down to the

ferry crossing. Online booking is preferred and since there are no shops nearby it is best to bring food with you.

The only other accommodation option is *The Henley Hotel* (☎ 01548-810240, 🖥 thehenleyhotel.co.uk; 1D/3T; 🐾; WI-FI; 🐾; mid Mar-end Oct). It was originally built as a smart Edwardian holiday cottage. **B&B** costs £79.50-95pp (sgl occ from £117); bookings must be for at least two nights.

For **food**, there is *Venus* (☎ 01548-810141, 🖥 lovingthebeach.co.uk; fb; 🐾; school summer holidays daily 9am-5pm, rest of year Mon-Fri 10am-4/5pm, Sat & Sun from 9am), a café in the car park down towards the beach, facing the island. It's actually a pretty decent place that's part of a chain, with several other branches along the path. Or there's *Beach Barista* (🖥 beachbarista.co.uk; summer weekends 8.30am-noon), serving coffee and croissants to campers up at Mount Folly Farm, with a couple of outlets on the beach (10am-4.30pm) serving ice-cream, hot and cold drinks, weather permitting.

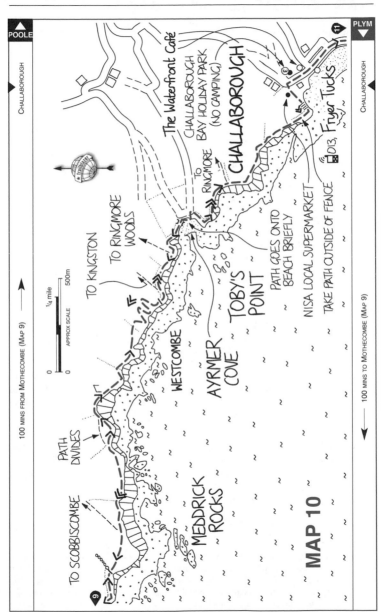

POOLE

CHALLABOROUGH

100 MINS FROM MOTHECOMBE (MAP 9)

¼ mile

500m

APPROX SCALE

0

0

TO SCOBBISCOMBE

PATH DIVIDES

TO KINGSTON

TO RINGMORE WOODS

MEDDRICK ROCKS

WESTCOMBE

AYRMER COVE

TOBY'S POINT

TO RINGMORE

CHALLABOROUGH

The Waterfront Café

CHALLABOROUGH BAY HOLIDAY PARK (NO CAMPING)

Fryer Tucks

D13,

NISA LOCAL SUPERMARKET

PATH GOES ONTO BEACH BRIEFLY

TAKE PATH OUTSIDE OF FENCE

PLYM

11

CHALLABOROUGH

100 MINS TO MOTHECOMBE (MAP 9)

MAP 10

ROUTE GUIDE AND MAPS

❑ **BURGH ISLAND**

Burgh Island is joined to the mainland at low tide by a lovely sand spit. However, if you wish to visit it when the tide's against you, you'll have to take the specially adapted sea tractor. There is good reason to visit, too, for not only does this small lump of grassy rock boast the remains of a chapel (possibly part of an ancient monastery) and an equally venerable pub but also, dominating the whole island, the exclusive and extortionate 1920s' Art Deco *Burgh Island Hotel* (☎ 01548-810514, ⌨ burghisland .com; 10D/15 suites; ✇; WI-FI; 🐾), which inspired the setting for Agatha Christie's *And Then There Were None*. Their more celebrated guests – Noel Coward, Josephine Baker, Amy Johnson and Gertie Lawrence – now each lend their names to one of the hotel's suites. With bed and breakfast from £405 (dinner B&B from £555) per room per night, it's out of reach for most trekkers – but that doesn't stop one from being able to admire it, if only from afar.

Frustratingly, because it could be such a wonderful pub, the *Pilchard Inn* is rather disappointing when it comes to serving walkers; much of the bar is given over for the sole use of the island's hotel residents and the café (Wed-Sun noon-3pm) only offers takeaway food and drinks. Such a shame for a place that's said to have been serving thirsty punters for more than 700 years. Maybe the new owners will have a different policy and walkers will be more welcome in the years to come.

BIGBURY-ON-SEA TO SALCOMBE [MAPS 11-16]

The coast path for this **13-mile (21km; 5hrs 5mins)** stage continues to be fairly remote and wild though there are more places on the way where you can get refreshments than on the previous stage.

The highlight – other than the scenery, of course, particularly during the latter half of the walk which is just unremittingly breathtaking – is the likeable village of Hope (or Outer Hope to give it its full title and to distinguish it from neighbouring Inner Hope, to the south). Overall, it's one of those stages where you should pray for fine weather; if your prayers are answered expect to spend a lot of time taking photos. However, before you set off make sure you have checked the ferry times for this section of the path.

The route

As before, the day begins with a crossing of a river, in this case the **Avon** (no, not *that* one). Getting to the ferry launch is a little tricky: from the beach at Bigbury, the path meanders close to – or on – the road out of the village up to **Mount Folly Farm**, which it cuts through on its way, via a sheep field or two, down to the ferry at **Cockleridge Ham**.

TACKLING THE AVON [Map 11; Map 11a, p116]

Ferry

The short ferry trip (☎ 01548-560897; early Apr-late Sep daily 10am-noon & 2-4pm; £4 one-way, contactless payment only) crosses the Avon from Cockleridge Ham in Bigbury to Bantham. The ferry runs by request and if the ferryman happens to be on the opposite bank to you, you have to signal to him by ringing the bell and waving that you are waiting for a lift. If you time things

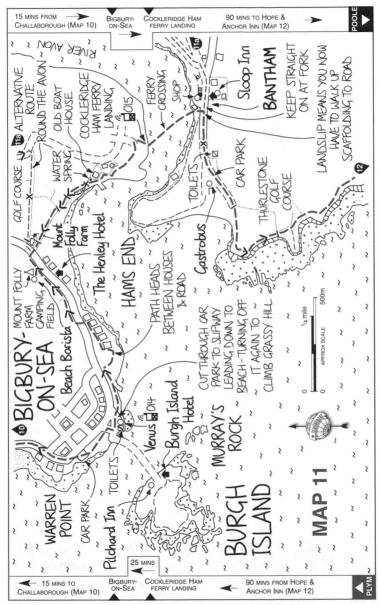

POOLE ▶

RIVER AVON

11a ALTERNATIVE ROUTE ROUND THE AVON

OLD BOAT HOUSE

COCKLERIDGE HAM FERRY LANDING

015

WATER SPRING

GOLF COURSE

Mount Folly Farm

11a

FERRY CROSSING

SHOP

Sloop Inn BANTHAM

KEEP STRAIGHT ON AT FORK

LANDSLIP MEANS YOU NOW HAVE TO WALK UP SCAFFOLDING TO ROAD

12

CAR PARK

THURLESTONE GOLF COURSE

The Henley Hotel

HAMS END

TOILETS

Gastrobus

MOUNT FOLLY FARM CAMPING FIELD

Beach Barista

PATH HEADS BETWEEN HOUSES & ROAD

10 BIGBURY-ON-SEA

Venus 014

Burgh Island Hotel

MURRAY'S ROCK

CUT THROUGH CAR PARK TO SLIPWAY LEADING DOWN TO BEACH – TURNING OFF IT AGAIN TO CLIMB GRASSY HILL

¼ mile   500m

APPROX SCALE

0   0

Pilchard Inn   TOILETS

WARREN POINT

CAR PARK

BURGH ISLAND

MAP 11

ROUTE GUIDE AND MAPS

25 MINS

PLYM ◀

wrong for the ferry, and you don't want to tackle the walk around the Avon, you could call a **taxi** (Arrow Cars ☎ 01548-856120).

Avon Estuary Walk – walking around the Avon

This pleasant **9-mile (13km; 3hrs) diversion** is easy on the eye without being stunning. The scenery is unsurprisingly verdant, there's a village at the halfway point where you can get a bite to eat, and it's very peaceful. Furthermore, though this trail has been officially designated as the Avon Estuary Walk, it's rare to find other people on it, giving you plenty of time to take in the lovely views and contemplate how much further along the coastal path you would be if only you had managed to catch the boat across the Avon.

The trail begins on the road just uphill from **Mount Folly Farm** (see p112) where a path off right takes you into the fields and across a **golf course**. The climb up the western side of the Avon is a little meandering but never more than a field or two away from the river, the path picked out with the blue 'heron' waymarkers of the Avon Estuary Walk. Undulating at first, towards its northern end the path flattens to cross the mudflats and creeks on its way to the only settlement on the route.

Aveton Gifford (🖳 aveton-gifford.co.uk) is not the prettiest of places but there is a pub here, *The Fisherman's Rest* (☎ 01548-550284, 🖳 thefisher

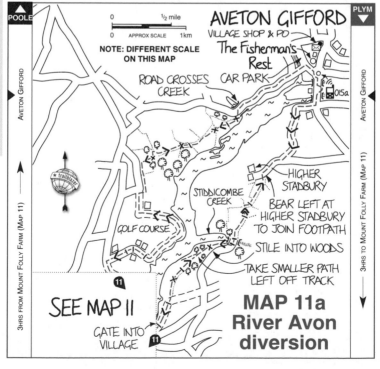

POOLE

PLYM ▼

AVETON GIFFORD

VILLAGE SHOP & PO

The Fisherman's Rest

0   ½ mile

0   APPROX SCALE   1km

NOTE: DIFFERENT SCALE ON THIS MAP

ROAD CROSSES CREEK

CAR PARK

015a

★ trailblazer

HIGHER STADBURY

STIDDICOMBE CREEK

BEAR LEFT AT HIGHER STADBURY TO JOIN FOOTPATH

GOLF COURSE

STILE INTO WOODS

TAKE SMALLER PATH LEFT OFF TRACK

11

SEE MAP 11

GATE INTO VILLAGE

11

MAP 11a River Avon diversion

SEE MAP 11

R O U T E   G U I D E   A N D   M A P S

AVETON GIFFORD

AVETON GIFFORD

3HRS FROM MOUNT FOLLY FARM (MAP 11)

3HRS TO MOUNT FOLLY FARM (MAP 11)

mansrest.co.uk; **fb**; WI-FI; 🐾 on lead; food school summer holidays daily noon-2pm & 7-9pm though hours may be extended, rest of year Tue-Sun noon-2pm & 7-9pm) and, 400 metres further along the road, a community-owned **village shop & post office** (☎ 01548-550996; **fb**; generally Mon-Wed 9am-5pm, Thur & Fri to 5.30pm, Sat to 1pm, Sun to 11am) which sells groceries, sandwiches, baked goods and ice-creams.

Stagecoach's No 3 **bus** (see pp53-5) passes though on its way to Dartmouth & Kingsbridge from Plymouth.

It's just outside the village that the path changes direction, crosses the Avon, and starts to head back south towards the coast again. A steep climb takes you away from the riverbank, before the path stumbles back down to cross **Stiddicombe Creek**. A lovely stretch follows through the woods and fields leading eventually to the village of **Bantham**, where you'll find food (Mon-Sat noon-2pm & 6-9pm, Sun noon-4pm & 6-9pm), beer and accommodation at the 14th-century *Sloop Inn* (☎ 01548-560489, 🖳 thesloop.co.uk; 4D/2Tr; ☞; WI-FI; 🐾; from £60pp, sgl occ room rate; summer months minimum two-night stay). There's also a small **village store** (☎ 01548-560645, 🖳 www.banthamstores.co.uk; **fb**; summer daily 9am-2.30pm, Thur-Sat 5-7pm; rest of year contact them for details) here with a *café* serving breakfasts (9-11.30am) and lunches (noon-2pm).

From the inn it's a few steps to the top of the road leading down to the ferry point – and a reunion with the coast path.

From the ferry point the path heads up to a car park, thereafter bending west then south and skirting the edge of **Thurlestone Golf Course**. There's often Gastrobus, a **seasonal snack van**, in the car park at Bantham, but the first proper eatery on this stage is the slightly pricey, but very good *Beachhouse Café* (☎ 01548-561144, 🖳 beachhousedevon.com; food Apr-July daily 9.30am-5pm, Thur-Sat to 8.30pm, July-Sep daily 9.30am-8.30pm), looking out towards the holed **Thurlestone Rock** which stands, sea-battered but proud, nearby. From here, a relatively straightforward stroll on low cliffs brings you to **Outer Hope**.

OUTER HOPE
[Map 12, p118 & Map 13, p119]
Given its remote location, it won't surprise you to discover that Hope Cove was once a favourite haunt of smugglers. You perhaps also won't be too shocked to discover that the wild and rugged coast around here has also seen its fair share of shipwrecks; as a result, the village is something of a mecca for divers.

The focus of interest on the cove for trekkers is Outer Hope. Facilities are minimal though there is a **village store** (daily 8am-4 or 6pm) that sells pasties and takeaway coffee as well as groceries, and has a **post office** inside it.

Tally Ho's 162 **bus service** travels between Outer Hope, Inner Hope (p120)

and Kingsbridge, where you can connect with other services; see pp53-5.

For **accommodation**, the main place in town is *Cottage Hotel* (☎ 01548-561555, 🖳 hopecove.com; 2S/27D or T/1T; ☞; WI-FI; 🐾; dinner B&B £75-140pp, sgl from £75, sgl occ pp rate + £35-50; closed Jan to early Feb), a smart old pile dating back to the 19th century, though the hotel only opened in the 1920s and its décor certainly harks back more to that era. Note that the rate includes dinner but £16 is deducted for just B&B.

Below Cottage Hotel, *Hope & Anchor Inn* (☎ 01548-561294, 🖳 www.hopeandanchor.co.uk; 8D/3Tr/1Qd; WI-FI; 🐾; from £75pp, sgl occ room rate) offers some of

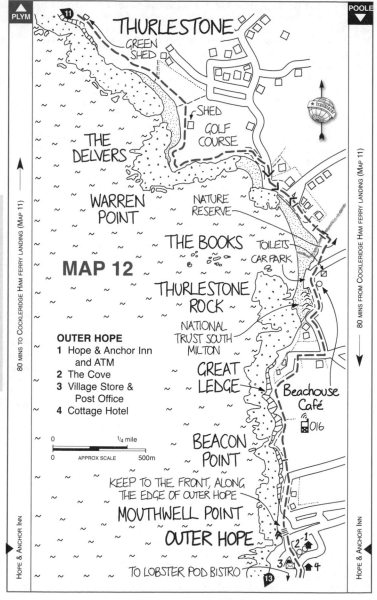

THURLESTONE

GREEN
SHED

SHED

GOLF
COURSE

THE
DELVERS

NATURE
RESERVE

WARREN
POINT

THE BOOKS

TOILETS

MAP 12

CAR PARK

THURLESTONE
~ ROCK ~

NATIONAL
TRUST SOUTH
MILTON

OUTER HOPE
1 Hope & Anchor Inn
  and ATM
2 The Cove
3 Village Store &
  Post Office
4 Cottage Hotel

GREAT
LEDGE

Beachouse
Café

016

0   1/4 mile

0   APPROX SCALE   500m

BEACON
POINT

KEEP TO THE FRONT, ALONG
THE EDGE OF OUTER HOPE

MOUTHWELL POINT ~

~ OUTER HOPE ~

2-1

3 ✉   4

TO LOBSTER POD BISTRO

13

80 MINS TO COCKLERIDGE HAM FERRY LANDING (MAP 11)

80 MINS FROM COCKLERIDGE HAM FERRY LANDING (MAP 11)

HOPE & ANCHOR INN

HOPE & ANCHOR INN

ROUTE GUIDE AND MAPS

the best accommodation in the village; the prices reflect this though they do vary so it is worth checking and they accept bookings for single-night stays. It is a large, smart, gastro-pub (food daily noon-3pm & 5-9pm) and has plenty of outdoor seating.

There are two other main places to eat convenient for passing walkers. Next door *The Cove* (☎ 01548-561376, 🖥 thecovedevon.co.uk; **fb**; WI-FI; 🐕; food daily noon-9pm) is a café-bar and live music venue spread over two floors that knocks

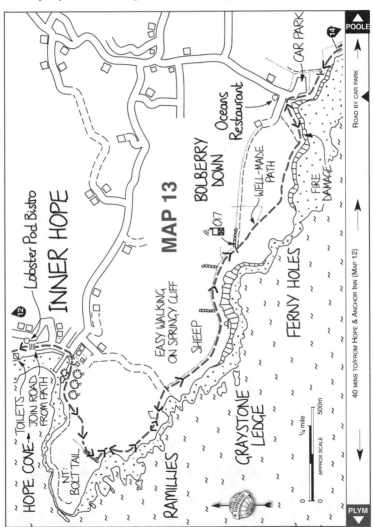

MAP 13

INNER HOPE

Lobster Pod Bistro

BOLBERRY DOWN

Oceans Restaurant

WELL-MADE PATH

FIRE DAMAGE

HOPE COVE — TOILETS

JOIN ROAD FROM PATH

NT: BOLT TAIL

EASY WALKING ON SPRINGY CLIFF

SHEEP

RAMILLIES

CRAYSTONE LEDGE

FERNY HOLES

POOLE

ROAD BY CAR PARK

CAR PARK

40 MINS TO/FROM HOPE & ANCHOR INN (MAP 12)

PLYM

¼ mile

500m

APPROX SCALE

out some great burgers (£12-16) and pizzas (£11-16) and has a good selection of craft-beer.

The third option is the slightly curious *Lobster Pod* (Map 13; 🖥 www.lobster-pod .co.uk; 🐾; food Wed-Sun noon-9pm), where diners sit inside glass pods so they can enjoy the view without the weather ruining the experience. It's certainly novel. Their speciality is lobster, of course (£5 for 100g) but they also offer stone-baked pizzas (from £11.50) and burgers, including a lobster and hake burger (£25).

From Outer Hope the path meanders past seafront residences to its Siamese twin, **Inner Hope**, from where a wooded path once again leads away from civilisation. This stretch from Inner Hope to Salcombe is book-ended by two promontories, **Bolt Tail** (Map 13) and Bolt Head (Map 15). Bolt Tail comes first, a lovely westerly-facing headland which the path contours round before describing a hairpin bend south-east through fields to **Bolberry Down**. The whole stretch is owned by the National Trust and, despite the car park, the path feels quite remote though there is now an eatery right by the path.

Oceans Restaurant (☎ 01548-562467, 🖥 oceansrestaurant.co.uk; food Wed-Sat 10-11.30am, noon-2pm & 6-8pm, Sun 10am-3pm; WI-FI; 🐾; Feb-Dec) serves breakfast baps (from £6.95), and lunch and dinner mains (£13-24), as well as coffee, cake and ice-cream, with the majority of the ingredients locally sourced. Or you could choose to detour off the path slightly earlier (see Map 14) to visit **East Soar Farm** (Map 15; ☎ 01548-561904, 🖥 eastsoaroutdoorex perience.co.uk). Their accommodation is for group bookings only – you can't pitch your own tent here – but they also run the huge *Walker's Hut* (daily Apr-Sep 10.30am-5pm, Feb, Mar & Oct 11am-4pm, closed Nov-Jan; 🐾) which offers hot drinks, snacks and shelter to campers and passing hikers alike. Note that this is an 'honesty hut' that is usually unstaffed, so do bring plenty of small change.

The third option, of course, is just to keep on walking. The approach to **Bolt Head** is marked by increasingly severe gradients, ensuring that by the time you reach civilisation again, at the twin millionaire hamlets of **South Sands** and **North Sands** you'll be ready for a drink again.

The very busy beach café *Winking Prawn* (Map 15; ☎ 01548-842326, 🖥 winkingprawn.co.uk; **fb**; WI-FI; 🐾 on lead; hours vary so check in advance but generally Mon-Thur 10am-7.30pm, Fri-Sun 9am-7.30pm) does sandwiches, wraps and baguettes (£6.50-11) as well as main meals (£13-30), and has garden BBQs in good weather. Most people, however, will probably want to continue to **Salcombe**, where further options await.

❑ **IMPORTANT NOTE – WALKING TIMES**

Unless otherwise specified, **all times in this book refer only to the time spent walking**. You will need to add 20-30% to allow for rests, photography, checking the map, drinking water etc. When planning the day's hike count on 5-7 hours' actual walking.

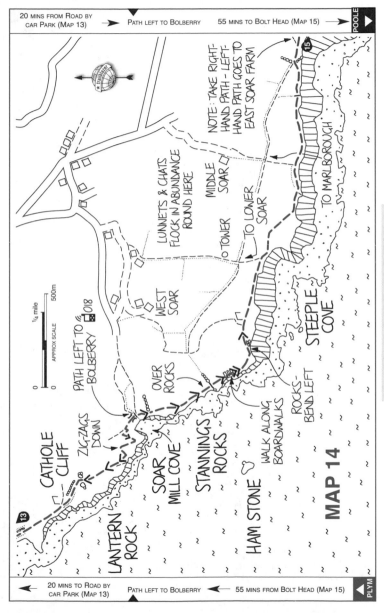

NOTE: TAKE RIGHT-HAND PATH – LEFT-HAND PATH GOES TO EAST SOAR FARM

LINNETS & CHATS FLOCK IN ABUNDANCE ROUND HERE

MIDDLE SOAR

TO TOWER

TO LOWER SOAR

WEST SOAR

TO MARLBOROUGH

STEEPLE COVE

¼ mile

500m

APPROX SCALE

PATH LEFT TO BOLBERRY 018

CATHOLE CLIFF

ZIG-ZAGS DOWN

OVER ROCKS

ROCKS – BEND LEFT

SOAR MILL COVE

STANNINGS ROCKS

WALK ALONG BOARDWALKS

HAM STONE

LANTERN ROCK

MAP 14

ROUTE GUIDE AND MAPS

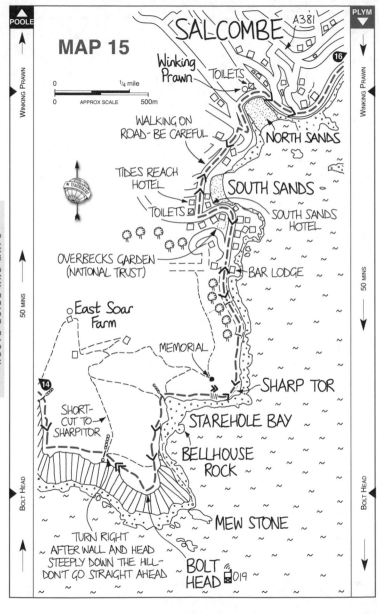

POOLE

WINKING PRAWN

50 MINS

BOLT HEAD

PLYM

WINKING PRAWN

50 MINS

BOLT HEAD

MAP 15

0   1/4 mile
0   APPROX SCALE   500m

SALCOMBE

A381

16

Winking Prawn

TOILETS

WALKING ON
ROAD - BE CAREFUL

NORTH SANDS

TIDES REACH
HOTEL

SOUTH SANDS

TOILETS

SOUTH SANDS
HOTEL

OVERBECKS GARDEN
(NATIONAL TRUST)

BAR LODGE

East Soar
Farm

MEMORIAL

14

SHORT-
CUT TO
SHARPITOR

SHARP TOR

STAREHOLE BAY

BELLHOUSE
ROCK

MEW STONE

TURN RIGHT
AFTER WALL AND HEAD
STEEPLY DOWN THE HILL-
DON'T GO STRAIGHT AHEAD

BOLT
HEAD 019

SALCOMBE [map p125]

Sophisticated, seafaring Salcombe sits at the mouth of Kingsbridge Estuary, its condos, penthouses, hotels and holiday homes stretching up the steep surrounding hills. Its written history harks back only as far as 1244, making it a positive youngster compared to some of the settlements around here and, in this respect, it very much sits in the shadow of neighbouring Dartmouth, whose past is indubitably both longer and richer. Salcombe followed the well-trodden path of many villages around here, eking out a living from the industries of fishing, smuggling and piracy. However, in 1764, the first holiday home, 'The Moult', was built by a Mr John Hawkins between Salcombe and North Sands (and still stands there); and Salcombe has been thriving on holidaymakers pretty much ever since.

A second income stream, from shipbuilding, started up at the same time and ensured the town's prosperity for much of the next century. In particular, Salcombe specialised in building fruit schooners – light and rapid craft required by traders to hurry their cargo of perishable fruit back from Spain and the Azores before it spoilt. The invention of ships made of iron and steel spelt the end of the industry in Salcombe and while its reputation as a seafaring centre remains to this day, its sailors now tend to come from the retired and wealthy rather than the ambitious and intrepid.

There's a lot to like about the town, not least **Salcombe Maritime Museum** (🖳 salcombemuseum.org.uk; Easter-end Oct daily 10.30am-12.30pm & 2.30-4.30pm; free), at the Market St end of Fore St, and below the tourist office. It has a number of displays recounting the town's history; the friendly staff are also a good source of local knowledge.

Services

At the time of writing the **tourist information centre** (☎ 01548-843927, 🖳 salcombe information.co.uk)had just been taken over by a new person and the opening days/ hours were undecided. The **post office** is in the Spar **supermarket** (Mon-Sat 7am-9pm, Sun 8am-9pm) on Loring Rd, though if it's

groceries you want the **Co-op** (daily 7am-11pm), opposite the end of Island Terrace, is more convenient. There's a free-to-use **ATM** in the car park beside The Kings Arms (see Where to eat) and in the Co-op. For a **pharmacy** there's a Boots (Mon-Fri 9am-1pm & 2-5pm, Sat 9am-5pm) on Fore St and there's a trekking shop, Mountain Warehouse (Sun-Fri 10am-4pm, Sat from 9.30am), at No 60.

Transport

[See also pp53-5] The town is connected to Kingsbridge & Totnes via Tally Ho's 164.

For a **taxi**, try Salcombe and District Taxi Company (also known as Taxi Mike; ☎ 0771-451 2516, 🖳 www.salcombeanddis tricttaxico.co.uk).

Where to stay

Campers need to walk about 1½ miles out of town to reach *Ilton Farm Campsite* (☎ 01548-843635, 🖳 iltonfarmcampsite.co .uk; WI-FI; 🐕 on lead) – take the pavement alongside the A381 and you'll eventually see a signpost for the campsite on your right. A basic pitch costs £15/20-24 for a tent and one/two adults, depending on the season, and there are free showers.

Finding a **B&B** that allows you to book in advance for one night only, and isn't a long trudge from town, is not as easy as you'd hope. One option is the pub, *Victoria Inn* (☎ 01548-842604, 🖳 victoria innsalcombe.co.uk; 1D/1D or T; WI-FI; 🐕; room only £50-70pp, sgl occ room rate), on Fore St, although it doesn't provide breakfast. The two rooms do have character, though, having been built in the grounds of the pub and together christened 'The Hobbit House' – watch your head as you enter through the front door! Another pub with rooms is *The Fortescue Inn* (☎ 01548-842868, 🖳 thefortsalcombe.co.uk; 6D; 🛏; WI-FI; 🐕; from £70pp, sgl occ from £130); rates here include a full English breakfast.

Rocarno (☎ 01548-842732, 🖳 www .rocarno.co.uk; 2D or T; WI-FI; from £41pp, sgl occ £78) is more central than some and welcomes coast-path walkers. Not far away is *Waverley* (☎ 01548-842633 or ☎ 07980 012608, 💻 waverleybandb.co.uk; 1D/3D or T/2Tr; WI-FI; 🐕; Mar-Nov) which charges £45-55pp (sgl occ from £65).

A stiff walk up from the centre, *Fo'c'sle* (☎ 07813-913213, ☎ 01548-843243, 💻 bedandbreakfastsalcombe.co .uk; 1D/2D or T; ☞; WI-FI; 🐕), on Onslow Rd, charges from £47.50pp (sgl occ £65) or room-only from £40pp (sgl occ £55).

Where to eat and drink

Salcombe is awash with eateries, most of which are on or just off Fore St. Note, however, that staff shortages are really having an impact, and at the time of research several places were unable to serve food simply because they can't get the workers. It's a knock-on effect from having little in the way of cheap housing in the area, so workers on low wages (eg waiters, bar staff etc) can't afford to live in this part of Devon.

Delis & takeaways If a quick sandwich and a sit down on a bench is what you're after, *Salcombe Delicatessen* (☎ 01548-842332, 💻 salcombedeli.co.uk; fb; Mon-Tue & Thur-Sat 9am-4.30pm, Sun to 3.30pm), at 52 Fore St, is just the ticket. They also do pasties and takeaway tea and coffee. Further on, at 10 Clifton Place, *The Salcombe Yawl* (☎ 01548-288380; fb; daily 10am-3pm), does sandwiches from £4.50, though a crab meat one is £9, while just up Fore St a little way is *The Bakehouse* (💻 www.bakehousesalcombe.co.uk; fb; daily 7.30am-5pm), where you can pick up a tasty pasty for £4.15. *Salcombe Original Takeaway* (☎ 07803 842527, 💻 www.sal combeoriginaltakeaway.co.uk; Feb half-term to end Oct daily noon-2.30pm & 5-9pm, rest of year noon-2pm & 5-8pm) is a popular takeaway chippy (though they also do pizza) on Fore St, which has a sit-down restaurant section too.

Where to stay: the details
Unless specified, B&B-style accommodation is either en suite or has private facilities.

Cafés, pubs & restaurants There's good grub to be had at *The Salcombe Coffee Company* (☎ 01548-842319, 💻 www.salcombecoffeecompany.com; fb; WI-FI; 🐕; summer daily 9.30am-4pm, winter hours variable), on Fore St, too. They do a great range of cakes and sandwiches (including bacon sandwich 'as it should be', ie non-white bread; £6.95) but the real attraction is their spicy and meat-filled chilli bowl (£12.95).

Sticking with Fore St, at No 19, through Crew Clothing shop, is *The Ward Room* (☎ 01548-843333; fb; WI-FI; 🐕; Mon-Sat 9am-5pm, Sun 10am-4pm) where drinks, cakes, cream teas and views over the harbour are all on offer.

For **pub food** next to the ferry passenger terminal (and thus the path) *The Ferry Inn* (☎ 01548-844000, 💻 www.theferry innsalcombe.com; fb; 🐕; food daily noon-3pm & 6-9pm, winter hours variable) is hard to beat in terms of location, especially if you take advantage of the waterside back terrace. Mains start at around £14.

Other pubs include the charming *Victoria Inn* (see Where to stay; WI-FI; 🐕; food daily noon-3pm & 5-9pm) which welcomes dogs and has a great beer garden, *The Kings Arms* (☎ 01548-842202; fb; WI-FI; 🐕; food daily noon-2.30pm & 5.30-8.30pm, though coffee and cake served from 10.30am), which also has outdoor seating, and *The Fortescue Inn* (see Where to stay; food daily noon-9.30pm), on Union St, which is the place to go for stone-baked pizza.

SYMBOLS USED IN TEXT

☞ Bathtub in, or for, at least one room; WI-FI means wi-fi is available
🐕 Dogs allowed; for accommodation subject to prior arrangement (see p313)
fb signifies places that have a Facebook page (for latest opening hours)

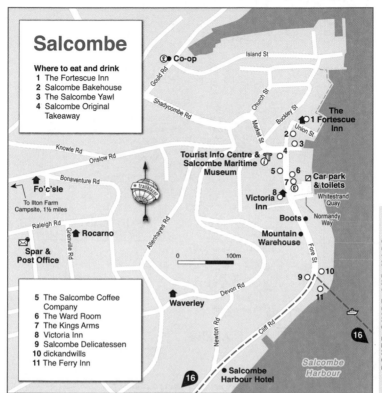

Salcombe

Where to eat and drink
1 The Fortescue Inn
2 Salcombe Bakehouse
3 The Salcombe Yawl
4 Salcombe Original Takeaway

Ⓔ Co-op

Island St

Gould Rd

Shadycombe Rd

Church St

Buckley St

The
1 Fortescue
Inn

Union St

2 ○

○ **3**

○ **4**

Tourist Info Centre &
Salcombe Maritime
Museum ℹ️

Market St

○

5 ○

○ **6**

○ **7**

☑ Car park
& toilets
Ⓔ

8 ○

Victoria
Inn

Whitestrand
Quay

Boots ●

Normandy
Way

Knowle Rd

Onslow Rd

Bonaventure Rd

★ trailblazer

Fo'c'sle

To Ilton Farm
Campsite, 1½ miles

Raleigh Rd

Grenville Rd

🏠 Rocarno

✉ Spar &
Post Office

Allenhayes Rd

0   100m

Mountain ●
Warehouse

Fore St

○ **10**

9 ○

○
11

5 The Salcombe Coffee
   Company
6 The Ward Room
7 The Kings Arms
8 Victoria Inn
9 Salcombe Delicatessen
10 dickandwills
11 The Ferry Inn

Devon Rd

Waverley

Newton Rd

Cliff Rd

16

● Salcombe
Harbour Hotel

Salcombe
Harbour

16

For a **restaurant** meal, head to ***dick andwills*** (☎ 01548-843408, 🖥 dickand wills.co.uk; food daily 5.30pm-9.30pm), a smart waterside brasserie and bar where top-quality evening mains start at £17.95 for the vegetarian mushroom burger.

SALCOMBE TO SLAPTON TURN   [MAPS 16-22]

Another stage, another lovely walk; this time consisting of **14¼ reasonably untaxing miles (23km; 4hrs 35mins)**, a few of which are actually iron flat – though there are just enough sharp ascents, too, to keep you honest.

This stage also boasts several places to stop and get some refreshments on the way and some great places to bed down for the night should you come to the justifiable conclusion that the scenery along this stretch is just too good to be hurrying through. These settlements include the idiosyncratic, camping hotspot of East Prawle and the one-street seafront villages of Beesands and Torcross. These places are undoubtedly charming in their own way; but it's the

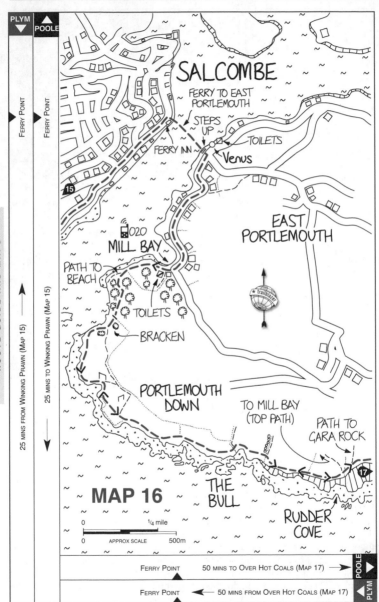

PLYM ▼

POOLE ▲

FERRY POINT

FERRY POINT

ROUTE GUIDE AND MAPS

25 MINS FROM WINKING PRAWN (MAP 15) →

← 25 MINS TO WINKING PRAWN (MAP 15)

SALCOMBE

FERRY TO EAST PORTLEMOUTH

STEPS UP

TOILETS

FERRY INN

Venus

15

📱020

MILL BAY

EAST PORTLEMOUTH

PATH TO BEACH

TOILETS

BRACKEN

PORTLEMOUTH DOWN

TO MILL BAY (TOP PATH)

PATH TO GARA ROCK

17

MAP 16

THE BULL

RUDDER COVE

0 ... ¼ mile
0 ... 500m
APPROX SCALE

countryside around here that truly makes the heart soar and stays in the memory long after you've finished this walk.

The route

As has become traditional on this trek, before you even begin walking you have to cross a stretch of water, in this case by catching the boat to **East Portlemouth**. The **ferry** (Mon-Fri 8.30am-6pm; Sat, Sun & Bank Hols 9am-6pm; £2; 🐕 free) shuttles back and forth continuously all day (although only half-hourly or hourly during quiet periods). In summer (Apr-Oct) it leaves from beside The Ferry Inn. In winter (Nov-Mar) it leaves from Whitestrand Quay.

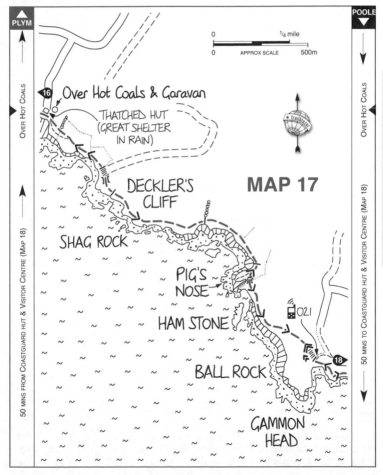

MAP 17

PLYM
POOLE

¼ mile
APPROX SCALE   500m

Over Hot Coals

16 Over Hot Coals & Caravan

THATCHED HUT
(GREAT SHELTER
IN RAIN)

DECKLER'S CLIFF

SHAG ROCK

PIG'S NOSE

HAM STONE

BALL ROCK

GAMMON HEAD

021

18

50 MINS FROM COASTGUARD HUT & VISITOR CENTRE (MAP 18)

50 MINS TO COASTGUARD HUT & VISITOR CENTRE (MAP 18)

ROUTE GUIDE AND MAPS

Back on *terra firma*, on your left is ***The Venus*** (☎ 01548-843558, 🖥 www
.lovingthebeach.co.uk/east-portlemouth; daily 10am-5pm), another outlet of
The Venus chain, where you can buy hot drinks, paninis and pasties as well as
cakes and ice-creams. Turn right when you step off the ferry, however, and
you'll pick up the trail along the tree-shaded tarmac leading to **Mill Bay**.

The woods mark the start of a relatively easy, largely flat, very pleasant and
pretty spectacular south-easterly amble. The path takes on a decidedly porcine
theme, passing **Pig's Nose** and **Ham Stone** before reaching (after one of the
larger climbs of the day) **Gammon Head**.

On the way you'll pass, on your left, an empty conical **thatched hut** (a
great shelter in rain), behind which you'll find **Gara Rock** (☎ 01548-845946,
🖥 gararock.com), a smart holiday complex. The restaurant here, *Over Hot
Coals* (daily noon-2.30pm), is open at lunchtime to anyone (residents only in
the evening), though it's too swish, perhaps, for the average sweaty walker and
they usually require reservation in advance. However, they also have the
Garavan, a van serving snacks and drinks at weekends in the summer school
holidays (11am-3pm), but subject to the weather.

More largely flat walking follows before a steady ascent leads to the
Coastguard Hut at **Prawle Point**, complete with its own small **Visitor Centre**
(daily 9am-5pm). Descending from here, there is now a very flat section that
hugs the coast, contouring round fields, passing the turn-off to **East Prawle**.

EAST PRAWLE   [Map 18]

It's a steep climb up from the path to
Devon's southernmost village – but for
campers (in July and August at least) and
for those who take delight in ancient, isolated and offbeat pubs, the exertions are
worth it. Note, however, that at the time of
writng there was no B&B in East Prawle.

The centre of this idiosyncratic village
is the eccentric *The Pigs Nose Inn* (☎
01548-511209, 🖥 pigsnoseinn.co.uk; bar
open all day except Sep-Jun Mon-Fri noon-
3pm & 6-11pm; WI-FI; 🐾). Overlooking the
village green, this 500-year-old establishment used to be a haunt of smugglers who
would store their booty here. Complete with
board games, live music, a pool room, and
paraphernalia galore, it's the kind of quirky
place you'll be telling your friends about
long after you've returned home. As well as
serving a fine choice of local ales (from
behind an unusually low bar) they offer
food (daily noon-2.30pm & 6-9pm; mains

£13-26). As if that's not enough, in high season they even have self-service **laundry
facilities** and possibly **showers** for passing
hikers and campers.

Directly opposite is the well-stocked
Piglet Stores (🖥 pigletstores.co.uk; daily
9am-5pm) and *Piglet Café* (same hours),
which does breakfast muffins (£6-8), and
light lunches (£5.50-11.50) and has a couple of picnic tables beside the village green.

During the summer East Prawle is
something of a Mecca for **campers** with a
number of fields opened up informally for
basic tent pitches: at *East Prawle Farm
Holidays* (☎ 07856 897053, 🖥 eastprawle
farmholidays.co.uk). 'Little Hollaway' is for
tents (from £7/10 one-/two-man tent; 🐾 if
tethered; end May-early Sep) – online booking preferred. There are portacabin toilets, a
washing-up sink, simple showers and drinking taps. Another option is *East Prawle
Camping* (🖥 eastprawlecamping.co.uk).

Those sticking to the path will continue past Maelcombe House before
emerging at ***Lannacombe Farm*** (☎ 01548-511158) and its lovely beach, where
camping (£10 per pitch) may be available outside the school holidays, though

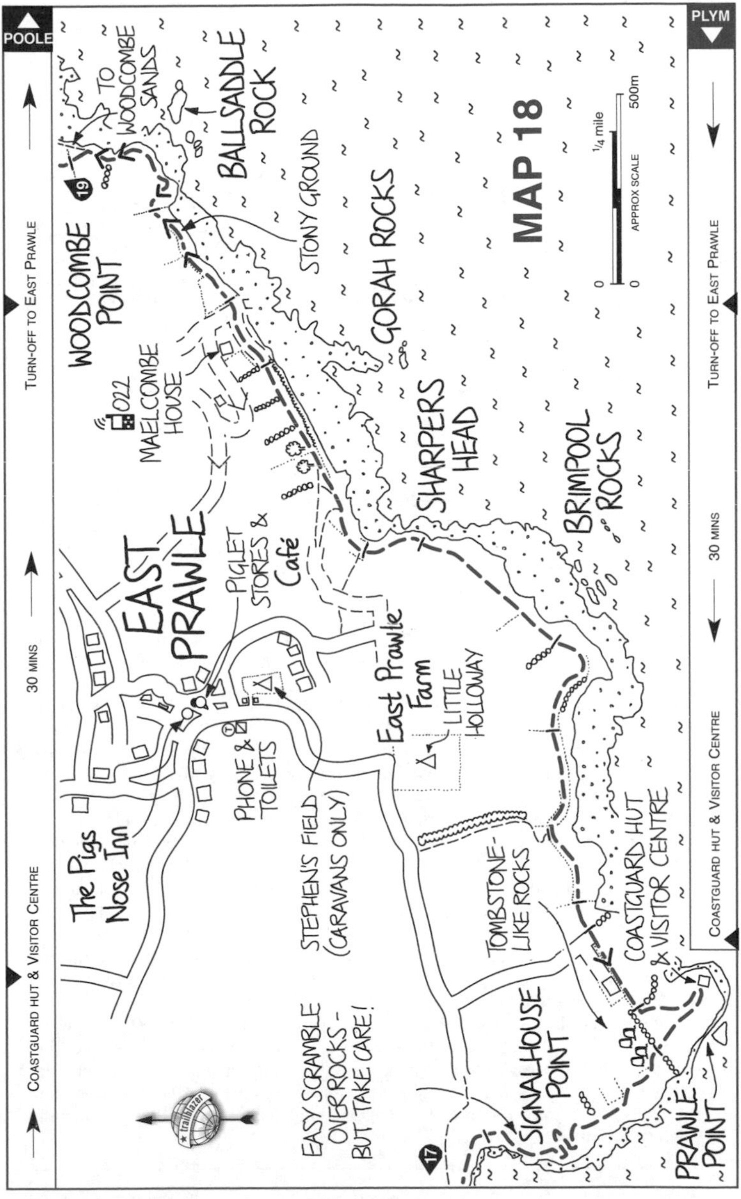
POOLE
PLYM
TURN-OFF TO EAST PRAWLE
30 MINS
COASTGUARD HUT & VISITOR CENTRE
WOODCOMBE POINT
TO WOODCOMBE SANDS
BALLSADDLE ROCK
STONY GROUND
GORAH ROCKS
MAP 18
1/4 mile
500m
APPROX SCALE
MAELCOMBE HOUSE
022
EAST PRAWLE
PIGLET STORES & Café
SHARPERS HEAD
BRIMPOOL ROCKS
East Prawle Farm
LITTLE HOLLOWAY
The Pigs Nose Inn
PHONE & TOILETS
STEPHEN'S FIELD (CARAVANS ONLY)
TOMBSTONE-LIKE ROCKS
COASTGUARD HUT & VISITOR CENTRE
EASY SCRAMBLE OVER ROCKS - BUT TAKE CARE!
SIGNALHOUSE POINT
PRAWLE POINT
trailblazer
17
19

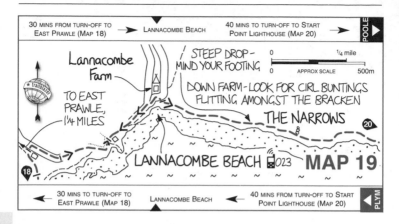

30 MINS FROM TURN-OFF TO EAST PRAWLE (MAP 18) → LANNACOMBE BEACH 40 MINS TO TURN-OFF TO START POINT LIGHTHOUSE (MAP 20) → POOLE

Lannacombe Farm

STEEP DROP - MIND YOUR FOOTING

TO EAST PRAWLE, 1¼ MILES

DOWN FARM - LOOK FOR CIRL BUNTINGS FLITTING AMONGST THE BRACKEN

THE NARROWS

0 | ¼ mile
0 | APPROX SCALE | 500m

LANNACOMBE BEACH 023 **MAP 19**

30 MINS TO TURN-OFF TO EAST PRAWLE (MAP 18) ← LANNACOMBE BEACH ← 40 MINS FROM TURN-OFF TO START POINT LIGHTHOUSE (MAP 20) PLYM

ROUTE GUIDE AND MAPS

❑ THE DESTRUCTION OF OLD HALLSANDS

Set precariously between sea and cliff, the existence of Hallsands (or Old Hallsands as we must call now it to distinguish it from the clifftop village that still stands) was always a perilous one. Its eventual demise, however, became the subject of controversy and legal disputes that rumble on even to this day.

Originally founded sometime in the 18th century, by the time of its destruction there were 37 houses in Old Hallsands and, according to the 1891 census, 159 inhabitants living in them, most of whom made their living by fishing. The pebble beach was all that separated the village from the often tempestuous tides that pounded the shoreline of southern Devon.

That beach, however, was largely removed in the 1890s by Sir John Jackson Ltd, a huge engineering firm that had recently received permission to dredge for shingle along the shoreline between Hallsands and Beesands. The locals were very unhappy with the granting of this licence, complaining that the dredging would cause damage to their crab pots, disturb the fish and might also cause damage to their houses.

Little did they know the full extent of that damage. To ameliorate their tempers, Sir John Jackson Ltd agreed to pay the villagers £125 for every year the dredging continued. It wasn't until 1900, however, that it dawned on everyone how slight this reward was. By then, the sea wall had washed away and the locals were complaining to their MP about the damage being caused. By this time the beach had also fallen by an estimated 7-12ft because of the dredging work, and a report concluded that '*in the event of a heavy gale from the East...few houses will not be flooded, if not seriously damaged*'. The work was only stopped in 1902, however, when the villagers decided upon direct action and prevented the dredgers from landing.

Unfortunately, by then, the damage had been done and in 1903 the engineers were forced to compensate the owners of six houses that had been lost to the sea, since the newly lowered beach was no longer an effective barrier against time and tide. Further huge storms in 1917 washed the village away, leaving only one building standing. Miraculously, however, no-one in the village was killed during these storms – though the village itself never recovered.

there are no toilet or shower facilities. However, there is access to spring water, the same water they get in the farm.

After leaving pretty Lannacombe Beach, a steady ascent through the nature trail of 600-year-old **Down Farm** follows, the trail passing through an area specifically preserved for the benefit of the declining population of **cirl buntings** (see p70).

After a few ups and downs, the path soon climbs steadily towards **Start Point Lighthouse** (closed at the time of research but check 🖳 www.trinity house.co.uk and click on Lighthouses; £5), though walkers will probably be more interested in photographing the nearby signpost that states that there are 168 miles left to Poole (or, for those heading in the other direction, 462 miles to Minehead in Somerset).

The path now heads towards and then through a car park on its way to **Hallsands**; it's worth pausing here awhile to look over the devastated and abandoned village of Old Hallsands (see box opposite), standing hard against the cliffs below. There's a fascinating **information board** here, detailing the village's harrowing story. It's then a relatively easy stroll from here to Beesands – and its pub.

BEESANDS   [Map 21, p133]

Derived from 'Bay Sands', Beesands is a typically tiny Devonian settlement, consisting of around 50 houses, 100 people, a church, snack shack and a good pub.

The Cricket Inn (☎ 01548-580215, 🖳 thecricketinn.com; **fb**; 4D/2Tr/1Qd; WI-FI; 🐾 bar only; £67.50-110pp, sgl occ room rate) is the social centre of the village, a fine place that dates back to the 19th century but is thoroughly up to date, with modern rooms named after English cricket grounds or famous English cricketers; they don't, however, take one-night bookings at weekends. The award-winning **food** (daily

noon-2.30pm & 6-8.30pm) focuses on fresh and local seafood.

Just a little way along the seafront is *Britannia @ The Beach* (☎ 01548-581168, 🖳 britanniaatthebeach.co.uk; **fb**; WI-FI; 🐾; Apr-end Oct Tue-Sat noon-2.15pm & 5.30-8.15pm, Sun noon-2.15pm), a friendly **café** specialising in locally caught seafood and shellfish, but also serving sandwiches and the like. There's a **takeaway** window (Apr-end Oct Tue-Sat 10am-9pm, Sun to 4pm) for those in a hurry. Their winter hours for both vary so check their website or Facebook page.

A reasonably sharp up-and-downer brings you to the next settlement on the route, **Torcross**, with more places at which to eat.

TORCROSS   [Map 21, p133]

Tiny Torcross consists of a busy promenade lining the sea wall – but very little behind. Even the **post office** & store has disappeared (though the former has remerged, in reduced form, in Start Bay Inn, on Fridays 2-6pm), leaving just a **bus stop** (Stagecoach's No 3 Plymouth–Dartmouth **bus service** stops here; see pp53-5) and, incongruously, a **WWII tank** (see box p136) of interest behind the seafront houses.

But it's on the promenade that the action happens. Here you'll find several

places to eat including the thatched pub, *Start Bay Inn* (☎ 01548-580553, 🖳 start bayinn.co.uk; **fb**; WI-FI; 🐾 top bar only; food daily 11.30am-9pm) where you can scoff on any number of fish specials plus pub-grub favourites such as veggie chilli (£10.90).

Next door, *Boat House* (☎ 01548-580747, 🖳 torcrossboathouse.com; 🐾; daily noon-7.30pm later in summer) is a family-friendly café serving fish & chips, burgers and pizza and takeaway.

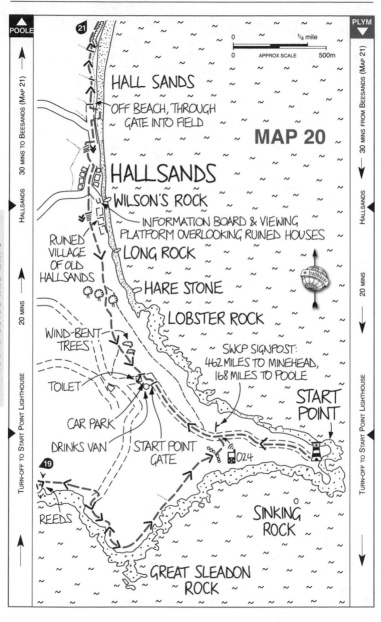

0   1/4 mile
0   APPROX SCALE   500m

HALL SANDS

OFF BEACH, THROUGH GATE INTO FIELD

MAP 20

HALLSANDS

WILSON'S ROCK

INFORMATION BOARD & VIEWING PLATFORM OVERLOOKING RUINED HOUSES

RUINED VILLAGE OF OLD HALLSANDS

LONG ROCK

HARE STONE

LOBSTER ROCK

WIND-BENT TREES

SWCP SIGNPOST: 462 MILES TO MINEHEAD, 168 MILES TO POOLE

TOILET

CAR PARK

DRINKS VAN

START POINT GATE

024

START POINT

SINKING ROCK

REEDS

GREAT SLEADON ROCK

30 MINS TO BEESANDS (MAP 21)

HALLSANDS

20 MINS

TURN-OFF TO START POINT LIGHTHOUSE

30 MINS FROM BEESANDS (MAP 21)

HALLSANDS

20 MINS

TURN-OFF TO START POINT LIGHTHOUSE

ROUTE GUIDE AND MAPS

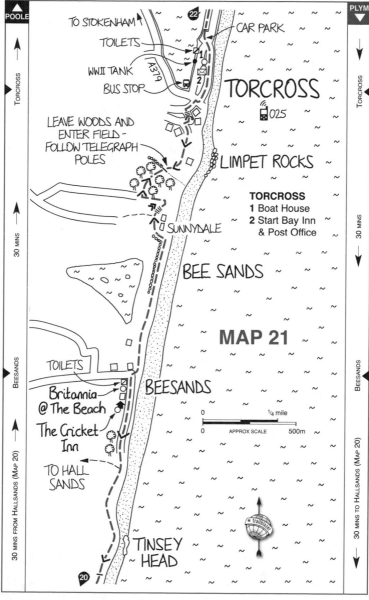

POOLE

TORCROSS

30 MINS

BEESANDS

30 MINS FROM HALLSANDS (MAP 20)

PLYM

TORCROSS

30 MINS

BEESANDS

30 MINS TO HALLSANDS (MAP 20)

ROUTE GUIDE AND MAPS

TO STOKENHAM

TOILETS

WWII TANK

BUS STOP

A379

CAR PARK

22

1

2

TORCROSS

025

LIMPET ROCKS

LEAVE WOODS AND
ENTER FIELD –
FOLLOW TELEGRAPH
POLES

SUNNYDALE

TORCROSS
1 Boat House
2 Start Bay Inn
  & Post Office

BEE SANDS

MAP 21

TOILETS

Britannia
@ The Beach

The Cricket
Inn

BEESANDS

TO HALL
SANDS

0   ¼ mile

0   APPROX SCALE   500m

TINSEY
HEAD

20

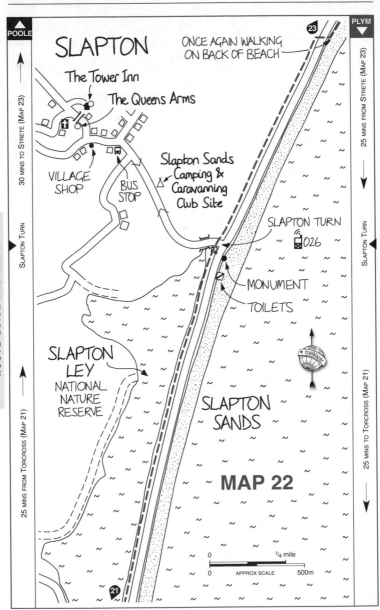

SLAPTON

The Tower Inn
The Queens Arms

VILLAGE SHOP

BUS STOP

Slapton Sands Camping & Caravanning Club Site

ONCE AGAIN WALKING ON BACK OF BEACH

SLAPTON TURN
026

MONUMENT

TOILETS

SLAPTON LEY
NATIONAL NATURE RESERVE

SLAPTON SANDS

MAP 22

0   1/4 mile
0   APPROX SCALE   500m

POOLE

PLYM

30 MINS TO STRETE (MAP 23)

SLAPTON TURN

25 MINS FROM TORCROSS (MAP 21)

25 MINS FROM STRETE (MAP 23)

SLAPTON TURN

25 MINS TO TORCROSS (MAP 21)

ROUTE GUIDE AND MAPS

For those who want to push on still further, an entirely horizontal 1½-mile stroll leads to **Slapton Turn**, the name given for the turn-off to the pretty village of **Slapton**, about three-quarters of a mile inland.

SLAPTON   [Map 22]

A quiet little huddle of historic buildings, Slapton (💻 slapton.org) lies about a mile off the coast path on the other side of the Ley from the beach which shares its name. The village is perhaps most famous for being evacuated to allow American GIs to stay (see box p136) in WWII. Facilities-wise, there's not much to the place other than the **village shop** (Mon-Sat 8am-6pm, Sun to noon), but it does boast a couple of fine pubs, with one also offering accommodation, and a very good campsite.

Transport-wise, Stagecoach's No 3 **bus service** is easily accessed from Slapton Turn and also less frequently from the village itself; see pp553-5 for details.

On the way into the village is *Slapton Sands Camping & Caravanning Club Site* (☎ 01548-580538, 💻 campingandcaravanningclub.co.uk; from £10pp; wi-fi; 🐾; Mar/Apr to end Oct/early Nov), a well-run, clean site with a laundry, a small shop and marvellous sea views.

There's **accommodation** at the other end of the village at the fascinating *Tower Inn* (☎ 01548-580216, 💻 www.thetowerinn.com; **fb**; 2D; wi-fi; 🐾; from £50pp, sgl occ £70), a 14th-century building which sits under the shadow of a striking, half-ruined tower that was once part of a

monastery linked to the nearby church via a bridge spanning the village road. The inn was built to house the workers who built the monastery, so is actually older than the tower itself, which sadly is no longer safe to enter, but still retains a mysterious charm. The accommodation is self-catering; each room has a small kitchenette and, for £10pp, they will supply you with breakfast ingredients. Rooms are available even if the pub is closed. A devastating fire meant that they didn't have a kitchen so the only hot **food** was cooked in their wood-fired oven. However, there should (also) be a kitchen by the time you are there; check their Facebook page or website for details.

Also dating back to the 14th century, though less dramatic in appearance, is *The Queens Arms* (☎ 01548-580800, 💻 queensarmsslapton.co.uk; food Tue-Sun noon-2pm & 5.30-8.30pm, pub closed 2.30-5.30pm; wi-fi; 🐾 on lead) a small, old and exceptionally friendly pub – especially to (well-behaved) dogs, who sometimes outnumber the human patrons. The food here is excellent too, though the pub's popularity (and small size) means you sometimes have to wait a while for both a seat and your meal.

❑ SLAPTON LEY NATIONAL NATURE RESERVE   Map 22

Separated from the sea by only the narrowest sliver of beach and tarmac, Slapton Ley can boast of being the largest freshwater lake in the South-West. A national nature reserve (💻 www.field-studies-council.org/locations/slaptonleynnr), the area plays host to badgers, dormice, bats and otters; unsurprisingly, however, it's the birdlife for which the reserve is famous, with the lake a natural staging post for migrants.

One resident of Slapton Ley is **Cetti's warbler** (*Cettia cetti*), which can occasionally be seen from the old stone bridge near Slapton Turn, though it's a very shy bird. As an insect-eating non-migrant, the warbler can suffer during very cold winters but at Slapton the population is stable at around 35-45 pairs. **Greater crested grebes** (*Podiceps cristatus*) and **cirl buntings** (*Emberiza cirlus*) also live near the lake. See also pp66-71.

SLAPTON TURN TO DARTMOUTH   [MAPS 22-25]

This lovely **8¾-mile (14km; 3½hrs)** stage is full of interest and, given the rugged nature of much of this coastline, surprisingly straightforward too. True, there are several climbs – but they are uniformly short and nearly always gentle. Indeed, the only difficulty with this stage is the brief stretch after the tourist beach at Blackpool Sands, much of which is undertaken on a busy and pavement-less main road. As with the previous stage, there are several places to stop and eat at including the villages of Strete and Stoke Fleming – as well as a beach or two where you can kick off your boots and feel the sand between your toes.

The route
This stage starts with a stroll beside the road at Slapton Sands. With the nature reserve on one side and a lovely pebbled shore on the other, it's hard to know on which side of the road to walk, though the official coast path sticks to the nature reserve side.

❏ **OPERATION TIGER**

As tranquil and picturesque as Slapton Sands and its namesake village may appear today, during World War II this whole area was converted into a 'practice ground' for 30,000 American troops prior to the Normandy landings. The site was chosen because of its similarity to Utah Beach in Normandy – namely a gravel beach followed by a thin ribbon of land and a lake – where the plan was that the troops would land during D-Day. As a result of this likeness, the 3000 residents of Slapton and Torcross – some of whom had never left their village before – were forced to evacuate.

While the landings were, of course, ultimately successful, the rehearsal itself was marred by tragedy on a huge scale. Despite protection from the Royal Navy, a convoy of eight Allied ships heading to this 'rehearsal' was attacked by nine German E-Boats, leading to the loss of 638 servicemen. Worse was to follow: when the remaining boats reached land, a further 308 personnel were killed by – unbelievably – friendly fire, following an order by Dwight Eisenhower to use live ammunition to harden the troops! As a result of the tragedy the landings were almost cancelled altogether. Ten men were unaccounted for following the Battle of Lyme Bay (as it became known) and with the generals afraid that they may have been picked up by the Germans and forced to reveal the plans, the invasion was close to being cancelled until the bodies of each of these 10 men were found.

Those who witnessed the tragic events of April 28th, 1943, were sworn to secrecy and indeed the incident was pretty well covered up by the authorities. Indeed, if it wasn't for local resident Ken Small, who used to find evidence of Operation Tiger while beachcombing in southern Devon in the '70s, it's uncertain whether there would be any memorial to the battle at all. Ken made it his ambition to find out exactly what had happened that day and, having done so, decided to try to commemorate the event.

The Sherman DD tank at the eastern end of Torcross was bought by Ken and raised from the seabed in 1984, and now stands as a tribute to the 946 US servicemen who died that day. A second memorial, the obelisk-like **monument** by Slapton Turn, was erected to thank the people of the local area for abandoning their homes whilst the American GIs moved in. In recent times people have placed stones at its base emblazoned with messages and memorials for those serving in contemporary wars.

At the end, as the road bends left to climb up to Strete, the path crosses the road to begin its own climb up to the village by the excellent *Lime Coffee Company van* (Easter to end Oct daily 10am-5pm, but weather dependent), serving, in our opinion, the best coffee east of Plymouth! Their baps are delicious, too, with bacon baps from £4.60, and halloumi, avocado & sweet chilli (£5).

The gentle climb eventually stiffens into a series of steep switchbacks that brings you up onto the road leading into **Strete**.

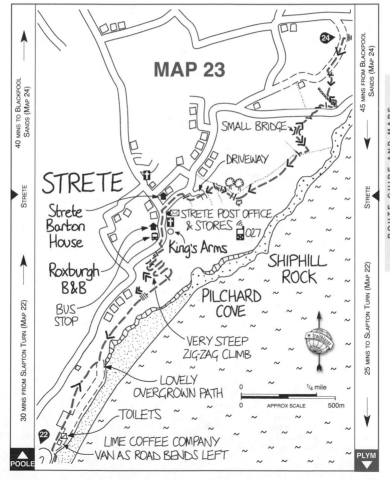

40 MINS TO BLACKPOOL SANDS (MAP 24)

STRETE

30 MINS FROM SLAPTON TURN (MAP 22)

45 MINS FROM BLACKPOOL SANDS (MAP 24)

STRETE

25 MINS TO SLAPTON TURN (MAP 22)

ROUTE GUIDE AND MAPS

MAP 23

SMALL BRIDGE

DRIVEWAY

STRETE

Strete Barton House

Roxburgh B&B

BUS STOP

STRETE POST OFFICE & STORES

027

King's Arms

SHIPHILL ROCK

PILCHARD COVE

VERY STEEP ZIG-ZAG CLIMB

LOVELY OVERGROWN PATH

TOILETS

LIME COFFEE COMPANY VAN AS ROAD BENDS LEFT

0   1/4 mile
0   APPROX SCALE   500m

ROUTE GUIDE AND MAPS

STRETE   [Map 23, p137]

Strete was another settlement where the residents were evacuated for Operation Tiger (see box on p136) during WWII and if you walk through here in the low season, it can feel as if they never came back. It's a sleepy place at the best of times, the only activity – save for the occasional inhabitant emerging to mow their lawns or tend to their begonias – focusing around **Strete Post Office and Stores** (☎ 01803-770225; shop Mon-Fri 8am-4pm, Sat & Sun 8am-noon, post office from 9am but closed on Sun).

Stagecoach's No 3 **bus service** (see pp53-5) passes through Strete en route between Plymouth and Dartmouth.

For **B&B**, there are two central options. **Roxburgh B&B** (☎ 01803-770870, ☎ 07818 208721, ☐ roxburgh house.co.uk; 1D/1T; from £42.50pp, sgl occ £65; WI-FI; ✷) is a lovely Victorian property; the double room is in the house and the twin room in a converted barn in the walled garden. They now accept bookings for a minimum of two nights. Nearby, **Strete Barton House** (☎ 01803-770364, ☐ stretebarton.co.uk; 4D/1D or T/1D in a self-contained cottage; ✿; WI-FI; ✷ in cottage; June-Sep; £75-100pp, sgl occ room rate) is a 16th-century manor house with a splendid garden in which to relax after a long day's slog. This is a top-end B&B, with prices to match, and unfortunately they usually take two-night bookings only – though it can't hurt to ask.

The charming village pub, **King's Arms** (☎ 01803-770027, ☐ kingsarmsat strete.co.uk; ✷; food Wed-Sat noon-2.30pm & 5.30-8.30pm, Sun noon-5pm), with its ornate first-floor balcony jutting out over the pavement, is back open though with limited times. Still, it's now community run, serves local ales and cider and the **food**'s homemade. Oh, and the views are just wonderful too!

From Strete the path passes through several fields which may or may not be filled with cows when you visit, before traversing the vertiginous dip in the earth's surface separating you from the road; it's steep but it's also mercifully short and, having rejoined the road, you cross it then hug it, strolling alongside the tarmac in lush fields of livestock.

The path leaves the line of the road briefly to cut down to **Blackpool Sands**, yet another gorgeous stretch of sand and home to **Venus Café** (☎ 01803-770209, ☐ www.lovingthebeach.co.uk/blackpool-sands; WI-FI; Mon-Fri 10am-5pm, Sat & Sun from 9am), a licensed café with an extensive restaurant menu as well as takeaway items which you can enjoy at tables on the decking overlooking the beach. Stagecoach's No 3 **bus** service calls at Blackpool Sands (see pp53-5).

From here the path continues along the main road before forking off to the left to follow a quieter lane, past the church into **Stoke Fleming** by The Green Dragon pub.

STOKE FLEMING   [Map 24]

Recorded in the Domesday book as 'Stoc', Stoke Fleming is an ancient village dominated by a church, **St Peter's**, that's almost as old as the village itself, with written references dating back to 1272; George Parker Bidder, the famous engineer who worked with George Stephenson in the early days of steam railways, is buried in the graveyard.

Facilities are limited to the **village shop and post office** (☎ 01803 771119; **fb**; shop Mon-Fri 8am-5.30pm, Sat 8.30am-3pm, Sun 9am-3pm, winter till noon; post office Mon-Tue & Thur-Fri 8am-5pm, Wed to 1pm, Sat 9am-1pm).

The only **bus service** to call here is Stagecoach's No 3 (Plymouth to Dartmouth); see also pp53-5.

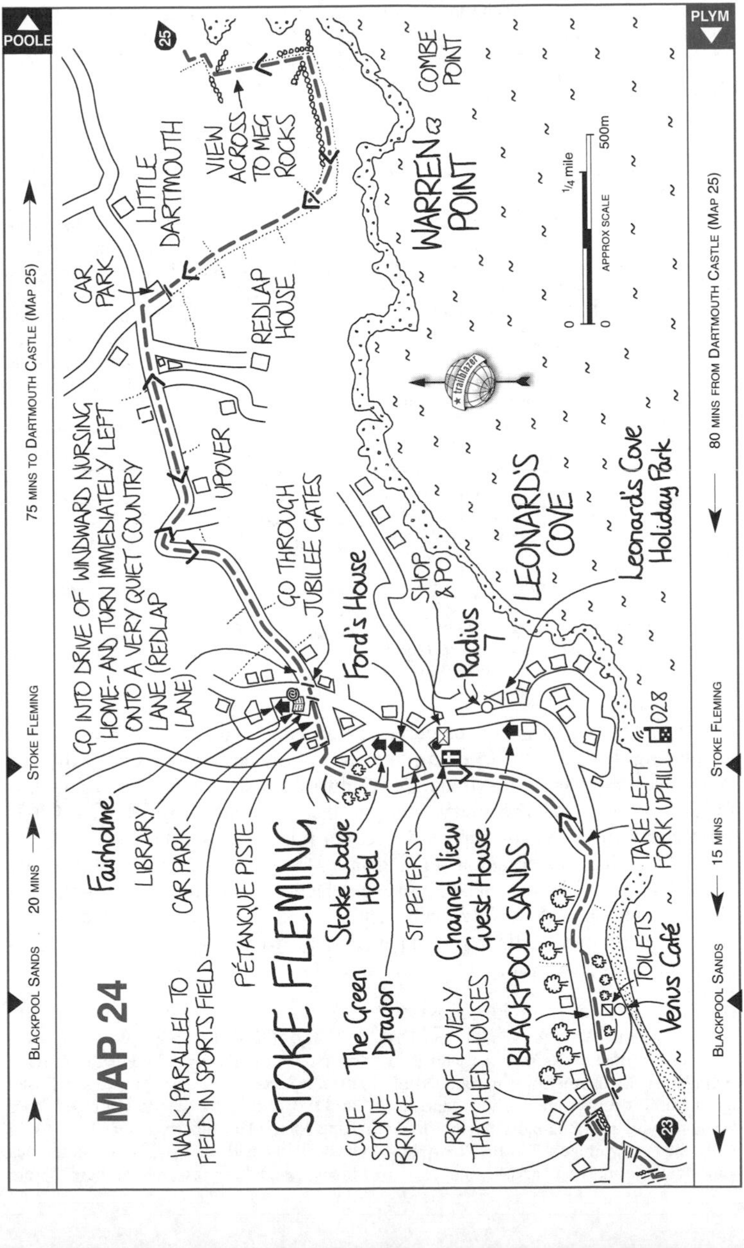

MAP 24

STOKE FLEMING

POOLE

PLYM

GO INTO DRIVE OF WINDWARD NURSING HOME - AND TURN IMMEDIATELY LEFT ONTO A VERY QUIET COUNTRY LANE (REDLAP LANE)

GO THROUGH JUBILEE GATES

LITTLE DARTMOUTH

CAR PARK

REDLAP HOUSE

UPOVER

VIEW ACROSS TO MEG ROCKS

COMBE POINT

WARREN POINT

Ford's House

SHOP & PO

Radius 7

LEONARD'S COVE

Leonard's Cove Holiday Park

¼ mile

500m

APPROX SCALE

WALK PARALLEL TO FIELD IN SPORTS FIELD

Fairholme

LIBRARY

CAR PARK

PÉTANQUE PISTE

The Green Dragon

Stoke Lodge Hotel

ST PETER'S

Channel View Guest House

CUTE STONE BRIDGE

ROW OF LOVELY THATCHED HOUSES

BLACKPOOL SANDS

Venus Café

TOILETS

TAKE LEFT FORK UPHILL

028

25

23

75 MINS TO DARTMOUTH CASTLE (MAP 25)

80 MINS FROM DARTMOUTH CASTLE (MAP 25)

BLACKPOOL SANDS ← 20 MINS → STOKE FLEMING

STOKE FLEMING ← 15 MINS → BLACKPOOL SANDS

ROUTE GUIDE AND MAPS

Stoke Fleming (*cont'd*) **Accommodation** includes a good **campsite** behind Radius 7 restaurant (see column opposite). *Leonard's Cove Holiday Park* (☎ 01803-770206, 🖳 leonardscove.co .uk; WI-FI; Apr-Oct) charges hikers from £15pp. It's well equipped with clean shower blocks, laundry facilities and flat grassy pitches with sea views.

You can get **B&B** at *Channel View* (☎ 01803-770389, 🖳 channelviewguesthouse .com; 3D/1D or T; WI-FI; 🐾; from £57.50pp, sgl occ £95), a dog-friendly establishment standing opposite the entrance to the campsite. Note that advance bookings for a one-night stay may not be accepted here between April and October.

There is also the smart *Ford's House* (☎ 07891 284636, ☎ 01803-770105, 🖳 www.fordshouse.co.uk; 2D; 🐾; WI-FI; Mar-Oct; from £50pp, sgl occ £90), on Dartmouth Rd, while up by the library, *Fairholme* (☎ 01803-770356, 🖳 fairholme dartmouth.co.uk; 2D/1T; WI-FI; £47.50-52.50pp, sgl occ £75-85) has smoked salmon and scrambled eggs on the breakfast menu.

Near Ford's House, but a fair way up the price scale, stands *Stoke Lodge Hotel* (☎ 01803-770523, 🖳 www.stokelodge.co

.uk; 2S/1D/21D or T; 🐾; WI-FI; 🐾 but not in public rooms; £59-70.50pp, sgl £88-91, sgl occ £99-110), a smart place set in three acres of gardens, with indoor and outdoor pools and a giant chess set.

The local pub, *The Green Dragon* (☎ 01803-770238; WI-FI; 🐾; **fb**) is a lovely old snug with a stone floor, big fireplace and comfy old sofas to fling your tired frame onto at the end of the day. They stock a selection of West Country ales, and their **food** (Mon & Tue 5.30-8.30pm, Wed-Sat noon-2pm & 5.30-8.30pm, Sun 1-5pm) can best be described as proper homemade pub grub at proper pub grub prices (eg if on the menu ham, egg & chips for around £10 and lamb's liver & bacon for £12.50) though prices are likely to go up.

Alternatively, you could try *Radius 7* (☎ 01803-770007, 🖳 radius7.co.uk; WI-FI; 🐾 bar only; food summer Mon-Sat 5-9pm, winter hours variable), a very popular restaurant-bar run by Leonard's Cove campsite in high season. The name comes from the fact that they try to source all their ingredients from within a seven-mile radius! You can also eat at the smart *Stoke Lodge Hotel* (see column opposite) either at lunch or book a table for their three-course dinner (set £37.50).

The path continues past the pub to a wooded alleyway and then out across the playing fields and their **pétanque piste**. Follow the signposts carefully and you'll eventually leave the village by Windward Nursing Home. The route now follows a very quiet country lane to the National Trust owned **Little Dartmouth** (look out for hares), where you finally get to enjoy a little bit of clifftop walking – once again fairly gentle – as you stroll round **Blackstone Point** (Map 25) before heading up the Dart via **Dartmouth Castle** and **Warfleet** and on to the lovely town itself.

Note that by the castle the coast path drops down through the church to continue along the riverfront.

DARTMOUTH [map p143]

Dartmouth is friendly, fascinating and has some lovely medieval streets as well as a rich history. Its prosperity was founded on the natural deep-water harbour and its accompanying port, the latter having originally been developed by the Normans almost a thousand years ago.

By 1147 that harbour was being used as a muster point for the 164 ships leaving for the Second Crusade – a role it reprised in 1190 during the Third Crusade under King John. (The suburb of Warfleet is said to be so named because of the numerous times fleets have assembled here before heading off to battle.) Home to the Royal Navy since Edward III's reign (1327-77), unsurprisingly the town has often been the target of attacks by foreign foes, a problem exacerbated by the town's secondary reputation as a centre for privateers (officially sanctioned pirates). The twin castles of Dartmouth (see box p142) and Kingswear were built at the end of the 14th century to defend against such assaults, and a chain once stretched across the narrow river

mouth to prevent invaders sailing straight up to the port.

With such a rich maritime heritage, it's no surprise that the town is home to the only naval college in Britain. **Britannia Royal Naval College** occupies a glorious hilltop building that dates back to the turn of the 19th century; prior to this, the college was based on two large hulks moored in the Dart itself. The college is famous for its royal links: kings George V and VI, the

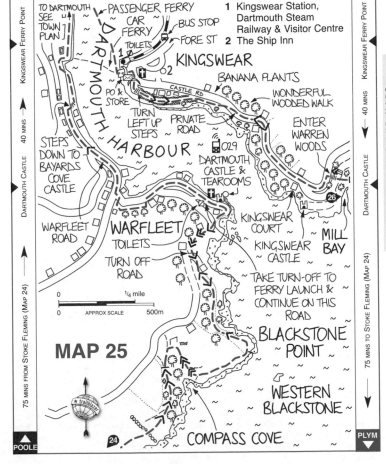

current king, Charles III, and the Duke of York all trained here, as did Prince Philip, the late Duke of Edinburgh; indeed, it is said that Prince Philip first met Princess Elizabeth (now the late Queen Elizabeth II), while a student here.

Given its long history and worldwide fame, it comes as something of a surprise to discover just how small the town actually is, with a permanent population of fewer than 6000. Nevertheless, there's enough here, including some great old buildings, to warrant a rest day should time and inclination allow. A significant number of the historic buildings here are listed, including **Butterwalk**, a terrace of rich merchants' houses built in 1640. Their intricately carved wooden fascia is supported on granite columns. Charles II held court here whilst sheltering from storms in 1671 in a room which now forms part of the small but fascinating **Dartmouth Museum** (☎ 01803-832923, 🖥 dartmouthmuseum.org; daily 11am-3pm; £4.50, concs £3.50).

Dart Music Festival (🖥 www.dart musicfestival.co.uk) is held here in May and **Dartmouth Food Festival** (🖥 www .dartmouthfoodfestival.com) in October; see p14 for details.

Services

Dartmouth's centre is a compact place and it doesn't take long to get your bearings.

Facilities in the centre include a **tourist information centre** (🖥 discoverdart mouth.com; Mon-Sat 10am-4pm, Sun to 3pm, winter hours may vary) in the Engine House on Mayor's Ave, and a Spar **supermarket** (Mon-Sat 7am-9pm, Sun 8am-9pm) with a **post office** inside on Victoria Rd.

There's also a larger Co-op supermarket (daily 7am-10pm) on Fairfax Place, a Boots **pharmacy** (Mon-Sat 9am-5.30pm, Sun 10am-4pm), a **launderette** (daily 8am-8pm, service wash 9am-1pm only), on Market St, and an **arts centre**, Flavel, which doubles as the local **cinema**.

There are also plenty of **banks** with **ATMs**. For **hiking and camping gear**, try Mountain Warehouse (Mon-Sat 9am-5.30pm, Sun 10am-4.30pm) on Duke St, or Trespass, just a few doors down (Mon-Sat 9.30am-5.30pm, Sun 10am-4pm).

Transport

Stagecoach's No 3 **bus** service connects the town with Kingsbridge and Plymouth as well as a number of coastal locations along the way; see pp53-5. For destinations to the east it is usually necessary to take the Dartmouth & Kingswear ferry to Kingswear; see p146.

Greenway Ferries operate services from here to Greenway (see box p164) hourly and the journey is shorter than going from Torquay.

❑ **DARTMOUTH CASTLE**   [Map 25, p141]

Built in 1388 to protect the town from invasion from the sea, Dartmouth Castle was in use right up to the Second World War. Features include the gun tower – the first, so it is believed, purpose built to carry heavy cannon big enough to sink ships – a Victorian gun battery and, unusually, a church, St Petrox. Doubtless the one aspect of the castle that will linger longest in the memory, however, is the beautiful view it provides of the Dart and the wooded slopes beyond.

The castle (🖥 english-heritage.org.uk; Apr-Oct daily 10am-5pm, Nov-Mar Sat & Sun only 10am-4pm; £8.10, EH members free) is today owned by English Heritage, which means it's in a fine state of preservation, the displays are interesting and well presented, and the story of the castle is clearly and imaginatively presented.

Outside the castle is ***Dartmouth Castle Tearooms*** (☎ 01803-833897, 🖥 dart mouthcastletearooms.co.uk; WI-FI; **fb**; Mar-end Oct daily 9am-4pm, Nov-Feb Thur-Sun 9am-3pm), known as the Castle Light in the mid 19th century when it was built and acted as a form of lighthouse, providing light to ships sailing up the Dart. Now it provides all-day breakfasts, light lunches and fabulous views.

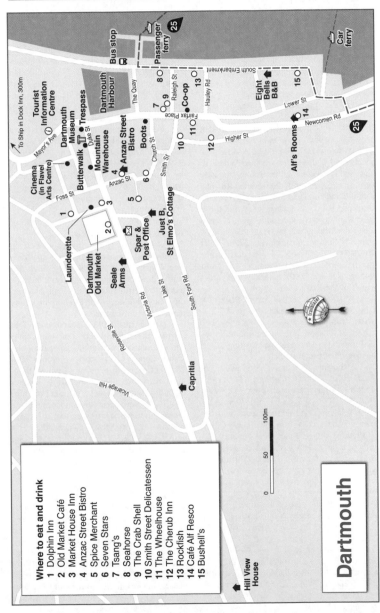

Where to eat and drink
1 Dolphin Inn
2 Old Market Café
3 Market House Inn
4 Anzac Street Bistro
5 Spice Merchant
6 Seven Stars
7 Tsang's
8 Seahorse
9 The Crab Shell
10 Smith Street Delicatessen
11 The Wheelhouse
12 The Cherub Inn
13 Rockfish
14 Café Alf Resco
15 Bushell's

Dartmouth

Hill View House

Capritia

Seale Arms

Dartmouth Old Market

Launderette

Spar & Post Office

Just B, St Elmo's Cottage

Alf's Rooms

Eight Bells B&B

Boots

Anzac Street Bistro

Mountain Warehouse

Butterwalk

Dartmouth Museum

Trespass

Cinema (in Flavel Arts Centre)

Tourist Information Centre

To Ship in Dock Inn, 300m

Dartmouth Harbour

The Quay

Co-op

Bus stop

Passenger ferry

Car ferry

South Embankment

Vicarage Hill
Rosseville St
Victoria Rd
Lake St
South Ford Rd
Foss St
Mayor's Ave
Duke St
Anzac St
Smith St
Church St
Fairfax Place
Raleigh St
Hauley Rd
Higher St
Lower St
Newcomen Rd
South Embankment

25
25

0   50   100m

Where to stay

There's a decent choice of **B&B** accommodation in Dartmouth (though no campsites or hostels). Unfortunately, by the time you've weeded out those that don't take single-night bookings in advance or are at the upper end of town (and thus quite far for weary walkers), the selection is relatively scant.

On the approach into town, and right by the coast path, *Alf's Rooms* (☎ 01803-835880, 🖳 cafealfresco.co.uk; 2D/room with a bunk bed; WI-FI; 🐾; from £47.50pp, sgl occ room rate), is run by the same people behind Café Alf Resco (see Where to Eat) and is accessed either through the café on Lower St, or via 47 Newcomen Rd. The rate includes breakfast in the café (see column opposite) – which is great for those who want an early start, as it opens at 7am. Just round the corner, and right on the coast path on South Embankment, *Eight Bells B&B* (☎ 07813-803472, 🖳 dartmouthbandb.com; 1D/1Qd; 🐾; WI-FI; from £45pp, sgl occ £60) naturally has great views of the River Dart.

Very central, *Anzac Street Bistro* (☎ 01803-835515, 🖳 anzacbistro.co.uk; 2D; WI-FI; from £70pp, sgl occ room rate), at 2 Anzac St, is another tempting option, especially with the sweet aromas wafting in the air from the restaurant below.

A short walk from here, on Lake St, is *Just B/St Elmo's Cottage* (☎ 07973 452669, 🖳 justbdartmouth.com; 3D; WI-FI; from £37.50pp, sgl occ £67.50); it provides three self-contained doubles, each with its own private access, in a townhouse called St Elmo's Cottage. Rates are room only and although the set-up has a hostel feel to it, the rooms are far from basic and promise a very comfortable stay. Just B also has some self-contained apartments in town; see the website for details.

Most of the rest of the town's B&Bs are centred on nearby Victoria Rd. Closest to the amenities are *Seale Arms* (☎ 01803-833833, 🖳 sealearms.co.uk; 3D/1Tr/one room sleeping up to five; 🐾; WI-FI; from £50pp, sgl occ room rate), at No 10; and *Capritia* (☎ 01803-833419, 🖳 capritia .com; 2D/1T; WI-FI; £52.50-67.50pp, sgl occ rates on request), at No 69, although

these two don't usually accept advance bookings for a one-night stay in the main season or at weekends.

As you wander further along Victoria Rd you will also come across *Hill View House* (☎ 01803-839372, 🖳 hillviewdart mouth.co.uk; 1S/2D/1T; WI-FI; from £40pp, sgl £52, sgl occ £70) at No 76 – whose continental breakfast may include croissants and banana smoothies.

Finally, if you want to sleep in a bit of history in such a historical town, the down-to-Earth *Ship in Dock Inn* (☎ 01803-839614, 🖳 theshipindockinn.co.uk; 4D; 🍺; WI-FI; from £55pp, sgl occ room rate) dating back to 1656, is very welcoming, and lies just a two-minute stroll to the north of the centre.

Where to eat and drink

Cafés & delis Handy for hikers walking into town on the coast path, *Café Alf Resco* (see Where to stay Alf's Rooms; WI-FI; 🐾; daily 7am-2pm) has a slightly Bohemian feel with graffitied walls and a roadside terrace that's bursting with punters on sunny days. Great coffee too.

Dating from 1823, **Dartmouth Old Market** is lovely collection of shops, cafés and stalls, clustered around a large cobblestone square. Its eateries include *Old Market Café* (Sun-Fri 10am-3pm, Sat 9am-4.30pm), which does some lovely lunches including smoked mackerel, salad & chips for £7.50. Other great delis in town include *Smith Street Delicatessen* (Tue-Sat 9.30am-4.30pm), which also doubles as a café, and *The Crab Shell* (Mon-Sat 10.30am-2.30pm, Sun 11am-2.30pm) a seafood-sandwich specialist on Raleigh St, with crab sandwiches for £9.25.

Pubs Of all the venerable buildings in town, *The Cherub Inn* (☎ 01803-832571, 🖳 the-cherub.co.uk; WI-FI; 🐾; food daily noon-2pm & 6-9.30pm) is the oldest (c1380) of them all. It's a small and cosy, welcoming place and they do some reasonable value traditional pub classics (from £14.95) and burgers (£16.95). It retains many of the original features – old ship timbers, wonky staircase, low beams – though the pub has actually only been here since the '70s! Still, for my money it has more character and feels more atmospheric than the 'oldest' (ie longest-running) pub in town, *The Seven Stars* (☎ 01803-839635, 🖥 www.quality-inns.co.uk/pubs/the-seven-stars-dartmouth; **fb**; 🐾 bar area; food Thur-Mon noon-4pm & 5-9pm, bar Thur-Mon noon-10pm). Food-wise, mains are tasty and well cooked but slightly overpriced, starting at £16 for the vegetarian beetroot burger or, for example, gammon & chips.

The green-tiled *Dolphin Inn* (☎ 01803-833698; **fb**; WI-FI; 🐾; bar daily noon-11pm) is a 19th-century pub now serving beers from its own brewery (Bridgetown). It welcomes walkers and is probably the busiest pub in town, though for food they serve only pork pies (from £3.20) and baps (£4) till they are gone.

Market House Inn (☎ 01803-839150; WI-FI; 🐾; bar Tue-Sun noon-10.30pm), on Market St, is a sports bar but they only serve bar snacks.

Restaurants On the coast path, and right beside the river, *Bushell's* (☎ 01803-833540, 🖥 www.bushellsdartmouth.co.uk; food Tue-Sat 10am-4pm & 6-9pm, Sun noon-3pm) is a bijou place with just five tables, serving locally sourced British food (mains £14-20), including seafood such as scallops (£13.50 for 3) and crab sandwiches (£11), right on the quayside, with outdoor seating until 5pm (weather dependent).

A short walk along the river is *Rockfish*

(☎ 01803-832800, 🖥 therockfish.co.uk; daily noon-4pm & 5-9pm), a smart fish restaurant with a takeaway (daily noon-9pm) on Lower St opposite the Lower Ferry. More than just a chippy (though they perform that role very well too), they have some unusual items including rock lobster (£38.95). Further along South Embankment, and perhaps the smartest place on the waterfront, *Seahorse* (☎ 01803-835147, 🖥 seahorserestaurant.co .uk; Tue-Sat noon-2.30pm & 6-9.30pm), does some lovely fish dishes, but it's pricey. Mains cost £17-42; even a starter will set you back more than £15.

A couple of streets inland, *Anzac Street Bistro* (see Where to stay; food Tue-Sat 6-8.30pm) which serves an eclectic menu including chicken supreme served with scallops & leeks (£25) or *spanakopita* (Greek spinach pie) for £20.

Tsang's (☎ 01803-832025; Wed-Mon 5.30-10.30pm), on Fairfax Place, meanwhile, has all your Chinese-food cravings covered, while for Indian food *Spice Merchant* (☎ 01803-832211, 🖥 www.spice merchantdartmouth.uk; Sun-Wed 4.30-10.30pm, Thur-Sat to 11.30pm) is a BYOB place on Anzac St that also offers takeaway and a delivery service.

For an ordinary chippy, try *The Wheelhouse* (☎ 01803-834446, 🖥 wheel housedartmouth.co.uk; takeaway Mon-Thur noon-2pm & 5-8.45pm, Fri & Sat noon-2pm & 4.30-9pm; restaurant shuts 30 mins earlier) opposite the Co-op.

DARTMOUTH TO BRIXHAM   [MAPS 25-29]

Once you've crossed the river, this **11-mile (17.5km; 4hrs)** stage starts and ends with some flat and easy walking which book-end a rather strenuous middle section.

After the simple stroll to Inner Froward Point, a particularly enjoyable wooded amble leads you to Pudcombe Cove and the marvellous views it offers out to sea. The shaded pathways here offer a splendid contrast to the long cliff-top walk that follows, a walk that's interrupted only by the need to descend to two gloriously quiet beaches. Your eventual arrival at Berry Head is an important point on your coastal journey as you now enter the area called the English Riviera (see box on p146) and also the English Riviera Global Geopark (see box p150), an area of international geological importance, and a powerful magnet for tourists.

ROUTE GUIDE AND MAPS

Note that refreshment options are limited to the towns that sandwich your walk; carrying plenty of water and a picnic to enjoy at one of the many beauty spots en route is highly recommended. However, before you set off make sure you have checked the ferry times for this section of the path.

The route

To cross the river Dart take **Dartmouth to Kingswear Passenger & Car Ferry** (☎ 01803-555872, 🖥 dartmouthrailriver.co.uk/boats; Mon-Sat 7.30am-1pm & 1.30-6.55pm, Sun 9am-1pm & 1.30-6.55pm; £2), a shuttle service that departs every 15 minutes year-round from just south of the main town centre. If that's not running, the car ferry runs later (Mon-Sat 7am-10.55pm, Sun from 8.10am, winter more limited service), costs less (£1.50; card only) and is quicker.

Kingswear then causes a brief distraction ...

KINGSWEAR [Map 25, p141]

Lying on the eastern bank of the River Dart, the peaceful little settlement of Kingswear (🖥 kingswear-devon.co.uk) has historically been – and remains today – a transport hub.

The earliest mention of a ferry crossing the Dart was in 1365; prior to that it had been used as a landing point for pilgrims heading to Canterbury following the death, in 1170, of Thomas à Becket (for whom the village church was built and dedicated).

The arrival of the railway in 1864 further boosted Kingswear's reputation as a transport centre and it became part of the then Great Western Railway in 1876. Though the line was closed in 1968, the tracks were purchased privately and you can still access the national rail network in Paignton and Torquay courtesy of

Dartmouth Steam Railway (🖥 www.dartmouthrailriver.co.uk; Apr-Oct daily 6 trains per day each way; Paignton return ticket £19.95, inc ferry to and from Dartmouth). There's a small **visitor centre** (Apr-Oct 10am-5pm; free) in the railway station, and just outside is a **post office and store** (fb; Mon-Sat 8am-6pm, Sun to 5pm).

Stagecoach's 18 and 120 **bus services** (see pp53-5) call here.

There's nowhere to stay here now, but there is a food option in addition to what's on offer at the railway station. *The Ship Inn* (☎ 01803-752348, 🖥 theshipinnkingswear.co.uk; bar daily noon-11pm; food Thur-Sat 6.30-8.30pm; WI-FI; 🐕) is a 15th-century establishment, nicely tucked away on Higher St. There are two open log fires and the menu includes pizzas (from £11).

If continuing straight on after the ferry crossing, turn immediately right to go underneath an archway (with the post office to your right) before turning left up Alma Steps. A brief jaunt along a wooded road follows before the houses are left behind and you are once again left with just nature for company – banana

---

❏ TORBAY, TOR BAY, OR THE ENGLISH RIVIERA

Torbay is an area which endears itself to the patriot, the naturalist and the artist'

Charles Kingsley

The 'English Riviera' is the Victorian nickname given to the Torbay area of South Devon that encompasses the three main towns of Brixham, Paignton and Torquay, the title deriving from the area's plentiful beaches and mild climate. Torbay is the council's name for the area; the actual bay is called Tor Bay.

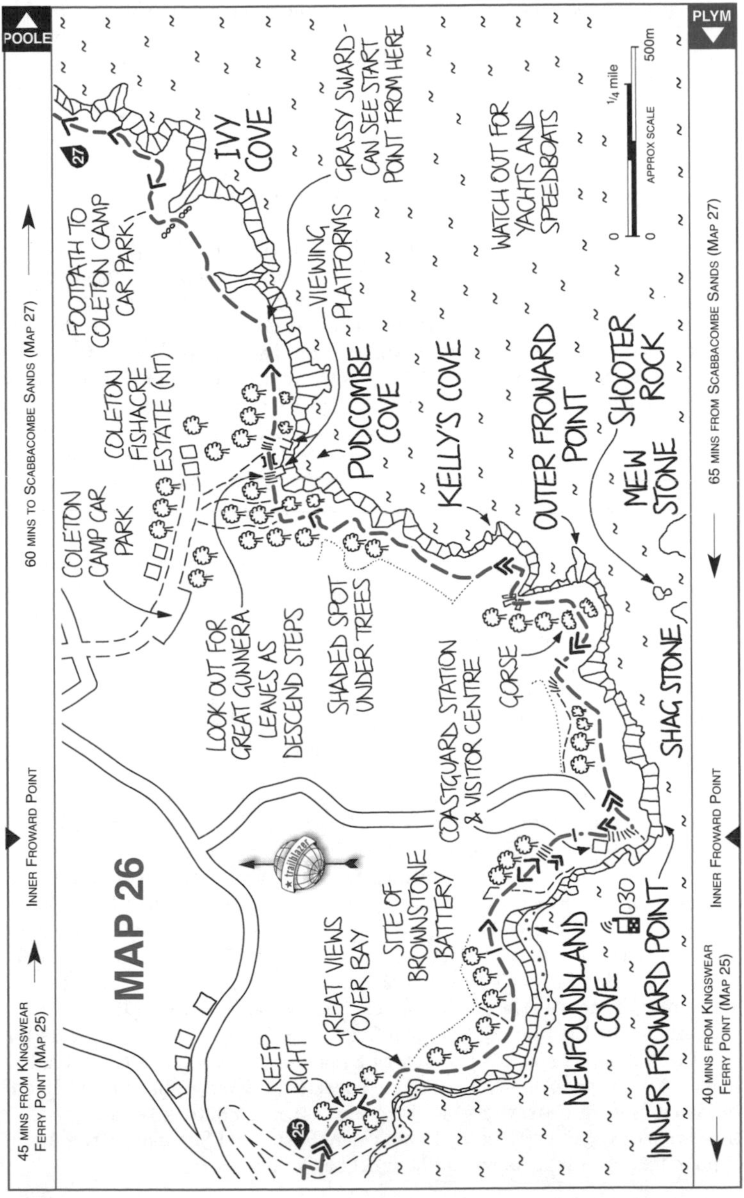

MAP 26

INNER FROWARD POINT

45 MINS FROM KINGSWEAR FERRY POINT (MAP 25)

INNER FROWARD POINT

60 MINS TO SCABBACOMBE SANDS (MAP 27)

KEEP RIGHT

GREAT VIEWS OVER BAY

SITE OF BROWNSTONE BATTERY

NEWFOUNDLAND COVE

INNER FROWARD POINT

COASTGUARD STATION & VISITOR CENTRE

GORSE

SHAG STONE

OUTER FROWARD POINT

MEW STONE

SHOOTER ROCK

KELLY'S COVE

PUDCOMBE COVE

COLETON FISHACRE ESTATE (NT)

COLETON CAMP CAR PARK

LOOK OUT FOR GREAT GUNNERA LEAVES AS DESCEND STEPS

SHADED SPOT UNDER TREES

FOOTPATH TO COLETON CAMP CAR PARK

IVY COVE

VIEWING PLATFORMS

GRASSY SWARD – CAN SEE START POINT FROM HERE

WATCH OUT FOR YACHTS AND SPEEDBOATS

500m

¼ mile

APPROX SCALE

0

0

40 MINS FROM KINGSWEAR FERRY POINT (MAP 25)

INNER FROWARD POINT

65 MINS FROM SCABBACOMBE SANDS (MAP 27)

plants and date palms turn to pine and other coniferous trees, while (with a bit of luck) sun-rays scatter sporadically through the branches. A right turn off the path will take you to **Kingswear Castle**, built in 1502 to complement Dartmouth Castle (see box p142) on the other side of the river. It's now owned by The Landmark Trust (☎ 01628-825925, 🖥 landmarktrust.org.uk) and used as a holiday let (1D/1T; ☞; 🐾; minimum stay three/four nights weekend/mid week).

As you leave the minor road a sign welcomes you into **Warren Woods**, whilst below you shelter **Mill Bay** and **Newfoundland coves**.

Eventually, after a strenuous climb or two (looking back there are great views over Dartmouth Castle and the bay), you arrive at the **site of Brownstone Battery**, an extensive WWII coastal defence position that is now managed by the National Trust. Its scattered collection of gun batteries, store huts and observation posts reaches right up to **Inner Froward Point**, from where both Start Point and Stoke Fleming church can still be seen. The site also contains a **coastguard station** housing a small **visitor centre** (daily 9am-5pm, winter 10am-4pm). The path now zig-zags steeply down, its route etched along the cliff and hillsides in front of you. There is the occasional tree amongst the gorse but little else for cover should the weather turn against you. The larger of the rocks you see out at sea is **Mew Stone** and its smaller companions are **Shag Stone** and **Shooter Rock**: seals may occasionally be seen resting on these lonely outcrops.

Arriving at picturesque **Pudcombe Cove**, behind you in the woods is **Coleton Fishacre Estate** (☎ 01803-752466, 🖥 www.nationaltrust.org.uk/coleton-fishacre; Mar-Oct daily 10.30am-5pm, Nov & Dec Sat & Sun 11am-4pm; £13, NT members free), the 1920s 'Arts and Crafts' holiday home of the D'Oyly Carte family with a lovely 30-acre garden.

The path again becomes exposed as it tacks its way along the hillside to **Scabbacombe Sands**, a pretty pebble beach worthy of a stop – the crystal-clear water certainly appears inviting on a hot summer's day. Note that the beach is also open to naturists.

The trail now begins on the first of two substantial ascents in this stage, the initial descent presenting a large **lime kiln** on the right at **Man Sands**. The views back over the valley as you clamber away from the beach are wonderful.

Following the edge of **Southdown Cliff** you arrive at **Sharkham Point National Nature Reserve** which, along with the nearby 100-acre Berry Head National Nature Reserve (see below), plays host to a colony of guillemots, greater horseshoe bats and eight species of orchid. There are more wildlife treats at nearby **St Mary's Bay** where, out at sea, dolphins and porpoises can sometimes be spotted. The path passes close to the campsite, Wall Park Touring Caravan and Centry Touring Camping Site (see p153).

The walking is now easy. Reaching a road, the entrance to **Berry Head** – home to two Napoleonic-era forts – appears to your right. **Berry Head National Nature Reserve** (NNR; Map 29; ☎ 01803-882619, 🖥 countryside-trust.org.uk/explore/berry-head; visitor centre Easter-end Sep daily 10am-4pm) is no longer open year-round but the toilet block is.

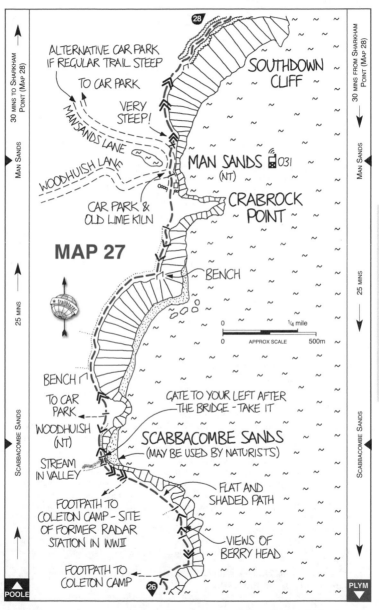

30 MINS TO SHARKHAM POINT (MAP 28)

MAN SANDS

25 MINS

SCABBACOMBE SANDS

30 MINS FROM SHARKHAM POINT (MAP 28)

MAN SANDS

25 MINS

SCABBACOMBE SANDS

POOLE

PLYM

ALTERNATIVE CAR PARK IF REGULAR TRAIL STEEP

TO CAR PARK

VERY STEEP!

MAN SANDS LANE

WOODHUISH LANE

SOUTHDOWN CLIFF

MAN SANDS 031 (NT)

CRABROCK POINT

CAR PARK & OLD LIME KILN

MAP 27

BENCH

BENCH

TO CAR PARK

WOODHUISH (NT)

STREAM IN VALLEY

FOOTPATH TO COLETON CAMP - SITE OF FORMER RADAR STATION IN WWII

FOOTPATH TO COLETON CAMP

GATE TO YOUR LEFT AFTER THE BRIDGE - TAKE IT

SCABBACOMBE SANDS (MAY BE USED BY NATURISTS)

FLAT AND SHADED PATH

VIEWS OF BERRY HEAD

0   1/4 mile
0   500m
APPROX SCALE

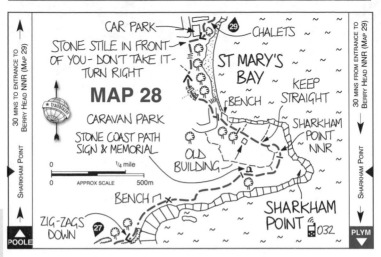

The award-winning *Guardhouse Café* (☎ 01803-855778, 🖥 guardhouse cafe.com; **fb**; intermittent WI-FI; 🐾 on lead; daily 9am-4pm, hot food to 3pm) has a fabulous cliff-top location close to the **lighthouse** on Berry Head which, at 58m above sea level, is located at the highest altitude of any British lighthouse. Probably as a result of its lofty location, it is also the smallest lighthouse in Britain, being just 5m high.

❑ **THE ENGLISH RIVIERA GLOBAL GEOPARK**

The English Riviera Global Geopark straddles the area called The English Riviera (see box p146), its coastal borders being at Sharkham Point (Map 28) and just north of Maidencombe Beach (see Map 36, p173).

A geopark is a site recognised and protected by UNESCO because of its unique geological significance. There are only 177 of these in the entire world, seven of which are in the UK, though the English Riviera is unique in being the only one that is largely urban. In addition to the Riviera's diverse geology, covering a number of periods, and its contribution to our understanding of the subject, the area is also a rich source of fossils, wonderful examples being those of a **woolly rhinoceros** and a **cave lion** that were both discovered at Kent's Cavern near Torquay. The **oldest human fossil** (a jawbone) yet to be found in the UK was also discovered in this cavern.

The park includes 32 **geosites** (geological sites of international importance) in total, though not all are open to the public. However, **Berry Head NNR**, guarding the southern entry to Tor Bay, **Petit Tor** and **Hope's Nose Site of Special Scientific Interest**, the latter at the geopark's northern extremity, are all visitable and on the path. Look out for the information boards that give further details on their geological importance.

The park also has **visitor centres** at Berry Head NNR (see p148) and Kent's Cavern (see p169), near Torquay.

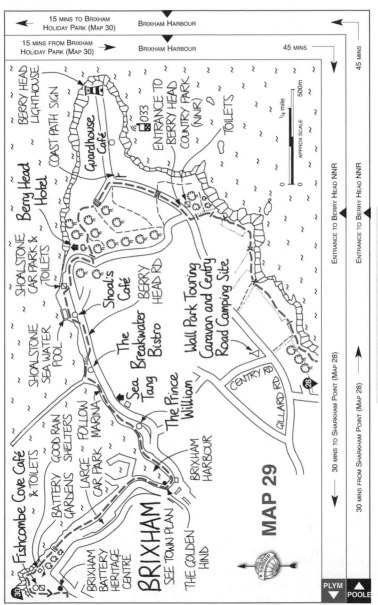

Gentle walking continues as you amble to **Berry Head Hotel** (see p154), where the trail leads into Shoalstone car park before reaching the wonderful **Shoalstone Sea Water Pool** (🖳 shoalstonepool.com), a free-to-use (though donation of £2.50 requested), open-all-hours, Art Deco lido with changing rooms beside it and a fine **café** – *Shoals* (☎ 01803-854874, 🖳 shoalsbrixham .co.uk; **fb**; WI-FI; 🐾 daytime only; early Feb to mid Dec daily noon-3pm & sittings at 6pm and 8pm) – overlooking it. Booking is essential in the evening.

The path as you enter Brixham is not wonderfully signed: look out for the steps shortly before the harbour-arm for an easy walk along the marina. You soon pass *The Breakwater Bistro* (☎ 01803-856738, 🖳 brixham-restaurant .co.uk; **fb**; WI-FI; 🐾; daily 10am-8 or 9pm), which is a takeaway but offers alfresco seating, and arrive at Brixham Harbour.

BRIXHAM [map opposite]

Sitting at the southern end of Tor Bay, Brixham, or *Briseham* as it is recorded in the Domesday Book (when it had a population of 39!) is the first of the three main towns of the English Riviera (the other two being Paignton and Torquay). Not quite as busy as Paignton, and far smaller than Torquay, the old harbour area may nevertheless feel a little too crowded for some walkers, particularly after the peace of the previous stage.

Synonymous with fishing, Brixham was the largest fishing port in South-West England during the Middle Ages. By the early 19th century there were over 200 trawlers operating out of the town and by 1850 it had become the largest fishery in England. Even today it remains the nation's foremost fishing port, landing a staggering £20 million worth of fish every year.

The harbour is dominated by an impressive 50-year-old replica of *The Golden Hind* (☎ 01803-856223, 🖳 golden hind.co.uk; Easter to end Oct generally daily 10am-4.30pm but the opening hours vary and they close some days so check their website before going; £7.95), the ship with which Francis Drake became the first Englishman (and the second person in the world) to circumnavigate the globe.

Behind the replica is the **statue of William, Prince of Orange**. Invited by Protestant English politicians concerned by King James II's Catholicism, William landed his 20,000-strong Dutch army at Fishcombe Cove, just outside Brixham, in 1688. From there he went on to overthrow James – in what became known as the Glorious Revolution – and become William III of England.

The social and maritime history of the town is celebrated at **Brixham Heritage Museum** (☎ 01803-856267, 🖳 brixham museum.uk; **fb**; Easter-Oct Tue-Sat 11am-2pm; free) in the Old Police Station at Bolton Cross, where there are two floors of galleries and displays housed inside an old police station.

Brixham Pirate Festival (see p14), held here at the end of April and beginning of May, features a variety of events including 'record attempts' for the 'Biggest gathering of pirates' (2010 saw the town gain – briefly – the world record).

Services

There's a **tourist information point** inside Ula! (daily 10am-5pm), an 'interior gifts' shop; it's just a table with leaflets on it so it is not much use, although shop staff will help you if they can.

There's a Co-op **supermarket** (daily 7am-11pm) near the harbour on Fore St, with an **ATM** outside it, and Brixham's **post office** (Mon-Sat 9am-5.30pm) within it. There's also a branch of Tesco (daily 7am-10pm) near the top of the same street where you'll also find Boots **pharmacy** (Mon-Sat 9am-1pm & 2-5pm).

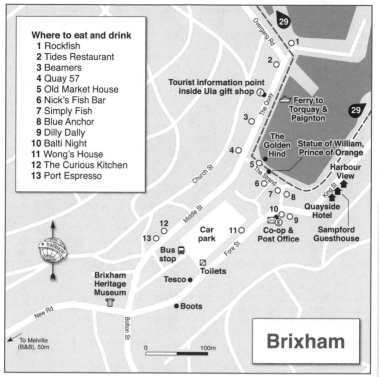

Where to eat and drink
1 Rockfish
2 Tides Restaurant
3 Beamers
4 Quay 57
5 Old Market House
6 Nick's Fish Bar
7 Simply Fish
8 Blue Anchor
9 Dilly Dally
10 Balti Night
11 Wong's House
12 The Curious Kitchen
13 Port Espresso

Tourist information point
inside Ula gift shop ⓘ

Ferry to
Torquay &
Paignton

The
Golden
Hind

Statue of William,
Prince of Orange

Harbour
View

Quayside
Hotel

Co-op &
Post Office

Sampford
Guesthouse

Car
park

Bus
stop

Toilets

Brixham
Heritage
Museum

Tesco

Boots

To Melville
(B&B), 50m

Brixham

0   100m

ROUTE GUIDE AND MAPS

Transport
The town is connected to the rest of the Riviera (and Kingswear) via Stagecoach's 12 & 18 **bus** services; see pp53-5.

Assuming the weather and tides are OK, Paignton Pleasure Cruises (☎ 01803-529147, boat ☎ 07768 014174, 🖳 www .paigntonpleasurecruises.co.uk; Apr-Oct daily hourly 10.30am-4.30pm; about £6/10 single/return) operate a **ferry** to Torquay and Paignton; see p159.

Where to stay
As you follow the path into Brixham you'll find **camping** at *Wall Park Touring Caravan and Centry Road Camping Site* (Map 29; ☎ 01803-856389, 🖳 centrytour ing.co.uk; tent plus up to two people costs

£16-29; 🐾; early Apr-end Oct) where Centry Rd meets Gillard Rd. Booking is recommended for August and there's a two-night minimum stay for Fri & Sat nights.

The first **B&B** you'll see as you enter town along Berry Head Rd is *Sea Tang* (Map 29; ☎ 01803-854651, 🖳 seatang-guesthouse.com; 2S/2D or T/1D/1Qd; WI-FI; £47.50-60pp, sgl/sgl occ from £70/75), at No 67, from where there are tremendous views over the bay and marina.

Overlooking the harbour from 65 King St is *Harbour View* (☎ 01803-853052, 🖳 harbourviewbrixhambandb.co.uk; 9D/1T; ☞; WI-FI; 🐾; £39.50-74.50pp, sgl occ room rate). Previously it was the residence of the harbourmaster and is grade II listed. Further down King St, at Nos 57-59, there is ***Sampford Guesthouse*** (☎ 01803-857761, 🖳 sampfordhouse.com; 4D/1T; 🥣; WI-FI; 🐕; £42-48pp, sgl occ from £74), which unfortunately does not accept advance bookings for one-night stays in the summer.

At the back end of town on New Rd there's another decent option. ***Melville Guesthouse*** (☎ 01803-852033, 🖳 the melvillebrixham.co.uk; 5D; WI-FI; £43.50-54pp, sgl occ room rate; Mar-Dec) is at No 45. Two of the rooms are suites with lounges and all the rooms have a mini-fridge. They also only accept advance bookings for a two-night stay or longer.

For **hotel** accommodation, ***Berry Head Hotel*** (Map 29; ☎ 01803-853225, 🖳 berryheadhotel.com; 3S/29D, some can be T; 🥣; WI-FI; 🐕; £78-94pp, sgl from £78, sgl occ £136-196) is a splendid – though not cheap – option to consider. Dinner can be provided but beware they do not accept advance bookings for one-night stays at weekends in summer.

Otherwise, there is ***Quayside Hotel*** (☎ 01803-302967, 🖳 quaysidehotel.co.uk), which overlooks the harbour from King St. However, it closed for renovation in November 2022 and work may take up to a year.

Where to eat and drink

It comes as no surprise, given the fact that the town can boast of one of the largest and newest fish markets in the UK, that seafood is something of a speciality. You don't have to stray too far from the path to sample it, either, with restaurants standing cheek by gill on the western side of the harbour – paradise for piscivores.

Cafés The best located cafés are on the coast path surrounding Brixham (see Map 29), but in the town itself, there's the friendly and award-winning ***DillyDally Tearoom*** (☎ 01803-431151, 🖳 www.dilly dallytearoom.co.uk; Tue-Sat 10am-3.30pm, Sun to 2pm; WI-FI; 🐕), just off the harbour on King St, where a double-sconed cream tea is just £6.95.

If you fancy exploring a little further into town, there are a few other excellent options. ***Port Espresso*** (☎ 01803-411120, 🖳 www.portespresso.com; **fb**; 🐕; Mon-Sat 9am-3pm) is another dog-friendly place, specialising in coffee, cake and brunches (from £4.50 for a bacon bap up to £10 for their version of the 'full English'), all housed, like many establishments on this stretch, in its own separate cave carved out of the cliffs. Just a couple of doors away, ***Curious Kitchen*** (☎ 01803-854816, 🖳 thecuriouskitchen.co.uk; **fb**; WI-FI; 🐕 daytime only; food daily 9am-3pm & Thur-Sat 7-9pm, winter Fri & Sat 7-9pm) is on Middle St. It's a modern place, with a rustic feel, serving healthy food and top-notch coffee – as well as a great line in donuts. Evenings are by prior booking only.

Despite the name, ***Tides Restaurant*** (☎ 01803-411150; WI-FI; 🐕; daily 8am-3pm) is really more of a greasy-spoon café; an unfussy place, with good-value lunchtime mains (£5.10-9.10). It's most popular, however, at breakfast (fry-ups from £7.50).

Pubs On the approach into town, you'll pass ***The Prince William*** (Map 29; ☎ 01803-854468, 🖳 theprincewilliam.co.uk; 🐕; food daily noon-3pm & 5-9pm) right on the coast path. It's somewhat soulless inside, but everyone sits outside, at tables overlooking the harbour. The Sunday carvery is popular.

In the heart of the harbour, ***Blue Anchor*** (☎ 01803-854575; **fb**; WI-FI; 🐕; food Mon-Sat noon-3pm & 5.30-9pm, Sun noon-4pm) is a more traditional, dog-friendly, real-ale pub with a decent pub-grub menu. Overlooking The Golden Hind, ***Old Market House*** (☎ 01803-856891, 🖳 www.oldmarkethousebrixham.co.uk; **fb**; WI-FI; 🐕 on ground floor only; food daily noon-3pm & 6-9pm, winter Wed-Sun only) is a gastro-pub with standard pub mains plus numerous seafood options. There's plenty of outdoor seating, including a first-floor terrace with unmatched views of the famous galleon moored beside it.

Restaurants Dominating the northern end of the harbour is a huge branch of the well-regarded seafood chain, ***Rockfish*** (☎

01803-850872, 🖥 therockfish.co.uk; daily noon-4pm & 5-9pm), with a large terrace looking out over Brixham's fishing fleet.

Nearby, *Beamers* (☎ 01803-854777, 🖥 beamersrestaurant.co.uk; Wed-Mon from 6.30pm) is another fish-centric establishment, though more refined. Seafood mains cost around £22-25, but there's also some fine cuts of steak here. Continuing down the street, *Quay 57* (☎ 01803-852937; **fb**; food Mon & Thur-Sat 10am-2pm & 5-8.30pm, Sun to 2pm; WI-FI; 🐾) sits on the corner of the quay opposite the *Golden Hind* (it even has some seating on the quay). Mains (£13-20) are delicious, but it's the light bites, such as the fish tacos (£9.95), that prove the most popular.

For more down-to-earth seafood dining, walk round the harbour to *Nick's Fish Bar* (☎ 01803-853357; summer Mon-Thur 11.30am-7.30pm, Fri & Sat to 8pm, Sun to 6.30pm; takeaway till 8.30pm, winter hours variable), an excellent takeaway chippy with some indoor seating too; or just round the corner to *Simply Fish* (☎ 01803-883858, 🖥 robertsfisheries.com; daily noon-9/9.30pm, winter 11.30am-3pm & 5-9pm).

Just opposite there's *Balti Night* (☎ 01803-882040, 🖥 www.thebaltinightbrixham.co.uk; Sun-Thur 5.30-11pm, Fri & Sat to 11.30pm) for Indian cuisine, and *Wong's House* (☎ 01803-856314; summer daily 5-11pm, winter closed Tue) for Chinese.

BRIXHAM TO TORQUAY [MAPS 29-33]

For many, this is a stage to endure rather than enjoy. Involving vast stretches where you'll be plodding on pedestrian promenades, this easy (though hard-on-the-ankles) 8½-mile (13.6km; 3¼hrs) stretch starts with an interesting section of sylvan walking that passes by pretty coves and through ancient woodland. After Broad Sands, however, the walk has little to excite unless beach huts and Brunellian railway lines are your thing.

That said, and in spite of this stage's shortcomings, there are plenty of options for refreshment on the English Riviera. So we advise you not to hurry through. Instead, take your time, spoil yourself with snacks, have your fill of fish & chips and conduct some in-depth research into what flavour ice-cream is your favourite. In doing this, you'll be saving your legs for tomorrow's stage – a stretch which does not allow for such frivolities.

The route

Having left Brixham via the large car park to the east of the harbour, you follow a set of steps that disappear into woodland. Continue on the path through **Battery Gardens** ready to defend England since the 16th century and one of the best-preserved WW2 Emergency coastal defence batteries.

At **Fishcombe Cove** there is a **seasonal** *café* (Easter-Oct Tue-Sun 10am-4pm, weather permitting), with a lovely perch above the cove, and good-value food, but only outdoor seating. The path climbs up behind the café to reach **Brixham Battery Heritage Centre** (☎ 01803-852449, 🖥 www.brixhambattery .net; Wed, Fri & Sun 2-4pm; free). Note the fierce snout of the 1950s Humver 'pig' and twelve-pounder gun that guard the centre.

Following the Battery you soon leave the road again by **Brixham Holiday Park** and enter **Elberry** and **Marridge** ancient woods (aka **The Grove**). The walk is wonderful and the woods friendly as you pass by the peaceful little **Elberry Cove** (look out for wild campers) before climbing over **Churston**

ROUTE GUIDE AND MAPS

Point to arrive by the multicoloured beach huts at **Broad Sands**. Note the rich red colour of the earth (an indication of iron-rich soil) and watch the trains as they chug along the railway line on the approaching cliffs. It is that railway line you now follow, first passing underneath it – where you can join the road to get to *Beverley Holidays campsite* (p159) in **Goodrington** – and later passing **Saltern Cove** – an SSSI and nature reserve that's unique in Britain as its boundaries extend underwater for 376 metres further than the low-water mark due to its unusual geology.

Goodrington Sands is the next stop, essentially a larger version of the previous beach and the home of *South Sands Café* (daily 9am-4pm, up to 7pm weather permitting). The beach at Goodrington Sands is partitioned by the rocky spit of **Middle Stone** where, nearby, you'll find the popular *Inn on the Quay* (☎ 01803-559754; breakfast Mon-Fri 6.30-10.30am, Sat & Sun 7-11am, meals daily noon-9.30pm; WI-FI) pub, part of the Brewers Fayre chain. Dogs are not allowed in the restaurant but there is an area where they can be left, and there is a lot of outdoor seating too.

Off to the left of the path is the UK's biggest outdoor waterpark, **Splashdown Quaywest** (☎ 01803-555550, 🖳 splashdownwaterparks.co .uk/quaywest; Mar-Sep daily 10am-5pm, till 7.30pm in peak times; £15.50-18), but the coast path passes in front of the pub and more beach huts to another seasonal café, *The Devon Ice Cream Shop* (daily 10am-5pm). It then climbs away from the beach to skirt the edge of **Roundham Head** where there is the possibility of spotting peregrine falcons and bottlenose dolphins. From here it's a road walk into **Paignton** via the harbour, where there are various eateries.

PAIGNTON [map p160]

Paignton is, it must be said, a rather run-down seaside town, though it's not entirely without its charms, boasting a fine pier, a pleasant harbour area and a massive promenade where the pavement is separated from the traffic by a large empty sward of grass. What's more, the B&Bs nearer the centre offer some of the cheapest accommodation along the whole of the South-West Coast Path.

Originally a Celtic settlement and first mentioned in the Domesday Book of 1086, 'Peynton' or 'Paington' (note the spelling) was a small fishing village until the Paignton Harbour Act of 1837 initiated the construction of a safe haven for craft in the village; the modern-day spelling, 'Paignton', arrived simultaneously. The town boomed with the construction of the railway in 1859 that linked the Riviera with London. The national rail network no longer goes as far as Brixham or Kingswear, though **Dartmouth Steam**

Railway (☎ 01803-555872, 🖳 dartmouth railriver.co.uk) provides a fun substitute. The ticket office is beside the main railway station and it has a gift shop and *café*. A return ticket to Dartmouth, including ferry across the Dart, costs £19.95.

Paignton Pier (🖳 paigntonpier.co.uk; pier free, charges for the attractions) was built in 1879 and was a popular attraction for holidaying Victorians until a fire all but destroyed it in 1919. A major redevelopment in 1980 brought it back to life and these days it houses the usual collection of arcade games, ice-cream stalls and children's fairground rides.

If you fancy a spot of **sea fishing** while you're here, head to the harbour to find Paignton Pleasure Cruises (see Transport p159) who also run a ferry service to Torquay and Brixham.

Paignton Festival (see p14) is held here in July.

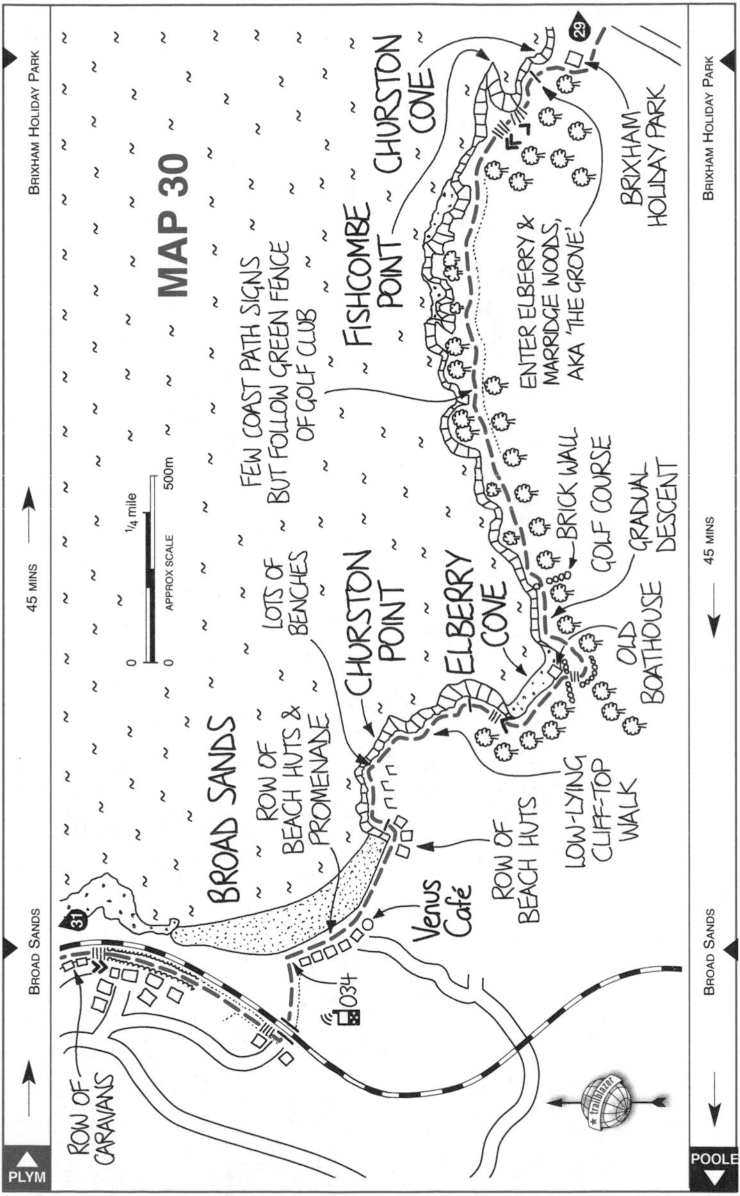

BRIXHAM HOLIDAY PARK

45 MINS

MAP 30

FEW COAST PATH SIGNS
BUT FOLLOW GREEN FENCE
OF GOLF CLUB

¼ mile

500m

APPROX SCALE

BROAD SANDS

LOTS OF
BENCHES

CHURSTON
POINT

ROW OF BEACH HUTS & PROMENADE

ROW OF CARAVANS

ROW OF
BEACH HUTS

Venus
Café

034

LOW-LYING
CLIFF-TOP
WALK

ELBERRY
COVE

OLD
BOATHOUSE

GOLF COURSE

GRADUAL
DESCENT

BRICK WALL

FISHCOMBE
POINT

CHURSTON
COVE

ENTER ELBERRY &
MARRIDGE WOODS,
AKA 'THE GROVE'

BRIXHAM
HOLIDAY PARK

BROAD SANDS

45 MINS

BRIXHAM HOLIDAY PARK

PLYM

POOLE

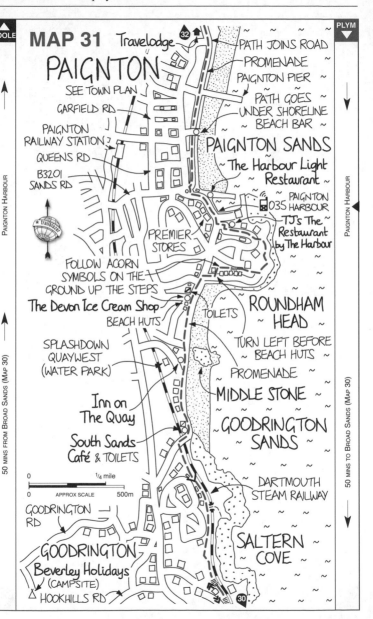

MAP 31

PAIGNTON

Travelodge

32

PLYM

POOLE

PATH JOINS ROAD

PROMENADE

PAIGNTON PIER

SEE TOWN PLAN

GARFIELD RD

PATH GOES
UNDER SHORELINE
~ BEACH BAR ~

PAIGNTON
RAILWAY STATION

PAIGNTON SANDS

QUEENS RD

~ The Harbour Light
Restaurant ~

B3201
SANDS RD

PAIGNTON HARBOUR

035 PAIGNTON
HARBOUR

PREMIER
STORES

~TJ's The ~
Restaurant
by The Harbour

FOLLOW ACORN
SYMBOLS ON THE
GROUND UP THE STEPS

The Devon Ice Cream Shop

BEACH HUTS

TOILETS

ROUNDHAM
~ HEAD

TURN LEFT BEFORE
~ BEACH HUTS

SPLASHDOWN
QUAYWEST
(WATER PARK)

~ PROMENADE ~

MIDDLE STONE ~

Inn on
The Quay

~GOODRINGTON
~ SANDS ~

South Sands
Café & TOILETS

0   1/4 mile

0   APPROX SCALE   500m

DARTMOUTH
STEAM RAILWAY

GOODRINGTON
RD

GOODRINGTON

SALTERN
~ COVE ~

Beverley Holidays
(CAMPSITE)

HOOKHILLS RD

30

PAIGNTON HARBOUR

50 MINS FROM BROAD SANDS (MAP 30)

50 MINS TO BROAD SANDS (MAP 30)

ROUTE GUIDE AND MAPS

Services

Paignton Library & Information Centre has free WI-FI, and a **tourist information point** (Mon & Fri 9.30am-5pm, Tue & Thur to 6pm, Wed to 1pm, Sat to 4pm). There are **banks** with **ATMs** around town – try Victoria St – and there is a **post office** (Mon-Sat 9am-5.30pm) on Torquay Rd.

For **provisions** there is a Premier Stores (Mon-Sat 7am-9pm, Sun 8am-8pm), by the harbour; a Tesco (daily 6am-11pm) at the western end of Victoria St, and a Lidl supermarket (Mon-Sat 8am-8pm, Sun 10am-4pm) a little further into town on Parkside Rd.

A **chemist**, Boots (Mon-Sat 9am-5.30pm) is on Victoria St. Nearby, **outdoor and camping gear** can be bought at Mountain Warehouse (Mon-Sat 9am-5.30pm, Sun 10am-4pm).

Transport

Stagecoach's No 120 **bus** connects the town to Kingswear; Kingswear and Dartmouth are connected by ferry. To access Brixham or Torquay you will need to catch their No 12 service and for Dawlish Warren and St Marychurch their No 22. Stagecoach's Gold service (to Plymouth) also calls here; see pp53-5 for details. All services call at the bus station as do National Express's NX102, 404 & 501 **coach** services (see box p51).

Paignton is a stop on both GWR's (see box p51) and Dartmouth Steam Railway's (see p156) **train** services.

Paignton Pleasure Cruises (see p153; boat ☎ 07768-014174; **fb**) operate a regular **ferry** service from the harbour to both Torquay and Brixham, though it is dependent on the weather, the sea and the tides. It is best to call the boat to check if the service is operating.

Where to stay

For **camping**, you need to come off the coast path before you reach Paignton, to find ***Beverley Holidays*** (Map 31; ☎ 01803-843887, 💻 beverley-holidays.co.uk; WI-FI; 🐕; late Mar to end Oct), a large, well-equipped holiday park with pitches from around £19.50 for a tent and up two people. Note that prices rocket to up to £40 per tent in peak periods. The main entrance is off Goodrington Rd.

Paignton is almost overrun with **B&B** accommodation, particularly along the three parallel streets of Kernou Rd, Beach Rd and Garfield Rd. However, as with most places on the Riviera (and beyond) the main issue facing walkers will be a reluctance to take one-night bookings in advance. If you're struggling to find somewhere, your best option may be the Travelodge (see p160).

Near to the harbour on Sands Rd there are a few decent options. ***Seaways*** (☎ 01803-551093, 💻 seawayshotel.com; 4D/2D or T/3D with bunk beds/1Qd; WI-FI; 🐕; from £42.50pp, sgl occ generally room rate), No 30, has a licensed bar. Indeed, having a licensed bar is actually quite a 'thing' in Paignton, with ***The Sands*** (☎ 01803-551282, 💻 office@thesandhotel.co.uk; 2S/2T/5D/2Tr; WI-FI; £42.50-57.50pp in high season, sgl/sgl occ £45-60), No 32, also having one. ***The Briars*** (☎ 01803-557729, 💻 briarshotel.co.uk; 1S/10D/1T; ●; WI-FI; £42.50-55pp, sgl £55-70, sgl occ room rate), is at No 26.

The town centre is surrounded by swinging 'vacancy' boards. To the north of Torbay Rd along Garfield Rd you'll find ***Kingswinford*** (☎ 01803-558358, 💻 www.thekingswinford.co.uk; 3D/2Tr/1Qd; WI-FI; £30-40pp, sgl occ £27-40, No 32; and ***Rosemead*** (☎ 01803-557944, 💻 rosemead paignton.co.uk; 2S shared facilities, 1D private bathroom, 4D/1D or T/1Tr all en suite; ●; WI-FI; £35-45pp, sgl/sgl occ from £40/50) at No 22. There's also ***Belle Dene*** (☎ 01803-559645, 💻 belledeneguest house.co.uk; 1S private facilities, 1T/4D all en suite; WI-FI; £35-40pp, sgl £45-50, sgl occ room rate), at No 25, which has a great sun-trap front garden.

Further good-value places are available on Beach Rd, where you'll find ***Barbican Hotel*** (☎ 01803-551332, 💻 barbicanhotelpaignton.co.uk; 5D/2T/2Qd; WI-FI) at No 5, which has a unique charging system: everyone pays £35 per head, except for children under 14 who pay their age (eg a ten-year-old will be charged £10).

Finally, right on the path, if a few minutes from the centre, *Travelodge* (Map 31; ☎ 0871 984 6393, 🖥 travelodge.co.uk; ☞; WI-FI; 🐾) have now opened a branch in Paignton; it's just off the seafront on Marine Drive. See p21 for more details.

Where to eat and drink

Paignton's residents are nicknamed 'Puddin' Eaters', a moniker that comes from the huge Paignton Pudding, which originated in the 13th century and is historically baked to celebrate local events. Thousands turning up for a piece of the one baked in celebration of the railway's arrival almost caused a riot, such was the desire for a chunk! You'll struggle to find any on a Paignton menu today, at least when there aren't any special occasions being celebrated; but if you do find some for sale somewhere, you'd be foolish to miss the chance.

Cafés Near the railway station, *Urban Edge* (☎ 07806 706645; **fb**; WI-FI; daily 10am-4pm) is the most stylish café in town, and the best for food, although nearby *Coffee #1* (☎ 01803-663795, 🖥 coffee1.co.uk; WI-FI; 🐾; Mon-Sat 7.30am-5.30pm, Sun 9am-5pm) also does an excellent brew.

As cute as the name suggests, *Cupcake* (☎ 01803-431506, 🖥 cupcakecafepaignton.co.uk; WI-FI; 🐾; Mon-Sat 9am-5pm, Sun 10am-2pm) is perfect for a quick pit stop. It does soups and sandwiches as well as its signature homemade cupcakes.

Restaurants & pubs Overlooking the harbour, the excellent *TJ's The Restaurant by The Harbour* (☎ 01803-527389, 🖥 tjsrestaurant.co.uk; **fb**; Wed-Sat 6-9pm, Sun 6-8pm; school summer hols daily 6-9pm; occasional summer lunchtimes) offers an imaginative menu including some decent

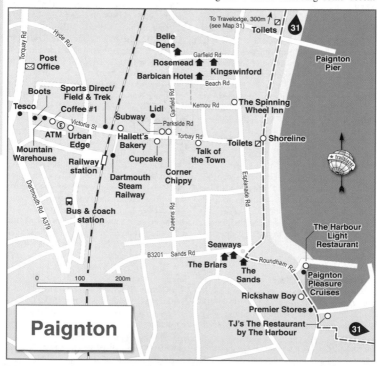

Paignton

vegetarian and vegan options such as pan-fried halloumi with beetroot purée & rosa pesto (£17.75) and a vegan pakora made with cauliflower and spring onions. Nearby, the seafood-led menu at *The Harbour Light Restaurant* (☎ 01803-229000, 🖥 harbourlightpaignton.co.uk; daily noon-9pm) includes mussels (£17), fish dishes as well as a Malaysian laksa curry (£13).

The best pub at the seaside end of town, though, is *The Spinning Wheel Inn* (☎ 01803-555000, 🖥 spinningwheelinn.co.uk; 🐾 on lead; food daily noon-4pm & 5.30-9pm) with an oak-beam interior, a large front garden, good-value pub grub (mains from £9.95) and a strong selection of real ales on tap. They also have live music most nights. Rivalling them in terms

of value is the *Talk of the Town* (☎ 01803-668070, 🖥 www.jdwetherspoon.com; WI-FI; food daily 8am-9pm) on Torbay Rd, though as with all Wetherspoons pubs, dogs are not allowed inside.

Snacks & takeaways For fish & chips, try *Corner Chippy* (Mon, Tue, Thur & Sun 11.45am-7.30pm, Wed, Fri & Sat to 8pm), at 49 Torbay Rd. Nearby, *Hallett's Bakery* (🖥 www.hallettsthebakers.co.uk; summer Mon-Sat 8.30am-4.30pm, Sun 9am-4pm) has baked goods and pastries covered.

For a Chinese takeaway, head to the harbour where you'll find *Rickshaw Boy* (☎ 01803-559901; daily 5-10pm) at 55 Roundham Rd.

The path through Paignton pursues the promenade, passing the pier and then the pretty, pastel-coloured beach huts at **Preston Sands**. A brief dalliance with tranquil **Hollicombe Park** – a refreshing respite from the roads and promenades – leads, eventually, to **Corbyn's Head**, where (if local folklore is to be believed) the pirate Samuel Corbyn was hanged for his swashbuckling crimes.

Passing **Abbey Park**, the beach at **Torre Abbey Sands** and **Princess Theatre** (🖥 atgtickets.com/venues/princess-theatre-torquay), you soon arrive at Torquay Marina.

TORQUAY   [map p167]

The largest and most central of the three Riviera towns, Torquay's population swells from somewhere around the 65,000 mark to nearer 200,000 at the height of summer. At these times you'll either have to embrace it or continue to the far more peaceful suburb of St Marychurch – or even, if stamina allows, the blink-and-you'll-miss-it village of Maidencombe.

As with Brixham, Torquay has its origins as a fishing village (though one with an important abbey – see column opposite) but secured an advantage in the tourism stakes during the Napoleonic Wars. With the Royal Navy spending a lot of time anchored in Tor Bay, it became a chic (if rather exclusive) seaside resort, where the relatives of the boats' officers would visit. It was during the Victorian era that Torquay and its environs earned the nickname of the English Riviera, with its mild and healthy climate being part of the attraction for holidaymakers as well as

those wishing to convalesce. The opening of the railway stations here (in 1848 and 1859) further accelerated Torquay's popularity.

Torre Abbey (☎ 01803-293593, 🖥 torre-abbey.org.uk; Tue-Sun 10am-5pm; £9.50, under-18s £3.70), the first building of note in the town, was a Premonstratensian (a Catholic order of canons founded at Premontre) monastery founded in 1196. Today it houses an art collection, runs tours and invites you to explore its exotic gardens. The *tea room* (daily 9am-4pm; 🐾) is a lovely spot for a light lunch or cream tea.

The area's most famous discovery, a prehistoric human jawbone, which was found at Kent's Cavern (Map 34; see p169), can be seen in **Torquay Museum** (☎ 01803-293975, 🖥 torquaymuseum.org; school summer holidays daily 10am-4pm, rest of year Tue-Thur & Sat 10am-4pm; £9). The museum also tells the story of the caves and houses an Agatha Christie gallery (see box p164).

The **International Agatha Christie Festival** (see p14) is held in and around the town during September. Some of the events in Torbay's **Festival of Poetry** (see p14) are also held here in October.

Services

The **English Riviera Visitor Information Centre** (☎ 01803-211211, 🖳 www.english riviera.co.uk; mid Feb-end Dec Mon-Sat 9.30am-5pm, Sun & Bank hols 10am-2pm) is conveniently placed in the marina.

There are plenty of **banks** with **ATMs** around town.

For **trekking and camping gear**, Trespass (Mon-Sat 9am-5.30pm, Sun 10.30am-4.30pm) is on Fleet St.

Further up, on Union St, is the **pharmacy**, Boots (Mon-Sat 9am-5pm, Sun 10am-4pm), while further down the road is the **post office** (Mon-Sat 8.30am-5.30pm, Sun 10am-2pm), hidden away in the local branch of WH Smith, and the **supermarket** Co-op (daily 7am-11pm) just back from the marina, as well as a Tesco (Mon-Sat 7am-11pm, Sun 11am-5pm) on Union St.

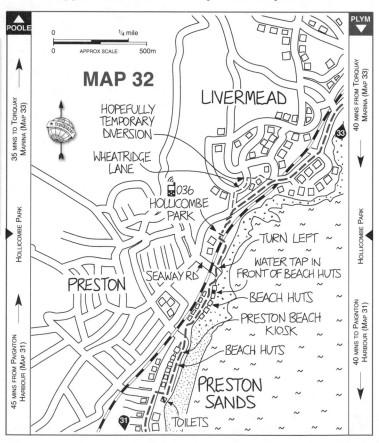

POOLE

PLYM

MAP 32

LIVERMEAD

HOPEFULLY TEMPORARY DIVERSION

WHEATRIDGE LANE

036

HOLLICOMBE PARK

TURN LEFT

WATER TAP IN FRONT OF BEACH HUTS

SEAWAY RD

PRESTON

BEACH HUTS

PRESTON BEACH KIOSK

BEACH HUTS

PRESTON SANDS

TOILETS

31

33

35 MINS TO TORQUAY MARINA (MAP 33)

HOLLICOMBE PARK

45 MINS FROM PAIGNTON HARBOUR (MAP 31)

40 MINS FROM TORQUAY MARINA (MAP 33)

HOLLICOMBE PARK

40 MINS TO PAIGNTON HARBOUR (MAP 31)

ROUTE GUIDE AND MAPS

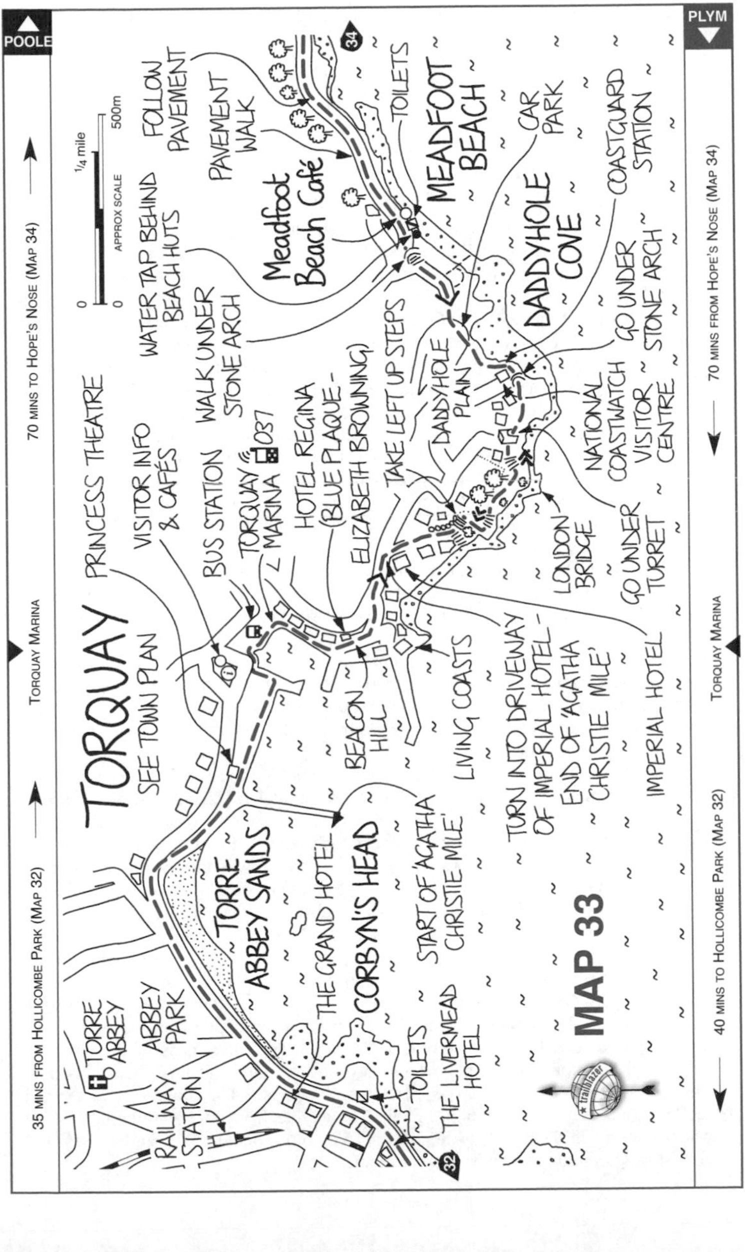

POOLE

TORQUAY MARINA

35 MINS FROM HOLLICOMBE PARK (MAP 32)

70 MINS TO HOPE'S NOSE (MAP 34)

PLYM

70 MINS FROM HOPE'S NOSE (MAP 34)

TORQUAY MARINA

40 MINS TO HOLLICOMBE PARK (MAP 32)

TORQUAY

SEE TOWN PLAN

PRINCESS THEATRE

VISITOR INFO & CAFÉS

BUS STATION

WALK UNDER STONE ARCH

WATER TAP BEHIND BEACH HUTS

FOLLOW PAVEMENT

PAVEMENT WALK

TOILETS

34

Meadfoot Beach Café

MEADFOOT BEACH

CAR PARK

DADDYHOLE COVE

COASTGUARD STATION

GO UNDER STONE ARCH

NATIONAL COASTWATCH VISITOR CENTRE

DADDYHOLE PLAIN

TAKE LEFT UP STEPS

GO UNDER TURRET

LONDON BRIDGE

HOTEL REGINA (BLUE PLAQUE – ELIZABETH BROWNING)

Torquay Marina 037

¼ mile

APPROX SCALE

500m

BEACON HILL

LIVING COASTS

TURN INTO DRIVEWAY OF IMPERIAL HOTEL – END OF 'AGATHA CHRISTIE MILE'

IMPERIAL HOTEL

THE GRAND HOTEL

START OF 'AGATHA CHRISTIE MILE'

CORBYN'S HEAD

~ TORRE ABBEY SANDS ~

TORRE ABBEY

ABBEY PARK

RAILWAY STATION

TOILETS

THE LIVERMEAD HOTEL

32

MAP 33

Transport

Stagecoach's 12 & 22 **buses** call at the bus station and travel as far west as Brixham and east as Shaldon and Teignmouth; see pp53-5 for details.

Frequent GWR **trains** connect Torquay with Exeter; see box p51.

For a **taxi** try 1st Class Cars (☎ 07778 287949), or Torbay Taxis (☎ 01803-211611, 🖥 torbaytaxis.co.uk).

❑ TORQUAY'S MOST FAMOUS DAUGHTER: AGATHA CHRISTIE

No-one can accuse Torquay of under-exploiting the legacy of its most famous daughter. In addition to the Agatha Christie Literary Trail and the Agatha Christie Mile (see below), the town also hosts an annual Agatha Christie Festival (see p14) every September. But who exactly was Agatha Christie – and what precisely was her connection with the town?

Ms Christie's biography is, of course, fairly well documented. During a spectacularly successful career she tried her hand at a variety of formats and genres, from short stories to plays and even romances (under the pseudonym Mary Westmacott). But it is, of course, her crime fiction, and particularly those stories involving the detectives Miss Marple and Hercule Poirot, that gave her worldwide fame and even earned her the sobriquet the 'Queen of Crime'. Her novels have sold a staggering 2-4 billion copies, a figure that puts her joint-first with William Shakespeare on the world's all-time bestsellers' list. What's more, her play *The Mousetrap*, having opened in November 1952, is still running in London's West End to this day, and having ratcheted up more than 28,500 performances in over 70 years is by far the longest-running West End show in history.

There is no doubt that Agatha's Christie's links with Torquay are numerous. Born in the town on 15th September, 1890, she also honeymooned here in 1914, worked as a nurse in the local hospital during the First World War and – though she travelled widely between the wars – in 1938 she and her second husband, the archaeologist Max Mallowan, purchased a holiday home on the nearby River Dart. Perhaps more importantly, however, Christie was greatly inspired by the rugged moors, cliffs, beaches, villages and islands of South Devon, many of which are recognisable (albeit under different names) in much of her work. Indeed the best-selling mystery novel of all time, *And Then There Were None* (1939), takes place on fictional Soldier Island which Agatha Christie based on Burgh Island (see box on p114) in Bigbury Bay. The island also features (though this time it's called Smugglers' Island) as Poirot's holiday destination in *Evil Under the Sun* (1941), the super sleuth's vacation being rather rudely interrupted by the discovery of an actress's strangled body in a nearby cove.

Today, Christie-philes – of which, to judge by the crowds that swarm in summer around all things Agatha, there are many – have plenty of ways of indulging their passion in her hometown. The holiday home she bought with her second husband, **The Greenway Estate** (☎ 01803-842382, 🖥 nationaltrust.org.uk/greenway; mid Feb-end Oct daily 10.30am-5pm, Nov-Dec weekends only; £13), is open to the public. You can reach the estate by **ferry** from Dartmouth (☎ 01803-882811, 🖥 greenwayferry .co.uk; Mar-Oct daily 10am-3pm, five services each way; £10 return).

There's also the **Agatha Christie Literary Trail**, stretching from Greenway on the River Dart to Babbacombe (north of Torquay), that links many of the writer's novels with locations that are believed to have influenced or inspired them. And the **Agatha Christie Mile** (see Map 33, p163) which begins at The Grand Hotel – where she honeymooned – and continues along Torquay seafront to The Imperial Hotel, which features in a number of her novels. For more details, the English Riviera Tourist Board produces a leaflet on both trails.

Where to stay

It will be no surprise that Torquay is full of accommodation aimed at the holidaying masses, though there are no campsites or hostels. Behind Abbey Park and along Belgrave Rd there are numerous B&Bs and hotels; once again, however, finding one willing to accept an advance booking for a one-night stop, particularly in July and August and at weekends, can be problematic though most will if they have availability near the time.

Options on Belgrave Rd include *The Wayfarer* (☎ 01803-299138, 🖳 wayfarer torquay.com; 4D/1D or T; WI-FI; from £37.50pp, sgl occ £60), at No 37; *Kethla House* (☎ 01803-473767, 🖳 kethlahouse .co.uk; 5D/1Tr/1Qd; WI-FI; £40-47.50pp, sgl occ room rate), No 33, who will cater for any special dietary requirements if requested in advance; and *Cranborne* (☎ 01803-211660, 🖳 cranbornetorquay.co.uk; 1S/5D/1T; ➟; WI-FI; £32.50-40pp, sgl from £50, sgl occ room rate), at No 58, which serves breakfast at 9-10am and check-in is 2.30-7pm.

On Scarborough Rd, just off Belgrave Rd, you'll come across *South View* (☎ 01803-296029, 🖳 thesouthview.com; 5D; WI-FI; £37.50-42.50pp, sgl occ room rate), at No 12, and *Southbank Townhouse* (☎ 01803-296701, 🖳 southbanktownhouse torquay.co.uk; 1S/1T/10D; ➟; WI-FI; £42.50-67.50pp, sgl £60-75, sgl occ room rate), Nos 15-17. Southbank is licensed (bar Mon-Sat 6.30-8pm). Note that neither of these places accepts children.

Nearer to the town centre, on Babbacombe Rd, is *Ravenswood* (☎ 01803-292900, 🖳 ravenswoodhotel.co.uk; 6D/1T; WI-FI; £44.50-54.50pp, sgl occ rates on request), at No 535.

Still on Babbacombe Rd, are: *Kingsholm* (☎ 01803-297794, 🖳 www .kingsholmhotel.co.uk; 1S/8D; WI-FI; £42-52.50pp, sgl from £55, sgl occ £79-93;

Mar-Nov) at No 539; *Hotel Peppers* (☎ 01803-293856, 🖳 hotel-peppers.co.uk; 2S/6D/2D or T all en suite; WI-FI; £35.50-39.50pp, sgl £50-69, sgl occ room rate), at No 551, which has an honesty bar and is happy to put walkers up for a solitary night; and, between them, *Hotel Hudson* (☎ 01803-203407, 🖳 www.hudsonhotel.co .uk; 2S/6D/2Tr; WI-FI; £30-47.50pp, sgl £45-70, sgl occ room rate), No 545, which does not take advance bookings for a one-night stay.

At the top of the hill (74 Braddons Hill Rd East) is the dog-friendly *Robin Hill Hotel* (☎ 01803-214518, 🖳 robinhillhotel .co.uk; 5D/5T/1Tr/2Qd; WI-FI; 🐕; £40-65pp, sgl occ £70-100). It's a great place to stop although it's a fair old march from the path itself (however, Stagecoach's No 22 bus service (see box pp54-5) stops near the top of Babbacombe Rd and leaves from The Strand.

Larger **hotels** available in Torquay include *Abbey Sands* (☎ 01803-294373, 🖳 richardsonhotels.co.uk/abbey-sands-hotel; 23D/15D or T/6T/2Qd; ➟; WI-FI; 🐕; £22-100pp, sgl occ rates on request), on Belgrave Rd. Note that rates vary widely and are usually for room only. Breakfast is available (from £10).

There is also a branch of the *Premier Inn* (☎ 0333-321 9097, 🖳 www.premierinn .com; 143D or T; ➟; WI-FI) chain (see p21 for more details; it is just a short distance from the seafront and path at the bottom of Belgrave Rd. *Travelodge* (☎ 08719-846412, 🖳 travelodge.co.uk; ➟; WI-FI; 🐕; see p21 for more details) incidentally, also

ROUTE GUIDE AND MAPS

SYMBOLS USED IN TEXT

➟ Bathtub in, or for, at least one room;   WI-FI means wi-fi is available
🐕 Dogs allowed; for accommodation subject to prior arrangement (see p313)
fb signifies places that have a Facebook page (for latest opening hours)

advertise a 'Torquay Hotel' but their establishment is actually around three miles away on Newton Rd in Torre. That said, the railway station in Torquay stands near the coast path and it's only a three-minute journey to Torre, where it's another two-minute walk to the hotel.

Where to eat and drink

Cafés Close to the coast path you can get sandwiches and pastries on Torwood St at the rather unimaginative titled but friendly *Food* (Mon-Fri 7.30am-3pm). Opposite you'll find the large *Boston Tea Party* (☎ 01803-921700, 🖥 bostonteaparty.co.uk; WI-FI; 🐾; daily 8am-5pm), a swish and slick affair that's just one link in a large West Country chain. The wide range of breakfasts are slightly overpriced (£2.75 for two slices of toast and up to £13 for the 'Boss Breakfast') but the service is exceptionally speedy, the welcome warm and there are plugs to charge your phones etc.

For a Devon cream tea with a dash of history, try *Torre Abbey Tea Rooms* (see p161). You don't have to pay to get into the abbey to visit the tea room.

Pubs Hugely popular, thanks largely to its prime location overlooking the harbour, *Offshore* (☎ 01803-292108, 🖥 offshoretorquay.co.uk; food daily 10am-9pm) is a bar-restaurant that's great for a pint of ice-cold lager on a sunny summer's evening, but also does very good food, including seafood.

Nearby *Shiraz* (☎ 01803-200002, 🖥 www.shiraztorquay.co.uk; food summer daily 9am-7.30pm, winter to 6pm) is a gastro-pub with a similar location, although the food (standard pub grub including fish & chips) isn't of the same standard. Both places are also open for breakfast.

Torquay's best traditional pub is also its oldest, the discreet *Hole in the Wall* (☎ 01803-200755, 🖥 holeinthewalltorquay.co.uk; WI-FI; 🐾 bar area only; food daily noon-2.30pm & 5.30-9pm), a 16th-century inn (c1540) located up a dead-end alley called Park Lane. They have as many as seven real ales on tap at any one time and also do decent pub grub.

Back down the bottom of the hill, *Apple & Parrot* (☎ 01803-214446, 🖥 www.appleandparrot.com; **fb**; daily noon-2/3am) can be a lively place. It is the unofficial home of live music in Torquay and boasts a large range of rums and local ciders. If you have the energy left for a sweaty night out, there are worse places to spend it.

Restaurants There's an eclectic mix of restaurants to choose from here, many of which are on or close to the marina.

Prezzo (☎ 01803-389525, 🖥 prezzorestaurants.co.uk; daily noon-10pm) is a branch of a reasonably smart nationwide pizza chain (pasta and pizza mains from £10) at the northern end of the marina.

For traditional British seaside fare, head to the chippy on the other side of the marina, *Harbour Fish Café* (daily noon-7pm, till 10/11pm during summer school hols), which has indoor seating as well as tables and chairs scattered around the pavement outside. Wonderfully, they serve alcohol here – a great accompaniment to fish & chips on a hot day.

Moving to Torwood St, there's a world of cuisines awaiting you. *Ephesus* (☎ 01803-294466, 🖥 ephesustorquay.co.uk; daily 4.30pm to late) specialises in Turkish and Greek cuisine; *Tang Tang* (☎ 01803-213344, 🖥 tangtangrestaurant.godaddysites.com; Sun-Fri 5-10.30pm, Sat to 11pm) is a large and well-regarded Chinese restaurant, *Maha-Bharat* (☎ 01803-215541, 🖥 maha-bharat-torquay.co.uk; daily 5pm to midnight) is an Indian restaurant with an emphasis on Bengali cuisine and some excellent Balti dishes, and *Smokey Joe's* (☎ 01803-214444, 🖥 www.smokeyjoestorquay.co.uk; Tue-Thur & Sun 5-9.30pm, Fri & Sat to 10pm), an American bar and grill with plenty of burgers and steaks. While across the road is *Amici* (☎ 01803-201770, 🖥 amici-torquay.co.uk; summer daily noon-10pm, rest of year may close earlier), another Italian with an outside eating area.

Finally, there are two upmarket options as you leave the town on the Coast Path. For fine dining, *The Elephant by Simon*

Torquay

Where to eat and drink
1 Torre Abbey Tea Rooms
2 Prezzo
3 Shiraz
4 Offshore
5 Harbour Fish Café
6 The Elephant
7 No 7 Fish Bistro & Wine Bar
8 Boston Tea Party
9 Apple & Parrot
10 Food
11 Hole in the Wall
12 Amici
13 Ephesus
14 Tang Tang
15 Maha-Bharat
16 Smokey Joe's

Robin Hill Hotel

Ravenswood
Kingsholm
Hotel Hudson
Hotel Peppers

Torquay Museum

Tusker Lodge

Babbacombe Rd

Museum Rd

Bus station

Hill Road East

Braddons

Co-op

Strand

Fleet St

The Imperial Hotel

Parkhill Rd

Beacon Hill

Living Coasts

Hotel Regina

Victoria Parade

Torquay Marina

037

English Riviera Visitor Information Centre

Trespass

Princess Theatre

Toilets

WHSmith & PO

Tesco

Boots

Castle Circus

Union St

Abbey Rd

Tor Hill Rd

Kethla House
The Wayfarer
Cranborne
South View
Southbank Townhouse

Lucius St

Scarborough Rd

Falkland Rd

Belgrave Rd

Premier Inn

Abbey Sands Hotel

Chestnut Ave

Abbey Park

Torre Abbey
1

The King's Drive

Avenue Rd

Rathmore Rd

Railway station

The Grand Hotel

New Harbour

Tor Bay

250m

0

Torquay

ROUTE GUIDE AND MAPS

Hulstone (☎ 01803-200044, 🖳 www.ele phantrestaurant.co.uk; Tue/Wed-Sat noon-2pm & 6.30-9pm) is as good as it gets and was the first place in town to be awarded a Michelin star. Cooking is taken very seriously here – it has its own farm from where many of the ingredients are sourced, and while it's as eye-wateringly expensive as you might expect, their set lunch menu (£31.50 for three courses) represents good value given the quality of the food.

Just above it (geographically, at least), *No 7 Fish Bistro & Wine Bar* (☎ 01803-295055, 🖳 no7-fish.com; Wed-Sat 12.15-1.45pm, also Mon-Sat 6-9.45pm) surprisingly claims to be Torbay's only seafood restaurant. The menu sounds delicious, with mains (from £13.75) including scallops simmered with mushrooms, vermouth & lemon.

TORQUAY TO TEIGNMOUTH   [MAPS 33-37]

This is a strenuous **11¼-mile (18km; 4hrs 35mins plus 5 mins for the ferry crossing to Teignmouth)** walk: after the concrete monotony of the previous stage it's time to open your lungs again and get back out into the wilds.

Having passed Hope's Nose, Torbay is finally left behind and although you'll be sucked back into civilisation briefly at St Marychurch, for most of this stage you'll find yourself enjoying some beautiful walking and mesmerising views interrupted only by the occasional and pleasantly isolated public house or seasonal café. With a ferry crossing (before you set off make sure you have checked the ferry times) from Shaldon to Teignmouth at the end of the day and numerous twists and turns, ascents and descents along the way, this stage should not be underestimated. Planning for rest-stops would be wise as well as carrying ample food and water.

The route

Leaving Torquay can take a little concentration: look for acorns on the ground and stickers on lamp posts – as well as more orthodox signage – and you should be fine. Eventually, after turning right at **The Imperial Hotel** (the path actually enters the car park of the hotel before skirting the hotel's grounds), the path finally finds some space and freedom from humanity through a stone archway leading to **Daddyhole Plain**, where you'll also find a small **National Coastwatch Visitor Centre** with displays on the history of Torbay, CCTV footage of the coastline, and a pair of binoculars for visitors to use. Due to its Devonian limestone, the accompanying cove here is one of the Riviera's geosites (see box on p150).

The path now passes through woodland overlooking **Meadfoot Beach** where there is *Meadfoot Beach Café* (☎ 01803-213988; **fb**; WI-FI; 🐾; daily 9am-5.30pm, winter to 4pm, though food until 3pm only) with baguettes, soups, jacket potatoes and wonderful sea views. Note, you can fill up your water bottle from the **water tap** behind the beach huts beside the café.

A short climb and some road rambling soon sees you rounding **Thatcher Point** and brings you to a junction where, officially at least, the coast path turns right down to **Hope's Nose** – an SSSI (note that because it is an SSSI you can't hammer the rock in search of fossils or take specimens; you can only photograph any fossils you see) and the northern promontory of Tor Bay –

before following a path above the road to continue. Wonderful woodland walking now follows as you continue along **Black Head** past **Anstey's Cove**.

Kent's Cavern (☎ 01803-215136, 🖥 kents-cavern.co.uk; daily 10am-4.30pm, café 10am-4pm; entrance ticket £14-15), a prehistoric cave system where in 1927 the oldest human fossil – an upper jawbone – yet to be discovered in the UK was unearthed, can be accessed by turning left and heading inland here; it is about a 10-minute walk.

The coast path, however, continues above **Redgate Beach** to **Long Quarry Point**. The signage is particularly poor here but look out for a wooden signpost leading off into the trees shortly after the mock-Roman shelter. Descending

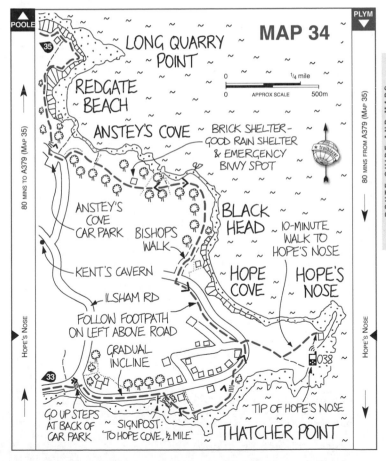

POOLE

PLYM

MAP 34

LONG QUARRY POINT

35

REDGATE BEACH

ANSTEY'S COVE

BRICK SHELTER – GOOD RAIN SHELTER & EMERGENCY BIVVY SPOT

trailblazer

ANSTEY'S COVE CAR PARK   BISHOPS WALK

BLACK HEAD

10-MINUTE WALK TO HOPE'S NOSE

KENT'S CAVERN

HOPE COVE

HOPE'S NOSE

ILSHAM RD

FOLLOW FOOTPATH ON LEFT ABOVE ROAD

GRADUAL INCLINE

038

33

GO UP STEPS AT BACK OF CAR PARK

SIGNPOST: 'TO HOPE COVE, ½ MILE'

TIP OF HOPE'S NOSE

THATCHER POINT

80 MINS TO A379 (MAP 35)

HOPE'S NOSE

80 MINS FROM A379 (MAP 35)

HOPE'S NOSE

0   ¼ mile

0   APPROX SCALE   500m

ROUTE GUIDE AND MAPS

steep wooded steps you eventually arrive at the upmarket but charming *Cary Arms* (☎ 01803-327110, 🖳 caryarms.co.uk; 7D/1Qd; ➥; WI-FI; 🐾; £97.50-225pp, sgl occ room rate), where the steak, mushroom & Devon ale pie (£18.50) may well prove too tempting to resist; **food** is served daily noon-3pm & 6.30-8.45pm.

From the pub you can see where, in 2010, a 5000-tonne rockfall occurred at the northern end of **Oddicombe Beach** near **Petit Tor Point**. The path avoids this by climbing steeply beside the fabulously fun, 90-year-old **Babbacombe Cliff Railway** (🖳 babbacombecliffrailway.co.uk; daily 9am-4.45pm; sgl/return £2.20/3; card only) and on, eventually, to the A379. Here you can either turn right to continue along the coastal path, or left to St Marychurch.

ST MARYCHURCH [Map 35]

Strictly speaking an outer suburb of Torquay, St Marychurch has a village-like vibe and is one of the oldest settlements in south Devon, dating back to around AD1050. The Saxon font at the **church of St Mary the Virgin** dates from AD1110, although the main part of the church was destroyed on May 30, 1943, by a German WWII bomb that killed 26 people, including 21 children who were attending a Sunday School service at the church. A simple plaque above the door commemorates the tragic event.

Fore St is home to **Bygones Museum** (☎ 01803-326108, 🖳 bygones.co.uk; daily Nov-Mar 10am-4pm, Apr-Jul & Sep-Oct to 5pm, Aug to 6pm; £11.50), where there are numerous displays relating to the Victorian era as well as a life-size Victorian street.

There is also a Co-op **supermarket** (daily 7am-11pm) with an **ATM** outside it, a **pharmacy**, Boots (Mon-Fri 9am-5.30pm, Sat to 1pm), and a **post office** (Mon-Fri 8.30am-5.30pm, Sat 9am-1pm).

Stagecoach's 22 (Dawlish Warren to Paignton) **bus** (see pp53-5) calls here.

For a **B&B** you could try *Babbacombe Palms Guest House* (☎ 01803-327087, 🖳 babbacombepalms.com; 3D/3D or T/1D plus bunk beds; WI-FI; 🐾; £41.25-50.62pp, sgl occ room rate), a small hotel with a licensed bar at 2 York Rd.

Food-wise, at the top of the railway is *Cliff Railway Café* (☎ 01803-324025, 🖳 yellands.com; **fb**; daily generally 9am-4.30pm, hot food till 3pm), with ice-cream, scones, paninis and cold beer, as well as fabulous views, available 364 days a year.

At 55 Fore St, *Driftwood Café* (☎ 01803-314057; **fb**; WI-FI; 🐾; Mon-Fri 9.30am-4pm, Sat to 2pm) does similar fare at slightly higher prices. Opposite, *Halletts Bakery* (Tue-Sat 8.30am-4pm) does pastries, pasties and the like.

For evening dining, sticking with Fore St, *Memories Bistro* (☎ 01803-322224, 🖳 www.memoriesbistro.co.uk; WI-FI; Tue-Sat 6-9pm) serves some lovely meals with ingredients sourced locally where possible. Try the fillets of sea bass with white wine, cream, lemon, ginger, garlic, parsley, and butter sauce (£17.95).

There are two pubs on Fore St too: *Molloys* (☎ 01803-311825; **fb**; WI-FI; 🐾; daily 11am-11.30pm) doesn't do food, but has real ales on tap; *The Dolphin Inn* (☎ 01803 323725, 🖳 www.dolphininntorquay .co.uk; WI-FI; 🐾; **fb**; food Mon & Wed-Sat noon-8pm, Sun noon-2pm; mains £9-11) does incredible value food and shows sport on the telly.

The other pub is round the corner, back towards the coast path: at the time of research the *Crown & Sceptre* (☎ 01803-361408; **fb**; WI-FI; 🐾; food daily noon-8/9pm) had just been taken over by new owners and they were only serving light bites but by 2023 they expect to be serving standard pub meals.

For takeaway, there's a branch of the pizza chain *Papa Johns* (☎ 01803-310000, 🖳 www.papajohns.co.uk; Mon-Thur 4-11pm, Fri-Sun 11am-11pm) at the bottom of Fore St.

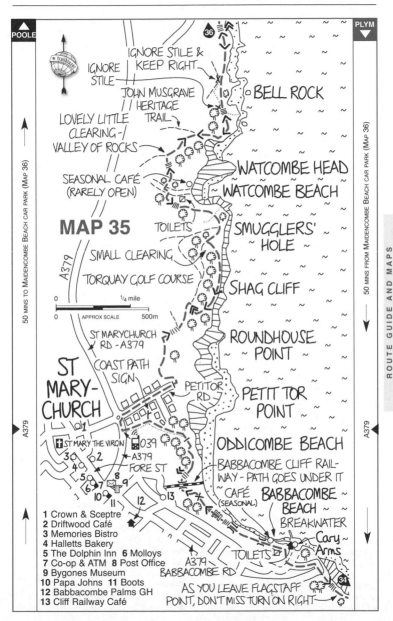

POOLE

PLYM

36

IGNORE STILE &
KEEP RIGHT
IGNORE
STILE

JOHN MUSGRAVE
// HERITAGE
TRAIL

BELL ROCK

LOVELY LITTLE
CLEARING -/
VALLEY OF ROCKS

SEASONAL CAFÉ
(RARELY OPEN)

WATCOMBE HEAD
WATCOMBE BEACH

MAP 35

TOILETS

SMUGGLERS'
HOLE

A379

SMALL CLEARING

TORQUAY GOLF COURSE

SHAG CLIFF

0   ¼ mile
0   APPROX SCALE   500m

ROUNDHOUSE
POINT

ST MARYCHURCH
RD - A379

COAST PATH
SIGN

ST
MARY-
CHURCH

PETITOR
RD

PETIT TOR
POINT

ST MARY THE VIRGIN

ODDICOMBE BEACH

039

3
4
5 8
6 7
10

A379
FORE ST

BABBACOMBE CLIFF RAIL-
WAY - PATH GOES UNDER IT
CAFÉ
(SEASONAL)   BABBACOMBE ~
~ BEACH ~

2

1
9

11
12
13

BREAKWATER
Cary ~
Arms

1 Crown & Sceptre
2 Driftwood Café
3 Memories Bistro
4 Halletts Bakery
5 The Dolphin Inn 6 Molloys
7 Co-op & ATM 8 Post Office
9 Bygones Museum
10 Papa Johns 11 Boots
12 Babbacombe Palms GH
13 Cliff Railway Café

A379
BABBACOMBE RD

TOILETS

34

AS YOU LEAVE FLAGSTAFF
POINT, DON'T MISS TURN ON RIGHT

ROUTE GUIDE AND MAPS

You stay with the A379 only until the roundabout, where Petitor Rd takes you to the back of the tor. Passing through the woods that decorate **Shag Cliff** you cross the track leading to **Watcombe Beach** where you'll find a *seasonal café* (that's rarely open these days) and a public **toilet**. More woodland wandering brings you to Maidencombe via a beautiful little glade called **Valley of Rocks** and a junction with the John Musgrave Heritage Trail (see p39).

MAIDENCOMBE [Map 36]

A quiet and remote cluster of houses, the centre of focus here is the delightful *Thatched Tavern* (☎ 01803-327140, 🖳 the thatchedtaverndevon.co.uk; **fb**; WI-FI; 🐾), a pretty, thatched-roofed country pub that serves excellent **food** (Tue-Sat noon-3pm & 6-8.45pm, Sun noon-4.45pm), and also has a delightful garden.

Nearer the beach is *Café Rio* (🖳 www.caferio-maidencombe.co.uk; **fb**; Apr-Oct daily 9am-6pm in peak periods, to 4pm otherwise) which also does kayak hire.

You need to walk up to Maidencombe Cross to catch Stagecoach's 22 **bus** (Dawlish Warren to Paignton), see pp53-5.

A gravel path takes you away from Maidencombe; following the copper-coloured cliffs it careens its way past **Blackaller's** and **Mackerel coves**, never seeming to find a straight (or horizontal) line until arriving at **Labrador Bay Nature Reserve** (🖳 rspb.org.uk, click on Reserves and events). Purchased by the RSPB in 2008 the reserve's aim is to help protect the **cirl bunting** (see also p70 and p135), a rare bird which is almost unique to South Devon. Other species regularly spotted include buzzards, peregrines and yellowhammers.

The path continues to dip and rise steeply via several combes, rejoining the A379 briefly before heading back into the fields. As you climb over **Bundle Head**, Teignmouth comes into full view – as does Shaldon Golf Course below you. Exmouth can also be seen – just – in the distance. A flat amble by the golf course brings you to a pleasant walk through woods. A bench offers a tremendous view across Teignmouth Pier as well as the delights that await you over the next few days.

Dropping down through the woods you arrive at a pub, *The Ness* (see p174 and p176), on the outskirts of the charming village of **Shaldon**.

SHALDON [map p174]

The quiet Georgian village of Shaldon offers a peaceful alternative to staying over the water in Teignmouth (not that it's especially boisterous there either).

It's a pity that most people hurry over the Teign as Shaldon is much more than just a commuter village. For a start, it has a few decent accommodation options, including a campsite, as well as a couple of very likeable boozers serving hearty food in an amiable atmosphere. It also boasts a **botanical garden** (**Homeyards**; built by the late widow of William Homeyard, the inventor of Liqufruta cough medicine; open all year,

free) with its own ruined castle, a **limekiln** (Map 37; behind The Ness pub) and even a small zoo: **Shaldon Zoo** (Map 37; ☎ 01626-872234, 🖳 shaldonwildlifetrust.org .uk; daily Apr-Sep 10am-5pm, Oct-Mar 10am-4pm; £9.95) is set in one acre of woodland on Ness Drive.

The village also has its own **classical music festival** in June and a **water carnival day** in August; see box p14 for both.

Services

The **tourist information centre** (Map 37; ☎ 07546-995623, 🖳 shaldon-village.co.uk;

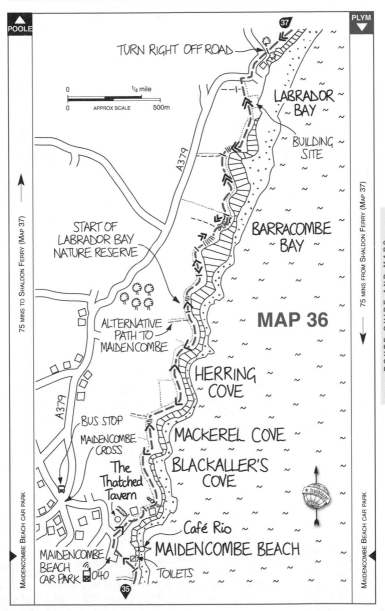

POOLE

PLYM

TURN RIGHT OFF ROAD

37

LABRADOR
~ BAY ~

~ BUILDING
~ SITE

A379

0   ¼ mile
0   APPROX SCALE   500m

75 MINS TO SHALDON FERRY (MAP 37)

75 MINS FROM SHALDON FERRY (MAP 37)

START OF
LABRADOR BAY
NATURE RESERVE

BARRACOMBE
~ BAY ~

MAP 36

ALTERNATIVE
PATH TO
MAIDENCOMBE

HERRING
~ COVE

A379

MACKEREL COVE ~

BUS STOP

MAIDENCOMBE
CROSS

BLACKALLER'S
~ COVE ~

The
Thatched
Tavern

Café Rio ~

MAIDENCOMBE BEACH CAR PARK

MAIDENCOMBE BEACH CAR PARK

MAIDENCOMBE
BEACH
CAR PARK   040

MAIDENCOMBE BEACH

TOILETS ~

35

trailblazer

ROUTE GUIDE AND MAPS

late May to late Sep daily 10.30am-4.30pm) stands in its own building in the car park opposite The Ness pub. Note that it's run by volunteers, so times are a little unreliable sometimes.

Everything else is down by the water in the village centre, including the well-stocked **village store** (☎ 01626-873426; Mon-Sat 7.30am-8pm, Sun 8.30am-7pm), a **post office** (Mon-Wed & Fri 9am-1pm & 1.30-4pm, Thur to 1pm, Sat to noon) and a **pharmacy** (Mon-Wed & Fri 9am-1pm & 2-6pm, Thur & Sat to 1pm).

Transport

Stagecoach's 22 (Dawlish Warren–Paignton) **bus** calls here; see pp53-5.

For a **taxi** try TQ14 in Teignmouth (see p177). See p176 for details about the **ferry** to Teignmouth.

Where to stay

For **camping**, you need to walk about a mile (1.2km) beyond the village to *Long Meadow Farm* (☎ 01626-872732, 🖳 long meadowfarm.co.uk; 🐾; £10-15 for a hiker & tent plus £5 for each extra person; Easter to end Sep), a very welcoming family-run campsite with five flat grassy pitches and various farm animals (chickens, pigs, goats and ponies) to keep young campers amused. Shepherd's huts (Good Friday to end Sep min two nights bedding not provided) are available – one sleeps up to two (£55-60) and the cabin sleeps 2 adults two children (£65-75). If you don't fancy the walk back into Shaldon, you can eat at the large holiday park opposite the farm entrance, which has a restaurant and a pub with a riverside terrace. To get to Long Meadow Farm, walk past the Shipwrights Arms on Ringmore Rd (which becomes Coombe Rd) and you'll see the farm entrance on your left.

For **B&B**, it's possible to stay at the super-smart pub *The Ness* (Map 37; ☎ 01626-873480, 🖳 theness.co.uk; 7D/2D or T; 👝; WI-FI; 🐾; £90-105pp, sgl occ room rate), right on the coast path. All the rooms have balconies, but not all have clear views over the estuary. Rates are higher for sea-view rooms.

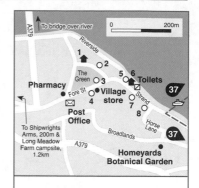

Shaldon

Where to stay, eat and drink

1 Potters Mooring
2 The London Inn
3 Village Fish & Chips
4 Shaldon Bakery
5 Clipper Café
6 Shaldon Beach Huts
7 Ferry Boat Inn
8 The Strand Café

Away from the shoreline and facing onto the picturesque village green is the dog-friendly *Potters Mooring* (☎ 01626-873225, 🖳 pottersmooring.co.uk; 4D/1T/1Tr plus a cottage – 1D & 1T; WI-FI; 🐾; from £72.50pp, sgl occ rates on request), at No 30. Unfortunately, they are unlikely to be able to accept advance bookings for one-night stays at weekends in July and August.

Maybe, instead, you'd like to rent a **beach hut**! *Shaldon Beach Huts* (🖳 shal donbeachhuts.co.uk; WI-FI; from £138 per hut per night for a single-night stay; rates reduced for longer stays) have just the one hut sleeping two to four. There is under-floor heating and it has a terrace which lead out on to the beach, as well as a shower and its own little kitchen. Booking is online.

Where to eat and drink

Cafés The award-winning *Shaldon Bakery* (☎ 01626-872401; **fb**; summer Mon-Sat 8am-3pm, winter to 2pm) sells

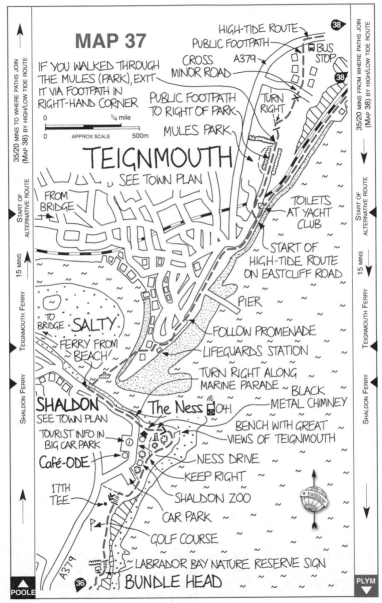

breads and cakes as well as local preserves for souvenirs and hot drinks to take away. Look out for their speciality 'uglibun' (£2); an oversized, oddly shaped, but ever-so-tasty currant bun that's so popular it has its own social media accounts.

With a prime location overlooking the estuary, *Clipper Café* (☎ 01626-873747, 🖥 theclippershaldon.co.uk; WI-FI; 🐾 ground floor only; daily 8am-9pm) is a popular, modern café with good coffee, a riverside terrace out the back and some good sharing platters (eg Mediterranean meat platter £17 for two). Across the road, *The Strand Café* (☎ 01626-872624, 🖥 thestrandcafebistro .co.uk; 🐾; Mon-Fri 10am-4pm, Sat & Sun 9am-4pm) is a café-bistro that specialises in brunches (£9-13).

Up near the zoo, *Café ODE* (Map 37; ☎ 01626-873427, 🖥 odetruefood.com/ cafe; fb; 🐾; WI-FI; Wed-Fri 10am-4pm, Sat & Sun to 5pm, occasionally open in the evenings) is an award-winning café-restaurant that sells craft beers and ciders. Its ever-changing menu may include delights such as venison bao bun with sweet sesame soy glaze and Asian salad or panko-crumbed pollock in brioche bun & crisp little gem lettuce (both £10.95).

Pubs & restaurants Shaldon is blessed with numerous pubs of distinction. The largest and swishest of these is *The Ness* (see Where to stay; food daily noon-8.30pm; WI-FI; 🐾), a Hall & Woodhouse property – so more of a restaurant than a traditional pub – but the food is good value and top quality, and the sea views from the tables on the terrace are superb.

A close rival to The Ness, *Ferry Boat Inn* (☎ 01626-872340, 🖥 www.theferry boatinn.co.uk; bar Mon-Sat noon-11pm, Sun to 10pm; 🐾; WI-FI) is an atmospheric place, though food is restricted to their summer barbecue (mid Apr-late Sep Fri-Sun noon-8pm), held on their lovely patio across the road overlooking the water.

Another pub that's worthy of your consideration is *The London Inn* (☎ 01626-872453, 🖥 londoninnshaldon.co.uk; WI-FI; 🐾 bar area only; food Mon-Sat noon-2.30pm & 6-8.30pm, Sun noon-5.30pm); it serves real ales and plenty of decent walker-sized meals such as roast lamb (£17.95) and pie & mash (£15.95).

A little further from Shaldon's centre, on Ringmore Rd, *The Shipwrights Arms* (☎ 01626-439226, 🖥 www.shipwrights-arms.co.uk; WI-FI; 🐾 on lead; food summer Tue-Sun noon-8pm, winter Tue & Wed 5-8pm, Thur-Sat noon-8pm, Sun noon-3pm) is less popular, but welcoming nonetheless, and serves good-value pub grub (mains £10-20) as well as a selection of real ales.

For a simple honest takeaway there's *Village Fish & Chips* (summer Tue-Thur 5.30-8pm, Fri & Sat to 8.30pm, winter days/hours variable) with a couple of tables inside.

The cute **ferry to Teignmouth** (☎ 07896-711822, 🖥 teignmouthshaldon ferry.co.uk; fb; summer daily 10am-5/6pm, winter hours vary – check all via Facebook page; £2, 🐾 free) leaves from the beach itself. Note that they take cash only. If you happen to arrive when there's no ferry, the alternative is to walk up to the road bridge and cross there (about 30 mins in total).

Note that, having arrived in Teignmouth, the coast path is less well signed, but if you walk up to the road from the ferry drop-off and keep following Teignmouth's promenade you can't go wrong.

❏ **IMPORTANT NOTE – WALKING TIMES**

All times in this book refer only to the time spent walking. You will need to add 20-30% to allow for rests, photography, checking the map, drinking water etc.

TEIGNMOUTH [map p179]

The last place in mainland England to have been successfully invaded by a foreign foe (in this instance the French in 1690), Teignmouth (pronounced 'Tinmouth') is a fun, friendly and compact place and one that's mercifully less hectic than its cousins down the coast. Lively cafés and proper pubs abound but sadly these days there's a dearth of tourist accommodation.

Visitors started to frequent the town in great numbers during the Georgian era (1714-1837) and many of the streets are adorned with architecture from this time.

Teign Heritage Centre (☎ 01626-777041, 🖥 teignheritage.org.uk; summer Tue-Sat 11am-3.30pm; £5), at 29 French St, houses **Teignmouth & Shaldon Museum** which has a number of collections celebrating the area's maritime links; the **Victorian pier** is charming.

The octagonal **St James Parish Church**, at the junction of Exeter Rd and Bitton Park Rd, has a 13th-century sandstone tower.

Hot hikers can cool off with an outdoor swim in **Teignmouth Lido** (🖥 www .teignbridgeleisure.co.uk/swimming/teign mouth-lido; May-early Sep daily; £6/5.50 adults/concs), right by the coast path as you leave the town. However, this wasn't open in 2022 so check in advance.

Teignmouth Folk Festival (see p14) is held here in June and the **Jazz Festival** (see p14) in November. Details of other local events can also be found on 🖥 love teignmouth.co.uk.

Services

There's a **tourist information point** (Mon-Sat 10am-3pm) with leaflets inside the reception area of the theatre, Pavilions Teignmouth. Theatre box office staff are also usually on hand to help with local information queries but it is also worth looking at 🖥 loveteignmouth.co.uk.

On Den Rd is the **post office** (Mon-Fri 9am-5.30pm, Sat 9am-12.30pm), while the Co-op **supermarket** (daily 7am-10pm) is close by on Bank St where, unsurprisingly, you'll find **banks** with **ATMs**.

Quayside **Bookshop** (Mon-Sat 10am-5pm) is in the old part of town on Northumberland Place. The **pharmacy**, Boots, is on Regent St (Mon-Fri 9am-6pm, Sat 8.30am-5pm).

There's a **launderette** (daily 7am-6pm) on Brunswick St.

Transport

Stagecoach's 2 **bus** (Newton Abbot to Exeter) calls here and as does their 22 (Dawlish Warren to Paignton) service; see pp53-5 for details.

GWR **trains** (see box p51) call here regularly en route between Exmouth and Paignton.

For a **cab** try TQ14 Taxis (☎ 01626-776011).

Where to stay

No more than a few hundred metres from the path and great value for money is the dog-friendly *Seaway* (☎ 01626-879024, 🖥 seawayteignmouth.co.uk; 2S/3D/1T; ☛; WI-FI; 🐾; from £45pp, sgl £55, sgl occ rates on request), at 27 Northumberland Place.

Slightly cheaper is *Lynton House* (☎ 01626-774349, 🖥 stay@lyntonhouseteign mouth.com; 2S/3D/3T/3Qd, one room sleeping up to five; ☛; WI-FI; 🐾; B&B from £43pp, in all rooms; Mar-Oct), at 7 Powderham Terrace. Most of the rooms have great views over either the sea or river but they do not take one-night bookings in advance between June and August.

Centrally, at 5 Brunswick St, is *Brunswick House* (☎ 01626-774102, 🖥 brunswickhouseteignmouth.co.uk; 2S/2D/1Qd; WI-FI; £40-47.50pp, sgl £45-55, sgl occ room rate). They have a budget single room which has an en suite shower but the toilet is a little way down the corridor.

Where to eat and drink

The oldest part of town near the mouth of the river is undoubtedly the best place to search for food, with some idiosyncratic cafés as well as several characterful old pubs that have watched over the comings and goings on the Teign for centuries.

ROUTE GUIDE AND MAPS

Cafés Our favourite café is *Oystercatchers* (☎ 01626-774652; WI-FI; 🐾; daily 8.30am-2pm, Sun 9am-2pm), 12 Northumberland Place, a fully licensed place with a mellow vibe and some terrific food; breakfasts cost £7.50-12 and paninis around £9. Just along the way, *Relish* (☎ 07770 938204; Tue-Sat 9.30am-1.30pm) is an unassuming café with some whopping great burgers from just £4 though it has limited opening hours. Next door, *Shaldon Bakery* (daily 8.30am-3pm) serves a range of pasties, with the traditional steak option for £3.60, or for something different try butternut and feta (£3.80).

The small but delightful *Crab Shack* (🖥 crabshackonthebeach.co.uk; **fb**; WI-FI; mid Feb to Dec Wed-Sun noon-3pm & 5.30-9pm) is a licensed café-restaurant tucked away on the waterfront beside Ship Inn and has its own fishing boats. The menu changes according to the catch, though you can usually rely on there being some delicious crab sandwiches. The views towards Shaldon are lovely too.

Down to earth *Sea View Diner* (☎ 01626-777888; 🐾; summer daily 8am-7pm, may close earlier in winter) has cheap treats, such as spag bol (£6.50) and is friendly, central and has long opening hours in the summer; in fact, it has everything except a sea view.

The plant-based café *Nourish* (☎ 01626-392326; **fb**; WI-FI; 🐾; Tue-Sat 9am-3.30pm), serves some delicious meat-free fare.

As you leave town, and right on the trail, *Teign Bean* (🖥 teignbean.co.uk; daily 8am-6pm in summer, variable hours in winter) is a coffee house but one that also serves scotch eggs, pasties, rolls and ice-cream.

Pubs & restaurants As good as some of the cafés are here, it's the pubs that really bring in the crowds. *Ship Inn* (☎ 01626-772674; **fb**; 🐾; food Mon-Sat noon-2.30pm & 6-9pm, Sun noon-3pm), an historical establishment built in the 1830s, is arguably the most popular. The food is just what you want from pub grub, being massive and tasty, and there are four or five cask ales on tap. Also has patio seating overlooking the harbour. Note the list of 14 men who served in the Battle of Trafalgar on the exterior wall facing the sea.

Virtually next door is *New Quay Inn* (☎ 01626-774145; **fb**; WI-FI; 🐾 bar area only), established way back in 1661. It has real ales, some harbour-side seating on its own little beach outside.

Snacks & takeaways For Chinese, head to *Hung Le* (☎ 01626-773495; Thur-Tue 5-11pm) on Teign St. For Indian, try *Bombay Delights* (☎ 01626-773824; daily 5.30-11pm) at No 38. *Ally's* (☎ 01626-777911; daily 4-11pm) is a kebab house at 11 Somerset Place, while *Harbour Fish Bar* (☎ 01626-775906; Wed-Sat noon-2pm & 4-8pm) is Teignmouth's best chippy.

For quick snacks on-the-go, the local butcher, *Lloyd Maunder* (**fb**; Mon-Fri 8am-5.30pm, Sat to 5pm) doubles up as a deli, while the bakery *Mini Heaven* (**fb**; daily 8.30am-4pm) is good for pastries, pasties and cakes. *Jane's Ice Cream* (Mon-Sat 9.30am-5pm, Sun 10am-4pm) should have all your ice-cream cravings covered.

TEIGNMOUTH TO EXMOUTH [MAPS 37-41]

This short and easy **8-mile (13km; low-tide route 3hrs, high-tide route 3¼hrs; times include the ferry journey)** section will likely be welcome following yesterday's exertions.

For this stage you need to consult a **tide-timetable**, though, as there is the possibility of having to follow two high-tide routes. Neither results in a lengthy detour, but both are inferior routes compared to the official coast-hugging path. You will also need to get to Starcross in time for the last ferry (before you set

Teignmouth

Where to eat and drink
1 Hung Le
2 Bombay Delights
3 Ally's Kebab Shop
4 Harbour Fish Bar
5 Mini Heaven
6 New Quay Inn
7 Ship Inn
8 Crab Shack
9 Oystercatchers
10 Shaldon Bakery
11 Relish
12 Lloyd Maunder
13 Sea View Diner
14 Jane's Ice Cream
15 Nourish
16 Teign Bean

off make sure you have checked the ferry times) across to Exmouth. Otherwise you certainly will have a lengthy detour to negotiate (an extra 14 miles!).

As long as you take the low route the terrain on this section is generally flat as you follow Brunel's railway along the sea-walls. Refreshments are also in ample supply, both in Dawlish and Dawlish Warren, and there are two really cracking pubs in Cockwood. Once at Starcross, if the ferry's not running you need to consider your options: Exmouth can be reached by public transport

❏ **THE LEGEND OF THE PARSON AND THE CLERK**

East of Teignmouth stand two huge rock stacks – and as you probably would expect from such prominent features, there are various legends surrounding the formation of these outcrops. The best known is this gothic morality tale:

Once upon a time the Bishop of Exeter was lying in bed in Dawlish, severely ill and close to death. An ambitious local parson, spying an opportunity to succeed the bishop, contrived to visit him on a regular basis to try to persuade him of his suitability for the promotion. Accompanying him on these visits was his clerk, who was tasked with guiding the parson across the local moor to Dawlish.

One evening, having received news that the bishop's health had rapidly declined, the parson decided to leave for Dawlish immediately despite the lateness of the hour. The two men galloped as fast as they were able, whipping their horses and stabbing them with their spurred heels in their attempt to get to the bishop's deathbed. The weather, however, turned against them, and a huge storm rose as the sun descended. The rain lashed down so heavily that the two men became lost in the gloom. The parson, furious that he could miss the bishop's demise, turned on his clerk and sneered the ominous words: 'May Satan take us to Dawlish for we shall never get there ourselves.'

Strangely enough (or maybe not, for those who are familiar with such legends), it was shortly after this that the two men were surprised by the sound of galloping hooves and a peasant on a moor pony approached and offered to be the two men's guide. In desperation, the two men paid little attention to the fact that both pony and rider were as black as the darkest night and followed the man to Dawlish. On the way they came to a well-lit mansion that neither the parson nor the clerk had noticed before. With the weather still against them, their guide, claiming to be the mansion's owner, invited them in, promising that he would guide them to Dawlish first thing in the morning instead.

Once inside, the pair were greeted by the sight of a large group of wild-looking folk indulging in an orgy of gorging and drinking and partying – a scene of unfettered hedonism to which the parson and the clerk were soon willing participants.

The next morning it was reported that the bishop had died, news that caused the two men to dash out of the mansion and mount their horses with the intention of continuing on their journey, realising that the parson's chances of promotion were slipping away. Their horses, however, would not move. To the backdrop of peals of laughter coming from the party within, the parson cursed 'Devil take the brutes'. It was at this point that their peasant guide appeared and thanked them – before ordering the horses to gallop into the sea, their cruel masters rooted in the saddles.

The following morning, when the god-fearing population of Dawlish left their homes to survey the damage caused by the storm, they saw that the red cliffs had been broken into two halves; and that on one half lay the lifeless body of the parson – while on the other lay that of his faithful clerk.

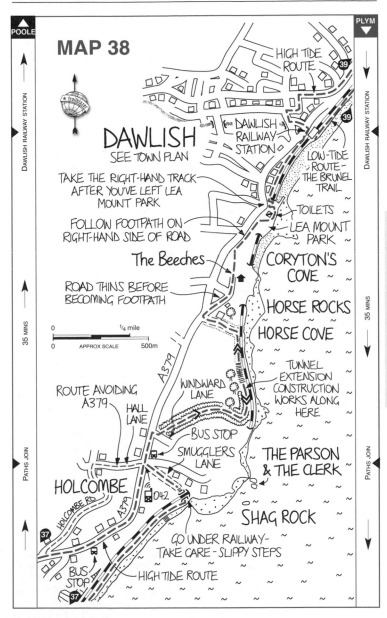

POOLE

PLYM

MAP 38

★ trailblazer

DAWLISH
SEE TOWN PLAN

DAWLISH RAILWAY STATION

HIGH TIDE
ROUTE
39

39

DAWLISH
RAILWAY
STATION

LOW-TIDE
ROUTE -
THE BRUNEL
TRAIL

TAKE THE RIGHT-HAND TRACK
AFTER YOU'VE LEFT LEA
MOUNT PARK

TOILETS

LEA MOUNT
PARK

FOLLOW FOOTPATH ON
RIGHT-HAND SIDE OF ROAD

The Beeches

CORYTON'S
COVE

ROAD THINS BEFORE
BECOMING FOOTPATH

HORSE ROCKS

HORSE COVE

0   ¼ mile
0   APPROX SCALE   500m

A379

WINDWARD
LANE

TUNNEL
EXTENSION
CONSTRUCTION
WORKS ALONG
HERE

ROUTE AVOIDING
A379

HALL
LANE

BUS STOP

SMUGGLERS
LANE

THE PARSON
& THE CLERK

HOLCOMBE

HOLCOMBE RD

A379

042

SHAG ROCK

37

GO UNDER RAILWAY -
TAKE CARE - SLIPPY STEPS

BUS
STOP

37

HIGH TIDE ROUTE

DAWLISH RAILWAY STATION

35 MINS

PATHS JOIN

ROUTE GUIDE AND MAPS

35 MINS

PATHS JOIN

from Starcross (see p188), though ambling addicts will probably prefer to tighten their bootlaces and stroll along a section of the attractive Exe Estuary Trail (see pp190-2). Doing so will add another eight miles to your walk if you're able to connect with the small ferry at Topsham, or another 14 miles if you miss all the ferries and have to walk all the way up to the nearest pedestrian bridge at Bridge Rd.

The route

There are two alternative trails leaving Teignmouth which divide near Teign Bean Café (see map p179) at the eastern end of the seafront. If the tide is in your favour you can walk straight along the sea wall with the railway to your left, towards the two giant rock stacks that loom in front of you. These are the **Parson** and the **Clerk**, said to have once been human until the devil turned them into stone (see box p180).

Just out to sea another rock formation, the finger-like rock that appears like Neptune's digit poking out of the waves, is **Shag Rock**. At the end, and having dipped underneath the railway line to ascend **Smugglers Lane**, the path meets up with the high-tide route on the busy A379.

> ### High-tide route: Teignmouth–Smugglers Lane (35 mins)
> Just before Teign Bean (see map p179) take the road on the left – Eastcliff Rd – to **Mules Park** (which you can either walk through or continue straight following the public footpath that runs to the right). At the top of the park you cross a field and minor road, continuing down the footpath until you reach the A379.
> For a more pleasant walking experience, however, turn left at the **Holcombe** sign and head down Holcombe Rd, with the pink, crenellated and thatched **Minadab Cottage** on your right. Follow Holcombe Rd, a quiet country lane surrounded by hedgerows, until you walk down into a dip, coming to a minor crossroads. Take Hall Lane on your right and this will reacquaint you with the A-road, the official high-tide route – and indeed the low-tide route too.

With all the paths reunited, a short walk up a hill brings you to **Windward Lane**, from where a path leads back to the railway, though it's not long before you're back on the A379 again. Don't follow this but instead take Old Teignmouth Rd on the right that leads past *The Beeches* (☎ 01626-866345, 🖳 thebeechesbandb.co.uk; 2D/1T; 🛏; WI-FI; £45-50pp, sgl occ room rate), at No 15A. However, they now only accept bookings for a minimum of two nights.

Another encounter with the A379 follows before the path heads through **Lea Mount Park**, sandwiched between the noisy A-road and **Coryton's Cove**, with its wonderful little beach (off the path). The path descends sharply now, zig-zagging its way down to the railway and **Dawlish**.

DAWLISH

Dawlish is a pleasant-enough place though the crowds in summer can be suffocating. Originally a little fishing community, Dawlish's name is thought to come from the Celtic 'Deawlisc', meaning 'Devil Water' – possibly because torrential rains are thought to have saturated the area's red cliffs, turning Dawlish Water – the stream

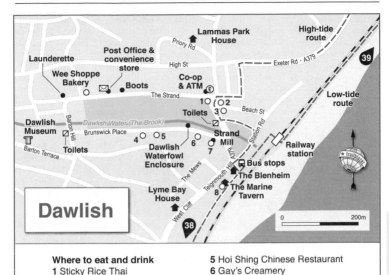

Dawlish

Where to eat and drink
1 Sticky Rice Thai
2 Home Kitchen
3 Bombay Delights
4 Brunswick Arms

5 Hoi Shing Chinese Restaurant
6 Gay's Creamery
7 Old Mill Tearoom
8 The Marine Tavern

ROUTE GUIDE AND MAPS

which runs through the town's centre – a satanic red (see box p180). Another hypothesis suggests that it comes from the Welsh 'du(g)lais', meaning 'black stream' as today the brook is known for its black swans that paddle happily in the very heart of the town.

Dawlish is famous in fiction as the birthplace of Charles Dickens' *Nicholas Nickleby*, and if you're interested in the town's history you may wish to visit **Dawlish Museum** (☎ 01626-888557; **fb**; mid May to late Sep Wed-Fri 11am-3pm, Sat 10am-1pm; £2) at the top of Barton Terrace.

Strand Mill is one of the country's largest mill wheels (15m in diameter). Originally built in 1717, when it would have stood alone, beside a brook in the middle of a meadow, it was rebuilt in 1825 after being destroyed in a fire, and continued to be in use until 1959. Attached to the mill is The Old Mill Tearoom; see Where to eat.

Services
Most services lie along The Strand that runs parallel and east of the stream. They include a Co-op **supermarket** (Mon-Sat 7am-10pm, Sun 10am-4pm), a **post office** (daily 7am-10pm), which is inside One Stop convenience store, and a branch of Boots the **pharmacy** (Mon-Sat 9am-6pm) between them.

There are **banks** with **ATMs** dotted around, including an ATM inside the Co-op. Just beyond the top of The Strand is a **launderette** (daily 7am-7pm).

Transport
[See also pp51-5] Stagecoach's 2 **bus** connects the village with Teignmouth, Dawlish Warren, Starcross and Exeter. GWR **trains** call here regularly en route between Exmouth and Paignton via Exeter.

For a **taxi** try Dawlish Cabs (☎ 01626-888111).

Where to stay

Rooms are thin on the ground in Dawlish. On the walk into town, **B&B** is available at *The Marine Tavern* (☎ 01626-865245, 🖥 marinetaverndawlish.com; **fb**; 1Tr/1D with bunk beds for children; ☛; WI-FI; from £32.50pp, sgl occ room rate), 2 Marine Parade. However, at the time of research the building was up for sale so this may have closed by the time you are there.

Close by, on the corner of Marine Parade and Teignmouth Hill, is *The Blenheim* (☎ 01626-862372, 🖥 www.the blenheim.uk.net; 1S/7D/1T/2Tr; WI-FI; £45-57.50pp, sgl/sgl occ from £70), 1 Marine Parade, from which there are great views out to sea and along the immediate stretch of coastline.

At 34 West Cliff, *Lyme Bay House* (☎ 01626-864211, 🖥 lymebaydawlish.co.uk; 8D/1T; ☛; WI-FI; 🐾; £47.50-57.50pp, sgl occ £85-105) is a short walk up the hill from the centre of town.

For top-notch B&B accommodation, try the wonderfully elegant *Lammas Park House* (☎ 01626-888064, 🖥 lammaspark house.co.uk; 2D/1T/1Qd; ☛; WI-FI; £50-75pp, sgl occ £80-140; mid Feb to end Dec), at 3 Priory Rd. The rooms are spacious, beautifully appointed and come with sea views; the 'quad' is a suite with a sitting room in between.

Where to eat and drink

Cafés, restaurants & takeaways The trickling brook known as **Dawlish Water** makes the perfect café setting for *Old Mill Tearoom* (☎ 07804-348637; **fb**; 🐾; summer Mon-Thur 10am-4pm, Fri & Sat to 6pm,

Sun 9.30am-4.30pm, winter hours variable so contact them for details); the menu includes a cream tea (£5.95) as well as sandwiches, panini, ploughman's lunch and cakes. *Gay's Creamery* (Mon-Sat 7.30am-6pm, Sun 8.30am-6pm) is really a gift shop but one that also does takeaway coffee, tea, pastries and ice-creams, as well as delicious cream teas. Best of all, customers can use their picnic tables over the road to sit right by the brook.

On the other side of Dawlish Water at the top of The Strand is the *Wee Shoppe Bakery* (Mon-Sat 8.30am-3pm). At the bottom end of The Strand is *Sticky Rice Thai* (☎ 01626-437343, 🖥 stickyriceonline .com) with food to eat-in (Mon-Tue 4-10pm, Wed-Sun noon-10pm) or takeaway. While nearby *Home Kitchen* (☎ 01626-895192, 🖥 homekitchendawlish.co.uk; WI-FI; 🐾; Feb-Dec Thur-Tue 8.30am-4pm) specialises in gluten-free products.

When it comes to **takeaways**, for Chinese head to *Hoi Shing* (☎ 01626-865351; Wed-Sun 5.30-10pm), a licensed restaurant and takeaway. For Indian, try the takeaway-only *Bombay Delights* (☎ 01626-773824; daily 5.30pm-midnight).

Pubs *Brunswick Arms* (☎ 01626-862181, 🖥 thebrunswickarms.co.uk; WI-FI; 🐾; food daily noon-3pm, Mon-Fri 5-8pm) is probably the best pub in town, with local ales on tap, decent pub grub and even a skittles alley.

Handiest for the coast path, and with sea-facing terrace seating (albeit beside a road), *The Marine Tavern* (see Where to stay; food Fri-Sun noon-3pm & 6-9pm; WI-FI; 🐾) has three or four real ales on tap.

Dawlish to Dawlish Warren (35 mins)

If you're sure that the tide is sufficiently low, begin this stretch by heading under the railway bridge to follow the path, also known as **The Brunel Trail** (Map 38), alongside the railway. It's a straightforward stroll that leads, eventually, to **Langstone Rock**. Cross the next pedestrian railway bridge and follow the path towards the road and into Dawlish Warren (see p186).

High-tide route: Dawlish to Dawlish Warren (35 mins)

At Dawlish railway station turn left to follow the A379 – Exeter Rd – as it winds its way out of town. The road has a pavement but it regularly switches

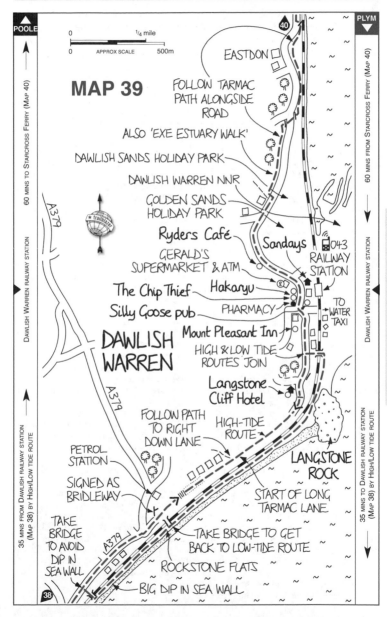

0   ¼ mile

0   APPROX SCALE   500m

MAP 39

EASTDON

FOLLOW TARMAC
PATH ALONGSIDE
ROAD

ALSO 'EXE ESTUARY WALK'

DAWLISH SANDS HOLIDAY PARK

DAWLISH WARREN NNR

GOLDEN SANDS
HOLIDAY PARK

Ryders Café

GERALD'S
SUPERMARKET & ATM

The Chip Thief   Hakaryu

Silly Goose pub   PHARMACY

Sandays

RAILWAY
STATION

043

TO
WATER
TAXI

**DAWLISH
WARREN**

Mount Pleasant Inn

HIGH & LOW TIDE
ROUTES JOIN

Langstone
Cliff Hotel

FOLLOW PATH
TO RIGHT
DOWN LANE

HIGH-TIDE
ROUTE

PETROL
STATION

LANGSTONE
~ ROCK

SIGNED AS
BRIDLEWAY

START OF LONG
~ TARMAC LANE

TAKE
BRIDGE
TO AVOID
DIP IN
SEA WALL

TAKE BRIDGE TO GET ~
BACK TO LOW-TIDE ROUTE ~

~ ROCKSTONE FLATS ~

~ BIG DIP IN SEA WALL ~

A379

38

40

60 MINS TO STARCROSS FERRY (MAP 40)

DAWLISH WARREN RAILWAY STATION

35 MINS FROM DAWLISH RAILWAY STATION
(MAP 38) BY HIGH/LOW TIDE ROUTE

60 MINS FROM STARCROSS FERRY (MAP 40)

DAWLISH WARREN RAILWAY STATION

35 MINS TO DAWLISH RAILWAY STATION
(MAP 38) BY HIGH/LOW TIDE ROUTE

sides – take care. Rather tediously, you remain on the road for half a mile, before turning right and entering a grassy area called **Rockstone Flats** (if you reach the petrol station you have gone too far). Keep to the left and follow what is signed as a bridleway. Passing some bungalows on your left you join a tarmac path that seems to roll out endlessly in front of you.

The path gradually descends past *Langstone Cliff Hotel* (☎ 01626-249685, ☐ langstone-hotel.co.uk; 12D/1T/48Qd, one room sleeps up to six; ☞; WI-FI; ☒; B&B £34.50-77pp, sgl occ room rate; dinner bed & breakfast rates also available), where passing walkers are welcome to stop for a coffee, some lunch or a cream tea, before eventually arriving in **Dawlish Warren**.

DAWLISH WARREN [Map 39, p185]

Essentially a railway station – with a few amenities dotted here and there to service the area's numerous holiday parks – Dawlish Warren has little to warrant a lengthy stop.

Dawlish Warren National Nature Reserve is absorbing and sometimes plays host to rare vagrant birds including the greater sand plover, elegant tern and great spotted cuckoo. However, it's located on the sand-spit on the opposite side of the railway tracks and thus a walk away from the trail, which will deter all but the most determined twitcher.

Refreshments are available in the village, as is limited accommodation. There is a **pharmacy** (Mon-Fri 9am-6pm) and a **supermarket**, Gerald's (daily 8am-10pm), with an **ATM** (£1.55).

Note that there is the option of a (seasonal) **water taxi** between Dawlish Warren and Exmouth Docks (sgl/rtn £3/5): ExePlorer Water Taxis Ltd (☎ 07970-918418, ☐ exeplorerwatertaxis.co.uk; **fb**; Apr-early Sep daily on the hour 9am-5pm, no dogs as they are not allowed on the beach!) will come and collect you from the beach. The taxi leaves from near the end of the sand spit that juts out from Dawlish Warren. From the railway station, walk to the end of the amusements past the Visitor Centre; keeping on the left-hand side (ie on the opposite side to the sea), continue past the golf course and through the dunes until you see the sign stating: 'Pick Up Point'. The walk will take approximately half an hour.

Stagecoach's Nos 2 and 22 **bus** services call here as do Riviera line **trains** (Exmouth to Paignton via Exeter); see pp51-5.

Sandays B&B (☎ 01626-888973, ☐ sandays-devon.co.uk; 2D/1T; WI-FI; from £43.50pp, sgl occ £60; Feb-Dec), on Warren Rd, accepts single-night bookings; the twin room is nice, however, and has its own sitting room overlooking the garden.

Mount Pleasant Inn (☎ 01626-863151, ☐ mountpleasantinn.com; WI-FI; ☒ on lead) is a pub that's a short walk up the hill but means it has great views overlooking the bay. It's the best spot in town (as far as it goes in Dawlish). It does **food** (summer daily noon-2pm & 6-9pm, winter hours variable), with sandwiches at lunch costing £8-11 or it's £13-15 for hot dinners (up to £32 for steaks) on the more extensive evening menu, which includes tapas, seafood, curries and steaks. There is a separate afternoon menu for the school summer holidays.

Silly Goose (☎ 01626-438781; ☒ on lead; food Mon-Sat 10am-9pm, Sun noon-9pm, winter hours variable) is a cheaper, family-friendly pub right on the path. They do food every day and in the summer breakfasts every day except Sundays.

Also right on the trail, *Ryders* (daily 8am-5pm) is a bakery-café that's convenient for a quick coffee and pastry.

Takeaway options include Chinese food at *Hakaryu* (☎ 01626-888388, ☐ hakaryu.net; daily 5-11pm), 3 Warren Rd, and fish & chips at *The Chip Thief* (☐ thechipthief.co.uk; daily 11.30am-2pm & 4-9pm) next door.

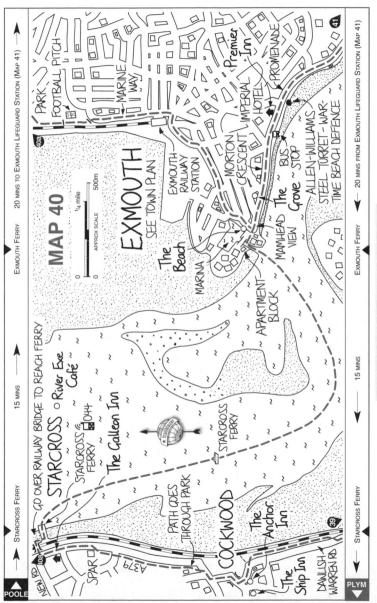

MAP 40

EXMOUTH
SEE TOWN PLAN

APPROX SCALE

0   ¼ mile

0   500m

STARCROSS
GO OVER RAILWAY BRIDGE TO REACH FERRY

River Exe Café

STARCROSS
FERRY

The Galleon Inn

STARCROSS FERRY

PATH GOES THROUGH PARK

STARCROSS FERRY

COCKWOOD

The Anchor Inn

The Ship Inn

DAWLISH-WARREN RD

SPAR

A379

NEW RD

PARK

FOOTBALL PITCH

MARINE WAY

The Beach

MARINA

APARTMENT-BLOCK

EXMOUTH RAILWAY STATION

MORTON CRESCENT

IMPERIAL HOTEL

Premier Inn

PROMENADE

MAMHEAD VIEW

The Grove

BUS STOP

ALLEN-WILLIAMS STEEL TURRET - WAR-TIME BEACH DEFENCE

★ trailblazer

STARCROSS FERRY

Exmouth Ferry

15 MINS

20 MINS TO EXMOUTH LIFEGUARD STATION (MAP 41)

Exmouth Ferry

15 MINS

20 MINS FROM EXMOUTH LIFEGUARD STATION (MAP 41)

ROUTE GUIDE AND MAPS

POOLE

PLYM

The path leaves Dawlish Warren along the road, bypassing holiday parks and chippies before joining the Exe Estuary Walk opposite Dawlish Sands Holiday Park. Following this trail, aka Cycle Track 2, you soon arrive in Cockwood.

COCKWOOD [Map 40, p187]

This small harbour village is blessed with two great pubs. The warm and friendly *Ship Inn* (☎ 01626-890373, 💻 shipinn cockwood.co.uk; WI-FI; 🐾 on lead; **food** daily noon-2.30pm & 6-9pm), on Church Rd, serves up delicious food (mains £10.95-22.75) and cask ales.

Close by, and right on the harbour-front on Dawlish Warren Rd, *The Anchor Inn* (☎ 01626-890203, 💻 anchorinncock wood.com; 🐾; food summer Mon-Sat noon-9pm, Sun to 8.30pm, winter hours variable) is over 450 years old and specialises in seafood, particularly mussels.

Follow the road over the bridge and out of the village. A brief interlude in a park follows before, in short order, you arrive in Starcross, from where you can board the Starcross to Exmouth **ferry**; for details, see below.

STARCROSS
[Map 40, p187; Map 40a]

This is the main departure point for the ferry across the Exe, but there are a few amenities in the village.

On The Strand you will find a Spar **supermarket** (Mon-Sat 7am-9pm, Sun 7.30am-9pm) and Boots **pharmacy** (Map 40a; Mon-Fri 9am-5.30pm, Sat to 1pm).

The Galleon Inn (☎ 01626-890412, 💻 www.galleoninn.co.uk; bar daily noon-10pm) offers **accommodation** (1S/3D/1Tr/1Qd; WI-FI; 🐾; room from £35pp, sgl £60, sgl occ room rate) but no food at all.

Pub food is available opposite the railway station at *The Atmospheric Railway Inn* (Map 40a; ☎ 01626-906290, 💻 www.atmosphericrailwayinn.co.uk; WI-FI; 🐾; food Mon-Sat noon-9pm, Sun noon-5.30pm; closed on Mon Oct-Mar/Apr); you can enjoy a meal (mains £13-20) whilst supping an ale in their beer garden.

Stagecoach's 2 **bus** connects the village with Teignmouth, Dawlish, Dawlish Warren and Exeter. GWR **trains** call here regularly en route between Exeter and Paignton. See pp51-5 for more details.

Tackling the Exe [Map 40, p187]

● **The Starcross to Exmouth Ferry** For a river that is crossed by no fewer than three ferry services, it can be surprisingly difficult crossing the Exe sometimes. The easiest way – and which is on the official coast path route – is the main Starcross to Exmouth Ferry (☎ 07934-461672; **fb**; Apr-end Oct daily, leaves Starcross hourly from 10.10am to 4.10pm & Exmouth 10.40am to 4.40pm, plus 5.10pm from Starcross & 5.40pm from Exmouth between mid May and mid Sep; 15-20 mins; single £5, day return £7; well-behaved 🐾 on lead); the ferry no longer has its own website, but you can find up-to-date news on its official Facebook page (💻 www.facebook.com/StarcrossExmouthFerry). Cash is safest (essential) as their card machine doesn't always get mobile/wi-fi reception.

As you cross the Exe look for out for avocets and ospreys in the skies above and grey seals from the waves below you.

For Exmouth and the continuation of the route see p192.

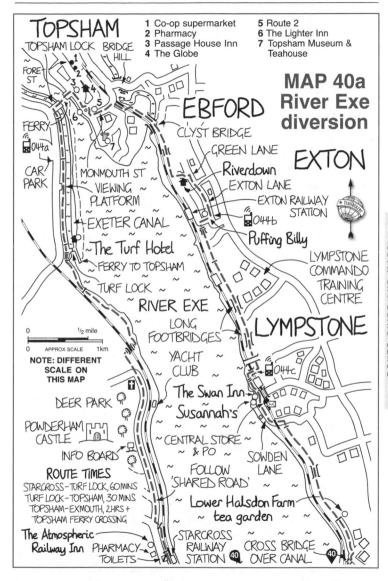

TOPSHAM

1 Co-op supermarket
2 Pharmacy
3 Passage House Inn
4 The Globe
5 Route 2
6 The Lighter Inn
7 Topsham Museum & Teahouse

MAP 40a
River Exe diversion

TOPSHAM LOCK BRIDGE HILL
FORE ST
EBFORD
CLYST BRIDGE
GREEN LANE
Riverdown
EXTON LANE
EXTON
FERRY
044a
CAR PARK
MONMOUTH ST
VIEWING PLATFORM
EXETER CANAL
The Turf Hotel
FERRY TO TOPSHAM
TURF LOCK
RIVER EXE
LONG FOOTBRIDGES
YACHT CLUB
The Swan Inn
Susannah's
CENTRAL STORE & PO
FOLLOW 'SHARED ROAD'
Lower Halsdon Farm
tea garden
EXTON RAILWAY STATION
044b
Puffing Billy
LYMPSTONE COMMANDO TRAINING CENTRE
LYMPSTONE
044c
SOWDEN LANE

0   ½ mile
0   APPROX SCALE   1km
NOTE: DIFFERENT SCALE ON THIS MAP

DEER PARK
POWDERHAM CASTLE
INFO BOARD
ROUTE TIMES
STARCROSS-TURF LOCK, 60 MINS
TURF LOCK-TOPSHAM, 30 MINS
TOPSHAM-EXMOUTH, 2 HRS +
TOPSHAM FERRY CROSSING
The Atmospheric Railway Inn PHARMACY
TOILETS
STARCROSS RAILWAY STATION 40
CROSS BRIDGE OVER CANAL 40

ROUTE GUIDE AND MAPS

● **Ferries further upstream** If you can't take the Starcross ferry you'll have to head inland to get across the Exe. There are **two further ferry services** that operate upstream of Starcross and Exmouth: the first leaves from **Turf Lock** (2½ miles from Starcross), the second from **Topsham Lock** (4 miles from Starcross), with both heading to the launch at **Topsham**; details of these services can be found below. Taking either of these will save you having to walk all the way up to Bridge Rd and back again. **Note with either service it is recommended that you phone beforehand to make sure they're operating and at what times**.

To get to either ferry, you need to join the **Exe Estuary Trail**, which heads north inland from Starcross round the pretty estuary, an SSSI with an abundance of wildlife including avocets and curlew. This is the route described below.

● **Public transport** Should there not be any ferries running when you plan to cross the Exe, there is a strong case to be made for taking public transport rather than walking all the way towards Exeter and back. From Starcross you can either take a GWR train or Stagecoach's No 2 **bus** service (see pp51-5) to Exeter; and from Exeter a train or Stagecoach's No 56 back south to Exmouth.

● **Walking (14 miles; 4½hrs)** If you really do want to walk it, you'll have to follow the Exe Estuary Trail a further three miles beyond Topsham Lock, pass under the M5 motorway bridge (which you can't cross on foot) and **cross the bridge at Bridge St**, before walking south to Exmouth.

Along the Exe Estuary Trail on the River Exe Diversion [Map 40a]
The way (**8 miles, 12.8km; 3½ hours plus 10 mins for Topsham ferry crossing**) is well-signed from Starcross railway station. The path soon says a welcome farewell to the A379 as you follow a very quiet lane along the river and railway, your attention eventually being diverted away from the water by the estimated 600 fallow deer residing in the grounds of impressive **Powderham Castle** – the historic home of the Earls of Devon – on your left.

Passing **Starcross Yacht Club** to your right and a church on your left, you cross the railway line to follow the edge of the estuary to **Turf Lock** and *The Turf Hotel* (☎ 01392-833128, 🖳 turfpub.net; WI-FI; 🐾; Mar-Oct), a very popular pub with cracking **food** (Wed-Sat noon-3pm & 5.30-8.30pm, Sun noon-3pm; bar open daily), fine local ales and a huge riverside beer garden. They also have two lovely **B&B** rooms (1D/1T shared bathroom; 🛏; 🐾; from £62.50pp, sgl occ £70).

Running from the back of the pub, **Turf Lock Ferry** (☎ 07778-370582, 🖳 www.topshamturfferry.com; sgl/rtn from £5/8, 🐾 50p; Apr-end June Wed-Sun 11.30am-8.30pm, July to mid Sep daily and to 9.30pm, mid Sep to end Oct Wed-Sun to 5.30pm or so). Ferries depart Turf Lock every hour on the half hour and from Topsham on the hour. Note that times are subject to low tides and weather conditions. They offer bird-watching cruises in winter.

If you wish to (or have to) continue to the next ferry, keep to the left-hand side of **Exeter Canal** for just over a mile to **Topsham Lock** where **Topsham Lock Ferry** (☎ 07801-203338; Apr-Sep Wed-Mon 9.30am-3.30 up to 5.30pm, Oct-Mar weekends & bank hols only 10am-5pm or dusk; £1.50; 🐾) – basically a man and his boat – takes about two minutes to cross to Topsham. Note that the ferry doesn't operate in bad weather conditions, or at low tide; for the latter check the tide times (🖳 easytide.ukho.gov.uk). It also doesn't run for one month a year for the boat to be repaired and the ferryman to have a holiday, though this is likely to be in winter so won't affect many walkers.

Remember that you need to phone either ferry beforehand to make sure it's running.

Topsham   On Fore St you'll find a Co-op **supermarket** (daily 7am-10pm) and a **pharmacy** (Mon-Fri 8.30am-6pm, Sat 9am-1pm). Stagecoach's 57 **bus** service calls here as do GWR **trains** between Exmouth and Exeter; see pp51-5 for details.

Should Topsham's considerable charms compel you to stay longer, hotel-style accommodation can be found at *The Globe* (☎ 01392-873471, 🖳 www.theglobetopsham.co.uk; 24D or T; ☛; WI-FI; 🐾; £60-70pp, sgl occ room rate), at 34 Fore St.

Topsham has some great pubs and eateries. Shortly after the ferry slipway you will come to *Passage House Inn* (☎ 01392-873653, 🖳 passagehouseinn topsham.co.uk; WI-FI; 🐾; food daily noon-9pm) with terrace seating over-looking the quay. Also doing pub meals is *The Lighter Inn* (☎ 01392-875439, 🖳 lighterinn.co.uk; **fb**; WI-FI; 🐾; food Mon-Sat noon-9pm, Sun to 4pm).

On the corner of Monmouth Hill is an excellent café, *Route 2* (☎ 01392-875085, 🖳 route2topsham.co.uk/cafe; **fb**; WI-FI; 🐾; daily 8am-5pm); it's a friendly, comfortable place, with some of the best breakfasts you'll taste any-where on the trail – the scrambled eggs (from £5.45) are to die for.

There's also a small *teahouse* inside the grounds of the charming **Topsham Museum** (🖳 topshammuseum.org.uk; Apr-Oct Wed-Sun & Bank Hols 2-5pm; free).

Having disembarked from either ferry in Topsham, turn right and walk along Ferry Rd until you meet Fore St where you turn right. Cross a mini round-about, follow the thin lane up Monmouth Hill and after just over 100 metres turn left along **Monmouth St**; having followed this for about a quarter-of-a-mile you arrive on Bowling Green Rd. Turn right here, then after 200 metres turn left over the railway line and follow the long, sweeping Clyst Bridge over the marshy expanses surrounding the River Clyst. Coming off the bridge, continue straight along the footpath-cycle lane until it turns left, bringing you out onto Green Lane. Turn right here and follow this and then Exton Lane as far as the junction with Station Rd where, turning right, you pass *The Puffing Billy* (☎ 01392-877888, 🖳 thepuffingbilly.co.uk; **fb**; WI-FI; 🐾; food Mon-Sat 10-11.30am, noon-2.30pm & 6-8.30pm, Sun noon-4.30pm), an upmarket gastro-pub. Exton **railway station** is a stop on GWR's Exeter–Exmouth line; see box p51.

For **B&B**, *Riverdown* (☎ 01392-873852, 🖳 riverdownbedandbreakfast.co .uk; 1D/1D or T; ☛; WI-FI; £40-52.50pp, sgl occ £70-95) is on your right, just before you turn right onto Green Lane. They don't accept advance bookings for a single-night stay other than in the winter months.

Having followed Station Rd for approximately 200 metres you pass through a gate on your left and arrive at the railway line. Gigantic wooden boardwalks now become your pathway and you follow them to **Lympstone** where, having crossed the railway line, you arrive opposite Central **conven-ience store & post office** (daily 7am-9pm). The pub to your right is *The Swan*

Inn (☎ 01395-270403, 🖳 theswaninn-lympstone.co.uk; **fb**; WI-FI; 🐾; food Mon-Sat noon-2.30pm & 5-7.45pm, Sun noon-2.30pm). Open at 10am, their kitchen doesn't open until midday though they can serve coffee before then.

Stagecoach's Nos 56, 57 & 58 **bus** services call in Lympstone.

Turn right at the road here and you'll soon come to *Susannah's* (☎ 01395-487220, 🖳 susannahs-tearoom.business.site; daily 10am-4pm) which does a great cream tea (£4). Follow the road through the village, with Exmouth finally appearing on the horizon. Follow **Sowden Lane**, turning sharp left to pass under the railway line before taking a footpath on your right, which is then followed for a further two miles into **Exmouth**.

Just before you reach Exmouth, you'll pass the beautiful grounds of the dog-friendly **Lower Halsdon Farm** and its rustic *tea garden* (**fb**; 🐾; Easter-May & Sep weekends & bank hols only 11am-4.30pm, Jul & Aug open daily).

EXMOUTH

Exmouth is a decent-sized town with all the amenities required and a good supply of accommodation, all (apart from the campsite) within easy walking distance of the ferry terminal and coastal path. Called Lydwicnaesse, or 'The point of the Bretons' in the 11th century, the town's name today is somewhat more self-explanatory, with 'Exe' a Celtic word for 'fish'. The town grew with the construction of permanent docks in the 19th century, its popularity as a destination for holidaymakers increasing exponentially as a result.

If you are interested in the town's history and social development **Exmouth Museum** (☎ 01395-260339, 🖳 www .exmouthmuseum.co.uk; Apr-end Oct Mon-Thur 10am-4pm, Sat to 1pm; £2.50) is on Sheppards Row.

Exmouth Festival (see p14) is held here in May or June.

Services

After several years of sharing its office with a taxi company, the **tourist information centre** (☎ 01395-830550, 🖳 www.visitex mouth.org; Apr-Oct Mon-Sat 10am-4pm, Oct-Apr Mon-Sat to 2pm, but subject to the availability of volunteers) finally has its own office again and it's right in the heart of the action on the main square at 45A The Strand.

The pedestrianised centre is not the most becoming of places but just about everything you need can be found within it. A **post office** (Mon & Wed-Fri 9am-5.30pm, Tue 9.30am-5.30pm, Sat 9am-12.30pm)

with its own ATM, is in WH Smith's on Magnolia Walk (the pedestrianised road that runs through Magnolia Centre, a shopping precinct). There is also a **pharmacy**, Boots (Mon-Sat 9am-5.30pm, Sun 10am-4pm), a branch of the **trekking/camping chain** Mountain Warehouse (Mon 9am-5.45pm, Tue-Sat 9am-5.30pm, Sun 10am-4pm) and a Co-op **supermarket** (Mon-Sat 7am-10pm, Sun 10am-4pm). There's also a Tesco (daily 6am-11pm) on Rolle St and a large M&S supermarket (Mon-Sat 8am-8pm, Sun 10am-4pm) beside the railway station.

There's a **launderette** (daily 8am-8pm) at 6 High St.

There are plenty of **banks** with **ATMs** around town. Indoor **Exmouth Market** (Mon-Sat 9am-5pm) is good for souvenirs.

Transport

[See also pp51-5] Stagecoach's No 56, 57 & 58 **bus** services connect the town with Exeter via different routes. Meanwhile, their No 157 goes to Sidmouth via Budleigh Salterton and their No 357 to Budleigh Salterton.

GWR **trains** run regularly to Exeter.

For a **cab** try AJ's Taxis (☎ 01395-222655).

See p188 for details of the Starcross to Exmouth Ferry.

Where to stay

Camping is an option, but the nearest site, *Prattshayes Campsite* (Map 41; ☎ 01395-

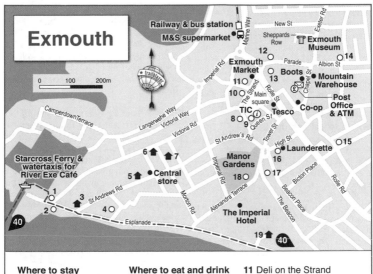

Exmouth

0   100   200m

Railway & bus station
M&S supermarket

New St

Sheppards Row

Exmouth Museum

12

Parade

14

Albion St

Exmouth Market

11

Boots

13

Mountain Warehouse

10

Main square

Post Office & ATM

TIC

Tesco

Co-op

8   9

Camperdown Terrace

Langenwehe Way

Victoria Way

Victoria Rd

St Andrew's Rd

Manor Gardens

Launderette

15

6   7

16

Starcross Ferry & watertaxis for River Exe Café

5   Central store

18   17

1

3   St Andrews Rd

Alexandra Terrace

The Imperial Hotel

2   4

Esplanade

19

40

Where to stay
3 Ash Hotel
5 Summer Wind
6 Dolphin Hotel
7 Breken Guest House
19 Premier Inn Exmouth Seafront

Where to eat and drink
1 The Beach
2 Rockfish
4 The Grove
8 The Bamboo Restaurant
9 Spoken
10 Crusty Cob

11 Deli on the Strand
12 The Mexican
13 Powder Monkey
14 Brunch, Lunch & Munch
15 Bicton Inn
16 Namaste Himalaya
17 Golden Dragon
18 Bumble & Bee

276626, 🖳 exmouthcountrylodge.com; 🐕 on a lead; from £20 for a tent and up to two hikers; Apr-end Oct) is a two-mile walk from the town centre and one mile from the path; either turn off the path at Maer Lane, just as you leave Exmouth, or you can continue on the coastal trail past Orcombe Point to a small path signposted to Gore Lane, which in turn leads to Maer Lane. This is a decent campsite, though, with good showers and a small shop and even a bar ('The Cabin').

Exmouth now has a branch of the **Premier Inn** (☎ 0333 321 9294, 🖳 premier inn.com; 🍴; WI-FI; see p21) chain. Located on the seafront, there's no denying that, for all its identikit blandness, it can be a great-value place to stay, with rooms starting at about £45 (sgl occ room rate).

The arrival of the Premier Inn is one of the reasons cited for why the number of **bed and breakfasts** in Exmouth seems to be diminishing. That said, there are still a few that are well located for both the trail and town centre.

On Morton Rd (Nos 2-6) is **Dolphin Hotel** (☎ 01395-263832, 🖳 dolphinhotel exmouth.co.uk; 3S share facilities, 3S/5T/8D/5D or T/2Qd, all en suite; 🍴; WI-FI; 🐕; £50-75pp, sgl £50-70, sgl occ £70-110), which has its own bar (daily from 6pm) but they don't serve food.

Close by is **Breken Guest House** (☎ 01395-269800; 2S/2D/1T; WI-FI; from £45pp inc sgl, sgl occ from £70), at No 13, but stays must be a minimum of two nights.

St Andrews Rd is home to some establishments, such as: **Ash Hotel** (☎ 01395-

224983; 1S/6D/1T; ☞; WI-FI; £42.50-45pp, sgl from £60, sgl occ £75-80), by the junction with Esplanade; *Summer Wind* (☎ 07786-375317, 🖳 summerwindguesthouse .co.uk; 1D/1T; WI-FI; room only from £40pp, sgl occ room rate), at No 64, which doesn't provide breakfast but provides a fridge and kettle in the room. Note they require a minimum 2-night stay all year.

Where to eat and drink
For most of Exmouth's eating options you have to walk five minutes from the path into the town centre. This is dominated by the main square, around which are dotted numerous eateries.

Cafés The most pleasant café is nestled into one corner of Manor Gardens. *Bumble and Bee* (☎ 07791-229741, 🖳 bumbleand bee.co.uk; fb; Apr-Sep daily 9am-5pm, rest of year check in advance) does healthy breakfasts, light lunches, and unusual honey and lavender scones. It's good value and is licensed too.

Of the places on the main square, *Deli On The Strand* (☎ 01395-279977, 🖳 www.delionthestrand.com; Mon-Sat 9am-4pm) is a good choice, with seating spilling out onto the pavement. It does well-made and delicious sandwiches and paninis, plus pies, soups and cream teas. Nearby, and cheaper, *The Crusty Cob* (☎ 01395-267634, 🖳 www.thecrustycob.com; Mon-Fri 7am-5pm, Sat to 4pm, also Sun in summer school holidays) is a bakery with some good-value sandwiches.

For good-value grub at lunchtimes do head to 14 Albion St and the highly rated *Brunch, Lunch and Munch* (☎ 01395-487466; fb; 🐾; daily 8am-3pm), with 'phat pasties' for £2.60-4.20, as well as jacket potatoes, burgers, sandwiches (from £4.35) and baguettes. Good food and nice people.

Pubs Almost as soon as you step off the Starcross Ferry you come to *The Beach* (☎ 01395-272090; fb; WI-FI; 🐾; food school summer holidays daily noon-9pm, rest of year variable), a vibrant place with some good food and a great atmosphere.

Continuing along the Esplanade, *The Grove* (☎ 01395-272101, 🖳 www.groveex mouth.co.uk; fb; WI-FI; 🐾; food Mon-Sat noon-9pm, Sun to 8pm), part of the Young's chain, offers a similar menu (mains £14-16, though the sirloin steak is £29), and has a large beer garden plus a first-floor terrace with sea views. Dogs are very welcome here too.

Near the railway station is the Wetherspoon's pub, *Powder Monkey* (☎ 01395-280090; food daily 8am-11pm), a hugely popular place with a large front patio. The food is cheap, but again it lacks a genuine pub atmosphere, and doesn't welcome dogs. The name, incidentally, commemorates the career of local girl Nancy Perriam who, unusually for a woman, worked on the naval ships as a powder monkey (ie someone who filled shells and cartridges with powder – a task usually done by boys). Nancy lived nearby in

---

❑ DINING OUT ON THE WAVES

A rundown of the eating options in Exmouth wouldn't be complete without mention of the multi award-winning *River Exe Café* (Map 40; ☎ 07761-116103, 🖳 riverexe cafe.com; Apr-end Sep Tue-Sat noon-10.30pm), the town's most unusual eatery. Situated on a barge floating on the River Exe, you have to get a water taxi to get to it; bookings for a meal are essential and include a booking for the water taxi – they allow two hours for a meal.

The water taxi leaves on the hour (£7 return from the Marina) and takes 20 minutes. Mains cost £16-32.50, while two-person seafood-sharing platters are £75 or £120. The mussels (£19.95 for a main dish including crusty bread) are a delicious speciality, while some of the fish is delivered from local fishing boats directly to the café – it doesn't get much fresher than that!

Tower St where she died in 1865 aged 98. *The Bicton Inn* (☎ 01395-272589, ☐ bictoninn.co.uk; **fb**; WI-FI; daily 11am to midnight), on the corner of Bicton St and South St, is a friendly community pub with a good selection of beers (though no food) and free live music – folk/blues/covers – every Thursday, Saturday and Sunday as well as other events during the week.

Restaurants Right on the coast path, *Rockfish* (☎ 01395-272100, ☐ therockfish.co.uk; daily noon-4pm & 5-9pm) is a modern seafood restaurant with ceiling-to-floor windows and terrace seating overlooking the sea. Mains, including traditional fish & chips (£8.95), cost between £9 and £20 (though the lobster is the outlier at £38.95), and they have an ever-changing local fish menu too.

Inland a bit, *The Bamboo Restaurant* (☎ 01395-267253, ☐ www.bambooexmouth.com; Wed-Mon 5-9pm) is a large but discreet place by the main square, with some tantalising Chinese dishes including sliced duck with fresh ginger & spring onions (£7.50). For more bog-standard Chinese cuisine, try *Golden Dragon* (☎ 01395-264027; daily 6-10pm), on The Beacon, with a menu which includes crispy seaweed (£4.40) and various hotplates (£9.90-10.50). *Namaste Himalaya* (☎ 01395-222831, ☐ www.the namastehimalaya.com; Tue-Thur & Sun 5-11pm, Fri-Sat to 11.30pm) serves Nepalese and Indian cuisine, while up by the railway station is *The Mexican* (☎ 01395-223388, ☐ eatmexican.co.uk; Mon-Sat 11.30am-2pm & 5-9.30pm, Sun 5-9pm; winter hours may vary) where evening mains cost around £14-15.

EXMOUTH TO SIDMOUTH [MAPS 40-46]

[MAPS 40-46]

Today's **12½-mile (20km; 4½hrs)** stage begins with a saunter through Exmouth on what, at approximately two miles, is said to be the longest seafront in Devon, and ends within the borders of a World Heritage Site (see box p196).

The cliff-top-walking involved in this stage is pretty relentless at times and there are a couple of moderately strenuous climbs. However, the views from West Down Beacon and Brandy Head more than make up for any aches and pains, while Otter Estuary Nature Reserve and the spectacular sea-stacks at Ladram Bay add plenty of wonder and variation to the day.

Budleigh Salterton makes a pleasant lunch stop. There are also a few cafés on the coast path (albeit some are linked to monstrous caravan parks) and of course, plenty of options for a cream tea or evening meal once you arrive in the elegant Regency town of Sidmouth.

The route

Disembarking from the ferry in Exmouth, follow the promenade (Esplanade) parallel with the road all the way along the seafront. It's quite a pleasant stretch, with seawall, beach, windsurfers and volleyballers to your right and **The Maer**, a nature reserve, on the opposite side of the road. If it's windy beware the gusts blowing sand off the beach and directly into your eyes. On your way look out for the **Allen Williams turret**, like a dalek's 'head', a relic not of time-travel but of WWII.

> ❏ **IMPORTANT NOTE – WALKING TIMES**
> All times in this book refer only to the time spent walking. You will need to add 20-30% to allow for rests, photography, checking the map, drinking water etc.

At **Exmouth Lifeguard Station** you have two options: turn left up to the roundabout then right to walk above the beach; or continue along the seafront to virtually the end of the tarmac and **Foxholes Beach**, where a steep path zig-zags upwards to rejoin the other path.

The trail is easy as it crosses the pastures of the National Trust-owned **High Land of Orcombe** and the views of the sea and back along the coast are occasionally magnificent. The strange **Geoneedle monument** marks the beginning of the **Jurassic Coast** which now spreads out, daunting and yet inviting in equal measure, in front of you. The path hugs the coast through **Devon Cliffs Holiday Park** (caravans only), where you can stop at *South Beach Café* (Map 42; Mar-Oct daily 11am-10pm), before reaching **Straight Point Rifle Range**. Below to your right as you pass along the edge of the park is **Littleham Cove** – home to swallows, falcons, kittiwakes and grey seals.

Eventually leaving the caravan park, the trail clambers over the spectacular terracotta cliffs to reach **West Down Beacon** (129m/423ft), from where you descend along foliage-enveloped trails through **Jubilee Park** (keep your eyes open for linnets, falcons and clouded yellow butterflies) to the Promenade in **Budleigh Salterton**.

BUDLEIGH SALTERTON [map p201]

Situated just to the west of the River Otter (Map 43), the genteel town of Budleigh Salterton was appropriately called Ottermouth until the name was changed to reflect what, at the time, was the town's primary industry: salt-panning.

Apart from picking up a sandwich – there are some nice cafés here – or resting on the town's quiet little seafront there is little to keep you in Budleigh Salterton, though the thatched **Fairlynch Museum** (☎ 01395-442666, 🖳 fairlynchmuseum.uk;

❑ THE UNESCO JURASSIC COAST WORLD HERITAGE SITE

The Jurassic Coast World Heritage Site (aka the Dorset and East Devon Coast World Heritage Site) stretches for 95 miles (155km) from Orcombe Point, just outside Exmouth in East Devon, to Studland Bay and the chalk stacks of Old Harry Rocks in Purbeck, Dorset.

In order to get some sort of handle on the complicated geology (see also pp58-63) of this region, it's useful to remember that, if walking from west to east along the coast path, the rocks on which you tread are getting ever younger the further you go. Starting with the red rocks of the **Triassic Period** (from 250 million years old) between Exmouth and Lyme Regis, the coast path then clambers over the younger stones of the **Jurassic Period** (from 200 million years old) between Pinhay Bay and White Nothe, before finally entering the **Cretaceous Period** (from 145 to 65 million years old) as you climb round Ringstead Bay. (As you probably expect, the division isn't quite as neat as this – many of the cliffs between Durdle Door and Studland, for example, are often still Jurassic due to various geological folds and the land tilting in the mid Cretaceous Period (see p62) – but for non-geologists this simple rule is a good place to begin.

It is due to this incredible and – unusually – very visible geology that the coastline was designated England's first UNESCO World Heritage Site in 2001, thereby placing it alongside sites such as the Great Barrier Reef and the Grand Canyon.

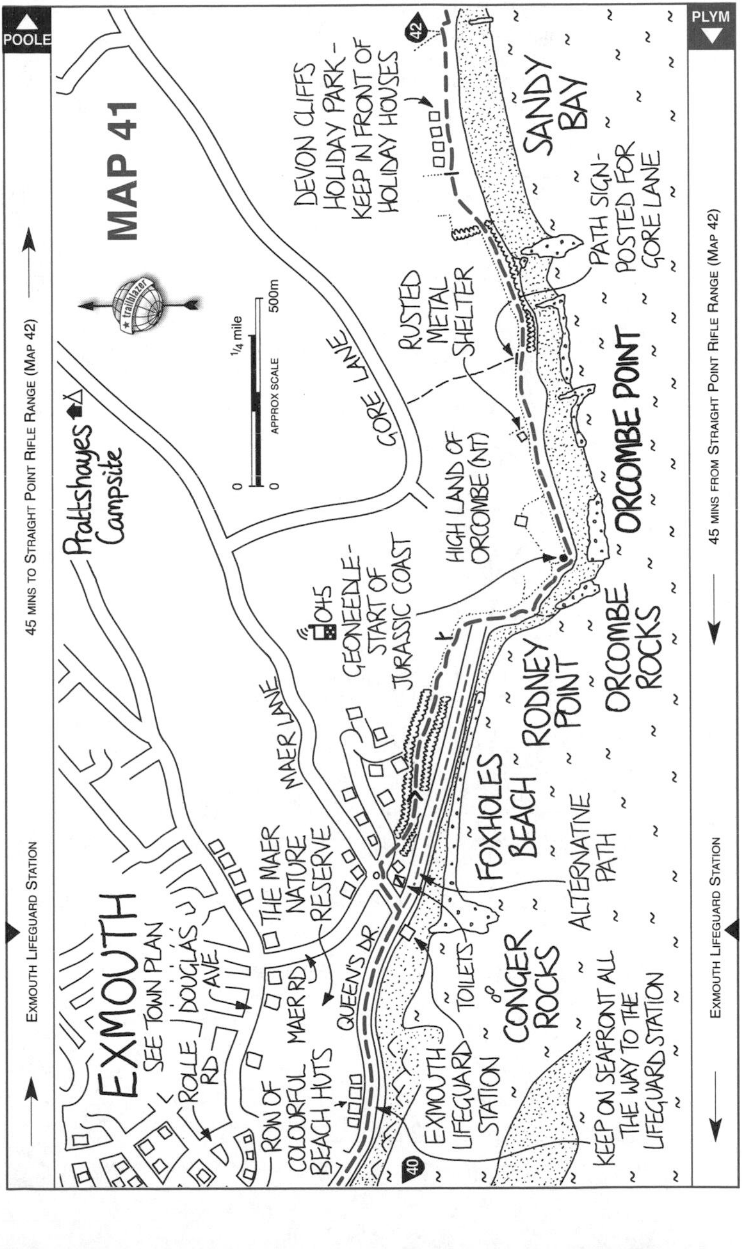

POOLE

PLYM

MAP 41

45 MINS TO STRAIGHT POINT RIFLE RANGE (MAP 42)

Prattshayes Campsite

DEVON CLIFFS HOLIDAY PARK – KEEP IN FRONT OF HOLIDAY HOUSES

42

SANDY BAY

GORE LANE

RUSTED METAL SHELTER

PATH SIGN-POSTED FOR GORE LANE

HIGH LAND OF ORCOMBE (NT)

GEONEEDLE – START OF JURASSIC COAST

ORCOMBE POINT

MAER LANE

EXMOUTH LIFEGUARD STATION

EXMOUTH SEE TOWN PLAN

THE MAER NATURE RESERVE

ROW OF COLOURFUL BEACH HUTS

ROLLE RD

DOUGLAS AVE

MAER RD

QUEEN'S DR

RODNEY POINT

FOXHOLES BEACH

ORCOMBE ROCKS

CONGER ROCKS

ALTERNATIVE PATH

EXMOUTH LIFEGUARD STATION

TOILETS

KEEP ON SEAFRONT ALL THE WAY TO THE LIFEGUARD STATION

40

APPROX SCALE

0   500m
0   ¼ mile

EXMOUTH LIFEGUARD STATION

45 MINS FROM STRAIGHT POINT RIFLE RANGE (MAP 42)

ROUTE GUIDE AND MAPS

Easter-Oct Tue-Sun & bank hols 11.30am-4.30pm; £2.50) is a nice distraction, with Bronze Age and geological displays, a room devoted to local celebrity Sir Walter Raleigh, and an impressive collection of some 4000 items of clothing, some dating back to the early 18th century.

Just past the museum, look for the **blue plaque** on the whitewashed walls of a house known as The Octagon. It celebrates the fact that John Everett Millias was staying in the house in 1870 when he painted his famous *The Boyhood of Raleigh*. The great adventurer Sir Walter Raleigh, the

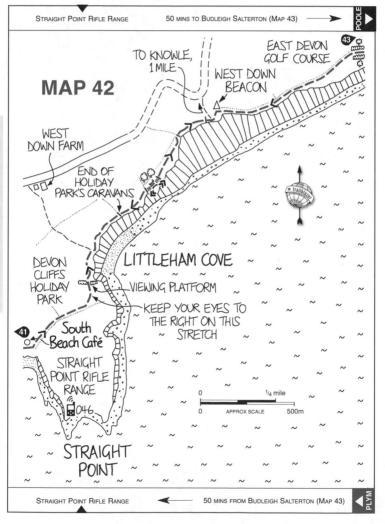

EAST DEVON
GOLF COURSE

43

TO KNOWLE,
1 MILE

WEST DOWN
BEACON

MAP 42

WEST
DOWN FARM

END OF
HOLIDAY
PARK'S CARAVANS

★ trailblazer

DEVON
CLIFFS
HOLIDAY
PARK

LITTLEHAM COVE

VIEWING PLATFORM

KEEP YOUR EYES TO
THE RIGHT ON THIS
STRETCH

41

South
Beach Café

STRAIGHT
POINT RIFLE
RANGE

0   ¼ mile
0   APPROX SCALE   500m

STRAIGHT
POINT

ROUTE GUIDE AND MAPS

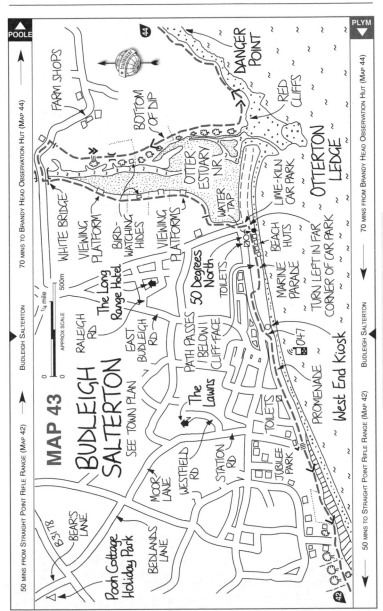

50 MINS FROM STRAIGHT POINT RIFLE RANGE (MAP 42)

BUDLEIGH SALTERTON

70 MINS TO BRANDY HEAD OBSERVATION HUT (MAP 44)

FARM SHOPS

DANGER POINT

RED CLIFFS

BOTTOM OF DIP

OTTER ESTUARY NR

OTTERTON LEDGE

WHITE BRIDGE

VIEWING PLATFORM

BIRD-WATCHING HIDES

VIEWING PLATFORMS

WATER TAP

LIME-KILN CAR PARK

MAP 43

BUDLEIGH SALTERTON

SEE TOWN PLAN

The Long Range Hotel

RALEIGH RD

EAST BUDLEIGH RD

50 Degrees North

TOILETS

BEACH HUTS

MARINE PARADE

TURN LEFT IN FAR CORNER OF CAR PARK

APPROX SCALE

¼ mile

500m

0

0

PATH PASSES BELOW CLIFF FACE

The Lawns

WESTFIELD RD

MOOR LANE

STATION RD

JUBILEE PARK

TOILETS

PROMENADE

West End Kiosk

B3178

BEAR'S LANE

BEDLANDS LANE

Pooh Cottage Holiday Park

50 MINS FROM STRAIGHT POINT RIFLE RANGE (MAP 42)

BUDLEIGH SALTERTON

50 MINS TO STRAIGHT POINT RIFLE RANGE (MAP 42)

BUDLEIGH SALTERTON

70 MINS FROM BRANDY HEAD OBSERVATION HUT (MAP 44)

subject of the painting, was actually born a couple of miles inland in East Budleigh. The very keen eyed might be able to spot a **smaller blue plaque** slightly further on, fastened to the low **sea wall** on the opposite side of the road. It claims that this is the wall that features in the painting itself.

Budleigh Music Festival runs for a week in July, while its more bookish cousin **Budleigh Salterton Literary Festival** is held every September. See box p14 for details.

Services
Though the town makes a good lunch stop and has several services, there is little accommodation here; as a result, most trekkers continue to Sidmouth where more beds are available. The friendly **tourist information office** (☎ 01395-445275, 🖳 www.lovebudleigh.co.uk; Mar/Apr-Oct Mon-Sat 10am-4pm, rest of year check in advance), on Fore St, however, have information about accommodation.

Near the tourist office is both a Spar **supermarket** (daily 7am-10pm), and there's also a Tesco (daily 6am-11pm) just up the road; the Co-op (daily 7am-10pm) in the middle of the High St has a **post office** (Mon-Sat 9am-5.30pm) housed within it. Nearby is a Lloyds **pharmacy** (Mon-Fri 9am-6pm, Sat 9am-4pm). There is an **ATM** outside the Co-op.

Transport
[See also pp53-5] For **buses**, Stagecoach's 157 and 357 connect the town with Exmouth and the 157 also with Sidmouth.

For a **taxi** contact Andrew Pelosi (☎ 01395-443122).

Where to stay
Camping is available relatively nearby at the small but well-equipped *Pooh Cottage Holiday Park* (Map 43; ☎ 01395-442354, 🖳 poohcottage.co.uk; £12.50-15 for tent and one hiker; WI-FI; 🐾; mid Mar to Oct), just one mile from the High St.

B&Bs are rather thin on the ground, though you could try *The Lawns* (☎ 01395-442862, 🖳 the-lawns.co.uk; 3D; 🍺; WI-FI) which is a fine place but they accept only those staying for a minimum of two nights. They offer a continental breakfast and charge from £55pp (sgl occ £90).

The Long Range Hotel (☎ 01395-443321, 🖳 thelongrangehotel.co.uk; 2S/4D/3T; 🍺; WI-FI; £59-84.50pp, sgl from £82.50, sgl occ rates on request) is away from the centre on Vales Rd, but only a few hundred metres from the coast path. It's a friendly and efficiently run place with a lovely conservatory looking over the garden.

Where to eat and drink
If you're just after a **café**, there's the *West End Kiosk* (Mon-Sat 9am-4pm, Sun 11am-3pm) on the seafront before you even hit the town, which does some lovely crab sandwiches and ice-cream. But for great value, you can't really beat the friendly *Village Emporium and Café* (🐾; daily 9am-6pm), which is the cheapest (hot baps from £3.50, cream tea £5.50, takeaway hot drinks £2) and possibly the cheeriest in town too.

For a more substantial **restaurant** meal, there's a bistro, a couple of restaurants and a pub. The pub, *The Feathers* (☎ 01395-708852; WI-FI; 🐾; food Mon-Sat noon-2.30pm & 6-8.30pm, Sun noon-4pm), which originally dates back to the 16th cen-

---

❏ A PEBBLE'S TALE

Budleigh Salterton is known for its Lower Triassic pebble beds. For thousands of years the predominantly oval shaped and extremely hard pebbles have been spilling out from the local cliffs as sea and time take their toll. Four hundred million years old, they are identical to rocks found in Northern France, both being made of hard quartzite. They are thought to have been transported to their two respective homes via one of the giant rivers that flowed through the Triassic period's arid and scorching red deserts (see Geology pp58-63).

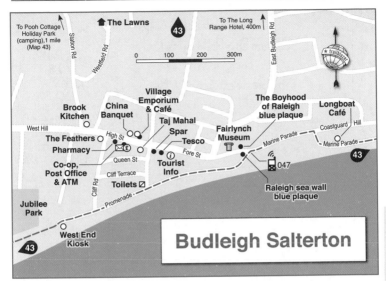

Budleigh Salterton

tury but has been heavily worked on since, offers a fairly standard pub-grub menu but has a specials board and they're a very amiable bunch.

At the top of town, ***Brook Kitchen*** (☎ 01395-911313, 🖥 www.brookkitchen .co.uk; WI-FI; 🐾; Mon-Sat 9am-5pm, Sun 9am-3pm) is the trendiest place in town, with cocktails on some Thursdays (to 8pm), live music some Sat nights (to 10pm) and tapas on Fri evenings (to 10pm). But it's the quality of the coffee, and the food, particularly the breakfasts – with everything from a three-rasher bacon sarni for £6.90 to a plate of avocado, feta & *dukkah* (a Middle

Eastern mix of herbs, nuts and spices) on sourdough for £9.50 – that stands out.

For Indian food, head to nearby ***Taj Mahal*** (☎ 01395-446093, 🖥 tajmahal budleigh.co.uk; daily noon-2pm & 5.30-11pm), at 1B High St; while for Chinese there's ***China Banquet*** (☎ 01395-445546; Wed-Mon 5-10pm).

As you leave the town on the coast path, ***Longboat Café*** (☎ 01395-443080, 🖥 www.longboatcafe.com; 🐾 on lead; Easter-end Oct daily 9.30am-3.45pm but to 6pm in peak season, winter weather permitting) is a cheery, popular beachside establishment with a scattering of tables outside.

Leaving Budleigh Salterton along the Promenade, past seemingly endless commemorative benches, eventually you hit the River Otter and there is a brief but pleasant sojourn round **Otter Estuary Nature Reserve**. Don't get too excited by the name, however, for mink are more common than otters and any paw prints you come across are more likely to belong to a Jack Russell. As compensation, however, in the skies above soar merlins and red kites, and kingfishers sometimes work the riverbanks.

Having left the reserve and rejoined the coast, you are now confronted by the ominously named cliffs **Danger Point** and **Black Head**, the trail here making for a majestic stroll on a sun-soaked summer's afternoon. **Brandy Head**,

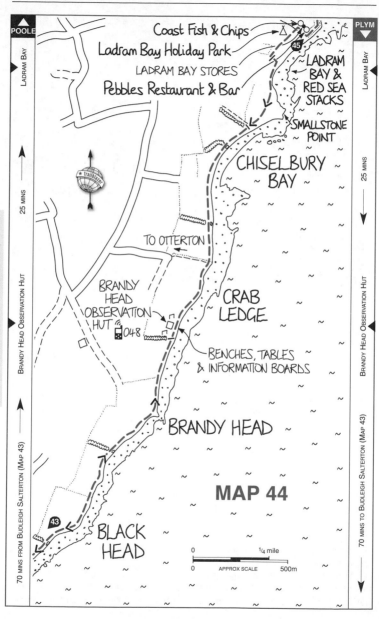

POOLE

LADRAM BAY

25 MINS

BRANDY HEAD OBSERVATION HUT

70 MINS FROM BUDLEIGH SALTERTON (MAP 43)

PLYM

LADRAM BAY

25 MINS

BRANDY HEAD OBSERVATION HUT

70 MINS TO BUDLEIGH SALTERTON (MAP 43)

Coast Fish & Chips
Ladram Bay Holiday Park
LADRAM BAY STORES
Pebbles Restaurant & Bar

45

LADRAM
BAY &
RED SEA
STACKS

SMALLSTONE
POINT

CHISELBURY
BAY

TO OTTERTON

BRANDY
HEAD
OBSERVATION
HUT 048

CRAB
LEDGE

BENCHES, TABLES
& INFORMATION BOARDS

BRANDY HEAD

MAP 44

43

BLACK
HEAD

0   1/4 mile

0   APPROX SCALE   500m

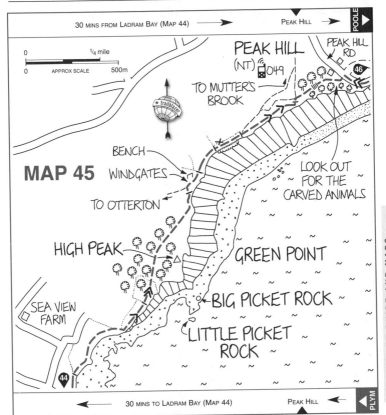

named after the contraband that was smuggled here, is topped by an **Observation Hut** that was used to test weapons and gun sights during WW2.

Continuing past **Chiselbury Bay** and **Smallstone Point**, you soon come to **Ladram Bay** with its impressive display of red sandstone sea stacks and the gigantic *Ladram Bay Holiday Park* (☎ 01395-568398, 🖳 ladrambay.co.uk; WI-FI; 🐾 but restricted areas; mid Mar-end Oct), home to *Pebbles Restaurant & Bar* (daily noon-9pm), *Coast Fish & Chips* (Thur & Sun-Tue 5-9pm, Fri & Sat 5-10pm), and the very well-stocked **Ladram Bay Stores** (Sun-Thur 8am-8pm, Fri-Sat to 9pm); note that these days/hours are different out of the peak season so check in advance. They do allow some *camping* here but, particularly for advance bookings, there's a two-night minimum stay (three nights in peak season); rates vary so contact them for details.

Following Ladram Bay you arrive at what initially appears to be a daunting climb. This is **High Peak** (157m) and the haul begins quite leniently, but becomes tough, once you enter the woods.

Once at the top take a deep breath; the reward for your efforts is a gradual descent through the trees and a dramatic view of the coastal cliffs ahead before you need to climb again, this time up the steeper slopes of **Peak Hill**. Descending through woodland once more (look out for the rabbits and mice carved into tree stumps) you arrive with some relief at **Peak Hill Rd**. Leaving it to inspect the ranks of **commemorative benches**, you soon come to a right turn leading down to **Jacob's Ladder Beach**.

As you round the cliff, *Clock Tower Café* (☎ 01395-515319, 🖥 clocktow ersidmouth.com; **fb**; 🐾 in conservatory; summer Wed-Mon 10am-5pm, winter hours may vary) stands above you, a restored 17th-century lime kiln and pseudo-do-fort that serves great breakfasts including a *shakshuka* – two poached eggs served with a subtly spiced tomato sauce with granary bread (£8.50).

Clifton Walkway and its rockfalls are now all that separate you from the end of the stage. Survive and you'll soon be strolling on **Sidmouth** seafront with all the other sunkissed sightseers.

SIDMOUTH [map p207]

'A town caught still in a timeless charm'
John Betjeman
Nestling quietly in the Sid Valley, with red cliffs soaring on either side, Sidmouth is, as the former poet laureate suggests, a lovely place. Winner of numerous awards for its gardens, floral displays abound throughout the town centre. A touch too old-fashioned and genteel for some, Sidmouth is ideal for the average walker who simply seeks shelter and sustenance without too much razzmatazz.

Featuring in the Domesday Book as 'Sedemuda', Sidmouth began life as a small fishing community. Its geographical location prevented the town from successfully constructing a decent harbour, as a result of which Sidmouth didn't really grow in earnest until tourism took off during the Georgian and Regency eras (1714-1837); much of the town's architecture still dates from this time. The young Queen Victoria holidayed in the town as a baby in 1819 and the town's growth and popularity as a resort continued throughout her reign.

Sidmouth Museum (🖥 www.sid mouthmuseum.co.uk; Apr-Oct Mon-Fri 10am-4pm, Sat 10am-1pm; £2.50), on Church St, houses exhibitions describing the town's development from a fishing village through to Regency and Victorian times as well as an exhibition on the town's lacemaking industry and the Sid Valley's biodiversity. They also offer guided walks (£2.50) to various parts of the town, each informative amble lasting approximately two hours.

Sidmouth Folk Week (see p14) is held here in late July/August.

Services

The **tourist information centre** (☎ 01395-516441, 🖥 www.visitdevon.co.uk/sid mouth; May-Sep Mon-Sat 10am-5pm, Sun 10am-4pm, Oct Mon-Sat 10am-1pm & 1.30-4pm, Nov-Apr Mon-Sat 10am-1.30pm) stands at the eastern end of town on Ham Lane.

There are two **trekking/camping shops** on Fore St, one that's a branch of a national chain – Mountain Warehouse (Mon-Sat 9am-5.30pm, Sun 10am-4pm) – and one that's not: Sidmouth Outdoor Co (☎ 01395-513747; Mon-Sat 10am-4pm). Nearby there's a **pharmacy**, Boots (Mon-Sat 9am-5.30pm, Sun 10am-4pm).

Much of what a trekker traditionally needs lies in from the seafront at the top

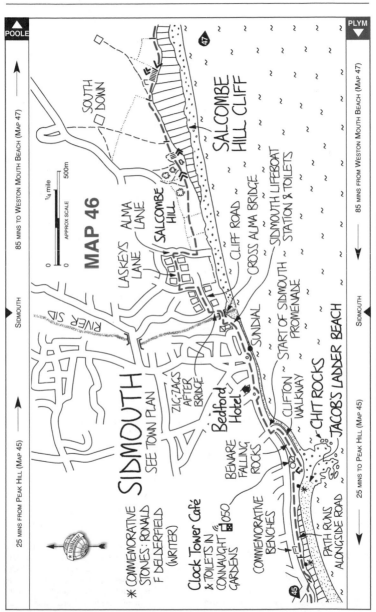

POOLE

PLYM

47

SALCOMBE HILL CLIFF

SOUTH DOWN

MAP 46

APPROX SCALE

¼ mile

0   500m

LASKEYS LANE

ALMA LANE

SALCOMBE HILL

CLIFF ROAD

CROSS ALMA BRIDGE

SIDMOUTH LIFEBOAT STATION & TOILETS

RIVER SID

SIDMOUTH
SEE TOWN PLAN

ZIG-ZAGS AFTER BRIDGE

Bedford Hotel

BEWARE FALLING ROCKS

SUNDIAL

START OF SIDMOUTH PROMENADE

CLIFTON WALKWAY

CHIT ROCKS

JACOBS LADDER BEACH

* COMMEMORATIVE STONES: RONALD F DELDERFIELD (WRITER)

Clock Tower Café & TOILETS IN CONNAUGHT GARDENS

050

COMMEMORATIVE BENCHES

PATH RUNS ALONGSIDE ROAD

45

25 MINS FROM PEAK HILL (MAP 45)

SIDMOUTH

85 MINS TO WESTON MOUTH BEACH (MAP 47)

25 MINS TO PEAK HILL (MAP 45)

SIDMOUTH

85 MINS FROM WESTON MOUTH BEACH (MAP 47)

ROUTE GUIDE AND MAPS

end of Fore St (by which point it's actually called High St), including a Co-op **supermarket** (daily 7am-10pm), Tesco (daily 7am-10pm) and, nearby, the **post office** (Mon-Fri 9am-5pm, Sat 9am-1pm). There are also some **banks** with **ATMs**.

Transport
[See also pp53-5] Stagecoach's No 157 **bus** travels east to Budleigh Salterton and Exmouth; the No 9A meanwhile connects the town with Seaton, Lyme Regis and Exeter, and the No 9 with Honiton and Exeter. First's X52 (Exeter to Lyme Regis) calls here and Axe Valley's 899 journeys to Seaton.

For a **taxi** try Sid Valley Cars (☎ 01395-577633).

Where to stay
Though there are numerous hotels on the seafront, annoyingly all of Sidmouth's **B&Bs** are a short jaunt from the centre. The closest, on Salcombe Rd, are *Canterbury House* (☎ 01395-513373, 🖳 canterbury-house.com; 1S/4D/2D or T; WI-FI; £47.50-52.50pp, sgl £60-65, sgl occ £70-80) which will accept single-night stays but these are more likely in the quieter season, and *Berwick House* (☎ 01395-513621, 🖳 www .berwick-house.co.uk; 5D/1T; WI-FI; from £47.50pp, sgl occ rates on request) which has two rooms in a separate annex and offers a good full English at breakfast as well as other choices. Note that between Easter and the end of September they ask for a minimum of three nights and two nights for the rest of the year. If there was a gap for a single-night stay they may charge an additional £15 per room.

A little further from the centre and on Vicarage Rd are: *The Groveside* (☎ 01395-513406, 🖳 thegroveside.com; 1S/6D/2T; WI-FI; £45-50pp, sgl from £65, sgl occ £77-85; Easter-Oct), an Edwardian boutique guest-house that serves locally sourced and organic food for breakfast plates; and *Southcombe* (☎ 01395-513861, 🖳 south combeguesthouse.co.uk; 5D/2T/1Tr; WI-FI), which charges from £42.50pp (sgl occ £60).

The seafront is lined with **hotels**. Two of the first that you come to are *Bedford*

Hotel (☎ 01395-513047, 🖳 bedfordhotel sidmouth.co.uk; 11S/27D or T/2Tr; WI-FI; 🐾; £90-112.50pp, sgl £100-125.50, sgl occ room rate, DB&B rates also available); and *Hotel Riviera* (☎ 01395-515201, 🖳 hotel riviera.co.uk; 7S/3D/16D or T; 🛏; WI-FI; small 🐾; mid Feb-end Dec; £118-146pp, sgl occ rates on request), where food is available all day but the restaurant is only open 12.30-2pm & 7-9pm. The top rates are for rooms with sea views.

Also on The Esplanade are three hotels owned by the same company, Sidmouth Hotels (toll free ☎ 0800-048 1731, 🖳 hotels-sidmouth.co.uk). Both *The Kingswood* (11S/17D/17T/3Tr; 🛏; WI-FI; 🐾; closed early Dec to mid Feb; B&B £111-128.50pp, sgl £73-82, sgl occ rates on request) and *The Elizabeth* (1S/11D/16T; 🛏; WI-FI; B&B £70-98pp, sgl £71-79, sgl occ rates on request; closed early Jan to mid Feb) also offer dinner, bed and breakfast rates (additional £15pp for a 3-course meal if booked in advance). The cheapest of the three is *Dukes Inn* (🖳 dukessidmouth .co.uk; 3S/4D/5Tr; 🛏; WI-FI; B&B £66-92pp, sgl £64-72, sgl occ from £135).

Away from the seafront, *Woodlands Hotel* (☎ 01395-513120, 🖳 woodlands-hotel.com; 3S/2D/13D or T/1Qd; WI-FI; 🐾; £80-125pp, sgl from £100, sgl occ room rate) is on the corner of Station Rd and Cotmaton Rd, a 10-minute walk inland.

Where to eat and drink
It's surprising more people in Sidmouth don't suffer from obesity, given the temptation placed before them every day by the huge range of eateries on offer.

Cafés & delis The first café you come on the seafront is also one of the best: *Fort Café* (☎ 01395-512200, 🖳 thefortcafesid mouth.co .uk; **fb**; WI-FI; 🐾; summer daily 10am-4.30pm, winter hours variable) is welcoming and does toasties and home-made ice-cream. Also convenient for the front are the bakers *Upper Crust* (Mon-Sat 8am-2.30pm) and *Coffee#1* (☎ 01395-514371, 🖳 www.coffee1.co.uk; Mon-Sat 6am-6pm, Sun 9am-5pm) both branches of national chains, both on Fore St and both

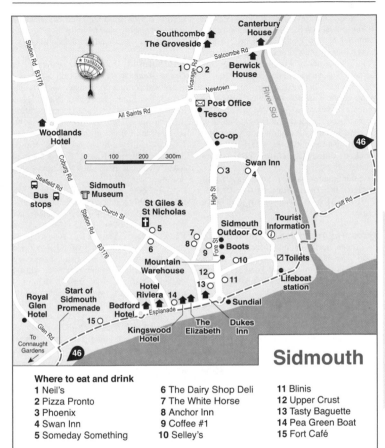

Where to eat and drink

1 Neil's
2 Pizza Pronto
3 Phoenix
4 Swan Inn
5 Someday Something

6 The Dairy Shop Deli
7 The White Horse
8 Anchor Inn
9 Coffee #1
10 Selley's

11 Blinis
12 Upper Crust
13 Tasty Baguette
14 Pea Green Boat
15 Fort Café

Sidmouth

ROUTE GUIDE AND MAPS

popular and also close to the seafront and the path. Nearby there's the dog-friendly *Selley's* (Mon-Sat 9am-4.30pm, Sun 11am-4pm; 🐾), tucked away discreetly in **Libra Court**. Most of the seating is in the pleasant courtyard, though there are a couple of cosy tables inside.

On the other side of Fore St, beside St Giles & Nicholas Church, is the narrow corner café *Someday Something* (☎ 01395-515829, 🖥 somedaysomething.co.uk; WI-FI; 🐾; Feb-Dec Tue-Sat 9am-4pm). Again

it's a bit of a squeeze inside, but tables spill out onto the pavements, making this a nice spot for a cream tea (£5.95).

Opposite is *The Dairy Shop Deli* (☎ 01395-513018, 🖥 thedairyshop.co.uk; WI-FI; 🐾; summer Mon-Sat 9/10am-5pm, winter to 4pm), a deli-cum-café serving lovely meals and snacks – most made with the local produce they sell in the shop – including crab sandwiches (£7.50) as well as plenty of vegetarian and gluten-free options.

Round the corner, on Old Fore St, *The White Horse* (☎ 01395-514271; summer Mon-Sat noon-6.30pm, Sun noon-3.30pm, winter hours variable), sounds like a pub but is more of a no-frills licensed café serving fish & chips, jacket potatoes and burgers.

Another licensed place, though far more swish, is *Blinis* (☎ 01395-572920, 🖳 blinis-cafe-bar.co.uk; WI-FI; Mon-Sat 9am-5pm; closed Jan), a stylish bar-café on Fore St. The speciality, naturally, are blinis – a type of pancake; try the scrambled egg, smoked salmon & chives blini (from £8.50).

For made-to-order takeaway sandwiches, try *Tasty Baguette* (☎ 01395-577575; Mon-Sat 9am-3pm), on Dove Lane.

Pubs *The Anchor Inn* (☎ 01395-514129, 🖳 theanchorinn-sidmouth.co.uk; WI-FI; food Tue noon-2.15pm, Wed-Sat noon-9pm, Sun to 8pm), on Old Fore St, does a fair fish pie (£13.95) as well as ham, egg & chips.

Despite its drawbacks (the lack of wi-fi and the fact that you will probably have to book in advance to get a table), *The Swan Inn* (☎ 01395-512849, 🖳 www.swan innsidmouth.co.uk; 🐾 in bar on lead; **fb**; food daily noon-2pm & 6-9pm) is perhaps the best pub in town, a smart but cosy place with friendly staff and good food. It's a

minute's walk from the High St but make sure you reserve your table for they're often booked out – especially in the evening.

Restaurants Down on the seafront, *Pea Green Boat* (☎ 01395-514152, 🖳 thepea greenboat.com; food summer daily noon-2pm & 5-8.30pm, winter hours variable), is a small but smart place with terrace seating looking out to sea. The menu focuses on seafood and varies but may include monkfish tail, chilli salsa, chicory salad, orange dressing & French fries (£26) and battered hake, alongside hand-cut chips, pea purée & tartare sauce (£19).

The best seafood place in town – in fact, probably the best restaurant in town – is *Neil's* (☎ 01395-519494, 🖳 neilsrestaurant.com; Tue-Sat 6.15-8.30pm) on Radway Place (Vicarage Rd). As they justifiably put it, they turn seafood into great food (though other, non-fishy dishes are also available). Mains include whole, grilled, Brixham lemon sole with homemade tartare sauce. A three-course meal is £39.95.

Also up this end of town are *Pizza Pronto* (☎ 01395-516319; daily 5-10pm). Down the road slightly is the Chinese restaurant, *Phoenix* (☎ 01395-514720; **fb**; July & Aug daily noon-2pm & 5-10pm, rest of year closed on Tue).

SIDMOUTH TO SEATON   [MAPS 46-50]

Today's **10¼-mile (16.5km; 4¼hrs)** stage is tough, but rewarding. As far as Branscombe Mouth it is a trail of very steep and largely wooded pathways, but one where the lucky walker gets to cross pretty combes on the way to barren and sparsely populated beaches. Only the occasional periods of level cliff-top walking show any mercy to the knees today, but the scenery, particularly gorgeous Lincombe, offers ample consolation.

There is also a decent café at Branscombe Mouth (note, this is the only place to get refreshments before Beer, unless you detour to The Fountain Head), whereafter the terrain changes drastically as you begin a spectacular walk below Hooken Cliffs, formed by a landslip in 1790. At windy Beer Head there are great views over Seaton Bay, where one finds both the friendly, photogenic fishing village of Beer, offering plentiful food and accommodation, and Seaton, this stage's destination. With the distance between Beer and Seaton being only 1½

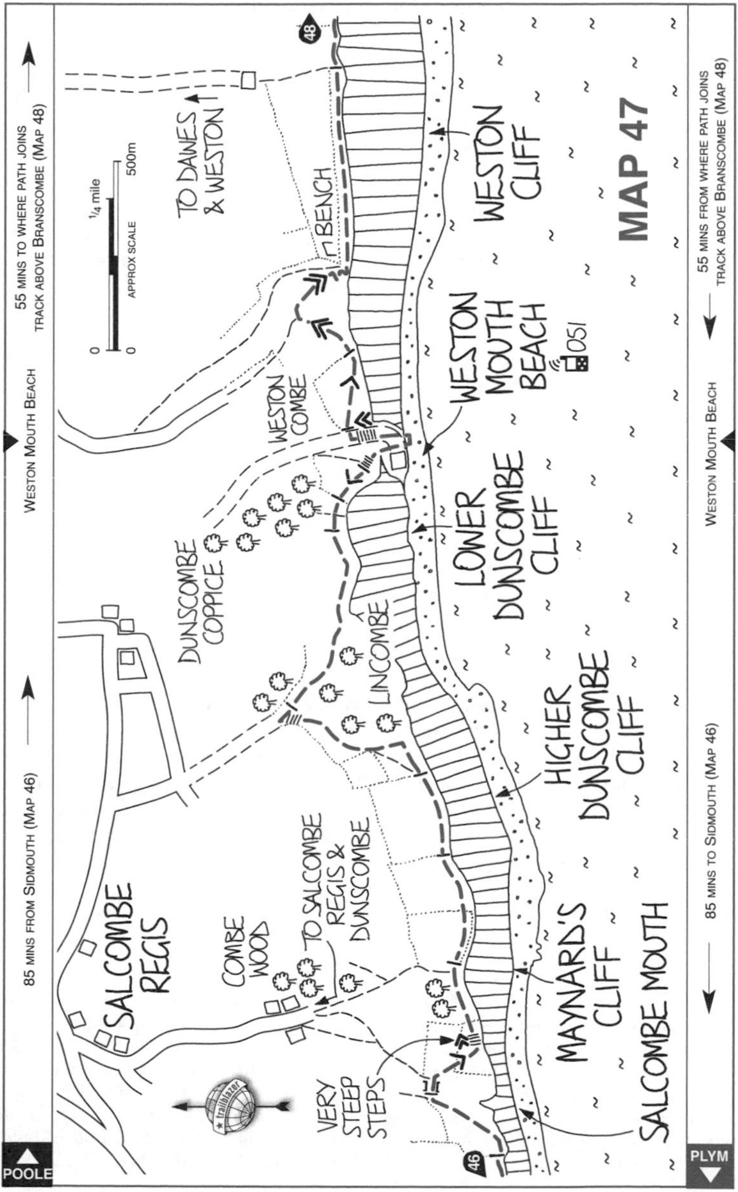

MAP 47

TO DANES & WESTON

T. BENCH

WESTON CLIFF

WESTON COMBE

WESTON MOUTH BEACH

051

LOWER DUNSCOMBE CLIFF

DUNSCOMBE COPPICE

LINCOMBE

HIGHER DUNSCOMBE CLIFF

SALCOMBE REGIS

COMBE WOOD

TO SALCOMBE REGIS & DUNSCOMBE

VERY STEEP STEPS

MAYNARD'S CLIFF

SALCOMBE MOUTH

46

¼ mile

500m

APPROX SCALE

48

POOLE

PLYM

ROUTE GUIDE AND MAPS

miles, the former is a viable overnight stop, especially as the next stage is relatively short.

The route

Your first task, having left Sidmouth, is to climb up steep **Salcombe Hill Cliff**, an ascent that bears more than a passing similarity to a couple of yesterday's climbs: the path begins gently in a field before winding up the steep slope to some woods that sit on the summit like a toupee.

Following the path along the cliff-tops, you then drop sharply into **Salcombe Mouth** and skirt round **Combe Wood** before climbing the immense **Maynard's Cliff** and the even steeper **Higher Dunscombe Cliff**. Note the colours of the cliffs with the pastel reds and dirty oranges of the Triassic era topped, on occasion, with the lighter-hued Cretaceous Upper Greensand – the Jurassic-era rock having been eroded away entirely (a phenomenon that geologists call an 'unconformity').

Afterwards, the path flirts with **Lincombe**, the calf muscles enjoying a lucky escape as the trail for once passes around the back of the combe rather than dropping into it. Keep your eyes peeled for green woodpeckers, painted lady butterflies and the rare marsh helleborine (*Epipactis palustris*) orchid as the trail continues to tackle the undulations before descending through **Dunscombe Coppice** to **Weston Mouth**'s undisturbed pebble beach. Climbing out – and it is some climb! – you now find yourself amongst the wild flowers on the rim of **Weston Cliff**, the way sticking to the cliff edge before heading inland across farmland on **Coxe's Cliff**.

Passing the site of **Berry Camp**, an Iron-age (or possibly Roman) hill-fort, you now follow a wooded path with ash trees to your right heading above the small village of **Branscombe** where, if you need a break, you'll find a wonderful, dog-friendly, real-ale pub, *The Fountain Head* (Map 48; ☎ 01297-680359, 🖥 fountainheadinn.com; food Tue 6-7.45pm, Wed-Sat noon-3pm & 6-7.45pm, Sun noon-2pm, pub closed Sun 5pm-Tue 5pm; 🐾) that does great food and serves ales (and ciders) from the local Branscombe Vale Brewery, and is signposted half a mile from the path. The path itself carries on to the National Trust owned **West Cliff**, from where you continue through the steep woods to **Branscombe Mouth**.

BRANSCOMBE MOUTH
[Map 49, p213]

Branscombe Mouth reached the headlines back in 2007 when a container ship, *MSC Napoli*, ran aground offshore while being towed to Portland, having been badly damaged in a storm off Lizard Point. The cargo that was subsequently washed ashore – including brand-new BMW motorbikes, perfumes, nappies and car parts – was gratefully (and illegally, as it turned out) taken by scavengers, who had collected on the beach, until the police intervened a few days later.

Though there aren't any motorbikes on offer these days, there's just enough to Branscombe Mouth to keep walkers happy. For **food**, there's *Sea Shanty Beach Café* (☎ 01297-680107, 🖥 www.seashantybeach cafe.com; **fb**; WI-FI; 🐾; Apr-Oct daily 9am-5pm, winter Thur-Sun only) with some great outdoor seating. They do full breakfasts (from £10.95), sandwiches (£7.95-9.95)

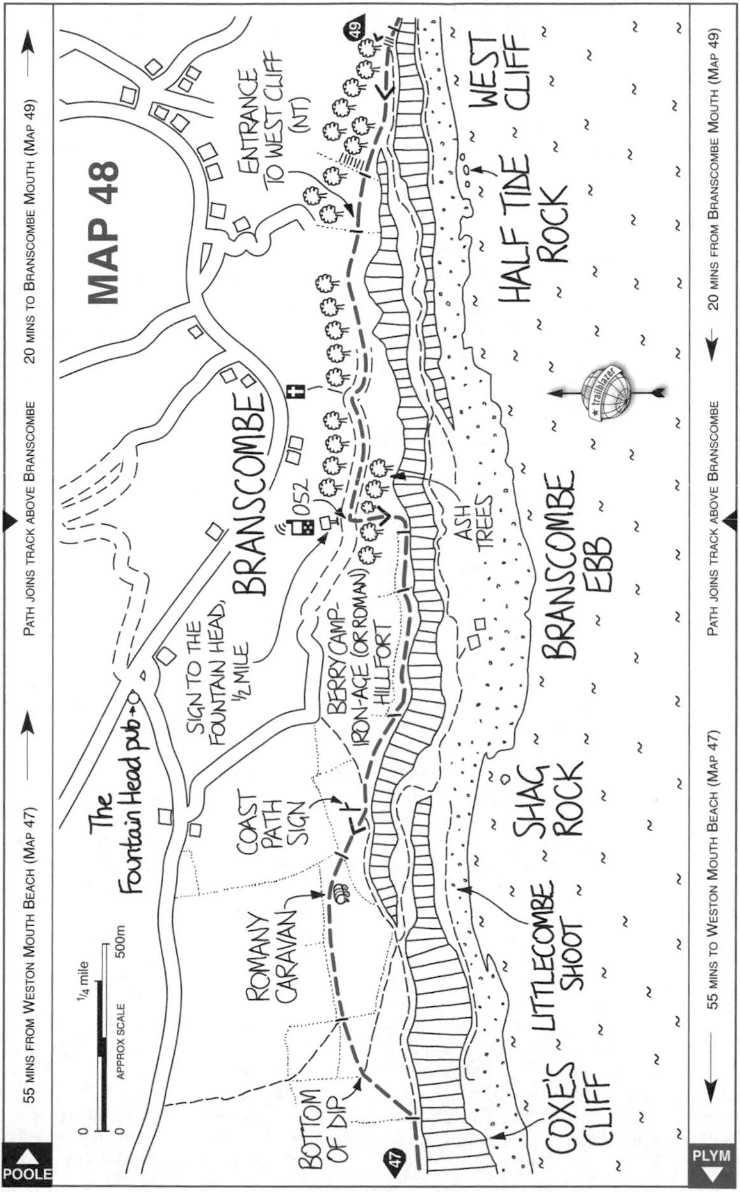
MAP 48
55 mins from Weston Mouth Beach (Map 47)
Path joins track above Branscombe
20 mins to Branscombe Mouth (Map 49)
55 mins to Weston Mouth Beach (Map 47)
20 mins from Branscombe Mouth (Map 49)
POOLE
PLYM
47
49
1/4 mile
0
500m
APPROX SCALE
The Fountain Head pub
Sign to the Fountain Head, 1/2 mile
BRANSCOMBE
052
Entrance to West Cliff (NT)
Coast Path sign
Romany caravan
Bottom of dip
Berry Camp – Iron-Age (or Roman) hillfort
Ash trees
Coxe's Cliff
Littlecombe Shoot
Shag Rock
Branscombe Ebb
Half Tide Rock
West Cliff
trailblazer

Branscombe Mouth (*cont'd*) and substantial lunchtime mains (£11-15), and stock beer from the local micro-brewery. The attached **shop** (same hours) sells basics such as newspapers and pasties.

Less than 200 metres (about 180 yards) up the road from Branscombe Mouth, **B&B** is provided at *Great Seaside* (☎ 01297-680470, 🖳 greatseaside.co.uk;

1Tr/1Qd both private facilities; 🛁; WI-FI; £62.50-67.50pp, sgl occ £110-125). It is a 16th-century farmhouse, the first written evidence of which dates from 1339 (!), and is now surrounded by National Trust land.

Axe Valley's 899 **bus service** (from Branscombe Village Hall) travels between Sidmouth, Beer and Seaton; see pp53-5 for details.

From Branscombe Mouth head up **East Cliff** to follow the path through Sea Shanty Caravan Park. (Alternatively, you can climb up over the top of **Hooken Cliffs**, the two paths reconvening shortly before Beer Head.) The time spent amongst the caravans is brief and you're soon back on a pleasant if rugged path that twists and turns its way through foliage sandwiched between Hooken Cliffs and Hooken Beach.

A steep climb presents marvellous views back over a collection of **chalk pinnacles** before a field takes you to **Beer Head** – and the most westerly chalk cliffs in England.

From here you then skip down to and over **Arratt's Hill** before a short road walk into the pretty fishing village of **Beer**.

BEER [map p214]

Devon villages don't come much more quintessential than cosy Beer, an ancient thatched village nestled on the county's south coast.

Along with the village called Hope, Beer seems to be one of those places that was named after something that most trekkers need to function properly. However, the name actually derives from the Anglo-Saxon word 'Bearu', meaning 'Grove', referring to the woodlands that originally cloaked the area.

The main joy of Beer can be had simply by strolling along its lovely main street, which follows a trickling brook down to the harbour, but the village also has some quirky sights. Behind Jimmy Green's clothes shop you'll find the **Bomb Shelter** (daily 10am-5pm; free), which rather than being an underground wartime bunker, is actually an exhibition room which displays and recounts the story of an unexploded 500kg WWII German bomb that landed safely in a field nearby, rather than destroying the village, thanks to the selfless heroics of Luftwaffe pilot Gunther Blaffert.

Down by the harbour, **Beer Fine Foundation Centre** (🖳 beervillageheritage.org.uk; free) celebrates the history and natural environment of Beer.

At the top end of town, half a mile beyond the turning to the YHA (turn left up Quarry Lane), are **Beer Quarry Caves** (☎ 01297-680282, 🖳 beerquarrycaves.co.uk; Easter to end Oct 10am-4pm; £10) which have a history stretching back over two millennia. 'Beer stone' was used in the construction of Exeter and Winchester cathedrals as well as Westminster Abbey and the Tower of London – where no doubt some of those smugglers who hid contraband in this vast underground complex feared they may end up. Beer Quarry Caves are also a stop on Axe Valley's 899 **bus** service; see box pp53-5.

Beer Rhythm & Blues Festival (see box p14) is held here in October.

Services

Assuming you have an account accepted by the post office you can withdraw money for free at the **post office** (Mon-Fri 10am-1pm

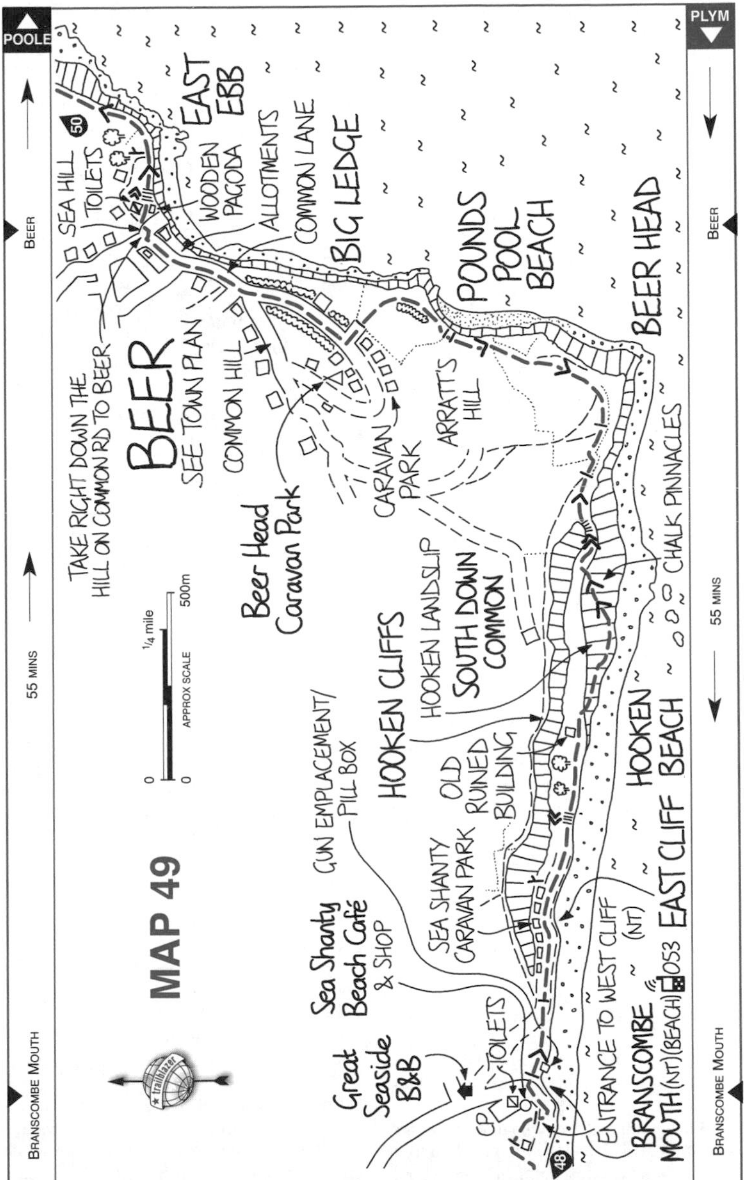

MAP 49

POOLE

PLYM

BRANSCOMBE MOUTH

BEER

55 MINS

TAKE RIGHT DOWN THE HILL ON COMMON RD TO BEER

EAST EBB

SEA HILL
TOILETS
WOODEN PAGODA
ALLOTMENTS
COMMON LANE
BIG LEDGE
POUNDS POOL BEACH
BEER HEAD

BEER
SEE TOWN PLAN

COMMON HILL

Beer Head Caravan Park

CARAVAN PARK
ARRATT'S HILL

HOOKEN CLIFFS
HOOKEN LANDSLIP
SOUTH DOWN COMMON
CHALK PINNACLES

¼ mile
500m
APPROX SCALE

GUN EMPLACEMENT/PILL BOX

SEA SHANTY CARAVAN PARK
OLD RUINED BUILDING

HOOKEN BEACH
EAST CLIFF BEACH

Sea Shanty Beach Café & SHOP

Great Seaside B&B
TOILETS

ENTRANCE TO WEST CLIFF
BRANSCOMBE MOUTH (NT)(BEACH) 053

ROUTE GUIDE AND MAPS

& 2-5.30pm, Sat 10am-1pm), which is inside a village shop called Rock Villa, which also sells some cracking craft beers.

There's also a **pharmacy** (Mon-Wed & Fri 9am-5.30pm, Thur & Sat 9am-1pm) and **Beer Village Stores** (Mon-Sat 7am-6pm, Sun 7am-5pm).

Transport
[See pp53-5] Axe Valley's No 885 & 899 **bus services** call here en route between Axminster/Sidmouth and Seaton.

Where to stay
Budget travellers are well catered for here. **Camping** is available at the excellent *Beer Head Caravan Park* (Map 49; ☎ 01297-21107, 🖳 beer-head.com; wi-fi; 🐾; end Mar-end Oct; £12-15pp), with great sea views from its flat grassy pitches and its own shop and bistro.

There's also a **hostel** (which offers camping as well): *YHA Beer* (☎ 0345-371 9502, 🖳 yha.org.uk/hostel/yha-beer; 3 x 4-/3 x 5-/2 x 6-bed rooms; dorm beds from £15pp, private rooms from £39; wi-fi social areas only) provides meals and has 24hr access. There are spacious **dorms** as well as private **rooms**; one of the 6-bed rooms is en suite. **Camping** (from £16pp; 🐾) is allowed in the garden with full use of the hostel's facilities, which includes a laundry and drying room, and a self-catering kitchen. They also have a couple of bell tents (🐾; £69-159 per night) The hostel is a short walk out of town; follow Causeway until it bends sharply round to the right at which point you should go straight on before turning right down Bovey Lane.

There are also some particularly impressive **B&Bs** in the village.

On Fore St you'll find *Durham House* (☎ 07816-526871, 🖳 durhamhouse.co.uk; 6D/1D or T; wi-fi; £42.50-47.50pp; sgl occ rates on request), where breakfast includes a Full English but they can cater for vegetarian, vegan and gluten-free diets. They also accept single-night stays for coast-path walkers.

On Dolphin Rd is upmarket *Belmont House* (☎ 01297-24415, 🖳 www.belmont housebedandbreakfast.com; 5D; 🍷; wi-fi;

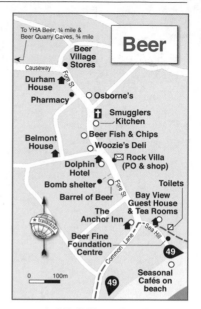

room only £40-62.50pp, sgl occ from £80); they don't serve breakfast.

Closest to the beach, and with sea views from most of its eight rooms, *Bay View Guest House* (☎ 01297-20489, 🖳 bayviewguesthousebeer.com; 8D; wi-fi; mid Feb-end Nov; from £55pp, sgl occ £80) is right on the coast path and has its own tea room (see Where to Eat).

Both pubs also do B&B. All the rooms at *The Anchor Inn* (☎ 01297-20386, 🖳 www.greenekinginns.co.uk/hotels/anchor-inn; 5D/1T; 🍷; wi-fi; 🐾; £33.75-70pp, sgl occ room rate) have a sea view. *Dolphin Hotel* (☎ 01297-20068, 🖳 dolphinhotel beer.co.uk; 3S/12D/4T/3Tr, one room sleeping up to five; 🍷; wi-fi in public areas; 🐾; £44.50-65pp, sgl occ room rate), meanwhile, has rooms ranging from singles to a room that sleeps up to five though that is over the bar so may be noisy.

Where to eat and drink
Almost everything is on Fore St, where you'll find a surprisingly wide choice of cuisines to cater for all budgets. For lunch-

box fillers, *Woozie's Deli* (Mon 9am-4pm, Wed-Sat 9am-5pm, Sun 10am-5pm) does a good line in pasties. Next door, *Beer Fish & Chips* (☎ 01297-625774; Tue-Thur noon-2.30pm & 5-8pm, Fri & Sat to 8.30pm) is the local chippy, where you can take away (hake & chips £8.50) and possibly also eat in though not at the time of research.

Cafés are thin on the ground, though there is *Bay View Tea Rooms* (see Where to stay; summer daily 10am-4pm) part of a gift shop overlooking the harbour, and there are *seasonal cafés* down on the beach.

The smartest **restaurant** in town (though still fairly informal) is *Smugglers Kitchen* (☎ 01297-22104, 🖥 thesmugglers kitchen.co.uk; **fb**; Tue-Sat 5.30-9pm), which focuses on West Country cuisine and stocks some fine wines and ales. Slightly further up Fore St, *Osborne's* (☎ 01297-24989; food Wed-Sat 6-10pm) is an equally popular tapas and wine bar.

Disappointingly, given the name of the village, Beer doesn't have any stand-out

pubs. Those it does have are ok, but are outclassed by many other pubs you'll have come across on your walk. There's a good selection of bottled ales in **Rock Villa** (the post office-cum-off-licence), however, so perhaps grab a bottle to sip down on the beach? Of the pubs, *Dolphin Hotel* (see Where to stay; food Mon-Sat noon-2.30pm & 5-8.30pm, Sun noon-6pm) does good food, but is less popular for a drink, probably on account of not being so close to the harbour. *The Anchor Inn* (see Where to stay; food daily noon-9pm, earlier in winter; WI-FI; 🐾) has a nice sea-view beer garden which is separated from the main building by the coast path.

Between the two, *Barrel of Beer* (☎ 01297-22824; **fb**; WI-FI; 🐾; Mon-Sat 10am-midnight, Sun 11am-11pm) is a new addition and, while it may lack the atmosphere and history of the other two, is a family run place, does food (school summer holidays noon-2.30pm; sandwiches from £7.95) and is your best bet if you want to watch some football on the telly.

To continue to Seaton, there are two routes – one with steps, one without – that lead up **East Ebb** and out of Beer. The path takes you around East Ebb's white cliffs and along a minor road which ends at the base of **Beer Hill**.

There are further alternatives here: **at low tide** turn right to walk along Seaton Hole Beach. **At high tide**, turn sharp left, along Old Beer Rd. After about 200m turn right up a wooded footpath (signposted), and then right again onto Beer Rd (the B3172), and right a third time along a footpath opposite Wessiter's Rd, which takes you back to the seafront. Follow the beach past another seasonal café, *Jane's Kiosk* (where there are some toilets), some beach huts and old-style lampposts, to the sleepy seaside town of **Seaton**.

SEATON [map p218]

While lacking the Regency splendour of Sidmouth or the olde-worlde charm of Beer, Seaton's plentiful amenities and accommodation make it a good option for a stop. Known as Fleet ('Creek') in Saxon times, its location near the mouth of the River Axe once made it an important port, and so it remained up until about the 14th century, when fierce storms caused parts of Haven Cliff to subside into the estuary and a shingle bank to form. The town has also dabbled in shipbuilding and salt-panning

down the years, the latter having been practised since the Iron Age.

The banks and flood plains that flank the Axe Estuary now host a number of nature reserves. **Seaton Tramway** (☎ 01297-20375, 🖥 tram.co.uk; daily Easter-Oct 10am-4/5pm, check website for other times of the year; 3/hr; Seaton to Colyton £7.70/10.90 single/return, 🐾 £1 each way; allow at least two hours) is a good way to see them as it meanders for three miles through the Axe Valley to Colyton, following the old Seaton & Beer Railway line that closed in 1967.

Other sites in town include **Seaton Labyrinth** (Map 50) in **Cliff Field Gardens** – a 60ft diameter spiral. Its half-a-mile turf pathways are lined with stones taken from different areas of the Jurassic coast to help explain the region's fascinating 185-million-year-old geological history. Residing on the top floor of the Town Hall in Fore St, **Axe Valley Heritage Museum** (🖳 www.devonmuseums.net/ Axe-Valley-Heritage-Museum/Devon-Museums; late May to Oct Mon-Fri 10.30am-12.30pm & 2.15-5pm; free) has an interactive display on the Jurassic coastline as well as an old smuggler's shawl from the mid 19th century.

Services
The **tourist information centre** (☎ 01297-21388; Apr-Oct Mon-Fri 9am-3pm, Sat & Sun 10am-noon, Nov-Apr Mon-Fri 10am-1pm) has a new home on the Esplanade, right on the coast path.

Other facilities in town include the **post office** on Harbour Rd (Mon-Fri 8.30am-5pm, Sat 8am-2pm), a Lloyds **pharmacy** (Mon-Sat 9am-5.30pm) on Queen St, a **launderette**, Launderama (daily 7am-7pm), at the top of Fore St, and a huge Tesco **supermarket** (Mon-Sat 7am-midnight, Sun 10am-4pm) set back off Harbour Rd with an **ATM** outside it.

Transport
[See pp53-5] For **buses**, Stagecoach's No 9A connects the town with Sidmouth and Exeter; Axe Valley's 378, 885 & 899 services go to Lyme Regis/Sidmouth/ Axminster and Dartline's No 20 goes to Taunton.

Where to stay
Campers should head to the very friendly *Axmouth Campsite* (Map 50; ☎ 01297-24707; tent & one/two hikers from £14; 🐾; mid Mar-mid Oct), less than three-quarters of a mile from the path. There is a **shop** and **launderette** plus (mostly) flat pitches, great views and two pubs by the entrance.

Seaton used to have plentiful **B&B** accommodation, all of which was within a few hundred metres of the path, though the Covid pandemic and the arrival of the *Premier Inn* (☎ 0333 234 6482, 🖳 premierinn.com; mix of 77D or T; 🐾; WI-FI; from £39; see p21 for more details) has forced many of them to close. While you may not be a fan of these chain hotels, they do at least accept bookings for just one night – something the other accommodation in town won't do.

For accommodation right on the seafront's eastern side try *Mariners* (☎ 01297-20560, 🖳 marinershotelseaton.co .uk; 3D/3D or T; WI-FI; Mar-Oct; from £57.50pp, sgl occ £110) .

In the same vicinity you will find *Redcliffs* (☎ 01297-20926, 🖳 redcliffs-seaton.co.uk; 1D/2T; WI-FI; from £47.50pp, sgl occ £70-75) at 3 Beach Rd. They now require a minimum 2-night stay all year,

For pub-based B&B consider *Eyre Court Hotel* (☎ 01297-21455, 🖳 eyrecourt seaton.co.uk; 4D/1T/2Tr/1Qd; WI-FI; from £55pp, sgl occ room rate) on Queen St.

Where to eat and drink
Cafés The best-located eateries, and the most convenient for the coast path, are the two cafés strung out along the seafront: *Terrace Arts Café* (☎ 01297-20225, 🖳 www.terracearts.co.uk; WI-FI; 🐾; Tue-Sat 10am-3pm) is a dog-friendly vegetarian place with a good selection of teas and smoothies as well as some decent food. There is also local art for sale. It does, however, have the road between it and the sea. The same problem affects nearby *Pebbles Café* (☎ 01297-441970; **fb**; WI-FI; 🐾; daily 9am-4pm), which is a slightly scruffy but friendly place, and one that's popular with the elderly – a bit like Seaton itself, really. It's good for all-day breakfasts and more substantial lunchtime mains, but doesn't have sea views.

Beano's (**fb**; daily 9am-5pm) is a no-nonsense takeaway kiosk with a bit of outdoor seating and a large and inexpensive menu (eg steak & onion bap for just £4.50).

Moving away from the front, *Barista* (Mon & Fri 10am-4pm, Tue-Thur 10am-

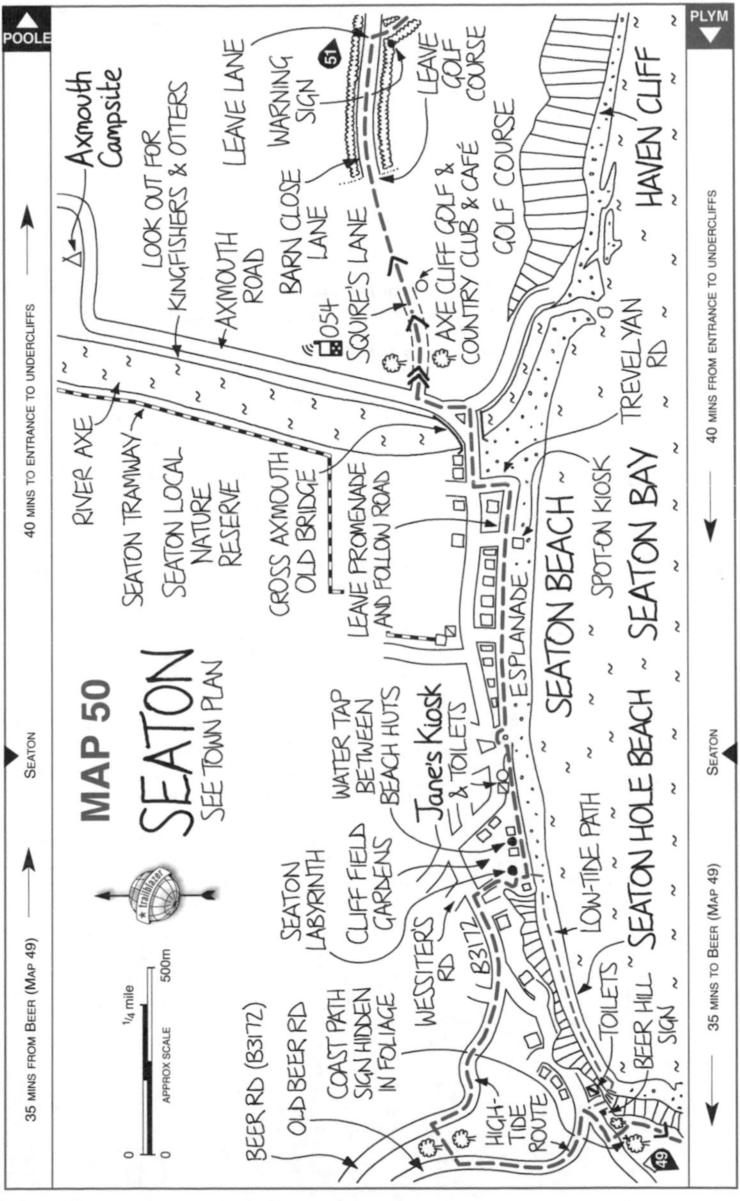
MAP 50
SEATON
SEE TOWN PLAN
POOLE
PLYM
35 MINS FROM BEER (MAP 49)
SEATON
40 MINS TO ENTRANCE TO UNDERCLIFFS
35 MINS TO BEER (MAP 49)
40 MINS FROM ENTRANCE TO UNDERCLIFFS
0
1/4 mile
0
500m
APPROX SCALE
trailblazer
Axmouth Campsite
LOOK OUT FOR KINGFISHERS & OTTERS
AXMOUTH ROAD
LEAVE LANE
WARNING SIGN
LEAVE GOLF COURSE
BARN CLOSE LANE
SQUIRE'S LANE
AXE CLIFF GOLF & COUNTRY CLUB & CAFÉ
GOLF COURSE
054
51
HAVEN CLIFF
TREVELYAN RD
RIVER AXE
SEATON TRAMWAY
SEATON LOCAL NATURE RESERVE
CROSS AXMOUTH OLD BRIDGE
LEAVE PROMENADE AND FOLLOW ROAD
SPOT-ON KIOSK
SEATON BEACH
SEATON BAY
ESPLANADE
WATER TAP BETWEEN BEACH HUTS
Jane's Kiosk
& TOILETS
SEATON LABYRINTH
CLIFF FIELD GARDENS
WESSITER'S RD
B3172
LOW-TIDE PATH
SEATON HOLE BEACH
BEER RD (B3172)
OLD BEER RD
COAST PATH SIGN HIDDEN IN FOLIAGE
HIGH-TIDE ROUTE
TOILETS
BEER HILL SIGN
49

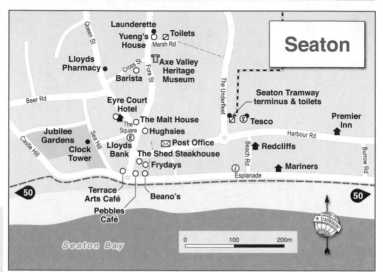

2pm, Sat 9.30am-5pm) is tucked away on Cross St and does a decent full English (£10.95) as well as baps, sandwiches etc.

It's a pleasant place but for a real monster feed, just a short stroll from the seafront try *Hughsies* (Tue-Sat 9am-1.45pm) a no-frills greasy-spoon café that describes itself as the home of the Jurassic Breakfast: three sausages, three pieces of bacon, two eggs, three hash browns, mushrooms, fried bread and beans for £11.50.

Restaurants, takeaways & pubs
Completely ignoring its seaside location, *The Shed Steakhouse* (☎ 01297-625926, 🖥 theshedsteakhouse.co.uk; summer Tue-Sat 5pm to late, Sun noon-7pm, winter hours variable) stands with its back to the coast on Harbour Rd. Expect to pay from £25.50 for 10oz rump steak and up to £52.50 for 16oz ribeye. Other dishes are available and more affordable, with burgers from £14.95.

Just back from the seafront, *Frydays* (☎ 01297-23911, 🖥 frydays.eu; Tue-Thur noon-2.30pm & 4.30-7.30pm, Fri & Sat to 8pm, Sun noon-3pm takeaway only) is your best bet for fish & chips. They do takeaway and have a comfortable restaurant area.

There's Chinese cuisine (takeaway only) at *Yeung's House* (☎ 01297-625559, 🖥 www.yeungshouseseaton.co.uk; Mon & Tue 5-10pm, Wed-Tue noon-1.30pm & 5-10pm, Fri & Sat noon-1.30pm & 5-10.30pm), on Fore St.

For **pub** food, try *The Malt House* (☎ 01297-22695, 🖥 malthouseseaton.co.uk; WI-FI; 🐾; food Mon & Thur-Sun noon-3pm & 5-8pm), on The Square, with a refreshingly simple menu where mains are all £10-15; or head up Queen's St to *Eyre Court Hotel* though at the time of research they didn't have a chef so weren't serving food.

SEATON TO LYME REGIS   [MAPS 50-53]

This **7-mile (11.5km; 3hrs)** section of the coastal path is like no other and will be, without any doubt, one of the highlights of your walk.

The day mainly comprises walking through the remarkable Axmouth to Lyme Regis Undercliffs National Nature Reserve (see box p220), shaped and moulded by landslides then left to its own devices to create that most unique and wonderful of landscapes: an English jungle. However, as with all jungles the terrain underfoot may cause problems, added to which there are some steep ascents to be tackled. Furthermore, the trail winds constantly up and down and back and forth, and is pockmarked with roots and interrupted by the odd fallen tree, so it is a day to be wary of your ankles.

It's also a day for carrying supplies as refreshments are not available in the reserve. Despite the tribulations, though, for most people this day is one of unfettered joy. And should you struggle against all the difficulties, at least comfort yourself in the knowledge that at the end of this stage lies Lyme Regis, a smashing town that's used to catering – from royalty downwards – to those in need of a well-earned rest.

The route

Leaving Seaton via the Esplanade – where, once upon a time, both a Tudor fort and a Martello tower stood – you make your way to **Axmouth Old Bridge**, a pedestrian bridge which was built in 1877 and is thought to be the oldest concrete bridge in Britain. Lying one mile inland, the village of Axmouth and the harbour were of great importance during Roman times and are situated at the end of a Roman road, The Fosse Way, which, running from Lincoln to Exeter was, following the Roman invasion in AD43, the western frontier of the Roman Empire.

A bit of tarmac-treading follows as you make your way to – and then up – Squire's Lane before bisecting **Axe Cliff Golf Club** (☎ 01297-21754, 🖳 axe cliff-fgolfclub.com), where there is a walker-friendly *café* (WI-FI; 🐕 on lead; daily 8.30am-4pm-ish but closed to non members during events, matches and tourna-

---

❏ LANDSLIDES

The geology of the Jurassic coast makes the cliffs and beaches along this stretch particularly susceptible to landslides, especially after periods of prolonged rainfall. Remember to tread carefully when walking on top of the cliffs and **always avoid walking and sitting directly below them where possible**. Remain aware of the edges, particularly in conditions that may leave you vulnerable to sudden gusts of wind and keep your dog on a lead at all times on clifftops.

Despite being relatively rare, landslides are occasionally responsible for fatalities, most recently in July 2012 when 400 tonnes of rock slid from the cliffs on to Hive Beach, near Burton Bradstock. In 2017, a huge landslide by West Bay saw more than 1500 tonnes of East Cliff fall into the sea. Thankfully it happened at night and nobody was hurt. A further large landslide in April 2021 near Seatown, caused by a naturally occurring geomorphological event known as a rotational slump, led to the re-routing of the South-West Coast Path (see p230).

ments), to join **Barn Close Lane**. The turn-off to the nature reserve is marked by a notice warning visitors of the strenuous and remote nature of the path; approach the cliff-edge by negotiating your way along hedgerows and across fields.

After an unspectacular stroll over the fields atop **Haven Cliff**, what follows next is nothing short of extraordinary as you enter an area where nature, as a rule, is definitely in charge: welcome to **Axmouth to Lyme Regis Undercliffs** (see box below). Apart from the occasional information board and the odd ruined building camouflaged amongst the leaves and vines – such as **Landslip Cottage** near **Downlands Cliff**, from which the Victorian owners used to sell afternoon teas to tourists, a **sheep wash**, just 50 metres off the path, or the **old chimney** (Map 52; part of a 19th-century freshwater pumping station) at the approximate halfway point – there is nothing to distract you away from the natural beauty of the forest. *(cont'd on p224)*

❏ AXMOUTH TO LYME REGIS UNDERCLIFFS NNR

Designated a National Nature Reserve (NNR) in 1955, the Axmouth to Lyme Regis Undercliffs are the result of numerous landslips. They are just one of many areas along the south coast to have suffered from this natural phenomenon, which occurs when long spells of wet weather saturate permeable Cretaceous rocks. As these rocks lie on impermeable clay, they eventually give way to the pressure exerted on them by the sheer volume of water and break away from the cliffs, leading to great scars in the landscape called undercliffs.

The 750-metre-wide **Whitlands Undercliff** (Map 52, p222) is actually the result of two landslips, in 1765 and 1840. However, the vicinity's most spectacular geological collapse happened at **Bindon Cliffs** (Map 51, opposite), to the west of Whitlands, on Christmas Eve 1839, when what became known as 'The Great Landslip' occurred. The first landslide ever to be scientifically documented – having been witnessed by the vicar of Axminster, William Conybeare, and William Buckland, a professor of geology at Oxford – where once there had been pasture there was now a gigantic chasm, 100m wide, 50m deep and 1km long. In the process, **Goat Island**, a piece of land forced off the top of the cliffs, formed a new plateau closer to the sea – the wheat and turnips that were grown on it surviving to produce another crop the following year which became popular souvenirs. Following such a remarkable event, the Undercliffs became a Victorian tourist attraction, regularly visited by paddle steamer; they even inspired a piece of music, *Landslide Quadrille*, which would be played on the boats as they passed.

What makes the Undercliffs so special is the fact that the land was left to its own devices during the 20th century, having been deemed too dangerous to graze sheep. Myxomatosis, too, has lent a hand, culling most of the local rabbits. As a result, the Lyme Regis Undercliffs are now one of the most significant wilderness areas in Britain, protected as part of the West Bay Special Area of Conservation and the East Devon AONB. A safe habitat for much **flora and fauna**, the Undercliffs provide sanctuary to green woodpeckers, bullfinches and Dartford warblers amongst many other birds. Many variations of flower thrive here too, including the pink pyramidical and the autumn ladies tresses orchid. Shrews and mice, lizards, grass snakes and newts scurry and slither in the undergrowth, whilst butterflies such as the wood white, silver-washed fritillary and chalk-hill blue flit from plant to plant. And all the while, flying high above you, ravens and peregrine falcons menacingly eye the ground. It's a magical place – and a splendid arena for the walker.

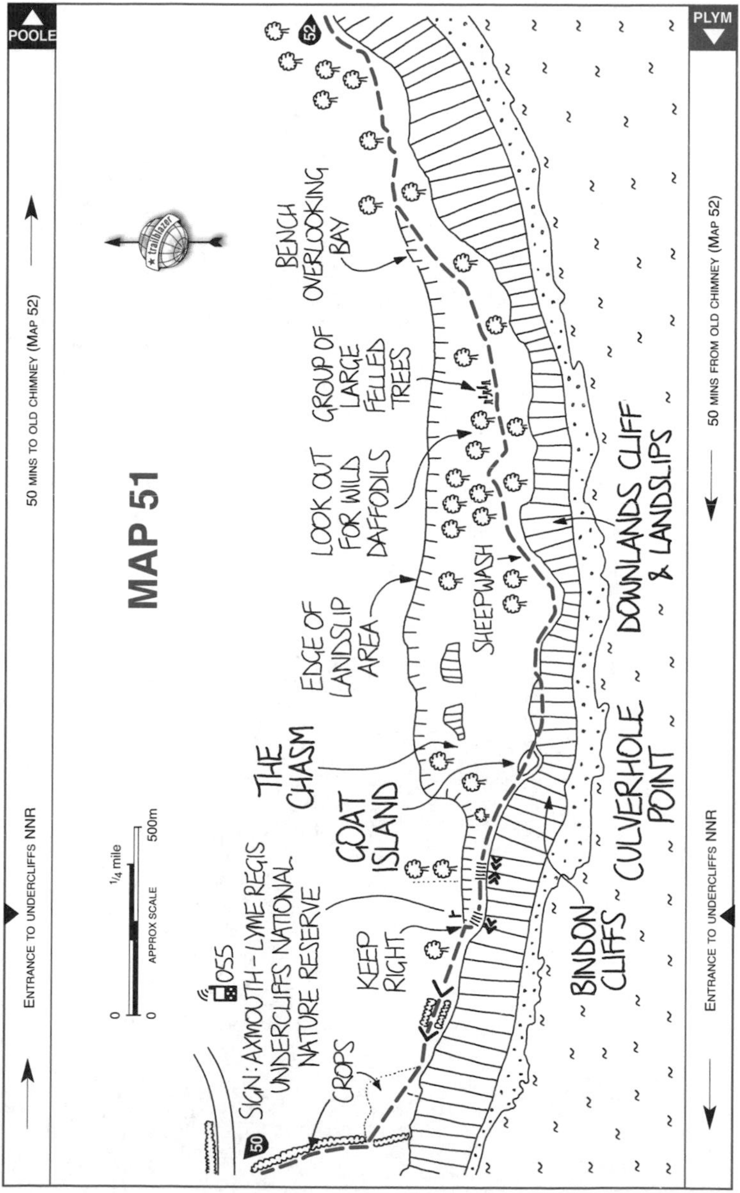
MAP 51
50 MINS TO OLD CHIMNEY (MAP 52)
ENTRANCE TO UNDERCLIFFS NNR
POOLE
PLYM
50 MINS FROM OLD CHIMNEY (MAP 52)
ENTRANCE TO UNDERCLIFFS NNR
0 1/4 mile
0 APPROX SCALE 500m
trailblazer
50
52
055
SIGN: AXMOUTH–LYME REGIS UNDERCLIFFS NATIONAL NATURE RESERVE
CROPS
KEEP RIGHT
GOAT ISLAND
THE CHASM
EDGE OF LANDSLIP AREA
LOOK OUT FOR WILD DAFFODILS
GROUP OF LARGE FELLED TREES
BENCH OVERLOOKING BAY
SHEEPWASH
DOWNLANDS CLIFF & LANDSLIPS
CULVERHOLE POINT
BINDON CLIFFS

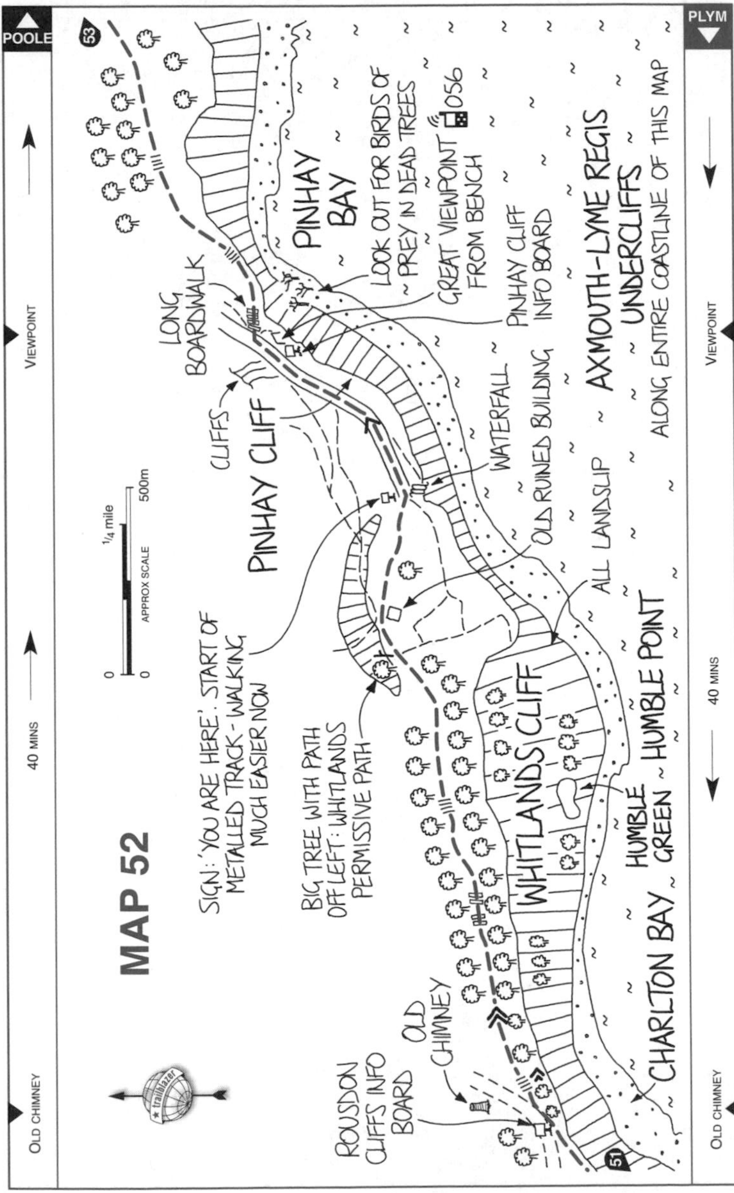

POOLE

53

PLYM

40 MINS

VIEWPOINT

OLD CHIMNEY

OLD CHIMNEY

VIEWPOINT

40 MINS

MAP 52

SIGN: 'YOU ARE HERE'. START OF METALLED TRACK - WALKING MUCH EASIER NOW

BIG TREE WITH PATH OFF LEFT: WHITLANDS PERMISSIVE PATH

LONG BOARDWALK

CLIFFS

PINHAY CLIFF

PINHAY BAY

LOOK OUT FOR BIRDS OF PREY IN DEAD TREES

GREAT VIEWPOINT 056 FROM BENCH

PINHAY CLIFF INFO BOARD

WATERFALL

OLD RUINED BUILDING

ALL LANDSLIP

AXMOUTH-LYME REGIS UNDERCLIFFS

ALONG ENTIRE COASTLINE OF THIS MAP

WHITLANDS CLIFF

HUMBLE POINT

HUMBLE GREEN

CHARLTON BAY

ROUSDON CLIFFS INFO BOARD

OLD CHIMNEY

51

0   ¼ mile
0   500m
APPROX SCALE

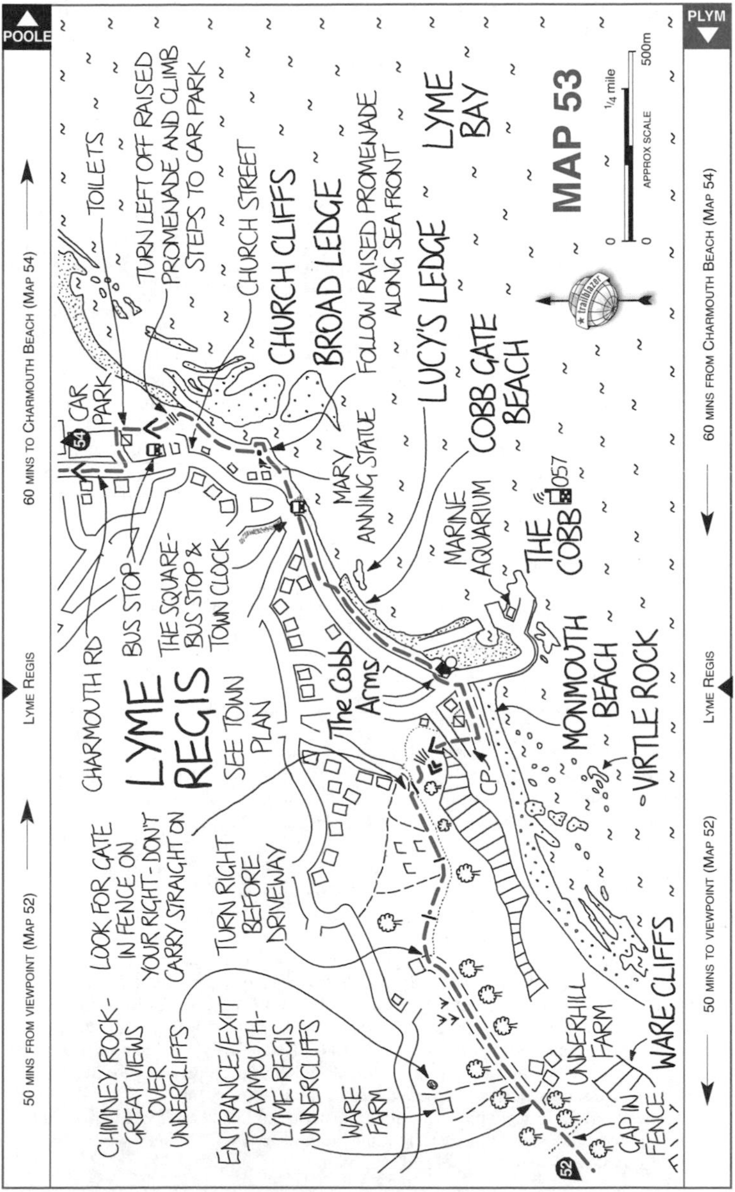

POOLE

PLYM

50 MINS FROM VIEWPOINT (MAP 52)

LYME REGIS

60 MINS TO CHARMOUTH BEACH (MAP 54)

TOILETS

TURN LEFT OFF RAISED PROMENADE AND CLIMB STEPS TO CAR PARK

CHURCH STREET

CHURCH CLIFFS

BROAD LEDGE

FOLLOW RAISED PROMENADE ALONG SEA FRONT

LUCY'S LEDGE

LYME BAY

MAP 53

1/4 mile   500m

0   APPROX SCALE   0

CAR PARK

MARY ANNING STATUE

COBB GATE BEACH

CHARMOUTH RD

BUS STOP

LYME REGIS

SEE TOWN PLAN

THE SQUARE - BUS STOP & TOWN CLOCK

MARINE AQUARIUM

THE COBB 057

The Cobb Arms

MONMOUTH BEACH

VIRTLE ROCK

CHIMNEY ROCK - GREAT VIEWS OVER UNDERCLIFFS

LOOK FOR GATE IN FENCE ON YOUR RIGHT - DON'T CARRY STRAIGHT ON

ENTRANCE/EXIT TO AXMOUTH - LYME REGIS UNDERCLIFFS

TURN RIGHT BEFORE DRIVEWAY

CP

WARE FARM

UNDERHILL FARM

GAP IN FENCE

WARE CLIFFS

52

50 MINS TO VIEWPOINT (MAP 52)

LYME REGIS

60 MINS FROM CHARMOUTH BEACH (MAP 54)

(cont'd from p220) At **Pinhay Cliff** things get a little more civilised as you join a sealed track; but the moment is brief and soon the wilds embrace you once more. From the viewpoint below Pinhay Cliff, Portland Bill can be seen as – on occasion – can peregrine falcons.

Continuing on, and having left the convoluted pathways near **Underhill Farm** (Map 53), you eventually arrive at **Ware Cliffs**, from where a wide grass path is followed that leads, eventually, to **The Cobb** – Lyme Regis's harbour.

LYME REGIS

Following the granting of a royal charter by King Edward I in 1284, the port-town that had previously simply been known as Lyme added the term 'Regis' in celebration ('regis' merely signifying that it has some sort of royal connection or endorsement). 'The Pearl of Dorset', as Lyme likes to be known, sits just inside the county border and has all that the walker could desire including several sights and attractions.

The town's main landmark is its harbour-wall, **The Cobb**, built in a curved shape in the 13th century to protect the resident boats. It famously features in Jane Austen's *Persuasion* and the book (and, subsequently, film) of John Fowles' *The French Lieutenant's Woman*. Austen and the crooked harbour aside, what Lyme Regis is best known for is fossils, with famed local palaeontologist Mary Anning making numerous discoveries of great importance hereabouts in the early 19th century (see box pp226-7).

Boosted by its £1.5m Mary Anning Wing extension in 2017, **Lyme Regis Museum** (☎ 01297-443370, 🖥 lymeregis museum.co.uk; Mar-end Oct Tue-Sat 10am-5pm, Sun 10am-4pm; £6.95) is now more modern and more accessible than ever. The museum, which organises expert-led **fossil walks** most days (see website for schedules), is built on the site of Anning's birthplace and includes exhibits and displays explaining the local geological and paleontological finds. The town celebrates Mary Anning Day in May each year when there are talks and displays of recently discovered fossils. Her grave, within the grounds of **St Michael the Archangel Church** (to the left of the church as you

---

❑ THE LASSIE OF LYME REGIS

Most people are familiar with Lassie, the collie dog who, in a succession of hugely popular films and TV series from the '40s right up to the '70s (and there was even a remake as recently as 2006), saved various hapless humans from the bottom of wells/cliff-faces/disused mine shafts, usually by barking at her owner who, somehow, managed to understand exactly what the problem was and help Lassie to effect a rescue. What is less well-known, however, is that the fictional bitch who first appeared in a novel in 1940 called *Lassie Come Home* by Eric Knight, was based on a real-life rough-haired crossbreed whose owner was the landlord of the Pilot Boat Inn in Lyme Regis. Though the breed may have been different, the heroic qualities that made the fictional Lassie so endearing were very much in evidence. According to popular legend, in the First World War the Royal Navy battleship *HMS Formidable* was struck by a torpedo off the coast of South Devon with the loss of over 300 men. One of the life rafts was eventually washed up on the coast off Lyme Regis. Having been brought ashore, it was found that everybody within had seemingly perished too, and the corpses of the sailors were laid on the tables of the Pilot Boat Inn.

Lassie, curious to see what was going on, started to lick at the feet of one of the cadavers – and the landlord noticed that the body responded! The man was revived, his life was saved – and thus a legend was born.

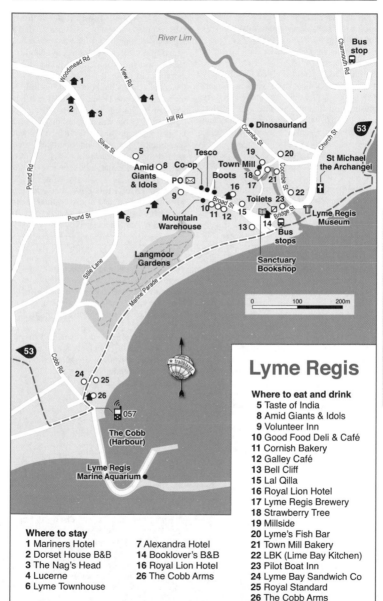

Lyme Regis

Where to eat and drink

5 Taste of India
8 Amid Giants & Idols
9 Volunteer Inn
10 Good Food Deli & Café
11 Cornish Bakery
12 Galley Café
13 Bell Cliff
15 Lal Qilla
16 Royal Lion Hotel
17 Lyme Regis Brewery
18 Strawberry Tree
19 Millside
20 Lyme's Fish Bar
21 Town Mill Bakery
22 LBK (Lime Bay Kitchen)
23 Pilot Boat Inn
24 Lyme Bay Sandwich Co
25 Royal Standard
26 The Cobb Arms

Where to stay

1 Mariners Hotel
2 Dorset House B&B
3 The Nag's Head
4 Lucerne
6 Lyme Townhouse

7 Alexandra Hotel
14 Booklover's B&B
16 Royal Lion Hotel
26 The Cobb Arms

face it), can also be visited. The church itself is of considerable antiquity, with its tower dating from Saxon times.

Fossils are also a major component of **Dinosaurland** (☎ 01297-443541, 🖥 dino saurland.co.uk; mid Feb-end Oct daily 10am-4pm, opening hours vary in winter; £6), a small, privately run natural history museum on Coombe St. The museum has more than 16,000 specimens on display and is housed in a Grade I listed building in what was once a church.

For more animated exhibits, **Lyme Regis Marine Aquarium** (☎ 07903 955300, 🖥 lymeregismarineaquarium.co .uk; mid Feb-end Oct daily 10am-4.30pm; £8) has starfish and sea scorpion as well as a display on the history of The Cobb on which it is situated.

Lyme Regis's **Town Mill** (🖥 town mill.org.uk; summer galleries daily 10.30am-4.30pm, miller-guided tours 11am-4pm subject to volunteer availability, check website for winter hours; free entrance but £8 for a guided tour), just off the main strip at the bottom of the hill, is mentioned in the Domesday Book (1086) and can be visited. The water mill closed down in 1926 but was restored in 2001 and is once again producing flour for the local community. The cobbled courtyard area around the mill is pleasant to visit, with a tearoom, a restaurant, a bakery and even a local brewery.

Both **Lyme Regis Fossil Festival** (see p14; mostly free) and a jazz festival, **Jazz Jurassica**, (see p14) are held here in April/May and June respectively.

❏ MARY ANNING AND THE FOSSIL COAST

Born in Lyme Regis in 1799, Mary Anning rose from a poor and uneducated background to become one of the world's leading and most revered fossil collectors and palaeontologists. She was introduced to fossil-hunting by her father, who sold his locally collected curios to tourists to supplement his income as a cabinetmaker, but his early death in 1810 at the age of 44 forced Mary and the rest of her large family to continue his work just to put food on their plates.

Mary's extraordinary ability to make significant discoveries, however, and her increasing knowledge on the subject coincided with the 19th-century's fledgling obsession with geology and evolution. In fact, Charles Darwin was a student of one of her earliest customers and some of her discoveries assisted in proving the extinction of some species – an idea previously given little credence as it suggested that God's Creation was somehow imperfect.

Mary collected her fossils along the coastal cliffs that surround Lyme Bay and some of her finds remain some of the most significant in the palaeontological field. She made the first of several important discoveries with her brother Joseph

Ichthyosaurus

in 1811 at the tender age of 12, unearthing a 17ft-long **ichthyosaurus** ('fish lizard') under the cliffs between Lyme and Charmouth. The family sold it for £23 and it was soon exhibited in London, the skull remaining the property of the Natural History Museum to this day. Down the years, Anning's reputation grew with each spectacu-

Plesiosaurus

lar new find: in 1823 she discovered a complete **plesiosaurus** ('near lizard') and in 1828 a pterodactyl skeleton, the first of its type to be found outside Germany. By the age of 27 she had opened Anning's Fossil Depot in which she exhibited and sold her finds.

Services

There's no tourist office but ⌨ www.visit-dorset.com/lyme-regis is worth a look.

For amenities, most things are at the top of Broad St including the **post office** (Mon-Fri 9am-5pm, Sat 9am-1pm), Co-op (daily 7am-10pm) and Tesco Express (daily 7am-11pm) **supermarkets** and a branch of Boots the **Chemist** (Mon-Fri 9am-1pm & 2-5.30pm, Sat to 5pm). There are a couple of **banks** with **ATMs** on Broad St. The street also plays host to Sanctuary (☎ 01297-445815, ⌨ lyme-regis.com; daily 10.30am-5.30pm), a second-hand **bookshop** that is full of character. For **trekking gear** there's a branch of Mountain Warehouse (Mon-Thur 9am-5pm, Fri & Sat to 5.30pm, Sun 10am-4pm).

Transport

[See also pp53-5] The most useful **bus** services throughout the Dorset section of the coast path are First's X51 & X53 (both Axminster to Weymouth) as they stop at numerous locations useful to walkers, including of course Lyme Regis. Another service calling here is Axe Valley's 378 to Seaton.

Where to stay

Although it's not possible to camp within Lyme Regis itself, *Wood Farm Holiday Park* (Map 54; ☎ 01297-560697, ⌨ park holidays.com; pitch £8.50-15 plus £5-10 per adult; 🐾; WI-FI £3 for two hours; Easter to end Oct) is only a short distance off the path (though approximately two miles from

Visiting geologists from all over Europe and America flocked to the shop. Unfortunately, the great social inequality of the time meant that a woman of her background was never going to be given the plaudits she deserved; indeed, many of her finds were credited to (male) palaeontologists who had purchased the items from her. However, in 2010 she was included in a list of the 10 British women to have most influenced the history of science and she is also thought to have been the inspiration for the tongue twister 'She sells seashells on the seashore'.

Mary is buried with her brother Joseph in the grounds of St Michael the Archangel Church (p224). Visitors sometimes leave fossils beside her gravestone.

Fossil hunting today Although a few ichthyosaur skeletons are still discovered each year, it seems rather unlikely that you will find one whilst strolling along the coastal path. However, the Jurassic coast is still a treasure trove for fossil-hunters and there are many great sites for hunting and collecting along the way. Most accessible are the beaches at Seatown and Charmouth but there are several other great spots including Church Cliffs (accessed from Lyme Regis harbour), Thorncombe Beacon, Burton Bradstock, Kimmeridge Bay and Eype. Note that **you must always be wary of the tides**. You should also always **be aware of the stability of any cliffs and do your hunting from the beach**; do not hammer into the cliffs themselves. (Anning herself lost her faithful dog Tray in a landslip in 1833.)

The most common finds are **ammonites** – the spiral-shaped shells of extinct marine molluscs (some of which can be up to a metre in diameter) – and **belemnites** – once called 'Devil's thunderbolts' due to their shape but in reality part of an internal shell in what was a squid-like animal. Occasionally hunters do discover more significant finds including the brown or black bones of an extinct marine reptile.

A good website to consult, particularly if you want to know where to look and whether there is any specific safety advice, is ⌨ ukfossils.co.uk; you can also pick up free pamphlets in local tourist offices. Charmouth Heritage Coast Centre (see p230), Lyme Regis Museum (see p224) and the museum at Kimmeridge (The Etches Collection, see p294) also have good displays on the fossils unearthed nearby.

Lyme Regis, between the town and Charmouth). There is a good *café* (daily 9am-6.30pm; WI-FI free for 15 mins) and a well-stocked **shop** (daily 8.30am-7pm) on site, as well as an indoor swimming **pool** (£2.50; daily 10am-7pm).

A night above one of the local **pubs**, all of which are dog-friendly, is also an option. The first you arrive at on your way into town is *The Cobb Arms* (☎ 01297-443242, 🖳 thecobbarms.co.uk; 2D/1T; ☞; WI-FI; 🐾; from £77.50pp, sgl occ room rate), Marine Parade, which also serves food (see Where to eat). However, note that a cooked breakfast isn't available before 9am though they can provide cereal and other foods earlier.

Meanwhile, high up on Silver St and at the back of the town is *The Nag's Head* (☎ 01297-442312, 🖳 www.nagsheadlymereg is.com; 1S/1T/4D; WI-FI; £57.50-60pp, sgl occ room rate), No 32, but they don't offer breakfast. There is live music most Saturday nights and if there's an event on Sky or BT Sports that brings in a crowd.

Booklover's B&B (☎ 01297-445815 or ☎ 01297-443653, 🖳 bookloversbb.co .uk; 2D; ☞; WI-FI; from £30pp, sgl occ £45-60) sits above The Sanctuary **bookshop** (see p227) and the rooms – not en suite but with private bathrooms – are suitably book-lined. It's a smashing, characterful 300-year-old Grade 2 listed place run by a smashing, characterful couple, and is located right in the heart of the action at the bottom of Broad St.

Others that are also close to the amenities can be found on Pound St, including the swish *Lyme Townhouse* (☎ 01929-400252, 🖳 www.lyme-townhouse.co.uk; 7D; WI-FI; £60-92.50pp, sgl occ room rate), at No 8.

Further uphill, though still within a short stroll of the centre, are: *Lucerne* (☎ 01297-443752, 🖳 www.lucernelyme.co .uk; 1S/2D/1D or T; WI-FI; £41-60pp, sgl from £80, sgl occ rates on request) on View Rd, but they only accept bookings for two-night stays; the very smart *Dorset House B&B* (☎ 01297-442055, 🖳 dorsethouse lyme.com; 2D/2D or T/1Tr; WI-FI; from £62.50pp, sgl occ £115) is at the junction of Silver St and Pound Rd.

Those wishing to add a little style to their stay may like to opt to go a **hotel**. Centrally located and hard to miss as you walk up Broad St is *Royal Lion Hotel* (☎ 01297-445622, 🖳 royallionhotel.com; 29D or T; ☞; WI-FI temperamental; B&B £85-125pp, sgl occ room rate); this old coaching inn, built in 1601 and now part of the Hall & Woodhouse chain, is so regal it even has a swimming pool!

Nearby is upmarket *Alexandra Hotel* (☎ 01297-442010, 🖳 hotelalexandra.co.uk; 1S/3D/19D or T; ☞; WI-FI; £105-152.50pp, sgl from £100, sgl occ room rate), while further up the hill, on Silver St, is *Mariners Hotel* (☎ 01297-442753, 🖳 hotellyme regis.co.uk; 1S/10D/2T/1Qd; ☞; WI-FI; 🐾; £65-80pp, sgl/sgl occ £130-150), which was also built in the 17th century as a coaching inn. The rates vary so look at their website for special offers.

Where to eat and drink

Always a pretty genteel and civilised place, over the past couple of decades Lyme Regis has also become rather trendy and sophisticated. As a result, the town now boasts several cute cafés, some good delis for takeaway food and a wide variety of cuisines offering food from all over the world.

Cafés One of the most popular cafés is *Town Mill Bakery* (☎ 01297-444754, 🖳 townmillbakery.co.uk; WI-FI; summer Thur-Mon 8.30am-3pm, closes earlier in winter). It's an informal, atmospheric, family-friendly place where customers sit and are served at long wooden tables and there is no booking. The food is excellent and sourced locally wherever possible.

Even closer to The Town Mill is *Strawberry Tree* (☎ 01297-445757, 🖳 strawberry-tree.co,uk; **fb**; 🐾 daytime only; Thur-Mon noon-3pm & 6-9.30pm), which serves tapas and coffee and cakes during the day and has a tapas menu in the evening. It faces Lyme Regis Brewery (see box p25) from across a cobbled courtyard.

Another popular spot is *Galley Café* (☎ 01297-445008, 🖳 galleycafe.co.uk; WI-FI; 🐾; daily 9am-5pm), a comfortable, fully licensed café on Broad St.

Also dog-friendly is *Bell Cliff* (☎ 01297-442459; **fb**; 🐾; daily 9am-5pm), a pleasant place with some lovely outdoor seating. For what is widely regarded as the best coffee, however, you need to continue up the slope to 59 Silver St and *Amid Giants & Idols* (☎ 07898-074305; **fb** @giantsandidols; WI-FI; 🐾; Tue-Sat 10am-4pm, Sun to 3pm, Nov-end Feb closed Mon & Thur), which also serves lovely cakes and sandwiches.

Pubs *Royal Lion Hotel* (see Where to stay; food daily noon-8.30pm) exudes venerability with its wood-panelled walls, oak beams and log fire.

The Volunteer Inn (☎ 01297-442214, 🖥 thevolunteerlymeregis.com; WI-FI; 🐾; food Wed-Sat noon-2.30pm & 6-8.30pm, Sun noon-2.30pm) is a cracking Irish pub, with a good selection of real ales and ciders served alongside their Guinness. This is a drinkers' pub, but they do still serve good food, all pub classics (£12.50-23.50) including locally caught seafood and a Sunday roast.

Championing locally brewed ales are *Lyme Regis Brewery* (see box p25; ☎ 01297-444354, 🖥 lymeregisbrewery.com; daily 11am-10pm; WI-FI; 🐾; no food), a small brewery-bar beside The Town Mill.

Drinkers have a few choices down at The Cobb too. *The Cobb Arms* (see Where to stay; food daily noon-3pm & 5-9pm) has a good menu starting at £13.50 for honey-glazed ham & eggs; fish & chips (£16.50) are always on the menu.

Nearby, *Royal Standard* (☎ 01297-442637, 🖥 www.theroyalstandardlyme regis.co.uk; WI-FI; 🐾; food Mon-Fri noon-2.45pm & 5.30-9pm, Sat & Sun noon-9pm) is a 400-year-old-plus establishment with a relaxed attitude to dogs and a menu (mains mostly £15-17) that includes mussels, scampi, steaks and burgers.

Restaurants Lyme Regis also boasts some decent restaurants.

Millside (☎ 01297-445999, 🖥 themill side.co.uk; summer Tue-Sat coffee 10.30am-noon, food noon-2pm & 6-8pm, winter days/hours variable) makes a fine choice and is a great place to sit outside on a sunny afternoon with a beer. The evening menu may include pea & mint ravioli (£19.75) and a fillet of turbot in seaweed butter for £33.

For a sit-down Indian meal, try *Taste of India* (☎ 01297-444224, 🖥 tasteofindia lyme.co.uk; Wed-Mon noon-2pm & 5.30-11pm), at the top of Broad St. It's BYO (bring-your-own alcohol) so works out cheaper than most.

Down a little further, the centrally located *Pilot Boat* (☎ 01297-443157, 🖥 thepilotboat.co.uk; food daily 9am-8pm) is the original home of Lassie the wonder dog (see box p224). The original inn has been thoroughly renovated inside and out and is now a rather fancy but family-friendly restaurant with a large menu including breakfasts, fish dishes, pizzas, pasta and burgers. The handpicked local crab sandwich is expensive (£14) but lovely.

Delis and takeaways On Broad St is the excellent *Good Food Deli & Café* (🖥 www.thegoodfoodcafe.co.uk; Mon-Sat 9am-5pm, Sun 10am-4pm) with great-value breakfasts, pastries and baguettes, as well as loads of lunch-box fillers.

Nearby, *Cornish Bakery* (☎ 01297-445885, 🖥 thecornishbakery.com; daily 8am-6pm) does excellent pasties (£4.80), as you'd expect, but also bakes good pastries and serves great coffee too.

For a takeaway supper there's an Indian, *Lal Qilla* (☎ 01297-442505, 🖥 lal qillalyme.co.uk; daily noon-2pm & 6-9pm), which also has an excellent BYO restaurant, and *Lyme's Fish Bar* (🖥 www.lymesfishbar.com; summer Mon-Thur 10.30am-2.30pm & 4.30-9pm, Fri to 9.30pm, Sat & Sun 10.30am-9pm, winter variable), the best of several chippies in town.

Down on The Cobb, *Lyme Bay Sandwich Co* (☎ 01297-444299; **fb**; Easter-Oct Thur-Tue 11am-3.30pm) does a filling baguette for £4.95.

LYME REGIS TO SEATOWN (& CHIDEOCK)   [MAPS 53-56]

Very different from yesterday – but just as dramatic – today's **7¼-mile (11.75km; 3hrs)** stage has much to offer including some wonderful cliff-top walking and an ascent to the highest point of the UK's southern coast: Golden Cap (191m/627ft).

Landslides just after Lyme Regis have forced the official trail to divert inland, only rejoining the coast at Charmouth (which is also the last place to pick up any supplies that you may need). From there you hug the cliffs, the scenery as mesmerising as the gradients are tough, with the views from the summit of Golden Cap and the long descent from it rounding off a fantastic day's walk. Seatown has limited accommodation so it may be worth planning for a night in Chideock, three-quarters of a mile inland.

Note that it is possible to walk to Charmouth from Lyme Regis straight along the beach, which may appeal to fossil hunters. However, this is not the official route and a **tide-timetable must be closely consulted** before embarking on such an adventure. It is also imperative not to walk too close to the cliffs due to the danger of falling rocks.

The route

Continue from the centre of Lyme Regis along the seawall past the theatre, museum and **statue of Mary Anning**, until you come to a flight of steps (from where you get a great view of the Black Ven landslip). Follow these steps uphill to Charmouth Road car park, and cross the car park to reach Charmouth Rd. Turn right (north), and walk past Lyme Regis Football Club. Just beyond the club a gate on the right takes you into the first of a series of fields, on the edge of **Timber Hill,** that you cut across to arrive at a patch of woodland.

Continue through the woods, climbing steeply upwards to a diversion (caused by further landslips). The path now goes left to continue amongst the trees, descending leisurely to a B-road where you turn right to pass the entrance to Lyme Regis Golf Club, before arriving at the A3052. This road you desert to follow the **white markers** through the golf course and the rhododendron wood at **Fern Hill**; a path that eventually leads you down Old Lyme Hill to the outskirts of Charmouth.

Turn right down **Higher Sea Lane**, which eventually arrives at **Charmouth Beach** and **Charmouth Heritage Coast Centre** (see below). If camping, however, don't take the path through the golf course but instead keep on the road, where *Wood Farm Holiday Park* (see p227) is signed to your left.

CHARMOUTH   [map p232]

For those not wanting a night in Lyme Regis, the village of Charmouth has the necessary amenities to make a stop possible and also provides an ample head-start for those wishing to get to Seatown (not to be confused with Seaton), or beyond, the next day.

The centre of interest for tourists in the village – and on the coast path – is the excellent **Charmouth Heritage Coast Centre** (☎ 01297-560772, 🖳 charmouth .org; Apr-Oct daily 10.30am-4.30pm, winter hours variable, see website for details), which displays recent fossil finds from

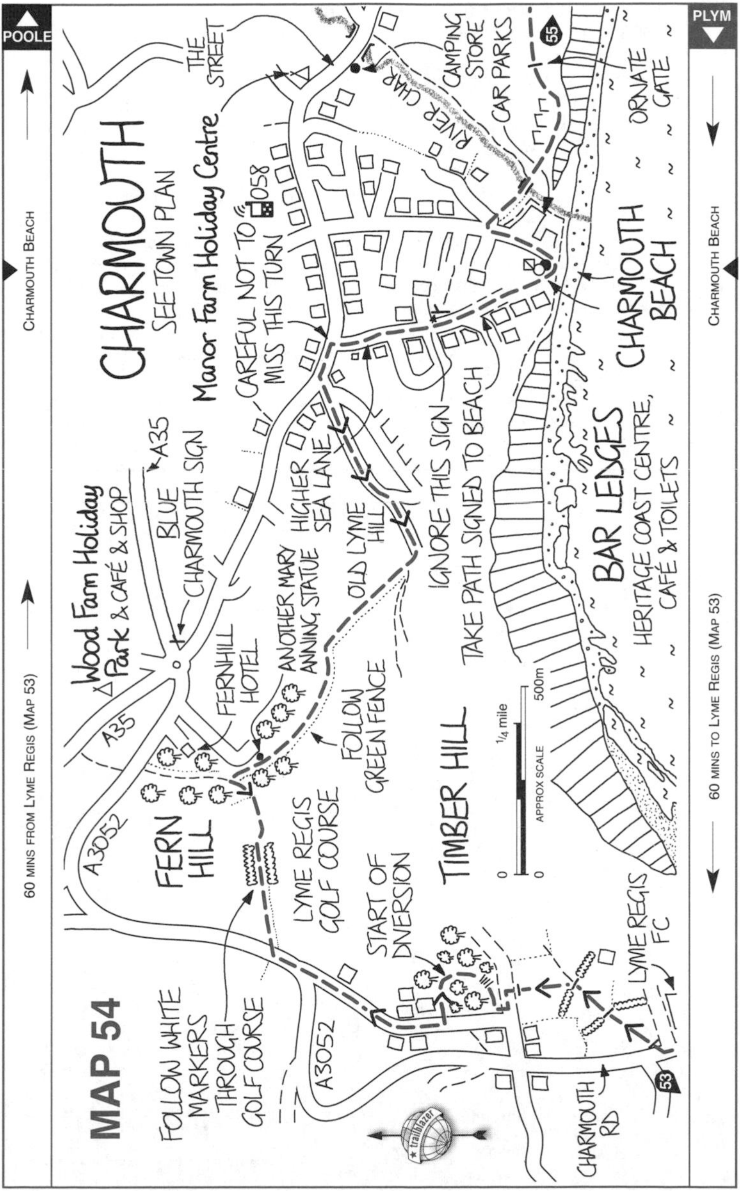
MAP 54
POOLE
PLYM
60 mins from Lyme Regis (Map 53)
Charmouth Beach
60 mins to Lyme Regis (Map 53)
Charmouth Beach
FOLLOW WHITE MARKERS THROUGH GOLF COURSE
A3052
A3052
FERN HILL
LYME REGIS GOLF COURSE
START OF DIVERSION
TIMBER HILL
LYME REGIS FC
CHARMOUTH RD
53
Wood Farm Holiday Park & CAFÉ & SHOP
A35
A35
BLUE CHARMOUTH SIGN
FERNHILL HOTEL
ANOTHER MARY ANNING STATUE
FOLLOW GREEN FENCE
HIGHER SEA LANE
OLD LYME HILL
IGNORE THIS SIGN
TAKE PATH SIGNED TO BEACH
BAR LEDGES
HERITAGE COAST CENTRE, CAFÉ & TOILETS
CHARMOUTH BEACH
CHARMOUTH
SEE TOWN PLAN
Manor Farm Holiday Centre
CAREFUL NOT TO MISS THIS TURN
058
THE STREET
RIVER CHAR
CAMPING STORE
CAR PARKS
ORNATE GATE
55
APPROX SCALE
0
1/4 mile
0
500m
trailblazer

ROUTE GUIDE AND MAPS

local beaches and organises 'fossil' and rockpooling events. It also has a *café* (Beach Café; see p234).

Most **services** can be found on The Street, the main road running along the back of Charmouth. **Provisions** are available from Charmouth Stores (Mon-Sat 7am-9pm, Sun 8am-9pm), and there is also a **pharmacy** (Mon-Fri 9am-1pm & 2-5.30pm, Sat 9am-1pm). You can get camping equipment from a large **camping store** (Map 54; ☎ 01297-560473, 🖳 www.dorsetleisurecen tre.co.uk; generally Mon-Sat 9.30am-5pm, Sun 10am-4pm but best to check) as you leave the village on The Street.

Transport

[See pp53-5] First's X51 and X53 (Axminster to Weymouth) **bus services** stop here.

Where to stay

As well as nearby Wood Farm Holiday Park (see p227), **campers** can pitch tents at ***Manor Farm Holiday Centre*** (☎ 01297-560226, 🖳 manorfarmholidaycentre.co.uk; WI-FI (additional charge); 🐾; £20-36 per tent and up to two adults), a pricey, but well-equipped holiday park right on the coast path and accessed from The Street.

There are also a few **B&Bs** scattered about the village although finding one willing to do a one-night stop, particularly during peak times, can be an issue.

Close to the beach, in Hammonds Mead, which is off Lower Sea Lane, you'll find ***The Beach Rooms*** (☎ 07890-629117, ☎ 01297-560030, 🖳 thebeachrooms.co.uk; 1Qd; ☞; WI-FI; room only from £70pp, sgl occ room rate); it offers a self-contained double suite with its own living room and

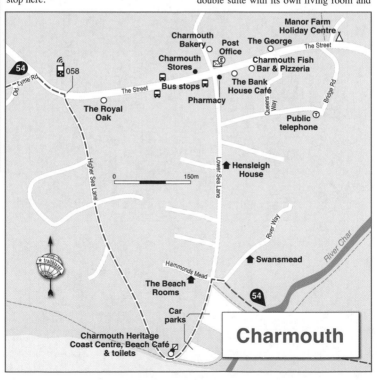

Charmouth

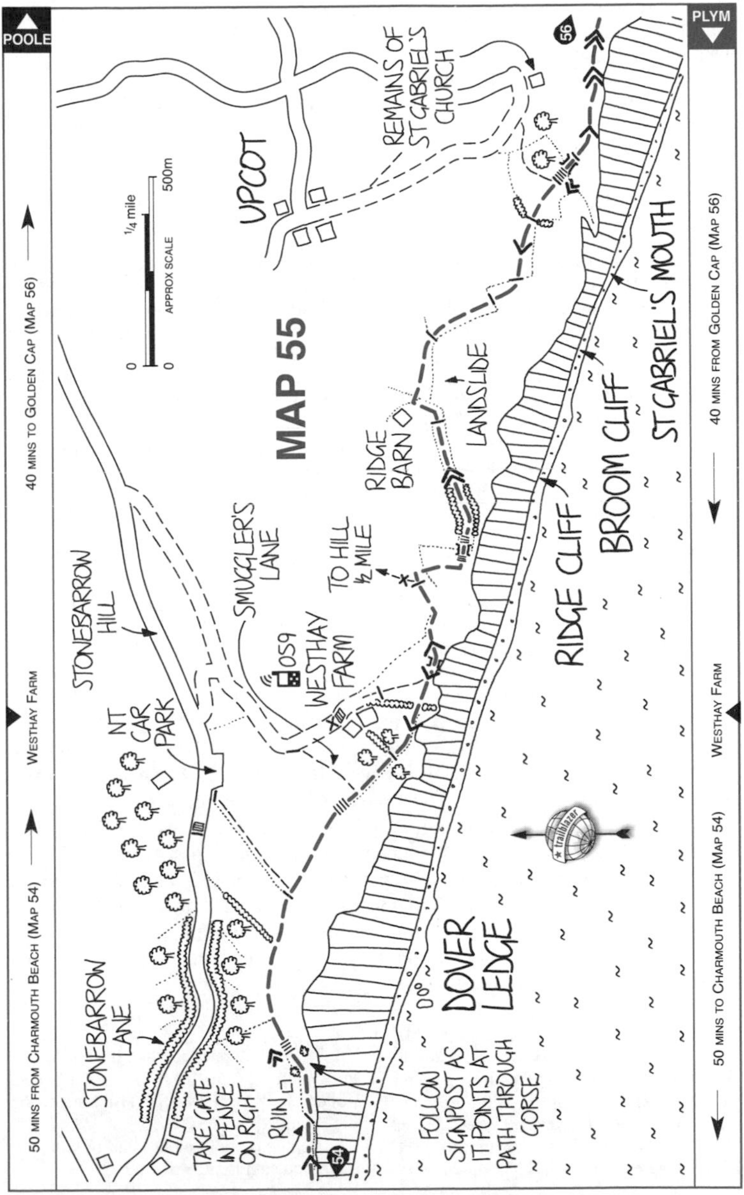

POOLE

50 MINS FROM CHARMOUTH BEACH (MAP 54) →

WESTHAY FARM ►

40 MINS TO GOLDEN CAP (MAP 56) →

STONEBARROW LANE

TAKE GATE IN FENCE ON RIGHT

RUIN

FOLLOW SIGNPOSTS AS IT POINTS AT PATH THROUGH GORSE

DOVER LEDGE

NT CAR PARK

STONEBARROW HILL

SMUGGLER'S LANE

TO HILL ½ MILE

WESTHAY FARM

OS9

MAP 55

¼ mile

500m

0   0
APPROX SCALE

RIDGE CLIFF

BROOM CLIFF

ST GABRIEL'S MOUTH

RIDGE BARN

LANDSLIDE

UPCOT

REMAINS OF ST GABRIEL'S CHURCH

56

PLYM ▼

50 MINS TO CHARMOUTH BEACH (MAP 54) ←

WESTHAY FARM ◄

40 MINS FROM GOLDEN CAP (MAP 56) ←

ROUTE GUIDE AND MAPS

Charmouth (*cont'd*) an extra double sofa bed. However, they only accept stays of a minimum two nights.

Also off Lower Sea Lane, but in the opposite direction along River Way, is *Swansmead* (☎ 01297-560465, 🖳 swansmead.co.uk; 1Qd; ➘; WI-FI; July-end Aug; from £50pp, sgl occ £81). There is a great view from the airy and clean room. However, they now accept stays for a minimum of two nights.

Further up Lower Sea Lane is *Hensleigh House* (☎ 01297-560830, 🖳 www.hensleighhouse.co.uk; 1S/2T/3D/ 2Qd; WI-FI; from £61.50pp, sgl £95, sgl occ £113).

Where to eat and drink

Charmouth Bakery (☎ 01297-560213; **fb**; their days/hours vary a lot so check on **fb** or Google before going), on a lane off The Street, is worth popping into if you're after lunchbox fillers. There's been a bakery on this site since the 1830s and they do some great pastries as well as sandwiches and takeaway tea and coffee.

For a proper sit-down café, *The Bank House* (☎ 01297-561600; **fb**; WI-FI; Mon, Tue, Thur & Fri 10am-3pm, Sat & Sun from 9am), on The Street, is a family-run

place (with some roadside patio seating) serving breakfast, hot and cold food and drinks, cakes and cream teas. As with the bakery, however, the café is away from both the sea and, now the SWCP has been rerouted back to the cliffs, the path too. If you're missing the roar of the tide there's also *Beach Café* (end Mar to end Oct Fri-Mon 10am-4pm, hours may vary according to the weather) down at Charmouth Heritage Coast Centre.

Back away from the coast, next door to The Bank House, fish 'n' chips are available at *Charmouth Fish Bar & Pizzeria* (☎ 01297-560220, 🖳 charmouthfishbar.co.uk; **fb**; school holidays daily noon-2pm & 5-9pm, summer generally Tue 5-9pm, Wed-Sat noon-2pm & 5-9pm but days/hours vary so check before going). They also have patio seating out front and do takeaways.

For *pub grub* head to *The George* (☎ 01297-560280, 🖳 thegeorgecharmouth .com; WI-FI; 🐾 on lead; food Tue-Sun noon-2pm & 6-9pm) or *The Royal Oak* (☎ 01297-560277, 🖳 www.royaloakcharmouth.co.uk; WI-FI; 🐾 lower bar; food Mon & Wed-Sat noon-2pm & 5-8pm, Sun 4-7pm), both of which have a selection of real ales on tap.

From Charmouth Heritage Coast Centre, with Portland Bill in the distance – you can clearly make out the path that leads off up the next cliff. It's a fairly strenuous trail and the path undulates dramatically, before you ascend the mighty **Broom Cliff**, with the ruins of 13th-century **St Gabriel's Church** (which lies on The Monarch's Way – see p39) lying to your left.

Back on the path, a few hundred calf-popping paces further will bring you atop that star of book covers and photoshoots, **Golden Cap** (191m/627ft) – the south coast's highest point. With Portland Bill to the east and the cliffs of Devon to your west, you now descend. Should you do this at dusk, the waning sun will turn the eastward cliffs a brilliant orange – it's just marvellous.

A brief dalliance with both woods and farmland eventually brings you to a road that bends down to **Seatown**.

SEATOWN   [Map 56]

Regarded as one of Dorset's prime fossil-collecting spots, Seatown has little to offer save for a pub, a campsite and some precious tranquillity. However, Chideock (see p236) is only a 15- to 20-minute stroll inland, where there is slightly more on offer.

To walk there either take the bridleway, Mill Lane, to the east of Golden Cap Holiday Park, or follow Sea Hill Lane to the site's west.

Details on both places can be found at 🖳 chideockandseatown.co.uk.

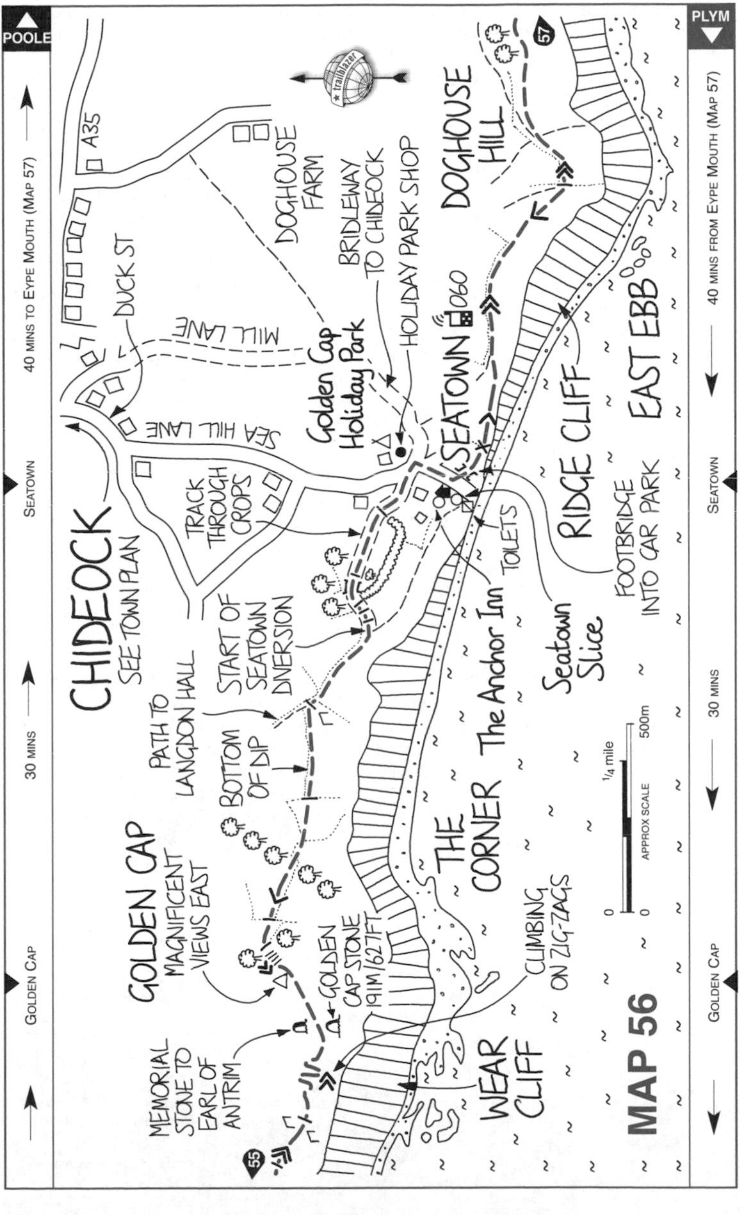

POOLE

PLYM

40 MINS TO EYPE MOUTH (MAP 57)

A35

Trailblazer

DUCK ST

DOGHOUSE FARM

BRIDLEWAY TO CHIDEOCK

HOLIDAY PARK SHOP

DOGHOUSE HILL

MILL LANE

SEA HILL LANE

Golden Cap Holiday Park

40 MINS FROM EYPE MOUTH (MAP 57)

57

CHIDEOCK
SEE TOWN PLAN

TRACK THROUGH CROPS

PATH TO LANGDON HALL

START OF SEATOWN DIVERSION

SEATOWN 060

EAST EBB

30 MINS

Seatown

RIDGE CLIFF

BOTTOM OF DIP

The Anchor Inn

TOILETS

Seatown Slice

FOOTBRIDGE INTO CAR PARK

GOLDEN CAP
MAGNIFICENT VIEWS EAST

GOLDEN CAP STONE
191M/627FT

THE CORNER

30 MINS

1/4 mile

500m

0

0

APPROX SCALE

SEATOWN

MEMORIAL STONE TO EARL OF ANTRIM

CLIMBING ON ZIG-ZAGS

WEAR CLIFF

GOLDEN CAP

55

MAP 56

GOLDEN CAP

ROUTE GUIDE AND MAPS

Campers can find accommodation at *Golden Cap Holiday Park* (☎ 01308-426947, 🖳 wdlh.co.uk/holiday-parks/golden-cap; £26-40 per pitch with electricity for up to two adults, mid July-end Aug grass pitch £25-27; WI-FI but not free; 🐾; camping mid Mar-Oct), right by the beach. It has a **shop** (summer daily 9am-5pm) that is well stocked and sells camping gas as well as hot drinks, snacks and even takeaway pizza. The showers are tremendous. They don't have that many grass pitches for most of the year and can sometimes fill up (be sure to call ahead to check they have space), but they open up a large camping field in late July and August to meet the extra demand. Note that like most of the B&Bs round here, they don't allow you to book for less than two nights – but contact them a day or two in advance and they may have availability.

For **B&B** and **food**, you're even closer to the beach at *The Anchor Inn* (☎ 01297-489215, 🖳 theanchorinnseatown.co.uk; WI-FI; 🐾 bar only; food daily noon-8.30pm), a lovely old smugglers' haunt with a great menu (mains £16-19) and a good selection of local ales. Note that between May and October they operate on a first come first served basis and accept card payment only. They have three very smart rooms (3D; 🛏; WI-FI; from £65pp, sgl occ room rate), but online bookings can only be for two nights (as that is what they prefer). However, if you call near the time they may be able to accept a single-night stay.

CHIDEOCK

Up in Chideock (pronounced Chidock) there's a well-stocked Spar **store** (daily 8am-6pm) which also has a **post office** (same hours).

For **buses**, First's X51 and X53 (see pp53-5) services stop here, connecting the village with places such as Lyme Regis, Abbotsbury and Weymouth.

Chideock has a couple of **B&Bs**: *Chideock House* (☎ 01297-489242, 🖳 chideockhouse.co.uk; 2D/1T; 🛏; WI-FI; 🐾; £47.50-50pp, sgl occ from £75), and the lovely *Rose Cottage* (☎ 01297-489994, 🖳 rosecottage-chideock.co.uk; 1T/1D; WI-FI; from £47.50pp, sgl occ £80), which accepts single-night stays.

For **food**, the two local pubs won't disappoint: Home to more than 150 clocks, *The Clock* (☎ 01297-489423, 🖳 clock chideock.co.uk; food daily noon-2.30pm & 6-9pm; WI-FI; 🐾 welcome in the bar) is a quirky, thatched 16th-century village freehouse that suffered a devastating fire in 2015 but has since reopened. They serve good-value pub grub (with regular and large portions) and have a selection of real ales.

Also thatched, *The George Inn* (☎ 01297-489419, 🖳 georgeinnchideock.co .uk; 🐾 on a lead and in the bar/on the terrace; WI-FI; food Wed-Mon noon-2.30pm & 6-8.15pm, Tue 6-8.15pm, Sun noon-2.30pm) is a more upmarket traditional Dorset pub, serving good-quality food (mains £14.50-23) as well as Palmers' ales. Thursday night is pizza night (from £11).

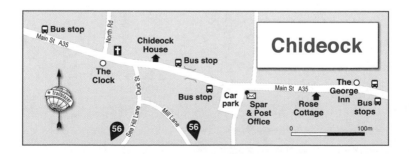

SEATOWN TO ABBOTSBURY [MAPS 56-62]

This is a stage of two halves: initially consisting of undulating cliff-top walking (with some steep climbs), this **12½-mile (20km; 4¼hrs)** stage passes through several small coastal hamlets on its way to Burton Freshwater and the outer extremities of Chesil Beach. From here, however, things get much flatter and easier as you pass by nature reserve, mere and common before turning inland to circle Chapel Hill and arrive at one of Dorset's many highlights: the village of Abbotsbury. Refreshments are available every couple of miles or so, as is accommodation should it become required.

(Note that those who are either running out of time to complete their trek, don't fancy walking through Weymouth, or just want a change of scenery from all this seaside, should consider taking the South Dorset Ridgeway. This leaves the main coast path at West Bexington; details can be found on pp247-50.)

The route
The first ascent of the day occurs on leaving Seatown and the climb up **Ridge Cliff**. This is quickly followed by an even more strenuous one which takes you up the interestingly named **Doghouse Hill**, where the path leads along the top of a ridge, traversing rolling cliffs until arriving at **Thorncombe Beacon**.

From the beacon the official path initially turns left and heads inland briefly. However, many people go straight down from the beacon as it is more direct. If you follow the official route you will see signs for *Downhouse Farm Garden Café* (☎ 01308-421232, 💻 downhousefarm.org; Mar-end Oct Thur-Sun and bank hol Mons 10am-5pm; 🐾, water bowl provided), a hidden gem that's only a five-minute detour from the path. They do breakfasts, sandwiches and delicious cream teas in a cosy garden courtyard. For accommodation, they also have two simple but comfortable **shepherd's huts** (1D; from £37.50pp, sgl occ rates on request) with a small double bed and a single solar-powered light, but no electricity. A shower and toilet are available behind the farmhouse. The rates do not include breakfast.

The official path turns back towards the cliffs at **Hope Corner**. There's a spring here, situated in a giant dip and surrounded by a stone wall. The path then descends to **Eype Mouth**.

EYPE MOUTH [Map 57, p239]
Situated in the dip between two cliffs ('Eype' meaning 'A Steep Place' in Old English) at the mouth of the River Eype, there are limited amenities for walkers here. **Boathouse Visitor Centre**, by the entrance to the car park, is unmanned (and rarely open) but it has some leaflets regarding local tourist attractions as well as panels with information about the geology and flora and fauna in the area.

Camping can be arranged just off Mount Lane at the friendly *Eype House*

Caravan & Camping Park (☎ 01308-426947, 💻 eypehouse.co.uk; £20-35 for tent and one/two hikers; WI-FI but not free; 🐾; campsite Easter to mid Oct). They have a *tea garden* and **shop** (both peak season daily 9am-4pm, rest of season hours variable also depending on the weather) stocking basic necessities (including camping gas) and serving cream teas, ice-creams and snacks. They also have a **log pod** which sleeps up to four people; bedding is not provided and there is a minimum two-night booking (£35-50 per night).

Hotel rooms can be had a little further up the lane at *Eype's Mouth Country Hotel* (☎ 01308-423300, 🖳 eypesmouthhotel.co .uk; 3S/10D/3T; 🛁; WI-FI; 🐾; £70-80pp, sgl/sgl occ from £102.50/127.50). Note that the hotel is unlikely to accept advance bookings for one-night stays at weekends between March and October but nearer the time it is worth calling. If going here it is nicest to walk along the path heading inland from the eastern side of the stream at Eype Mouth. The restaurant is for residents only save for the winter months (food daily noon-2.30pm & 6.30-8.30pm).

Crossing a stream by the beach, you again take off upwards to conquer **West Cliff** (another strenuous climb), at the top of which to the left is *Highlands End Holiday Park* (☎ 01308-426947, 🖳 wdlh.co.uk/holiday-parks/ highlands-end; pitch and up to two people £22-41; WI-FI but not free; 🐾; mid Mar-Oct). There is a **shop** (daily 9am-5pm) which stocks a good range of basic foods and has a **tourist information point**. There's also a restaurant, a bar and a leisure club with swimming pool (£4). All the pitches have electricity but at weekends in the peak season they open a field and charge from £20 for up to two in a tent.

The path then goes downhill to **West Bay** – an unprepossessing town that resembles, from this aspect, something out of the old Soviet Union. Continue towards it, however, and you'll find it is an amiable place with a decent harbour.

WEST BAY   [map p241]

At the furthest western point of Chesil Beach, West Bay (🖳 westbay.co.uk) is a working harbour but one that also thrives on the passing tourist trade, with several places to stay and eat. The town used to be known as Bridport Harbour and actually falls within the boundaries of Bridport, a couple of miles away. The arrival of the railway in Bridport caused the name change when, in an early example of rebranding, the harbour was renamed West Bay to make it sound more attractive to tourists.

Fans of classic television comedies may want to stand on the beach, remove all their clothes and walk into the sea in homage to the memorable opening scene of *The Life and Times of Reginald Perrin*, which was shot here. More recently scenes from the ITV drama *Broadchurch* were also filmed on the beach here and in parts of the town.

Services

Although there are more services in Bridport, a couple of miles up the road and a stop on both the X52 & X53 bus services, there is enough for most passing walkers here in West Bay, including a small supermarket: Nisa Local (Mon, Fri & Sat 8am-7pm, Tue-Thur & Sun to 6pm).

There is an **ATM** (£1.85 per transaction) on the wall by the entrance to West Bay Holiday Park.

Transport

[See pp53-5] First's X52 (Bridport to Wool station) & X53 (Axminster to Weymouth) **bus** services stop here.

Where to stay

Much of the accommodation in West Bay can be found on West Bay Rd, the lengthy thoroughfare which runs all the way to Bridport.

In July and August only **campers** are in luck as *Britt Valley Campground* (off map p241; ☎ 01308-897239, 🖳 brittvalley .co.uk; around £15 for a tent and one/two hikers inc use of shower; 🐾) occupies two of the local fields for eight weeks around the school summer holidays. Follow West Bay Rd out of town for about 300m, and the site will soon appear on your left.

One of the nearest **B&Bs** to the path is *The Durbeyfield* (☎ 07973 769432, 🖳 www.thedurbeyfield.co.uk; 1T/1D shared

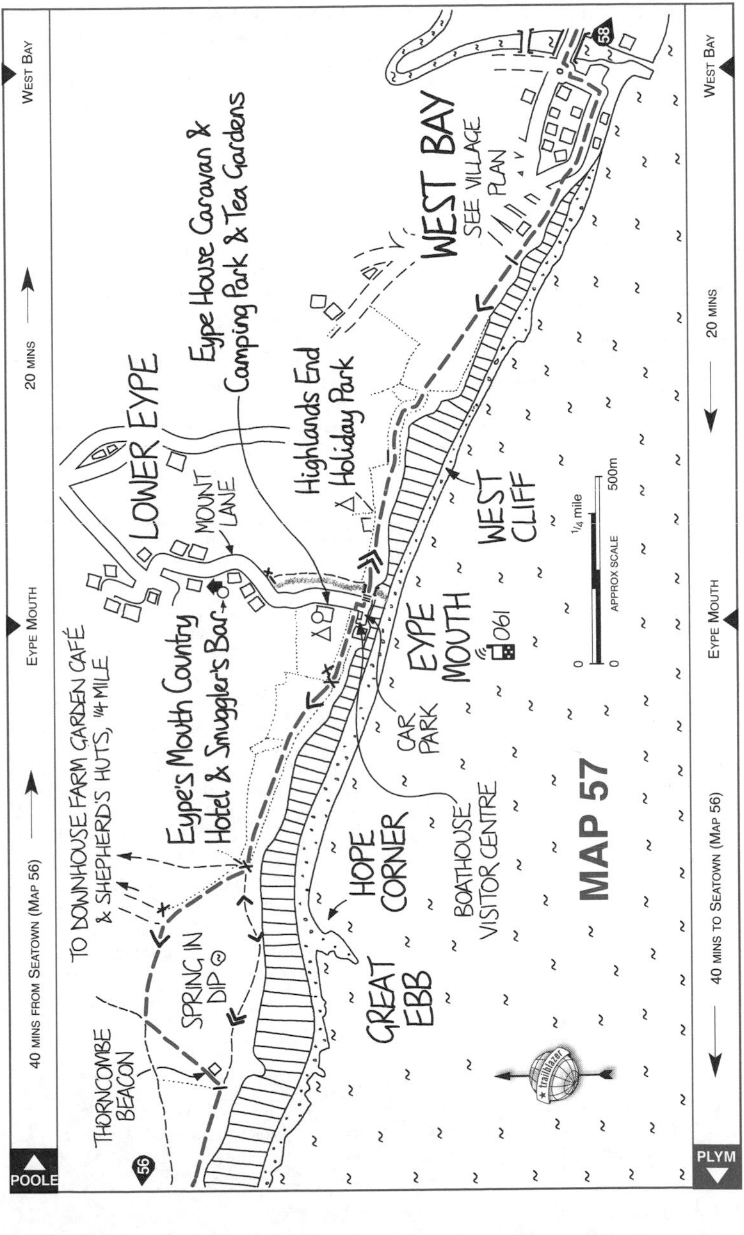

WEST BAY

20 MINS →

EYPE MOUTH

← 40 MINS FROM SEATOWN (MAP 56)

THORNCOMBE BEACON

56
POOLE

SPRING IN DIP

TO DOWNHOUSE FARM GARDEN CAFÉ & SHEPHERD'S HUTS, ¼-MILE

Eype's Mouth Country Hotel & Smuggler's Bar

MOUNT LANE

LOWER EYPE

Eype House Caravan & Camping Park & Tea Gardens

Highlands End Holiday Park

WEST BAY

SEE VILLAGE PLAN

58

GREAT EBB

HOPE CORNER

BOATHOUSE VISITOR CENTRE

CAR PARK

EYPE MOUTH

061

WEST CLIFF

MAP 57

¼ mile

APPROX SCALE

0   500m

WEST BAY

20 MINS →

EYPE MOUTH

40 MINS TO SEATOWN (MAP 56) →

PLYM

ROUTE GUIDE AND MAPS

facilities, 1T/3D/1Tr/1Qd; ♥; WI-FI; 🐕;
£47.50-67.50pp, sgl occ room rate), at 10
West Bay Rd. Happy to take one-night
bookings and with their own bar
(Quarterdeck; Thur-Sun only) where you
can eat a takeaway meal, this place could
hardly be more convenient.

On the other side of the harbour,
Heatherbell Cottage (☎ 07812 041377, 💻
heatherbellcottage.com; 3D; WI-FI; from
£50pp, sgl occ room rate), in Hill Close, is
also conveniently placed for the path and
can be reached from it. Alternatively walk
along Forty Foot Way past S&E (see Where
to eat) and turn right.

The other centrally located options are
rooms above a pub, **The George** (☎ 01308-
423191, 💻 georgewestbay.com; 4D/1Tr/
1Qd; ♥; WI-FI; from £63.25pp, sgl occ
£116.50), and in a hotel, **Bridport Arms
Hotel** (☎ 01308-422994, 💻 thebridport
arms.co.uk; 2T/8D/1Tr; ♥; WI-FI; 🐕;
£72.50-77.50pp, sgl occ £125), which is a
16th-century flower-fronted inn right on the
harbour with smart rooms. More upmarket
is **West Bay Hotel** (☎ 01308-422444, 💻
westbayhotel .co.uk; 1D/ 2Qd; WI-FI; 🐕;
£67.50-132.50pp), a Palmers pub that has
recently been renovated.

The remaining options are all strung
out along West Bay Rd. **Haddon House
Hotel** (☎ 01308-423626, 💻 hotelsbridport
.co.uk; 7D/6D or T; ♥; £65-86.25pp,
sgl occ £82-139) is the first place you come
to, just 100m or so out of town, and one of
the most charming and smartest places
you'll find. They will only accept advance
bookings for a single-night stay between
end October and March. Further along, at
No 117, **Eypeleaze** (☎ 01308-423363, 💻
eypeleaze.co.uk; 1D/1T; ♥; WI-FI; £40-
42pp, sgl occ rates on request) is willing to
accept one-night stops depending on other
bookings.

Where to eat and drink

Whatever you think of West Bay, you've
got to admit − you're not going to go hungry here! In addition to the established
eateries − of which there are many − the
harbour is dotted with **food stalls** selling
fish & chips, ice-cream and takeaway cof-
fees, especially in high season.

On the way into the village, on the
west side of the harbour, is the modern,
glass-fronted **Windy Corner Café** (☎
01308-459221, 💻 windycornercafe.co.uk;
WI-FI; 🐕; daily 9am-4pm), with reasonably
priced food and sea views. Round the corner from here is **S&E** (☎ 01308-427787;
Tue-Thur 5-8pm, Fri & Sat noon-2pm & 5-
8pm, winter hours variable), a decent local
chippy with both a restaurant and a takeaway. Between the two, **Catch of the Day**
(daily 8am till when it gets quiet) does a
huge Full English for a tenner but they specialise in fish.

Most of the best places to eat are on the
other side of the harbour, including several
good **cafés**: Right on the sand, **Watch
House Café** (☎ 01308-459330, 💻 watch
housecafe.co.uk; WI-FI; 🐕; Sun-Thur
10am-5pm Fri & Sat to 7pm), sister to both
Hive Beach Café and Club House (see
p244), has extensive outdoor seating and a
menu (breakfasts £7-13, lunch mains £14-
18) that includes numerous seafood options.

Inland slightly, is the tranquil **Sladers
Yard Art Café** (☎ 01308-459511, 💻 sladers
yard.wordpress.com; 🐕; Wed-Sun 10am-
4.30pm), which uses local produce and
organic ingredients as much as possible.
They offer sandwiches (from £10, rising to
£18 for the crab sandwich), salads and mains
such as chunky fish stew (£20). It occupies a
lovely space inside a small art gallery and
there's seating in the courtyard too.

Opposite, is **West Bay Tea Rooms** (☎
01308-455697, 💻 westbaytearooms.co.uk;

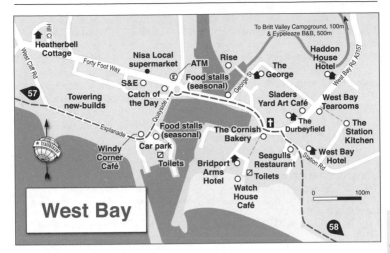

West Bay

Mon-Tue & Fri 10am-4pm, Sat & Sun to 4.30 or 5pm) which has a wide tea selection and a good choice of baguettes; note that dogs are not allowed here.

Surprisingly, despite all the competition, the eatery we were most taken by was *The Cornish Bakery* (☎ 01308-458256, ☐ thecornishbakery.com; WI-FI; ✖; daily 8am-6pm). Not only are they the first to open in the village, but the welcome is warm when they do, they are extremely dog-friendly, the locals clearly love the place – and the flat white I was served was the best on the entire trail. They also serve pasties, pastries as well as interesting breads to take away.

For **restaurants**, dominating the harbour, *Bridport Arms Hotel* (see Where to stay; food daily noon-2.30pm & 6-8.30pm) has mains ranging from pub classics such as cheeseburger and fries (£15) to more substantial fare like rump steak (£22).

Just up the road, *Haddon House Hotel* (see Where to stay; daily noon-2pm & 6.15-8.30pm) offers one of the more refined dining experiences in the village. Their two-course lunch (Mon-Sat, £14.95) is good value, particularly as you get a minimum choice from six dishes for each course.

Rise (☎ 01308-422011, ☐ risecafe bar.co.uk; ✖; Sun-Thur 9am-10pm, Fri &

Sat to 11pm) has a cracking location, seemingly perched on a river island, overlooking the village and the waterway. They serve upmarket burgers (£14-17.50), various fish and meat dishes and a luxurious crab sandwich (£16).

More affordable, but still a nice place for seafood, *Seagulls Restaurant* (☎ 01308-425099, ☐ seagullsrestaurant.co.uk; Feb-Nov Tue-Sat 6-9.30pm, Sun noon-3pm) is another smart choice for an evening meal, and it also does a great Sunday roast (£15.95).

For **pubs**, try *The George* (see Where to stay; daily noon-2.30pm & 5-8.30pm; ✖), which serves pub classics including steak pie (£12) and Dorset ham, egg & chips (£12). *West Bay Hotel* (see Where to stay; WI-FI; ✖; food Mon-Thur noon-2pm & 6-9pm, Sat noon-3pm & 6-9pm, Sun noon-3pm) has good ale and classic pub-grub mains (from £12).

Top of the pile, however, is *The Station Kitchen* (☎ 01308-422845, ☐ www.thestationkitchen.co.uk; Wed 5-8.30pm, Thur-Sat noon-2pm & 5-8.30pm); it's a quirky, gorgeous restaurant, housed inside West Bay's disused railway station and a train carriage. The contemporary British menu focuses on locally sourced food, including fresh fish.

At the eastern end of West Bay there is more climbing to be done to get over **East Cliff**. There was a dramatic cliff fall here in June 2017 (and another smaller one in 2021), but the path has reopened again, a few metres inland. Be sure to stick to the path here, and not to wander too close to the cliff edge.

From East Cliff, the path follows the cliff line along the edge of a golf course down to the beach at **Burton Freshwater**, where you'll find Freshwater Beach Holiday Park (see below) before climbing up **Burton Cliff**. From the top of this cliff you can, by gazing inland, catch your first glimpse of the Saxon settlement of Burton Bradstock. Straight ahead, the terrain flattens out, the ominous edge of Portland's Underhill getting ever closer.

To access **Burton Bradstock** turn left up Cliff Rd (see Map 58).

BURTON BRADSTOCK　[Map 58]

This unspoilt historic stone village is very pleasant, with lovely old buildings, many of them topped with thatch, particularly the old cottages around **St Mary's Church**, a number of which date back to the 16th and 17th centuries. That said, it is probably not worth diverting from the path just to see the village unless you plan to take advantage of its services or to grab a pub lunch. Many of the events in **Burton Bradstock's Festival of Music and Art** (see p14), held in August, take place in the church.

Close to the church you'll find the **Village Stores** (☎ 01308-897243, 🖥 may downfarmshop.com; **fb**; Mon, Wed & Fri 8.30am-5pm, Tue, Thur & Sat to 12.30pm) which sells local farm produce and houses the **post office** (same hours as store).

Down on the main road out of the village is a petrol station with a Central **convenience store** (daily 6.30am-11pm) that sells coffee and has an **ATM** (£1.85) outside it.

First's X53 **bus service** (see pp53-5) calls in en route between Axminster and Weymouth.

Should you wish to **camp** in the area *Freshwater Beach Holiday Park* (☎ 01308-897317, 🖥 freshwaterbeach.co.uk; Mar to end Nov; £8-22 for a tent and up to two hikers; 🐾; WI-FI) is the large family-orientated caravan park at the back of Burton Freshwater. It has a Spar **supermarket** (daily 9am-5pm, closes later in peak season), and campers can use both the indoor swimming **pool** (which has a Jacuzzi, steam room and sauna!) and the

outdoor pool free of charge. Be sure to tell them you are a hiker in order to get the cheapest rate for a tent pitch.

On top of Burton Cliff, you can find sumptuous double rooms at *Seaside Boarding House* (☎ 01308-897205, 🖥 the seasideboardinghouse.com; 9D; 🍷; WI-FI; 🐾; from £122.50pp, sgl occ £225), right on the path before it drops down to Hive Beach. Seaside has a bar and a quality restaurant too (food Tue-Sun noon-3pm & 6.30-9.45pm).

Further beyond the village, *Chesil Beach Lodge* (Map 59; ☎ 01308-897428, 🖥 chesilbeachlodge.co.uk; 1D/2D or T; WI-FI; 🐾; £65-117.50pp, sgl occ room rate) is on the coast road (B3157). The best way for walkers to reach it is to continue along the coast path for just under half a mile before turning inland before Old Coastguard Holiday Park and following the footpath.

For **food**, there are two excellent pubs on the main road in the centre of the village. The menu at *The Anchor Inn* (☎ 01308-897228, 🖥 www.anchorinn.pub; 1D or T/1Qd; WI-FI; 🐾; food Mon-Sat noon-2pm & 5.30-8.30pm, Sun noon-3pm) changes frequently but focuses on fish and shellfish, though they also have meat and vegetarian options. You sometimes need to book here for evening meals.

Just down the hill, *The Three Horseshoes* (☎ 01308-897259, 🖥 three horseshoesburtonbradstock.co.uk; 🐾 bar area; food summer Tue-Sat noon-8.30pm, Sun noon-3pm, winter Tue-Fri noon-2pm & 5.30-8.30pm, Sat noon-8.30pm, Sun

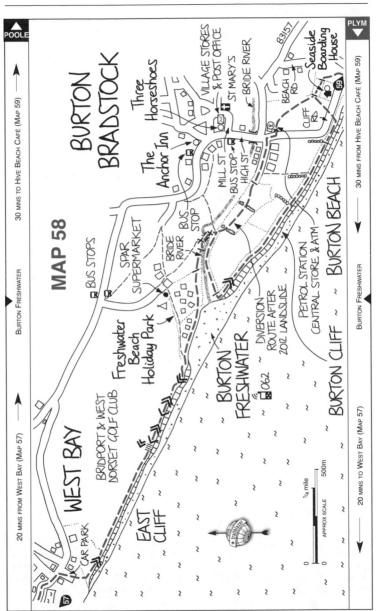

MAP 58

BURTON BRADSTOCK

Three Horseshoes

The Anchor Inn

VILLAGE STORES & POST OFFICE

ST MARY'S

BRIDE RIVER

B3157

Seaside Boarding House

BEACH RD

CLIFF RD

MILL ST

BUS STOP

HIGH ST

BUS STOP

BRIDE RIVER

SPAR SUPERMARKET

BUS STOPS

Freshwater Beach Holiday Park

Bridport & West Dorset Golf Club

WEST BAY

EAST CLIFF

CAR PARK

BURTON FRESHWATER

DIVERSION ROUTE AFTER 2012 LANDSLIDE

PETROL STATION CENTRAL STORE & ATM

BURTON CLIFF ~ BURTON BEACH

POOLE

30 MINS TO HIVE BEACH CAFÉ (MAP 59) →

BURTON FRESHWATER

← 20 MINS FROM WEST BAY (MAP 57)

PLYM ▼

30 MINS FROM HIVE BEACH CAFÉ (MAP 59) →

BURTON FRESHWATER

20 MINS TO WEST BAY (MAP 57) →

¼ mile
500m
APPROX SCALE
0

noon-3pm) is more down-to-earth, and welcomes muddy hikers as well as dogs. They offer good homemade food (mains £12-23) with a particular flair for desserts and have

Palmers' ales on tap. Note the pub is closed in the afternoon in winter (Tue-Thur 3-5pm).

The walking is easy as you pass Burton and then **Hive Beach** where *Hive Beach Café* (☎ 01308-897070, 🖥 hivebeachcafe.co.uk; WI-FI; 🐾 ; daily 10am-5pm plus summer sometimes Mon-Sat up to 7pm and winter Thur-Sat to 7pm) has grown from a seasonal beach shack into a gourmet café-bistro with plastic awnings sheltering diners from the elements. The food's good, but it's not cheap (lunchtime mains from £18).

More caravan parks and cliffs follow before **Cogden Beach** spreads out on your right and **Burton Common** appears bleak and endless to your left, looking in many ways like Dartmoor (its tors are around 50 miles south-west). The path slices between the two, their contrasting charms changing with each season.

Passing behind **Burton Mere**, you walk through scrub and farmland along the back of a pebble ridge – the sea isn't always visible but the sound of the waves remains therapeutic enough.

Having passed through **West Bexington Nature Reserve** – of importance due to the rare shingle habitat that thrives here – you arrive at the car park at **West Bexington Beach**. This is also the start of the **South Dorset Ridgeway** (see p247). For the continuation of the main route see p250.

WEST BEXINGTON   [Map 60, p246]

It is hard to imagine that contemporary West Bexington was, before the Romans came, inhabited by the feared and belligerent Durotriges tribe that once occupied much of Dorset; indeed, what with a French raiding party burning and pillaging the tiny village (and destroying its church) in the 15th century, it's fair to say that this sleepy hamlet has had more than its fair share of excitement down the centuries. All this violence in what is now such a tranquil location.

Unfortunately, Tamarisk Farm **shop** (☎ 01308-897781, 🖥 tamariskfarm.co.uk/wp/shop; Tue 4-6.30pm, Fri 8.30-11am), the only shop here, has very limited hours.

The only place to stay is at *Manor House* (☎ 01308-897660, 🖥 manorhotel dorset.com; 10D/4D or T; ☞ ; WI-FI in public areas; from £57.50pp, sgl occ £110), a 16th-century manor-house hotel with well-appointed bedrooms. The **restaurant** (Mar-end Oct daily noon-2.15pm & 6-8.15pm, rest of year probably Thur-Sun only), which has garden seating on pub

benches, and the **bar** (daily 11.30am-10pm), which serves real ales (Otter; see box p24), are both open to non-residents and passing walkers are welcome just to pop in.

Down at the beach is *The Club House Restaurant* (☎ 01308-898302, 🖥 theclub housewestbexington.co.uk; food Wed & Sun 9.30am-4pm, Thur-Sat 9.30-11.15am & noon-7.30pm), a fine-dining establishment (evening mains from £16) with a lovely sea-facing location that, despite its upmarket reputation, is a friendly place to stop for coffee and cake. However, dogs are only permitted in the covered area outside and they must be on a lead.

The nearest **bus stop** is at Swyre, about 1¼ miles/2km from The Club House. First's X53 **bus** (Axminster to Weymouth; see pp53-5) service stops off by The Bull Inn there. The route is also very handy for the South Dorset Ridgeway (aka The Inland Route), which follows the course of the B3157 road for much of its length.

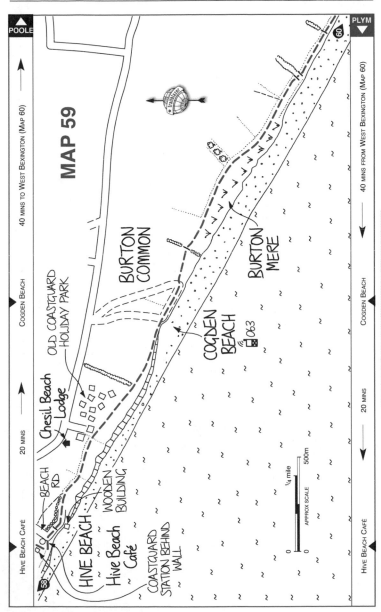

MAP 59

POOLE

PLYM

40 MINS TO WEST BEXINGTON (MAP 60)

40 MINS FROM WEST BEXINGTON (MAP 60)

COGDEN BEACH

COGDEN BEACH

20 MINS

20 MINS

HIVE BEACH CAFÉ

HIVE BEACH CAFÉ

OLD COASTGUARD HOLIDAY PARK

BURTON COMMON

BURTON MERE

COGDEN BEACH

063

Chesil Beach Lodge

BEACH RD

WOODEN BUILDING

HIVE BEACH

Hive Beach Café

COASTGUARD STATION BEHIND WALL

1/4 mile

500m

APPROX SCALE

0

0

60

58

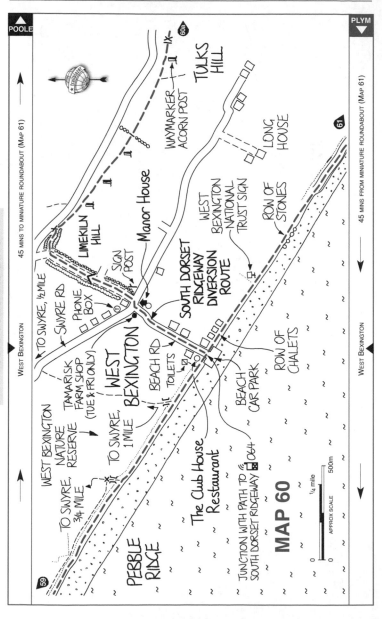

POOLE

PLYM

45 MINS TO MINIATURE ROUNDABOUT (MAP 61)

TRUEBARR

TULKS HILL

WAYMARKER ACORN POST

LONG HOUSE

LIMEKILN HILL

SIGN POST

Manor House

WEST BEXINGTON NATIONAL TRUST SIGN

ROW OF STONES

61

SOUTH DORSET RIDGEWAY DIVERSION ROUTE

45 MINS FROM MINIATURE ROUNDABOUT (MAP 61)

WEST BEXINGTON

TO SWYRE, ½ MILE

SWYRE RD

PHONE BOX

WEST BEXINGTON

BEACH RD

TAMARISK FARM SHOP (TUE & FRI ONLY)

TOILETS

WEST BEXINGTON NATURE RESERVE

TO SWYRE, 1 MILE

BEACH CAR PARK

ROW OF CHALETS

TO SWYRE, ¾ MILE

The Club House Restaurant

JUNCTION WITH PATH TO SOUTH DORSET RIDGEWAY ✆ 064

MAP 60

PEBBLE RIDGE

59

¼ mile

500m

APPROX SCALE

0

0

South Dorset Ridgeway (aka Inland Route)

[Map 60, Map 60a & 60b, p248; Map 60c, p249; Map 73, p277]
At its most basic, this walk could be seen as nothing but a short cut, saving the weary trekker about 19¼ miles on the standard route via Weymouth and Portland. Thus those short on stamina and shoe leather, the fatigued and the fed-up, may appreciate this reducing of their expedition. But this **17-mile (27.4km; 5¼hrs)** saunter, **which has been part of the SWCP since its inception in 1978** (and thus 25 years before Portland), offers so much more than just a saving of time. For the South Dorset Ridgeway takes you through one of the most ancient landscapes in the UK. Very few – if any – walks in the UK will take you past such a wealth of **Neolithic, Bronze Age and Roman sites**, from burial chambers and barrows to stare holes and stone circles, not to mention a rash of tumuli like geological pimples pockmarking the ground. (For details of these various sites, see Appendix B, p310.)

It is an incredibly beautiful walk too. Those who have walked on the South Downs Way will find several similarities as they stroll along a chalk ridge with gigantic sweeping views over a terrain that falls away on either side of the trail; indeed, curiously, there are more views of the sea on this route than on the coast path. There is the wildlife, too, particularly birdlife, with raptors especially ubiquitous, including an abundance of buzzards, kestrels and even the odd kite soaring and swooping. There are skylarks aplenty, too, performing a vertical lift-off from the fields as if powered, seemingly, by nothing but song.

Of course, the 'official' coast path is not without its attractions too and we recognise that most people will stick to the seaside route, especially as it takes in the idiosyncratic isthmus of Portland which was added to the official trail in 2003. But we do urge you, if you have the time, to try to fit in at least a section of the Ridgeway as well. Weymouth is a good base, with First X53's **bus** to Swyre for West Bexington in the morning and More Damory's No 30 back from Osmington in the late afternoon and evening; see pp53-5 for details.

Note that there are **no refreshments** on the South Dorset Ridgeway until Osmington, less than a mile from the end of the trail, though a side-trip to Abbotsbury, three-quarters of a mile down the hill, is a viable option. Note, too, that just about the entire trek is on an **exposed ridge** so bring suitable raingear and sunblock to cover all weather possibilities.

The route

Leave West Bexington from the beach car park next to The Club House and follow the road up the hill, passing Manor House on your right. Where the road bends away keep heading straight up on a farm track to the summit of **Limekiln Hill** where the path meets and follows the B3157. Crossing several fields, you soon pass the first of a myriad of tumuli, or barrows, on the trail.

Traversing **Tulks Hill**, you cross the road to climb the western end of the ridge up to **Abbotsbury Castle**. Sitting proudly above the surrounding landscape, this triangular hill-fort is the most prominent of the Iron Age sites on the route, one of a string of such fortifications that include nearby Eggardon Hill Fort and much larger Maiden Castle, both of which are visible from here.

Excavations have also yielded evidence of a Roman signal tower that was built on this site, and this location also played host, for centuries, to a warning beacon, used, for example, during the nation's wait for the arrival of the Spanish Armada.

ROUTE GUIDE AND MAPS

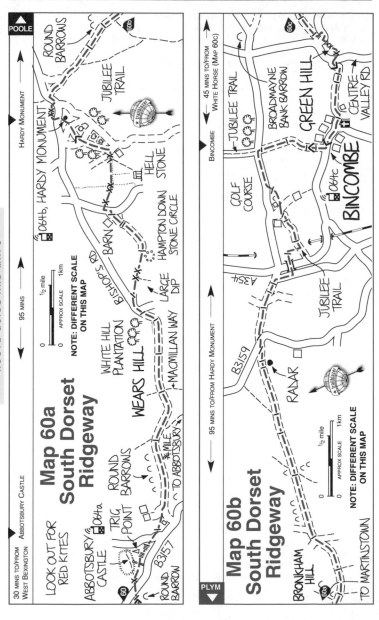

Map 60a
South Dorset Ridgeway

POOLE ▲

30 MINS TO/FROM WEST BEXINGTON ▶ ABBOTSBURY CASTLE

◀ 95 MINS ▶ ◀ HARDY MONUMENT ▶

LOOK OUT FOR RED KITES

ABBOTSBURY CASTLE 064a

TRIG POINT

ROUND BARROWS

B3157

ROUND BARROW

60

TO MARTINSTOWN

WEARS HILL

MACMILLAN WAY

WHITE HILL PLANTATION

¾ MILE TO ABBOTSBURY

LARGE DIP

HAMPTON DOWN STONE CIRCLE

BARN

BISHOP'S RD

HELL STONE

064b, HARDY MONUMENT

ROUND BARROWS

JUBILEE TRAIL

60b

NOTE: DIFFERENT SCALE ON THIS MAP

0   ½ mile
0   APPROX SCALE   1km

Map 60b
South Dorset Ridgeway

PLYM ▼

95 MINS TO/FROM HARDY MONUMENT ▶

◀ BINCOMBE ▶ ◀ 45 MINS TO/FROM WHITE HORSE (MAP 60c) ▶

BRONKHAM HILL

60a

RADAR

B3159

JUBILEE TRAIL

A354

GOLF COURSE

JUBILEE TRAIL

BINCOMBE

064c

BROADMAYNE BANK BARROW

GREEN HILL

CENTRE VALLEY RD

60c

NOTE: DIFFERENT SCALE ON THIS MAP

0   ½ mile
0   APPROX SCALE   1km

Crossing a minor road after the castle, the trail dodges through numerous barrows as it heads to the summit of **Wears Hill**, with the western side of The Fleet ever increasing in size below you. St Catherine's Chapel (Map 62) comes into sight and a path offers access to Abbotsbury.

Cross the Macmillan Way (see p39) and continue past **White Hill Plantation** to Bishop's Rd from where you should follow the path to **Hampton Down Stone Circle**. This ancient monument is thought to have been used for rituals and is believed to be over 4000 years old.

An even more impressive prehistoric site lies nearby, just south of the path after Hampton Barn Farm. This is the dramatically named **Hell Stone**, a burial chamber or dolmen built around 6000 years ago that was restored, incorrectly by all accounts, in the 19th century. Hell Stone stands just to the south of the path: just before you enter the woods leading up to the Hardy Monument, turn south through the farm gate and walk across the field to the dolmen.

From here it's only a woodland walk to the **Hardy Monument** (🖥 nation altrust.org.uk/hardy-monument; inside currently open for two days in May & Oct only), which commemorates Rear Admiral Sir Thomas Masterman Hardy (1769-1839), captain of *HMS Victory*, part of the fleet that won the Battle of Trafalgar in 1805 and, more famously, the man from whom Admiral Nelson requested a kiss as he lay dying from his wounds (Hardy complied with his friend's wishes, kissing his dying friend on the forehead). Built in 1844-5 the monument stands 22 metres (72ft) high and is owned by the National Trust.

After the monument the Ridgeway joins the Jubilee Trail (see p39) to reach **Bronkham Hill**, passing yet more prehistoric earthworks, before a 3¼-mile stroll amongst numerous barrows brings you to the Roman road between Dorchester and Weymouth, now known, more prosaically, as the **A354**. Excavations near here uncovered a mass grave of some 50 decapitated Scandinavians dating back to the Saxon Age.

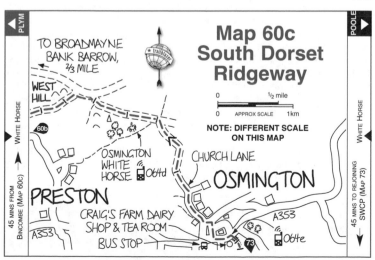

Map 60c
South Dorset
Ridgeway

Crossing the busy road via a bridge, you follow a gravel path before the Jubilee Trail is again joined briefly, the two trails following the same route as they make their way to a minor road.

The spell on tarmac is brief and you soon leave the road, turning right – and south – on to a farm's driveway, finally leaving the Jubilee Trail behind as it veers away to the north. The path descends to the end of another minor road and on to the settlement of **Bincombe**, leaving it after the church to go through more fields to **Green Hill**.

Carrying on to **West Hill** and back on to the ridge, tumuli again rise from the earth as you pass a trig point and above the famous **Osmington White Horse** (see p278). From here you make your last descent to pass through farmland leading to the end of Church Lane in **Osmington**. First's X54 and More's No 5 and No 30 **bus** services stop here; see pp53-5.

On the way out of the village, *Craig's Farm Dairy Shop & Tea Room* (☎ 01305-834591, 🖳 craigsfarmdairy.co.uk; 🐾 tearoom only; Mar-late Sep food Mon-Fri 9am-5pm, Sat to 4pm, Sun 10am-4pm, shop open till later, rest of year variable so contact them to check) is a decent little farm shop that sells fruit, cheeses, meats, ice-cream and coffee.

To reach the SWCP from here, head east along the A353, turning right off the road and passing through four fields on your way to **Osmington Mills** and a reunion with the coast path (see p278).

(Main route continued from p274) After more horizontal hiking the pebbles disappear and you're left to stroll on a four-wheel drive track, the scrub hemming you in on both sides.

After you've passed **The Old Coastguards**, once a haunt of Thomas Hardy, a minor road (complete with **pill box**) ensues, the epic expanse of **Chesil Beach** now beginning to dominate the view in front of you.

Before you hit the western end of **The Fleet** (the lagoon behind Chesil Beach), and just after you pass *Beach Café* (daily 10am-5pm), a small café shack, which is open all year and sells bacon baps, pasties, cakes, coffee and a reasonable selection of lunches (£8.50-12), the path takes a left and climbs as if heading towards the 15th-century **St Catherine's Chapel** (Map 62). St Catherine, incidentally, is the patron saint of spinsters and women are said to visit the church in desperate search of husbands. Gentlemen trekkers – you have been warned. The climb towards the chapel affords your first views of **West Fleet** – and, if you're lucky, the mute swans of **Abbotsbury Swannery** (see p252).

Rounding the hill, the path veers off to the right and you arrive at a junction of two paths: turn left for the village or turn right to cross over a small stream and arrive at a stile next to an impressive plane tree. Turning left here will also lead you into **Abbotsbury** itself; or you can turn right and follow the road onwards along the coastal path, past the entrance to the swannery.

❏ **IMPORTANT NOTE – WALKING TIMES**

All times in this book refer only to the time spent walking. You will need to add 20-30% to allow for rests, photography, checking the map, drinking water etc.

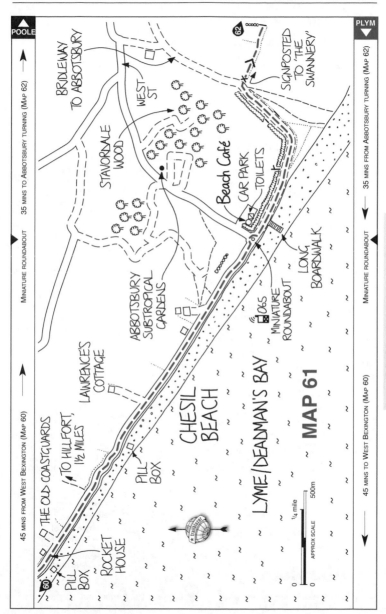

POOLE

PLYM

45 MINS FROM WEST BEXINGTON (MAP 60)

MINIATURE ROUNDABOUT

35 MINS TO ABBOTSBURY TURNING (MAP 62)

BRIDLEWAY TO ABBOTSBURY

WEST ST

STAVORDALE WOOD

Beach Café

CAR PARK

TOILETS

SIGNPOSTED TO 'THE SWANNERY'

ABBOTSBURY SUBTROPICAL GARDENS

LONG BOARDWALK

LAWRENCE'S COTTAGE

TO HILLFORT, 1½ MILES

THE OLD COASTGUARDS

PILL BOX

ROCKET HOUSE

PILL BOX

B3157

MINIATURE ROUNDABOUT

CHESIL BEACH

LYME/DEADMAN'S BAY

MAP 61

¼ mile

500m

APPROX SCALE

0

0

45 MINS FROM WEST BEXINGTON (MAP 60)

MINIATURE ROUNDABOUT

35 MINS FROM ABBOTSBURY TURNING (MAP 62)

45 MINS TO WEST BEXINGTON (MAP 60)

ROUTE GUIDE AND MAPS

ABBOTSBURY [map below]

Rich in English history, the pristine little village of Abbotsbury (🖳 abbotsbury.co .uk) is one of the highlights of the whole walk – there's nowhere else along the whole of the coast path quite like it. There is a reasonable amount of accommodation – although booking ahead, especially in summer, is advisable – and it's a great place to stop for lunch, a coffee or a cream tea.

Sight-wise, the most important buildings are the **remains of the Benedictine Abbey of St Peter**, which was founded in the 11th century; the accompanying **Tithe Barn**, which at 272ft is the longest in England (indeed, when they rethatched the roof in 2006, so enormous was the task that it took three years to complete); and **St Catherine's Chapel** (Map 62; see p250), which, like Tithe Barn, was a 15th-century addition to the village.

Having survived the Black Death and other invasions, the abbey finally met its match in the Dissolution under Henry VIII and was destroyed in 1538. The barn, however, supposedly resisted the same fate due to its multitude of uses, while the chapel survived due to its importance as a navigational aid to those sailing in Lyme Bay. Dotted amongst them are several **cottages** that date back to the 16th century or earlier, with many of them incorporating materials from the demolished abbey.

The monks were also responsible for the **Swannery** (Map 62; ☎ 01305-871858, 🖳 abbotsbury-tourism.co.uk/swannery; mid Mar to Oct daily 10am-5pm; £12; strictly no dogs), established in the 11th century to supply the fare for their tables. The swans are somewhat luckier today and hundreds reside here. If you're a sucker for a cygnet plan your trip for between mid May and late June when they are hatching. There's a *café* (daily 10.30am-4.30pm) by the entrance, which is handy if you're passing through without visiting Abbotsbury.

In the centre of the village, the 14th-century **Church of St Nicholas** remains scarred by the English Civil War – the Grade-I listed tower still bearing the marks of musket fire, shot whilst the Cavaliers had the Roundheads under siege within its walls. Along West St, is the unusual **Clock Work Shop** (☎ 01305-873852, 🖳 dorset antiqueclocks.co.uk; Mon-Fri 10am-5pm), which has a first-floor showroom displaying dozens of elegant and largely very rare pieces, including a 1650 balance-wheel lantern clock that is valued at £12,500.

About half a mile further west (turn left off West St into Cleverlawns), the

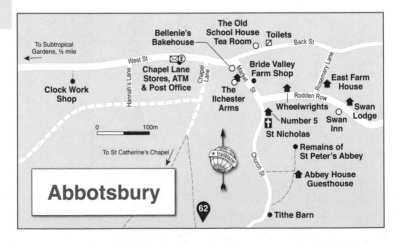

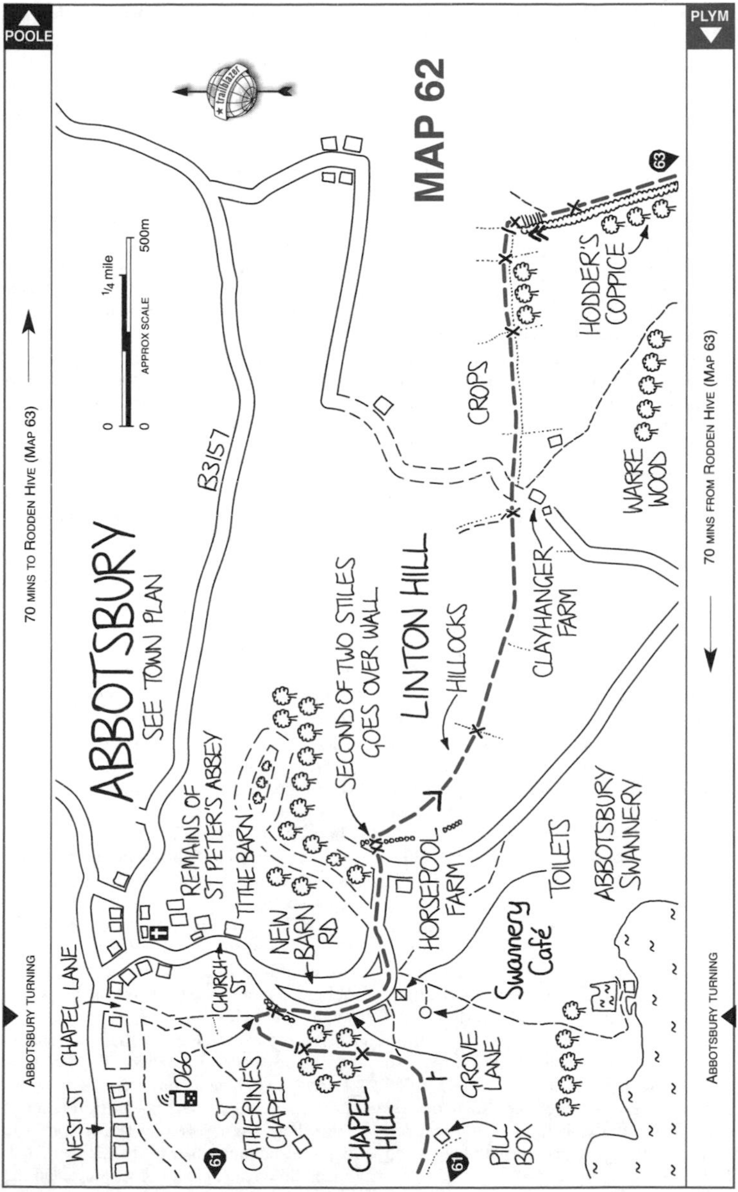

MAP 62

ABBOTSBURY TURNING

ABBOTSBURY TURNING

POOLE

PLYM

¼ mile

500m

0

0

APPROX SCALE

ABBOTSBURY

SEE TOWN PLAN

B3157

REMAINS OF
ST PETER'S ABBEY

TITHE BARN

NEW
BARN
RD

CHURCH
ST

WEST ST

CHAPEL LANE

1066

ST
CATHERINE'S
CHAPEL

CHAPEL HILL

PILL
BOX

GROVE LANE

HORSEPOOL
FARM

Swannery
Café

TOILETS

ABBOTSBURY
SWANNERY

SECOND OF TWO STILES
GOES OVER WALL

LINTON HILL

HILLOCKS

CLAYHANGER
FARM

CROPS

WARRE
WOOD

HODDER'S
COPPICE

61

61

63

ROUTE GUIDE AND MAPS

Subtropical Gardens (Map 61; ☎ 01305-871387, 🖥 abbotsbury-tourism.co.uk/gardens; Mar-Oct daily 10am-5pm, Nov-Mar to 4pm, closed mid to end Dec; 🐾 if on a lead; £12), on Bullers Way, were originally established in 1765 as the first Countess of Ilchester's kitchen garden.

Today the 20 acres are filled with rare and exotic plants – and a *café* (☎ 01305-871732; daily 10am-4.30pm, winter to 3.30pm) which offers soups, sandwiches and savouries.

Services
The **post office** (Mon-Sat 8am-6pm, Sun 9am-1pm) is inside the well-stocked **Chapel Lane Stores** (☎ 01305-871080; fb; generally Mon-Sat 7am-7pm, Sun 8am-6pm). There's also a free-to-use **ATM** inside.

You can also get supplies such as local cheeses, cold meats, honey and jam, at **Bride Valley Farm Shop** (☎ 01305-871235, 🖥 dorsetlonghorn.co.uk; Tue-Sat 8.30am-2pm).

Transport
[See pp53-5] First's X52 & X53 **bus** services pass through.

Where to stay
Abbotsbury has several **B&Bs**, some of which are surprisingly affordable. Those walking with a dog should try *Number 5* (☎ 01305-871882, 🖥 candcrawlings@gmail .com; 1D, private facilities; WI-FI; 🐾; from £37.50pp, sgl occ room rate).

Abbey House Guest House (☎ 01305-871330, 🖥 theabbeyhouse.co.uk; 2T/3D; 🛏; WI-FI; £37.50-62.50pp, sgl occ room rate) is typical of the kind of accommodation available in the village, being both gorgeous and ancient. The place actually dates back to the 15th century when it was part of the abbey's infirmary and overlooks the abbey today, its grounds (parts of which are now given over to the tearoom – see Where to eat) sloping down to the duck-filled millpond. Do settings get any better? Rooms are individual, as you'd expect, with one attic room and all with king-sized beds.

Not too far away is *Wheelwrights* (☎ 01305-871800, 🖥 wheelwrights.co.uk; 1D or T; WI-FI; from £50pp, sgl occ £90; Mar-end Oct), a thatched cottage at 14 Rodden Row. However, they only accept bookings for a minimum of two nights.

With a long and interesting history (an arch that can be seen in one of the walls is thought by some to date back as far as the 11th century!), *The Ilchester Arms* (☎ 01305-873841, 🖥 theilchester.co.uk; 7D/2T; 🛏; WI-FI; 🐾; from £54.50pp, sgl occ £59.50) is an old pub with rooms on Market St in the very heart of the village. Food is also provided (see Where to eat).

Further east the 17th-century Dorset longhouse at *East Farm House* (☎ 01305-871363, 🖥 eastfarmhouse.co.uk; 2D/1T; WI-FI; from £50pp, sgl occ £95) has chickens and ducks roaming the farm while ponies occupy the stables in the back courtyard, and on the eastern extremity of the village is *Swan Lodge* (☎ 01305-871249, 🖥 swaninabbotsbury@gmail.com; 2T/3D; 🛏; WI-FI; 🐾; from £47.50pp, sgl occ £75) across the road from – and owned by – Swan Inn (see Where to eat).

Where to eat and drink
Two tearooms face each other in the centre of the village. *The Old School House Tea Room* (☎ 01305-871808; Mar-mid Dec Tue-Sun 10.30am-4pm but can vary in the winter months; 🐾) offers sandwiches (from £6.50), scones, light lunches and always has a great display of cakes to choose from. It has a lovely little patio garden out back, a delightful hostess and dogs are welcome. A standard cream tea costs from £6.80.

Bellenie's Bakehouse & Tea-Room (🐾; Wed-Mon 7am-3.30pm) proudly boasts of its award-winning cakes such as a delicious farmhouse fruitcake but also has a magnificent cream tea.

The pubs and inns are the most reliable places to head for dinner. *The Ilchester Arms* (see Where to stay; food daily noon-2.30pm & 6-8pm; 🐾) is the focal point of the village come evening and has an à la carte restaurant (mains £14-22) with fish specialities, plus plenty of real ales. On the outskirts of town, *Swan Inn* (see Swan Lodge, Where to stay; food generally daily noon-8pm; ✹) has a wide range of fairly

simple but filling fare such as braised pork in cider and apple sauce with veg.

ABBOTSBURY TO FORTUNESWELL [MAPS 62-68]

This **13-mile (21km; 4hrs 20 mins)** day starts with a 3-mile hike along a ridge and through fields that, at times, can feel a long way from the sea. It is however, good walking. There are great views over the surrounding countryside as you make your way through the farmland, eventually arriving at the western end of The Fleet – the great expanse of water that separates the mainland from the large pebble ridge of Chesil Beach and also a nature reserve.

The rest of the stage is largely spent on the flat. Following the lakeshore, interrupted only by Chickerell Rifle Range (should target practice forbid your passing there is an easy alternative), you eventually arrive at Ferrybridge in Wyke Regis, from where you can either cross the *tombolo* (sand bar) to the Isle of Portland (round hike from Ferrybridge and back 13 miles/21km; 5½hrs), or continue on into Weymouth (3 miles/5km; 1hr 10 mins). There is accommodation in both places and to get to both there are buses.

This may not be the most exciting stage and the relative lack of refreshments until you reach the suburbs of Weymouth/Portland is irksome. Luckily, there are plenty of places along the banks of The Fleet that make great locations for a picnic. Accommodation-wise, there are numerous options for campers, and a pricey manor-house hotel, but little else.

The route

To leave Abbotsbury village head down Church St, passing St Nicholas Church and Tithe Barn, before turning off down a minor road – Grove Lane – signed to The Swannery. Carry on straight down the lane and you are soon on the coastal path again by the gorgeous plane tree .

Passing the entrance to The Swannery (see p252), you leave the road on a bend to cross a stile then, almost immediately cross another to get over a wall, before following the path up over fields with St Catherine's Chapel watching your progress from the rear and the western end of The Fleet now clearly visible to your right. The path follows a ridge with an idyllic pastoral landscape to the right that gently recedes towards Chesil Beach. This ridge is followed until a sharp turn sends you down and right, briefly along the outskirts of **Hodder's Coppice**, before more fields take you to the edges of **Wyke Wood**. Having briefly followed Bridge Lane you pass a house marked 'private' on your right and, crossing a few more fields, you reach **Rodden Hive** and **Fleet Lagoon Nature Reserve**.

Despite the path's occasional brief diversion away from the water's edge (such as at **Herbury**; Map 64) you never stray too far from The Fleet and its flapping feathery frequenters. Much of the walking is along the edge of farmland, interrupted only by the odd field boundary.

Campers are spoilt for choice along this stretch. They can find a pitch at *Bagwell Farm Campsite* (off Map 63; ☎ 01305-782575, 🖳 bagwellfarm.co.uk;

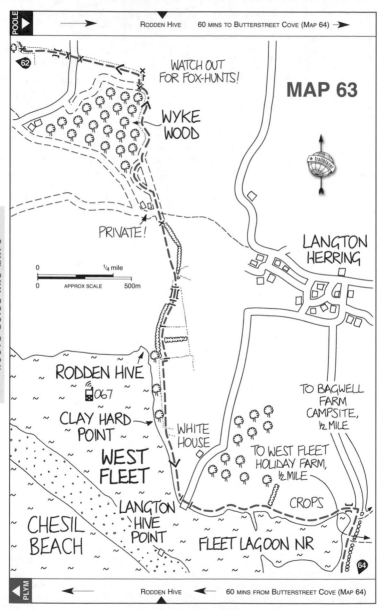

WATCH OUT
FOR FOX-HUNTS!

MAP 63

62

WYKE
WOOD

★ trailblazer

PRIVATE!

LANGTON
HERRING

0 ¼ mile
0 APPROX SCALE 500m

RODDEN HIVE
☏ 067

CLAY HARD
POINT

WEST
FLEET

WHITE
HOUSE

TO BAGWELL
FARM
CAMPSITE,
½ MILE

TO WEST FLEET
HOLIDAY FARM,
½ MILE

CROPS

CHESIL
BEACH

LANGTON
HIVE
POINT

FLEET LAGOON NR

64

WI-FI; 🐾; £16-25/19-28 for a tent and one/two adults), which has its own **restaurant** (Easter-Oct daily 5-9pm) and **shop** (daily 9am-5pm) and offers £2-5 discounts for sloping pitches. It's signposted half a mile from the path. Close by, and also half a mile from the path, is *West Fleet Holiday Farm* (off Map 63; ☎ 01305-782218, 🖥 westfleetholidays.co.uk; WI-FI; 🐾 on lead at all times; Easter-Sep; £14-28/17-33 for a tent and one/two adults), which has a heated outdoor pool (seasonal).

Just beyond this is *Sea Barn Farm* (Map 64; phone as for West Fleet; 🖥 www.seabarnfarm.co.uk; 🥤; WI-FI; 🐾 on lead at all times; mid Mar-early Oct) which charges the same as West Fleet but has better views. Follow the 'farm path' signs from the coast path just after the racecourse. Booking (at least 24hrs in advance) for both is essential.

A little further along, *East Fleet Farm Touring Park* (☎ 01305-785768, 🖥 eastfleet.co.uk; SWCP hikers pay from £10 for a pitch; 🐾; mid Mar-end Oct) is right on the path and also very well equipped. It is run by Away Resorts (🖥 www.awayresorts.co.uk).

Just before the racecourse you'll pass *Moonfleet Manor Hotel & Restaurant* (☎ 01305-786948, 🖥 moonfleetmanorhotel.co.uk; 36 rooms inc 3D/14D or T and rooms sleeping up to six people; 🥤; WI-FI; 🐾; £70-162.50pp, sgl occ from £125), a 17th-century manor house that's been converted into a hotel. While you may find it a touch too expensive to stay here, passing walkers are welcome to swing by for lunch (daily noon-2.30pm), afternoon tea (2-4.15pm) or dinner (5-8.45pm). They even have their own pizza tipi now (summer school holidays Thur-Sat noon-8pm, Sun 4-9pm); or you even just pop in for a coffee or a cold beer.

Chickerell Rifle Range is eventually reached. **If the red flags are flying do not enter** but follow the short detour to the north instead. You then pass by a caravan park before heading towards an **army training centre**, after which the path turns east by the water's edge to cross level grassland and pasture with the eastern end of Chesil Beach in your sights and with Portland becoming ever clearer. There's a **campsite** right on the path, *Seaview* (☎ 07805 924721, 🖥 www.seaviewfarm.co.uk; 🐾; £20 for up to four people), that opens up for 28 days in August. Booking is recommended.

Strolling past chalets on your left you arrive at a minor road where over your left shoulder you'll see the popular *Crab House Café* (☎ 01305-788867, 🖥 crabhousecafe.co.uk; WI-FI; Feb-mid Dec Wed-Sat noon-2.30pm & Wed-Thur 6-9pm, Fri-Sat 6-9.30pm, Sun noon-3pm), which specialises in seafood.

From here it's a short hop to **Ferrybridge** where a choice needs to be made; for Portland and the continuation of the path (see p259), or to continue onwards from Ferrybridge, crossing the road and heading into Weymouth. There are **buses**, too, to both Portland and Weymouth from Ferrybridge: First's No 1 (Weymouth–Portland) and their No 501 (Weymouth–Portland Bill); see pp53-5. For the trek into Weymouth, see p269.

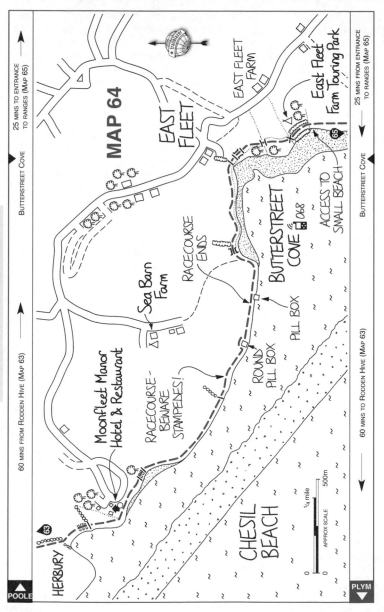

MAP 64

25 MINS TO ENTRANCE TO RANGES (MAP 65)

BUTTERSTREET COVE

25 MINS FROM ENTRANCE TO RANGES (MAP 65)

BUTTERSTREET COVE

60 MINS FROM RODDEN HIVE (MAP 63)

60 MINS TO RODDEN HIVE (MAP 63)

EAST FLEET FARM

EAST FLEET

EAST FLEET FARM

East Fleet Farm Touring Park

65

ACCESS TO SMALL BEACH

BUTTERSTREET COVE 068

Sea Barn Farm

RACECOURSE ENDS

PILL BOX

ROUND PILL BOX

PILL BOX

Moonfleet Manor Hotel & Restaurant

RACECOURSE – BEWARE STAMPEDES!

CHESIL BEACH

HERBURY

63

POOLE

PLYM

¼ mile

500m

0

0

APPROX SCALE

For the continuation to Portland, turn right and follow the tombolo on a dreary 2-mile roadside trudge – it's well worth breaking the journey, either at **Billy Winters** (☎ 01305-774954, 💻 billywinters.co.uk; **fb**; summer food Sun, Wed & Thur 11am-7pm, Fri & Sat to 8pm, winter Wed & Thur 10am-6pm, Fri & Sat to 8.30pm, Sun to 5pm) with all-day breakfasts, pizzas and burgers (both from £12.50); or, on the other side of the road, at the excellent **Chesil Beach Visitor Centre** (Map 67; ☎ 01305-206191, 💻 chesilbeach.org/cbvc; daily 10am-4pm), which houses the award-winning *Taste Café* (☎ 01305-206196, 💻 tastecafeatchesilbeach.co.uk; WI-FI; 🐾; same hours), a gift shop, and numerous interactive displays detailing the unique coastline here. *(cont'd on p262)*

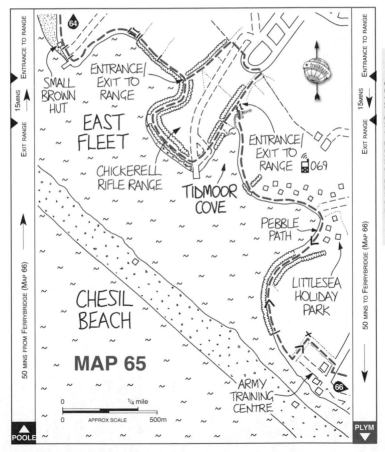

ROUTE GUIDE AND MAPS

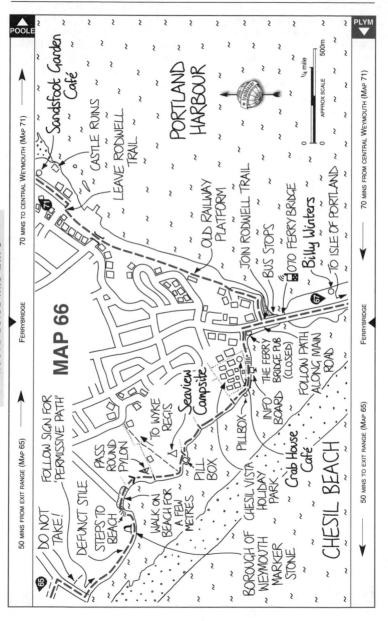

MAP 66

50 MINS FROM EXIT RANGE (MAP 65) →

FERRYBRIDGE

70 MINS TO CENTRAL WEYMOUTH (MAP 71) →

← 50 MINS TO EXIT RANGE (MAP 65)

FERRYBRIDGE

← 70 MINS FROM CENTRAL WEYMOUTH (MAP 71)

POOLE

PLYM

DO NOT TAKE!

FOLLOW SIGN FOR 'PERMISSIVE PATH'

DEFUNCT STILE

STEPS TO BEACH

PASS ROUND PYLON

WALK ON BEACH FOR A FEW METRES

TO WYKE REGIS

Seaview Campsite

PILL BOX

PILLBOX

INFO BOARD

THE FERRY BRIDGE PUB (CLOSED)

FOLLOW PATH ALONG MAIN ROAD

CHESIL VISTA HOLIDAY PARK

Crab House Café

BOROUGH OF WEYMOUTH MARKER STONE

CHESIL BEACH

Sandsfoot Garden Café

CASTLE RUINS

LEAVE RODWELL TRAIL

PORTLAND HARBOUR

OLD RAILWAY PLATFORM

JOIN RODWELL TRAIL

BUS STOPS

TO FERRY BRIDGE

Billy Winters

TO ISLE OF PORTLAND

¼ mile

0   500m

0

APPROX SCALE

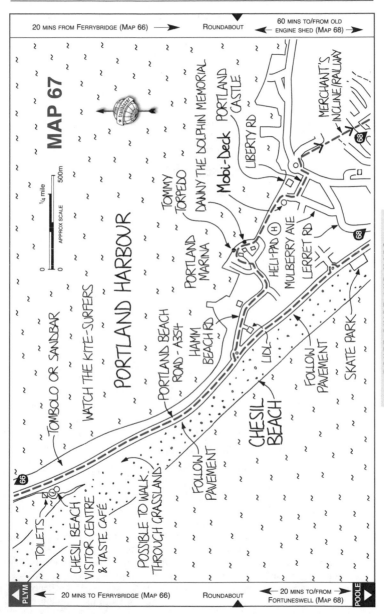

MAP 67

PORTLAND HARBOUR

¼ mile

500m

0

0

APPROX SCALE

TOMBOLO OR SANDBAR

WATCH THE KITE-SURFERS

PORTLAND BEACH ROAD - A354

HAMM BEACH RD

PORTLAND MARINA

TOMMY TORPEDO

DANNY THE DOLPHIN MEMORIAL

Mobi-Deck

PORTLAND CASTLE

LIBERTY RD

MERCHANT'S INCLINE RAILWAY

HELI-PAD (H)

MULBERRY AVE

LERRET RD

LIDL

FOLLOW PAVEMENT

SKATE PARK

CHESIL BEACH

FOLLOW PAVEMENT

TOILETS

CHESIL BEACH VISITOR CENTRE & TASTE CAFÉ

POSSIBLE TO WALK THROUGH GRASSLAND

66

68

68

ROUTE GUIDE AND MAPS

(cont'd from p259) They also have a free-to-use telescope and visitors can hire a backpack with binoculars (for use in/around the centre only) for £3.

Back on the path towards Portland, three roundabouts are eventually crossed, the third furnished with a bus stop and The Little Ship pub.

Back on the main road, continue a little way along before turning right into Pebble Lane, following it as far as **Chiswell** and *The Cove House Inn* (Map 67; ☎ 01305-820895, 🖥 thecovehouseinn.co.uk; 🐾; food summer Mon-Fri noon-2.30pm & 6-9pm, Sat noon-4pm & 5.30-9pm & Sun noon-4pm, winter closed on Mon), a friendly pub which serves decent pub grub and real ales; customers spill out onto the promenade on sunny evenings.

From here continue to **Fortuneswell**.

FORTUNESWELL   [Map 68]

Scruffy Fortuneswell isn't the most charismatic of stops on the path. For a night it's fine, but it's much more atmospheric – and prettier – to stay at Portland Bill if you can.

Services on Fortuneswell (the road that runs through the village) include a Co-op **supermarket** (Mon-Sat 7am-11pm), a Boots **pharmacy** (Mon-Fri 9am-5.30pm, Sat 9am-1pm), and a **post office** (Mon-Sat 5am-5.30pm, Sun 6am-1pm).

At 2-4 Fortuneswell, is the very smart *Queen Anne House* (☎ 01305-820028, 🖥 queenannehouse.co.uk; 4D; 🍽; WI-FI; £50-55pp, sgl occ room rate), while higher still, and overlooking the town below, is *The Heights Hotel* (☎ 01305-821361, 🖥 heightshotel.com; 6S/48D or T; 🍽; WI-FI; £45-100pp, sgl £90-100, sgl occ room rate), on Yeates Rd. It's a modern place which serves decent café and bistro food all day

(Mon, Tue & Thur 8am-6pm, Fri-Sun 8am to 'late'; WI-FI) and has panoramic windows to make the most of the great views.

There are numerous other choices for food, but perhaps the most popular for coast path walkers is *The Cove House Inn* (see above). At the end of the promenade is the tiny, but very popular *Quiddles* (☎ 01305-820651; daily 9am-sunset but meals only served to 2.30pm, after that only snacks and cakes), which has a choice location on the promenade, overlooking West Weare beach. All the seats are outside on the patio or roof terrace. They specialise in seafood, but do normal café fare too.

For **buses**, First's No 1 service travels regularly between Weymouth and Portland. First also operates a seasonal service (501) between Weymouth and Portland Bill. See pp53-5 for details.

FORTUNESWELL TO WEYMOUTH   [MAPS 68-71]
(VIA THE ISLE OF PORTLAND CIRCUIT)

Today's multifaceted **14¾-mile (23.75km; 5½hrs)** walk around the wild and intriguing Isle of Portland (see box p264) is an adventure like no other on this trek. Connected to the mainland by two miles of road, the isle feels somehow estranged from the rest of Dorset as if cast away – without ever truly being able to free itself from the mainland's grasp.

With a landscape that encompasses lonely clifftops, surreal boulders, disused quarries, housing and industrial estates, MoD compounds, prisons and institutions, nature reserves, a 13th-century church and three lighthouses, there is little likelihood of you becoming bored on this great slab of limestone. Wildlife abounds too, with over half of Britain's 57 butterfly species in residence and birdlife visiting the isle in such numbers that one of the three lighthouses has

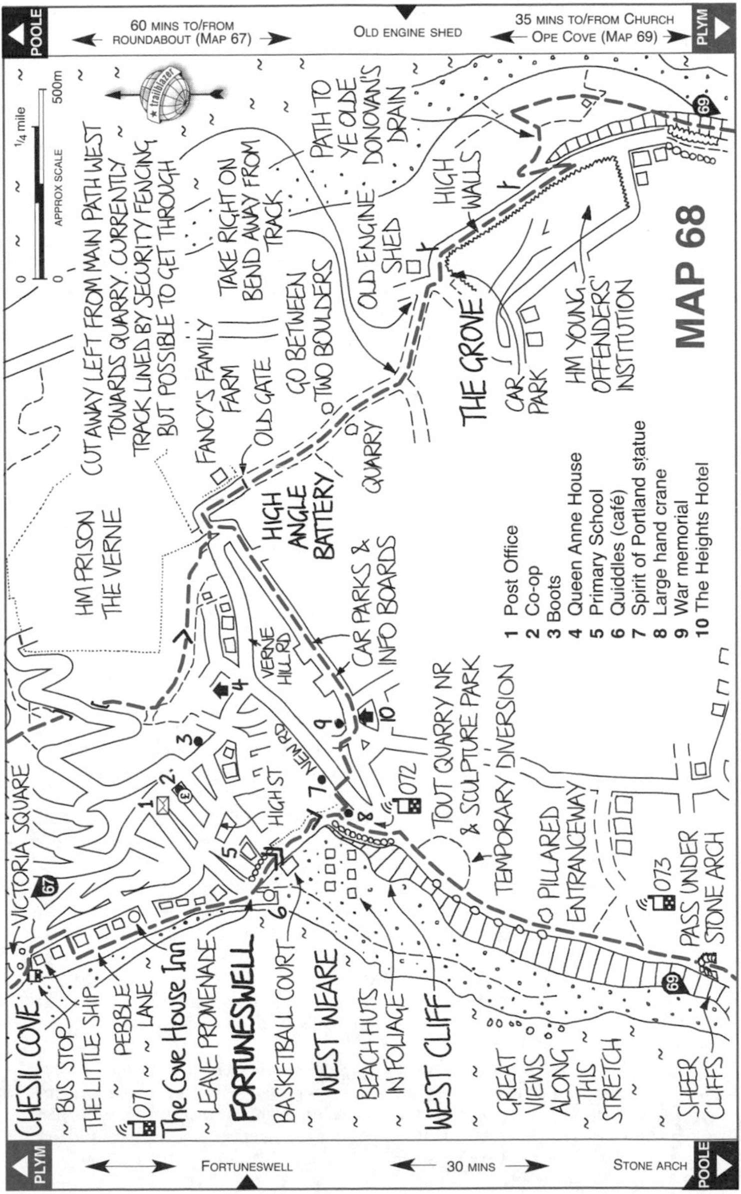
POOLE
60 MINS TO/FROM ROUNDABOUT (MAP 67)
OLD ENGINE SHED
35 MINS TO/FROM CHURCH OPE COVE (MAP 69)
PLYM
0
1/4 mile
0
APPROX SCALE
500m
trailblazer
CUT AWAY LEFT FROM MAIN PATH WEST TOWARDS QUARRY. CURRENTLY TRACK LINED BY SECURITY FENCING BUT POSSIBLE TO GET THROUGH
TAKE RIGHT ON BEND AWAY FROM TRACK
PATH TO YE OLDE DONOVAN'S DRAIN
OLD ENGINE SHED
HIGH WALLS
FANCY'S FAMILY FARM
OLD GATE
GO BETWEEN TWO BOULDERS
QUARRY
THE GROVE
CAR PARK
HM YOUNG OFFENDERS' INSTITUTION
MAP 68
HM PRISON THE VERNE
HIGH ANGLE BATTERY
CAR PARKS & INFO BOARDS
VERNE HILL RD
1 Post Office
2 Co-op
3 Boots
4 Queen Anne House
5 Primary School
6 Quiddles (café)
7 Spirit of Portland statue
8 Large hand crane
9 War memorial
10 The Heights Hotel
VICTORIA SQUARE
67
HIGH ST
NEW RD
072
TOUT QUARRY NR & SCULPTURE PARK
TEMPORARY DIVERSION
PILLARED ENTRANCEWAY
073
PASS UNDER STONE ARCH
69
CHESIL COVE
BUS STOP
THE LITTLE SHIP
PEBBLE LANE
071
The Cove House Inn
LEANE PROMENADE
FORTUNESWELL
BASKETBALL COURT
WEST WEARE
BEACH HUTS IN FOLIAGE
WEST CLIFF
GREAT VIEWS ALONG THIS STRETCH
SHEER CLIFFS
69
PLYM
FORTUNESWELL
30 MINS
STONE ARCH
POOLE

been turned into a bird observatory. Basking sharks, dolphins and seals also inhabit the waters offshore.

The path is generally easy on the legs, but with a couple of short ascents around the Underhill area, and there are some places to stop for food, including a café near the isle's southern tip, where you can also find two places with hostel-type accommodation and a pub with rooms and a campsite. To return to the mainland the coast path suggests you need to walk the tombolo twice – though buses also cross the tombolo frequently between Fortuneswell and Ferrybridge.

The route

From The Cove House Inn the path now briefly follows the edge of Chesil Cove, turning left and then right to head up the steep path to **West Cliff**, with the beach huts and boulders of **West Weare** below you.

At the very top of the steps turn back for a great view over Portland Harbour: one of the largest man-made harbours in the world, it was formed by the construction of huge stone breakwaters between 1848 and 1905.

❏ THE ISLAND OF PORTLAND

Six kilometres long, two-and-a-half kilometres wide and made of limestone, the Isle of Portland is what is known as a **tied island**, connected to the mainland by a sandbar, or tombolo – which, in Portland's case, is better known as the A354. The island today is most famous for Portland stone, a durable, good-looking material used in the building of Buckingham Palace and St Paul's Cathedral (the latter, incidentally, designed by Christopher Wren who was once MP for Weymouth and controlled the quarries on Portland). The stone was also used for thousands of gravestones during the two world wars.

The isle is divided into two main areas: the northern, steeply sloping **Underhill** (which has been visible for many miles) and the flatter, plateau-like southern expanse of **Tophill**. The isle slopes down from approximately 150 metres above sea-level near **The Verne**, atop Underhill, to just above sea-level by the time you reach Portland Bill. There are eight settlements, the most relevant to the walker being Chiswell, Fortuneswell (for both see p262) and Castletown. Although the first two sit close enough to be almost indistinguishable, Chiswell consists of the flatter area near Chesil Cove and the sea (ie the home of The Cove Inn) whilst Fortuneswell is made up of the sloping streets that lead up from the hill. Castletown lies to the east of Chiswell.

The most prominent tourist attraction on the island – save, perhaps, for the lighthouse at Portland Bill – is **Portland Castle** (Map 67; ☎ 01305-820539, 💻 english-heritage.org.uk/visit/places/portland-castle; daily Apr-end Oct 10am-5pm, closed Nov-Mar; £7.80). Known as a 'Device Fort' or 'Henrician Castle', it was constructed (using Portland Stone, of course) on the orders of Henry VIII in 1540 in order to defend Weymouth from attack by the French and Spanish. Possibly due to the quality of the stone it is one of the best-preserved castles from this era. The SWCP passes right in front of the castle.

One final tip: whilst a guest on the isle be wary of using the word 'rabbit'. Records suggest that superstitious quarry workers would always see a bunny emerging from its burrow immediately before a rockfall. Such was their superstition, they often refused to work if one was spotted! The unusual moniker 'underground mutton' is how the locals are said to refer to our furry friends.

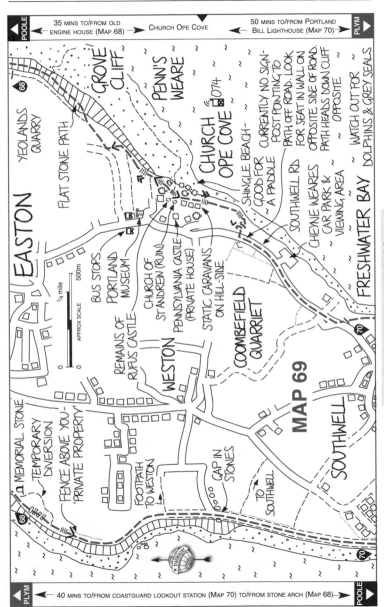

POOLE

PLYM

GROVE CLIFF

PENN'S WEARE

YEOLANDS QUARRY

68

FLAT STONE PATH

CHURCH OPE COVE

074

CURRENTLY NO SIGN-POST POINTING TO PATH OFF ROAD. LOOK FOR SEAT IN WALL ON OPPOSITE SIDE OF ROAD. PATH HEADS DOWN CLIFF OPPOSITE

SHINGLE BEACH – GOOD FOR A PADDLE

SOUTHWELL RD

CHEYNE WEARES CAR PARK & VIEWING AREA

WATCH OUT FOR DOLPHINS & GREY SEALS

FRESHWATER BAY

EASTON

BUS STOPS

PORTLAND MUSEUM

CHURCH OF ST ANDREW (RUIN)

PENNSYLVANIA CASTLE (PRIVATE HOUSE)

STATIC CARAVANS ON HILL-SIDE

REMAINS OF RUFUS CASTLE

¼ mile

500m

APPROX SCALE

0

COOMBEFIELD QUARRIET

MAP 69

SOUTHWELL

WESTON

70

MEMORIAL STONE

TEMPORARY DIVERSION

FENCE ABOVE YOU– 'PRIVATE PROPERTY'

FOOTPATH TO WESTON

GAP IN STONES

TO SOUTHWELL

68

70

PLYM

POOLE

Via a short, signposted, diversion the path now heads through disused **Tout Quarry**, a nature reserve and sculpture park. As you walk alongside the boulders, under stone archways and with some sheer drops to your right, there are marvellous views back down along the whole of Chesil Beach. This exposed cliff-top path contrasts starkly with yesterday's agrarian amble.

After another small diversion, the path gradually bends south and widens, with housing estates interrupting the scenery on the left and a **business park** doing similar work straight ahead. Passing this, you descend gradually across grasslands; watch out for the odd sprouting of barbed wire lying in wait in the scrub to snare the unwary.

On the way you come to a **coastguard's lookout station** and the **Old (Higher) Lighthouse** – the light from which first guided sailors in 1716 – one of three lighthouses at Portland Bill. Just after this you'll pass *Portland Bunkhouse* (☎ 07776-054720, 🖳 portlandbunkhouse.com; 38 beds in 7 bunkbed rooms each sleeping 4/8 people, 1D, shared facilities; from £20pp, sgl occ in double room £25; WI-FI), a former transmitter station. The new owners have done their hardest to overcome the flaws that used to mar the place; windows have now been placed in a couple of rooms, and those that still lack natural light now have fans at least which make it feel fresher. The self-catering kitchen is fine, the owners are friendly, and the place now regularly scores highly on review sites.

Continuing downhill, you soon get to *The Pulpit Inn* (☎ 01305-561089, 🖳 www.pulpitinnportland.co.uk; 2D/1T; intermittent WI-FI; 🐾 bar only), which

---

❑ TOUT QUARRY SCULPTURE PARK

One of the more curious attractions on Dorset's coastal path – indeed, on the entire South-West Coast Path – is the Tout Quarry Sculpture Park. Over sixty artworks have been sculpted from the bare Portland stone, and a wander around it is quite fascinating. Some of the sculptures are quite subtle – indeed, at first glance you may think that some of the works have just been weathered by the wind and rain to create the patterns upon them. Others, however, such as the grinning Roy Dog, which emerges from the bare rock as if looking out from its den, are more obvious.

As you might have guessed from the sheer variety of the work, the sculptures are not the work of one person. Instead, the park started in 1983 when it was decided to open the former quarry up to artists' residencies and allow each artist to respond to the 40-acre site as they saw fit. Previous artists at the quarry have included Anthony Gormley, creator of the *Angel of the North* and probably Britain's most famous living sculptor. His work, *Still Falling*, depicts a man falling head-first down a cliff-face.

The residency program continues to this day and it's not uncommon to see artists practising their masonic skills on the local geology today. But even if the art itself doesn't appeal, it's fascinating to see how nature is slowly encroaching and reclaiming the site once more, with rarities such as rock stonecrop and Portland spurge thriving in the quarry, while butterflies flit from sculpture to sculpture.

The sculpture park is free to visit but, unless one of the many temporary diversions to the Coast Path divert you into the quarry, it can be easy to miss. Do your best not to: it's a fascinating place.

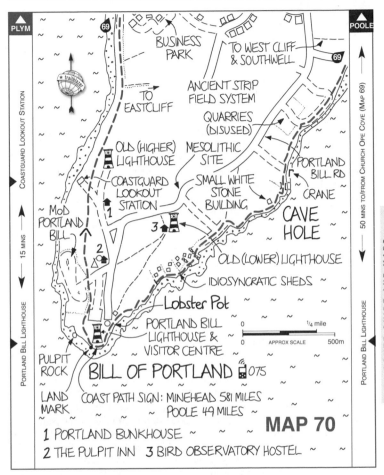

PLYM

POOLE

BUSINESS PARK

TO WEST CLIFF & SOUTHWELL

69

TO EASTCLIFF

ANCIENT STRIP FIELD SYSTEM

QUARRIES (DISUSED)

OLD (HIGHER) LIGHTHOUSE

MESOLITHIC SITE

PORTLAND BILL RD

COASTGUARD LOOKOUT STATION

SMALL WHITE STONE BUILDING

CRANE

1

MoD PORTLAND BILL

CAVE HOLE

2

3

OLD (LOWER) LIGHTHOUSE

IDIOSYNCRATIC SHEDS

Lobster Pot

PORTLAND BILL LIGHTHOUSE & VISITOR CENTRE

0   ¼ mile

0   500m
APPROX SCALE

PULPIT ROCK

BILL OF PORTLAND 📱075

LAND MARK

COAST PATH SIGN: MINEHEAD 581 MILES
POOLE 49 MILES

MAP 70

1 PORTLAND BUNKHOUSE
2 THE PULPIT INN 3 BIRD OBSERVATORY HOSTEL

Coastguard Lookout Station

15 MINS

Portland Bill Lighthouse

50 MINS TO/FROM CHURCH OPE COVE (MAP 69)

Portland Bill Lighthouse

ROUTE GUIDE AND MAPS

charges £39.50-55pp (sgl occ room rate) for **B&B** and now does **camping** (£10 per tent up to two people). They also do **food** (summer Mon-Sat noon-9pm, Sun noon-3pm & 5-9pm, call for winter opening days/times). Their pub-grub mains cost £13-17, although they also have fish specials, and do sandwiches and jackets (£6-9) before 5pm. Opening times can be a bit hit and miss, especially in bad weather, so it's worth calling ahead.

From the pub, you soon reach the highlight and focal point of most people's Portland Isle tour: the striking, red-and-white painted **Portland Bill Lighthouse** (☎ 01305-821050, 🖥 trinityhouse.co.uk/lighthouses; **fb**; visiting hours vary but generally Easter-end Sep daily 10am-5pm, Oct-Mar Sat & Sun 11am-3pm; visitor centre £3/2.50 adults/concs, centre and lighthouse £8.50/7.50 adults/concs), which was built between 1905 and 1906, is still a working lighthouse and now houses Portland's **Visitor Centre**. A stone's throw away is **Pulpit Rock**, a remarkably square-looking rock stack, formed during quarrying in the 1870s and which can be climbed.

Close to the lighthouse, and commanding a fabulous seaview location, is the excellent café-restaurant, *The Lobster Pot* (☎ 01305-820242, 💻 lobsterpot restaurantportland.co.uk; WI-FI; daily 9.30am-4.30pm), a great spot for breakfast, lunch or just a coffee and ice-cream. It's a bright, big-windowed space and they have picnic tables outside.

A little further along the path the old (lower) lighthouse, built in 1716 (although re-built in 1869), houses an important **bird observatory** and also provides fabulous-value *hostel accommodation* (☎ 01305-820553, 💻 www.port landbirdobs.com; 9 bunk-bed rooms each with 2-4 beds, sleeps 25; shared facilities; from £20pp, sgl occ £20; WI-FI) for ramblers, twitchers, climbers and artists. Meals are not provided but there's a large, well-equipped self-catering kitchen, a lounge area with huge bird-watching bay windows, a small, but well-stocked reading room and simple, but neat and tidy rooms with very comfortable wooden-framed bunk beds and clean shared bathrooms. Most of the rooms are in the ground-floor base of the lighthouse, but three are in the tower itself, at the top of which is an observatory with 360° views. There's a wonderfully laidback atmosphere and outside the main bird-watching seasons (spring and autumn), when it's best to book ahead, you'll often have a dorm to yourself. As well as the dorms, there is also a self-contained **lighthouse keeper's cottage** (1T and a room with a bunk bed; shower; 🐾; £80 for up to four people, sgl occ rates on request). However, you would need to book very early for that as it is extremely popular; it is also highly unlikely there will ever be a single-night vacancy for it. First's seasonal 501 **bus** service calls here; see pp53-5.

Keeping to the right of Portland Bill's **idiosyncratic 'sheds'**, you pass through disused and deserted quarries and out of sight of any civilisation. The path gradually rises away from the shoreline to a road, until a second path winds downwards through rocks and scrub to the **remains of Rufus Castle** (Map 69) – also known as Bow and Arrow Castle and built in the late 15th century. The ruins now constitute a Grade-I listed building and unfortunately are deemed too fragile for the public to freely wander. Close by (though off the path) is the site of the 13th-century **Church of St Andrew**, Portland's parish church until the 18th century. Its graveyard remains the eternal resting place of seafarers; the gravestones, made of course of local stone, are worth a look.

Not too far away (and also off the path), **Portland Museum** (☎ 01305-821804, 💻 portlandmuseum.co.uk; Easter-Oct Sat-Thur 10.30am-4pm, rest of year variable as opening days/hours depend on the availability of volunteers so check their website; £4.50/3.50 adults/concs) has display sections that include Stone, Sea and Shipwrecks and Famous Portland People.

The path continues through the scrub, above the quarries and boulders of **Penn's Weare** and **Grove Cliff** and through a gate at the far end of the huge **Yeolands Quarry**, with Portland goats grazing nearby. This leads to a Young Offenders' Institution and the **Old Engine Shed**, that housed the locomotives that were used in the quarries. Continue onwards along the road passing **Fancy's Family Farm** and the entrance to **HM Prison The Verne**: formerly a fortress and a barracks for a thousand troops, the Verne Citadel became a prison in 1949, the interior being completed by prisoners themselves. The prison holds an unwanted world record thanks to ex-inmate John Hannan who escaped (by tying bedsheets together to make a rope) in 1955, despite only being given a 21-month sentence in the first place. Assuming he is still alive, he has now been on the run for longer than any person in history. Behind you is **High Angle Battery**, built in 1892 to defend Portland Harbour.

Just past Fancy's Family Farm the path divides and you have a choice to make. Either continue along the road back to Fortuneswell, where you pass car parks, information boards and a war memorial on the right and *The Heights Hotel* (see p262) on the left. Or you can take the path that leaves the road on the bend, a path that follows the perimeter of the prison as it makes its way to the top of the arrow-straight path known as the **Mariner's Incline**. This leads fairly steeply down to **Portland Castle** (see box p264), opposite which you'll find the great value and dirt-cheap snack van *Mobi-Deck* (☎ 077721 60925; **fb**; daily 10am-3pm, weather permitting) and around the Marina to the **Tombolo**.

All that's left to complete your Portland Odyssey is to head back across the Tombolo and continue your saunter into Weymouth ...

Into Weymouth

For the walk to the centre of Weymouth you join **The Rodwell Trail**, which begins by Ferrybridge (see Map 66, p260). The coast path leaves The Rodwell just before *Sandsfoot Garden Café* (**fb**; weather permitting summer daily approx 9am-4.30 or 5pm; winter weekends only) near the **remains of Sandsfoot Castle** (🖳 www.sandsfootcastle.org.uk; free), one of Henry VIII's fortifications which, together with Portland Castle (over on the island), defended the harbour. Most of the ruins have now fallen into the sea but some remain and lottery funding has enabled it to be opened to the public.

From the café follow the road for a distance to **Belle Vue Rd**, where you turn right, then **Bincleaves Rd** where another right turn and then an almost immediate left leads into a park. That leads, via a bridge, to **Nothe Gardens**, passing the Victorian **Nothe Fort** (☎ 01305-766626, 🖳 nothefort.org.uk; Easter-end Oct daily 10.30am-4pm, closed mid Dec to mid Feb and weekends only 11am-3pm the rest of the year; £9.50) on your right. The gardens lead around the pretty little **harbour** where, crossing **Town Bridge**, you follow the coast path signs down the steps and along the eastern edge of the harbour. You then take up the tram lines, passing **Weymouth Harbour Cargo Stage** on the right, the smell of fish pungent in the air. At the end of the road there's the Pavilion theatre in front of you to the right – and the promenade (Esplanade) along Weymouth seafront ahead.

It's a lovely stroll along the seafront, with arcades and fairground rides on your left and kid-laden donkeys panting in the sun to your right. The promenade is adorned with statues and memorials aplenty to the great and the good including: the grand **George III statue** (situated by the bus stops), a **Jubilee Clock**, a tribute to Queen Victoria, as well as more solemn ones to American GIs, ANZAC forces and home-grown Tommys who perished in World War II. From the Pier Bandstand, follow the blue Coast Path signs and continue along Brunswick Terrace and out of town.

WEYMOUTH   [map p273]

Dubbed 'the Naples of England' by the Victorian tourism industry, and more recently chosen to host the sailing events at the 2012 Olympics, Dorset's fourth largest town was once the favourite holiday destination of His Royal Highness George III following the decision of his brother, the Duke of Gloucester, to build a huge residence here.

Though the townsfolk didn't follow the lead of their fellow south-coast resorts, Lyme and Bognor, in changing their name to celebrate the royal patronage bestowed upon them, there is no doubting they are just as proud of their regal links. Not only are there plaques and place names aplenty in Weymouth that commemorate George's visits, but there's also the rather gaudy statue of him in the centre and a large white chalk depiction of him atop a horse etched into the hillside just outside the town near Osmington (see p278).

Perhaps, given that Weymouth's prior claim to fame was as the place where the Black Death entered the country in 1348, the locals' desire to celebrate the king's choice of holiday destination is understandable.

There's plenty for walkers to enjoy in the town – including a wonderful sweep of sand that stretches for miles, a great harbour with some lovely cafés and restaurants as well as all the services and facilities you'd expect of a town this size.

Wessex Folk Festival is held here in June and **Dorset Seafood Festival** (Seafest) in September; for details of both see p14.

Services

Since late May 2022 Weymouth has had its own **tourist information centre** (🖥 www .weymouthinformationshop.co.uk; Mon-Sat 10am-4pm); it is at 98 St Mary St. The **post office** (Mon-Fri 9am-5pm, Sat 9am-1pm) is on St Thomas St and there are plenty of **banks** with **ATMs** around town.

The town centre also has a branch of Boots the **chemist** (Mon-Sat 8.30am-5.30pm, Sun 10am-4pm), on St Thomas St. **Camping suppliers** Mountain Warehouse and Trespass are within a couple of hundred yards of each other on St Mary St and both have the same opening hours (Mon-Sat 9am-5.30pm, Sun 10am-4.30pm).

There's a Tesco Metro **supermarket** (Mon-Sat 7am-10pm, Sun 10am-4pm) on nearby St Thomas St.

If you struggled to find your own ammonites on the beaches around Lyme Regis, you can buy **fossil souvenirs** at a shop called Fossil Beach (daily 9.30am-5pm), at the top of St Thomas St.

Summer walkers should take note of the numerous **water taps**, located at the back of the beach as you leave town heading north.

Transport

Weymouth is very well connected by **bus**: First (Nos 1, 8, 10, X51, X52, X53, X54 & 501) and More Bus (No 5 & 30) operate services to and from surrounding towns and villages. However, the only bus to Durdle Door and Lulworth is More's seasonal Breezer 30 service. See pp53-5 for details.

South Western Railway operates **train** services here from London Waterloo and

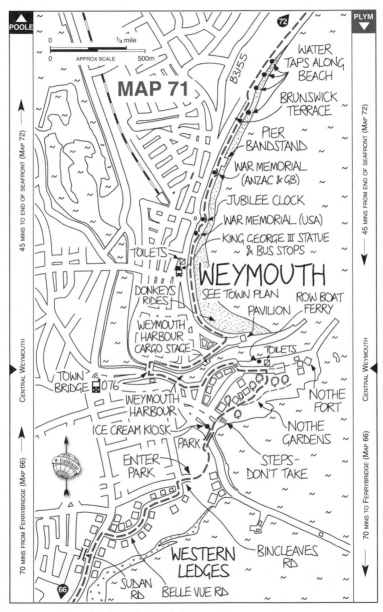

72

MAP 71

¼ mile

APPROX SCALE

0   500m

B3155

WATER TAPS ALONG BEACH

BRUNSWICK TERRACE

PIER BANDSTAND

WAR MEMORIAL (ANZAC & GB)

JUBILEE CLOCK

WAR MEMORIAL (USA)

KING GEORGE III STATUE & BUS STOPS

TOILETS

WEYMOUTH

SEE TOWN PLAN

DONKEYS RIDES

PAVILION

ROW BOAT FERRY

WEYMOUTH HARBOUR CARGO STAGE

TOILETS

TOWN BRIDGE 076

WEYMOUTH HARBOUR

NOTHE FORT

ICE CREAM KIOSK

PARK

NOTHE GARDENS

ENTER PARK

STEPS- DON'T TAKE

trailblazer

WESTERN LEDGES

BINCLEAVES RD

SUDAN RD

BELLE VUE RD

66

45 MINS TO END OF SEAFRONT (MAP 72)

45 MINS FROM END OF SEAFRONT (MAP 72)

CENTRAL WEYMOUTH

CENTRAL WEYMOUTH

70 MINS FROM FERRYBRIDGE (MAP 66)

70 MINS TO FERRYBRIDGE (MAP 66)

ROUTE GUIDE AND MAPS

GWR from Bristol. To get to Exeter, Torquay or Plymouth by train you need to change in Castle Cary. See box p51.

> **Where to stay: the details**
> Unless specified, B&B-style accommodation is either en suite or has private facilities.

Where to stay

Weymouth has approximately 150 **B&Bs** so there shouldn't be too many issues with finding a bed though many places require stays of at least two nights, if not three, in the peak season but even sometimes all year. However, they can be fairly helpfully divided into three categories: the few that will allow people to book well in advance for one night only; those that do so but not at weekends and/or in the peak season (July and August); and those that don't. Ever. That said, most will accept people for just one night if they have availability and you turn up on the day.

Old Harbour View (☎ 01305-774633, 🖳 oldharbourviewweymouth.co.uk; 1D/1D or T; WI-FI; from £65pp, sgl occ £90) only accepts stays of a minimum of two nights. It is on the way into town and is perfectly located near harbour-side pubs; it is not cheap but the location is ideal.

Moving north to the string of establishments on The Esplanade are: ***The Roundhouse Hotel*** (☎ 01305-761010, 🖳 roundhouse-weymouth.com; 1T/5D; WI-FI; £47.50-77.50pp, sgl occ room rate) at No 1; at No 2, ***Aaran House*** (☎ 01305-766669, 🖳 aaranhouse.co.uk; 4D/2T; 🛁; WI-FI; £47.50-60pp, sgl occ room rate), which is the only one of the three which accepts advance bookings for a single-night stay in the main season; and their neighbour at No 3, ***Beach View Guest House*** (☎ 01305-570046, 🖳 beachviewguesthouse.com; 5D; 🛁; WI-FI; from £37.50pp, sgl occ £65).

Still on The Esplanade, ***The Anchorage*** (☎ 01305-782542, 🖳 theanchorageweymouth.co.uk; 1S/4D/1D or T/1Tr; WI-FI; £42.50-50pp, sgl from £50, sgl occ rates on request), at No 7, accepts a minimum advance booking of three nights March to end September and two nights the rest of the year.

Still good value are ***Bay View Hotel*** (☎ 01305-782083, 🖳 bayview-weymouth.co.uk; 6D/2Tr; WI-FI; £32.50-35pp, sgl occ from £60), No 35, which provides fridges in its rooms as they serve a continental-style breakfast and guests eat in their rooms. They accept a minimum booking of two nights year-round.

Langham Hotel (☎ 01305-782530, 🖳 langham-hotel.com; 6D/3Tr/3Qd; 🛁; WI-FI; Apr to early Nov; £45-60pp, sgl occ £68-90), at No 130, requires a minimum stay of three nights between June and September. Some rooms can sleep children.

In contrast and before leaving The Esplanade altogether, right at its heart sits ***Gloucester House*** (☎ 01305-785191, 🖳 gloucesterhouseweymouth.co.uk; 2S/6D/2T/2Tr/2Qd; WI-FI; £47.50-97.50pp, sgl £62-100, sgl occ rates on request) at No 96, where one-night bookings are usually allowed if there is a gap.

The Esplanade isn't the only street stuffed with accommodation; at the opposite end of town there is another string of B&Bs on Brunswick Terrace. Most of them are great value and some accept one-night stops, at least outside the peak seasons of July and August. ***Whitecliff*** (☎ 01305-785554, 🖳 whitecliffweymouth.co.uk; 1S/4D/1T/1Tr; 🛁; WI-FI; £40-67.50pp, sgl from £60, sgl occ generally room rate), at No 7, is a decent and well-run place.

> **SYMBOLS USED IN TEXT**
> 🛁 Bathtub in, or for, at least one room; WI-FI means wi-fi is available
> 🐕 Dogs allowed; for accommodation subject to prior arrangement (see p313)
> **fb** signifies places that have a Facebook page (for latest opening hours)

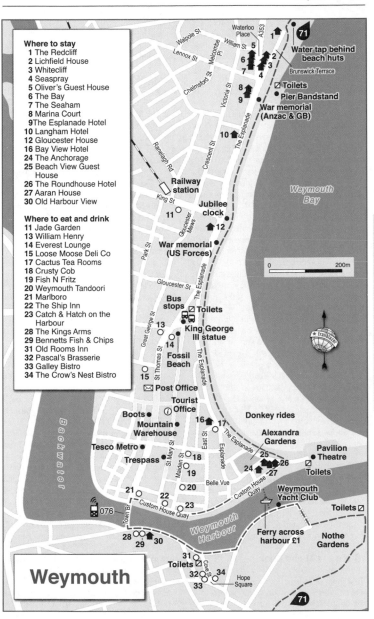

Where to stay
1 The Redcliff
2 Lichfield House
3 Whitecliff
4 Seaspray
5 Oliver's Guest House
6 The Bay
7 The Seaham
8 Marina Court
9 The Esplanade Hotel
10 Langham Hotel
12 Gloucester House
16 Bay View Hotel
24 The Anchorage
25 Beach View Guest House
26 The Roundhouse Hotel
27 Aaran House
30 Old Harbour View

Where to eat and drink
11 Jade Garden
13 William Henry
14 Everest Lounge
15 Loose Moose Deli Co
17 Cactus Tea Rooms
18 Crusty Cob
19 Fish N Fritz
20 Weymouth Tandoori
21 Marlboro
22 The Ship Inn
23 Catch & Hatch on the Harbour
28 The Kings Arms
29 Bennetts Fish & Chips
31 Old Rooms Inn
32 Pascal's Brasserie
33 Galley Bistro
34 The Crow's Nest Bistro

Walpole St
Lennox St
Waterloo Place
A353
William St
Melcombe Pl
Chelmsford St
Victoria St
5
6
1
2
7
4
3
Water tap behind beach huts
Brunswick Terrace
8
☑ **Toilets**
9
● **Pier Bandstand**
● **War memorial (Anzac & GB)**
10
The Esplanade
Crescent St
Ranelagh Rd
Railway station
King St
Gloucester Mews
Jubilee clock
11
12
Park St
War memorial (US Forces)
The Esplanade
Gloucester St
Bus stops
🚌 ☑ **Toilets**
King George III statue
13
Great George St
St Thomas St
14
Fossil Beach
The Esplanade
15
✉ **Post Office**
Tourist Office ⓘ
Boots ●
Mountain Warehouse ●
16
17
Donkey rides
East St
Tesco Metro ●
Trespass ●
St Mary St
Maiden St
18
19
Belle Vue
20
The Esplanade
Esplanade
Alexandra Gardens
25
Pavilion Theatre ●
24
26
27
☑ **Toilets**
Weymouth Yacht Club
⚓
21
22
23
Custom House Quay
Town Br
📱 076
Custom House Quay
28
29
30
Ferry across harbour £1
Toilets ☑
Nothe Gardens
31
Toilets ☑
32
33
34
Hope Square
Cove St
Weymouth Harbour

Weymouth
Weymouth Bay

0   200m

Backwater

71

ROUTE GUIDE AND MAPS

Also very good value are *Lichfield House* (☎ 01305-784112, 🖥 lichfieldhouse .net; 2D/1T/2Tr; WI-FI; £39-57.50pp, sgl occ rates on request), at No 8, and *Seaspray* (☎ 01305-786943, 🖥 www.seaspray-wey mouth.co.uk; 4D/1Qd; WI-FI; £40-62.50pp, sgl occ £72-92) at No 6. However, both accept a minimum stay of two nights and in July and August three or four nights.

Further down the street, *The Redcliff* (☎ 01305-784682, 🖥 redcliffweymouth.co .uk; 4S/6D/2Tr; WI-FI; 🐾; £55-67.50pp, sgl from £65, sgl occ room rate), at No 18-19, accept advance bookings for a one-night stay during the week in summer but not at weekends. They are also happy to do laundry.

One block behind Brunswick Terrace, so fronted with a road rather than the sea, Waterloo Place is home to another line of B&Bs. *Oliver's Guest House* (☎ 01305-786712, 🖥 oliversguesthouse.co.uk; 1S/4D all en suite, 1T/1D share facilities; WI-FI; £45-52.50pp, sgl occ room rate), at No 12, though the minimum stay is two nights; *The Bay* (☎ 01305-786289, 🖥 thebay guesthouse.co.uk; 3D/2D or T; WI-FI; £39.50-60pp, sgl occ rates on request) at No 10, where the minimum stay in summer is three nights but they will accept single-night stays if they have a gap near the time and their rooms have fridges; and *The Seaham* (☎ 01305-782010, 🖥 theseaham weymouth.co.uk; 5D; WI-FI; £45-52.50pp, sgl occ room rate) at No 3. This last, incidentally, has some great breakfast options, with kippers, poached haddock and salmon on their menu.

Also in this area is *Marina Court* (☎ 01305-782146, 🖥 marinacourt.co.uk; 8D/1D or T/1Tr/2Qd; WI-FI; room only £40-52.50pp, sgl occ £70-95; continental/ cooked breakfast £7/12.50; Mar/Apr-end Oct), at No 142 The Esplanade. However, at the time of research they were uncertain if or when they would re-open.

Where to eat and drink
The historic harbour area is your best bet for a meal or a drink, but the most pleasant place to eat is just off it, to the south, in a small, quiet, partly tree-shaded plaza called Hope Square, where several lovely café-restaurants create a Mediterranean-like atmosphere with tables spilling out onto the pavements.

Cafés & delis Right on the Esplanade, *Cactus Tea Rooms* (🐾; Mar-Nov daily from 10.30am, they close when it is quiet or the weather is bad, latest they stay open is 6.30pm) has been going for almost 20 years and does brunches and lunches (sandwiches £5-7, jacket potatoes £7.50, mains £10) as well as a lovely Dorset apple cake.

For sandwich fillers, try *Loose Moose Deli Co* (☎ 01305-774941; Mon-Fri 7am-3.30pm, Sat 9am-2.30pm), on School St just off St Thomas St; or there's a branch of the local bakery chain *The Crusty Cob* (Mon-Sat 8.30am-4pm).

Restaurants On a sunny summer's day, you can't beat Hope Square, where three charming European-inspired eateries vie for your attention: best of the lot, thanks largely to its tree-shaded terrace, is *The Crow's Nest Bistro* (☎ 01305-786930, 🖥 crowsnestweymouth.com; Thur-Sat 6-10.30pm) which has an extensive tapas menu (£6-7.50).

Across the square, *Galley Bistro* (☎ 01305-784059, 🖥 thegalleybistro.co.uk; food Wed-Sat noon-2pm & 5.30-9pm, Sun noon-3pm) offer lunches (£7-18) and evening mains (£13-23), while *Pascal's Brasserie* (☎ 01305-777500; fb; Mar-end Oct Wed-Mon 9.30am-4pm, winter Thur-Mon) serves nothing but home cooking, much of it French (the owner hails from Paris), and specialises in dishes such as 'canard confit' (duck confit), though doesn't ignore the cuisine of its new homeland either, baking cakes and scones daily and conjuring up a mean Dorset apple cake.

For Chinese food, *Jade Garden* (☎ 01305-778844, 🖥 jadegarden-weymouth .co.uk; Wed-Mon 5-11pm), on King St near the railway station, is a sit-down restaurant as well as a takeaway. They do some Malay and Thai dishes too.

For fresh seafood, two fine establishments operate out of Weymouth's Old Fish Market on the harbour front. *Catch* (☎

01305-590555, 🖳 www.catchattheoldfish
market.com; Tue-Thur 5.30-9pm, Fri & Sat
noon-2pm & 5.30-9pm) is a local seafood
restaurant where a two-course dinner is
£55, or it's £65 for three.

The front of the building, however, is
largely taken up with its little brother,
Hatch on the Harbour (☎ 07789-136722,
🖳 www.hatchonthehar bour.com; Apr-Oct
daily noon-9pm), a more informal, 'street-
food' style fish place serving such delights
as three oysters (£7.50); scallops in salsa
verde and grilled lobster are also frequently
available.

Pubs & takeaways There are numerous
harbourside pubs including: *The Kings
Arms* (☎ 01305-772200; **fb**; Mon-Sat
noon-11pm, Sun to 9pm), which doesn't
serve food but allows customers to take
food in as long as they buy a drink; *The
Ship Inn* (☎ 01305-773879, 🖳 shipwey
mouth.co.uk; food daily noon-9pm; 🐾);
and *Old Rooms Inn* (☎ 01305-771130;
food daily 11am-9pm; 🐾), which is part of
the Greene King chain. Old Rooms Inn has
an extensive outdoor seating area. All three
serve a selection of real ales.

Away from the harbour, *William
Henry* (☎ 01305-763730; food daily 8am-
10pm) on Frederick St near the bus station,
is the local Wetherspoons.

Of the plethora of **fish & chip shops**, a
few stand out: *Fish N Fritz* (🖳 www.fish
nfritz.co.uk; daily 11.30am-7pm) does its
best to promote less popular fish to try to
save the diminishing stocks of cod and
other favourites. Similarly, *Bennetts Fish
& Chips* (☎ 01305-781237, 🖳 bennettsfish
andchips.co.uk; Sun-Thur 11.30am-10pm,
Fri & Sat to 10pm); its speciality is its fisherman's bap (cod in a brioche bun with
salad; £7.65). *Marlboro* (☎ 01305-785700,
🖳 marlbororestaurant.co.uk; daily
11.30am-9pm) is one of the most established chippies in town and has been going
since 1974.

For an Indian takeaway, try *Weymouth
Tandoori* (☎ 01305-776744, 🖳 thewey
mouthtandoori.co.uk; Tue-Sun 5.30-
10.30pm) on Maiden St. *Everest Lounge* (☎
01305-784 988, 🖳 www.theeverestlounge
.com; Sun-Thur 5.30-10.30pm, Fri & Sat
from 5pm), near the seafront bus station at
9-10 Thomas St, serves very good Indian
and Nepalese cuisine (mains from £10.50).

WEYMOUTH TO LULWORTH COVE [MAPS 71-76]

This **11-mile (17.75km; 4¾hrs) stage** is as splendid as it is strenuous.
Reckoned by many to be the most beautiful on the trail, it takes you to the pure
white chalky cliffs leading to Lulworth Cove – similar to the chalky cliffs
prevalent further east at Beachy Head and the South Downs of Sussex.

Apart from their distinctive colour, the other characteristic of this type of
cliffs is the way they rise and fall, sometimes relentlessly so – and this is certainly true of this trail, which starts off with an iron-flat walk along Weymouth
seafront (complete with several places serving refreshments) and ends with a
real rollercoaster along the cliffs leading to Durdle Door – perhaps the Dorset
coastline's most iconic feature. From there it's a comparatively small hop to
Lulworth Cove – one of the county's more famous olde-worlde villages, where
even the bus shelter is thatched!

The route
The first gradient on this strenuous stage is a small one. Having finally divert-
ed from the seafront at *Café Oasis* (🖳 www.cafeoasis.co.uk; daily 8am-4.30pm,
occasional evenings too), you climb up **Bowleaze Coveway**, passing in front of
The Lookout Café (**fb**; daily 9am-4.30pm), with its fine views, and up over
Jordan Hill. *(cont'd on p278)*

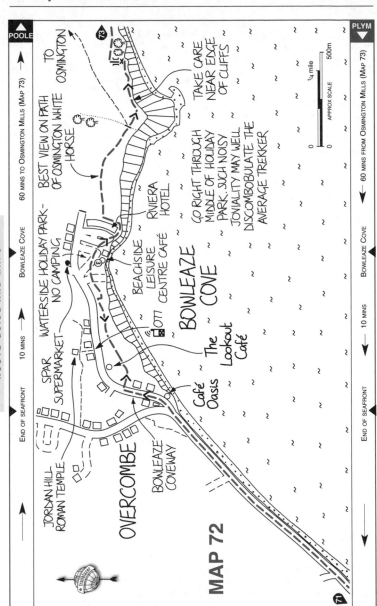

POOLE

PLYM

60 MINS to Osmington Mills (MAP 73)

TO OSMINGTON

BEST VIEW ON PATH OF OSMINGTON WHITE HORSE

TO OSMINGTON

TAKE CARE NEAR EDGE OF CLIFFS

BOWLEAZE COVE

60 MINS FROM OSMINGTON MILLS (MAP 73)

WATERSIDE HOLIDAY PARK – NO CAMPING

RIVIERA HOTEL

BEACHSIDE LEISURE CENTRE CAFÉ

GO RIGHT THROUGH MIDDLE OF HOLIDAY PARK. SUCH NOISY JOVIALITY MAY WELL DISCOMBOBULATE THE AVERAGE TREKKER

BOWLEAZE COVE

SPAR SUPERMARKET

10 MINS

10 MINS

The Lookout Café

END OF SEAFRONT

BOWLEAZE COVEWAY

OVERCOMBE

Café Oasis

¼ mile

APPROX SCALE

0   500m

JORDAN HILL ROMAN TEMPLE

MAP 72

END OF SEAFRONT

71

73

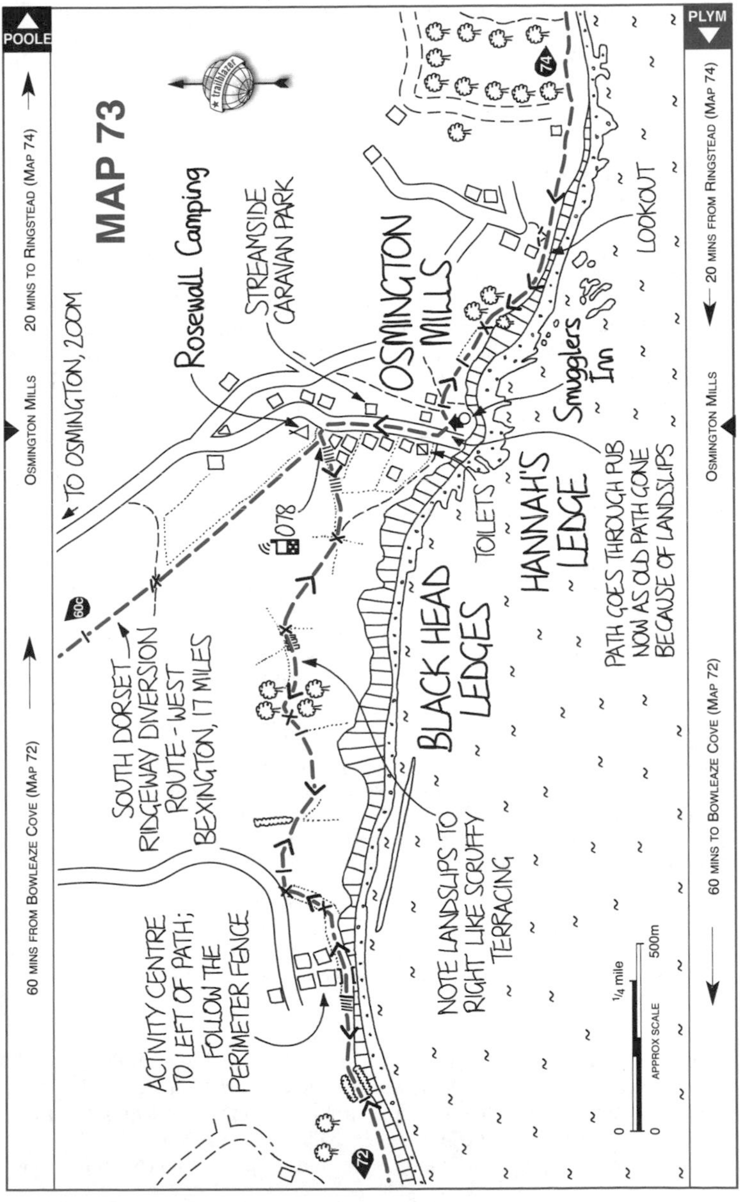

MAP 73

60 MINS FROM BOWLEAZE COVE (MAP 72)

OSMINGTON MILLS

20 MINS TO RINGSTEAD (MAP 74)

★ trailblazer

TO OSMINGTON, 2.00M

Rosewall Camping

STREAMSIDE CARAVAN PARK

SOUTH DORSET RIDGEWAY DIVERSION ROUTE - WEST BEXINGTON, 17 MILES

ACTIVITY CENTRE TO LEFT OF PATH; FOLLOW THE PERIMETER FENCE

OSMINGTON MILLS

Smugglers Inn

HANNAH'S LEDGE

TOILETS

078

BLACK HEAD LEDGES

NOTE LANDSLIPS TO RIGHT LIKE SCRUFFY TERRACING

PATH GOES THROUGH PUB NOW AS OLD PATH GONE BECAUSE OF LANDSLIPS

LOOKOUT

PLYM

74

72

¼ mile

500m

APPROX SCALE

0

0

60 MINS TO BOWLEAZE COVE (MAP 72)

OSMINGTON MILLS

20 MINS FROM RINGSTEAD (MAP 74)

(cont'd from p275) At the top of the hill – and thus largely ignored by the path, though it's a only one-minute detour off it, are the remains of a **Roman temple**. Not much is known about this once-sacred place other than that it was built in around the 4th century; there's not much now save for the simple square outline of the temple's foundations in the ground.

The path continues down to another temple of sorts, this one dedicated to the practice of arcades and sun worshipping: Beachside Leisure Centre with its amusement-park children's rides and several cafés. The path actually cuts right through it, but unless you need to visit the handy Spar **supermarket** (daily 8am-8pm), at the entrance to Waterside Holiday Park (which doesn't allow camping), there's not much need to stop.

Climbing out of the dip, the path passes round the Art Deco splendour of **Riviera Hotel**, once again closed to the public. You soon climb into the fields at the end of the road – look to your left for the best view from the path of the **Osmington White Horse** (see Map 60c, p249) at Osmington Hill. The figure on the horse is George III and it was done in the early 1800s.

Having crossed some fields the path now saunters along – or near – the cliffs and below the perimeter of an activity centre, before dropping, after some simple meandering, to a reunion with the South Dorset Ridgeway (see p250), just before it meets the road running down to **Osmington Mills**.

OSMINGTON MILLS   [Map 73, p277]

There's little to the village save for a place to have lunch but it's perfectly located – and there are some options for accommodation should you wish to linger longer.

For **campers**, the very welcoming *Rosewall Camping* (☎ 01305-832248, 🖳 weymouthcamping.com; Easter-Oct, weather dependent; 🐾; tent & 1/2 hikers from £8/10) has a **shop** (peak season daily 8am-5/6pm, rest of season hours vary) which is well stocked in the high season – and even serves hot drinks – but has a more limited selection in the low season. The site is right on the path and has a lovely spacious shower block.

At the bottom of the village – and yet also its very heart – is the charming *Smugglers Inn* (☎ 01305-833125, 🖳 smugglersinnosmingtonmills.co.uk;   4D;

🐾; WI-FI; 🐾; £67.50-107.50pp, sgl occ room rate), a lovely thatched place with origins dating back to the 13th century. It's a Hall & Woodhouse pub and bears the same smart-traditional style of the others in the chain. It has great **food** (Mon-Sat noon-9pm, Sun to 8pm), a large beer garden, and Badger ales on tap. Get here early on a hot summer's day, however, or you'll be waiting a while for your dinner.

As for transport, First's X54 **bus** services stop in Osmington village (see Map 60c) – a 15-minute walk from Osmington Mills – en route between Poole and Weymouth. More's Damory 5 service operates to Dorchester and in summer their Breezer 30 between Weymouth and Swanage. See pp53-5 for details.

Heading round behind Smugglers Inn, more field walking follows, the path squeezed between fence and cliffs, with a couple of brick shelters as the only significant features before the path cuts through the houses of **Ringstead Bay**, where you'll find *Ringstead Bay Kiosk* (☎ 01305-852427; Mar-end Oct generally daily 9am-5 or 6pm, occasionally up to 8pm) waiting to serve you food and

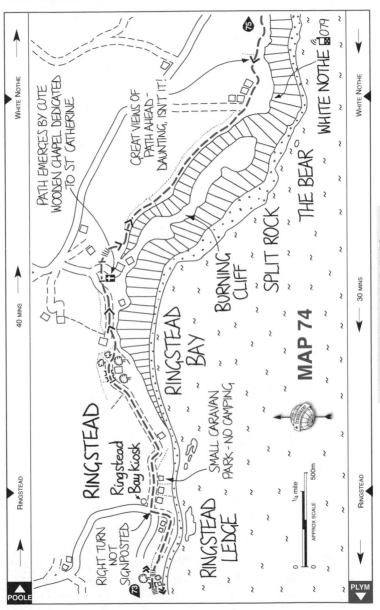

RINGSTEAD

Ringstead Bay Kiosk

RIGHT TURN NOT SIGNPOSTED

RINGSTEAD LEDGE

SMALL CARAVAN PARK - NO CAMPING

RINGSTEAD BAY

PATH EMERGES BY CUTE WOODEN CHAPEL DEDICATED TO ST CATHERINE

GREAT VIEWS OF PATH AHEAD - DAUNTING, ISN'T IT!

BURNING CLIFF

SPLIT ROCK

THE BEAR

WHITE NOTHE

MAP 74

¼ mile
500m
0
0
APPROX SCALE

POOLE

RINGSTEAD

40 MINS

WHITE NOTHE

RINGSTEAD

30 MINS

WHITE NOTHE

PLYM

hot drinks (depending on the weather). Turning right along a lane just before the kiosk, you walk round the back of some homes and on, up past the landslips that lie to your right like scruffy terracing, to the tiny wooden **chapel**, dedicated to St Catherine. Some more easy climbing brings you to the remote houses at **White Nothe**. (Note you can also walk along the landslips, known as **Burning Cliff**, though you do so at your own peril and you may not be able to ascend to White Nothe so you may have to return before continuing on the path. The cliff is so-named after a band of bituminous shale caught fire in 1826.)

The tough stuff begins here. Most of the climbs on this section to Durdle Door are both lengthy and steep. The first descent, down to **Middle Bottom**, is typical. Passing a **stone obelisk** (which, along with a second obelisk nearby, is a 19th-century navigational aid used by sailors), the path descends quickly along the cliffside before climbing, equally rapidly, out of it.

A second descent down to the beach by the **Bat's Hole** rock formation and a third to the wonderfully named **Scratchy Bottom** (which features in the book *Rude Britain: The 100 Rudest Place Names in Britain* by Ed Hurst and Rob Baile) follow in short order before you are finally rewarded with your first view of the famous natural arch at **Durdle Door** (see box below).

At the time of research there was a diversion just after Durdle Door, which took walkers inland slightly, up to the car park by the entrance to *Durdle Door Holiday Park* (see p282) before rejoining the original path soon after, as it climbed over **Hambury Tout**. As with other SWCP diversions, this temporary alteration to the path may well turn out to be permanent as erosion continues to eat away at the original trail. From the car park it's a gentle descent to the elegant arc of lovely **Lulworth Cove**.

❏ DURDLE DOOR

Geologically speaking, Durdle Door is nothing more than an arch of limestone rock set out at sea but joined to the mainland by a narrow sliver of land or isthmus. Derived from an Old English word *thirl* meaning 'to drill', the door is part of the 12,000-acre Lulworth Estate.

Though it appears to have been here forever, the arch was of course formed by the tides eroding the rock away – the same force that now threatens to destroy it and which UNESCO are attempting to counteract to prevent it falling into the sea altogether. (Incidentally, to see what Durdle Door might have looked like once upon a time, neighbouring Stair Hole – Map 76 – is an 'infant' cove, the waves having broken through to form an arch and the Wealdon clays behind that which were once protected are now rapidly being eroded.)

So far, so prosaic. Plenty of artists down the years have been inspired by Durdle Door, however, and this curiously carved lump of rock features in many works, from music videos (step forward Billy Ocean, Cliff Richard and Tears for Fears who all shot promotional videos here), to films (Emma Thompson's *Nanny McPhee* and *Wilde*, the biopic of Oscar Wilde starring Stephen Fry, both had scenes filmed here), and, perhaps most famously, it was also used as a location for the 1967 film adaptation of Thomas Hardy's novel *Far from the Madding Crowd*, starring Julie Christie.

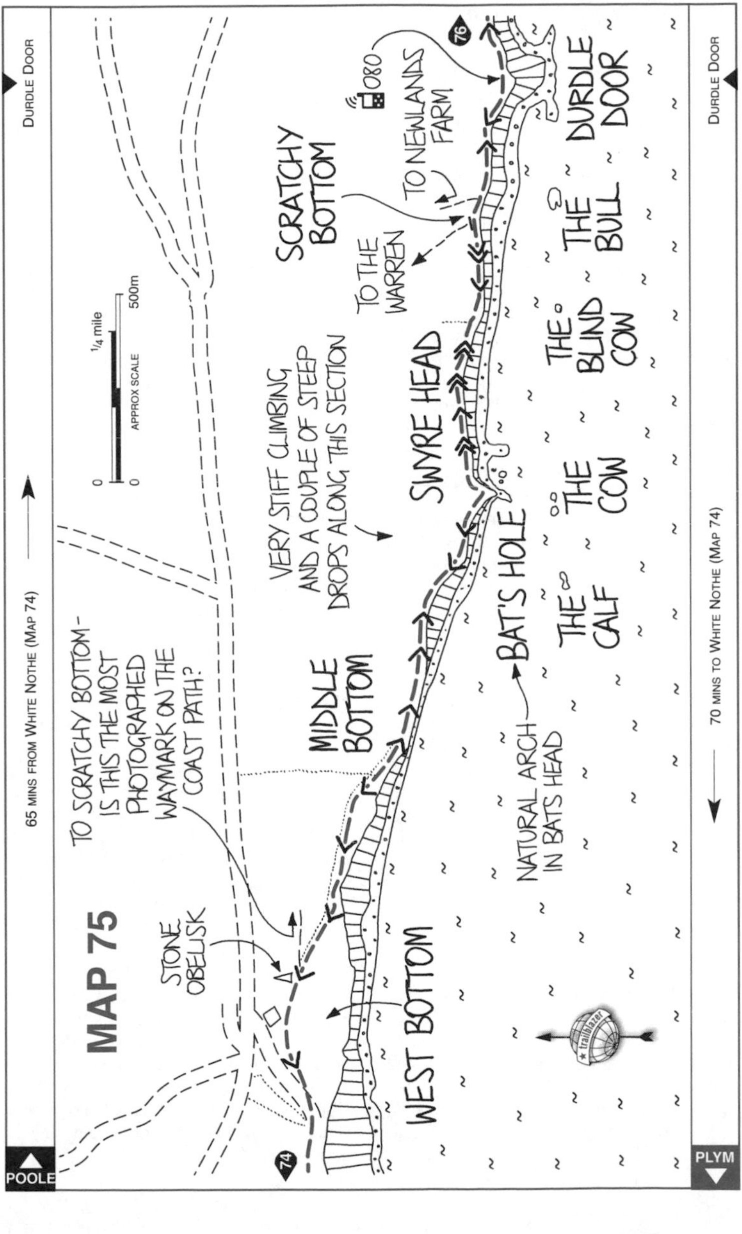

MAP 75

DURDLE DOOR

DURDLE DOOR ◀

65 MINS FROM WHITE NOTHE (MAP 74)

70 MINS TO WHITE NOTHE (MAP 74)

TO SCRATCHY BOTTOM -
IS THIS THE MOST
PHOTOGRAPHED
WAYMARK ON THE
COAST PATH?

VERY STIFF CLIMBING
AND A COUPLE OF STEEP
DROPS ALONG THIS SECTION

SCRATCHY
BOTTOM

TO NEWLANDS
FARM

TO THE
WARREN

SWYRE HEAD

MIDDLE
BOTTOM

BAT'S HOLE

THE
BLIND
COW

THE
BULL

DURDLE
DOOR

STONE
OBELISK

THE
CALF

THE
COW

NATURAL ARCH
IN BATS HEAD

WEST BOTTOM

¼ mile

APPROX SCALE

0   500m

0

POOLE ▲

PLYM ▼

76

74

ROUTE GUIDE AND MAPS

WEST LULWORTH AND LULWORTH COVE [Map 76 & map p284]

One of the most picturesque coves on the south coast, inland of which is one of the walk's most idyllic villages, Lulworth Cove, and its accompanying village, West Lulworth, virtually demand that you spend a night here. However, there is something of a contradiction facing SWCP trekkers. The path virtually demands that you visit at weekends, as that is when the nearby ranges are open to allow you to continue on the path. However, to visit Lulworth on a weekend, particularly a hot one, is to see the village at its absolute worst, when the whole place is swamped by day-trippers and the surrounding fields are converted into one enormous car park. It's enough to put you off the entire human race. That said, there is still some charm to the place; the wonderful nearby scenery, fantastic pubs, great B&Bs and absorbing **visitor centre** (Apr-end Sep daily 10am-6pm, Oct-Mar to 5pm but all depend on the weather) are all still there if you can fight your way through the throng.

Services

There isn't much in the way of amenities in either the cove or the village. There is a **shop**, The Lulworth Stores (Easter to end Oct daily 9am-8pm, starting from 8am in high season), on Church Rd on the edge of the village, that has a good selection of groceries and baked goods. It's slightly away from the action on the seafront, but the coast path passes almost in front of it. The visitor centre has an **ATM**, a gift shop and a café.

For **tourist information** try the Lulworth Estate 🖳 lulworth.com.

Transport

[See pp53-5] In summer, More's Breezer 30 (Weymouth to Swanage) & 31 (Wool to Lulworth Cove) and First's X52 **bus** services call at Durdle Door, West Lulworth and Lulworth Cove.

For a **taxi** try Silver Cars (☎ 07811-328281 or ☎ 01929-400409, 🖳 www.silvercars.co.uk).

Where to stay

There is **camping** just a few minutes back from Durdle Door, immediately behind the car park at the top of the hill. ***Durdle Door Holiday Park*** (Map 76; ☎ 01929-400200, 🖳 durdledoor.co.uk; Mar-end Oct; 🐕) has a café/bar, a shop and a wonderful location. A standard pitch (for up to four people) costs up to £40, but walkers may get a discount; booking is recommended. Note that they will probably ask you to camp in the 'rookery', so-called because it's where rooks always nest. If you're a light sleeper, bring earplugs. One reader said that it is possible to sleep in a different part of the park away from them – it might be worth asking to see if it's possible when you are there. They also have **camping pods** (£68-96, sleep 4, bedding not included).

Lulworth also boasts a **hostel**, though it's a little way out of the village. ***YHA Lulworth Cove*** (☎ 0345-371 9331, 🖳 yha.org.uk/hostel/yha-lulworth-cove; 3 x 4-/2 x 5-/2 x 6-bed rooms; dorm beds from £13pp, private rooms from £29) is a pleasant place with helpful staff. One of the four-bed rooms is en suite. Meals are available but there is also a self-catering kitchen. They also allow **camping** (Mar-Oct; from £13pp; 🐕). To get here follow the road to West Lulworth along the coast path, to a signpost on the right pointing the way to the hostel.

Other accommodation includes ***The Castle Inn*** (☎ 01929-500566, 🖳 butcombe.com/the-castle-inn-dorset; 8D/4Tr; 🥣; WI-FI; 🐕; £75-125pp, sgl occ rates on request), a beautiful, thatched 17th-century establishment with lovely rooms decorated in unvarnished wood and neutral hues.

The village also has a number of charming **B&Bs**. On Main Rd you'll find ***Downalong*** (☎ 01929-400300, 🖳 downalong.co.uk; 1D/1T private facilities; WI-FI; 🐕; from £52.50pp, sgl occ £90-105), with a continental breakfast, and ***The Old Barn*** (☎ 01929-400305, 🖳 theoldbarnlulworthcove.com; 3D/1D or T/1Qd; WI-FI; 🐕; £45-65pp, sgl occ room rate), who do not accept advance bookings for a one-night stay at the weekend.

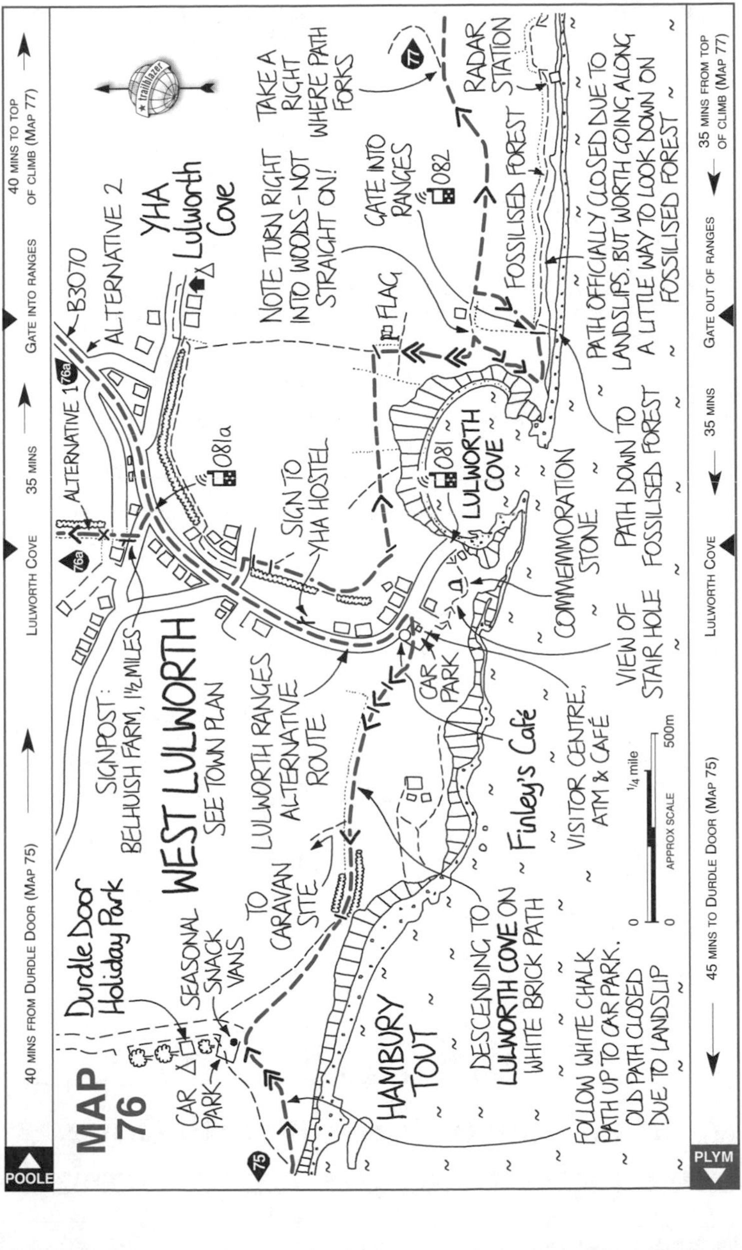

MAP 76

▲ POOLE

40 MINS FROM DURDLE DOOR (MAP 75)

Durdle Door Holiday Park

CAR PARK

SEASONAL SNACK VANS

SIGNPOST: BELHUISH FARM, 1½ MILES

WEST LULWORTH
SEE TOWN PLAN

TO CARAVAN SITE

LULWORTH RANGES ALTERNATIVE ROUTE

Finley's Café

DESCENDING TO LULWORTH COVE ON WHITE BRICK PATH

HAMBURY TOUT

FOLLOW WHITE CHALK PATH UP TO CAR PARK. OLD PATH CLOSED DUE TO LANDSLIP

75

0
0   500m
¼ mile
APPROX SCALE

VISITOR CENTRE, ATM & CAFÉ

CAR PARK

COMMEMORATION STONE

VIEW OF STAIR HOLE

081 LULWORTH COVE

PATH DOWN TO FOSSILISED FOREST

081a

SIGN TO YHA HOSTEL

ALTERNATIVE 1

76a

ALTERNATIVE 1

76b

B3070

ALTERNATIVE 2

YHA Lulworth Cove

NOTE TURN RIGHT INTO WOODS – NOT STRAIGHT ON!

TAKE A RIGHT WHERE PATH FORKS

FLAG

GATE INTO RANGES

082

77

RADAR STATION

FOSSILISED FOREST

PATH OFFICIALLY CLOSED DUE TO LANDSLIPS, BUT WORTH GOING ALONG A LITTLE WAY TO LOOK DOWN ON FOSSILISED FOREST

40 MINS TO TOP OF CLIMB (MAP 77)

LULWORTH COVE ← | → 35 MINS ← | → GATE INTO RANGES ← | → 40 MINS TO TOP OF CLIMB (MAP 77)

45 MINS TO DURDLE DOOR (MAP 75) | LULWORTH COVE ← | → 35 MINS ← | → GATE OUT OF RANGES ← | → 35 MINS FROM TOP OF CLIMB (MAP 77)

PLYM ▼

The following B&B is also reluctant to accept one-night stays at the weekend and over summer but may do if there is space in their diary. The 400-year-old dog-friendly *Tewkesbury Cottage* (☎ 01929-400561; 2D/1T; ☞; WI-FI; 🐾; £47.50-52.50pp, sgl occ from £90) is at 28 Main Rd.

Apart from *Limestone Lulworth* (☎ 01929-400252, 🖥 www.limestonehotel.co .uk; 10D/1D or T; ☞; WI-FI; 🐾; £75-170pp, sgl occ room rate) which is in the centre of the village, most **hotel**-style accommodation can be found down in Lulworth Cove itself, just a couple of hundred metres or so from the path.

Lulworth Cove Inn (☎ 01929-400333, 🖥 lulworth-coveinn.co.uk; 9D/3D or T; ☞; 🐾; WI-FI; £62.50-115pp, sgl occ room rate) is a smart Hall & Woodhouse pub, with some lovely rooms, many with sea view, and accepts one-night bookings.

Further down, *Lulworth Lodge & Bistro* (☎ 01929-400252, 🖥 www.lulworth lodge.co.uk; 7D/5D or T; ☞; WI-FI; 🐾; £75-170pp, sgl occ room rate) is similarly stylish and is situated where the old mill once stood. It also has some fabulous views of the cove and is owned by the same people as Limestone Lulworth.

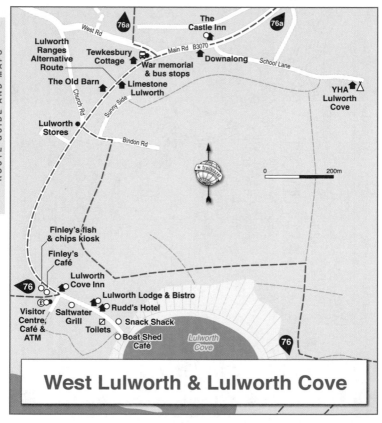

ROUTE GUIDE AND MAPS

West Rd · 76a · The Castle Inn · 76a

Lulworth Ranges Alternative Route · Tewkesbury Cottage · Main Rd B3070 · Downalong · School Lane

War memorial & bus stops

The Old Barn · Limestone Lulworth

Church Rd · Sunny Side

YHA Lulworth Cove

Lulworth Stores

Bindon Rd

trailblazer

0   200m

Finley's fish & chips kiosk

Finley's Café

76 · Lulworth Cove Inn

Lulworth Lodge & Bistro

£ · Rudd's Hotel

Visitor Centre, Café & ATM · Saltwater Grill · Toilets · Snack Shack

Boat Shed Café · Lulworth Cove · 76

West Lulworth & Lulworth Cove

Rudds (☎ 01929-400552, 🖳 ruddslul worth.co.uk; 6D/1Tr/1Qd; ➤; WI-FI; 🐾; £55-115pp, sgl occ room rate) is a lovely place with an outdoor swimming pool and some lovely views of the Cove from some of its rooms – the closest accommodation to the beach. However, they do insist on a minimum two-night booking at weekends in the peak season.

Where to eat and drink

The excellent *Castle Inn* (see Where to stay; food daily noon-3pm & 5-9pm; 🐾) has its own brewery, the products of which occasionally end up as ingredients in their food, such as their Butcombe Gold beer-battered haddock & thick-cut chips, minted peas & tartare sauce (small/large £14.50/18.50). Apart from the Castle, however, the rest of the eateries are clustered together, down towards the cove.

Next to the visitor centre, which itself has a small café, is *Finley's Café* (☎ 01929-400711, 🖳 finleyscafe.co.uk; 🐾; daily August 9.30am-5pm, rest of year 10am-4/5pm), which has a self-service canteen system, and is sometimes overrun with school groups, but is an OK choice nonetheless. It has an attached **fish & chips kiosk** (Mar-Oct daily noon-5.45pm) that's also very popular.

Walking downhill from here towards the cove you'll pass a trio of side-by-side establishments, including an ice-cream parlour, a fudge shop and the café-bistro *Saltwater Grill* (WI-FI; 🐾; daily 9am-4 or 5pm), with all-day breakfasts which are always popular as well as pizzas, burgers and sandwiches.

On the opposite side of the lane is *Lulworth Cove Inn* (see Where to stay; WI-FI; 🐾; food Mon-Sat noon-9pm, Sun to 8pm) which serves good-quality pub grub. Further down the lane are *Lulworth Lodge & Bistro* (see Where to stay; food daily noon-3pm & 6-9pm) and *Rudd's Hotel* (see Where to stay; food daily noon-4pm & 5-7.45pm), which both have bistro-style restaurants serving good food, including seafood specials, in a stylish atmosphere.

For something more affordable (not that the bistros are overly expensive) walk further down to *Snack Shack* (Mon-Fri 10am-5pm, Sat-Sun 9am-7pm), a takeaway kiosk that does burgers, baps, sandwiches and coffee. Right by the water is *Boat Shed Café* (☎ 01929-400810; 🐾 on lead; daily 8.30am-5pm, winter to 4pm and weather dependent), a tiny café housed in a former lock-up with a veranda overlooking the famous cove.

LULWORTH COVE TO KIMMERIDGE BAY [MAPS 76-79]

There's a bit of a military theme to this **7¼-mile (11.75km; 3hrs** 20 mins; **Alternative 1: 5hrs, p288; Alternative 2: 4½hrs, p290)** stage. In addition to the fact that today you'll be visiting both an Iron-Age fort (which was later used by the Romans) and various fortifications from the Second World War, there is also the small matter that, for almost its entire length, **you'll be walking through a very active firing range**. Indeed, the ranges provide the greatest obstacle to today's stage, for the path through them is open only occasionally (usually only at weekends). This is a shame, for the ranges are a delight, with fortifications, fossilised forests and fascinating flora abounding.

In short, **it's well worth timing your walk to ensure your arrival coincides with the weekend, which is when the ranges are usually open** (call ☎ 01929-404712; Mon-Thur 7.30am-5pm, Fri to 3pm, to double check when the ranges are open); and this is the trek we've described on p286. (If this isn't possible, however, don't despair, for we've also described the beautiful alternative routes around the ranges' perimeter, starting on p288.)

If you do manage to hike through the ranges you'll actually find this stage rather short – it can be completed in a (rather long) morning. That's not to say it's easy, however, for there are several painfully sharp gradients on the way. But being just over seven miles long does, of course, allow for the possibility – for the fit, at least – of combining this stage and the following one into one long (and exhausting) day to Swanage. This is no bad thing, for accommodation at Kimmeridge is both a little off the trail and in short supply. However, only the fit and fanatical should consider doing this – it's a lot of miles and gradients to squeeze into one day. If you do decide to combine the two stages you should certainly consider bringing lunch with you from Lulworth, unless you're willing to trek uphill to Kimmeridge village from the bay.

The route through the ranges

The day begins with a relatively untaxing stroll around the cove that brings you to the no-nonsense fence surrounding the firing range. Following it to the clifftop, you'll find the **gate** into the range itself.

At this point the authorities have made it clear that they now want you, on passing through the gate, to immediately turn left and head inland to the main track running through the ranges. That's a shame, for it means you no longer pass by one of the more unusual sights on this stretch of path: a **fossilised forest**. Don't expect to see stone trees 'growing' out of the cliff-ledge; instead, look for **thrombolites**, which are fossilised rings of algae that thrived around tree trunks when the forest was flooded 150 million years ago. The area used to be known as 'Vairy Vances' or 'Fairy Dances', in reference to these thrombolite rings. The 'forest' lies just a few minutes from the gate, at the bottom of the cliffs, though do make sure it's safe to take the old coast path to see them.

Back on the proper coast path, the walk within the ranges can best be described as two very stiff climbs and one long but gentle one, separated by some surprisingly unchallenging sections, all set amongst some fascinating (particularly if rusting military vehicles are your thing) and beautiful scenery.

The first of the big climbs lies about a mile from the fossilised forest; it's an exhausting haul up **Bindon Hill**, usually done to a soundtrack of crashing waves and whistling wind. That climb conquered, a lovely bit of gentle ridge-top rambling follows before a sharpish descent to **Arish Mell** – from where the lengthier climb up to **Flowers Barrow** begins. It's a wearying climb – you can see why Iron-Age man chose the summit of this hill as the location for a **fort** – and why the Romans subsequently used it for their own military purposes. The unexcavated remains of the fort explain the existence of the unusual bumps and

---

❏ KEEP TO THE PATH!

More than anywhere else on the coast path it is absolutely vital that you keep to the signposted path through Lulworth Military Range (the yellow posts traditionally point the way). As you can probably tell by all the metalware rusting in the fields, there's a fair bit of unexploded ordnance left lying hereabouts. So keep to the path – and make sure your dog keeps to the path too.

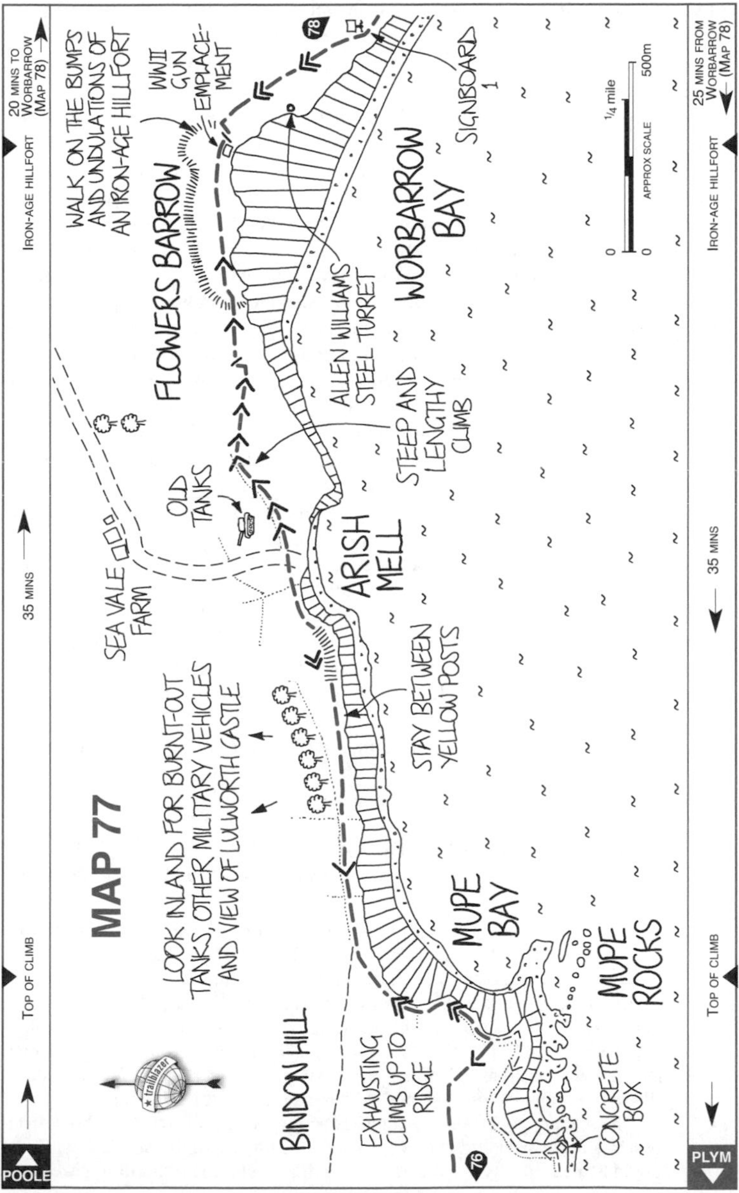

MAP 77

20 MINS TO WORBARROW (MAP 78)

IRON-AGE HILLFORT

WALK ON THE BUMPS AND UNDULATIONS OF AN IRON-AGE HILLFORT

WWII GUN EMPLACEMENT

78

FLOWERS BARROW

OLD TANKS

SEA VALE FARM

35 MINS

Allen Williams Steel Turret

STEEP AND LENGTHY CLIMB

WORBARROW BAY

SIGNBOARD

ARISH MELL

¼ mile

500m

0   APPROX SCALE   0

25 MINS FROM WORBARROW (MAP 78)

IRON-AGE HILLFORT

TOP OF CLIMB

LOOK INLAND FOR BURNT-OUT TANKS, OTHER MILITARY VEHICLES AND VIEW OF LULWORTH CASTLE

STAY BETWEEN YELLOW POSTS

35 MINS

BINDON HILL

MUPE BAY

MUPE ROCKS

EXHAUSTING CLIMB UP TO RIDGE

CONCRETE BOX

76

TOP OF CLIMB

POOLE

PLYM

folds in the summit. Amongst these remains are a couple of hut circles and a few ramparts; sadly, however, where the hill forts were designed to protect the inhabitants from invaders, they are helpless against the depredations of the elements and much of the site has fallen victim to erosion.

Also on the Barrow, an old **WWII gun emplacement** shows that, while weaponry and warfare may have changed in the 2500 years since the Iron Age fort was built, a hilltop location is still regarded as invaluable when it comes to looking out for enemy advances. Further down the slopes, the rust-coloured metal ball is actually a WWII **Allen Williams Steel Turret** – of which we've already seen an example in Exmouth.

The path passes more ruins at **Worbarrow** and its accompanying **Tout**, or hill, which resembles a giant geological apostrophe punctuating the sea. You then climb for a third time (though mercifully less steeply now) towards **Tyneham Cap** which, unusually, the path contours round rather than conquers, dropping gently, via unconcerned sheep, to the gate at the end of the ranges. Incongruously, next-door is a small **oil well** – indeed, Wytch Farm Oil Well is said to be the site of the oldest continually working oil well in the UK.

From here it's but a short stroll round to **Kimmeridge Bay**. At first sight there doesn't seem to be much here save for a large car park, some public toilets and a couple of old sheds down on the water's edge. However, these sheds provide the answer to why so many people come to this bay for they house the **Fine Foundation Wild Seas Centre** (Apr-Oct daily 11am-4pm, Nov weekends only) which provides an interactive explanation on the neighbouring bay, its ledges and rockpools, waters that together make up **Purbeck Marine Nature Reserve**. Britain's longest-established Voluntary Marine Nature Reserve is home to sea anemones, crabs, wrasse, mullet, lobster and blennies. The centre has a small souvenir shop and they've organised an underwater nature trail for snorkelers.

For the amenities of Kimmeridge (see p294) you have to walk for 10-15 minutes up the hill from the bay.

See p294 for the continuation of the route.

WHEN THE RANGES ARE CLOSED
[Map 76a, p291; Map 76b, p292]

Alternative 1
Yes, the walk through the ranges is the kind of stroll that causes writers to write, poets to eulogise, and atheists not only to believe in the existence of a God but also to believe that he loves us dearly and clearly wants us to be happy.

But if the ranges are shut when you arrive, there's no need to plunge headlong into a pit of despair and self-loathing (as long as you choose Alternative 1). Because, simply put, this **13½-mile (21.75km; 5hrs** yomp has more than enough compensations. It's much easier (though longer), with fewer of those roller-coaster undulations that are so characteristic of the coastal route.

The scenery, too, is often exquisite (and if you've followed this book from the start – and especially if you began at the beginning of the South-West Coast Path in Minehead – your eyes and ears will probably be grateful to gaze upon

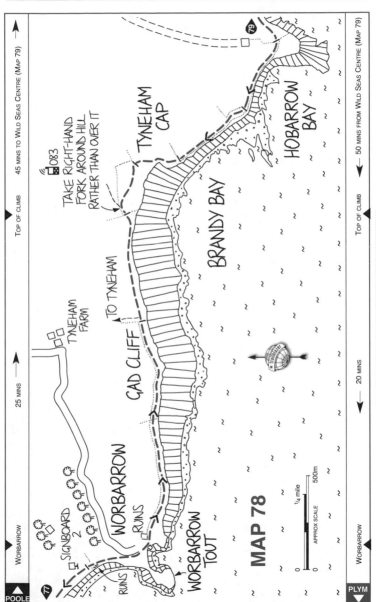

WORBARROW — TOP OF CLIMB — 45 MINS TO WILD SEAS CENTRE (MAP 79)

25 MINS

TYNEHAM FARM

TO TYNEHAM

TAKE RIGHT-HAND FORK AROUND HILL RATHER THAN OVER IT

☎ 083

TYNEHAM CAP

79

SIGNBOARD 2

WORBARROW
RUINS

RUINS

WORBARROW TOUT

GAD CLIFF

BRANDY BAY

HOBARROW BAY

MAP 78

¼ mile
500m
APPROX SCALE
0   0

20 MINS

TOP OF CLIMB — 50 MINS FROM WILD SEAS CENTRE (MAP 79)

WORBARROW

POOLE

PLYM

something other than the sea), with sumptuous bluebell woods, sweeping country estates, neatly cultivated fields, ancient farmhouses and some whopping great country manors to titillate the senses.

There's also more wildlife on this path too, with deer (both roe and the rarer sika, an immigrant from East Asia, thrive in the ranges), hares, pheasants and raptors all dropping by now and again to see who's passing. And overlaying everything is this comforting, life-affirming tranquillity and isolation. It's just lovely. And yes, while there is a good amount of this walk that is undertaken on roads (approximately four miles), much of it is on quiet country lanes edged with lovely cottages or rhododendron forests, where traffic is infrequent and there are grassy verges to hop onto if necessary.

So cease your wailing, silence those gnashing teeth, dry those tears from your eyes and wipe your nose on your Gore-Tex; because you have a lovely walk to complete – and you need to get going...

The route The day begins with a stroll from the official path up to **West Lulworth** (assuming you haven't already visited it), from where the first of the steep climbs begins up through fields to a brief union with the **Purbeck Way** (see p40), a route that you very quickly betray for the **Hardy Way** which leads you down past hare-inhabited pastures to **Belhuish Farm**. Reaching the end of their drive, after the B3071, the path then follows the edge of gorgeous **Burngate Wood**, filled with deer and bluebells, which you leave by its most easterly point to saunter eastwards on a rough track to **Park Lodge**, with Lulworth Castle (see p293) and its domed chapel to your right.

More woodland skirting occurs after crossing another road, with the idyllic looking lake and its '**fort**' to your left. Following a hedge-lined country track, it's not long before you hit the range (the border, as you'll soon discover, being marked by a red flag). Follow the path round the ranges' edge and you soon reach **Coombe Heath Nature Reserve** and from there more woodside wandering leading to a small country lane which, in turn, leads to **Holme Lane** (Map 76b), where you turn right.

While it's never a blessing to feel the thud of sole on tarmac, the road is pleasantly quiet and the bucolic views to Holme Priory – after you've passed the crossroads at **West Holme** – are distracting. You eventually leave this road, just after a signposted but badly maintained bridleway, for a road marked 'East Holme Rifle Range', which soon takes you past an unsightly quarry and on to **Dorey's Farm**, after which there's yet more sylvan strolling – at least until the road to Kimmeridge is reached. There now follows the least pleasant couple of miles on this walk, though with some lovely little cottages and the huge **Grange Farm** on the way, it isn't entirely horrid. The road-rambling ends with a steep, uphill gradient, your reward for conquering it being some wonderful sweeping views north and south over lovely, voluptuous Purbeck.

A steep descent, some more road walking, a bisection of *Steeple Leaze Farm* and its **campsite** (see p294), another small climb and descent and a traverse of four or five fields follows before Kimmeridge Bay is reached – and a reunion with the official trail.

Alternative 2
Definitely the inferior of the three routes, basically on this **12-mile (19.3km; 4½hrs)** option you are treading tarmac the whole way. The road in question is

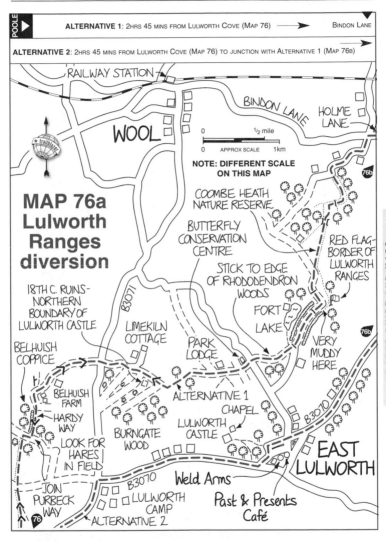

ALTERNATIVE 1: 2HRS 45 MINS FROM LULWORTH COVE (MAP 76) ⟶ BINDON LANE

ALTERNATIVE 2: 2HRS 45 MINS FROM LULWORTH COVE (MAP 76) TO JUNCTION WITH ALTERNATIVE 1 (MAP 76B)

RAILWAY STATION

BINDON LANE

HOLME LANE

WOOL

0 ½ mile
0 APPROX SCALE 1km

NOTE: DIFFERENT SCALE ON THIS MAP

COOMBE HEATH NATURE RESERVE

MAP 76a Lulworth Ranges diversion

BUTTERFLY CONSERVATION CENTRE

STICK TO EDGE OF RHODODENDRON WOODS

RED FLAG - BORDER OF LULWORTH RANGES

18TH C. RUINS - NORTHERN BOUNDARY OF LULWORTH CASTLE

B3071

LIMEKILN COTTAGE

FORT

LAKE

PARK LODGE

VERY MUDDY HERE

BELHUISH COPPICE

BELHUISH FARM

HARDY WAY

LOOK FOR HARES IN FIELD

BURNGATE WOOD

ALTERNATIVE 1

CHAPEL

LULWORTH CASTLE

B3070

EAST LULWORTH

JOIN PURBECK WAY

76

B3070 LULWORTH CAMP

ALTERNATIVE 2

Weld Arms

Past & Presents Café

POOLE

ROUTE GUIDE AND MAPS

the B3070 which is the same road that you join when you hit Lulworth Cove and which passes through West Lulworth and the ranges (but is open even when the ranges are usually shut). Given all the pavement-pounding, you should really consider this option only if you are after a pub, a café, or Lulworth Castle – all of which can be found in East Lulworth.

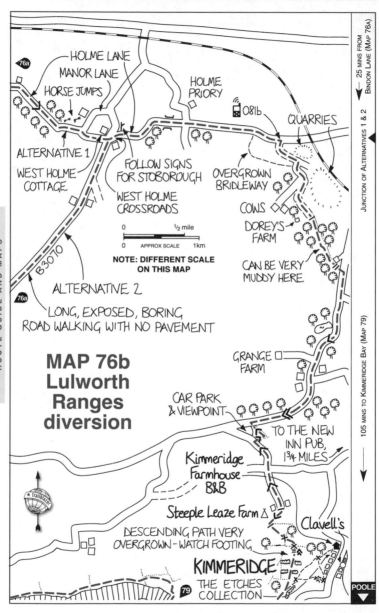

76a

HOLME LANE
MANOR LANE
HORSE JUMPS

HOLME PRIORY

📱 081b

QUARRIES

ALTERNATIVE 1

WEST HOLME COTTAGE

FOLLOW SIGNS FOR STOBOROUGH

OVERGROWN BRIDLEWAY

WEST HOLME CROSSROADS

COWS

DOREY'S FARM

B3070

0   ½ mile
0   APPROX SCALE   1km

NOTE: DIFFERENT SCALE ON THIS MAP

CAN BE VERY MUDDY HERE

ALTERNATIVE 2

76a

LONG, EXPOSED, BORING ROAD WALKING WITH NO PAVEMENT

**MAP 76b
Lulworth
Ranges
diversion**

GRANGE FARM

CAR PARK & VIEWPOINT

TO THE NEW INN PUB, 1¾ MILES

Kimmeridge Farmhouse B&B

Steeple Leaze Farm △

Clavell's

DESCENDING PATH VERY OVERGROWN – WATCH FOOTING

KIMMERIDGE

79

THE ETCHES COLLECTION

25 MINS FROM BINDON LANE (MAP 76A)

JUNCTION OF ALTERNATIVES 1 & 2

105 MINS TO KIMMERIDGE BAY (MAP 79)

POOLE ▼

The route From West Lulworth continue on the B3070 to **East Lulworth**. The pub here, *Weld Arms* (☎ 01929-400211, 🖥 www.theweldarms.co.uk; WI-FI; 🐾) is a goodie, with decent **food** (daily noon-8pm; mains £15-24) and a lovely beer garden. The only problem is that it is probably too near West Lulworth to consider it a lunchtime option; though if you visit the castle first it could fit in.

Just beyond here is *Past and Presents Café* (☎ 01929-400637; daily summer 10am-5pm, winter to 4pm; WI-FI; 🐾), housed in an old Catholic school, originally built in 1877. You can get tea, coffee and snacks here, and there's an art gallery to peruse and a gift shop selling locally produced handicrafts.

The road passes the entrance of **Lulworth Castle** (🖥 lulworth.com/visit/places-to-visit/castle-and-park; Sun-Thur 10.30am-5pm; £7, English Heritage members free); the castle was originally built as a hunting lodge in the early 17th century by Thomas Howard, 3rd Lord Bindon, to entertain hunting parties for the king and his court. Gutted by a fire in 1929, it was restored and is still maintained by English Heritage. Camp Bestival (see box p14), held here in July, is the little sister of the far larger Bestival, held on the Isle of Wight.

From East Lulworth, you now have to walk along the morale-sapping, pavement-less and seemingly never-ending B3070 to the **West Holme crossroads** where this route joins up with Alternative 1 (see p290).

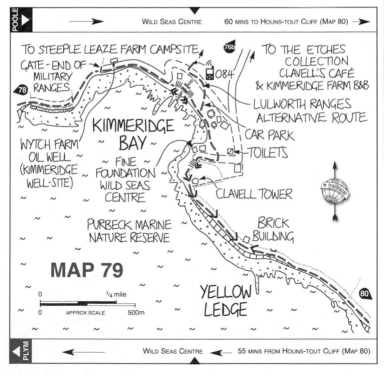

WILD SEAS CENTRE   60 MINS TO HOUNS-TOUT CLIFF (MAP 80)

TO STEEPLE LEAZE FARM CAMPSITE
GATE-END OF MILITARY RANGES
78
TO THE ETCHES COLLECTION
CLAVELL'S CAFÉ & KIMMERIDGE FARM B&B
76b
084
LULWORTH RANGES ALTERNATIVE ROUTE
KIMMERIDGE BAY
WYTCH FARM OIL WELL (KIMMERIDGE WELL-SITE)
FINE FOUNDATION WILD SEAS CENTRE
CAR PARK
TOILETS
CLAVELL TOWER
PURBECK MARINE NATURE RESERVE
BRICK BUILDING

MAP 79

0   ¼ mile
0   APPROX SCALE   500m

YELLOW LEDGE

80

WILD SEAS CENTRE   55 MINS FROM HOUNS-TOUT CLIFF (MAP 80)

POOLE

PLYM

ROUTE GUIDE AND MAPS

KIMMERIDGE [Map 76b, p292]

As well as the excellent fossil museum (The Etches Collection, see box below) which opened in 2016, there's a **B&B**, a nearby **campsite** and a good **café** here.

The **campsite**, at *Steeple Leaze Farm* (☎ 01929-480733; £8pp; Easter till Sep/Oct depending on weather; 🐾), is about 20 minutes out of Kimmeridge on the alternative route (see p290). It's a simple place with portacabin showers, toilets without toilet paper, and no food available on site, but it does allow open fires. Be warned, however, that it's a long schlep from the bay to the site and really is convenient only for those who took the alternative route around the ranges. They also accept cash only.

Kimmeridge Farmhouse (☎ 01929-480990, 🖳 kimmeridgefarmhouse.co.uk; 3D; 🖢; WI-FI; £55-62.50pp, sgl occ from £90) is a great big 14th-century pile with smart rooms. Note they accept stays of a minimum of two nights only. The café/restaurant, run by the daughter of the people who own the Farmhouse, is called *Clavell's* (☎ 01929-480701, 🖳 clavellsrestaurant.co.uk; 🐾; food daily July & Aug 10am-10pm, Easter-July & Sep-Oct Sun-Thur to 5pm, Fri & Sat to 8pm, rest of year days/hours vary). It's licensed and, while not cheap, has a good selection of sandwiches (from £8.95), baguettes, lunch-time mains (from £15.95) and desserts.

The nearest pub, *The New Inn* (off Map 76b; ☎ 01929-480357, 🖳 newinn-churchknowle.co.uk; 🐾 main bar only; food daily noon-2.15pm & 6-8pm, till 9pm in summer), is a couple of miles away, in Church Knowle.

KIMMERIDGE BAY TO SWANAGE [MAPS 79-84]

Just two stages to go, but by now it should have become clear that the coast path is not going to let you complete your trek without a struggle. For though in mileage terms this stage is not too daunting at **13½ miles (21.75km; 4hrs 50 mins)**, those bald statistics hide a couple of pretty hamstring-hammering, calf-creaking ascents. But there are compensations – as always – in the form of some delicious views, an ancient and remote chapel, the penultimate lighthouse on the path, a diverting nature reserve and the former tourist attraction of the Tilly Whim Caves (closed to the public for safety reasons since 1976).

The village of Worth Matravers, about a mile inland, is also a charming place with pretty limestone cottages, a great pub and a cute teahouse – well worth a detour if you're after refreshments. If you're not planning on visiting

---

❏ THE ETCHES COLLECTION – MUSEUM OF JURASSIC MARINE LIFE

Over the last 35 years, local amateur paleontologist and fossil hunter Steve Etches has assembled a unique collection of over 2000 specimens from the late Jurassic period. In 2016 a home was found for this superb collection in a purpose-built museum and workshop that opened in the centre of Kimmeridge.

The fossils are beautifully displayed and labelled; the CGI animations showing them swimming in the sea bring it all to life. Top exhibits include an ichthyosaur with a stomach full of fish, a squid complete with its ink sac, a lobster and a fossilised dragonfly wing. Through the big glass window at the end of the main gallery in the workshop you may see Steve Etches himself hard at work on a new specimen.

The museum (☎ 01929-270000, 🖳 theetchescollection.org; £9) is open daily (except 24-26 Dec) 10am-5pm. It's quite small but well worth a visit.

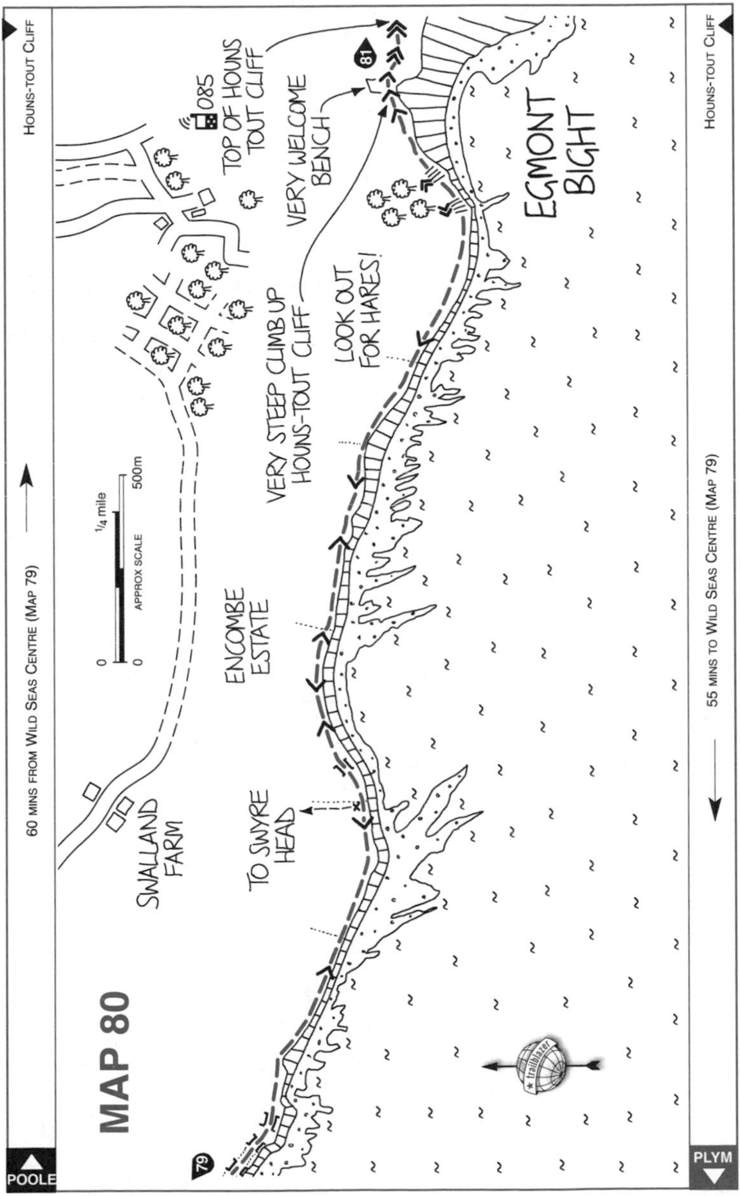
MAP 80
60 mins from Wild Seas Centre (Map 79)
Houns-tout Cliff
55 mins to Wild Seas Centre (Map 79)
Houns-tout Cliff
POOLE
PLYM
79
81
0
¼ mile
0
500m
APPROX SCALE
SWALLAND FARM
ENCOMBE ESTATE
TO SWYRE HEAD
VERY STEEP CLIMB UP HOUNS-TOUT CLIFF
LOOK OUT FOR HARES!
VERY WELCOME BENCH
085
TOP OF HOUNS TOUT CLIFF
EGMONT BIGHT
trailblazer

Worth Matravers, there's nowhere else to stop for food until Durlston, about a mile before Swanage, so make sure you bring your own!

The route

The path leaves Kimmeridge Bay via the 19th-century **Clavell Tower**, a folly built by the 70-year-old Reverend John Richards Clavell in 1830. It was moved back from the cliff edge at great expense and effort in 2002 to avoid the encroaches of the sea and the slips of land. The tower is now available as accommodation – though it's usually booked out years in advance and costs from £552 for a four-night stay! Contact The Landmark Trust (🖳 landmarktrust .org.uk) if you're interested.

The gradients are rather gentle for the first few miles (especially when compared to some of the giants of the previous two stages) but don't be lulled into a false sense of security; you'll soon have to tackle the hill of **Houns Tout Cliff** – the summit of which is only gained after a tough slog. Following the descent, a simple meander inland from **Chapman's Pool** brings you to the point where you could leave the coast path for **Worth Matravers**.

WORTH MATRAVERS   [off Map 81]

Lovers of quaint villages and quirky pubs may well be tempted to detour inland to the knot of thatched, limestone cottages built around a pond that makes up the beautiful stone-clad settlement of Worth Matravers.

Acton Field Campsite (☎ 01929-424184, 🖳 actonfieldcampsite.co.uk; from £12 for a one-person tent, £20 for a medium tent; shower costs 20p; ✄; Apr-end Oct) lies about a mile from the path. A mobile grocery visits during the summer school holidays.

For **B&B**, there's the gorgeous *Post Office Cottage* (☎ 01929-439442, 🖳 worth mytravels.co.uk; 2D/1T; WI-FI; from £50pp, sgl occ £85), a Grade II-listed building, built in 1750 and overlooking the village pond. There are three bedrooms, but they only rent to one guest (or group of guests) at a time, so even if you just book one room, you'll get sole use of the living and dining areas too. They are happy to provide evening meals for walkers if booked in advance.

Practically next door, *Worth Matravers Tea & Coffee Shop* (☎ 01929-439368; Easter-Sep Wed-Sun 10am-4pm,

rest of year Fri-Sun 10am-3.30pm but call or check on Google before going, especially for the winter months, as their opening days/hours can vary even weekly) offers picnic-type food (such as pasties, sausage rolls & tortilla) as well as hot and cold drinks, ice-creams, cakes and cream teas – takeaway only now.

Just up the road, *The Square & Compass* (☎ 01929-439229, 🖳 squareand compasspub.co.uk; ✄; food daily summer noon-11pm) is a unique village pub dating back to 1776. They don't have a typical food menu. Instead, their recipe for success is a selection of home-made pasties and pies, washed down with real ales or home-made cider (see box p25) and served inside, in an atmospheric low-ceilinged pub, or outside, on their chunky, stone-carved garden furniture. They hold a week-long festival here in July/August (see box p14), and there's a **fossil museum** attached to the pub. There's also live music most weekends.

Worth Matravers can also be reached from Map 82. To get to the coast path from Worth Matravers follow the signposted path to Winspit.

(route cont'd on p300)

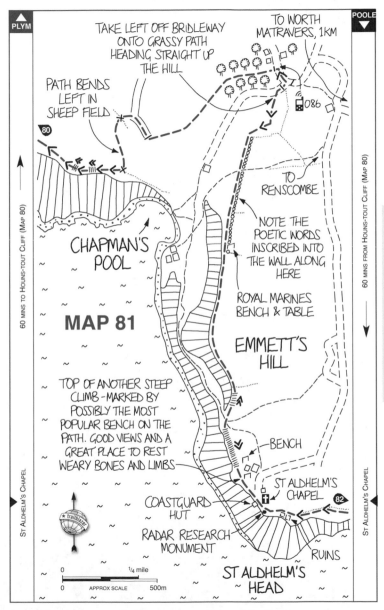

PLYM

POOLE

TO WORTH
MATRAVERS, 1KM

TAKE LEFT OFF BRIDLEWAY
ONTO GRASSY PATH
HEADING STRAIGHT UP
THE HILL

PATH BENDS
LEFT IN
SHEEP FIELD

80

086

TO
RENSCOMBE

CHAPMAN'S
POOL

NOTE THE
POETIC WORDS
INSCRIBED INTO
THE WALL ALONG
HERE

ROYAL MARINES
BENCH & TABLE

MAP 81

EMMETT'S
HILL

TOP OF ANOTHER STEEP
CLIMB - MARKED BY
POSSIBLY THE MOST
POPULAR BENCH ON THE
PATH. GOOD VIEWS AND A
GREAT PLACE TO REST
WEARY BONES AND LIMBS

BENCH

ST ALDHELM'S
CHAPEL

82

COASTGUARD
HUT

RADAR RESEARCH
MONUMENT

RUINS

ST ALDHELM'S
HEAD

trailblazer

0   ¼ mile

0   APPROX SCALE   500m

60 MINS TO HOUNS-TOUT CLIFF (MAP 80)

60 MINS FROM HOUNS-TOUT CLIFF (MAP 80)

ST ALDHELM'S CHAPEL

ST ALDHELM'S CHAPEL

ROUTE GUIDE AND MAPS

ROUTE GUIDE AND MAPS

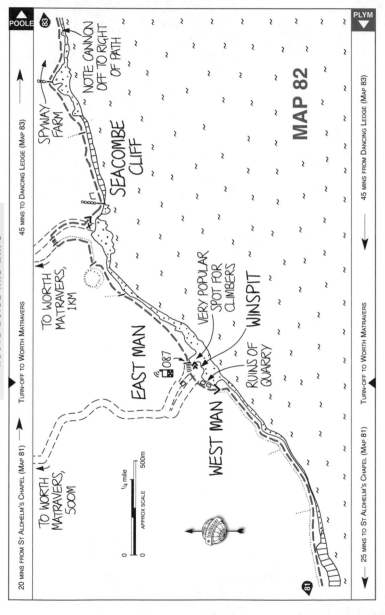

POOLE 83

NOTE CANNON OFF TO RIGHT OF PATH

SPYWAY FARM

SEACOMBE CLIFF

MAP 82

PLYM

45 MINS TO DANCING LEDGE (MAP 83)

45 MINS FROM DANCING LEDGE (MAP 83)

TO WORTH MATRAVERS, 1KM

EAST MAN

087

VERY POPULAR SPOT FOR CLIMBERS

WINSPIT

RUINS OF QUARRY

20 MINS FROM ST ALDHELM'S CHAPEL (MAP 81)

TURN-OFF TO WORTH MATRAVERS

TURN-OFF TO WORTH MATRAVERS

TO WORTH MATRAVERS, 500M

WEST MAN

¼ mile

500m

APPROX SCALE

0

0

Trailblazer

25 MINS TO ST ALDHELM'S CHAPEL (MAP 81)

81

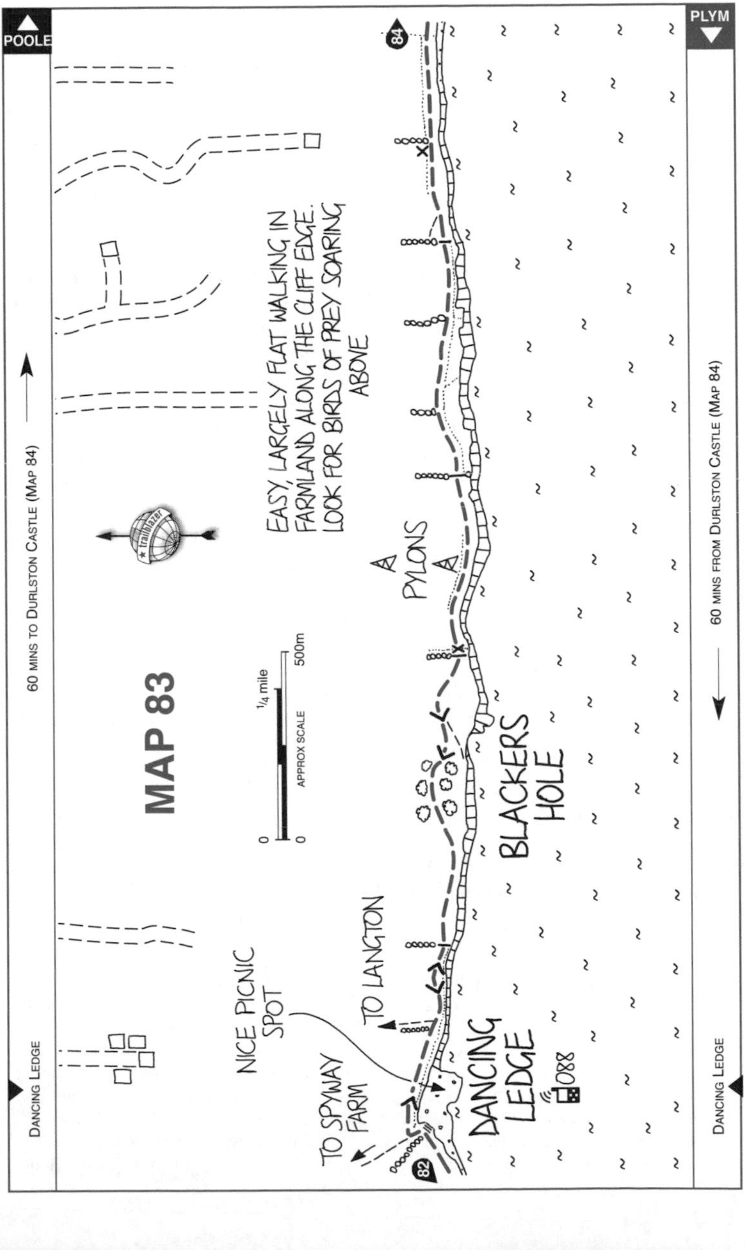

POOLE ▲

60 MINS TO DURLSTON CASTLE (MAP 84) →

DANCING LEDGE ◄

MAP 83

¼ mile
500m
APPROX SCALE
0
0

Trailblazer

EASY, LARGELY FLAT WALKING IN FARMLAND ALONG THE CLIFF EDGE. LOOK FOR BIRDS OF PREY SOARING ABOVE

NICE PICNIC SPOT

TO SPYWAY FARM

TO LANGTON

DANCING LEDGE

88

BLACKERS HOLE

PYLONS

84

PLYM ▼

← 60 MINS FROM DURLSTON CASTLE (MAP 84) →

DANCING LEDGE ◄

ROUTE GUIDE AND MAPS

(cont'd from p296) The slog up Houns Tout Cliff was not the last for, having climbed **Emmett's Hill**, a near-vertical descent and ascent follows to **St Aldhelm's Head** – home to a coastguard hut, a house or two, a radar research monument and a 12th-century chapel, dedicated to the eponymous saint, that's made of local Purbeck stone. If you missed the turning to Worth Matravers earlier it is also accessible by taking the track due north from St Aldhelm's Chapel.

It is no small relief to find that the haul up to St Aldhelm's really is the last major climb of the day, and though five miles separate you from Swanage, none of them, thankfully, is that taxing.

The path meanders past old quarries and cliffs – the latter a real draw for local climbers, for whom the region has plenty – and on via **Dancing Ledge** (Map 83) to the lighthouse at **Anvil Point** and so on to **Durlston National Nature Reserve**, home of butterflies, birds and plants galore. Here you will also find the Victorian **Durlston Castle** (💻 durlston.co.uk; daily Apr-Nov 10am-5pm, Nov-Mar 10.30am-4pm; free), with a visitor centre, gift shop and pleasant *café* (☎ 01929-421111, 💻 7eventhwave.com; daily 9.30am-4pm; 🐾). Outside it stands the 40-tonne **Great Globe**, constructed from Portland stone in 1891 and one of the largest stone spheres in the world. While beneath it are the **Tilly Whim Caves**, a set of three caves, formerly a limestone quarry, that were originally excavated during the Napoleonic era and enjoyed a heyday in the 1880 as a tourist attraction. The props used throughout the cave system, incidentally, all came from shipwrecks, of which there was a ready supply in the 19th century. Closed since 1976 due to safety concerns over rockfalls, visitors can at least now peer into the caves thanks to some new gates that are being installed, as well as improvements to the paths down to the caves.

Back on the Coast Path, the trail descends on pretty **Isle of Wight Rd** (yes, that is the island you can see ahead of you on a clear day) and out into the outskirts of **Swanage**, which you reach via a short detour along **Peveril Point**.

SWANAGE   [map p303]

The final town on the Jurassic coastline is actually rather a small and unassuming place. With a population of around 10,000 and lacking any major sights or attractions, Swanage is nevertheless the largest settlement on the Isle of Purbeck and another place that survives – and in high summer thrives – on the tourist hordes. What these tourists find when they arrive is a pleasant place with amiable people, a great sweeping arc of sand and just about every amenity a visitor could need as well as a **heritage railway** (💻 www.swanagerailway.co.uk).

Swanage Jazz Festival is held here in July and the **Folk Festival** in September; see box p14 for details of both.

Services

Swanage centre is a compact place with everything in easy reach. The **tourist information office** (☎ 01929-766018, 💻 visit-dorset.com/explore/towns/swanage; Mon-Fri 10am-4.30pm, Sat & Sun 9am-4.30pm) is on the seafront overlooking the beach.

On High St you'll find the local **launderette**, Purbeck Valet (Mon-Wed & Fri 9am-4pm, Thur & Sat 9am-1pm) and, at its eastern end, the **camping outlet** Jurassic Outdoor (☎ 01929-424366, 💻 jurassicoutdoor.com; Mon-Sat 10am-5pm, Sun 10am-4pm).

Moving to Station Rd you'll find Boots **pharmacy** (Mon-Sat 9am-5.30pm,

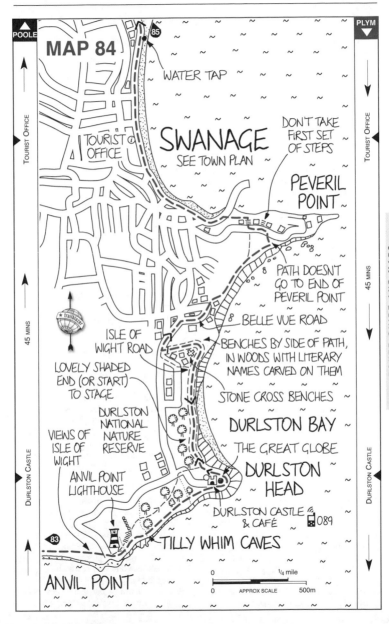

MAP 84

POOLE

PLYM

TOURIST OFFICE

TOURIST OFFICE

WATER TAP

TOURIST OFFICE

SWANAGE
SEE TOWN PLAN

DON'T TAKE
FIRST SET
OF STEPS

PEVERIL
POINT

45 MINS

45 MINS

PATH DOESN'T
GO TO END OF
PEVERIL POINT

BELLE VUE ROAD

ISLE OF
WIGHT ROAD

BENCHES BY SIDE OF PATH,
IN WOODS WITH LITERARY
NAMES CARVED ON THEM

LOVELY SHADED
END (OR START)
TO STAGE

STONE CROSS BENCHES

DURLSTON BAY

DURLSTON
NATIONAL
NATURE
RESERVE

THE GREAT GLOBE

VIEWS OF
ISLE OF
WIGHT

DURLSTON
HEAD

ANVIL POINT
LIGHTHOUSE

DURLSTON CASTLE
& CAFÉ

089

DURLSTON CASTLE

DURLSTON CASTLE

83

TILLY WHIM CAVES

ANVIL POINT

0   ¼ mile

0   APPROX SCALE   500m

ROUTE GUIDE AND MAPS

Sun 10am-4pm) and the **supermarket** Budgens (Mon-Sat 7am-10pm, Sun 11am-5pm), while at the end of the road, by the station, is a second and larger supermarket, Co-op (Mon-Sat 7am-10pm, Sun 10am-4pm) with an ATM.

Near here is the **post office** (Mon-Fri 9am-5pm, Sat 9am-1pm).

Transport
More's Breezer No 40 **bus** travels to Poole via Wareham whilst their No 50 goes to Bournemouth via Sandbanks and South Haven Point. In summer, their Breezer 30 service travels to Weymouth stopping at Lulworth Cove en route. See pp53-5 for details. National Express's 035 service also calls here (see box p51).

For a **taxi**, try Swanage Taxis (☎ 01929-421122, or ☎ 01929-425350, 🖳 www.swanagetaxis.com).

Where to stay
Swanage is blessed with a **hostel**. *YHA Swanage* (☎ 0345-371 9346, 🖳 yha.org .uk/hostel/yha-swanage; 101 beds in 2-/3-/4-/6-/7-bed rooms, some en suite; WI-FI in social areas; dorm bed from £18pp, private rooms from £49), is on Cluny Crescent. Meals are available but there is also a self-catering kitchen.

There are several particularly decent **B&Bs** scattered about town. However, note that during festivals (see box p14) and in the peak season many require a two- or three-night minimum stay, particularly for advance bookings.

Climbing the hill on Park Rd you will find *The Limes* (☎ 01929-422664, 🖳 limes hotel.net; 3S/6D/3Qd; ☛; WI-FI; 🐾; £60-75pp, sgl from £60, sgl occ room rate) at No 48. In the same vicinity but on Manor Rd, *Hermitage Guesthouse* (☎ 01929-423014, 🖳 hermitage-online.co.uk; 3D or T, private facilities; ☛; WI-FI ground floor only; Mar-end Oct; from £40pp, sgl occ room rate) overlooks the town.

Moving to the centre of town and closer to the bus and railway stations is *Firswood* (☎ 01929-422306, 🖳 firswood guesthouse.co.uk; 1S/2D or T/4D; ☛; WI-FI; from £50pp, sgl £51, sgl occ room rate),

29 Kings Rd, though they don't take credit or debit cards.

A short stroll away from the centre and opposite St Mary's Church on Kings Rd are *Millbrook* (☎ 01929-423443, 🖳 www.mill brookbedandbreakfast.co.uk; 6D/1T; WI-FI; £45-52.50pp, sgl occ £80-95), at No 56, who do not accept advance bookings for a one-night stay except in winter; and *Rivendell Guesthouse* (☎ 01929-421383, 🖳 rivendell-guesthouse.co.uk; 3D/2D or T; ☛; WI-FI; £42.50-67.50pp, sgl occ £68-100), No 58, who will take one-night bookings throughout July and August if their diary allows, but not for advance bookings. Note that the prices quoted are for room only, but they can provide breakfast (£7.50pp) if requested and it is served in guests' rooms.

If you'd rather stay in a pub there's the friendly *Red Lion* (☎ 01929-423533, 🖳 red lionswanage.com; 1S/1D/2T/1Tr; 🐾; from £50pp, sgl/sgl occ £50).

Northern Swanage (Map 85)
Just after the coast path leaves the beach, are more options: *The Sandhaven* (☎ 01929-422322, 🖳 thesandhaven.co.uk; 6D/2T; ☛; WI-FI; £45-60pp, sgl occ room rate) at No 5 Ulwell Rd. Nearby on Highcliffe Rd, *The Castleton* (☎ 01929-423972, 🖳 thecastleton.co.uk; 1S/6D/1T/1Tr/1Qd; ☛; WI-FI; £52.50-60pp, sgl from £75, sgl occ rates on request) at No 1, and *The Rookery* (☎ 01929-424224, 🖳 therookeryswanage.co.uk; 1S/3D/1T/1Tr/3Qd; ☛; WI-FI; from £50pp, sgl/sgl occ £80) at No 3, are also decent options. The latter is licensed. Note that none of the above accepts advance bookings for a one-night stay in the main season; generally the minimum is two or three nights.

Where to eat and drink
Cafés & delis The unusual *Gee Whites* (🖳 geewhites.co.uk; Easter-Oct daily 9am-9pm) is an open-sided affair whose extensive menu includes typical British-café fare (breakfasts, toasties, jackets and burgers), but there's also a decent seafood menu and they serve booze too. It can look bleak in overcast conditions, but pick a hot day in August and it's a lovely, bubbling place.

ROUTE GUIDE AND MAPS

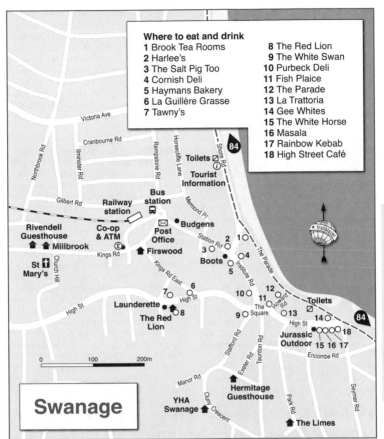

Where to eat and drink
1 Brook Tea Rooms
2 Harlee's
3 The Salt Pig Too
4 Cornish Deli
5 Haymans Bakery
6 La Guillère Grasse
7 Tawny's

8 The Red Lion
9 The White Swan
10 Purbeck Deli
11 Fish Plaice
12 The Parade
13 La Trattoria
14 Gee Whites
15 The White Horse
16 Masala
17 Rainbow Kebab
18 High Street Café

Swanage

ROUTE GUIDE AND MAPS

Nearby is the no-frills ***High Street Café*** (☎ 01929-781443; **fb**; WI-FI; 🐾; daily summer 7am-7pm, winter to 5pm), a good-value place with baps (£3.30) and all-day breakfasts (£4.50-9).

Keeping with the High St, ***La Cuillère Grasse*** (☎ 01929-427777; **fb**; daily 9am-1.30pm) is as cheap and no-frills as its name implies (it translates as 'The Greasy Spoon'), with a full English just a fiver and breakfast baps starting at just £2.

For a traditional café with a sea view, head to ***Brook Tea Rooms*** (Tue-Sat 8.30am-5pm) which has a good selection of pasties and pies as well as crab sandwiches and, of course, cream teas.

If you're just looking for better-than-average lunchbox fillers, ***Purbeck Deli*** (☎ 01929-422344, 🖥 www.thepurbeckdeli.co .uk; summer Mon-Fri 9.30am-4pm, Sat to 5pm, winter days/hours variable), on Institute Rd, is bursting with cheeses, chutneys, the perfect accompaniment to the freshly baked bread offered just down the road at ***Haymans Bakery*** (Mon-Sat 8.30am-4pm, Sun 9.30am-3pm).

Restaurants For fish & chips, two places stand close to each other: *Fish Plaice* (☎ 01929-423668, 🖥 fishplaice.co.uk; **fb**; generally Mon-Thur 11.30am-8.30pm, Fri & Sat to 9pm, Sun to 8.30pm but hours vary depending on the season and the weather) serves the usual battered fare – as well as some renowned homemade fishcakes (£2.70) – that has 'em queuing out of the door. They have also started some gluten-free frying nights – check the website for dates. Next door, *The Parade* (☎ 01929-422362, 🖥 theparadefishandchips.com; restaurant Mon-Thur 11.30am-2.30pm & 4.30-7.30pm, Fri & Sat 11.30am-7.30pm, Sun 11am-7pm; takeaway daily 11.30am-8pm) is a worthy rival as is *Harlees* (🖥 harlees.co.uk; 🐾; daily noon-7.30pm), a large place at the bottom of Station Rd that's actually part of a small local chain.

Pizza fans can head to *La Trattoria* (☎ 01929-423784, 🖥 latrattoria.co.uk; daily 5-9pm), an Italian restaurant that's been here since 1970.

Masala (☎ 01929-427299, 🖥 masalaswanage.wordpress.com; Sun-Thur 5-10pm, Fri & Sat to 11pm; curries £7.25-13.75), on High St, is a fairly standard Indian that does takeaway (though not deliveries). Close by is *Rainbow Kebab* (☎ 01929-427373; Sun-Thur 3-11pm, Fri & Sat to midnight). Further up High St, *Tawny's* (☎ 01929-422781, 🖥 tawnys-winebar.co.uk; Tue-Sat 6.30-9.30pm) is a sophisticated restaurant/wine bar with some hearty evening dishes (£18-36) such as crab linguine in a spiced creamy sauce (£22).

The Salt Pig Too (☎ 01929-550673, 🖥 www.thesaltpig.co.uk; WI-FI; 🐾; Mon-Sat 8am-6pm, Sun to 4pm) is a rustic, open-plan café-restaurant that shares its space with a butcher's. They serve tasty breakfasts and lunches. The burgers here are particularly good and they do a cracking Sunday roast (£16.95).

Pubs The best pub-food option is probably *The White Swan* (☎ 01929-423804; **fb**; food daily noon-9pm, to 8pm in winter; 🐾), a deceptively large place in the centre of town. It's a real-ale pub and the home of the popular Piddle Beer, but it's also a very welcoming place. The menu includes baguettes (£7.50-8.50) and pub-grub mains (from £13.50) throughout the day. Another fine real-ale pub is *The Red Lion* (see Where to stay; WI-FI; 🐾), further up High St. They serve food daily (noon-3pm & 6-9pm) including a Wednesday curry night (curry and a pint for £11.75), a Friday steak night (two rib-eye steaks and a bottle of wine for £31.75 and a Sunday roast (£9.95-10.95).

Also on High St, *The White Horse* (☎ 01929-422469, 🖥 www.thewhitehorseinnswanage.com; WI-FI; 🐾; food daily 9am-2.30pm & 5.30-9pm) does pub-grub classics such as steak & ale pie and has Sky Sports for the football.

SWANAGE TO SOUTH HAVEN POINT [MAPS 84-88]

And so to the last stage – and, at **7½ miles (12km; 2¾hrs)** a very pleasant one it is too. After all the ups and downs of the previous few days, it's also a relatively painless one, with only one protracted but gentle climb, an even more gentle descent – and then, for the first time in the book, a lengthy stretch of beachcombing along the flat sands of South Haven.

It's a lovely, serene end to your journey as you pick your way amongst the sun seekers, sand strollers, naked naturists and other daytrippers to South Haven Point and the finish line, where any aches and niggles that have haunted you for the past few days are suddenly soothed by the most effective balm known to man – the overwhelming sense of achievement and self-satisfaction.

The route

The stage begins with a simple stroll along Swanage seafront, the path eventually abandoning the coast to strike through the northern suburbs. Your last chance to buy **refreshments** before you climb Studland Hill is at Ballard Down Stores (Map 85; Mon-Fr 6am-5pm, Sat to 4.30pm, Sun to noon) on Redcliffe Rd. For accommodation options here see p302.

The path then embarks on the gentle climb up breezy **Studland Hill**. You don't stay up there for long, however – just long enough, perhaps, to get your first glimpse of Poole, and the Needles on the Isle of Wight some 15 miles away – before the even more gentle descent to **The Pinnacles** and **Old Harry Rocks**, where seagulls soar and falcons swoop.

Signposts for the Coast Path are non-existent around here but once you reach the bottom take a sharp left to take the large track heading into the trees, and then a small meadow, after which it divides; the right-hand (alternative) branch takes you to the beach and the friendly beach shack *Joe's Café* (Easter-Oct daily 10am-4pm up to 8pm depending on the weather; Nov-Easter weekends only); by keeping straight on you'll pass some toilets and the road that runs in front of award-winning 16th-century ***Bankes Arms*** (☎ 01929-450225, 🖥 bankesarms.com; 5D/2D or T/1Tr all en suite, 2D shared bathroom; ☛; WI-FI; 🐾; £30-67.50pp, sgl occ from £65, minimum two nights at weekends, three nights over bank holiday weekends), the home of the Isle of Purbeck brewery (see box p25), two log fires, some great **food** (Jun-Nov daily noon-9pm, Nov-May Mon-Fri noon-3pm & 6-9pm, Sat & Sun noon-9pm) and smart rooms. Wonderful, yes – but it's an unusual trekker who stops now when the finishing line is just a short trudge away, along Studland Beach.

ROUTE GUIDE AND MAPS

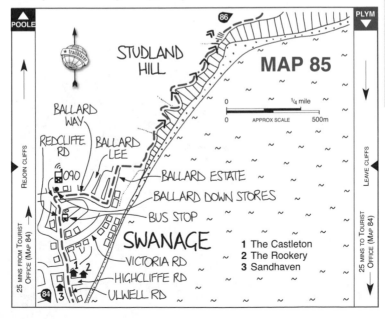

About 50 metres past Bankes Arms, turn right down a marked pathway to rejoin the coastline, from where your route is pretty self-evident, the path joining the sands of **Studland Bay** to continue its shoreside saunter. It is tempting here, especially on a hot day, to take off your hiking boots and finish your walk barefoot with the cool waves lapping over your aching feet, but be warned: walking barefoot on fairly rough sand for what amounts to around 4km, whilst carrying a heavy rucksack, is an invitation for some serious blisters. But if you have time do stroll barefoot for a while on the firm sand near the water's edge.

Passing the National Trust car park, home to a **visitor centre**, the large *Knoll Beach Café* (daily 9.30am-5pm) and gift shop, the route continues north through the **naturist beach** (the only one in the National Trust's extensive portfolio). Not even the sight of Dorset's finest in the buff can detract you from your task now, though, as you march ever onwards, rounding the bend to see, in the distance ahead, first the large ferry making the short trip between Sandbanks and **South Haven Point**; then, a few steps further on, the point you've probably been dreaming about for the past 217¼ miles (or, indeed, 630 miles if you've walked all the way from Minehead): the **Coast Path Sculpture**, marking the end of this stage, the end of the path – and the end of your walk. Congratulations!

● **Moving on** See p309 (Appendix A) for information about the ferry to Sandbanks and then bus to Poole and also More's 50 bus which stops here at South Haven Point (Shell Bay Ferry) and then goes to Bournemouth.

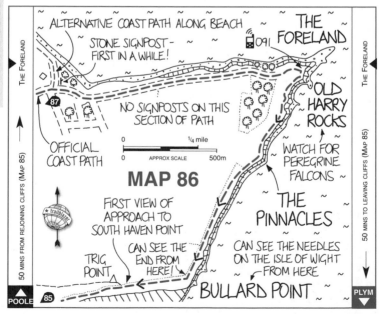

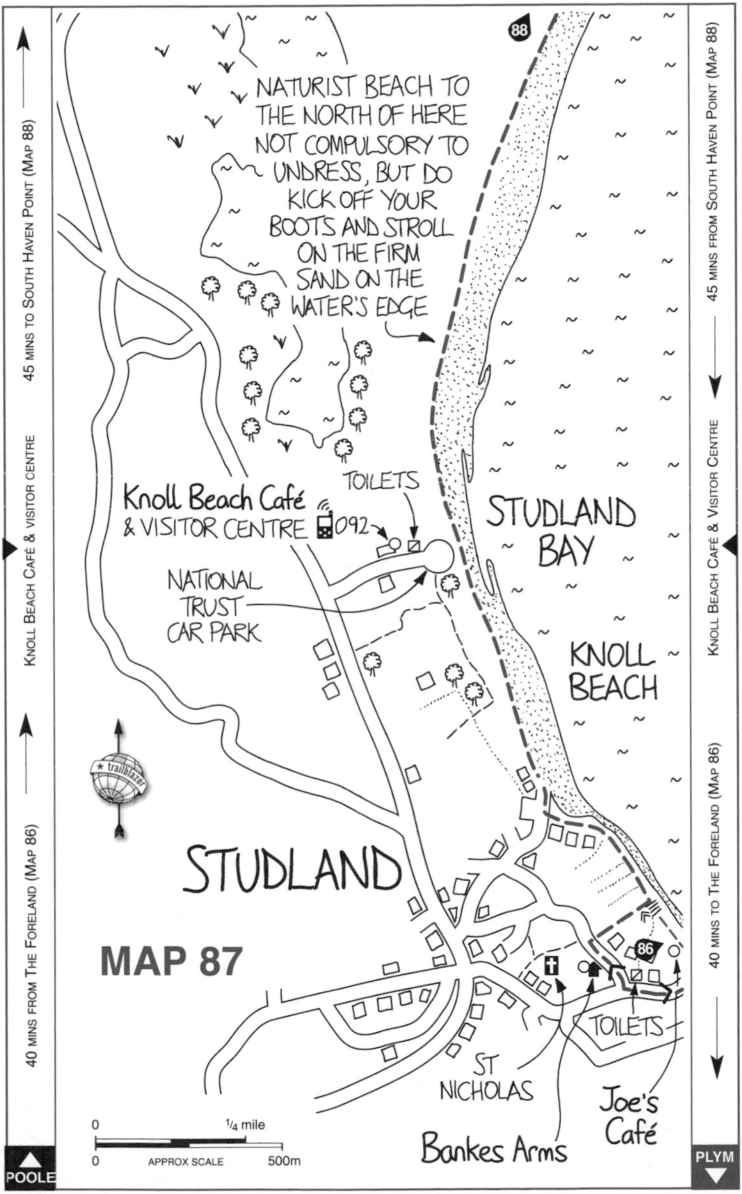

NATURIST BEACH TO
THE NORTH OF HERE
NOT COMPULSORY TO
UNDRESS, BUT DO
KICK OFF YOUR
BOOTS AND STROLL
ON THE FIRM
SAND ON THE
WATER'S EDGE

Knoll Beach Café
& VISITOR CENTRE 📱092

TOILETS

STUDLAND
BAY

NATIONAL
TRUST
CAR PARK

KNOLL
BEACH

STUDLAND

MAP 87

ST
NICHOLAS

TOILETS

Joe's
Café

Bankes Arms

0   ¼ mile

0   APPROX SCALE   500m

45 MINS TO SOUTH HAVEN POINT (MAP 88)

KNOLL BEACH & VISITOR CENTRE

40 MINS FROM THE FORELAND (MAP 86)

45 MINS FROM SOUTH HAVEN POINT (MAP 88)

KNOLL BEACH CAFÉ & VISITOR CENTRE

40 MINS TO THE FORELAND (MAP 86)

ROUTE GUIDE AND MAPS

POOLE

PLYM

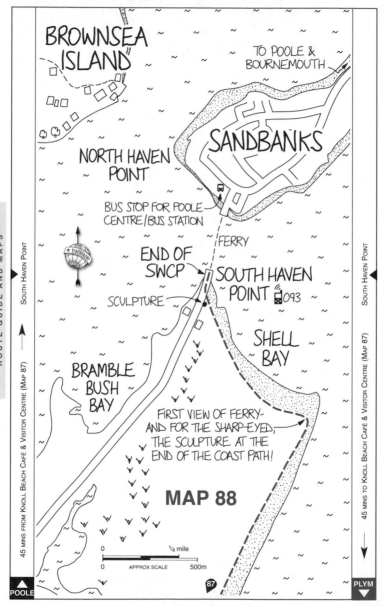

BROWNSEA ISLAND

TO POOLE & BOURNEMOUTH

SANDBANKS

NORTH HAVEN POINT

BUS STOP FOR POOLE CENTRE / BUS STATION

FERRY

END OF SWCP

SOUTH HAVEN POINT 🛟093

SCULPTURE

SHELL BAY

BRAMBLE BUSH BAY

FIRST VIEW OF FERRY AND FOR THE SHARP-EYED, THE SCULPTURE AT THE END OF THE COAST PATH!

MAP 88

0   ¼ mile
0   APPROX SCALE   500m

87

ROUTE GUIDE AND MAPS

SOUTH HAVEN POINT

45 MINS FROM KNOLL BEACH CAFÉ & VISITOR CENTRE (MAP 87)

SOUTH HAVEN POINT

45 MINS TO KNOLL BEACH CAFÉ & VISITOR CENTRE (MAP 87)

▲ POOLE

PLYM ▼

APPENDIX A: POOLE & BOURNEMOUTH

Though not on the path, there's a fair chance you'll be visiting Poole or Bournemouth at some point in your trip – probably at the end – in order to catch transport to/from the start/end of the trail. Both offer all the amenities you are likely to need.

Poole

To get to Poole bus station (20 mins), which is walking distance from Poole railway station, take the **ferry** (⌨ sandbanksferry.co.uk; daily 7am-11pm; 3/hr; £1) across to Sandbanks and jump on More's Breezer No 60 **bus** (this stops running at around 6pm in winter). First's X54 bus connects Poole with Weymouth. South Western Railway operates **train services** to London Waterloo.

For further details of these bus and train services see pp51-5.

To help you get around pay a visit to the **tourist information centre** (☎ 01202-128888, ⌨ pooletourism.com; Easter-Oct daily 10am-5pm, Nov-Easter Mon-Sat 10am-4pm, Sun noon-4pm) in the flashy modern Poole Museum, at 4 High St.

The most attractive part of town is the harbour area, where you'll also find some **B&Bs** including *Quayside* (☎ 01202-683733, ⌨ quaysidepoole.co.uk; 1S/2D/2T/2Tr; WI-FI; from £45pp, sgl/sgl occ £80), 9 High St, which is opposite the museum.

For **food**, there are lots of options along The Quay and the High St. *Guildhall Tavern* (☎ 01202-671717, ⌨ www.guildhalltavern.co.uk; WI-FI; 🐾; Mon-Sat 11.30am-9pm), at 15 Market St, is a French restaurant that is a good place for that end-of-trek celebration, pricey and indulgent (mains £18-23.95) but with suitably luxurious dishes.

Bournemouth

More's Breezer No 50 stops at South Haven Point (Shell Bay Ferry) on its way between Swanage bus station and Bournemouth railway station (45 mins; £3.60). The **bus**, which runs until around 9.30pm in the main season (rest of year to about 6.45pm), goes on the ferry (see above) itself, stopping to pick up passengers at the bus stops immediately before and after it. South Western Railway operates **train services** to London Waterloo and Cross Country Trains to Birmingham.

For further details of these bus and train services see pp51-5.

Bournemouth Tourist Information Centre (☎ 01202-123800, ⌨ bournemouth.co.uk; Apr-Jun & Sep-Oct daily 9am-5pm, July & Aug to 6pm, Nov-Mar 9am-4pm) is at Pier Approach on the seafront.

Bournemouth has no shortage of **accommodation** options. One place near the railway station is *Lea Hurst B&B* (☎ 01202-290136, ⌨ leahursthotel.co.uk; 4D/2T/2Qd; WI-FI), at 8 Frances Rd, charges £25-35pp (sgl occ £32-42) and is near the railway station. In the peak season they do not accept bookings for one night only. If you want a final night near the sea consider *The Cumberland* (☎ 01202-298350, ⌨ cumberlandhotel.oceana-collection.com; 11S/50D/15D or T, one suite, all en suite or with private facilities; ▼; WI-FI; small 🐾 but certain rooms only); it is a vast 1930s Art Deco hotel with a wide range of rooms, the best of which have a balcony and sea view. B&B costs £36.50-110.50pp (sgl/sgl occ from £48); room only rates also available.

For **food** again there is the usual range of chain restaurants and cafés but one place by the sea that is worth trying is *West Beach* (☎ 01202-587785, ⌨ west-beach.co.uk; WI-FI; 🐾 at lunchtime only; Mon-Fri 9am-10pm, Sat & Sun 8.30am-10pm); the menu focuses on fish but there are also daily specials and meat/vegetarian options.

APPENDIX B: THE RIDGEWAY'S PREHISTORIC SITES

Nobody is quite sure why there is such an abundance of prehistoric sites along the Ridgeway. Many think that this chalky ridge provided the easiest way to travel east–west through this part of Dorset, rather than trying to wade through the boggy forested ground present in the valleys below. The Ridgeway also provides a natural 'plinth', a perfect platform for these early people to design and display their temples, tombs and tumuli so their neighbours could see them. Whatever the reasons, the quantity and variety of prehistoric sites on the Ridgeway puts it on a par with the landscape around Stonehenge. Over 3000 sites have now been discovered, many of them only recently.

These sites fall into four main chronological categories. The oldest finds date back to the **Neolithic Age** (4000-2000BC – note the definitions of each of these ages is very fluid and different books may give different start and end dates for the various eras). These were the first farmers, who cleared the Ridgeway of its forests in order to plant crops and cultivate the land. The monuments they built tend to be found at the western end of the Ridgeway, where they had easy access to their building materials – rocks from the Valley of Stones. This valley lies to the west of the Hardy Monument (see Map 60a) and is where early man would source rocks and boulders for their burial chambers and stone circles that dot the landscape. There are only a couple of examples of these within easy reach of the path. The first is **Hampton Down Stone Circle**, constructed around 2000BC – though it has been moved and altered many times since. It is believed that the stone now sits in its original position, though with only 10 of the original stones (a photograph from 1908 indicates there were 16 at that time). On the other side of the Hardy Monument, and a little off the path, is the more impressive **Hell Stone**, a Neolithic stone burial chamber that resembles a kind of mini Stonehenge. Actually, the chamber was only one part of the structure, for from the chamber ran a mound of earth, the whole construction being known as a **long barrow**. Unfortunately, it is widely believed that the 19th-century antiquarians who restored this one rebuilt it incorrectly – though to the laymen it's still a powerful place and the chamber a mighty structure.

In addition to the 17 long barrows on the Ridgeway there are also three **bank barrows**, of which one, **Broadmayne Bank Barrow**, lies around 500m off the path to the north-east of Green Hill. While it is believed the long barrows had some sort of funerary function – the number of bones excavated within the burial chambers suggest they were used as communal burial places – the function of these bank barrows is unknown.

The practice of constructing barrows continued into the **Bronze Age** (2000-500BC) though the style changed as the mounds became more hemispherical. It is these Bronze Age **round barrows** that are the dominant feature of the path. Once again these definitely had a funerary purpose, the corpses of the deceased being placed within the mounds. **Bronkham Hill**, east of the Hardy Monument on the trail, has the finest collection of round barrows on the path. Some important archeological finds have been found in these tumuli including the beautiful Clandon Lozenge, a decorative gold 'plate' that is now on display in the County Museum in Dorset.

By around the 9th century BC the Britons were using a new metal for the first time, heralding in the **Iron Age**. On the Ridgeway, this epoch is best represented by the giant hillforts scattered hereabouts, of which **Abbotsbury Castle** is typical: there's little to cause the layman's jaw to drop when visiting this hilltop site today, though archaeologists will recognise the curves, folds and bumps in the land that are the telltale signs of such a construction. The castle is just one of three in the area, with Maiden Castle, just outside Dorchester, considered to be the most important Iron Age fort in the UK due to its size and history. By the middle of the 1st century AD, however, the Romans had arrived and the Iron Age was ending – and prehistory, too, with the Romans bringing their practice of writing official documents, notes and letters that recorded their time in Britain.

APPENDIX C: TAKING A DOG

The South-West Coast Path is a dog-friendly path and many are the rewards that await those prepared to make the extra effort required to bring their best friend along the trail. However, you shouldn't underestimate the amount of work involved in bringing your pooch to the path. Indeed, just about every decision you make will be influenced by the fact that you've got a dog: how you plan to travel to the start of the trail, where you're going to stay, how far you're going to walk each day, where you're going to rest and where you're going to eat in the evening.

The decision-making begins well before you've set foot on the trail. For starters, you have to ask – and be honest with – yourself: can your dog really cope with walking 10+ miles (16+km) a day, day after day, week after week? And just as importantly, will he or she actually enjoy it?

If you think the answer is yes to both, you need to start preparing accordingly. For one thing, extra thought needs to go into your itinerary. The best starting point is to study the Village & town facilities table on pp32-5 (and the advice below), and plan where to stop, where to eat, where to buy food for your mutt, etc etc.

Looking after your dog

To begin with, you need to make sure that your dog is fully **inoculated** against the usual doggy illnesses, and also up-to-date with regard to **worm pills** (eg Drontal) and **flea preventatives** such as Frontline – they are, after all, following in the pawprints of many a dog before them, some of whom may well have left fleas or other parasites on the trail that now lie in wait for their next meal to arrive. **Pet insurance** is also a very good idea; if you've already got insurance do check that it will cover a trip such as this.

On the subject of looking after your dog's health, perhaps the most important implement you can take with you is the **plastic tick remover**, available from vets for a couple of quid. Ticks are a real problem on the SWCP, as they hide in the long grass waiting for unsuspecting victims to trot past. These removers, while fiddly, help you to remove the tick safely (ie without leaving its head behind buried under the dog's skin).

Being in unfamiliar territory also makes it more likely that you and your dog could become separated. For this reason, make sure your dog has a **tag with your contact details on it** (a mobile phone number would be best if you are carrying one with you); since 2016 it's been a legal requirement to have your dog microchipped.

What to pack

You've probably already got a good idea of what to bring to keep your dog alive and happy, but the following is a checklist:
● **Food/water bowl** Foldable cloth bowls are popular with walkers as they are light and take up little room in the rucksack. It is also possible to get a water-bottle-and-bowl combination, where the bottle folds into a 'trough' from which the dog can drink.
● **Lead and collar** An extendable one is probably preferable for this sort of trip. Make sure both lead and collar are in good condition – you don't want either to snap on the trail, or you may end up carrying your dog through sheep fields until a replacement can be found.
● **Medication** You'll know if you need to bring any lotions or potions.
● **Tick remover** See above.
● **Bedding** A simple blanket may suffice, or you can opt for something more elaborate if you aren't carrying your own luggage.
● **Poo bags** Essential.
● **Hygiene wipes** For cleaning your dog after it's rolled in stuff.
● **A favourite toy** Helps prevent your dog from pining for the entire walk.

❏ **PACKING FOR YOUR DOG**

When it comes to packing, I always leave an exterior pocket of my rucksack empty so I can put used poo bags in there (for deposit at the first bin I come to). I always like to keep all the dog's kit together and separate from the other luggage (usually inside a plastic bag inside my rucksack). I have also seen several dogs sporting their own 'doggy rucksack, so they can carry their own food, water, poo etc – which certainly reduces the burden on their owner!

● **Food/water** Remember to bring treats as well as regular food to keep up the mutt's morale.
● **Corkscrew stake** Available from camping or pet shops, this will help you to keep your dog secure in one place while you set up camp/doze.
● **Raingear** It can rain a lot!
● **Old towels** For drying your dog after the deluge.

Dogs on beaches

There is no general rule regarding whether dogs are allowed on beaches or not. Some of the beaches on the SWCP are open to dogs all year; some allow them on the beach only outside the summer season (1st May to 30th Sep); while a few beaches don't allow dogs at all. (Guide dogs, by the way, are usually excluded from any bans.) If in doubt, look for the noticeboards that will tell you the exact rules.

Visit Dorset (💻 visit-dorset.com/ideas-and-inspiration/dog-friendly/dog-friendly-beaches) provide a comprehensive list of what beaches are dog friendly. Visit Devon used to do the same, but for some unconscionable reason have decided to replace it with an article about family-friendly beaches. So you'll just have to rely on the local noticeboards to discover where your pooch can play on the pebbles and saunter on the sands.

Where dogs are banned from a beach there will usually be an alternative path that you can take that avoids the sands. If there isn't an alternative, and you have no choice but to cross the beach even though dogs are officially banned, you are permitted to do so as long as you cross the beach as speedily as possible, follow the line of the path (which is usually well above the high-water mark) and keep your dog tightly under control **on a lead**.

Whatever the rules of access are for the beach, remember that your dog shouldn't disturb other beach-users – and you must always **clean up after your dog**.

Finally, remember that you need to bring drinking water with you on the beach as dogs can overheat with the lack of shade.

When to keep your dog on a lead

● **On cliff tops** It's a sad fact that, every year, a few dogs lose their lives falling over the edge of the cliffs. It usually occurs when they are chasing rabbits (which know where the cliff-edge is and are able, unlike your poor pooch, to stop in time).
● **When crossing farmland**, particularly in the lambing season (around May) when your dog can scare the sheep, causing them to lose their young. Farmers are allowed by law to shoot at and kill any dogs that they consider are worrying their sheep. During lambing, most farmers would prefer it if you didn't bring your dog at all.

The exception is if your dog is being attacked by cows. There have been deaths in the UK caused by walkers being trampled as they tried to rescue their dogs from the attentions of cattle. The advice in this instance is to let go of the lead, head speedily to a position of safety (usually the other side of the field gate or stile) and call your dog to you.

● **On National Trust land**, where it is compulsory to keep your dog on a lead.

● **Around ground-nesting birds** It's important to keep your dog under control when crossing an area where certain species of birds nest on the ground. Most dogs love foraging around in the woods but make sure you have permission to do so; some woods are used as 'nurseries' for game birds and dogs are only allowed through them if they are on a lead.

Cleaning up after your dog

It is extremely important that dog owners behave in a responsible way when walking the path and all excrement should be cleaned up. In towns, villages and fields where animals graze or which will be cut for silage, hay etc, you need to pick up and bag the excrement. In other places you can possibly get away with merely flicking it with a nearby stick into the undergrowth, thus ensuring there is none left on the path to decorate the boots of others.

If your dog is anything like others, it'll wait until you are 300m past the nearest bin – and about four miles from the next one – before relieving itself. Don't be tempted to leave it, but bag it up; this means you're likely to have to carry it for a couple of miles – just look on it as your own personalised little hand warmer.

Staying and eating with your dog

In this guide we have used the symbol 🐾 to denote where a hotel, pub or B&B welcomes dogs. However, this always needs to be arranged in advance – especially as many B&Bs etc have only one or two rooms suitable for people with dogs – and most places charge extra.

Hostels (both YHA and independent) do not permit them unless they are an assistance (guide) dog. Campsites (including holiday parks) tend to accept them as long as they are kept on a lead and they may only be accepted in certain areas.

Before you turn up always double check whether the place you would like to stay accepts dogs, whether there is space for them and what the charges and regulations are.

When it comes to eating, most landlords allow dogs in at least a section of their pubs, though few restaurants do. Make sure you always ask first and ensure your dog doesn't run around the pub but is secured to your table or a radiator.

APPENDIX D: GPS WAYPOINTS

MAP	REF	GPS WAYPOINT	DESCRIPTION
Map 1	001	SX 48376 54004	Start of walk/Mayflower Steps
Map 1	002	SX 48974 53954	Turn-off to Breakwater Hill
Map 2	003	SX 50643 53881	Oreston Rhino sculpture
Map 2	004	SX 50350 52914	Radford Castle
Map 3	005	SX 49140 52394	Jennycliff Café
Map 3	006	SX 49141 50716	Cliffedge Café
Map 4	007	SX 49744 48820	Heybrook Bay
Map 5	008	SX 51786 48489	The Old Mill Café (turn-off to Wembury)
Map 6	009	SX 54021 47711	Ferry at Noss Mayo
Map 6a	009a	SX 52858 49645	Knighton Stores & post office in Wembury
Map 6a	009b	SX 55377 52168	Brixton Gallery and post office
Map 6a	009c	SX 56655 52714	Join lane
Map 6a	009d	SX 57093 51067	Puslinch Bridge
Map 6a	009e	SX 54772 47658	The Ship Inn, Noss Mayo
Map 7	010	SX 54423 45979	Ruined signal station
Map 8	011	SX 59057 47243	St Anchorite's Rock
Map 9	012	SX 61415 47574	Crossing of Erme, Mothecombe side
Map 10	013	SX 64908 44880	Fryer Tucks fish & chips, Challaborough
Map 11	014	SX 65162 44158	Venus Café
Map 11	015	SX 66623 44045	Cockleridge Ham Ferry Landing (River Avon)
Map 11a	015a	SX 69261 47236	Roundabout into Aveton Gifford
Map 12	016	SX 67718 41556	Beachhouse Café
Map 13	017	SX 68734 38504	Turn-off for pathway by wall
Map 14	018	SX 69814 37608	Path left to Bolberry
Map 15	019	SX 72538 36200	Bolt Head
Map 16	020	SX 74148 38087	Mill Bay
Map 17	021	SX 76605 35829	Junction with path by Gammon Head
Map 18	022	SX 79156 36320	Maelcombe House
Map 19	023	SX 80192 37184	Lannacombe Beach
Map 20	024	SX 82456 37221	Turn-off to Start Point Lighthouse
Map 21	025	SX 82334 42016	Torcross
Map 22	026	SX 82888 44346	Slapton Turn
Map 23	027	SX 84075 46876	Strete Post Office & Stores
Map 24	028	SX 85935 47962	Take left fork, uphill to Stoke Fleming
Map 25	029	SX 88664 50280	Dartmouth Castle
Map 26	030	SX 90309 49635	Inner Froward Point
Map 27	031	SX 92234 53402	Man Sands
Map 28	032	SX 93514 54677	Sharkham Point
Map 29	033	SX 94030 56163	Entrance to Berry Head Country Park (NNR)
Map 30	034	SX 89516 57606	Path turns left between row of beach huts
Map 31	035	SX 89460 60284	Paignton Harbour
Map 32	036	SX 89787 62257	Hollicombe Park
Map 33	037	SX 91761 63385	Torquay Marina
Map 34	038	SX 94952 63682	Tip of Hope's Nose
Map 35	039	SX 92154 66031	Join A379
Map 36	040	SX 92656 68475	Maidencombe Beach Car Park
Map 37	041	SX 94041 71961	The Ness
Map 38	042	SX 95496 74828	High- and low-tide routes merge
Map 39	043	SX 97854 78532	Dawlish Warren railway station

MAP	REF	GPS WAYPOINT	DESCRIPTION
Map 40	044	SX 97689 81903	Starcross Ferry
Map 40a	044a	SX 96240 87947	Topsham Ferry
Map 40a	044b	SX 98275 86387	Junction of Exton Lane with Station Rd
	044c	SX 98875 84287	Lympstone, cross railway line
Map 41	045	SY 02079 79549	Geoneedle, start of Jurassic Coast
Map 42	046	SY 03594 79851	Straight Point Rifle Range
Map 43	047	SY 06365 81799	Budleigh Salterton; join Marine Parade
Map 44	048	SY 09047 83638	Brandy Head Observation Hut
Map 45	049	SY 10876 86735	Peak Hill
Map 46	050	SY 11977 86946	Clock Tower Café
Map 47	051	SY 16397 87962	Weston Mouth Beach
Map 48	052	SY 19210 88297	Path joins track above Branscombe
Map 49	053	SY 20684 88162	Branscombe Mouth
Map 50	054	SY 25368 90114	Squire's Lane (Axe Cliff Golf Club clubhouse)
Map 51	055	SY 27034 89627	Sign: Axmouth–Lyme Regis Undercliffs NNR
Map 52	056	SY 31690 90835	Viewpoint at Pinhay Cliff
Map 53	057	SY 33804 91656	The Cobb, Lyme Regis
Map 54	058	SY 36206 93612	Turn-off for Charmouth Beach – careful not to miss this turn
Map 55	059	SY 37885 93090	Path to National Trust car park, Stonebarrow Hill
Map 56	060	SY 42011 91776	Seatown
Map 57	061	SY 44782 91079	Eype Mouth
Map 58	062	SY 47487 89729	Burton Freshwater
Map 59	063	SY 50271 88161	Cogden Beach
Map 60	064	SY 53054 86511	Junction with path to South Dorset Ridgeway
Map 60a	064a	SY 55071 86596	Abbotsbury Castle
Map 60a	064b	SY 61306 87616	Hardy Monument
Map 60b	064c	SY 68352 84842	Bincombe
Map 60c	064d	SY 71520 84385	Osmington White Horse
	064e	SY 72839 82931	Turn off road after Craig's Farm Dairy Shop & Tea Room
Map 61	065	SY 55974 84614	Miniature roundabout
Map 62	066	SY 57576 84873	Junction with path to Abbotsbury
Map 63	067	SY 60535 82030	Rodden Hive
Map 64	068	SY 63457 79942	Butterstreet Cove
Map 65	069	SY 64638 78822	Entrance/exit to range (Tidmoor Cove)
Map 66	070	SY 66674 76290	Ferrybridge
Map 67	071	SY 68327 73505	The Cove House Inn
Map 68	072	SY 68639 72928	Large Hand Crane
Map 68	073	SY 68215 72084	Pass under stone arch
Map 69	074	SY 69712 71084	Church Ope Cove
Map 70	075	SY 67711 68279	Bill of Portland
Map 71	076	SY 67882 78756	Town Bridge, Weymouth Harbour
Map 72	077	SY 69910 81969	Turn-off to Jordan Hill Roman temple
Map 73	078	SY 73556 82056	Reunion with South Dorset Ridgeway
Map 74	079	SY 77221 80962	White Nothe
Map 75	080	SY 80595 80302	Path above Durdle Door
Map 76	081	SY 82425 79934	Lulworth Cove
Map 76	081a	SY 82450 80766	Alternative routes divide
Map 76b	081b	SY 90923 85489	Turn off road to quarries
Map 76	082	SY 82975 79720	Gate into Lulworth Ranges

MAP	REF	GPS WAYPOINT	DESCRIPTION
Map 78	083	SY 88895 79777	Take right-hand fork around hill, not over it
Map 79	084	SY 90803 79304	Stile near end of alternative routes
Map 80	085	SY 94996 77334	Top of Houns-tout Cliff
Map 81	086	SY 96129 77784	Turn-off for Worth Matravers
Map 82	087	SY 97722 76177	Gate at East Man, Winspit
Map 83	088	SY 99686 76962	Dancing Ledge
Map 84	089	SZ 03399 77253	Durlston Castle & café
Map 85	090	SZ 02989 80264	Turn-off Redcliffe Road to Ballard Way
Map 86	091	SZ 05441 82474	Old Harry Rocks
Map 87	092	SZ 03427 83558	Knoll Beach Café
Map 88	093	SZ 03620 86653	South Haven Point

Map key

⌂ Where to stay	📖 Library/bookstore	● Other
O Where to eat and drink	@ Internet	CP Car park
Λ Campsite	🏛 Museum/gallery	🚌 Bus station/stop
⊠ Post Office	✝ Church/cathedral	▭ Rail line & station
Ⓔ Bank/ATM	Ⓣ Phone box	⛴ Ferry
ⓘ Tourist Information	⊘ Public toilet	▭ Park
	□ Building	📟 082 GPS waypoint

South-West Coast Path	Sand dunes	Trees/woodland
Other path	Cliffs	Bog or marsh
4 x 4 track	Stone & earth wall	Sand
Tarmac road	Bridge	Stones
Steps	Fence	Lighthouse
Slope	Wall	Golf course
Steep slope	Hedge	NR Nature Reserve
Stile	Water	23 Map continuation
Gate	Stream/river	

INDEX

Page references in **bold** type refer to maps

TRAILBLAZER TITLE LIST

For more information about Trailblazer and our
expanding range of guides, for guidebook updates or
for credit card mail order sales visit our website:

trailblazer-guides.com

TRAILBLAZER'S BRITISH WALKING GUIDES

We've applied to destinations which are closer to home Trailblazer's proven formula for publishing definitive practical route guides for adventurous travellers. Britain's network of long-distance trails enables the walker to explore some of the finest landscapes in the country's best walking areas. These are guides that are user-friendly, practical, informative and environmentally sensitive.

● **Unique mapping features** In many walking guidebooks the reader has to read a route description then try to relate it to the map. Our guides are much easier to use because walking directions, tricky junctions, places to stay and eat, points of interest and walking times are all written onto the maps themselves in the places to which they apply. With their uncluttered clarity, these are not general-purpose maps but fully edited maps drawn by walkers for walkers.

'The same attention to detail that distinguishes its other guides has been brought to bear here'.
THE SUNDAY TIMES

● **Largest-scale walking maps** At a scale of just under 1:20,000 (8cm or 3¹/₈ inches to one mile) the maps in these guides are bigger than even the most detailed British walking maps currently available in the shops.

● **Not just a trail guide – includes where to stay, where to eat and public transport** Our guidebooks cover the complete walking experience, not just the route. Accommodation options for all budgets are provided (pubs, hotels, B&Bs, campsites, bunkhouses, hostels) as well as places to eat. Detailed public transport information for all access points to each trail means that there are itineraries for all walkers, for hiking the entire route as well as for day or weekend walks.

Cleveland Way *Henry Stedman*, 1st edn, ISBN 978-1-905864-91-1, 240pp, 98 maps
Coast to Coast *Henry Stedman*, 10th edn, ISBN 978-1-912716-25-8, 268pp, 109 maps
Cornwall Coast Path (SW Coast Path Pt 2) *Stedman & Newton*, 7th edn, ISBN 978-1-912716-26-5, 352pp, 142 maps
Cotswold Way *Tricia & Bob Hayne*, 4th edn, ISBN 978-1-912716-04-3, 204pp, 53 maps
Dales Way *Henry Stedman,* 2nd edn, ISBN 978-1-912716-30-2, 192pp, 50 maps
Dorset & South Devon (SW Coast Path Pt 3) *Stedman & Newton*, 3rd edn, ISBN 978-1-912716-34-0, 340pp, 97 maps
Exmoor & North Devon (SW Coast Path Pt I) *Stedman & Newton*, 3rd edn, ISBN 978-1-9912716-24-1, 224pp, 68 maps
Glyndŵr's Way *Chris Scott*, 1st edn, ISBN 978-1-912716-32-6, 220pp, 70 maps (**mid 2023**)
Great Glen Way *Jim Manthorpe*, 2nd edn, ISBN 978-1-912716-10-4, 184pp, 50 maps
Hadrian's Wall Path *Henry Stedman*, 7th edn, ISBN 978-1-912716-37-1, 250pp, 60 maps
London LOOP *Henry Stedman*, 1st edn, ISBN 978-1-912716-21-0, 236pp, 60 maps
Norfolk Coast Path & Peddars Way *Alexander Stewart*, 1st edn, ISBN 978-1-905864-98-0, 224pp, 75 maps
North Downs Way *Henry Stedman*, 2nd edn, ISBN 978-1-905864-90-4, 240pp, 98 maps
Offa's Dyke Path *Keith Carter*, 5th edn, ISBN 978-1-912716-03-6, 268pp, 98 maps
Pembrokeshire Coast Path *Jim Manthorpe*, 6th edn, 978-1-912716-13-5, 236pp, 96 maps
Pennine Way *Stuart Greig*, 6th edn, ISBN 978-1-912716-33-3, 272pp, 138 maps
The Ridgeway *Nick Hill*, 5th edn, ISBN 978-1-912716-20-3, 208pp, 53 maps
South Downs Way *Jim Manthorpe*, 7th edn, ISBN 978-1-912716-23-4, 204pp, 60 maps
Thames Path *Joel Newton*, 3rd edn, ISBN 978-1-912716-27-2, 256pp, 99 maps
West Highland Way *Charlie Loram*, 8th edn, ISBN 978-1-912716-29-6, 224pp, 60 maps

'The Trailblazer series stands head, shoulders, waist and ankles above the rest. They are particularly strong on mapping ...'
THE SUNDAY TIMES

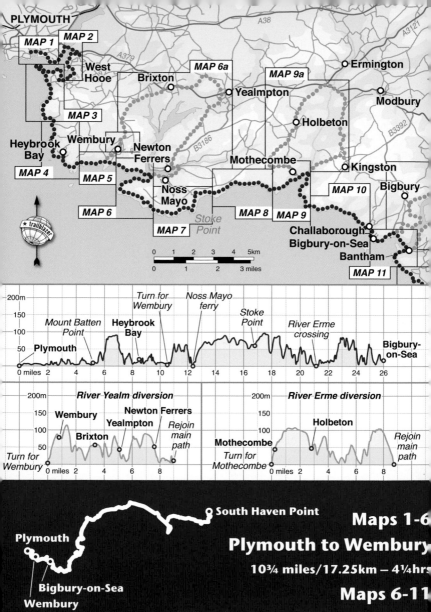

PLYMOUTH

MAP 1 MAP 2

West Hooe

Brixton

MAP 6a

MAP 9a

Ermington

Yealmpton

Modbury

MAP 3

Holbeton

Heybrook Bay

Wembury

Newton Ferrers

Mothecombe

Kingston

MAP 4

MAP 5

Noss Mayo

Bigbury

MAP 6

MAP 8 MAP 9

MAP 10

Stoke Point

MAP 7

Challaborough
Bigbury-on-Sea
Bantham

MAP 11

0 1 2 3 4 5km
0 1 2 3 miles

Elevation profile (main path):

200m
150
100
50

Plymouth

Mount Batten Point

Heybrook Bay

Turn for Wembury

Noss Mayo ferry

Stoke Point

River Erme crossing

Bigbury-on-Sea

0 miles 2 4 6 8 10 12 14 16 18 20 22 24 26

River Yealm diversion

200m
150
100
50

Turn for Wembury

Wembury

Brixton

Yealmpton

Newton Ferrers

Rejoin main path

0 miles 2 4 6 8

River Erme diversion

200m
150
100

Mothecombe

Turn for Mothecombe

Holbeton

Rejoin main path

0 miles 2 4 6 8

South Haven Point

Plymouth

Bigbury-on-Sea

Wembury

Maps 1-6

Plymouth to Wembury

10¾ miles/17.25km – 4¼hrs

Maps 6-11

Wembury to Bigbury-on-Sea

15¼ miles/24.5km – 5½hrs

NOTE: Add 20-30% to these times to allow for stops

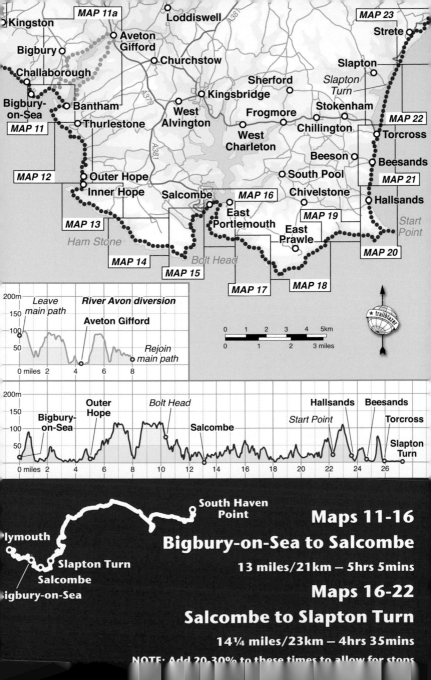

MAP 11a
Kingston
Loddiswell
Bigbury
Aveton Gifford
Churchstow
Challaborough
Sherford
Bigbury-on-Sea
Kingsbridge
MAP 11
Bantham
West Alvington
Frogmore
Thurlestone
West Charleton
Chillington
West Pool
MAP 12
Outer Hope
South Pool
Inner Hope
Salcombe
Chivelstone
MAP 13
MAP 16
East Portlemouth
East Prawle
MAP 19
Ham Stone
MAP 14
Bolt Head
MAP 15
MAP 17
MAP 18
MAP 20

MAP 23
Strete
Slapton
Slapton Turn
Stokenham
MAP 22
Torcross
Beeson
Beesands
MAP 21
Hallsands
Start Point

200m
150
100
80
Leave main path
River Avon diversion
Aveton Gifford
Rejoin main path
0 miles   2   4   6   8

0 1 2 3 4 5km
0 1 2 3 miles

trailblazer

200m
150
100
50
Bigbury-on-Sea
Outer Hope
Bolt Head
Salcombe
Hallsands
Beesands
Start Point
Torcross
Slapton Turn
0 miles 2   4   6   8   10   12   14   16   18   20   22   24   26

South Haven Point
Plymouth
Slapton Turn
Salcombe
Bigbury-on-Sea

Maps 11-16
Bigbury-on-Sea to Salcombe
13 miles/21km – 5hrs 5mins

Maps 16-22
Salcombe to Slapton Turn
14¼ miles/23km – 4hrs 35mins

NOTE: Add 20-30% to these times to allow for stops

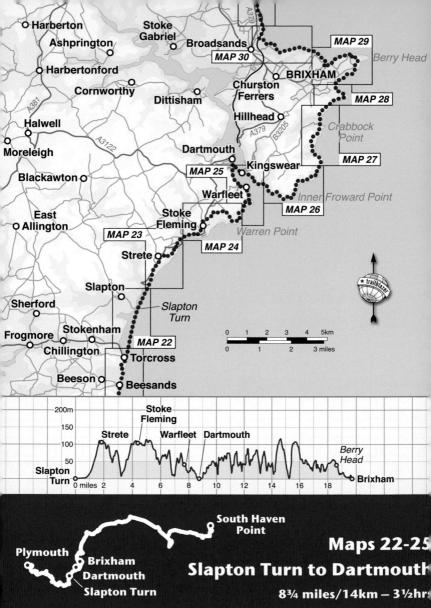

Maps 22-25
Slapton Turn to Dartmouth
8¾ miles/14km – 3½hrs

Maps 25-29, Dartmouth to Brixham
11 miles/17.5km – 4hr

NOTE: Add 20-30% to these times to allow for stop

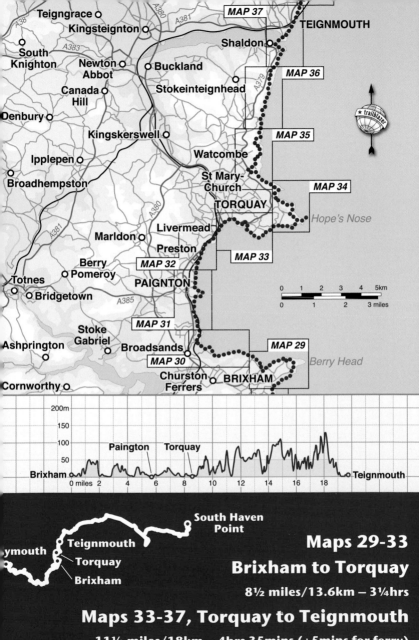

Maps 29-33

Brixham to Torquay

8½ miles/13.6km – 3¼hrs

Maps 33-37, Torquay to Teignmouth

11¼ miles/18km – 4hrs 35mins (+5mins for ferry)

NOTE: Add 20-30% to these times to allow for stops

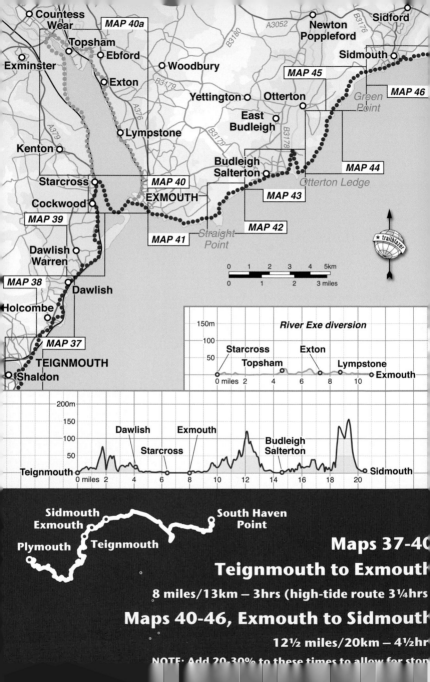

Countess Wear
MAP 40a
Topsham
O Ebford
Exminster
O Woodbury
Exton
Sidford
Newton
Poppleford
A3052
B3180
Sidmouth
MAP 45
Green
Point
MAP 46
Yettington
Otterton
East
Budleigh
MAP 44
Lympstone
Kenton
Budleigh
Salterton
Starcross
MAP 40
Cockwood
EXMOUTH
MAP 43
Otterton Ledge
MAP 39
MAP 42
Dawlish
Warren
MAP 41
MAP 38
Straight
Point
Dawlish
Holcombe
MAP 37
TEIGNMOUTH
Shaldon

0   1   2   3   4   5km
0   1   2   3 miles

River Exe diversion

150m
100
Starcross   Exton
50   Topsham   Lympstone
                                    Exmouth
0 miles 2   4   6   8   10

200m
150
100   Dawlish   Exmouth
50   Starcross   Budleigh
                                    Salterton
Teignmouth   Sidmouth
0 miles 2   4   6   8   10   12   14   16   18   20

Sidmouth   South Haven
Exmouth   Point
Plymouth   Teignmouth

Maps 37-4(

Teignmouth to Exmouth

8 miles/13km – 3hrs (high-tide route 3¼hrs

Maps 40-46, Exmouth to Sidmouth

12½ miles/20km – 4½hr

NOTE: Add 20-30% to these times to allow for stop

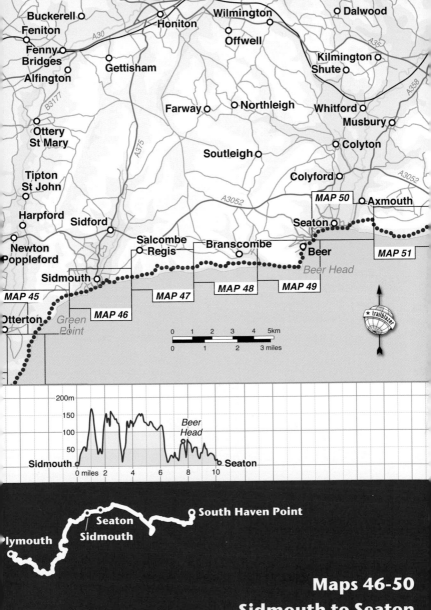

Maps 46-50

Sidmouth to Seaton

10¼ miles/16.5km – 4¼hrs

NOTE: Add 20-30% to these times to allow for stops

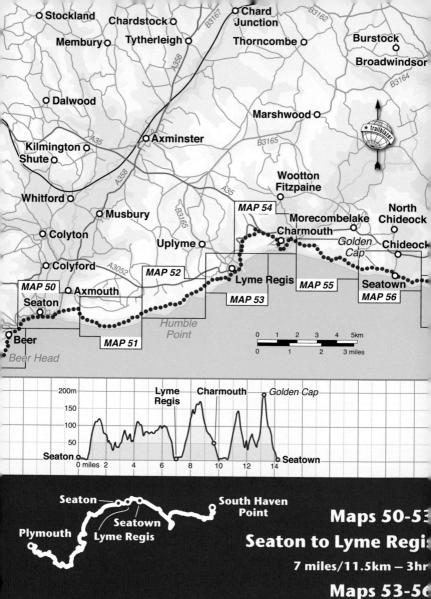

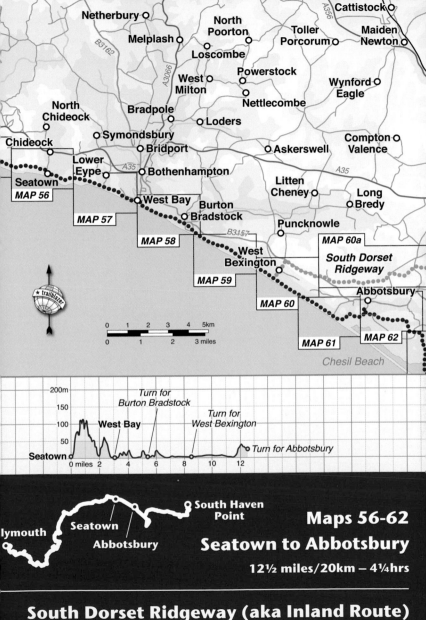

Netherbury
North Poorton
Cattistock
Toller Porcorum
Maiden Newton
Melplash
Loscombe
West Milton
Powerstock
Wynford Eagle
Nettlecombe
North Chideock
Bradpole
Loders
Compton Valence
Chideock
Symondsbury
Askerswell
Bridport
Lower Eype
A35
Bothenhampton
Litten Cheney
Long Bredy
Seatown
MAP 56
West Bay
Burton Bradstock
Puncknowle
MAP 57
B3157
MAP 60a
MAP 58
West Bexington
South Dorset Ridgeway
MAP 59
Abbotsbury
MAP 60
MAP 61
MAP 62
Chesil Beach

0 1 2 3 4 5km
0   1   2   3 miles

200m
150
100
50
Turn for Burton Bradstock
West Bay
Turn for West Bexington
Turn for Abbotsbury
Seatown
0 miles 2   4   6   8   10   12

lymouth
South Haven Point
Seatown
Abbotsbury

Maps 56-62

Seatown to Abbotsbury

12½ miles/20km – 4¼hrs

South Dorset Ridgeway (aka Inland Route)

West Bexington to Osmington Mills, 17 miles/27.4km – 5¼hrs

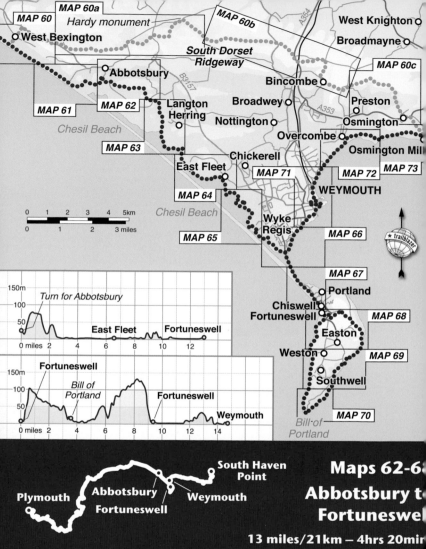

MAP 60

MAP 60a
Hardy monument

MAP 60b

West Knighton ○

Broadmayne ○

○ West Bexington

*South Dorset
Ridgeway*

MAP 60c

○ Abbotsbury

Bincombe ○

Preston ○

MAP 61

MAP 62

Broadwey ○

Langton
Herring

Nottington ○

Osmington ○

MAP 63

Overcombe ○

Osmington Mil

Chesil Beach

Chickerell
○

East Fleet

MAP 71

MAP 72

MAP 73

MAP 64

WEYMOUTH

Chesil Beach

Wyke
Regis

MAP 65

MAP 66

MAP 67

Portland ○

Chiswell ○
Fortuneswell ○

MAP 68

Easton
○

Weston ○

MAP 69

Southwell
○

*Bill of
Portland*

MAP 70

0 1 2 3 4 5km
0   1   2   3 miles

150m
100
50

Turn for Abbotsbury

East Fleet   Fortuneswell

0 miles 2   4   6   8   10   12

150m
100
50

Fortuneswell

*Bill of
Portland*

Fortuneswell

Weymouth

0 miles 2   4   6   8   10   12   14

South Haven
Point

Plymouth   Abbotsbury   Weymouth
              Fortuneswell

Maps 62-6

Abbotsbury t
Fortuneswel

13 miles/21km – 4hrs 20mir

Maps 68-71, Fortuneswell to Weymouth

(via Isle of Portland circuit) 14¾ miles/23.75km – 5½hr

South Dorset Ridgeway (aka Inland Route

West Bexington to Osmington Mills 17 miles/27.4km – 5¼hr

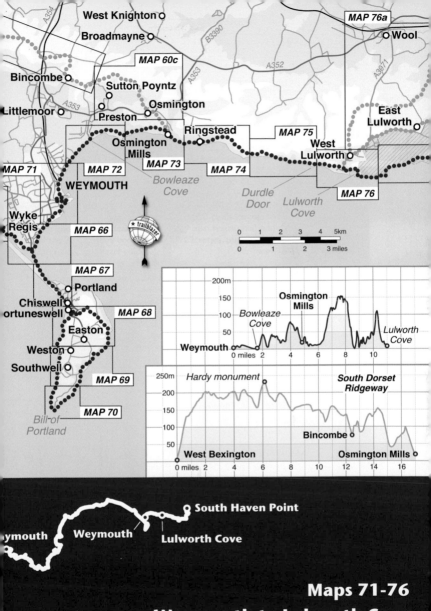

West Knighton
Broadmayne
MAP 76a
Wool

Bincombe
MAP 60c
Sutton Poyntz
Osmington
Littlemoor
Preston
A353

East Lulworth

Ringstead
MAP 75
West Lulworth

Osmington Mills
MAP 73
MAP 74

MAP 71

MAP 72

WEYMOUTH

Bowleaze Cove

Durdle Door *Lulworth Cove*

MAP 76

Wyke Regis

MAP 66

0 1 2 3 4 5km
0   1   2   3 miles

MAP 67

Portland

Chiswell
Fortuneswell

MAP 68

200m
150
100
50

Osmington
Mills

*Bowleaze
Cove*

Easton

Weston

Southwell

MAP 69

Weymouth
0 miles 2   4   6   8   10

*Lulworth
Cove*

MAP 70

250m
200
150
100
50

Hardy monument

*South Dorset
Ridgeway*

*Bill-of-
Portland*

Bincombe

West Bexington

Osmington Mills

0 miles 2   4   6   8   10   12   14   16

South Haven Point

ymouth   **Weymouth**

Lulworth Cove

Maps 71-76
Weymouth to Lulworth Cove
11 miles/17.75km – 4¾hrs
NOTE: Add 20-30% to these times to allow for stops

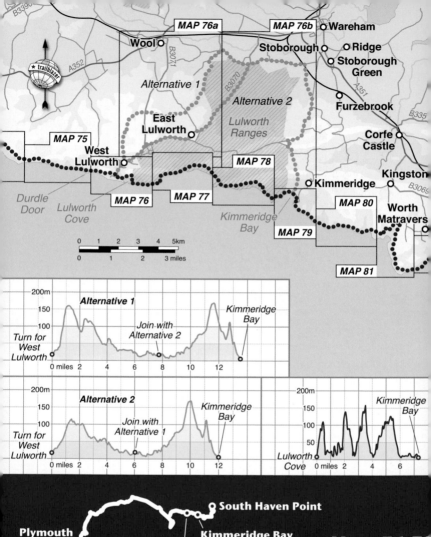

MAP 76a

MAP 76b ○ Wareham

Wool ○   Stoborough ○   ○ Ridge
                                        ○ Stoborough
                                          Green
Alternative 1

MAP 75   Furzebrook

West   East
Lulworth ○   Lulworth ○   *Alternative 2*
                                         *Lulworth
                                          Ranges*   Corfe ○
                                                          Castle

                        MAP 76   MAP 77   MAP 78   Kingston
                                                      ○
Durdle   ○ Kimmeridge   ○
Door   Lulworth   Worth
        Cove   *Kimmeridge*   MAP 80   Matravers
                                 Bay   ○

                                        MAP 79

                                        MAP 81

0   1   2   3   4   5km
0   1   2   3 miles

Alternative 1

200m
150
100
                                                    *Kimmeridge
                                                     Bay*
Turn for
West   *Join with
Lulworth ○   Alternative 2*

0 miles 2   4   6   8   10   12

Alternative 2

200m
150   *Kimmeridge
100   Bay*
Turn for   *Join with
West   Alternative 1*
Lulworth ○

0 miles 2   4   6   8   10   12

200m   *Kimmeridge
150   Bay*
100
50
Lulworth ○
Cove   0 miles 2   4   6

○ **South Haven Point**

Plymouth   **Lulworth Cove**   **Kimmeridge Bay**

Maps 76-79
Lulworth Cove to Kimmeridge Bay

7¼ miles/11.75km – 3hrs, via coastal route

13½ miles/21.75km – 5hrs, via Alternative 1

12 miles/19.3km – 4½hrs, via Alternative 2

NOTE: Add 20-30% to these times to allow for stops

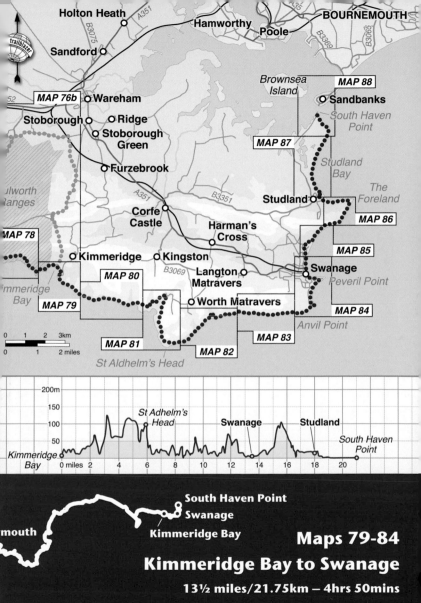

Holton Heath *A351*   **Hamworthy**   **Poole**   **BOURNEMOUTH**

Sandford

MAP 76b   **Wareham**

Stoborough   **Ridge**

Stoborough Green

Furzebrook

Brownsea Island   *MAP 88*   **Sandbanks**

South Haven Point

MAP 87

Studland Bay

Studland   *The Foreland*

MAP 86

Corfe Castle   **Harman's Cross**

Lulworth Ranges

MAP 78

Kimmeridge   **Kingston**   *B3069*

Langton Matravers

MAP 80

MAP 85

Swanage   *Peveril Point*

Kimmeridge Bay

MAP 79

Worth Matravers

MAP 81   *St Aldhelm's Head*   *MAP 82*   *MAP 83*   *Anvil Point*   *MAP 84*

0 1 2 3km
0 1 2 miles

200m
150
100   *St Adhelm's Head*   **Swanage**   **Studland**
50
Kimmeridge Bay   0 miles 2   4   6   8   10   12   14   16   18   20   *South Haven Point*

South Haven Point
...mouth   **Swanage**
Kimmeridge Bay

Maps 79-84

Kimmeridge Bay to Swanage

13½ miles/21.75km – 4hrs 50mins

Maps 84-88, Swanage to South Haven Point

7½ miles/12km – 2¾hrs

NOTE: Add 20-30% to these times to allow for stops

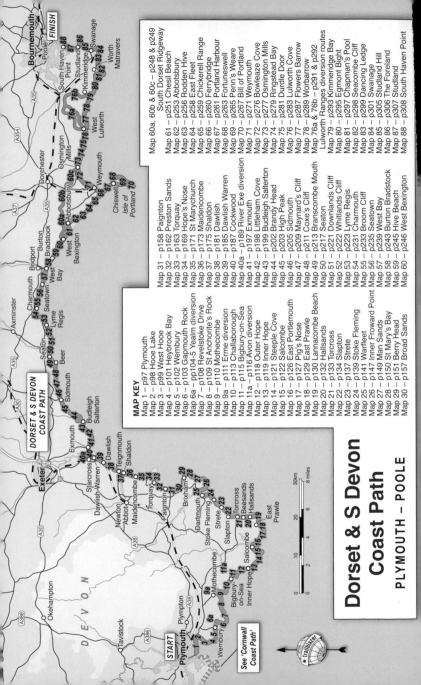

Dorset & S Devon
Coast Path
PLYMOUTH – POOLE

See 'Cornwall Coast Path'

START
Plymouth

DORSET & S DEVON
COAST PATH

FINISH
Bournemouth